W9-ADQ-342

CONTROVERSIES IN EDUCATION

DWIGHT W. ALLEN

SCHOOL OF EDUCATION
UNIVERSITY OF MASSACHUSETTS

JEFFREY C. HECHT

1974

W. B. SAUNDERS COMPANY - Philadelphia - London - Toronto

W. B. Saunders Company: West Washington Square
Philadelphia, PA 19105

12 Dyott Street
London, WC1A 1DB

833 Oxford Street
Toronto, Ontario M8Z 5T9, Canada

Controversies in Education   ISBN   0-7216-1130-3

Last digit is the print no.:   9   8   7   6   5   4   3   2   1

CONTRIBUTORS

CLARK C. ABT is founder and president of Abt Associates Inc. He was graduated from M.I.T. in engineering, received an M.A. in philosophy from Johns Hopkins and a Ph.D. from M.I.T. in social science. Dr. Abt has directed social science research, operations research, systems engineering and interdisciplinary analysis. He is the author of numerous articles and the book, *Serious Games.*

DWIGHT W. ALLEN is dean of the School of Education at the University of Massachusetts at Amherst, and a member of the Advisory Committee for Science Education. He has directed projects and published papers on a wide variety of topics, including microteaching, flexible scheduling, and differentiated staffing. He received his Ed.D. from Stanford University.

CHRIS ARGYRIS teaches at the Graduate School of Education, Harvard University. He has written extensively in the areas of interpersonal relationships and organizational change, including the following books: *Integrating the Individual and the Organization; Organization and Innovation;* and *Personality and Organization.*

BARBARA ARNSTINE is assistant professor of education at California State University, at Sacramento. She has taught at the Davis campus of the University of California, at the University of Tennessee, and at Boston University, and she served as Director of the Center for Action on Poverty at the University of Wisconsin.

DONALD ARNSTINE is professor of education at the University of California, Davis. He has written a book and several dozen articles in the philosophy of education, and has served as President of the John Dewey Society (1970-72) and of the Philosophy of Education Society (1972-73).

ISAAC ASIMOV has written over a hundred books on a wide variety of topics, including *Asimov's Guide to the Bible* and *The Genetic Code.* He is especially well known as a writer of science fiction and a popularizer of science, and holds a doctorate in biochemistry.

iii

KENNETH H. BLANCHARD is on the faculty of the Center for Leadership and Administration, School of Education, University of Massachusetts. He also works with and trains school administrators and teachers throughout the country in the areas of motivation, leadership, and change. He has written extensively in these areas and is co-author, with Paul Hersey, of *Management of Organizational Behavior: Utilizing Human Resources.*

MARION BLANK, a developmental psychologist, has been particularly interested in studying the role of language in learning difficulties and in developing programs to overcome such difficulties. She received her graduate training at Cambridge University in England and has subsequently worked in the Department of Psychiatry at the Albert Einstein College of Medicine of Yeshiva University.

JOHN BREMER is commissioner of education for British Columbia, Canada and was formerly Killam Senior Fellow at Dalhousie University, Halifax, Nova Scotia. He designed and founded Philadelphia's Parkway Program, was superintendent of one of the three decentralization districts in New York City, and is co-author of *School Without Walls* and *Open Education: A Beginning,* as well as several articles and reviews. He is also well known as a lecturer and consultant.

CHARLES H. BUZZELL is associate commissioner of occupational education of the Massachusetts Department of Education. He has served as a faculty member at Rutgers and as a consultant in career education. In Massachusetts, he has developed Project CAREER, a comprehensive computer-assisted career education plan. He is the author of numerous papers and articles on career education.

JAMES CARMODY, a native of New Zealand, is at present on the faculty of the School of Education, University of Massachusetts. He obtained his Ph.D. in educational psychology from the University of Iowa in 1971 and worked in the research and development division of the American College Testing Program.

PHILIP R. CHRISTENSEN is an assistant professor at the University of Massachusetts' School of Education. He is Project Director for the Flexible Curriculum, an innovative system of instructional packaging and record-keeping being tested by the School. His major professional interests include structural innovation in education, teacher training, and international education.

JOHN R. COYNE, JR., teaches in the Department of Mass Communications at Arizona State University, and was a writer on former Vice President Agnew's staff. He has attended Columbia, the University of Alaska, the University of Denver, and the University of California at Berkeley, and was for three years associate editor and feature writer on William F. Buckley Jr.'s *National Review.* He is the author of numerous articles and two books; *The Kumquat Statement* and *The Impudent Snobs.*

ELSIE Y. CROSS is the director of the Goddard College Masters Program in Philadelphia, Pa. She was an organizer for the Philadelphia Federation of Teachers, AFL-CIO, Local 3, served on its Executive Board for five years and was a member of the negotiating team for the first two contracts. She taught for seven years in a Philadelphia high school and was an administrator in the Office of Community Affairs, School District of Philadelphia for four years.

EVELYN PAYNE DAVIS is presently vice president of Community Education Services for the Children's Television Workshop. She has previously served as director of fund development and community relations for the New York Urban League, director for the USO, fund-raising and public relations director for the Harlem YMCA, and an executive assistant for HARYOU-ACT.

DAVID E. DAY is an associate professor and director of early childhood education at the School of Education, University of Massachusetts. His experience includes directing early education components of an urban education improvement project and research in the language development of preschool children. He is currently studying the nature and purposes of day care and early education programs.

CHRIS DEDE graduated from the California Institute of Technology, majoring in chemistry and English, and received his doctorate from the School of Education of the University of Massachusetts. He is currently an assistant professor and director of the Program for the Study of the Future in Education at the University of Massachusetts. He has published extensively in future studies, science education, and urban education.

M. DEL VECCHIO is a former student at "Smith Public High School." She is presently attending college and wants to pursue a career in art education on a college level.

LARRY L. DYE is an assistant professor of education at the University of Massachusetts, Amherst. He has done extensive work in the area of penal reform and juvenile delinquency prevention and control, and is involved with the phasing out of all juvenile correctional institutions in the Commonwealth of Massachusetts. He himself has been incarcerated in juvenile and adult correctional institutions.

TODD EACHUS is presently an assistant professor of education and associate director of the Northeast Regional Media Center for the Deaf at the University of Massachusetts, Amherst. His major interest is the application of behavioral procedures to education, with particular emphasis on the education of the deaf.

ARTHUR EVE has been a classroom teacher and a school administrator. He received his Ph.D. at the University of Chicago. Currently, he is associate director of the Institute for Governmental Services and an associate professor in the School of Education at the University of Massachusetts.

LOUIS FISCHER is a professor of education, University of Massachusetts, and holds degrees in both law and philosophy of education. His teaching experience ranges from second grade to graduate school. He has published many professional articles, and his volume, *The Civil Rights of Teachers,* with David Schimmel as co-author, appeared in the spring of 1973.

ALLAN A. GLATTHORN is presently director of teacher preparation at the Graduate School of Education, University of Pennsylvania. He has also been a director of an alternative schools project and the principal of a large suburban high school. He is a

v

member of the National Humanities Faculty and the National Council for the Humanities.

PAUL GOODMAN was an author and social critic whose concerns focused heavily on education. Among his works are *Growing Up Absurd, Compulsory Mis-education, The Community of Scholars,* and *People or Personnel.* He died in 1972.

WILLIAM PHILLIP GORTH is director of the Center for Educational Research at the School of Education, University of Massachusetts. His interests focus on building strong evaluation programs within public schools by using modern ideas in educational measurement, administration, and data processing. These interests have led to the development of Comprehensive Achievement Monitoring (CAM).

RONALD K. HAMBLETON is an associate professor of education and psychology at the University of Massachusetts. In 1971 he was awarded an American College Testing Program postdoctoral fellowship. He is the author of many papers in the areas of test theory and evaluation methodology. Currently, he is an advisory editor for the *Journal of Educational Measurement.*

WILFRID G. HAMLIN is a longtime member of the faculty of Goddard College, Plainfield, Vermont. He has been a teacher, a dean of the Adult Degree Program, and is presently an assistant to the president for special projects. He has published many articles about education and is co-author (with Margaret Skutch) of *To Start a School,* 1972.

GLENN HAWKES is an assistant professor of education at the University of Massachusetts, Amherst. He has also been director of the MAT program there, and has taught high school social studies. He has helped design and direct the U Mass/Malcolm X College Urban Elementary Teacher Education Program.

G. LOUIS HEATH is an assistant professor of education at Illinois State University, specializing in social foundations of education. He earned his doctorate in this specialty from the University of California at Berkeley, and is the author of numerous articles.

JEFFREY C. HECHT holds degrees in engineering from the California Institute of Technology and in education from the University of Massachusetts, Amherst, where he is a doctoral candidate. He is currently engaged in preparing instructional materials on computers, and doing free-lance writing on education and other areas.

PAUL HERSEY is director of the Center for Leadership Studies and professor of organizational behavior, College of Business Administration, Ohio University. A recognized educator, trainer, and lecturer, he has worked extensively in the training and development field in this country and abroad. He is best known for his book, co-authored with Kenneth H. Blanchard, *Management of Organizational Behavior: Utilizing Human Resources* which has already been translated into Japanese, Portuguese and Spanish.

JULIUS HOBSON is a civil rights activist and director of the Washington Institute for Quality Education in Washington, D.C. He was the successful plaintiff in a suit charging the Washington school administration with discrimination in the allocation of resources and assignment of teachers and students. He is a former member of the Washington school board.

SOPHIE S. HOLLANDER is senior supervisor of Resource Development and Information Dissemination of the Massachusetts Department of Education. She has been a supervisor of academic subjects, and taught English as a second language at the adult and community college level. She is also a journalist and free-lance writer, and author of *Impressions of the United States.*

EUGENE R. HOWARD has served as a teacher, administrator, author, and consultant. He is well known for his work as creator of the highly innovative Ridgewood High School in Norridge, Illinois, and as director of the Charles F. Kettering Foundation's Demonstration Schools program. He is currently superintendent of schools in Urbana, Illinois.

JACK HRUSKA is an assistant professor at the University of Massachusetts, where he teaches educational foundations and directs a teacher training program. He earned his Ph.D. from Michigan State University, and he has taught social studies and directed cooperative education programs for eight years in high school.

MADELINE HUNTER is principal of the laboratory school and lecturer in the UCLA Graduate School of Education. Her background as a psychologist provided the impetus for factoring the teaching process into decisions and competencies which can be predictably learned in preservice and in-service classes. The result is a new teacher appraisal instrument (T.A.I.).

IVAN ILLICH, philosopher born in Vienna, Austria, 1926; now lives in Cuernavaca, Mexico. In 1970 he published *Deschooling Society,* in which he questioned not only the need for universal schools but also the need for their product, namely, "education."

LORD JAMES OF RUSHOLME (Eric John Francis James), a British educator, is Vice Chancellor of the University of York. He was educated at Queen's College, Oxford, in chemistry, and has served on England's Social Science Research Council. He was head of a committee which recently studied teacher education in Great Britain and recommended extensive changes in existing practice.

DANIEL C. JORDAN is presently director of the Center for the Study of Human Potential, School of Education, University of Massachusetts at Amherst. He holds a Bachelor's of Music degree in applied piano from the University of Wyoming, a B.A. and M.A. in music from the University of Oxford, England, where he studied for three years on a Rhodes scholarship, and an M.A. and Ph.D. in human development from the University of Chicago.

DRAPER KAUFFMAN, JR., is co-director of the Future Studies Teacher Training Program at the University of Massachusetts. He has also been a coordinator of the Future Studies Program there, an education policy analyst for the Stanford Research

Institute, and a field ethnologist with the Ilongot, a tribe of headhunters in the Philippines.

EDWARD T. LADD was a professor of education at Emory University, where he specialized in the problems of discipline and students' rights in public schools. He was the consultant on children's rights in school to the 1970 White House Conference on Children, and was a co-founder of the National Committee to Abolish Corporal Punishment in Schools. He was killed in a bicycle accident in January, 1973.

R. A. LAFFERTY is a well-known writer of science fiction and fantasy, including *Past Master* and *The Devil is Dead.* He is a native of Oklahoma, and an electrical engineer by profession. The selection included in this volume originally appeared as a nonfact article in *Galaxy Science Fiction.*

MYRON LIEBERMAN is director of the Office of Program Development, Office of Teacher Education in the City University of New York. He received bachelor's degrees in law and education from the University of Minnesota and an M.A. and Ph.D. from the University of Illinois, from which he received a distinguished alumni award in 1967.

WILLIAM C. LINDHOLM is chairman of the National Committee for Amish Religious Freedom, which was formed at the University of Chicago in 1967 and successfully defended the Amish in the victory in the United States Supreme Court. He has a B.A. from Augustana College in Rock Island, Illinois and a Master of Divinity degree from the Lutheran School of Theology in Chicago. He is an ordained clergyman of the Lutheran Church in America and serves Holy Cross Lutheran Church in Livonia, Michigan.

MICHAEL MACCOBY is a psychoanalyst and a fellow at the Institute for Policy Studies in Washington where he is directing a project on technology, work, and character sponsored by Harvard University's Program on Technology and Society. He has co-authored a book with Erich Fromm, *Social Character in a Mexican Village.*

NEAL B. MITCHELL, JR., is a registered professional engineer and president of both Mitchell Systems, Inc. and International Construction and Marketing Company. He has been a professor and director of the Architectural Technology Workshop at the Harvard Graduate School of Design, and has won several prizes in building competitions.

ROBERT D. MOON is assistant secretary of evaluation, planning, and development, Council for Exceptional Children, Washington, D.C., and consultant on information systems, Hewitt Research Center.

DENNIS R. MOORE teaches in the Walnut Hills Community School, Cherry Creek, Colorado, and is a graduate student at the University of Colorado, Denver Center.

RAYMOND S. MOORE is chief executive officer, Hewitt Research Center, and professor of education, Andrews University, Berien Springs, Michigan. He has been a teacher, principal, and superintendent in California public schools and an administrator and professor in colleges and universities, including two in the Orient. His extensive research background includes initiation and direction of the first and only comprehensive nationwide study of interinstitutional cooperation in American higher education, 1965-67.

JAMES MORROW's main interests, besides education, are writing, cartooning, and film-making. He first became interested in the relationship between media and learning while making documentary films for the Philadelphia public schools. He recently co-directed a comedy featurette, *A Political Cartoon,* for Odradek Productions.

RICHARD J. NEUHAUS is pastor of the Church of Saint John the Evangelist (Lutheran), Brooklyn; associate editor of *Worldview;* author of *In Defense of People;* and co-author, with Peter Berger, of *Movement and Revolution.* His involvement with educational reform in New York City has included helping establish an experimental community-controlled school in the Williamsburg Bedford-Stuyvesant section of Brooklyn.

RICHARD MILHAUS NIXON was born in Yorba Linda, California on January 9, 1913, graduated from Whittier College in 1934, and won a full scholarship to the Law School of Duke University, from which he graduated in 1937 with honors. He served in the U.S. Navy from 1942 to 1946. He has held the offices of U.S. Representative, Senator, Vice President, and, finally, 37th President of the United States.

NOEL NOVINSON was born (1947) in Ithaca, N.Y., raised in North Miami Beach, Florida, received his B.A. in philosophy and psychology (1969), and is currently writing science-fiction, doing research on altered states of consciousness, and keeping involved with academia at the University of California at Santa Barbara.

LEON E. PANETTA has served as director of the Office for Civil Rights, Department of Health, Education, and Welfare, and as executive assistant to New York City mayor John Lindsay, with responsibility for civil rights and intergovernmental relations. He is the author of *Bring Us Together: The Nixon Administration and the Civil Rights Retreat.* He is currently an attorney in Monterey, California.

HOWARD A. PEELLE is presently an assistant professor and director of Instructional Applications of Computers at the University of Massachusetts' School of Education. He is interested in uses of artificial intelligence techniques in computer-assisted instruction and A Programming Language (APL) in teaching elementary school children.

PHILIP H. PHENIX teaches philosophy at Teachers College, Columbia University. He has written numerous books, including *Man and His Becoming, Philosophy of Education,* and *Realms of Meaning.*

NEIL POSTMAN is a professor of education at New York University, and is a prominent figure among those who criticize the heavy emphasis upon reading in modern education.

HARRY E. RANDLES is an associate professor of educational administration in the School of Education, Syracuse University. His teaching and research interest is Personnel. His doctorate was granted jointly by Miami University of Ohio and The

Ohio State University in 1964; he earned his master's degree at Miami University of Ohio, 1958.

BETTY REARDON taught secondary social studies for nine years. Since 1963, she has served as director of the School Program of the Institute for World Order in New York City, where she has worked on the development of curriculum materials, teaching strategies, and teacher education for peace education and world order studies.

OFRA REISMAN is a nursery school educator in Israel. After serving as a director of a nursery school for a period of ten years, she became interested in developing more formalized curricula for children of preschool age. Her work is currently being applied in a wide range of settings, including day care centers for children from disadvantaged backgrounds as well as residential settings for young children.

JOSEPH RHODES, JR., is a Pennsylvania state assemblyman from Pittsburgh. He has been a Junior Fellow at Harvard University, director of the Contemporary University Program, a member of the President's Commission on Campus Unrest, and a consultant to the Ford Foundation.

IRVING ROSENSTEIN is a visiting assistant professor of urban education at Temple University, and an associate education director of the Philadelphia Joint Board, Amalgamated Clothing Workers of America. An elementary and special class teacher in Philadelphia, he has also served on the Executive Board of the Philadelphia Federation of Teachers and been an organizer and negotiator for Local 3, AFT.

MASHA RUDMAN has been involved in teaching since 1953. She is currently the director of the Interstate Staff Development Cooperative. She holds the position of associate professor and is co-director of the Integrated Day Program at the School of Education, University of Massachusetts. She is the author of numerous publications in the field of education and is currently working on a book, *A Contemporary Approach to Children's Literature.* In 1972, she was the recipient of the Distinguished Teacher Award of the University of Massachusetts, and in 1973, she was elected to the Hunter College Hall of Fame.

DAVID SCHIMMEL is an associate professor at the University of Massachusetts School of Education. He received his J. D. from Yale University. He is a co-author of *The Civil Rights of Teachers* (1973) and is again collaborating with Louis Fischer on a new book on the civil rights of students.

HARVEY B. SCRIBNER, the first chancellor of the decentralized public school system of New York City, 1970-73, is professor of education at the School of Education, University of Massachusetts.

SIDNEY B. SIMON is a professor in the Center for Humanistic Education at the University of Massachusetts. He taught English, social studies, core, and dramatics for seven years in secondary schools before becoming a teacher-educator. His writings have been published extensively and include *Wad-Ja-Get?,* a novel attacking grading practices. His major concern is the area of value-clarification.

B.F. SKINNER has taught at Harvard University since 1948. He has been and continues to be a leading spokesman for the importance of operant conditioning as the prime factor in the shaping of human behavior. His research grew out of laboratory work but he has expressed its social implications in such books as *Walden II* and *Beyond Freedom and Dignity.*

MORTIMER SMITH is executive director of the Council for Basic Education in Washington, D. C. and editor of its *Bulletin.* He is the author or co-author of nine books in the fields of biography and education and has written for many magazines and contributed to several anthologies.

LEONARD B. STEVENS, special assistant to Dr. Scribner in New York City, is a writer and editor who is a graduate assistant at the School of Education, University of Massachusetts.

LINDLEY J. STILES is a former dean of two schools of education, the University of Virginia and the University of Wisconsin, Madison, and is well known for his leadership in the field of teacher education. His Massachusetts Study laid the foundation for the growing nationwide efforts to reform the system of certification for elementary and secondary school teachers.

MURRAY SUID is a staff writer at *Learning* magazine. He has taught at the secondary level. He co-authored *Painting with the Sun* (a first book of photography) and *Moviemaking Illustrated: The Comic Book Film Book.* His short film comedy, *The J-Walker,* won a Cine Eagle award.

ROBERTA KOCH SUID is the book reviews editor for *Learning* magazine. She has taught at the secondary level. She designed *Painting with the Sun* (a first book of photography), was managing editor of *k-eight* magazine, and was a co-author of *Interaction,* a k-12 language arts program.

DENNIS SULLIVAN was educated in philosophy and theology while a student for the Roman Catholic priesthood, and has travelled through South America as a Pulitzer Travelling Fellow. From September, 1969 to March, 1972, he coordinated a seminar on Alternatives in Education at the Intercultural Documentation Center (CIDOC) in Cuernavaca, Mexico. He now lives in London, England, where he works as a free-lance journalist and edits a series of working papers called *Ideas in Progress.*

DOROTHY WESTBY-GIBSON, an educator and sociologist, serves as chairman of the Department of Secondary Education, at San Francisco State University. Her professional experience includes social group work as well as public-school teaching and administration. She frequently has been a consultant with school districts and community projects, and has written extensively on the controversial subject of grouping.

DOXEY A. WILKERSON is vice president of Mediax Associates, Inc., Westport, Connecticut. He recently retired as professor of education, Ferkauf Graduate School, Yeshiva University, and has taught at four other institutions and served as research associate with several national studies of Negro education. Publications include several books and monographs and scores of journal articles.

GERALD S. WITHERSPOON is president of Goddard College, Plainfield, Vermont, and is also a member of the Board of Directors of the Union for Experimenting Colleges and Universities, and the Union Graduate School, and a trustee of Antioch College. He did graduate study in philosophy at the University of Paris and Princeton, and earned the J. D. degree from the University of Chicago Law School.

ALBERT H. YEE is dean of Graduate Studies and Research at California State University, Long Beach. He has a Stanford doctorate and was a postdoctoral research fellow at the University of Oregon. Among his many publications are *Social Interaction in Educational Settings* and *Perspectives on Management Systems Approaches in Education: A Symposium.* As a Fulbright-Hays professor in Japan during 1972, he conducted lectures on his major research interest, the social psychology of education. Dr. Yee recently visited the People's Republic of China to obtain firsthand information about China's psychologists, schools and universities, and exchange opportunities. He was formerly a professor in the School of Education at the University of Wisconsin, Madison.

JAMES CLAYTON YOUNG is an assistant professor in the Department of Early Childhood Education at Georgia State University. He has also served as director of the Head Start Leadership Development Program at the University of Massachusetts, from which he also received his doctorate. Earlier, he had taught in the Gary, Indiana public schools.

ACKNOWLEDGMENTS

Any volume like *Controversies in Education* owes a lot of thanks to a lot of people who helped make it possible. We owe special thanks to those who contributed articles to the volume—without them, this book simply would not exist.

Many people at the University of Massachusetts have given us invaluable help in the form of comments, criticism, and suggestions. Much of the initial development and organization of this volume was done by Lloyd Kline and Richard de Lone, who made our task much easier. Pat Sullivan, too, has given us assistance far above and beyond the call of duty. The Editorial and Managing Editorial Boards have made major contributions for which we are grateful. We also wish to thank Peter Wagschal for helping with our editorial tasks.

Baxter Venable of W. B. Saunders Company has shown remarkable patience with our many failings and foibles. And without much help from Susan de Lone, Teddy Dunbar, Lois Hecht, Linda Paririo, and Susan Theroux, *Controversies in Education* would never have been assembled between covers.

Dwight W. Allen
Jeffrey C. Hecht

CONTENTS

SECTION THREE   TEACHING AND TECHNOLOGY

SECTION SIX   TEACHERS

SECTION SEVEN   STUDENTS

SECTION EIGHT SCHOOL/SOCIETY

61

Julius Hobson

62

Harvey B. Scribner; Leonard B. Stevens

introduction

Dwight W. Allen
Jeffrey C. Hecht

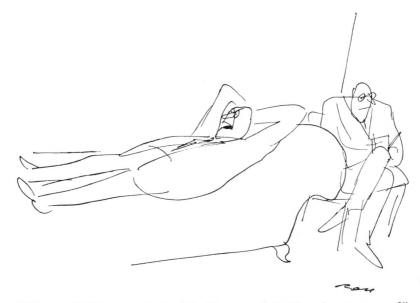

"Who am I? Where am I going? And how much is this going to cost me?"

There was a time—and not so very long ago—when it was a fairly simple matter to put together what seemed like a useful book on educational problems. As few as five years ago, in fact, virtually any educator could have compiled a sane and logical list of current problems in education, followed by an apparently reasonable set of programs aimed at solving those problems in a fairly straightforward manner.

But, as with so much else in the 1970's, the educational picture is changing with virtually every blink of the eyes. Solutions which seemed almost obvious five years ago, and which have been pursued in some quarters with a messianic fervor ever since, are now beginning to seem naive and even old-fashioned. Problems which loomed as crises and demanded immediate attention then have faded before a rising tide of public apathy or crumbled beneath the weight of more pressing, if less exciting, concerns. Five years ago, virtually everyone seemed to want to talk about education: everyone had an Answer and, if agreement on solutions was absent, at least the issues seemed to be clear to all. Now, the conversations have ebbed, no one even seems to have an appropriate Question, and it borders on the impossible to make a reasonable list of current issues in education.

What has *not* changed in the past five years is the very real sense of crisis in American education. Despite the growing apathy and confusion, there persists a strong conviction that *something* is desperately wrong with our educational institutions. As much as we may disagree on *what* is wrong and how to fix it, we do increasingly agree that something must be done, and soon, to restore public confidence in the educational process and to create institutions that are worthy of that trust. To put it all another way, we seem to be at a point in the history of American education where no one can make definitive statements even about the nature of the most crucial problems that we face; and yet, at the same time, we all realize that we are in the midst of what may well be an unprecedented educational crisis.

It is with this dual recognition of crisis and bewilderment that we have put together a volume on Controversies in Education. There is nothing definitive or messianic here. The collection of solutions and problems is temporary, and the controversies explored here are as diverse as our current crisis is confused. At worst, the reader will find here a random montage of current educational jargon. At best, he will find a vehicle for exploring the current state of the art in education as well as some of its future possibilities. What we hope to do in these pages is to provoke the reader into *thinking,* and learning more about education than he originally wanted to know.

It would probably be a mistake to read this volume from beginning to end, and it would certainly be an error to consider any article or chapter—much less the book as a whole—to be a complete treatment of any subject. Our intent is to suggest a variety of areas in which crucial issues might be defined and from which promising solutions might eventually be developed. We hope to ask more questions than we answer; to leave more avenues open than we close; to create more problems for the reader than we solve.

Furthermore, we have expectations of our readers. We hope that they are not looking for simple solutions to educational problems, for our experience has shown that learning is an enormously complex process. We hope that they will be critical and thoughtful enough to argue with themselves over every idea they find in these pages. Most importantly, we hope that they will have the tenacity and imagination to go far beyond this book in their pursuit of promising approaches to the current state of educational crisis.

Beyond the pages of this book, there is an enormously complex web of ideas, institutions, and individual people completely absorbed in the day-to-day tasks of defining and carrying out the educational process for a society in desperate need of new approaches. If this volume can succeed in getting its readers to immerse themselves in the intricacies of that process, with a growing understanding of the difficulty of the task at hand but a continued sense of urgency, we will have succeeded in producing the book we hoped to build.

WHAT SHOULD EDUCATION BE? PHILOSOPHIES/ PERSPECTIVES

"Just exactly what are you teaching these children, Miss Rawley?"

What should education be? Ask this question of any reasonably diverse group who are the least interested in the topic and they'll argue indefinitely. If they try to define the term "education" first, they probably won't even get to the question.

Critics of education have repeatedly noted the lack of a coherent philosophy or goal. Schools and school boards have attempted to fill this gap by writing official school philosophies, which, with rare exceptions, tend to be documents sufficiently vague that everyone can agree with them. Some private schools have had more success, largely because they have more freedom to choose their approaches. (It's very unlikely that any community would support either a military academy or a Summerhill-type school.) The public schools, however, usually must develop the goals of education implicitly—largely through administrative regulations, and partly by the individual teachers themselves.

What are the results? Some observers have attempted to analyze organizational practices to determine the philosophies behind them. In The Human Side of Enterprise (McGraw-Hill, 1960), MacGregor speaks of behavior as indicating implicit belief in Theory X or Theory Y. Briefly, Theory X assumes people are inherently lazy and seek to avoid work, while Theory Y assumes that people want to do meaningful work. Though these are probably oversimplifications, it is possible to classify many teachers as believers in Theory X or Theory Y. Other such analyses have found, among other items, many forms of institutional racism and a frequent tendency toward mindlessness in the schools.

"What should education try to do?" Historically, there have been many goals set forth. The Puritans thought it should teach children how to read the Scriptures. By the mid-nineteenth century, education was supposed to give every boy an equal opportunity. (That it was every "boy," and that an unstated modifier usually was "white" means that the vision was limited; it does not mean that the vision was an evil one.) There were other visions to follow. Schools were the "melting pot" for the American culture, making immigrants (German, Irish, Polish, or whatever) into Americans. Schools were to prepare children for life—to teach a boy a trade, to teach a girl housekeeping (and, as the vision expanded, to teach her business skills as well, if she desired). Schools were to impart moral training, to help build physical fitness, to build a happy, healthy person, and to teach the joy of learning.

This crazy quilt of visions is still with us today, in a multitude of courses, curricula, and approaches to education.

This is perhaps most obvious in the variety of courses, which generally evolved piecemeal from legislative requirements, local needs, and teacher interests. Thus driver training, physical education, and civics are offered because of state law; agriculture and Italian because of the specific community; and Far Eastern history and Japanese because a teacher happens to be qualified to teach them. Many critics feel that the result is far from a coherent whole—and that if it is to be effective, some unifying vision is needed.

The essays in this section speak primarily to two questions—what education should try to do and what it shouldn't. Lord James tells us we're limited by the law of "conservation of curriculum"; that education, for all its lofty goals, can only do a finite number of things. How many are worth doing, how much can we really accomplish, and how can we establish a hierarchy of values to aid in making decisions? Do we want a coherent curriculum concentrating on a few goals, or a cluttered one, trying to do more of the things that need doing? What role (if any) should the home, the society, and the child have in all this? Somehow, somewhere, we must study the alternatives and make the choices.

Though it is necessary to select the most important tasks education should attempt, it is also urgent to identify what it should not attempt. This is important at two levels. One is values: should (or can) schools be neutral in the area of values? Or is the result a "valueless" institution, at best peddling, in Richard Neuhaus' words, an inferior "bootleg religion"? If not, what values should the schools teach—and at what point does this become the "indoctrination" of which John R. Coyne Jr. warns us?

On another level, there have been many warnings that part of the educational process may be (or is) destructive. Ivan Illich holds that the very notion of schooling itself is dangerous. Glenn Hawkes warns that we may have "unconsciously planted in the heart of the 'new curricula' the seeds of massive social insanity." After all the unpleasant lessons that the environmental crisis has taught us about side effects, can we afford to ignore the possibility of mind pollution?

In a society as diverse as our own, it may never be possible to reach any real agreement on what education should be. Indeed, it may not even be desirable to reach an "official philosophy" for American education as a whole. But it is vital that each of us—especially those involved in education—have a real sense of what we think education should be.

1 transforming the curriculum: a deweyan reinterpretation

Barbara Arnstine
Donald Arnstine

When the curriculum of the public schools comes under heavy siege, it is not unusual for critics to call upon the ideas of John Dewey. Even *Newsweek* magazine, which normally associates the name of Dewey with "soft pedagogy," has recently paid obeisance to him in its own semiliterate way: ". . . philosopher John Dewey synthesized the ideas of Pestalozzi and Froebel with his own empirical concept that children would learn best if they were encourged to become involved with their own education" (May 3, 1971). Most of this sort of reference to Dewey seems intended as an invocation of authority in order to make a point. It is much more difficult—but in the long run far more valuable—to re-examine Dewey's thought in a serious effort to make some sense out of the curriculum.

There is a special reason for this difficulty, beyond the obvious one that reading a profound and original philosopher is more challenging than scanning a textbook or a popular journal. Dewey's philosophical posture was a contextual one: he argued typically that things could not be understood in isolation from other things, but that they made sense only in terms of their interrelations and transactions. An analysis of the curriculum from this viewpoint sees as hopelessly inadequate the familiar bookkeeper's approach which thinks in terms of so many credit hours of this or that subject.

A Deweyan approach to the curriculum cannot consider its content independent of how it is to be taught and who is to do the teaching and the learning. Thus for Dewey there can be no account of *just* the curriculum: that with which it interacts must also be considered. The discussion that follows will not attempt to reconstruct or summarize what Dewey wrote about the curriculum, but will instead re-examine contemporary curriculum approaches and possible options to them from a Deweyan point of view. Thus it will necessarily consider the interaction of curriculum content with instructional methods and with the social climate of classrooms. The discussion will be divided into three parts. In the first, the impact of the curriculum from the point of view of children will be considered. The second part will examine the purposes for which adults devise curricula, especially for secondary school youth. Finally, the third part will consider a wholly different approach to curriculum organization, based upon a Deweyan interpretation of learning and schooling.

THE CHILD AS LEARNER

The public school curriculum is seldom discussed or evaluated from the point of view of those who are subjected to it. We are interested in whether students like their teachers, but we seldom concern ourselves with whether they like what is being taught. Throughout his writings on education, John Dewey tried to look at the curriculum from the child's viewpoint. He was not, however, a romantic solely concerned with the child's happiness. His concern with the child was an outgrowth of his conception of learning. For Dewey, learning was a consequence of active experiencing, and it resulted in changes in attitudes, values, and degrees of competency—not merely in the acquisition of information or skills. Consequently, Dewey focused his attention on the child as the learner, and began his critical examination of the school curriculum from this focus. In order to understand some of the problems embedded in the present school curriculum, we will examine it first from the point of view of the child.

It is important to remember that a child's first contact with school is not his first contact with learning. He has been learning from the moment of birth. The informal "curriculum" to which he has been exposed has taught him very practical ways of managing his world and of relating to the people in it. Speech is an essential aspect of this informal curriculum because it is at once both practical and social. The child wants something, and he quickly learns that speech is an effective means of obtaining it. He also learns that talking adds a dimension to human contact that is pleasurable in itself—an extended form of emotional communication. As the child learns to speak in settings that are practical and social, the "methods" used are a direct outgrowth of his purposes and the content that he learns.

In his contact with the informal curriculum, the child's experiences as a learner are not essentially different from his experiences in any other learning environment. He learns through active participation, in a context that he perceives as practical, social, or both. The ongoing activities of home and play meet these criteria for learning and, as a consequence, most children learn an amazing amount from the informal curriculum experienced outside of school.

The informal curriculum that the child learns before he enters school has consisted of information, skills, and ideas that are of value to him. But just as he prizes his ability to talk, to play, and to know the direction to his friend's house, so he also values the conditions under which he has learned these things. The child learns in practical and social settings, and he prizes these settings as much as he values what he has learned in them. He likes human contact and he likes doing new things, not only for what results, but for their own sake. Thus the child *is* social and practical, not just for the ends that he wishes to achieve, but as a normal and pleasurable state of being. It is this state of being that the informal curriculum cultivates with its human intercourse and activity. For it is this state of being that is most conducive to learning.

Before we proceed to the child's experience with the formal curriculum of the schools, it may be necessary to clarify further the idea of "practical" that we have been using to describe the informal curriculum of the child's early experience. A practical setting is one in which the learner perceives the usefulness of the skills, information, or ideas presented. Since this practicality is a part of the learner's perception, it is a highly personal aspect of the situation. The effects of radiation to the atomic scientist and the art of balancing on a bicycle to the child are both practical in the context in which they learn them. While our society may value the scientist's efforts to a greater degree, it is important to remember that from a psychological point of view, both child and scientist are interested in and see the purpose of what they are doing. For them, their activities are practical.

When the child arrives at school, he encounters a formal curriculum, predetermined and prepackaged for his consumption. Since it is predetermined, this formal curriculum cannot partake of the social and practical experiences that have directed the child's learning up to this point. It is a curriculum that is both impersonal and irrelevant, because it exists independently of the child's needs, feelings, and problems. The child meets this curriculum as a practical and social human being. Its contents are seen as alien and useless; it lacks necessary relations to his personal life. Thus the child cannot be *both* a sociable and purposive human being *and* a learner of this curriculum. The two roles are so opposed that it is impossible for the child to continue functioning as a learner when he goes to school.

Given the child's point of view, it is easy to see that he cannot *learn* the formal curriculum of the schools. But the teacher, who is paid to accomplish something, must attempt to teach it anyhow. What the teacher can extract from the child is a set of performances which the schools will then call learning. These performances will be memorized and routinely delivered, and their contents will be quickly forgotten.

In his attempt to produce these performances, the teacher tries methods that will help him accomplish his task efficiently and humanely as well. The most efficient way to teach such a curriculum would be a training (or conditioning) system that produced the performances through rewards and punishments (or reinforcements).* But while this system is an appropriate outgrowth of the demands of the curriculum, most teachers are uncomfortable using it. They find such a system of teaching impersonal, authoritarian, and rigid and thereby reject the method of training that would be most effective, because they value social warmth, creativity, and democratic procedures. It is unfortunate that they do not reject the curriculum as well, for it inspires and perpetuates this method of teaching.

Having rejected the method that is most germane to the curriculum at hand, many teachers adopt a style of teaching that promotes other values. In their attempts to create conditions that foster self-respect, affection, and social responsibility in the classroom, these teachers mistakenly assume that the curriculum is reconstructed through their efforts.

But the method cannot transform the material, if it is conceived independently of that material. Teachers can make the tedium of "learning" for performances more palatable through games and freely given affection, and the child may learn important social values from the teacher's method. Yet the curriculum itself remains as meaningless as ever.

There is no clearer evidence for the discrepancy between methods and material than the inefficiency seen in teaching the present school curriculum. Though methods such as reward systems are found to be efficient, they are too similar to animal training techniques for teachers to use them comfortably. Consequently, a great deal of their time is spent in developing a style of teaching that impedes the curriculum's acquisition rather than fostering it. An inefficient method is beneficial because it is at least more humane

---

*The clearest and most thoroughgoing statement of such an approach to instruction is still to be found in B.F. Skinner, The science of learning and the art of teaching, *Harvard Educational Review,* 24:86-97, 1954. Skinner, of course, thought that the acquisition of discrete, behavioral performances was what teachers were after when they tried to foster learning.

and democratic, but it hardly attacks the problem of the curriculum itself. It remains inappropriate for human consumption despite all our ingenuity in helping students get it down. And the day of reckoning comes even for the most humane teacher when his students must meet the performance levels the curriculum requires. Time and again, he must abandon his values to accomplish the training the curriculum demands. He views these moments, usually related to testing, grading, and discipline, with a prolonged indecision and despair of his own ability to teach. What is inappropriate, however, is the material being taught. Until that is changed, the control of the teacher over the classroom environment is minimal. The best he can do is make the performance less painful and the punishment less harsh. In so doing, he must himself risk charges of inefficiency and poor performance.

The formal curriculum will have almost no consequences for the child's future behavior, since the rote and routine performances will be quickly forgotten. But what the child does learn as a consequence of subjection to this curriculum will make a great difference. For the child goes through school as a social and practical human being, and in doing so, he responds to all experiences, even unpleasant ones. Thus while the curriculum is trivial, the setting which supports, sustains, and tries to teach this curriculum has a tremendous impact on the child. The child may remain unmoved by the curriculum per se, but the school in which he spends a significant part of his youth will promote experiences from which he will learn.

Because the school is organized around and dedicated to teaching an irrelevant and impersonal curriculum, most of its impact on children will be negative. It is a place where significant social relationships involving the sharing of ideas have to be broken down in order to get individual performances that indicate success or failure. The child finds that normal human intercourse is called cheating in school, and that everything depends upon his success in competing with his peers. Thus he must learn to mistrust his fellow students and jealously guard his answers so that he can present them to the teacher for a reward at the proper time. Or he may learn to form an alliance with his peer group and either ignore the demands of adult authority or learn to satisfy them efficiently with a system of successful cheating.

The child will also learn that his value as a person and his sense of what matters here and now are constantly undermined. He will learn that what concerns him is of no consequence except as it can be used to extract the required performance. He will also learn to live in the future, since the rewards for the effort he is making will always occur in the future—promotion, graduation, college, a job. In the process of schooling, a child's social values and practical values will change. In order to succeed at the performances required by the formal curriculum, he must become less social, less practical. The child must abandon his role as learner which was developed in active social participation in the informal curriculum of the pre-school years. And as the child becomes less social and less practical, he becomes less fully human as well.

> In the schoolroom the motive and cement of social organization are alike wanting. Upon the ethical side, the tragic weakness of the present school is that it endeavors to prepare future members of the social order in a medium in which the conditions of the social spirit are eminently wanting (Dewey, "The School and Society," p. 39).

CURRICULUM IN THE SECONDARY SCHOOL

The selection of curriculum content by others at the elementary level is usually defended on the grounds that the child is too immature to do his own choosing. But since there is so great a gap between the child's experience and the content of the curriculum, the best he can do is to give a performance that will satisfy his teacher. Real learning would be quite another matter. Yet the case with the older student may be different. Since broader experience has helped him become more mature, it is claimed that he *can* acquire the content of an academic curriculum in such a way as to see its relevance to personal and social life.

If this is true, it would make sense to present the adolescent with a carefully selected, well-balanced set of studies as a means of rounding out his education. This in fact is just what is attempted in the comprehensive high school. To see whether the attempt has succeeded, and to examine other curricular options, we turn now to a consideration of secondary education.

The academic curriculum is intended to provide enough breadth and depth for anyone intending to go to college or simply wanting to be educated in a general sort of way. Presumably, one exposed to this curriculum should be able to read and write competently, speak articulately, and have a taste for good literature; he should calculate accurately and understand mathematical relationships; he should understand American history in the context of the development of other Western nations, one of whose languages he has mastered; and he should understand the fundamental interrelations in organic and inorganic nature, and the methods by which those interrelations are discovered. In short, this curriculum is intended to produce a generally educated person. Yet despite the intention, no such persons are produced by the schools. Few enough mature adults, let alone children and youth, possess the capacity, the interest, or the patience to become so broadly informed and competent.

The even "balance" of the academic curriculum presupposes either that learners have no particular interests of their own (which is absurd), or that their interests need not be served by schools, even when those interests are respectable, academic ones. Thus the ideal product of the academic curriculum would be a creature without special interests or with the ability and willingness to put his interests aside until weekends. Such a creature, stuffed with a broad sampling of information, would very likely be socially, politically, and sexually neutral: a mental and moral eunuch. Thus there is reason to be grateful for the schools' failing to achieve their academic aims.

If a student's grades are low, if he strongly dislikes academic studies, or if his interests do not extend beyond seeking a job after graduation, he is directed to the vocational (or sometimes the catch-all "general") curriculum. Along with a few students seriously interested in acquiring job skills go the educationally disaffected: the low IQs, the rebellious, the apathetic. Their lot in school is not a happy one. Low in prestige, they are excluded from most extracurricular activities because their grades are too low or because they lack the social background and skills which many of those activities demand.

The academic courses these students are required to take are often simplified. This simplification is effected by teachers and curriculum makers who prejudicially regard these students as stupid and incompetent. Thus what is left for them to learn is simple in the sense of simple-minded. It is even duller and more trivial than the material offered in the academic curriculum. Their vocational training is of equal value. Assigned tasks on obsolete equipment often donated to the school by a factory that had no more use for it, these students are prepared for jobs which in many cases will not exist when and if they graduate. The vocational curriculum thus prepares workers about as effectively as the academic curriculum prepares scholars.

It is not necessary to document the failure of the academic curriculum to capture the interest of the majority of students who lack scholarly inclinations. Unfortunately, even the scholarly few are ill-served, since they must curb their interests in biochemistry, poetry, colonial history, or whatever, and instead pursue *all* the studies, in the prescribed manner, and in a balanced way. Told that they may pursue their own projects *after* their regular work is done, their genuine scholarship is insensibly transformed into a bribe, and the schools' handful of scholars becomes debauched (Goodman, 1963).

The academic curriculum is thus an obstacle to academic study. Genuine scholars study what they find fascinating, raise uncomfortable questions, and risk defending unpopular opinions. Quite to the contrary, those who succeed in the academic curriculum have learned to do their assignments, adopt routines, and accept the beliefs of authorities. The reverse of scholarship, it is a comfortable way to behave once you get used to it:

> ... the mind, shut out from worthy employ and missing the taste of adequate perform-
> ance, comes down to the level of that which is left to it to know and do, and perforce
> takes an interest in a cabined and cramped experience.... An interest in the formal
> apprehension of symbols and in their memorized reproduction becomes in many pupils a
> substitute for the original and vital interest in reality... (Dewey, "The Child and the
> Curriculum," p. 108-109).

Before we ask what reasonable alternative exists to the standard academic and vocational curricula, one further consequence of funneling students into them must be mentioned. The curricular patterns of students closely coincide with their socioeconomic and racial backgrounds. Students bound for college in the academic curriculum predominantly come from the middle classes; students in general and vocational curricula come largely from low income and minority groups.* The former group, with promise in its future, comes to feel that hard work, obedience, promptness, and persistence will eventually lead to success. Students in the latter group, not sure of even getting a job and often lacking successful role models, come to feel powerlessness in their own fate, and often adopt attitudes ranging from quiet resignation to open rebellion (Coleman, 1966, pp. 319-320).

Since the curriculum patterns typical in comprehensive secondary schools cause students increasingly to associate only with others *like themselves,* the mental, moral, and social attitudes they form are reinforced by their peers. Thus the separation of students along lines which correspond to racial or socioeconomic status helps to maintain narrow and unrealistic attitudes in all students. The result widens the gulf between social classes and racial groups, hampers social mobility, and increasingly reduces mutual understanding. People separated from one another in this way have little sympathy for one another's problems, and little inclination to seek cooperative and mutually beneficial solutions. Such attitudes create and perpetuate slums and suburbs, and support wars whose tragic consequences for others are not seen at first hand.

A NEW APPROACH

The curriculum is usually taken to denote the content of instruction to which all school students should be exposed. It has been argued above that it is unwise to maintain separate curricula for separate groups of students. It has also been argued that a curriculum that is impersonal is not learned at all, only memorized. But we may still ask, is there

---

*Many studies show evidence of this. See, for example, Frank Cordasco, The Puerto Rican child in the American school. Congressional Record, Reprint 3: 195 (October 19, 1965).

some curriculum content so fundamental that *all* students should learn it? Literacy, of course, is an essential, but is there anything else? While theorists have spent much effort in trying to identify indispensable bodies of knowledge and skills, we might well abandon this search, for it regularly turns up content which is both debatable and obsolescent. Instead, we might attend—as Dewey advised—to content which is germane to problems confronting democratic social life. We cannot depend solely on experts to solve all *these* problems, for the outcome depends on what *all* the people do about them:

> The things which are socially most fundamental, that is, which have to do with the experiences in which the widest groups share, are the essentials. The things which represent the needs of specialized groups and technical pursuits are secondary. There is truth in the saying that education must first be human and only after that professional. But those who utter the saying frequently have in mind in the term human only a highly specialized class: the class of learned men who preserve the classic traditions of the past. They forget that material is humanized in the degree in which it connects with the common interests of men as men (Dewey, 1916, p. 225).

And, it might be added, with the common interests of children as children.

We have already seen that a preselected and relatively fixed set of studies fails to meet the needs and interests of students, and thereby confounds efforts to make it a functioning part of their experience. A curriculum so foreign creates the need for a variety of techniques, rewards, and threats, which are lumped together under the somewhat misleading term "methods." To avoid the artificialities that result, it is clear that the concept of *a* curriculum, or of finite curricula, must be abandoned altogether. In its place, in order to teach the "essentials" of which Dewey wrote, must be put topics and issues which meet both individual and more broadly social standards of relevance. These topics will vary in different classrooms and at different times, but they will serve as the focal point around which information and skill can be gathered. "A curriculum," Dewey wrote, "which acknowledges the social responsibilities of education must present situations where problems are relevant to the problems of living together, and where observation and information are calculated to develop social insight and interest" (Dewey, 1916, p. 226).

In today's highly rule-bound, bureaucratized schools, teachers practice "methods" of "getting across" selected bodies of knowledge and skills. Students, expected to do their "own" work, are cut off from fruitful interchange with one another, and are subject to the decisions, directions, and evaluations of their teachers, who themselves become mere appendages to the curriculum. Thus kept in their classrooms in a state of perpetual social and intellectual immaturity, students become accustomed to looking elsewhere for learnings that are valuable.

But the problem of curriculum cannot be solved simply by finding another one—some new, more up-to-date set of studies. Rather, the entire atmosphere of schooling must be reconceived. For the arid and sterile climate that is now so typical, substitute a school which is itself a genuine community made up of people different enough from one another to be able to learn from each other:

> In place of a school set apart from life as a place for learning lessons, we have a miniature social group in which study and growth are incidents of present shared experience. Playgrounds, shops, workrooms, laboratories not only direct the natural active tendencies of youth, but they involve intercourse, communication, and cooperation—all extending the perception of connections (Dewey, 1916, p. 416).

Participation in such a community makes the development of social sensitivity and insight functional rather than merely verbal. Teachers and other adults in such a learning community become learners themselves. But they are more than that, for their experience enables them to initiate and guide activities, and to help young people make their own evaluations. But they come armed with no curriculum to which all must be exposed.

That is half the story. The other half is to recover the connection between young people and their natural and social environment. Schools have driven a wedge between children and the world outside by extending the age of compulsory schooling, lengthening the school day and the school year, and assigning homework which serves as a constant reminder of school even when the child isn't there. This hothouse cultivation of the young has produced a generation of men and women full of schooling but insensitive to the social, economic, and political complexities of their own troubled society.

As long as young people are sheltered from the world, they will come to believe that "present day concerns are sordid and unworthy of attention" (Dewey, 1916, p. 417). Such attitudes may be a comfort to adults who have an interest in keeping things as they are, but they cannot satisfy anyone seriously concerned with education rather than mere habituation. Thus, however congenial the community becomes *within* the school, it is the responsibility of educators to introduce the young to the world outside. Not simply as observers, studiously taking notes like little hairless sociologists, but as participants—as workers in hospitals, sanitariums, storefronts, schools, vacant lots, reclamation areas, and the thousand other places where help is needed.

Curriculum reform, then, means giving up the ideal of a fixed set of academic studies good for all students. Instead, it means transforming the school into a genuine community, and joining that deliberately educative community with the world outside. People learn through interaction with that world, and the most significant part of it is the other people in it, even though they may not always be physically present. The truth of this, and the obvious failure of separately conceived and independently established curricula and teaching methods, suggest the value of enabling schools to function not only as models of community life, but also as active agents in the creation of far wider and more broadly public communities.

REFERENCES

Coleman, James S., et al.: Equality of Educational Opportunity. Washington, D.C., U.S. Department of Health, Education, and Welfare, Office of Education, 1966.

Dewey, John: The child and the curriculum. *In* Dworkin, Martin (ed.): Dewey on Education. New York, Teachers College Press, 1959.

Dewey, John: Democracy and Education. New York, Macmillan, 1916.

Dewey, John: The school and society. *In* Dworkin, Martin (ed.): Dewey on Education. New York, Teachers College Press, 1959.

Goodman, Paul: Why go to school? *The New Republic,* 1963; reprinted in Sexton, P.C. (ed.): Readings on the School in Society. Englewood Cliffs, N.J., Prentice-Hall, 1967.

2 roads and highways, learning and schools: alternatives in education

Ivan Illich
Dennis Sullivan

A good way to begin this discussion of alternatives to school is by thinking about the difference between a road and a highway. Roads are public utilities used for communication. The decision to build a road is a bold act of faith in the value of human interchange. Roads mean trade and travel, an exchange of fabrics and metals, the sharing of artistic patterns and technical devices. Roads connect.

The modern superhighway, on the other hand, is a specialized, exclusive accessory of the private automobile, without which it would make no sense. To build auto-paths which endure speeds both unsafe and impractical is absurd except from the viewpoint of the auto manufacturer. And in fact, it is the carmaker who is the architect of the highway.

Automobile manufacturers produce not only cars, but also the demand for cars. They sell the desire to control a machine and to race at high speeds in luxurious comfort, as well as the fantasy at the end of the road. As a result, they also sell souped-up engines, air-conditioning, safety belts, and exhaust controls. In addition to these list-price items, the driver must also pay for advertising and marketing, fuel, maintenance and parts, and insurance, as well as less tangible costs such as loss of time, temper, and breathable air in traffic-congested cities. The entire society, drivers and nondrivers alike, pays for polluted air and noise, and suffers the absence of an adequate system of public transportation.

Today, every poor country spends local taxes and scarce foreign exchange building highways which can be used only by the privileged minority of car owners. With each new investment in highway construction, the poor are further isolated. Yet, with each new highway, the desire for a private car increases.

The only way a Latin American country could shift from a transporation system based on velocity and individual comfort to a system planned for fluidity and destination would be to stop building highways and to expand the existing network of roads adequate for high-axle trucks. A necessary corollary would be strict legal limitations on imported vehicles. Practically speaking, the private car would have to be eliminated in favor of a sturdy, all-purpose vehicle with a built-in speed limit of perhaps 20 mph. Such a vehicle does not exist: it would have to be invented by creative modern technology to restore an "old fashioned" institution—roads.

A highway system, then, makes sense only if the private car makes sense. In like manner, the school system makes sense only if learning is really the result of curricular teaching. If, on the other hand, learning results from meaningful relationships with persons and things, then effective roadways connecting persons with things and other persons would serve learning better than do schools.

Highways do not serve the need of man to move from one place to another, except accidentally. The essence of a highway is its service to the automobile industry. Highways belong to a cluster of institutions defined by the elaboration of a product which serves its stated purpose badly. The cumulative cost of the cluster, both economic and social, is staggering.

Man loses control when his institutions do not serve him but define his needs and their satisfaction. This abdication of responsibility is costly in every sense. Once we accept the identification of transportation and the private car, we accept the huge expenses of the automobile and all its accessories. The identification of education and schooling is far more expensive financially, psychologically, and socially.

The car is successful because men have been sold on speed. Schools are successful because men have been sold on measuring and packaging their own development. "Education" has come to mean passage through an elaborate ritual wherein success can be measured against a scale common to all.

The school ritual is central to the maintenance of a society dedicated to constant consumption. In school we learn to consume packaged learning in the form of curriculum. Like other modern consumer products, the curriculum is scientifically designed and marketed, becoming ever more flexible in order to satisfy the greatest variety in taste. The curriculum, again typically, is always going out of date, so there is always a demand for the latest model.

As long as only a small group of exhibitionists wants to drive automobiles, society does not suffer much from their idiosyncrasies. When everyone begins to define his transportation needs in terms of a car, however, some portion of the society gets priced out of the institution which monopolizes the resources needed to provide transportation. Everyone feels entitled to that which is by its nature exclusive. No alternative is allowed to exist, and those who most need an alternative are those who most desire the existing arrangement.

Schools become fatal when they are made universally obligatory. Those who do not make it or who drop out not only feel inferior, but are also deprived of all the social and economic benefits dependent on success in the school ritual. There is simply no other way.

Institutions make themselves exclusive by the design of their basic product. Private cars come with deluxe accessories. It is take it all or leave it all—from seat cushions to oil fields and the depletion allowance, from stereo tape decks to poisoned air and highway casualties. Schools, too, are complex packages. As with cars, the frills are eliminated only with difficulty and the basic package is impenetrable. Today, most people in the world are legally bound to attend school for six years, and no country fails to make inordinate investments in higher education. The resulting distortion is grotesque, as the university graduate represents an investment as much as a thousand times greater than the median citizen, and large numbers of people are automatically made criminal by the impossibility of obeying compulsory education laws.

Schools are, in fact, far more discriminatory than highways. The bridge and highway systems are paid for partially, or sometimes even principally, by tolls and gasoline taxes extracted from drivers. Schools are, on the other hand, a perfect system of regressive taxation, in which the privileged graduate rides the back of the entire paying public. The underconsumption of highway mileage is not nearly as costly as the underconsumption of schooling. The man who does not own a car in Los Angeles may be almost immobilized, but if membership in a car pool will get him to work, he can get and hold a job. The school dropout has no alternate route. The suburbanite with his new Galaxie and his country cousin who drives a beat-up jalopy get the same basic use out of the speedway, even though one man's car is valued at thirty times the other's. Contemporary society evaluates a man's education much more rigidly, in terms of the number of years completed and the costliness of the schools attended. And participation in school is by forced draft. The law compels no one to drive, whereas it obliges everyone to go to school.

School belongs to a set of manipulative institutions which sets the tone of the times. All these institutions tend to develop effects contrary to their aims as the scope of their operations increases. This boomerang effect is clearest in the case of the military: the higher the body count of dead Vietnamese, the more enemies the United States has around the world. Social institutions use their therapeutic image to mask the same effect. Jails increase both the quantity and the quality of criminals; in fact, they often create them from mere nonconformists. Mental hospitals, nursing homes, and orphan asylums do much the same thing. All these institutions acquire members by commitment or by a system of selective service. They pursue social goals by forcing individuals to comply with the behavior patterns they set. Once a person is drafted into one of these manipulative institutions, he finds it almost impossible to get out, at least psychologically. There is always something more that can be done to him.

The task of institutional change is to free ourselves from institutions which do things for us and to create institutions which allow us to do things for ourselves. We must reject those institutions which exist for the sake of simultaneously producing both a product and a demand for a product, whether the product is called learning, health, or Chevrolet. All these institutions cost too much, since they must increase fringe benefits in order to keep their product in demand, until fringe items become central. They must manipulate, since free men would not stand for a world where poverty programs produce more poor, computerized warfare produces more enemies, technical assistance produces more underdevelopment, and schools produce more dropouts. The search for alternatives necessitates a shift—an about-face—in institutional style.

Desirable alternatives to discriminatory and degrading schooling will resemble a telephone exchange more than any existing educational institution. Yet such alternatives do not represent a leap into the unknown. The elimination of highways leads to a return to roads, this in turn requires, as we stated earlier, the invention of vehicles which do not exist. In the case of education, it is a matter of returning to the most natural ways of learning, but here also, today's technology must be used to make a return possible. Return is also, however, advance. Roads have never been universal and neither has education. Today, roads *could* be universal, and so too could the presently betrayed promise of equal educational opportunity be fulfilled.

The planning of desirable alternatives to school must not begin with the question, "What should a person learn?" but with the question, "What kinds of things and people might learners want to contact in order to learn?" Such a change in the nature of educational planning places great confidence in individuals, since it leaves them with all the initiative and responsibility for their own learning. This is a very hopeful position. But hope can be regained only by hoping, and hope has been almost completely replaced in today's world by the always more frustrated expectations of the benevolent remedies offered by monopolistic institutions.

Roads lost their liberating character when they became highways. Educational institutions will be liberating only when they do not pretend to produce education.

Consider the telephone exchange as an example of an institution which unites people with maximum ease and minimum censorship. The exchange is completely client initiated and controlled—both caller and receiver have the option of hanging up whenever they wish. Though telephone lines facilitate communication, they do not dictate the message. This does not mean that the telephone system cannot be abused; it does mean that it is not the nature of a telephone system to rule on its own success beyond the mere fact of established contact. To overcome existing problems in establishing contact would not require a change in its nature. The telephone system is relatively cheap, since it does not have to be sold by an elaborate advertising and marketing process. Bell advertises mostly to make her customers forget bad service.

What sort of resources does a learner need? Resources can be divided into things and persons. Persons can be divided further into those who can do something the learner wants to do, those who share his interest in learning this or that, and those who have more experience than he and wish to share it. The question can also be seen by looking at the distinction between information and critical response. Information can be stored in things and in persons. Access to things happens at the bidding of the learner, but access to informants requires the other's consent. Criticism can also be twofold: it can come from peers or elders. Peers can be colleagues with whom to raise a question, companions for playful and enjoyable reading or walking, and challengers at any type of game. Elders can be consultants on what skill to learn, which method to use, what company to seek at a given moment, or they can be guides to the right questions to be raised among peers.

There seem, then, to be four basic categories of physical and human resources, access to which must be relatively easy if a man is to learn what he wants to learn—things, skill models, peers, and elders (or teachers). Alternative educational institutions would be networks which maximize access to these resources. In this paper, these networks are described in the briefest fashion, without reference to various problems which could be handled in a fuller discussion.

THINGS (DIRECTORY OF EDUCATIONAL OBJECTS)

The man-made environment has become as inscrutable as were the forces of nature for the primitive. At the same time, schools monopolize specifically educational materials, making them into specialized tools for educators and inflating their cost by forcing them to simulate either environments or teachers. Simple educational objects have been expensively packaged by the knowledge industry. De-schooling, then, means making the general physical environment accessible and removing the sacred aura from those learning resources which have been reduced to teaching instruments.

In the sacred space of the classroom, the student uses the map, the laboratory, the paintbrush, and other artifacts only when the curriculum tells him to do so. Even the great classics become part of "sophomore year" instead of marking a new turn in a person's life. Just as the church removes objects from the profane world by having a priest bless them, so school takes materials out of everyday use by labeling them as educational tools whose use must be administered by certified teachers.

The money now spent on the sacred paraphernalia of the school ritual should be freed to provide all citizens with greater access to the real life of the city. Roads should be made safe for children to walk on. Special tax incentives should be granted to those who employ children between the ages of 8 and 14 for a couple of hours each day. We should return to the tradition of the bar-mitzvah, permitting a boy of 12 to become a man fully responsible for his participation in the life of the community.

Modern junk defies educational tinkering. Children used to take apart cars and radios. Now, mechanics with specialized manuals charge exorbitant fees to fix gadget-ridden automobiles, and a disassembled transistor radio is ready for the garbage heap. Other things and places have also become impenetrable, not only because they are private, but also because they are considered the special domain of professionals and therefore, dangerous to the uninitiated. The de-schooling of educational artifacts requires attention to the accessibility and educational value of all artifacts and processes.

Private cars should be banned from Manhattan. Every other cross-street should be closed to automotive traffic and parking forbidden everywhere. In a city opened up to people, teaching materials which are now locked up in storehouses and laboratories could be dispersed into independently operated storefronts. There would be tool shops, libraries, laboratories, and gaming rooms. Photographic labs and offset presses would support the flourishing of neighborhood newspapers. At one corner, the city dweller would find a store lined with viewing booths for closed circuit television, and at the next he would find another featuring office equipment for use and repair. Jukeboxes, with music suited to the taste of all types and all generations, would be commonplace. Museum outlets would circulate exhibits of originals and prints.

Such a network would not, of itself, change the fact that many of the world's things are controlled by business and government, but opening access to those objects which are not so controlled might remind men of their birthright to the world.

SKILL EXCHANGE

In principle, skill teachers should never be scarce. If a skill is in demand, there must be someone around who has acquired the skill and can demonstrate it. Yet converging self-interests conspire to stop the sharing of skills. The man with the skill profits from its scarcity, not from its reproduction. The teacher who specializes in transmitting the skill profits from the artisan's unwillingness to launch his own apprentice into the field. The public is indoctrinated to believe that skills are valuable and reliable only if they are the result of formal schooling. The job market depends on making skills scarce and on keeping them scarce, either by proscribing their unauthorized use or by making things which can be operated and repaired only by those who have access to tools or information which is difficult to acquire.

Schools produce shortages of skilled persons. They insist on packaging skill learning into a curriculum on an all-or-nothing basis so that only those who can afford the whole can get any part. Most fundamentally, they insist on the certification of all teachers. To guarantee access to an effective exchange of skills, we need legislation which generalizes academic freedom. The right to teach any skill should come under the protection of freedom of speech. Once restrictions on teaching are removed, they will quickly be removed from learning as well.

The skill teacher needs some inducement to grant his services to a pupil. One way to channel public funds to noncertified teachers would be to create skill centers with free public access. Payment could be made after passing a public test. Another approach would be to give certain groups within the population educational currency good for attendance at skill centers where other clients would have to pay commercial rates. A much more radical approach would be to create a bank for skill exchange. Each citizen would be given a basic credit with which to acquire fundamental skills. Beyond that minimum, further access would go to those who earn it by teaching. Only those who have taught others for an equivalent amount of time would have a claim on the time of more advanced teachers. Parents could also earn skill-credit for their children.

The freedom of the skill exchange would have to be guaranteed by two kinds of law. The first would forbid discrimination in hiring, voting, or admission to centers of learning on the basis of previous attendance at some curriculum. This would not exclude specific tests of competence but it would remove the present absurd privileges enjoyed by those persons who have learned skills with the largest expenditure of public funds. Additional legislation would have to limit those skills for which testing and certification would be admissible. Otherwise, it would be easy to surreptitiously reintroduce complex batteries of tests as a means of social selection. By allowing only the operation of specific machines or systems to be tested, objectivity would not be too hard to achieve.

PEER MATCH

Skill exchange is founded on complementary interests: one man has a skill, another wants to acquire it. A third learning network would be based on identity of interests. Most education now takes the form of common inquiry among peers. In school, peer groups officially form around the goals of teachers. A desirable educational system would let each person specify the activity for which he seeks a peer.

This network would be the simplest to operate. The user would identify himself by name and address and describe the activity he wishes to pursue. In its most rudimentary form, client and computer could communicate by return mail. In big cities, typewriter terminals could provide instantaneous responses. A complement to the computer could be a network of bulletin boards and classified newspaper ads, listing the activities for which the computer could not produce a match. No names would be given. Interested readers would then introduce their names into the system.

Peer matching of this type is merely a reaffirmation of the right to free assembly. This is one of many rights men have given over to manipulative institutions which make certain forms of assembly obligatory. Instead of waiting to be drafted into the company of others, men must take the initiative of calling one another together for the sake of original action.

PROFESSIONAL EDUCATORS

As men gain new choices because of easier access to learning resources, their willingness to seek guidance and leadership will increase. As they are liberated from manipulation by others, they learn to profit from the discipline others have acquired. The end of school would mean the end of schoolteachers. It would not mean a lack of demand for men of practical wisdom for sustaining the newcomer on his educational adventure.

Such a shift from institutionalized teaching to self-activated learning would require professionals who design and operate the kinds of networks described above. Only a few such people would be needed, but they would have to be gifted with a genius for staying out of other people's way. People who are excluded from administrative responsibility in school could easily do this kind of job. Many of those who do have a place in school, however, would not do at all. Student discipline, public relations, hiring, supervising, and firing of teachers would have neither place nor counterpart in the networks. Neither would curriculum-making, textbook purchasing, the maintenance of grounds and facilities, nor the supervision of interscholastic athletic competition. Babysitting, lesson planning, and record keeping, which now take up so much of a teacher's time, would also be superfluous talents for network architects.

Pedagogues would also find new prestige in humbler roles. They would be the priest-like officials of the public schools no longer but would be free to provide the individualized instruction which is now preached but seldom practiced. In a world of educational networks, each learner would be on his own, but the wise student would periodically seek advice about possible methods, help over difficult hurdles, and assistance in setting new goals. Even now, this is the kind of service which earns a teacher the most gratitude from his pupils.

Once it is no longer necessary for all teachers to pose as experts, those who have a real claim to superior insight and experience can once again become masters. The availability of the "elders" will depend on their willingness to let others associate with them, either in retracing the steps of development already accomplished or in present exploration on the borderline of the known.

The relationship of master and disciple is not restricted to intellectual discipline. It has its counterpart in the arts, physics, religion, psychoanalysis, and pedagogy. It fits mountain climbing, silverwork, politics, cabinet making, and personnel administration. What is always common to this relation is the awareness on the part of master and disciple alike that it is a privilege that is literally priceless.

These categories, though exclusive, are not absolute. A skill model for instance, can easily be a master as well. He need not be, however, and that is the point. There are more skill models available than skill masters, and they are fully adequate for most demands. They do not now teach for many reasons, most of which can be traced to the existence of schools. From a group of peers, both skill model-skill learner and master-disciple situations can emerge, but unless the distinctions are made, people will lose the initiative to get together on their own.

The four networks are nothing new. A good case could be made for the proposition that most learning now occurs because of the informal versions that already exist. But if schools were eliminated (both physically and psychologically), the channels could be opened to far more people. We now learn from things and people outside school, but we are taught to depreciate such learning and even to avoid it. Those who have greater barriers between them and the educational environment are kept from living in it and detoured through the impoverished atmosphere of school. It is time to beat new paths.

the case for organic-prophetic education

3

Glenn W. Hawkes

We are being increasingly bombarded with warnings that our schools are failing, that they are joyless and inhumane places, and that we had better do something about them. Few of us, I'm sure, would deny the validity of the concern. But the problem may not be merely that we are not meeting our goals or that we are not adequately individualizing our goals, as so many of these warnings imply. From my vantage point our educational system is doing a frighteningly effective job in meeting its goals—that is, teaching young Americans to view the world (and themselves) through the glasses of the various academic disciplines that, taken together, constitute the major frame of reference for education.

If there is one overriding social-educational problem today, it is this general frame of reference—the *Weltanschauung,* the paradigm—which enshrines various forms of analysis and discovery based upon the assumptions and methodology of subject-matter disciplines. We are enveloped by a general frame of reference which is devoid of the mystical, tragic, spiritual, personal, playful, hopeful, and historical dimensions of existence. The system of thought or paradigm through which we function is mechanistic and predictive; it denies the cultural and historical evolution of a Whole Being, of which each individual human is but a small, though important, creative part.

Most of us "moderns" function through a paradigm which is inorganic, or nonorganic, a *Weltanschauung* which promotes the 17th century Newtonian notion of the world-universe as a great *machine.* We may use the term body when referring to the human species or to all living things, yet we see ourselves as apart from, rather than a part of, a larger, living body; we do not think of our heartbeat as flowing in and from the pulsations of the entire planet and beyond. Thus we carry in our nervous system the idea of facing, confronting, or conquering nature, as if nature were *out there.* There is a little sign on the wall of the children's library in a local school which says it all:

600
Applied Science
How Do I Control Nature?

Thermodynamics can tell us that there is no such thing as a true closed system, sufficient in and of itself—except, perhaps, the entire universe—but we find this hard to understand, and, like physicists, we make "simplifying assumptions" so we can pretend there are closed systems. And then we proceed to accept such systems as absolute truths, forgetting that we were the ones who closed the systems. We have even gone so far as to construe the individual self as a closed system, and we are almost incapable of grasping "self" (and the broader manifestation of individualism, or individuation) as an historical-evolutionary phenomenon, interwoven in an unfolding Whole.

This essay is based on an organic paradigm, which defines the Body of Life—the Living Whole—as a macrocosm in which and through which each individual can be grasped as an ontogenetic particle in a phylogenetic wave of unfolding life, all within a larger, mysterious Whole. The present, mechanistic paradigm, shaped by the world-machine images of Newtonian "law," minimizes the meaning of those organic *things* that we like to do most: singing, dancing, eating, making love, sleeping, and so on. From the vantage point of organic integration, those same concerns emerge as central, vital to social and educational reforms. The organic viewpoint is prophetic, not predictive; the individual is located within history, not analysing it from without. Rather than starting with assumptions about laws which supposedly exist regardless of our presence, this paradigm begins with assumptions rooted in life processes that are both internal and external to our presence.

Ours is an age of analysis, largely because of the success of our educational system. Generally speaking, our educational process has produced the greatest number (and largest percentage) of analytical minds the world has ever known. We're so analytical that we even analyze our capacities to analyze. In the words of Noel F. McInnis:

> Our present teaching methods, at all levels of education, tend to foster a common intellectual skill: thinking the world to pieces. This skill is very essential. . . .
> But thinking the world to pieces is only half of understanding. We relate to our world in the manner that we perceive it. Having been taught mostly to *think* the world to pieces, it is any wonder that we are now tearing it to pieces? . . .
> The planet's program is one of synthesizing parts into wholes. Our educational program, and thus the subsequent behavior of those who go through it, is largely one of reducing wholes into parts . . . . if we continue our almost exclusive preoccupation with reducing wholes into parts, in our studies and tinkerings with the planet, *we* may become one of the parts not saved.
> We are desperately in need of perceiving the planet as a *gestalt* (McInnis, 1971).

Recent trends in education suggest that the newest object-subject of analysis is none other than the self. In the name of *integration,* educators teach children how to take the self apart. The "humanistic movement," stressing the affective and emotional dimensions of learning rather than the cognitive, grows out of theoretical research and findings in psychology. This movement may seem to be the ultimate in education, and *it is certainly founded on good motives;* however, in some respects it is actually perpetuating the worst kinds of fragmentation and self-estrangement. Thus today the analytical tools of humanistic psychology can supply us with three new domains (cognitive, affective, and psychomotor), and a whole host of subselves to go with Freud's id, ego, and super-ego.

The general message is clear. We learn by dividing up what we study into little pieces, analyzing each piece to try to understand it, and *then,* perhaps, putting them together again. We're supposed to do the same with *the self.* Certainly we can take apart an automobile, learn something about it, and put the pieces together again. But what about Humpty-Dumpty? What about people?

My point here is not that analysis is intrinsically damaging. Nor am I trying to minimize the importance of scientific discovery and understanding. Analysis, prediction, and disciplinary knowledge are vital, essential to human survival. My point is that a purely analytical view of world and self is a terrifying dead end, for by its own definition, *it* excludes the mystical, tragic, spiritual, personal, playful, organic, and prophetic dimensions of life.

We have succeeded, not failed, in teaching the young about the world in which we live, the world as viewed through the structures, processes, and organizing principles of the various disciplines of thought. Students today understand with analytical accuracy all of the *best* predictions which grow out of the *best* scientific disciplines. Yet, as Ernst Cassirer put it, we have a "wealth of facts," but hardly a "wealth of thoughts." Until we can move beyond our fragmented analyses, "we shall remain lost in a mass of discon-nected and disintegrated data which seem to lack all conceptual unity" (Cassirer, 1944, p. 22).

Therein lies the problem, the paradigm problem, which is so much interwoven with the way we view world and self that we can hardly appreciate the possibility of knowing the universe, and thus being in the universe, in any other way. Even the process of appreciation is itself one of "looking at," and "understanding" (standing under), rather than being in.

T. S. Eliot's "The Love Song of J. Alfred Prufrock" tells about an extremely well-educated man. He could analyze his world and himself with the greatest precision. He could view any given problem or issue from any number of scientific vantage points. He was tutored in "language arts," and was "cultured." He could also understand himself, his inner needs, his motives, and his frustrations (he would have had no trouble inventing techniques and games for "finding the self"). But he was afraid, lost in his own power to understand almost everything and believe in almost nothing. He was lost in a vision of the world of parts, and at best made wild guesses about any Whole or Wholes. He was virtually paralyzed in the face of action:

> Do I dare
> Disturb the universe?
> In a minute there is time
> For decisions and revisions which a minute will reverse.

Eliot wrote those lines in 1917. In 1970 a sensitive, senior high school student in Amherst, Massachusetts, wrote the following lines:

> Why bother?, nothing can be done.
> We know what's wrong, but as soon
> as you do one thing, someone will
> do something else—it's too late!

"It's too late!" Perhaps it is too late. Through careful analysis, through the best evidence that can be gathered from any number of scientific disciplines, we seem headed pell mell toward a most impressive oblivion. Again, no group is more aware of this than *the best* students. The Harvard biologist, George Wald, put it this way: "I know what is bothering the students. I think that what we are up against is a generation that is by no means sure it has a future" (*Boston Globe,* March 8, 1969).

Indeed, our analytical tools do point *toward* our impending doom, but let us not delude ourselves with the idea that we have a corner on the truth. There are many traditions of knowing the world, many of them quite different from our sanctified analysis. One of these, arising from the roots of Western history, is the prophetic tradition. Some of that tradition is alive and well, even in our age of predictive analysis. Prophecy does not rule out the findings of scientific inquiry; rather, it embraces them within a more general orientation—that of human hope, love, and freedom. It does not start from an assumption of self-separate-from-history; rather, it starts with the assumption of self-in-and-helping-to-determine-history.

The analytic orientation toward knowledge is predictive, rather than prophetic. Our orientation toward knowledge is just that, an orientation *toward,* whereby that which is to be understood is assumed to be apart from the dynamics of understanding, apart from the person seeking to understand. Our most cherished method of analysis is the scientific method, in which the scientist takes himself out of reality to make his predictions, and finds himself looking "toward" reality. For to be scientific (or objective—the terms are sometimes interchangeable) is to be separate from reality. A properly scientific article is written in the third person, totally divorcing the author from the results. Yet by this separation and the reduction of the sense of *in*volvement, we find that the world becomes a collection of objects, which in turn can be made into subjects, while we ourselves become more and more objective (objectified, that is, objects). (One of the fuzzy-minded claims of modern thinking is that the only reality is that which is real to each individual— that the only reality is subjective, a reality of the self. This absurd notion has developed as an overreaction to the equally absurd notion of the self-as-separate-from the dynamics of reality.) One thing stands out: the separate self, looking toward or at something or someone—with no sense of being-a-part-of, or perhaps with a feeling of being all-powerful—*but* in either case, feeling separate, cut-off, a-part-from the dynamics of history. So, whether by elevating the scientific disciplines or by elevating the separate self, today the *individual* is hard pressed to define his or her presence in the universe as a presence interwoven with a larger framework of Life.

This phenomenon is nowhere more evident than in the most progressive curriculum of our schools. In teaching the "new history," for example, we have lost the sense of being part of an unfolding drama of human life. Students are learning how to analyze, how to practice the methodology of the historical discipline. (Students are taught that all historical thought is relative except relativity itself, which is assumed to be an absolute.) Thus, historians and educators, most of whom already have an understanding of their role in history, have developed a curriculum that no longer presents students with a narrative of events, circumstances, and human actions of which their own lives are a part. Rather, students are asked to become apprentice historians of a particular type—the scientific, analytical type that looks at history through a microscope (a microscope, I should add, that many historians themselves do not use to find their own vision of historical meaning and their place within it). The students may indeed produce the required analysis, or some semblance thereof, that is good enough to pass the course. That doesn't mean they'll like it or benefit from it. Indeed, they may simply be confused.

In many respects the "new history" is a sophisticated response to the challenges which change and complexity have thrust upon us. The Enlightenment conceptions of human reason and historical progress (as found in many nineteenth century textbooks, and in some of our own day) have been correctly assessed and rejected by most of today's educators. Valid questions have been raised about the traditional treatment of American history, with its chauvinism, racism, and other evils.

The result, though, has been a subtle but far-reaching overreaction that leads many away from historical consciousness itself. This is manifested in our "instant lives" (from instant coffee to instant credit), and involves a certain "nowness" about everything. At one level this extends our nervous system in a McLuhanesque manner, facilitating a realistic conception of the "global village"; yet at another level it creates the illusion of living in a self-contained capsule of time, without causal connection to time past or time future. We are witnessing in the growth of the "now" generation a decline in the capacity to grasp events as unique phenomena in an unfolding of causal-linear sequences. We are witnessing a loss of the past. With the past lost, we cannot define reality so as to grasp the future with any kind of positive affirmation. Our best *predictions* tell us that our most important goals for the future are all negative—stop pollution, stop racism, stop killing, and so on—and who can live long without a positive sense of the future? We develop *futuristics* as a new discipline; scores of scenarios are flashed before our eyes, and we are told that we have a new disease, "future shock." Yet in all of this there is little organic-prophetic sense of our being in history, and of our possessing any long-range positive goals.

> The possession of long-range goals, regarded as central to one's personal existence, distinguishes the human-being from the animal, the adult from the child, and in many cases the healthy personality from the sick (Allport, 1955).

Perhaps we have unconsciously planted in the heart of the new curricula the seeds of massive social insanity.

And what of the question of happiness? We have adopted an economic model. MORE is the reward for effort. More! More knowledge, more money, more power, more goods and services, more education, more *self-fulfillment,* more of what N. O. Brown called the "shellfishness of selfishness." Happiness is *not* construed through concepts of service or sacrifice to some greater whole or greater good. The paradigm does not permit that kind of "sentimentality"—it's *passé.*

One of the most terrifying effects of the fragmentation-objectification-simple-location syndrome is the feeling that since we are somehow outside of history, others must be making it. We are powerless, but "they" are not. "They" are responsible for what's wrong with the world, and we don't know what to do to stop them. The blue-ribbon commissions established to find out exactly who "they" were, concluded (with Pogo) that "they" were "us": we were the makers of our own historical tragedy. But these findings did little to stop the paranoids in their urgent search for "they." The whole world, the universe, is a "we," but somehow we've lost touch with that primitive, animistic orientation. The hard and social sciences are more sophisticated than to believe the universe is alive!

A student may indeed learn to recognize H_2O and $NaCl$ and the nature of that lime which constitutes a seashell. But that same student (who may be an 800 college board achiever) may never know that his or her own body is organically made of the same H_2O and $NaCl$ and lime that have been analyzed so nicely in the laboratory; that same student may never know that the chalk used to write the formula on the blackboard is made also of the same lime. And what about the mystery of all of this, and the powers and mystery of human consciousness? It is all certainly better restricted to the moralizing of ministers, priests, rabbis, Eastern mystics, and crank educators.

Unlike prediction, organic prophecy demands an orientation *in* a living reality, not toward a static one or one in which "more" is the only future. Reality is thus living as both subject and object, with certain living manifestations, you and I, consciously choosing the ways in which we will manifest ourselves in future space and time. Prophecy is *self-group* fulfilling—there is a sense of partaking in the making of one's self and one's world, *and* in the larger Body of Life.

J. Alfred Prufrock could not embrace prophecy:

> I am no prophet—and here's no great matter;
> I have seen the moment of my greatness flicker,
> And I have seen the eternal Footman hold my coat,
>   and snicker,
> And in short, I was afraid.

If we embrace prophecy, we see prediction as a form of prophetic fulfillment in which we have removed ourselves from participating in life's unfolding. The predictive orientation is dangerous, fulfilling people only when they have emptied themselves, when they are objective objects. It is in this direction, by way of the academic disciplines, and most recently by way of the *self education* movement, that our elaborate system of formal education has propelled us into a world of powers and forces which, although we can analyze and understand ("stand under"), we cannot participate in, but at best can only simulate in a sterile, laboratory setting.

In a world of J. Alfred Prufrocks, we are looking *at* ourselves, our past, and our future; we are able to analyze, even synthesize on occasion, but we are unable to act because we have lost the power of prophecy. Our world is fragmented and objectified, instant and immediate to the extent that we are unable to identify ourselves as agents with both a past and a future; we have lost our prophetic dimension. During the past two decades we have ended a particular love affair with historical space and time. The danger is not in this fact per se, but rather in the possibility that we may convince ourselves that we do not need a new love affair. [Ironically, of all those seeking to reform education today, no group is more organically prophetic than black Americans. Unlike many mainstream reformers, those who seek to promote a black perspective have reinterpreted and reembraced historical meaning in a manner which defines individual freedom within a grand and dramatic unfolding of the whole. Beginning with African roots (which are in all probability the roots of the whole species), this perspective construes each individual in relation to a prophetic future, where, as Martin Luther King said, "No man will be free until all men are free."] *A major educational task is before us: to stimulate in ourselves a positive sense of our involvement in historical events and circumstances at the very time when events and circumstances have conspired to deprive us of our will to invent in an organic-prophetic manner.*

REFERENCES

Author's note: The following list of books and articles suggests some of the sources which might be pursued by those readers wishing to explore the organic-prophetic paradigm in greater depth.

Allport, Gordon: Becoming: Basic Considerations for a Psychology of Personality. New Haven, Yale University Press, 1955.
Brown, Norman O.: Life Against Death: The Psycho-Analytical Meaning of History. Middletown, Conn., Wesleyan University Press, 1959.
Buber, Martin: The Prophetic Faith. New York, Harper and Row, 1960.
Cassirer, Ernst: An Essay on Man. New Haven, Yale University Press, 1944.
De Unamuno, Miguel: The Tragic Sense of Life, J. E. Crawford Flitch, trans. New York, Dover, 1921.
Eiseley, Loren: The Immense Journey. New York, Random House, 1957.
Eliade, Mircea: Cosmos and History: The Myth of the Eternal Return, Willard Trask, trans. New York, Harper and Row, 1959 (Torchbook).
Eliot, T. S.: The Complete Poems and Plays. New York, Harcourt, Brace, Jovanovitch, 1952.
Fromm, Erich: Escape From Freedom. New York, Holt, Rinehart, and Winston, 1941.
Hawkes, Glenn W., and Trask, David F.: The case for prophetic history. World Order, 4:No. 4, Summer, 1970.
Heisenberg, Werner: Physics and Philosophy: The Revolution in Modern Science. New York, Harper and Row, 1962 (Torchbook).
Jaspers, Karl: The Origin and Goal of History, Michael Bullock, trans. New Haven, Yale University Press, 1953.
Kuhn, Thomas: The Structure of Scientific Revolutions. Chicago, University of Chicago Press, 1962.
McHale, John: The Future of the Future. New York, Braziller, 1969.
McInnis, Noel F.: Teach the earth whole. 1971. Available from Center for Curriculum Design, 823 Foster St., Evanston, Ill., 60204.
Montagu, Ashley: On Being Human. New York, Hawthorn Books, 1950.

Sinnott, Edmund W.: The Biology of the Spirit. New York, 1955.
Teilhard de Chardin, Pierre: The Phenomenon of Man. Bernard Wall, trans. New York, Harper and Row, 1959.
Theobald, Robert: An Alternative Future for America Two. Chicago, Swallow Press, 1968.

4 in defense of the liberal arts

Mortimer Smith

The liberal arts are what education is all about. To find them in need of defense indicates the present perilous state of education. They embody the heritage of transmissible knowledge, beginning, as far as formal educational institutions are concerned, at the lowest level with the rudiments of reading, writing, and figuring, and going on to the refinements of knowledge at the high school, college, and graduate levels. The role of the liberal arts is an essential, connective one. "Historic continuity with the past," said Mr. Justice Holmes, "is not a duty, it is only a necessity." It is the liberal arts that provide this necessary historic continuity.

We have reached the point in our debates about education when it is seriously argued that the liberal arts, the traditional subject-matter of education, are irrelevant, at least in the school and college setting. It is not always clear what function educational institutions are to serve in the future, but one gathers that they may survive as therapeutic agencies or as social-action organizations making war on middle-class values. In any case, schools and colleges, it is maintained, must not be narrowly concerned with literacy and the development of intelligence. It is significant that the critics of education whose views are now most widely heard are not those who believe the schools are failing to teach the basic subjects adequately—*they* are yesterday's critics. Today's critics do not have "knowledge" and "academic achievement" emblazoned on their banners but "feeling," "informality," and "freedom." Not intellect but emotion, not the cognitive aspects of education but the affective, are now the concerns of the critics. (If the new wave of critics had a little more of Holmes' sense of historic continuity they might feel the ghosts of William Heard Kilpatrick and the progressives of fifty years ago peering over their shoulders.)

As an unreconstructed critic of the older dispensation I propose to make an argument for the primacy of the liberal arts at all levels of education. These arts are not an adornment for an aristocracy but a necessity for democrats. I believe there is a body of basic knowledge that is essential for all students, although it is obvious that not all will travel the road of education at the same pace nor will all reach the farthest outposts. Let me preface the statement of my case by saying that I am concerned primarily with content. I am not wedded to any absolute method in teaching, any untouchable technique, except that I would maintain that authority, structure, and measurement are intrinsic components of the teaching function. It seems to me that the new critics—the romantic radicals or revolutionaries—have devised a doctrine of false opposites in pitting freedom, sympathy, and joy against authority, structure, and discipline. The good teacher who organizes his subject, asserts his authority in teaching it, and holds his students to some standard of achievement is not the unfeeling and unloving monster he is so often painted by the romantics. If he respects his students and feels a responsibility for teaching them something he will concentrate on his role of teacher and leave to others the roles of pal, confessor, or psychiatric counselor.

It may at first glance seem rather fanciful to include among the liberal arts what goes on, or should go on, in the early grades. The skills of reading, writing, and figuring might be considered simply rudimentary "tools" that will be needed later in pursuing more sophisticated subjects, but they are more than this. One of the better insights of the early progressives in education was that childhood should not be considered a temporary way station on the road to adulthood—the child exists *now* and his schooling should provide nourishment for the present as well as the future. What I have in mind when I speak of liberal arts in the early grades has been mentioned in a somewhat different context by George Santayana. He said that education might be regarded as a means toward a livelihood, with reading, writing, and arithmetic considered necessary for tradesmen, but he then went on to say: "But when they [reading, writing, and arithmetic] are taught and learned only for that purpose, they are diverted from their natural use, which is to merge into liberal arts and be intrinsically liberal, since they employ and liberate the spirit. They should be taught, even in their elements, as arts, as games, as occasions for delight; and then their utility in the business world will not prevent them from remaining essentially liberal" (Santayana, 1951, p. 424). Just as the basic skills are more than vocational assets for workmen, so they are more than rudimentary learning-tools for the very young. They can be true occasions for delight for children, as well as promises for the remote future.

What are the basic liberal arts of the elementary curriculum? It goes without saying that reading is the basis for all the arts—or *does* it go without saying? Some McLuhan-esque philosophers denigrate the usefulness of reading; some look to a future when the book will be obsolete. Norman Miller, chairman of the Department of Education at Beaver College, says: "For the vast majority of citizens reading may be totally unnecessary except in school. Printed matter is not the only way of ingesting information. In fact, it may be one of the least effective media today" (Miller, 1968, p. 62). Wayne O'Neil, professor of linguistics at the Massachusetts Institute of Technology, makes this startling observation: "Being able to read is not a necessary part of being civilized or uncivilized, useful or useless" (O'Neil, 1970, p. 260). In discussing "what reading is good for," Neil Postman, professor of education and English at New York University, doubts its vocational utility: "The number of jobs that require reading skill much beyond what teachers call a 'fifth-grade level' is probably quite small and scarcely justifies the massive, compulsory, unrelenting reading programs that characterize most schools" (p. 246).

This sort of antireading and antibook sentiment is, one hopes, a vision, or nightmare, for the future. Reading has not yet been abandoned in our schools although one could wish it better taught. Everyone, from United States commissioners of education on down, agrees that we are failing in the teaching of the essential first skill. Assuming for the moment, however, that we can hurdle the obstacle of reading retardation, let us return to the question of defining the basic liberal arts for the elementary school. "Elementary education," says Mark Van Doren, "can do nothing better for a child than store his memory with things deserving to be there. . . . They should be good things; indeed, they should be the best things, and all children should possess them" (Van Doren, 1943. p. 94).

In the field of reading, these things should be something better than the sanitary adventures of Dick and Jane and their dog Spot. Nowhere does the doctrine of "relevancy" do more harm than in the selection of the kinds of things children are to

read. To assume that they are interested only in what is current and familiar is a pedagogic error of the first magnitude, for children desire to rise above their environment. The
constructive power of a transcending imagination is surely one of the precious possessions
of childhood. All youngsters ought to read, or have read to them, classical myths, fairy
tales, poetry, and many of the children's books that have become classics. The list of such
works of the imagination may vary with individual teachers, but the basis of selection
must be the necessity of providing some elements of a common heritage. Teachers with
real spine, who are indifferent to current winds of doctrine and fashion, will even ask
their pupils to memorize some of the great works of the imagination. Again, individual
taste will decide what these are to be, but they might include the Gettysburg Address, the
preamble to the Constitution and the opening paragraphs of the Declaration, some
passages from the Bible, Shakespeare, Milton, and to come down a few pegs, Longfellow,
Whittier, and Poe.

This early exposure to the first-rate rather than the shoddy will train the child's ear
for the sounds and nuances and beauties of his language. In addition—and this will reveal
just how antediluvian I am—some effort should be made to teach the grammatical forms of
English. Prescriptive grammar need not be taught in the manner of the pedant or of the
rigid and unimaginative purist. The English language is a living and changing thing but, as
I have said elsewhere, there must be some semblance of a path through the jungle if we
are not to become hopelessly entangled in the wild linguistic underbrush. Many school
teachers, says Douglas Bush, seem to have been nourished on the doctrine that whatever
is used in English is right: "Thus, if two truck-drivers collide, the ensuing verbal
exchanges are good English because they are appropriate to the social situation" (Bush,
1961). I would like to see English usage taught in such a manner that students can
recognize the differences between the prose styles of John F. Kennedy and Dwight D.
Eisenhower and know which is superior.

What other "deserving" things, to use Mark Van Doren's term again—what other sets
of symbols and sets of facts—should store the memory of the child? Arithmetic and
elementary science, algebra and more advanced science and Latin if the school includes
seventh and eighth grades. Geography, in the sense of ordered knowledge of the physical
world—the location of states, countries, and cities. History—not the hybrid social studies,
but history taught as narrative. I agree with Samuel Eliot Morison when he says that
young people will learn more about the American Revolution by reading a classic
narrative of the event "than by attempting to penetrate the mental processes of George
III, George Washington, the House of Commons, and the Continental Congress through
successive 'bundles' of source material" (Morison, 1964, p. 44). History for children must
be taught as an art, not as a behavioral science. In the elementary school we must not
turn social studies into bull sessions in which children parrot the opinions of adults about
apartheid policy in South Africa or other vast and complex problems. Dean Rusk once
remarked that he doubted that the Kashmir question could be solved in the elementary
school.

I stress elementary education at such length because it is the foundation rock of the
whole educational edifice. To return to a point made earlier, elementary education is
important as preparation, as a means of providing the child with the framework of
fundamental knowledge he will need for all later learning; it is also important for his
present life, for providing him with Santayana's "occasions for delight." It is a unique
combination of practical skills and liberal arts, and when successful, it has a liberalizing
effect on the recipient of it.

Inspired by the ideas of the early progressives and sometimes by perversions of those ideas, elementary education in the last forty years or so has not been a notable success. What one might expect to be the byproducts of learning ("good citizenship," "emotional stability," "development of the personality") have too often become a substitute for learning itself. As I hinted earlier, I wish that the critics who now offer "revolutionary" solutions for the lower schools could see that many of our troubles stem from the fact that in the past we adopted strikingly similar "revolutionary" solutions. Today's "relevance" is only yesterday's "needs" in disguise.

A program of the liberal arts at the high school level would include history (ancient, European, American); English (composition and literature); languages (classical and modern); sciences (biology, chemistry, physics, mathematics); and music and art. Who takes precisely what from this catalogue of studies is a matter for the decision of the individual and the school, but every student should have a balanced program drawn from the two roads to knowledge, that of analysis (the sciences) and that of intuition or imagination (the humanities). And this program should be for all students, whatever their social background and academic ability. Any system that provides a curriculum for the intellectually elite that is radically different from the curriculum for those presumably destined to be hewers of wood and drawers of water is a travesty of education. At the Bronx High School of Science or at New Trier the methods and the pace may be different from those used at Comprehensive High, but there must be a common devotion to the ideal of the liberal arts. "To assume," says Francis Keppel, "that academic subjects are merely an obstacle course for college admission is to miss the whole point of liberal education. It is in the great tradition of our secondary schools that history and geography, literature and science and mathematics be made available to all of our citizens, that they have merit in and of themselves" (Keppel, 1965, p. 6).

Education at the college level continues to be based on the liberal arts, but now these arts have been transformed. They are one thing for the child, another for the teenager, still another for young adults. Now they are no longer rudimentary skills or aggregations of fact. They have become scientific and scholarly disciplines which the student uses for his own organization of ideas and knowledge, disciplines which he can employ also for dealing with the larger issues of meaning and value. Now the design begins to reveal itself; now, in Emerson's words from "The American Scholar," the student finds that "the world lies no longer a dull miscellany and lumber-room, but has form and order."

Alas, in our time the college student's world doesn't always have form and order. The college, like the high school, suffers from the sins of omission committed by the lower school, especially the failure to teach elementary literacy. It is difficult to grasp ideas if you have not yet grasped the rudiments of reading and writing. The late William Riley Parker, Professor of English at Indiana University, wrote: "Without the least exaggeration I can say that, as a teacher of graduate students in English, there is not a single assumption I can make about either knowledge or skill already acquired. I cannot assume a single book read by everyone in class; I cannot assume knowledge of the simplest Bible story or myth or fairy tale or piece of children's literature" (Parker, 1961). And here is Jacques Barzun of Columbia University on a related theme: "Speaking for myself, I can say that among the highly selected graduate students in the university where I teach I find about one in ten who needs coaching in the elements of literacy—spelling, punctuation, sentence structure, and diction. And these students cannot write because they cannot read" (Barzun, 1961, p. xiii).

Parker and Barzun were writing about the situation some years ago but there is good evidence for believing that the conditions they described have improved very little, if any. Many of the new critics of education are frank to say that formal learning may not be the first obligation of the school. An interesting example of this reasoning is provided by some remarks of Theodore R. Sizer, when he was Dean of the Harvard Graduate School of Education. Speaking at a conference on testing problems, Dean Sizer said that "we need not only 'intelligence quotients' but also 'bigotry quotients'—and remedial work for youngsters who are excessively bigoted. I am not being facetious here. The moral development of a youngster—his sense of justice and his use of justice—is perhaps more important than his cognitive development. This country has suffered excessively already from intellectually able but morally stunted people" (Sizer, 1970, p. 57).

Even for those of us who are against bigotry, this is a difficult statement to accept, especially in its blithe compartmentalizing of cognitive and moral development. One would suppose that learning—cognitive development—would be of help in dispelling the ignorance that causes bigotry. And I for one believe morally stunted people are much more apt to be found among the ignorant than among the intellectually able. Dean Sizer's argument is somewhat in the spirit of a remark made by a National Education Association official, quoted in a Washington newspaper, who, after saying that too much stress could be put on reading at the expense of creativity, then delivered this *non sequitur:* "Hitler was a good reader."

One result of the contemporary worship of youth-culture has been to downgrade the authority both of the teacher and of knowledge. The very nature of the educational process would suggest that the young person is in a position subordinate to the teacher, who presumably knows more than he does, and to the knowledge that he has not yet absorbed. But when we encourage the young to believe that everyone is intellectually equal, that one man's opinion is as good as the next man's, we must play down the disciplines of knowledge lest it be shown that the young are in fact ignorant. Some students, of course, welcome the opportunity to escape the rigorous course, preferring talk-fests to anything that requires listening, reading, and note-taking. Such share-the-ignorance sessions can be particularly depressing when, as so often happens, they involve essentially bright young people who have never grasped the truth of John Dewey's remark that "the achievements of the past provide the only means at command for understanding the present." Where the youth-culture is taken seriously, the liberal arts fade into the background, replaced by nonsubjects. A writer in the weekly magazine *New York,* reported a few years ago that a 17 year old freshman at the Columbia, Maryland, campus of Antioch took three courses—sexology, cartoons, and novel writing (O'Reilly, 1970).

Warnings of the dire consequences of the neglect of the liberal arts have been with us for a long time. Two of the most famous of these warnings were made over fifty years ago, when H. G. Wells told us that we were in a race between education and catastrophe, and Alfred North Whitehead said in *The Aims of Education:* "In the conditions of modern life, the rule is absolute. The race which does not value trained intelligence is doomed." I do not see how even the most casual observer of the scene around us can escape the conclusion that we edge closer and closer to catastrophe as we value trained intelligence less and less. Our times are marked by a retreat from reason, deification of feeling, preoccupation with irrational violence. Our public life, even our arts, are full of people who possess that most deadly combination of qualities, passion and ignorance.

I do not want to convey the idea by what I have written to this point that all we need do for salvation is to turn on a tap marked "the liberal arts" and education will be revived by the pure and living waters. The romantic anarchists are right when they deplore some of the things done in the past in the name of the liberal arts. It is easy to show that some teachers and some schools mismanage authority, subject matter, and discipline in ways that violate the humane ends of education. At the college level, professorial scholarship sometimes degenerates into a pedantry that can kill the love of learning and repel the students. Examples of pedantry abound, especially among professors of English. I sometimes think that the worst fate that can befall a dead writer is to have his remains worked over by a professor of English in an American college. Most such biographies are exercises in library browsing, usually containing more information about the victim than most readers care to know, the significant all jumbled up with the insignificant, and the whole convoyed by the inevitable and interminable footnotes.

Yes, the liberal arts have their weaknesses, and the temple is often guarded by those who are unworthy. The solution is not to follow the revolutionaries who want us to tear down the edifice and raise a new educational institution in which everything is unstructured and the teachers are the emotional buddies of their students. Our problem in education arises from two circumstances: a native American reluctance to build a philosophical framework for action and a perennial shortage of natural teachers. We have a desperate need for training schools that can turn nonteachers into teachers equipped with a firm philosophical and pedagogical base for teaching the liberal arts. Our salvation lies in the production of these good teachers, who can then devise their own innovations. At the moment we are operating in reverse order: devising the innovative machines without regard to the competence of the operators.

Throughout this essay I have tried to identify, in passing, some of the advantages that accrue to those who have been fortunate enough to be exposed to the liberal arts. I would like to sum up these advantages, to suggest what are the residual goods after twelve or fourteen, or more, years of formal education, or of self-education, for that matter. What is the end purpose of this long apprenticeship in listening, writing, reading, thinking?

Different people supply different answers to the question of the ultimate aims of education. Some believe that education is to be valued chiefly in terms of marketable skills, as something that is useful in vocational or professional training. Some regard it as an instrument of social mobility, enabling one to move from a lower social class to a higher. Some think of it as a sort of preservative, a means of buttressing entrenched social and economic viewpoints. Still others—and this is largely a contemporary phenomenon— find it a convenience in constructing a new, and presumably, braver social order. A few years ago when we were frightened by Russian accomplishments in science, many saw education as an instrument for advancing the national interest.

The liberal arts may have relevance to all these things, but I see their chief value in personal rather than in direct social terms. The aim of an education in the liberal arts is to produce good individuals who in the aggregate will improve society, but the process of education remains an intensely personal and private experience.

At its best, training in the liberal arts results in self-knowledge and self-realization, in developing intelligence that can be applied to solving, or at least understanding, personal and social problems. Such an education is truly liberating because it frees an individual from some of the prejudices and irrationalities that beset the uneducated. He can decide personal, social, and political issues by other means than tossing a coin or following TV pundits or the latest polls.

Such an education, firmly grounded on the record of man's history on earth, is not apt to result in notions of man's perfectability or in the illusion that social institutions can be made perfect. Reasonable people will see that men and institutions can be changed and modified; they will also see that men and institutions have natural flaws that are roadblocks on the path to utopia. Much of our social turmoil today stems from the faith of the naive and half-educated that social arrangements can be made perfect. When they discover that they are not being made perfect, nor likely to be made perfect, they react, often violently, in anger and disgust. Their cry of "Revolution now, or else!" prevents more reasonable souls from getting on with the task of realizable reform.

In a time when group action is the fashion, a liberal education can provide some inner resources so that a person may learn to live with himself. The power of concentration these days is becoming more and more difficult for some people, including educated people. Father Chevesta, missionary and explorer, who was one of the great authorities on the various tribes of pygmies, said that the dwarfs of the Congo completely lacked this power of concentration: "They are always absorbed by external impressions, whose continual change prevents them from withdrawing into themselves, which is the indispensable condition of any learning" (see Ortega y Gasset, 1957, p. 22). A proper education enables a person to withdraw into himself and to enjoy himself when he gets there. I think it was Pascal who said that education enables one to sit alone in a room and not perish.

Another thing I think a proper education can teach is compassion. Such an education shows us, through that vast panorama of struggle, courage, despair, good and evil, villainy and sainthood, which is mankind's record on earth, that we share a common humanity and a common destiny. Pity and compassion, one for another, arise out of knowledge and understanding, not out of ignorance and lack of comprehension.

I would mention one final advantage that accrues to those who have been educated in the liberal arts. In my judgment, one of the contributing factors in the disorganization and disorientation of youth is that in the present educational scheme of things there is a notable absence of form, of structure, of systematic inquiry and methodology. The liberal arts—the disciplines of English, mathematics, science, history, and foreign languages—are bodies of knowledge that have their own form and structure. Those who have experienced these arts in school and college are less likely than the uninitiated to permit aimlessness, lack of order, and chaos to determine their style of life, either on the personal or community level.

A fitting end to this defense of the liberal arts is this quotation from the text of Sir Kenneth Clark's remarkable series of television programs on the history of civilization:

> I hold a number of beliefs that have been repudiated by the liveliest intellects of our time. I believe order is better than chaos, creation better than destruction. I prefer gentleness to violence, forgiveness to vendetta. On the whole I think that knowledge is preferable to ignorance, and I am sure that human sympathy is more valuable than ideology. I believe that in spite of the recent triumphs of science, men haven't changed much in the last two thousand years; and in consequence we could still try to learn from history. History is ourselves. I also hold one or two beliefs that are more difficult to put shortly. For example, I believe in courtesy, the ritual by which we avoid hurting other people's feelings by satisfying our own egos. And I think we should remember that we are part of a great whole, which for convenience we call nature. All living things are our brothers and sisters. Above all, I believe in the God-given genius of certain individuals, and I value a society that makes their existence possible (Clark, 1969, pp. 346-347).

That is the credo of a civilized man. It can stand also as an eloquent statement of what the liberal arts are all about.

REFERENCES

Barzun, Jacques: Tomorrow's Illiterates. Boston, Atlantic-Little, Brown, & Co., 1961.

Bush, Douglas: Literary scholarship and criticism. *Liberal Education, 47:* 207-228, 1961.

Clark, Kenneth: Civilization. New York, Harper & Row, 1969.

Keppel, Francis: How should we educate the deprived child? *Occasional Paper No. 7,* Washington, D.C., Council for Basic Education, 1965.

Miller, Norman: Reading: Isn't It Really the Teacher? Danville, Ill., Interstate Printer and Publishers, Inc., 1968.

Morison, Samuel Eliot: Vistas of History. New York, Alfred A. Knopf, 1964.

O'Neil, Wayne, and Postman, Neil: Illiteracy in America: A special issue of the *Harvard Educational Review, 40:* No. 2, May, 1970.

O'Reilly, Jane: Notes on the new paralysis. *New York,* October 26, 1970.

Ortega y Gasset, Jose: Man and People. New York, W. W. Norton & Co., 1957.

Parker, William Riley: *NEA Journal,* November, 1961.

Santayana, George: Dominations and Powers. New York, Charles Scribner's Sons, 1951.

Sizer, Theodore R.: Education, U.S.A., 1970.

Van Doren, Mark: Liberal Education. New York, Henry Holt and Co., 1943.

5 the arts — neglected resources in education

Daniel C. Jordan

Can anyone reasonably argue that the arts hold second place to any other discipline of learning in heightening perception, sharpening the intellect, and strengthening conviction? The answer is they cannot because the qualities that the arts offer to educators are unique; they exist in no other discipline.

William Schuman, President,
Lincoln Center for the Performing Arts
New York City

Large numbers of critics, experts and laymen alike, have examined education in recent years and found it gravely ill. The specifics vary, but the general message is the same. Education is sick because it has lost sight of its legitimate purpose, which Jacques Maritain describes as "a conquest of internal and spiritual freedom to be achieved by the individual person, or, in other words, a liberation through knowledge and wisdom, goodwill, and love."

Schools today are not places where the human spirit is exalted and liberated. Why? There are no doubt a thousand reasons—structural, economic, bureaucratic, social, cultural, and political—each of which could generate the kinds of complexities and entanglements that guarantee paralysis. Yet, at least part of the solution seems somewhat obvious. First, one must ask the right question: what things have exalted and liberated the human spirit? Along with religion, the arts figure prominently as the highest expression of man's capabilities and among the noblest embodiments of his spirit. They mediate "visions of possibility," and when these visions connect with our consciousness, we burst with vitality and can achieve an awareness culminating in an exploration of our own potentialities leading to the exaltation and liberation of the human spirit.

In *The Aims of Education,* Whitehead says that education should be the guidance of the individual toward a comprehension of the art of life. He specifies the "art of life" as "the most complete achievement of varied activity expressing the potentials of that living creature in the face of its actual environment. This completeness of achievement involves an artistic sense (a sense of values), subordinating the lower to the higher possibilities of the indivisible personality" (Whitehead, 1950, p. 10). Progress toward that conception of education is highly unlikely without a heavy reliance on the arts and participation in the creative activities they can inspire. Without them the heart of education is empty and the school experience will be sterile and alienating.

A NEW EDUCATIONAL ROLE FOR THE ARTS

Despite such visions, the arts are feebly represented in the curriculum of our public schools. Whenever there is a budget squeeze, the arts, being lowest on the list of educational priorities, are always sacrificed. However, often the "sacrifice" is small. Some would even say we're better off without the arts as currently taught in school. The thirty or forty minutes of music on Tuesday afternoons every other week and the once- or twice-weekly art classes (in which a large part of the time is used for taking materials out and cleaning up the mess afterwards) usually have no connection with the student finding any "vision of possibilities" for himself. They would be better classed as anaesthetic than as aesthetic experiences. To millions of youngsters in American schools, art is only for hanging on the wall, choirs are for a Christmas concert, and the band is for football games. Dance and movement are at best physical education and the theatre is the junior and senior class play. The domination of this performance-product orientation makes art activities a bore for most and exciting for only a very few.

The role we have given the arts in education is one that contributes to sterility and alienation, and leaves their full worth unknown. Clearly we need to reconceptualize this role. The arts should be at the core of the curriculum and the heart of the educational experience rather than teetering precariously on the edge, longed for unconsciously by everyone, understood by few, and ignored or unsupported by most administrators.

ANTIDOTE FOR ALIENATION

When one is forced to do things of little value unconnected with critical needs and constructive purposes, irrelevance prevails and alienation begins. Hegel (who invented the term) used it to describe the psychological state of human beings whose faculties are no longer involved in natural processes. What is natural about screwing the same kind of bolt on the same kind of wheel for hours on end? What is natural about learning the correct grammatical structure of a sentence so you can write it down in a workbook for a grade? This noninvolvement of human faculties in natural processes induces what Herbert Read calls "the atrophy of sensibility" (Read, 1967, p. 21)—anaesthesia. If one is psychologically anaesthetized, how can he feel alive? His dead nerves can be penetrated only by violence in some form: violent action, violent sounds, violent colors. Such violence destroys all inclination to seek out what Jakob Burckhardt called the "mystery of beauty" (Burckhardt, 1943, p. 179). When we stop seeking out the mystery of beauty, we lose sight of the most beautiful mystery of all—the "possibilities" and potentialities within each of us that we must relate to in certain ways if they are to become manifest. Releasing these potentialities is, in essence, what education is all about (for a description of an educational model based on this definition, see Jordan and Streets, 1973). When one loses touch with them, impetus for growth wanes, vitality is replaced by apathy, and life loses its luster; a state of alienation prevails.

Wherever racism, crime, and mental illness are found, "identity problems" of the individuals involved will be found as well. These identity problems are almost always related to loss of contact with one's potentialities. Harry Williams, an English theologian, wrote recently that:

> The root of sin . . . is the identification of my total self with the self of which I am aware. Two consequences follow from this identification. First of all, the known self is

too narrow to be satisfying to me and is felt in its constriction to be intolerable. Secondly, the unknown self which, for mistaken reasons of security, I keep imprisoned and in exile, becomes a savage as a result, like a man locked for life in a dark dungeon, seeking nobody (Williams, 1963, p. 95).

Thus, if one denies the unknown potentialities within, the self that is presented to the world will be a mask—a false self. And, as Erich Fromm points out, this false self is deliberately created to gain approval, much like a marketed product.

The present curriculum of traditional school systems, the methods employed by teachers, and the system of grading contribute to the manufacture of the false self and the consequent loss of identity—that is, to alienation. The endless exercise of storing information only for retrieval for tests, rather than for application to real life situations (i.e., "natural processes" of living and working), is devastating. Ironically, it is those aspects of the curriculum that are most abstracted from natural processes that receive the greatest emphasis in our public school systems. The student who is creative or courageous enough to protest being subjected to such intolerable circumstances will be punished in one way or another, making it even more difficult for him to overcome his alienation.

The arts are grossly neglected as vital educational resources. Yet they can play a most critical role in the release of human potentialities and the consequent reduction of alienation and its concomitant pathology—social and personal. Practicing the arts can aid in this direction because the artist, professional or amateur, is always facing the unknown. He is perpetually seeking to express these potentialities, and the very process keeps him in intimate contact with them.

THE ARTS AND EARLY CHILDHOOD EDUCATION

Such investigators as Hess, Bloom, Piaget, Fowler, and Deutsch have accumulated an impressive amount of evidence that the most critical periods in human development occur between birth and age five. These findings have stimulated great interest in early childhood education and started a trend toward providing formal educational experiences for preschool age children.

The planning of such experiences must begin from an understanding of the developmental needs of children as they progress through different maturational stages. Selecting experiences from the arts to fill these needs seems particularly appropriate. For instance, psychomotor development is critical in the child's development because so many other things depend upon competence in that area. Yet, in many preschool and elementary school programs, very little systematically planned movement and dance take place. Instead, children are permitted to run around, waving their arms and kicking their feet at random. The natural tendency of young children to be in motion could be better utilized by a special curriculum in movement and dance, which could do much more than help develop muscular control and coordination.

Children begin to grasp a sense of space and time only by using their own body as a reference point. The ability to locate sounds in space, to concentrate visually on an object, and to estimate the distance between themselves and objects located visually, are all ultimately determined by the interplay between sensory input (originating from stimuli outside the body) and input from the kinesthetic senses (originating from within the body). Without the organization of space and time, almost all subsequent learning tasks will be extremely difficult. Thus it is surprising to find practically no movement and dance in the curriculum during the early years, and very little music on a regular basis.

Music can aid in the development of a child's ability to organize time, since rhythm itself is a way of organizing time. Furthermore, music helps directly in developing auditory acuity: discrimination of pitch, timber and amplitude—all of which are useful in a wide variety of subsequent learning tasks. Working with music involves grasping the basic notions of frequency, relativity, time, variation on a given pattern or theme, velocity, and a number of other dynamic concepts useful in organizing and understanding a wide variety of phenomena which the child will later encounter. The visual arts help to develop visual acuity: color discrimination, saturation discrimination, hand-eye coordination, and other perceptual and expressive skills that have a direct bearing upon learning to read and write. Sculpture develops the tactile senses in relationship to a growing capacity for the organization of space. In the theater arts, both ideas and feelings can be organized and tried out in dramatic form—literally a means of experimenting with new roles under relatively safe and nonthreatening circumstances. Such experience relates directly to the problems which inevitably arise in forming one's identity.

The practice of the arts relates to development of cognitive, affective, and moral competencies as well. Concept formation and utilization, symbolic transformation, analysis, synthesis, and general language development are part of artistic experiences. Furthermore, it is difficult to dramatize a story, experience the rhythm of music through dance, and create a design by the arrangement of color without having high levels of emotional involvement. Engaging in such experiences in groups also assists social development and the emergence of moral competence.

Finally, it is practically impossible to be a passive spectator in such experiences. The arts invite active involvement, thereby demonstrating their power to help the child first discover his potentialities and then express them.

William Schuman, President of the Lincoln Center for the Performing Arts in New York City, has made the point that the reason the arts have suffered in education generally is because their nature has been misunderstood. He says:

> More often than not, the arts are generally considered as avenues for emotional expression and the artist, as a person who is able to express himself only in emotional terms. In consequence, educators have assigned to artists the emotional provinces of man, while the schools have been given the intellectual territory. This has created an illogical dichotomy in which training and perception in the arts are minimized and left largely to chance while practical instruction in the intellectual disciplines is a recognized responsibility. Our blindness to the importance of the arts means that half of man's potentiality is consigned to an educational vacuum (Schuman, 1968, p. 11).

This "illogical dichotomy" underlies the divorce of feeling from thinking, which is another aspect of the alienation syndrome. It is important that children begin their educational experiences free from the effects of that dichotomy. The arts provide a unique means for integrating thinking, feeling, and acting.

FOSTERING CREATIVITY

The passive assimilation of facts involves very little creativity. In fact, the American educational system's preoccupation with its current conception of grading creates a climate and method of instruction that punishes creativity. A novel response on the usual type of test given in public schools will probably be scored as wrong. Thurstone once observed that the creative person "wishes to see a new idea work" while the uncreative person, wishing to conserve what is, tends to approach a new idea in terms of "why it won't or can't work." Traditional classroom management techniques tend to reflect the latter orientation and thereby discourage creativity.

Furthermore, characteristics associated with creative children usually go unappreciated by teachers and administrators. Creative children frequently have their own time schedule, which doesn't fit in with the regular scheduling of classes. They are impulsive and at the same time certain and confident, characteristics which teachers are apt to perceive as impertinence. They are attracted to strangers, thereby upsetting conservative adults. Often they like periods of disorder and tolerate ambiguity with little discomfort. Having their own ways of doing things, they always challenge authorities who insist there is only one way, particularly when that way is different from the child's.

This last tendency often leads to conflict between creative children and the kinds of persons usually certified to teach in traditional public schools. Any child who continues to insist on being his true creative self is very likely to be seen as a trouble-maker. Frequently, a teacher's response to such a child will cause the child either to withdraw or strike out. If he withdraws and conforms, all will be well from the teacher's viewpoint. If he strikes out, he will be punished. In due course, he will become a liability to himself and will grow increasingly uncomfortable in the formal learning situation.

In investigating factors which constitute the structure of the intellect, Guilford discerned two basic intellective modes. One, which might be considered the noncreative mode, emphasizes retaining the known, learning what has already been determined, and conserving what already has been established. The creative mode involves a revision of the known, an exploration of undetermined things, and a construction of what might be (Guilford, 1956).

What aspects of the curriculum attract the creative child, adolescent, or adult? Is it grammar, spelling, or mathematics? Or is it expression through art media: dance, music, theatre, and the visual and plastic arts? The answer is obviously the latter area. This is not to say that math and grammar are uncreative and have no aesthetic of their own. But they are symbolic systems, whose transformations are determined by specific rules, which, if violated, produce "wrong" answers or conclusions. The arts, because they offer so many equally acceptable alternatives and so few "right" answers, invite a freer expression and require a different kind of evaluation or grading. Furthermore, those dedicated to teaching the arts usually are committed to free expression and have a natural distaste for the kind of evaluation which punishes or inhibits creativity.

What about curiosity, speculation, imagination, and intuition? They accompany creativity and often are under-valued and unappreciated by educators and administrators. Again, the traditional academic curriculum has less chance of strengthening these creative elements than do the arts (Gordon, 1961; Osborne, 1967; Torrance, 1962; Maslow, 1962; Anderson, 1959; Gowan, 1967).

INTEGRATING THE ARTS AND THE CURRICULUM

The successful definition of the role of the arts in education, as briefly outlined above, will depend on a number of factors. Among the most important of these are the manner in which the arts themselves are integrated and the method by which they are related to the rest of the curriculum. Currently in most public school systems, musicians don't know what the visual artists are doing; neither of them knows what the dancers are doing, and none of these have any connection with the theater arts program. Theater sometimes does provide an integrating force, since sets have to be painted, music is sometimes employed, and occasionally there is need for a choreographer. But often even this does little good, and, in smaller school systems, theater arts usually do not exist at all.

There are several causes for this lack of integration. Teachers of the arts themselves have rarely experienced such integration. The idea of employing the arts to release human potential (rather than as just another way of turning out a product to grade) is also probably foreign to most. But even if these problems could be overcome, more time would have to be allotted for integration to take place on a regular basis.

The natural processes of life are not fragmented or compartmentalized the way knowledge in schools is divided into various disciplines, each of which is considered a separate field. The lack of integration within the curriculum itself and its lack of integration with life contribute to alienation. Thus the arts must be integrated with the rest of the academic curriculum before they can provide significant new resources.

The process of integration itself will necessitate a recognition of the importance of lateral transfer and divergent thinking—both sources of creative power. When faculty and students begin to think about the relationship of music to physics, biology, and history, for instance, new "visions of possibilities" are opened up. Lateral transfer—working with relationships across disciplines rather than within them—always produces new perspectives and insights. Such a transfer rests on acceptance of other disciplines as "kin" rather than as "foreigners." It rarely fails to mediate a creative achievement. There are many historically significant instances of what the kinship of lateral transfer will produce. Michael Polanyi eloquently expresses one of them in describing Pythagoras, who derived "the pleasing effect of a succession of musical notes from the integer ratio between the lengths of the chords struck in producing them. Sustained by this striking fact, the Pythagorean tradition maintained for centuries a musical appreciation of the mathematical laws controlling the celestial order" (Polanyi, 1958, p. 193).

Such cross-disciplinary appreciation can sustain the vitality of the educational enterprise because it can lead us to the threshold of new possibilities. Crises are generated when those "visions of possibilities" are punished, denied, or left to wither by the very institutions that should be encouraging them. Many such crises lie ahead for education in Western society. They will deepen swiftly if administrators, school committees, and educators continue to neglect the vital educational resource that the arts represent. "For educators not to grasp the vitality, the spirituality, and the intellectuality of art as central to an educated man is to ignore the measure by which our civilization will be judged" (Schuman, 1968, p. 13).

REFERENCES

Anderson, H. H. (ed.): Creativity and Its Cultivation. New York, Harper and Row, 1959.
Burckhardt, Jakob: Reflections on History. (Translated by Hottinger.) London, 1943.
Fromm, Erich: Alienation under capitalism. In Josephson, Eric, and Josephson, Mary (eds.): Man Alone: Alienation in Modern Society. New York, Dell Pub. Co., 1962.
Gordon, W. J. J.: Synectics. New York, Harper and Row, 1961.
Gowan, J. G., et al.: Creativity: Its Educational Implications. New York, Wiley, 1967.
Guilford, J. P.: The structure of intellect. Psychological Bulletin, 52, 267-293, 1956.
Jordan, Daniel C., and Streets, Donald T.: The ANISA Model: A new basis for educational planning. Young Children, 28, No. 5, 289-307, 1973.
Maslow, A. H.: Emotional blocks to creativity. In Parnes, S. J., and Harding H. S.: A Sourcebook for Creative Thinking. New York, Scribner, 1962.
Osborn, A. F.: Applied Imagination. New York, Scribner, 1967.

Polanyi, Michael: Personal Knowledge. Chicago, University of Chicago Press, 1958.
Read, Herbert: Art and Alienation: the Role of the Artist in Society. New York, Horizon Press, 1967.
Schuman, William: Cultivating student taste. *Today's Education, 57*: November, 1968.
Torrance, E. Paul: Guiding Creative Talent. Englewood Cliffs, N. J., Prentice-Hall, Inc., 1962.
Whitehead, Alfred North: The Aims of Education. London, Williams and Norgate, 1950.
Williams, Harry: Theology and self-awareness. *In* Vidler, A. R. (ed.): Soundings: Essays Concerning Christian Understanding. Cambridge, Cambridge University Press, 1963.

the role of 6
the educator in a
scientific world

Lord James of Rusholme

For the professional educator nothing is at once more flattering and more irritating than the frequency with which experts pass a whole succession of "bucks" to him. Whether it is a question of the supply of experts itself, or the right use of leisure, or the rise in juvenile delinquency—sooner or later the discussion ends with the phrase, "Ah, well, that's really a matter for education." Placing responsibility on the educational system in this way is something more than flattering or irritating, however—it is justified. If increased scientific knowledge is going to change the world in certain important ways, then the educational system must change, too, if it is to meet its new responsibilities.

The term educational system is, of course, very vague. Even as we normally use it, it includes institutions that range from the kindergarten to the research center. In a wider sense the family, the neighborhood, the methods of mass communication, and all the forces and pressures of society are educative in that they supply information, experiences, and attitudes to the young. But I shall ignore these and concentrate on the formal side of education.

Having made that reservation, let me try to map out the field I want to explore. The educator has, first, an obvious responsibility for the actual professional education he gives to the future specialist in science. Second, he has the duty to make the nonscientist aware of the contribution science is making and will make to the life of the individual and the community. Third, he is concerned with the very broad question of the general education of the scientist, with what Comenius called "that training in all that concerns their common humanity." Scientists, after all, are men and women who have to think and act within a framework of personal relationships and social obligation.

The first of these topics, the professional education of the scientist, presents what might be described as an insolvable but relatively straightforward problem—the "knowledge explosion." If we are to go on teaching a scientific subject in such a way that any of our students are to reach the boundaries of knowledge within a few years, we must examine and change our methods in the most ruthless way possible. Quite manifestly we

Adapted from a talk given at Caltech's 75th Anniversary Conference, Reprinted from *Scientific Progress and Human Values.* Published at the California Institute of Technology, 1967.

must use every conceivable device to save time in the retrieval and dissemination of information. But, much more importantly, we must scrutinize our syllabuses and methods of teaching with the utmost care to eliminate the purely factual and emphasize the fundamental, the general, and the creative.

Here we run into a major difficulty. The more we emphasize the underlying principles, the greater the intellectual demands we make upon our pupils. We must increasingly recognize the very great differences in mental endowments between them. Faced with this growing mountain of sheer knowledge, we must be more ready than we are to treat in quite different ways the individuals who can attain different heights upon it. The bulk of knowledge will only become manageable in so far as it is unified by broad, synthetic ideas, and it is precisely these ideas which are the most difficult for any but the best minds to originate or even to understand. The steps in the peak may be cut by reasonably gifted journeymen; it is ever more true that the peak itself will only be attained by the exceptional. It becomes, therefore, increasingly necessary for a society to be able to identify these exceptional synthetic minds capable of generalization and to possess exceptional institutions capable of educating them.

Having said something about the specialized education of the professional scientist, I can now approach the heart of my subject: Given the scientific revolution, what kind of general education can we give our students to help them understand the new world and meet its problems and its opportunities? In particular, what kind of education will enable them to make value judgments in a very rapidly changing material environment? Let me emphasize how great this revolution is by an example: The beginning teacher today is teaching children who will be adults in the year 2000. Their problems will not be our problems; their resources will not be our resources. In some ways, the framework of their moral and political judgments may well be utterly different. Not only will these pupils be men and women of 40 or 50 at that time, but the teacher himself will still be teaching.

The first conclusion that follows is obvious enough. In the days when the corpus of knowledge and the general fabric of society were fairly static, education was something that could reasonably be over with a degree or diploma of some kind. Today, it cannot. We must recognize the necessity of continuing adult education, both professional and nonprofessional, and in this attitude we in Britain lag far behind the United States.

But let us look beyond that specific technical point to the broad question of what a scientific revolution means in social and moral terms. We can take two or three examples, almost at random. The nature of politics was transformed for the educated by the invention of printing. The invention of the vacuum tube and the cathode ray tube transformed it yet more drastically, and for everyone. Without radio, a Hitler can appeal to a few thousand people at a time; with it, he can corrupt a nation. Without television, political confrontation can be at the level of the Lincoln-Douglas debates; with it, we are exposed to the dangers of a world made precarious by the statements of tired, dazzled men, stepping from airplanes, or the still greater dangers of one where the first require- ment of a statesman shall be a telegenic image. Again, the concentration of military and industrial power involved in the sheer cost of modern weapons and machines creates a new climate of political decision. An infallible contraceptive may relieve millions from the certainty of starvation; it may also entirely alter the sanctions for certain patterns of sexual behavior in civilized societies. The combined researches of geneticists, physicists, psychiatrists, and chemists will alter the context in which we make every kind of moral judgment. Such a rapidly changing environment imposes immensely heavy responsibilities on the general education of all our students. Yet such an education becomes increasingly more difficult to devise.

Compare the situation today with that of just over a century ago. It was possible then for the greatest of schoolmasters, Thomas Arnold of Rugby, to feel that he was preparing his pupils for the needs of society and the service of their fellow men by preaching to them on Sundays and seeing that on weekdays they were taught Latin, Greek, and ancient history, with a little mathematics from a teacher of inferior status and optional French from a visiting native.

Today, how is one to understand the modern world, let alone act in it, without some knowledge of subjects of which the curriculum of a century ago took no account—modern history and geography, modern languages and English and economics, and, above all, science? Yet, it was possible within living memory for one of the greatest of English schools to proclaim in its prospectus: "For those boys having no aptitude for classics or modern languages, a science course is provided."

The dilemma of education today is simply this: Whereas the growth of knowledge forces us to an ever greater professionalism and, hence, specialization, the demands on the breadth of information, responsibility, and awareness of the citizen of the world today press us to attempt an ever greater breadth in our education. I feel that I should like to be remembered as the discoverer of a law as simple as the law of conservation of mass but more unambiguously valid. It is called the law of conservation of the curriculum or, I should modestly hope, James's Law. It states that whenever you add anything fresh to the curriculum you must inevitably take something out, and state honestly what it is, and why it is being removed. Although modern techniques of teaching can sometimes save time, the essential dilemma remains: to prepare our students for the modern world we ought to teach them more things, but the growth of knowledge in each individual field makes it obligatory to teach them fewer. This is the essential paradox of general education.

One of the clearest demands of such an education is that no one should go out from our schools and universities utterly ignorant of any science at all. In England, at any rate, few educational platitudes have been so slow of acceptance. But we are all still very far from knowing *what* science a future lawyer or administrator should know to make his judgment more valid and his actions more rational.

We often seek to avoid this problem by saying that it is not factual knowledge that we want but sufficient exposure to science so that the nonscientist shall understand "how the scientist's mind works." Such an approach has something to be said for it, but it suffers from two difficulties. First, one cannot teach the scientific method, whatever that is, without teaching *about* something. Second, it is a mistake to maintain that a scientist's mind works in some quite different way from that of the historian or the economist—the fallacy underlying one of the most dangerous, if most publicized, heresies of our time, the two-culture theory.

Yet, we clearly cannot ignore this vital question altogether. We should make a more resolute attempt than we have done to define more precisely what *kind* of scientific knowledge the nonscientist wants to know and needs to know. We delude ourselves if we think that very elementary courses in our secondary schools are all that is required. What must follow are efforts at that most difficult kind of writing, really good popularization emphasizing the relevance of the particular field to social, political, and moral problems. Some excellent efforts have been made in this direction, particularly in the United States, but they must be continued and extended by some of our best minds.

If some kind of basic, general scientific education, even at a superficial level, is increasingly necessary, still more important is the nonscientific general education of the scientist—not that I subscribe to the view that proficiency in science is a condition requiring remedial treatment, whereas the study of nearly anything else is almost automatically broadening and humane. The prevalence of this attitude is revealed by a glance at the pages of any intellectual weekly. It is obviously assumed that the latest scholarly work on the fall of Byzantium or symbolist poetry is of interest to the educated man, whereas a new work on science is not. One of our major tasks is actually to convince people that an education centered on science is itself concerned with values, not only that it embodies a passionate belief in the value of truth, but that in the pursuit of scientific knowledge can be found the same impulses of creativity and the same pursuit of eternal order in the universe that characterizes the work of Piero or Mozart or Thucydides. At this highest level of experience, the springs of creation in every field rise in a common source. Nevertheless, it is easier for a run-of-the-mill scientist to omit altogether any acquaintance with the questions which enable him to make sound value judgments in the fields of aesthetic or social life than for some of his arts colleagues.

There are other reasons for believing that the general education of the scientist assumes ever greater importance as the years pass. First, there is the simple fact that scientists are increasing in number. Second, it is probable that they will increase not only in numbers but also in power. In a world increasingly dominated by science and technology, the politician or the social scientist has to depend on scientific knowledge for the answers to his questions and even for the realization that the questions exist. The scientist will almost certainly be recognized not simply as an answerer of questions; there will be, one hopes, a growing tendency for more scientists to move from the purely scientific field to positions of administrative and political power.

What kind of education, then, are we to give our scientists to equip them to be at home not only in their specialized fields but in those of moral, political, and social relationships? The often repeated demands for a compulsory broad general education have been, in my view, largely misconceived. The insistence, until recently, that every scientist or technologist entering the universities of Oxford and Cambridge should have an elementary knowledge of Latin was a particularly bizarre example of this misconception. Because we do not know what knowledge and what qualities we really desire our educated man to possess in the year 2000, we mistake the shadow for the substance and fall into the heresy that almost anything is broadening so long as it is not related to what the student really wants to do.

I believe that we are too much afraid of three words: relevance, specialization, and superficiality. By relevance I mean that since a student of science enjoys doing science, we must establish relationships between his science and the other things we teach him (a line of thought pursued by Sir Eric Ashby in his excellent book, *Technology and the Academics*). Second, it is of no avail to bemoan the growth of specialization. It is a necessity that is increasingly forced upon us. We will simply have to make more sure that from it spring some of the great values of any good higher education—the values of thinking hard, honestly, rigorously, and in depth about at least one field of learning.

Outside this hard core, our practices will be governed by the further conceptions that I include under the word superficiality: support, stimulus, and leisure. First, the mathematics or the Russian required by our chemists need not be taught as they would be to specialists. For scientists, such subjects are useful tools, and, like driving an automobile, they must be taught with this purely utilitarian point of view. Second, since we can no longer hope to teach everything, we must introduce our students at quite an openly superficial level to some of the great ideas and the great books, to make them realize the relevance of some of Plato or Homer or Matthew Arnold or Conrad for themselves as citizens and men. Our mistake has been trying to teach these things with the rigor we should use in teaching them to professionals. We have also concentrated such studies in general courses preliminary to professional studies, as though general education was a hurdle to be surmounted and passed, instead of a permanent stimulus to continuing self-education. And third, we have so filled our students' lives with requirements in their special fields, with examinations in ancillary subjects, with programs and tests of general studies, that we have denied them the leisure to think, read, and talk for themselves of what they learn. Our students may not be overworked; they are very often overtaught.

The idea of a hard core of specialization surrounded, as it were, by an aura of more general, more superficial, but highly stimulating, teaching will only work if we modify not only the content of our education but its methods and its organization. The kind of teaching we want in general education at the higher levels is less a matter of transmission of information and more one of dialectic. If this is true, it must be personal. And if the leisure I have spoken of is to be educative, the immediate environment must not be too large and too anonymous.

It becomes ever more necessary to reject methods of education directed entirely to transmitting information and to concentrate on those which encourage independent critical thought. In so far as transmission is necessary, we must learn to employ every new means which technology can put in our hands. But, associated with it, the more truly educative elements must be personal relationships between teacher and taught, and personal stimulus to discuss, to read, and to question ruthlessly—elements to be found in the tutorial and the seminar rather than in the teaching machine, the television screen, or even the lecture.

This I believe to be particularly true of moral education. In no part of education have we tried harder and with less certainty of success. Arnold with his great sermons, the 19th century English public school with its belief that ball games had something to do with character, and the permissive view that children are naturally good (rather than, as St. Augustine and many parents have believed, naturally bad): All are attempts to deal with a problem difficult even to define. Are we equating morality with social conformity? Let us hope not completely. With traditional beliefs? They are dissolving before our eyes. We have to reconcile apparent contradictions: how to produce tough and skeptical minds that are yet idealistic, and how to encourage a nonconformity that is responsible and creative, not merely antisocial. As Reisman has so preceptively shown, a technological revolution imposes increasing strains on the structure of morality. Yet we know that whatever the technical changes of the next 50 years, the basic moral problems will remain the same as those that Shakespeare or Henry James force us to think about; and we know, too, that the most important element in moral education is the contact of pupil and teacher.

The new emphasis on—or rather the rediscovery of—the role of the teacher is, in my view, associated closely with taking the sacred cow of higher education for a long, cold walk. I am talking, of course, about research. To say that there is too much research is one of those superficially absurd statements which, I believe, conceals an essential truth. In some ways the most important effect of the growth of science has been the value which we put on research. And the high valuation on research has been transmitted from the sciences to other fields of activity. Yet the position of research, especially of trivial researches, is probably different in science from that in the arts and the humanities.

In the sciences the research worker is carrying out an actual act of creation: he is, as it were, the poet or the sculptor, even if a very minor one. The new facts that he so patiently establishes may be tiny elements in an edifice from which man may ultimately view the universe in an entirely new light. In the arts, this is not so. Too often the researcher has copied the techniques of the natural sciences. Energy that would have been better spent reflecting on the already known is devoted to discovering the new but essentially trivial. Indeed, in the whole field of research, not only in the arts, we are approaching (if we have not already passed) the point at which we cannot regard research as a self-justifying activity. There will simply not be enough qualified individuals to pursue even a fraction of the profitable lines that open before us. We have to establish criteria of importance, a hierarchy of value among the possible things that we can find out, or even want to find out. We must have the courage to say that some things are simply not worth discovering, lest the pursuit of wisdom grind to a halt, stifled beneath a mountain of almost inaccessible and largely valueless truth.

Such a hierarchy of value is in many ways easier to establish in the arts than in the sciences, for in science it is well known that apparently trivial researches may have surprising and fundamental results, though under modern conditions of research this is far less likely than it was some years ago. But in the arts and humanities it is surely possible to say with some certainty that much of what is done in the name of research is not a genuine work of creation, that it is done to secure a qualification by pursuing something so trivial that it has not been done before simply because no one thought it worth doing.

I am anxious that I should not be too much misunderstood on this point, for I am no intellectual Luddite. Research, like any creative art, can be one of the supreme manifestations of the human spirit. With the contemporary decline of the novel, and to some extent of the visual arts, it may well be contended that today creativity and imagination are flowering most freely in the sciences. But there is a limit to the amount of manpower that can be devoted to research. There is a danger that its prestige may attract into it minds which would be better employed in the work of closer reflection on what is already known, at one end of the scale, or in the day-to-day work of teaching, at the other. There is the danger, too, that the prestige of the word *research* may distort our education system by diverting it from the tasks of the exploration, the transmission, and the reinterpretation of human values.

As we consider the kinds of questions raised by the speed of scientific development, we may be forgiven for having deep misgivings. These misgivings have led to fear and distrust of scientific advance as destructive of humane values. The kind of society which mass education and scientific technology together create, even if it does not destroy itself physically, may be one in which human values have declined—a candy-floss culture dominated by the standards of an uncritical majority and manipulated by the ad men. In other words, education may lose.

But that position, although intellectually tenable, is one that no educator can accept. For the whole enterprise of education rests on an optimism that we can make men a little more humane, a little more rational, a little better. If the growth of scientific knowledge offers obvious dangers in its capacity to destroy the body and degrade the spirit, it also offers new hope, not simply of material progress but of providing a framework in which we may live, in many respects, more humanely.

We have hitherto lived, and still live, in a world in which the life of the mind for the few presupposes a basis of slavery or near-slavery for the many. The life of the majority of men is not merely short, but squalid and unfulfilled. Our speculations on the good life have, as it were, rested on a fundamental disingenuity. From that dilemma science can set us free. Man does not live by bread alone, but without bread he cannot live at all, and with insufficient bread his life is usually unworthy of a man. We must not regard material advance as a danger to the good life but as an opportunity for enhancing it.

Nor is it only in material triumphs that science can be an ally in the pursuit of that ideal. In its devotion to truth and rationality, it can be the enemy of propaganda and intolerance. In its acts of creation, science takes its place among the great achievements of the spirit. In its revelation of the nature of the universe, it forces man to proclaim not only, in his moments of triumph, "What a piece of work is man!" but, in humility before the stellar immensities, "What is man that thou art mindful of him?" even if some of us can no longer address that cry to a personal deity.

If we are to realize these values from the growth of science, it must be part of an educational process that reveals their existence. Whether it be in the specialized education of the scientist himself, or in the general education that seeks to put the scientist's work in the context of other kinds of experience, or in making nonscientists aware of what this new knowledge can accomplish, the teacher must accept and prepare himself for the new responsibilities our time lays upon him. For lose we shall if the men of intellect treat their search for truth as a kind of intellectual game, or if, on the other hand, in their anxiety to respond to social needs, they simply give the community what it wants and lack the courage to help it to want the right things.

In short, we need more and better teachers. The only solution I can really offer is as difficult to achieve as it is simple to state. We delude ourselves if we think that new techniques can ever be more than aids, necessary and invaluable, but still aids. We delude ourselves if we believe that unlimited research in education will provide a series of simple answers for education in the new world. In the last resort, if our education is to be better, as it must, it will get better because it is carried on by more educated, more sensitive, and more humane people who are not afraid to emphasize the social and moral relevance of the subjects they teach. Nothing less than the future of mankind depends on our answers to these questions of education.

7 vocational education – all the way or not at all

Jack Hruska

GROWING DISENCHANTMENT

Despite an avalanche of criticism in recent years, now capped by Charles Silberman's *Crisis in the Classroom,* and despite a multitude of efforts by educators at change, schools remain essentially the same, children remain unhappy, and public education is in jeopardy. I contend that most of our efforts at change—e.g., team teaching, modular scheduling, differentiated staffing, and so on—do not alter the basic philosophical framework of education. They don't challenge the widely held idea that education is a "preparation for life." In so doing, they don't take kids seriously.

Schools are full of educators who have widely varying ideas of how students should be prepared for life. But there is something wrong with the approaches they suggest, whether academic or vocational. To the extent that we implement the preparation for life philosophy we imply that the young do not know how to live. Their rebellion at virtually all levels of education is in large part an indignant protest to this condescension and resultant manipulation. This idea of education as preparation for life is not malicious and very often not consciously adopted. Educators say and believe that education is a life-long process, "a way of life." But they operate the schools according to the contradictory tradition that education is a preparation for life.

For two decades reformers have devoted millions of foundation dollars and an untold amount of intellect to providing an academic education for more youngsters. As Cremin says of the reformers, "They simply refuse to honor the view that only twenty percent of our children can profit from academic courses and that the remaining eighty percent need either trade training or something called 'life adjustment education.' " With this goal in mind we have done noteworthy work in providing materials which attempt to draw on the ongoing interests of the student. But, as Cremin concludes, ". . . their sharpest challenge still lies ahead of them, namely, to design up-to-date curricula that make no compromise with truth or significance and yet prove attractive and comprehensible to dull or poorly motivated children" (Cremin, 1972, pp. 59-60).

The reform movement, whether it is addressed to the new math, new English, or new social studies, has at least two crucial unknowns: (a) how to arrange content, materials, teachers, discipline, and time in such a manner that it is palatable in an "intellectually honest way" to all students; and (b) is an academic education *desirable* for all students? It is this latter question, for which reformers assume a positive reply, that may be the real hooker. For it may be that we *can* in fact develop ways to continue our schools in some meaningful academic way for all students (although my hunch is that we can't). The question then would be: Ought we to do so? Is the academic life the good life for all people? It seems to me that there is mounting evidence against it, albeit the variables are such that causal relationships are difficult to establish. But, can we overlook the dissatisfactions which seem to occur when human beings begin to live in an abstract world? Are not the counterculture, the do-it-yourself craze, camping, sensitivity training, hobbies, perhaps even our infatuation with football, sex, and crime, evidence of an unfulfilled human need—the need for constant touch with reality, for authenticity, for concrete experience?

Again, there is no lack of authorities to warn us of the dangers of building an educational model on abstractions. Erich Fromm argues that schools teach children to be "... friendly, yet not deeply attached to anybody or anything." He sees the separation of theoretical knowledge as tending "to separate theory from practice, and to make it more difficult, rather than easier, for the individual to participate meaningfully in the work he is doing." He recommends:

> No youngster should graduate from school unless he has learned some kind of handicraft in a satisfactory and meaningful manner; no primary education would be considered finished before the student has a grasp of the fundamental technical process of our industry. Certainly high school ought to combine practical work of a handicraft and of modern industrial technique with theoretical instruction (Fromm, 1967, pp. 299-300).

William James applauded the introduction of manual training into the schools because of its effect on the *total* make-up of the person.

> The most colossal improvement which recent years have seen in secondary education lies in the introduction of the manual training schools; not because they will give us a people more handy and practical for domestic life and better skilled in trades, but because they will give us citizens with an entirely different intellectual fibre (James, 1958, p. 40).

And, of course, Dewey gave much of his life to healing the dichotomies that lesser minds insisted on concocting. He argued for concrete experiences and rigorously resisted the temptation to make education more efficient by formalizing and abstracting it. "Hence the need for restating into experience the subject matter of the studies, or branches of learning. It must be restored to the experience from which it has been abstracted" (Dewey, 1968, p. 22).

And Dewey might have been addressing himself to any number of modern day practices when he said about abstract material:

> The legitimate way out is to transform the material; to psychologicalize it—that is, once more, to take it and to develop it within the range and scope of the child's life. But it is easier and simpler to leave it as it is, and then by trick of method to *arouse* interest, to *make* it interesting; to cover it with sugar coating; to conceal its barrenness by intermediate and unrelated material; and finally as it were, to get the child to swallow and digest the unpalatable morsel while he is enjoying tasting something quite different. But, alas, for the analogy! Mental assimilation is a matter of consciousness; and if the attention has not been playing upon the actual material, that has not been apprehended, nor worked into faculty (Dewey, p. 30).

Thus, we may be idolizing a false god. Our hopes to save the schools by popularizing academic learning may further the anxieties, tensions, apathy, and alienation already

prevalent in our society. Kenneth Keniston, in *The Uncommitted,* claims that the young
search longingly for a cause in which they can gain a sense of personal identity, and to
which they can passionately commit themselves. We need to ask whether a formal and
bookish education can provide this need for more than a small minority.

TRADITIONAL VOCATIONAL EDUCATION AS AN ALTERNATIVE

Some educators, reacting to the shortcomings of an academic education, have come
down hard in favor of vocational education. In so doing they frequently narrow the
notion of "preparation for life" to preparation for a job. However, I believe this posture
flies in the face of certain realities: the average person will change jobs five times in his
lifetime, occupational skills are quickly out-dated, few teenagers are able rationally to
select an occupation, and on-the-job training may be the most efficient occupational
training for most jobs. (And I am at one with Robert Hutchins, who argues that the job
of the schools is so big that they should do nothing that another institution can do as
well.) Traditional vocational education programs are also subject to the criticisms that
they (1) are providing industrial training at public expense, (2) actually terminate a
child's search for his vocation and dead-end him into a slot, and (3) psychologically
condition him to accept himself as one type of human being, different from those who
find enjoyment in thinking, beauty, argument, books, surprise, uncertainty, poetry, or
whatever. (This may be the most tragic shortcoming resulting from the academic versus
vocational tracking system. As Robert Rosenthal, *Pygmalion in the Classroom,* and
Kenneth Clark, *Dark Ghetto,* have demonstrated, the self-fulfilling prophecy is a critical
variable in human behavior. When we separate kids into those who can continue to learn
and those who are preparing for immediate employment, we may, by our diagnosis,
preclude the latter from future learning.)

Nonetheless, many vocational educators believe that the quality of education is
correlated with the degree to which schoolrooms can be turned into facsimiles of
factories. The dedication of such educators is truly remarkable. They possess the zeal and
spirit that springs from singleness of purpose, clear-cut goals, and esprit de corps. This
zest has fathered an association (American Vocational Association), corralled millions of
federal dollars, energized congressmen, and neatly dichotomized education into camps,
each willing to let the other go its own way. Each, I believe, has been plagued by man's
historical quest for certainty. While some look for the ends of education in the quantifi-
able goals of college entrance, test scores, attendance, grades, and so on, these vocational
educators have turned to industry in an attempt to quantify their objectives. Thus job
preparation, the development of saleable skills and attitudes, and industrial manpower
needs have become for them the purposes for education.

This is not to argue that kids shouldn't learn vocational skills in school. I believe, in
fact, they should have opportunities to learn more. What they learn, and how well they
learn it, however, should be a function of their own growth needs. The ability to do
something well may provide the security necessary for the student to seek further growth.
However, to look to industry instead of to college entrance requirements for the
guidelines for educational decisions is to err as far in one direction as in the other. Thus,
both the academicians and the vocationalists have been overcome with the frustrations
that are part and parcel of thinking seriously about the ends of education. They have
taken opposite ways out, but neither route, I believe, holds much promise.

Vocational educators are certainly to be applauded for their development of materials, projects, and equipment which provide an alternative to books, lectures, and abstractions. The tragedy of this approach, however, has been the explicit shifting of the *end* of education for vocational students. Not only have we provided new methods for our less academic students, but we have given up, in effect, our goal of educating them and substituted a goal of training them. Thus, rather than conceiving of vocational education as another *method* of transmitting culture, socializing, developing identity, and helping students grow, we have conceived of it as an alternative objective. We justify such fuzzy thinking by arguing that all youngsters need a saleable skill. The substitution of vocational competency for a legitimate goal of education is a manifestation of Whitehead's observation that educators tend to lower their ideals to the level of their practices.

For to serve either college entrance requirements or industry is to prostitute what education is all about—the growth and development of people. There may well be times when a student's growth can best be furthered by providing him with job skills or college entrance requirements, but it is of critical importance that we recognize that these are means to this particular student's growth, and that his maximum growth may necessitate from time to time rescheduling his education away from skill training or studies required for college entrance. In short, if we focus on the student we may find that his needs and the needs of industry or college registrars are incompatible. The fact that college entrance requirements and industrial needs are far easier to discern than student growth needs is no excuse for us to shoot at the more clearly outlined target. It is illusory to believe that the needs of young people can be met by serving the interest of particular institutions.*

My argument boils down to this: Our society is showing many signs of wide-spread alienation, anxiety, and frustration, to which the schools are a contributing factor. Many talented educators, recognizing the need for reform, have concentrated on popularizing an academic approach. It is my contention that there is little evidence to suggest that an academic approach can be made palatable for all students, and there is much evidence to suggest that it would be unwise even if possible. Moreover, traditional vocational education, which does a lot of the right things for the wrong reasons, is not a viable alternative to serve the growth needs of our young.

VOCATIONAL EDUCATION AS A METHODOLOGY

What other alternatives are available? It is my faith, bolstered by the experience of scattered programs, that there is a rich and fertile ground somewhere between a sequentially contrived academic curriculum and career-oriented vocational education, and, furthermore, that there are reasonable choices between authoritarian subject-matter schools and Summerhill. It necessitates, however, a modification of our philosophical framework. That is, we must abandon the idea that schooling is a preparation for life and entertain the Deweyan proposition that educators should help the student "by extracting at each present time the full meaning of each present experience."

---

*I recently read a dissertation in which the author gathered information as to the philosophies underlying the alternative school movement. In response to the question "Have you conducted any follow-up studies on your graduates?" a principal wrote, "Hell, we are not preparing people for life—we live here." That principal understood that true "preparation for life" requires full attention to the reality of the present and to the students' needs in the here and now.

When we use preparation, in its treacherous sense, as our guide, we get all caught up in putting together a logically conceived, sequential curriculum from nursery school to graduate school. When that process known as schooling leads to violence, rebellion, or other disturbances, we vigorously manipulate the variables of time, staff, materials, student government, and so on, to temper the frustrations schools provoke. There is evidence that much of our societal troubles and suffering is the result of a widespread sense of powerlessness and alienation that occurs when people believe they are being used. This feeling is particularly acute in education. I believe that an educational system grounded in a "preparation" philosophy can only contribute to this alienation. Erich Fromm, in *The Sane Society*, writes of alienation:

> By alienation is meant a code of experience in which the person experiences himself as an alien. He has become, one might say, estranged from himself. He does not experience himself as the center of his world, as the creator of his own acts—but his acts and their consequences have become his masters, whom he obeys, or whom he may even worship (Fromm, 1967, p. 111).

Do not many of our students fall into this category? They attend schools so that *later on* they can contribute to democracy, help solve the shortage of technicians, engineers, doctors, teachers, shore up our national defense, stay off the welfare rolls, succeed in college, vote, be a responsible neighbor. When curriculums are rigorously preplanned to promote these *future* consequences, the student, because he does not identify with these goals, "is out of touch with himself." Even when this costly and benevolent preplanning is intended to enrich the life of the student, it is geared for a distant time. If the student does not identify with this value at the *present* time he is quite likely to consider it coercive, and even if he does not view it negatively, he is unlikely to pursue it with any of the force, intelligence, and joy of which human behavior is capable.

The evidence seems to be, regardless of how benevolent and noble our intentions, that our present systematic process is crumbling. While it may appear that vocational education is an alternative, it can also be considered merely as a less academic approach to preparing the child for some future end. In neither case do we offer the child alternatives that allow him to engross himself enthusiastically in whatever intrigues him and captures his attention simply because they are the types of experience that a 6, 12, or 18 year old finds fascinating. Lest I am accused of painting with too broad a brush, let me acknowledge that I do not accept the position that schools are detrimental to all children of all ages. Elementary schools are frequently oriented to the very activities that children find engrossing, and many of our academic students leave our schools having spent their years in activities that developed them aesthetically, academically, socially, and spiritually. It is my belief, however, that aside from the early elementary years and some programs for the academically inclined, schooling falls far short of the ideals which seem within our grasp.

Can we assume that children are like "big people" in some ways? Let's assume they, too, are included as referents when Maslow writes, "The only happy people I know are the ones who are working well at something they enjoy," and "Most people prefer no work at all to meaningless work, or wasted work, or made work" (Maslow, 1965, p. 28). It is crucial to understand that Maslow's argument rests on the idea that the worker, not some wiser and more experienced employer or curriculum builder, must decide whether the work is worthwhile. It is simply not enough to tell him that his dull and lifeless role on the assembly line will enable him to fulfill himself later, nor is it enough to tell a 14 year old that no matter how much it repels his natural tendencies, if he will "put forth a little effort" and "turn in his homework," he will be thankful someday. We need to take young people seriously—to postulate that their lives and life styles are inherently valuable at each age, that they wish to contribute to worthwhile activities at each age, *and* that the thing may be worth doing simply because they want to do it.

I believe that people find themselves when they lose themselves in activities which they find worthwhile, and that the current crisis in the schools is, in part, because we have been unable to systematically structure a curriculum that provides those work-centered growth-producing experiences for a large percentage of our young. In spite of the funds and talent of the National Science Foundation, enrollment in the physical sciences drops; in spite of modulars, team teaching, and learning centers, discipline increasingly commands our attention; in spite of inquiry, discovery, and sensitivity, students turn away. Perhaps we need to make a leap of faith. Maybe, regardless of our investments to the contrary, education *is* incidental; and maybe we can be imaginative enough to arrange or *permit* individual experiences that are shot through with growth-inducing activities.

If this process has a signpost, it might be "vocational education as a methodology." "Vocational," however, is used in its pregnant, perhaps romantic, sense, meaning that one is called to a vocation through an almost organic bond to the materials of that vocation. This notion runs through the writings of Plato, Dewey, Goodman, James, and Rogers, and literally saturates the works of Abraham Maslow and Erich Fromm.*

Perhaps by looking at the writings of our past scholars with one eye and casting the other eye on the alienation, anxiety, fear, hate, and mental sickness of our own society we can gain insights into what constitutes a healthy relationship between man and nature. One might conclude, for example, that most people learn by working with concrete materials, by molding them and shaping them for functional use or aesthetic appreciation. And further, that without that involvement with materials, man is less than he might be. Erik Erikson stresses this need for young people to work with materials.

> While all children at times need to be left alone in solitary play or, later, in the company of books and radio, motion pictures and television, and while all children need their hours and days of make-believe in games, they all, sooner or later, become dissatisfied and disgruntled without a sense of being able to make things and make them well and even perfectly: it is this that I have called the *sense of industry.* Without this, even the best-entertained child soon acts exploited. It is as if he knows and his society knows that now that he is psychologically already a rudimentary parent, he must begin to be something of a worker and potential provider before becoming a biological parent. With the oncoming latency period, then, the advancing child forgets, or rather quietly "sublimates"—that is, applies to concrete pursuits and approved goals—the drives which have made him dream and play. He now learns to win recognition by producing things. He develops perseverance and adjusts himself to the inorganic laws of the tool world and can become an eager and absorbed unit of a productive situation (Erikson, 1968, pp. 123-124).

If this is so, vocational education might have more to do with the fascination of materials, the seeking of identity, the relationship of man and things, or, in short, the growth and development of people, than with job getting and skill training. This is *not* to say that jobs

---

*Thomas Green offers the stimulating argument that we ought to separate conceptually a man's work from his job. His job is how he makes his living. His work, however, is his mode of fulfillment and identity. His work is what he does in his "off" hours, which now constitute the major part of his life. It is this conception of "work" or "vocation" that I believe schools can exploit into a meaningful curriculum. See Thomas F. Green, *Work, Leisure, and the American Schools,* New York, Random House, 1968.

and skills are unimportant, but rather that they are better regarded as outgrowths of an involvement with materials than as the specific ends sought. In this sense, vocational education is not for one *type* of child, but for all children. It is a wholistic and alternative way of looking at education. It is to argue that every child, if uncoerced, has deep and penetrating interests—*even though they may be short-lived*—that can be treated as temporary vocations, and that are shot through with growth opportunities.

These vocational interests are inherent in adolescence and we ignore them at our peril. Edgar Friedenberg puts it this way:

> But respect for competence in oneself and others is crucial in adolescence, for it is crucial to self-definition. In a world as empirical as ours, a youngster who does not know what he is good *at* will not be sure what he is good *for;* he must know what he can do in order to know who he is. The things he does well may not, of course, be things that win him the esteem of the community; some adolescents, when they get nervous and upset, steal cars and take joy rides in them the way an adult might work off his mood by gardening or a game of golf. But they must be skills that identify him to himself and others, and keep him from getting lost (Friedenberg, 1959).

Students make films, cook, build houses, publish newspapers, fix TV's, plant trees in the city, tutor younger children, raise crops, and build stereos, to mention a few examples, *not* because they have carpenters, farmers, TV repairmen, and so on as ends-in-view, but because those activities, if intelligently organized, are the kinds of activities that produce happy, confident, graceful, forceful, intelligent, and sociable people.

Some people may develop their ethical posture by a lecture/seminar/reading approach to Kant's Categorical Imperatives or Bentham's utilitarianism. Others, however, may better grapple with ethical considerations by building a house and deciding which materials to use in the foundation, attic, and other places which the owner is unlikely to inspect, or by publishing a small newspaper and wrestling with the ethical issues encountered there. My opinion is that a teacher grounded in ethics could make excellent use of these kinds of situations. This idea is also compatible with Dewey's position in *Art As Experience* that aesthetics ought to be an integral part of daily living, not set off as a separate discipline. Dewey contends that "The intelligent mechanic engaged in his job, interested in doing well, and finding satisfaction in his handiwork, caring for his materials and tools with genuine affection, is artistically engaged" (Dewey, 1958, p. 5). Most adults have "had art" throughout their schooling, yet a cursory examination of our ugly buildings, our shabby towns, our entire surroundings indicate that we have decided that art was, in fact, a course or, at best, a spare time hobby. Our environment might become more beautiful if young student-engineers were encouraged to think about greener trees, cleaner water, color combinations, and forms as they thought about stresses and strains or cost/benefit analysis in production.

This development of temporary vocations can be a wholistic—scientific, moral, aesthetic, spiritual—way of looking at the world. At one time, people learned skills for a job, an income, a livelihood. But our affluent, open society has radically altered the value structure of our young people. For, as Silberman writes,

> What these "new" students understand, far better than their parents, is that the choice of a career involves far more than a choice of how to earn a livelihood. They understood, viscerally if not intellectually, that the question, "What shall I do?" really means "What shall I do with myself?" or rather "What shall I make of myself?" And that means asking "Who am I? What do I want to be? What values do I want to serve? To whom and to what do I want to be responsible?" (Silberman, 1970, p. 23).

In short, vocational interests, when generated out of a student's needs and experiences, can lead to exploration, critical analysis, and moral searching. To reduce vocational preparation to skill development is to create the illusion of a bond from a relationship which has long been split by reality. Further reflection on this topic may encourage us to jettison our current concepts of vocations—lathe operator, carpenter, keypunch operator—and regard them as functions of human needs. Thus, we might think in broad terms such as communications, transportation, health, construction, government, or human relations. From this vantage point, educators, both teachers and others who teach, can help the student make connections between his temporary *here and now* vocation and the broader world with which it interacts.

This is not to deny that many students will select a career vocation as a result of exposure to these activities, but that outcome is only one result of the total process. Nor do we propose to abolish the formal academic approach, for, after all, the love of literature, history, mathematics, or French may be the most important vocation for a student at any given moment. In fact, the aim is to strengthen and enrich the scholarly approach by enabling its participants to concentrate their energies on the content and not on the administration and discipline required when all learners must be pushed, pulled, bullied, and bribed through that process. Educators may need to be reminded that, in the main, the scholarly endeavors which excited them were likely to have been those areas which they now teach, and which were and are vocational pursuits for them. There is no reason why educators have a right to expect youngsters to be excited about the *teacher's* vocational interests.

It is unfortunate that our schools have altered educators' concepts of human nature. For when education is conceived as being synonymous with courses, assignments, tests, and lessons, teachers invariably conclude that their most difficult task is motivation. It is as though they believed that the natural state of youngsters is rest, and to spur them into activity one must grade, test, entice, threaten, shame, punish, *or reward.* And of course they are right, as long as the activity the teacher demands is grounded in the curriculum committee, the syllabus, the principal, or because "it's always taught in the sixth grade." But, in another sense, "how to motivate children" poses the question badly. Reworded in a Deweyan way, the question asks "How can we utilize the inherent motivation of the child to enrich his experiences?" and puts the motivation into a different, and I believe more plausible, perspective.

This all-inclusive vocational approach would dispel the conventional wisdom that places vocational education in juxtaposition to academic education. This notion simply makes no sense whatever. (The Job Corps teachers found that the skill most desperately needed by their trainees was skill in communication. Woodworking courses in adult education are inundated with professional people who wish to work with their hands in off hours. Yet, traditionally, English is academic and woodworking is vocational.) It may be far more fruitful to think of education as a continuum, at one end of which would be education directly related to job requirements and on the other, education remotely related to job requirements. This does not imply major differences inherent among subjects—such thinking has no place with the concept of a "whole" person. For any student at any given time a given subject may fall anywhere on the continuum. Looking at education from this perspective we can discard the whole baggage of terminal education, track systems, general education, academic education, and vocational education. As educators we needn't be concerned with whether the student is interested in a course or module because he wants entry level skills, career advancement, a hobby, or merely because he wants to know or be able to do what we can teach. In public education it may not be any of the educator's business why a student has enrolled in his course.

If the foregoing makes any sense at all, it suggests that education might find a wealth of talent in people in industry who are having a love affair with electricity, fertilizer, cement, chemicals, space, oceans, clothing, food, medicine, films, newspapers, wood, international relations, metal, or whatever. It is not difficult to imagine that many of them may be (1) frustrated with the limited parameters imposed by their job situation, or (2) willing to share their romance on a part-time basis with young adults. If we could encourage these people to come into the schools and *continue* their involvement with their materials, we might find a remarkable student response. And if we can stretch our minds we might conceive of ways to involve these men and women with the young by using business and community facilities, thus reviving somewhat the generally discarded notion that education is a community affair.

This grounding of education in the temporary vocational interest of young people could have a most advantageous side-effect. If we broaden the base of education so that professionals, tradesmen, and craftsmen have an educational responsibility, the ensuing dialogue and interaction might call into question the ethical behavior of all occupations. Seldom does a person have to think as seriously about what he is doing and why he is doing it as when he must justify it to the idealistic morality of youth. And in these days of unfathomable weaponry, pollution, and consumer confusion due to the complex make-up of products, it might be healthy to let young people share in the role of being the nation's soul searcher.

There is a need, of course, to further refine the methodologies of building an educational endeavor around vocational interest. I resist the urge on two counts. First, I believe the know-how is readily available; I think we lack the faith. If we can come to rid ourselves of our "preparation for life" orthodoxies, I am confident we have the where-withal to educate people by capitalizing on their prime interests. Second, to spell out the details of implementation is to repeat the errors that, in part, have created the present crisis in education. If we have learned anything in recent years about innovative programs, it is that success, in the main, lies in the ability of parents, students, the community, and teachers to utilize local resources in a manner compatible with the local attitudes, desires, abilities, and personalities. The transportability of successful programs has been low, as one has every reason to expect.

For years vocational educators have been doing a lot of good things for the wrong reasons and in so doing have settled for far too little. They have been satisfied with more jobs and higher starting salaries for vocational school graduates. Yet, all the time, within that ethos of involvement, interest, creativity, self-expression, and skill development is the framework for an educational idea that is consistent with both rigorous ideals and contemporary learning theory.

REFERENCES

Cremin, Lawrence A.: The Genius of American Education. New York, Random House (Vintage Books), 1972.
Dewey, John: Art as Experience. New York, Capricorn, 1958.
Dewey, John: The Child and the Curriculum. Chicago, University of Chicago Press, 1968.
Erikson, Erik H.: Identity, Youth, and Crisis. New York, W. W. Norton, 1968.
Friedenberg, Edgar: The Vanishing Adolescent. New York, Dell Publishing Co., 1959.
Fromm, Erich: The Sane Society. New York, Fawcett Premier, 1967.
Green, Thomas F.: Work, Leisure and the American Schools. New York, Random House, 1968.
James, William: Talks to Teachers. New York, Norton Library, 1958.
Maslow, Abraham: Eupsychian Management. Homewood, Ill., Richard D. Irwin, Inc., 1965.
Silberman, Charles: Crisis in the Classroom. New York, Random House, 1970.

beyond nationalism: **8**
education
and survival

Betty Reardon

Prologue

> ... In the year 1980 a radio telescope picked up a message from a previously undis-
> covered planet in our solar system. ... It read: "Hello. Who are you? Describe
> yourselves. ..."
>   A world conference was called to prepare a reply. ... It was signed "The Nations of
> Earth."
>   After some weeks, a message came back. It consisted of two questions: "What are
> nations? Are they good for your species?" (Hanvey, 1972)

This scenario is futuristic, but the question is urgently contemporary; if it is not answered before 1980, the human species may not survive much beyond that date. Because men respond to major global events and problems as nations, we need a better understanding of the institution of nationalism. Indeed, the topic becomes a part of the public discussion of survival issues. There is an ever-increasing condemnation of "nationalism," but little recognition of the role played by schools in promoting and perpetuating it. Educators, more than any other group, must take a hard look at nationalism in our contemporary society, and at their responsibility for its growth and prostitution to the war system.

When we study human behavior and aggression to find answers to the problems of war and survival, we must note the role of the nation. In its present form, the "national security state" constitutes the major threat to human survival. Men do not make war as men; they do so as people organized into nation-states competing with other nation-states. It is not nationalism itself but the investment of feelings of identity and fellowship with members of one's own culture in the *nation-state* which makes it possible for nationalism to produce warfare.

Nationalism in its cultural sense has been a positive and powerful integrative force in human history. The federation of tribes with similar languages, value systems, and cultural patterns into nations made it possible for men to share resources more effectively. With basic survival needs met, they could turn their attention to the development of the mind—to science, art, philosophy, and politics. The nation-state has been the patron of education, and education, in turn, has served and supported its patron. In helping humans identify with other people, nationalism has been a significant step toward the ultimate unity of the human species.

Unfortunately, the trend toward the unification of the species has been outstripped by the revolutions in science and technology. The formation of the nation-state may have made it possible for men to turn their attention to scientific inquiry, but the resulting technological revolutions may not be in the best interest of mankind. This technological "progress" has resulted in such rapid changes that man's political institutions have been made dangerously obsolete. Mankind is caught in an institutional trap, the spring of which is the nation-state. The nation-state now possesses weapons able to destroy human life and civilization but lacks the institutional capacity to save them. It has been the most important force aborting productive and positive energies of nationalism and "fixating" political development at the nation-state level. Humankind faces a crisis in its development which will not be resolved until the fixation is transcended. Educators, who are largely responsible for this fixation, have a profound obligation to help society understand the problem, devise ways of dealing with it, and project possible solutions.

Educators have always seen the potential of nationalism as an integrative force. A primary aim of American social education has been the forging of immigrants from various national and cultural backgrounds into a single political unit. That function is still reflected in texts bearing such titles as *Americans All*. Social education has been based on strong national sentiments aimed at developing a national identity that assures citizen support of nation-state policies (particularly in its relations with other nation-states), as can been seen in recent studies of social studies textbooks around the world (Kyung-Soo Cha, 1971). Most of these books either imply or openly state the moral and cultural superiority of the nation producing the texts.

The influence of nationalism on social education may vary from nation to nation and may result from different immediate circumstances, but it is nevertheless very strong in all nation-states. This nationalistic theme is especially strong in former colonies, where "emerging nations" see that the major world powers are strongly integrated, forceful nation-states and pressure their educators to integrate tribal peoples into one cohesive political unit. Nationalistic education is devised in these nations, as it has been in the more politically "mature" states, to teach students that the interests of their nation-state involve conflict and competition with the interests of the other nation-states. This perception of the national interest forms the greatest barrier to the global, humanistic education which is now required for the survival of the human species.

In its early stages, integrative nationalism in the United States proved to be a positive force in two ways. It provided another dimension of identity for immigrants, who could refer to themselves as Irish-Americans, German-Americans, or Italo-Americans. This kind of identity did not require that they reject the culture, values, and identity of their origin; instead they could add to an original identity another and broader dimension. This experience is of no little significance for educators concerned with broadening the sense of identity to include groups beyond one's own nation.

Integrative nationalism also made possible that type of selflessness generally designated as "patriotism." In times of national emergency individuals willingly make great sacrifices for the national interests, which they perceive as an extension of their own self-interest. The ability to draw upon such sentiments among its peoples is essential to any nation in the stage of defining and developing itself. Now, as mankind seeks to identify its universal characteristics and common interests so that the human species may survive, educators from all nations must apply their skills to the task of defining and developing the "human community."

To do so, however, they should be aware of two problems inherent in integrative nationalism. The crisis in race relations we are currently experiencing is a severe manifestation of one of these problems. In the stage of positive integrative nationalism, minorities, for reasons which include physical characteristics that are obviously different, tend to be distinguished from the majority. These minorities come to be viewed almost as a threat to the integrity and cohesiveness of the state. In certain cases they are even seen as enemies, foreigners, so to speak, within its boundaries. If they do not conform, if they do not integrate, they are blamed. It generally takes a traumatic experience or a major crisis such as the series of events precipitated by the Watts riots in 1965 to make the integrated portion of the society see how the majority has abused the interests of minorities.

Minorities are almost always poorly served by most of the institutions which serve the rest of the nation, a fact which even such enlightened groups as educators usually do not see before a crisis erupts. This fact is shown by, for example, the rush to black studies programs that followed the onset of the racial crisis. In facing the task of community-building, educators must be forward-looking enough to attempt to avoid a similar situation on a world scale. Like most nation-states, the world system is controlled by powerful elites. If, in attempting to develop a "world community," these elites were to establish structures which did not serve all the diverse groups to be included in them, a worldwide struggle between the powerful and the "powerless" might destroy us as finally as any war among nation-states.

The other problem of integrative nationalism is the ease with which "patriotism" can be turned into a common hatred of an enemy, real or imagined. Since even friends outside the nation are nearly always perceived as somewhat less human than the people within it, an "enemy" is not human at all, and not deserving of human treatment. Thus, a man like Lieutenant Calley could come to feel that since his nation was in grave danger, acts against the enemy could not, under any circumstances, be considered crimes against human persons. This human tendency makes it infinitely more difficult for education to "rehumanize" former enemies and to make it possible for people of all nations to consider all others as human. Educators must consider whether or not ardent patriotism is indeed a desirable attribute in citizens of a world in conflict, where disputes are settled through deadly wars, any one of which might escalate into a worldwide holocaust.

Once established, the nation-state, like any other institution, seeks to maintain itself. It develops a concern for its security and is often preoccupied with threats from the outside. The destructive "enemy"-oriented aspect of patriotism is intensified and national-ism becomes a negative, exclusive force. National security often becomes the chief national concern, influencing all phases of life within the state, especially education.

Educators must examine such issues as war crimes and "anti-Communism" courses in order to fully understand the ways in which the nation-state has used education, and to consider the resulting problems for those educators trying to help build a world community. Education must, of course, contribute to national goals, but shouldn't we also reflect upon how such contributions are used by the nation-state? Our government considers national security to be in the realm of the Department of Defense, not the Department of Health, Education, and Welfare. Yet the most monumental effort made by the educational system of the United States in the twentieth century was made under the National Defense Education Act. That legislation was quite clearly a response to a power challenge from our major opponent in the international system, not to an intrinsic educational need.

Observing the programs which were supported by the NDEA further indicates the powerful effect which national security has had on educational policy. Funds allocated to the social sciences often supported programs designed to teach the United States how to be more powerful and influential in its dealings with other cultural areas. Other cultures were not studied as part of the common heritage of all mankind nor as a means of enriching our own culture, but rather as entities to be better "understood" and therefore more easily manipulated. Indeed, the major resource in world affairs education became the Department of State which regularly offers briefings to educators. As James Becker points out, these briefings are held "so that foreign policy and defense policy can be interpreted 'correctly' in our nation's classrooms." The state thus assures that its educational system will predispose its people to spend resources for national defense rather than for more humanly directed national purposes. Becker also points out the degree to which practices such as ROTC units and civil defense drills make the nation's schools part of the nation-state's defense system (Becker, 1973).

The issue of students' rights also shows how the national security takes precedence over all other national interests. Students were the first to identify ROTC as an intrusion of the defense system into the educational system. Further, expression of the dissent and protest many felt against the Vietnam war was prohibited in most schools. With the Tinker Case* this dissent became a major constitutional issue in which the rights of students were found to be violated by the school in its efforts to serve the interests of national security.

Social educators assert that schools should prepare students for constructive participation and intelligent decision-making in a representative democracy. Without open inquiry into these issues of national security, foreign policy, and the nature of national-ism, how can the schools do this? Under current conditions are students likely to examine whether national security means the security of the people—i.e., the individuals and groups of that nation—or the security of the state—i.e., the government as run by the defense elites? Is it possible to study carefully and objectively the costs of national security to the various groups within each nation, not only by outright taxation but also by the sacrifice of other public services, particularly to the deprived, the sick, the elderly, and dependent children?

If the nation-state continues to hold the same sacrosanct position in modern education as the pre-Reformation Church held in the educational system of that era, have we anything to look forward to but continued ideological and political conflicts leading to its gradual demise? Educators might, in fact, find it useful to have their students examine the nation-state-church analogy. Try, for instance, to substitute the word "heresy" for "treason" in some of the articles on the controversy over *The New York Times'* publishing of the Pentagon Papers. Does the functional meaning change very much? Compare some of the transcripts of the former House Un-American Activities Committee with hearings before the Inquisition. Which seem more enlightened or less reflective of superstition and fear?

Fortunately for the intellectual history of man, some of the restrictions the Church imposed on inquiry were removed by the Protestant Reformation. This event, however, did not have as fortuitous an effect on our social and political history. Europeans divided themselves into "us" and "them" by religion as we now do by ideology. "Us" are those who believe as we do and are governed by the same sort of elites. Social and political functions concerning "us" are separated from those concerning "them." In Europe this helped intensify the feeling of negative/exclusive nationalism. A series of national wars

---

Tinker v. the Des Moines Public Schools, 1969. See Nat Hentoff, Why Students Want Their Constitutional Rights, *Saturday Review,* May 22, 1971.

followed the religious wars and prevented, until the present century, the natural next step beyond nation-states to a multi-national geopolitical community. "Domestic" and "foreign" affairs were considered two different domains, a perspective which still prevails.

On a planet recognized as a single closed system, this situation contains the seeds of disaster. By reinforcing that division, the public education system helps maintain our present fixation on the nation-state. A curriculum like our own, which treats "American history" and "world history" as two different subjects, ill serves the goal of human survival. The most advanced content within the social studies these days is "international education," which, however, has done little to overcome this dysfunctional dichotomy. Even though there is a growing intention to use such education to help build a world community, the very terminology limits us. International education teaches primarily about the nation-state—its characteristics, its function, and its relations with other nation-states. Its presentation reinforces the view that the natural order of things is the present world political system of sovereign nation-states. It prevents a truly planetary perception of world problems and thereby impedes progress toward a global community, which will require *transnational* activity transcending the limits of nation-states.

International education implies that nation-states serve the interests of their people and says that any progress in the world political system will be made by these nation-states acting *"inter-nationally."* The present curriculum makes it almost impossible for students to view peoples in the world community acting within units other than nation-states. Under such conditions, how can students effectively examine such issues as limitations of sovereignty? How can a nation-state functionally participate in a world federation if it is only a nation-state when it is sovereign? Given the mounting evidence that problems such as war, environmental decay, and resource depletion cannot be resolved by the nation-state, what alternative political units can be proposed and considered?

A few educators have seen that the nation-state emphasis in international education is counterproductive and have suggested changes, such as shifting the focus to intercultural education, an idea advocated by Oliver Caldwell in the *Phi Delta Kappan:*

> A good case could be made for the idea that international education as a concept is obsolete. The name itself is wrong. Our basic interest is not in studying about other nation-states. Our basic and inescapable need is to learn how to understand and to communicate with peoples of other cultures. This problem begins right at home, among our own people in our fifty states. The militant blacks have managed to secure concessions from university administrations by demanding that black studies be taught in our colleges and universities. Americans of Puerto Rican and Mexican descent are making the same demands. The American curriculum should pay more attention to the "inner space" of our own mixed national cultural heritage. Learning to understand and communicate with our own cultural minorities will help us to understand our neighbors around the world (Caldwell, 1971, p. 544-45).

Indeed his suggestion does offer a positive alternative. But it does not come to terms with the institutional and perceptual fixation on the nation-state. Clearly, if we are to move beyond this fixation, the problems of the national security state must be faced. There is an urgent need to move beyond international, intercultural education, comparative studies, and all other such approaches to a serious consideration of the common problems of human survival and the development of new world institutions which can assure that survival.

The first step for the educational system should be to abjure its role as a tool of the national security state. Clearly, the interests of education are not served by the state, not only because of the limits placed on inquiry but also because of the limited percentage of national wealth left to education. All other public services suffer when the security system demands more than half the nation's treasury. Educators must demand a more equitable share. We must begin to take more seriously the responsibility assumed long since by many scientists—the necessity to disarm and demythicize the nation-state. Perhaps in so doing we risk more than the scientists, but do we have any less responsibility? If wars do "begin in the minds of men," we must shoulder an even greater share of the burden of eliminating the war system and the other threats to human survival. Ours is the task of helping to change attitudes and expand identities.

Educators may well begin this task by looking at their own attitudes, their own identities. How many of us truly believe and behave as part of the family of man, giving full respect and dignity to all our fellow humans, including students? Have we truly concerned ourselves with the problem of alienation among students, many of whom see more clearly than we the threat posed by the nation-state system? Have we examined the relationship of that system and all its inadequacies to their alienation? Certainly the amount of curricular attention and the openness of inquiry by educators into the problems of the nation-state system indicate precious little such examination.

More educators should be joining the students who deplore the lack of relevance in much of the current curriculum. The true test of relevance in our present circumstances is the contribution of a given subject or skill to human survival, including the survival of individuals in a society menaced by the swollen monster of the nation-state. This monster encourages no answer to the basic existential question of "Who am I?" other than: "an American" or "a Russian" or "a Frenchman." Educators must recognize that among the most basic of human needs is to know what it is to be human and to understand that quality as the foremost component of an emerging world community. Humanness is the first requisite of survival and, therefore, of relevance.

Understanding the common problems of humankind is the second requisite and should be the basic learning goal of education for survival. Throughout the world students should be inquiring into questions regarding war, racism, poverty, pollution, ignorance, disease, overpopulation, human dignity, and the possibilities for a future in which the first seven on that list have been drastically reduced in an effort to increase the eighth. Open inquiry into such issues will result in problems and controversies, as have less sophisticated world studies programs. But without such inquiry, how will students develop survival skills? And without such controversy, how will we involve all communities? It took courage and sacrifice to build nations. It may take even more to go beyond them. But what is the alternative?

Such efforts should be made by educators throughout the world, and steps should be taken to denationalize all curricula dealing with world problems. Materials originating within one nation should be replaced by new ones cooperatively designed by curriculum developers of different cultures working together on common problems, striving toward a human perspective. Several such projects, sponsored by The Institute for World Order, are currently under way.

Much of the difficulty in devising and introducing these materials will come from the threat they may pose to the identity of those who believe in the value of their nation-state, and who have deeply involved themselves in this belief. These difficulties must be faced with sympathy, intelligence, and professionalism. The skills traditionally used for political socialization should be transferred to the world community level. Educators must once again work toward the integration of various groups. Perhaps we may learn in the process some new techniques which will truly encourage cultural pluralism by stressing universals as much as differences and giving full value to both.

Such a task will require emphasis on valuing skills and on the development of techniques which will permit value clash without violence. Value education is vital in order to build a community of widely diverse cultures, conflicting ideologies, and a variety of races. To say that such a task is impossible to accomplish is to say that we will not survive. To say that it will not be both difficult and dangerous is to fail to understand the task. But if we can adequately meet the challenge of threat to identity, if we can, in the terms of Harold Lasswell, extend "the self-reference mechanism" of most educated people to include mankind, then we will not fail.

Three specific programs to facilitate the task could be undertaken immediately. First, let us implement the recommendation from the U.S. Office of Education study on international education that all programs in this area be organized from global and human species-centered perspectives (U.S. Office of Education, 1969). Second, let us replace traditional citizenship education with a "survival curriculum," such as that proposed by Michael Scriven "that education for survival is largely education for creation of and adjustment to revolution" (Scriven, 1969). And finally (and probably most importantly) let us begin to devise the urgently required changes in the world political system by initiating an inquiry into the present system of sovereign, competitive nation-states.

In our classrooms we must begin to ask some sharp and penetrating questions about the nature and behavior of nation-states. What is sovereignty? Why do nations cling to it? Who exercises it in the present nation-state system? Is the exercising of sovereignty very different in the United States from that in the Soviet Union? What is the relationship between elites and sovereignty within the nation-state structure? What is the relationship between the nation-state system and the continued exploitation of third world nations?

Why does the nation-state and no other institution have a monopoly on the use of organized violence? What does that monopoly mean in terms of rights of minorities and individuals who dissent from the policies of the nation-state or who hold values different from the prevailing value system embodied by the establishment which runs the state?

What are the functions and responsibilities of the nation-state? How have they changed over the years? For what reasons other than identity have people given their allegiance to the nation-state? Does the national security state really provide security? Can nation-states still answer those needs for mankind? Can it protect us all from the threats of war, poverty, and pollution? Should we entertain new institutional patterns other than the nation-state system? What relationship might such patterns have to human survival?

Education has always served the dual needs of preparing individuals to function within the social order and of improving and expanding that order. This is a natural and desirable service to society. Current educational practice, however, seeks not to prepare and to improve but to impose and preserve. In so doing, it becomes a maladaptive practice which ultimately contributes to the miseries of the individuals in the society and to the decline of the society itself. Preoccupation with the past and glorification of the traditional institutions, with the exclusion of critical evaluation of those institutions, make it impossible to plan and work for a carefully projected and commonly desired future for the members of the whole human race. This circumstance makes it absolutely necessary to change the current educational practice of glorifying the individual nation-state and encouraging the pursuit of its power and interests. If this change does not come, there may be little hope for other urgently needed institutional change.

Epilogue

> To the second message from the newly discovered planet the nations of the earth replied, "Our schools are looking into the questions you have asked about nations."
>   A third message was received by Earth. It said "What are schools? Are *they* good for your species?"

REFERENCES

Barnet, Richard: Farewell to the nation-state. *New York Times,* June 19, 1971.

Becker, James: International and cross-cultural experiences: 1973 ASCD Yearbook, Education for Peace: Focus on Mankind, Henderson, George (ed.), Association for Supervision and Curriculum Development, 1201 Sixteenth St. N.W., Washington, D.C. 20036.

Caldwell, Oliver J.: The need for intercultural education in our universities. *Phi Delta Kappan, 52*:No. 9, 544-545, May, 1971.

Falk, Richard: This Endangered Planet. New York, Random House, 1971.

Hanvey, Robert: The nation-state (sound filmstrip). Produced for the Institute for World Order. Published and distributed by Doubleday Multimedia, 1972.

Kyung-Soo Cha: A quantitative analysis of concepts and values in selected Korean and U. S. social studies textbooks. Syracuse University, 1971 (unpublished). Bibliography available from the Institute for World Order, 11 W. 42nd St., New York, New York 10036.

Lasswell, Harold: Multiple loyalties in a shrinking world. Paper delivered to the 1968 annual Convention of the National Council for the Social Studies.

Scriven, Michael: Education for survival. *In* Kinley, G. (ed.): The Ideal School. Willamette, Illinois. Kagg Press, 1969.

U. S. Office of Education: An examination of objectives, needs, and priorities in international education in U. S. secondary and elementary schools, 1969.

responsibility 9
and indoctrination

John R. Coyne, Jr.

The Most Depressing Innovation of the Year Award goes to the Berkeley Board of Education, which recently passed a resolution directing school administrators "to establish and carry out antiwar programs in all schools and classrooms" in support of nationwide anti-Vietnam demonstrations.

Now there is no doubt that it would be a better world if man eschewed war completely (although the conservative believes this can never happen, given man's flawed nature). But one suspects that the motivation behind the Berkeley resolution isn't quite this pure.

Most liberal, educated Berkeleyites probably oppose, as does their school board, the war in Vietnam. But probably a significantly smaller number opposes the notion of war under all circumstances. Some, for instance, probably believe that we were required to fight Hitler. Others no doubt feel that the Israelis had to go to war. Still others may justify the recent Indian attack on Pakistan. And there are probably some Berkeleyites who oppose our involvement in Vietnam but believe the North Vietnamese have the right to wage war on the South.

All of which, of course, adds up to a very elementary point—the Berkeley antiwar classes are directed not at the idea of war but rather at one war in particular, and this a war around which swirl ideological and political arguments.

The antiwar movement fascinates conservatives, for conservatives were the only opponents of expanding the war during the period when liberal Democrats like J. William Fulbright were cheering for the Gulf of Tonkin resolution and Kennedyite technocrats such as Robert McNamara and Daniel Ellsberg were drawing up contingency plans for bigger and better bombings and battles.

Conservatives remember also the Democratic convention in '68, when the peace plank was voted down, thanks mainly to the efforts of men like Edmund Muskie, men who later campaigned for the presidency on that same peace plank.

And conservatives now notice another strange change developing. Richard Nixon, in '68, at least, a conservative, won that election by promising to end the war. He was the peace candidate. And he has done just that—he has ended the war. But by some strange transmutation, the liberal Democratic war which Mr. Nixon ended in a way that Hubert Humphrey wouldn't have dared to attempt, suddenly, according to various presidential aspirants and the Ellsbergs, became Mr. Nixon's war, and by extension, the war of us conservatives, who never wanted it in the first place.

But I argue this way, not to make a political point of my own, but to attempt to demonstrate precisely what's wrong with taking a position on the Vietnam war in the classroom. For any position you take on this war automatically becomes a partisan political position, whether you intend it that way or not. If you speak out insistently against the situation in South Vietnam as it now stands, you are criticizing the Republicans who are presently charged with administering our involvement. If you defend our involvement there, you are in effect defending the incumbent administration and attacking the Democrats who are disputing with it.

The fact is that there is no consensus in the nation on the war. The war is still ideologically and politically ambiguous, and when you teach someone to take a definite stand, as at Berkeley, you also necessarily urge him to adopt certain ideological positions. You are, in other words, proselytizing and indoctrinating. It is not possible, especially when charged by the school board to teach antiwar courses, to do otherwise. (One might speculate on what would happen to that teacher who was *pro*-war. Would he find the school board's directive impossible to carry out? And what would be the consequences to his career?)

Many have characterized ours as the age of the new romanticism, the chief qualities of which are emotionalism and moral fervor. These can be especially dangerous qualities in a time when differences are deep and basic, for they are essentially subjective qualities, and as such cannot allow for objectivity. Thus the antiwar people *burn* with the intensity of their opposition, believing right down to the marrow that no one could *possibly* disagree with them. Anyone who purports to disagree must be stupid, insincere, or evil.

I come across this reaction daily, working as a conservative in a monolithically liberal profession. One professor of sociology, for instance, has just finished a book which proves that the firing of an Arizona State University professor is indicative of a national move toward the right, in the direction of Nazi type repression. The sociology professor is eloquent in his defense of his dismissed colleague, an avowed activist socialist, who was fired for dismissing classes in order to take part in a New Left rally.

The firing, insists the sociology professor, was a purely political act, carried out by a repressive board of regents. No man, he insists, should be fired for his political beliefs, the airing of which is each man's privilege, and indeed his duty, under our constitution.

Granted. But during the course of an interview, the sociology professor asked the interviewer, a leftward-inclined student reporter, if he knew me. The student replied that he did, that in fact we often discussed contemporary social and political issues.

"How could you talk to a man with that background?" asked the professor. (I had worked for William Buckley for three years as an associate editor of *National Review* and had worked briefly during the summer of '71 on the staff of Vice President Agnew.)

"There are people who have set out to murder half the world's population," the professor continued, "He's allied himself with those people."

The professor was then asked whether I should enjoy the same rights as the dismissed socialist professor. Of course not, he responded. The cases are not similar. Which means, I assume, that my right of free speech should be abridged—for the good of society, of course.

Free speech, then, but free speech for the left. Dissent also, but dissent from the left. In short, ideological absolutism, ironically enough preached by those who inveigh against the notion of absolute values.

The academy trains our leaders and those teachers who will teach our children and mold our future leaders. And our society is in trouble if these leaders and molders set out upon their careers with closed minds. And I fear they will do so, for they are trained in what often seem the most closed minded communities on earth.

Much lip service is paid in the academy to presenting two sides of each significant national issue. Yet there is only one side on most pressing national issues, and that side tends always to lie to the left of center. Thus, any meaningful debate between, say, conservative and liberal, is impossible, for one cannot debate with people whose initial premise is always that the other side is dead wrong and that, since we know this absolutely and believe it almost religiously, they can score only debater's points. Thus, William Buckley is successful only insofar as he dazzles his audience. Despite the fact that he is a deeply religious man with deeply held political convictions, he is seldom granted deep sincerity. Academic audiences like him because he is entertaining. Seldom, however, will they bother to consider the possibility that he just might be right. We conservatives, as my professor of sociology believes, are haters and murderers, our motives always suspect. The professor will simply not allow me good faith.

There is, then, in the intellectual community, a central ideological point, lying much farther to the left than the center of the national, noninstitutionalized, nonintellectual, ideological spectrum. Anyone standing to the right of that central point has no say in academe. Thus, incendiary orators like William Kunstler or Huey Newton are free to roam the campus lecture circuit, sure of a warm welcome wherever they speak. Yet Vice President Agnew cannot, although he deeply desires to do so, speak on any major non-Southern university campus. The reason: the university administrations cannot guarantee his safety. (Not long ago, the Vice President was asked by administrators at Harvard not to appear before students in a government class there. The administrators cancelled an invitation extended by a young professor because, they feared, there would be riots. When the instructor questioned the decision, a dean told him that it was all the Vice President's fault for creating such conditions in the first place.)

Now you may not be an admirer of Spiro Agnew (and I'm sure you're not if you're a typical university graduate), but can't you see the irony here? Any speaker who sets out to prove that the CIA assassinates presidents, that there is a conspiracy to murder Black Panthers, that Agnew would like to kill kids, that the Administration is preparing concentration camps, that ours is the most rotten and repressive system the world has ever seen (all such charges of violent repression and suppression of free speech always delivered at the top of the lungs)—any such views, no matter how crazed, are received enthusiastically. Yet the Vice President of the United States cannot get a hearing on any major northern campus.

But most important, of course, is what such an atmosphere does to students. I teach on one of the nation's least politicized university campuses. Yet when William Kunstler recently spoke here the turnout was dismayingly massive, a comprehensive cross-section of the student body giving Kunstler a hero's welcome. His speech was alarming, the reaction to it chilling. For these three thousand plus students, crammed standing-room only into the university auditorium, accepted every word as basic, unadorned truth. When Kunstler accused Governor Nelson Rockefeller of literal murder, the applause crackled. When Kunstler spoke of government conspiracies against black people, the nods were knowing. When he spoke of planned genocide, the charge was received as routinely as a weather report. Afterward, talking with students, reading student publications, listening to student conversations, I came across only two students willing to question the wildest of Kunstler's charges.

Lately many people, among them the editors of the *New York Times* and Edward Kennedy, have told us that the campuses have cooled off, that the radicals are no longer a threat, and that the campus revolution is over. It may be over, but has it failed? Some of us believe it is over because the campuses have become so radicalized that there are no revolutionary battles left to fight. Today, the typical assistant professor of English literature takes stands on issues ranging from Vietnam to black militants that a few years back would have been embraced only by the SDS. The campuses, some of us feel, have become so radicalized that even at a quiet place like Arizona State University, the views of an eccentric fanatic like William Kunstler, who tells us that Governor Rockefeller not only ordered him murdered but also directed authorities to cut the throats of prison guards held hostage in order to make it appear that the convicts had murdered them, are taken as the norm.

How did it happen? How did the process which we now see at work in the public schools of communities like Berkeley actually begin?

It began, of course, in the universities, where there has traditionally been no short supply of active indoctrinators like my dismissed socialist colleague. But these active indoctrinators, I believe, have been less effective than the unconscious indoctrinators. It's always much easier, after all, to judge a man who tells you where he stands than to analyze a man who stands in one place but actually believes he stands in another.

An example. Let me quote at some length, if I may, from a controversial section of a controversial book, *The Kumquat Statement,* which I wrote in 1970, The scene is the University of California at Berkeley. The character: a professor of English, from whom I took a course.

"The professor of a popular course at Berkeley in British literature was known to be a soft touch, meaning you could doze away the session, take no notes, write one of those subjective, top-of-the-head papers, scribble some sensitive little thoughts (preferably sexual ones) for the final exam, and get an easy B. An A came a bit harder, usually requiring the reading of a few introductions and the repetition on the final exam of some of the professor's choicer remarks.

"He was fiftyish, short and plump, and he liked girls, pretty ones. They knew this, of course—the student grapevine is one of the world's finest intelligence systems—and they'd grab the seats down front in the auditorium where he lectured to a couple of hundred students, both graduate and undergrad. He'd lean over the lectern, gaze at the girls in short skirts, who'd stretch becomingly, and talk about 'my wife's crumpled old body,' which he'd compare with 'your high breasts and firm thighs.' Now, it's inevitable that the subject of sex will come up in any discussion of literature, but not necessarily in connection with every single work since the death of Victoria. One can perhaps forgive this professor his daily bout of rather mild self-titillation, but unfortunately it went a good deal deeper, debasing not only the poor goatish old professor but also the literature to which, presumably, he'd dedicated his life. By debasing the literature, he debased the whole system of values that underlay literature.

" 'Principles and values make us unhappy,' he'd say, generalizing from the work under consideration. (It's an academic habit to use the occasion of analyzing the written word as an excuse to propound one's eclectic view of the nature of man, the universe, and the local water supply.)

" 'Religion [and] nationalism make us unhappy,' he tells a bunch of kids, many of whom have recently left religious homes and are still, in their rather simpleminded ways, somewhat proud to be Americans. 'Take care of matter and the spirit will take care of itself.' But apparently it's no easy job to take care of matter, for the mood suddenly changes. 'The only reality is the reality of loneliness,' he says, staring at those thighs. 'Man is trapped in a prison house of self and consciousness, living in metaphysical isolation.' Now he descends from the metaphysical. 'Life is dirty and vulgar,' he intones gloomily. Human existence is all 'bestiality and cannibalism. . . .'

" 'There is no authority in life or nature. Man is guilty of the general crime of being alive.' (Guilty by what authority? one wanted to shout.) Man's duty is 'just to drudge along.' Why? Because 'it's brave to live.' Although, of course, in a world without authority and standards, bravery must carry the same moral weight as girl ogling, sodomy, or chicken plucking.

"Thus it is in the 'liberal' classroom at many universities today—the standard liberal-arts eclectic blend of liberal flummery, a half-cooked combination of the early twentieth-century popularizations of Marx, Darwin, and Freud, stirred in with a healthy dose of the theory of relativity, imperfectly understood and dishonestly applied to human affairs. Add a pinch of existentialism, mix it all up, and watch the students get sick. How does one explain to these students that this posturing intellectual pretender in jacket and tie lives the most orthodox of middle class lives. . . .

"The brightest and most cynical students know this, of course. . . . But do the more naive know it's all just a game? What can there be to live for in a world of 'bestiality and cannibalism,' a world with no values and standards. . . . How about that confused girl from some hick town who loves her family and all they represent but comes to believe that their morality is artificial, their way of life hypocritical, their teachings baseless and corrupt? And how about that overly intense boy who gets the message loud and clear and follows it through to its logical conclusion by fire-bombing some campus building? I've seen it happen. Isn't his gesture essentially an admirable one, a gesture the professor, if he had any real convictions, would have to praise in the classroom, a blow for purity in a corrupt universe? Are teachers willing to accept responsibility for the rubble of these lives? Or will some professor shrug, as did Timothy Leary when one of his disciples, a teen-aged girl, drowned after an overdose of dope, and say, with Leary, why should I feel badly when so many people are dying in Vietnam?

"What is this professor doing? . . . by using his subject to score political points he undermines the beliefs and traditions of many of his students. He is no Marxist, just a typical liberal-leftist academic, and like most of his colleagues he probably has little idea of what he's done. And when those kids leave his classes, many of them with a whole belief system lying in rubble around their feet, they're prime material for conversion to a new system."

And thus, the radicalization of the American university. And now, as the Berkeley antiwar classes suggest, a generation of radicalized and deeply politicized teachers and administrators has left the campuses to carry on the work of indoctrination in the public schools.

When I call them radicalized, of course, I don't mean that they are radicals, by any stretch of the imagination. Rather, they have come to accept as norms the whole range of radical ideas which dominate the intellectual life of the academy. And now, in such places as Berkeley, they unthinkingly pass along these values to a few generations of school children. It is, of course, as in the case of the poor Berkeley professor, primarily a matter of fashion. Certain ideas, certain attitudes, certain ways of thinking are fashionable in the academic world, and most citizens of the academic world want to be with it. And to be with it, it is necessary to accept certain notions. Agnosticism, for instance, is always in vogue. Religion is asinine and superstitious, as is patriotism (except, of course, when it appears in North Vietnam or various African nations). Right and wrong—why, they're impossible to determine, of course, for their meaning is purely semantic. There are only shades of gray, no absolutes, except, of course, the war in Vietnam—that is *definitely* wrong. (Wrong by what standard? Well, it just *is.*)

Exaggerated? Perhaps. But I don't think so. Increasingly, it seems to me, the teachers who graduate from our radicalized campuses are bringing the same lessons to our school children as those that have long been standard fare for university students.

The primary function of a large group of liberal arts professors has long been, they sincerely believe, to "shake the kids up," to get them to question "those middle-class values."

Now, no matter that those "middle-class values" that we all so easily sneer at are the values that made this a great nation (if you're radicalized enough, of course, this assertion will be meaningless, for you won't accept the proposition that this is a great nation); that the term "middle-class values" is shorthand for all those social, philosophical, religious, and moral ideas that make up the Judaeo-Christian heritage; and that the people who preach most strongly against them are often the people who, like my Berkeley professor, live the most mundane of middle-class private lives.

But forget all these inconsistencies and concentrate on the result of this fashionable approach. The high school or college student meets such a teacher, who sincerely believes that the best thing he can do for the student is to "shake him up," to make him question those middle-class values. These values, instilled at home, have up to this moment been accepted unquestioningly. But now, suddenly, a learned, articulate teacher asks him to question them. In order to question them, of course, one must find arguments which attack them, and when these arguments are presented by a learned sophisticated teacher, the thing being argued against, a belief in God, for instance, usually embraced unquestioningly and therefore inarticulately, suddenly seems shallow. A new opposition often sets itself up in the student's mind—inarticulate or uncommunicative parents who dogmatically insist that the student accept certain truths versus an articulate, sympathetic teacher who invites them to question those supposed truths.

That the parents are inarticulate does not make these beliefs wrong. Nor does the glibness of the teacher do so. But it will often seem to the student that such is the case. The teacher teaches the value of eternal questioning, skepticism. But skepticism for many becomes an absolute in itself, leaving a moral and intellectual vacuum where once there had been values. The teacher forgets to teach that one should question the value of eternally questioning, and by so doing leaves his students unsatisfied.

The unsatisfied student, his first value system in rubble around his feet, finds a void in his life and seeks something to fill it. And that something, of course, tends most often to be that which is most fashionable among his peers. Thus a generation of students finds its new set of absolute values in the utterances of the new romantics.

And these are no longer just college students. That group who listened so happily to Kunstler was a very young group, a large percentage of them freshmen. Their automatic acceptance of the truths preached by Kunstler was the result of some experience earlier than the first year of college. One suspects, that like the current crop of high and grade schoolers at Berkeley, they are being indoctrinated at a very early age.

What to do about it? I suppose I'd begin by begging teachers to examine very carefully those attitudes and ideas they pass on in the classroom. How many of them are sincerely held? How many have been subjected to rigorous intellectual examination? And how many of them are simply reflexive, fashionable intellectual attitudes adopted by professors for much the same reason as pipe-smoking? Do you know what you mean when you talk about "shaking kids up?" Do you understand just how complex and how important to our society are those things we rather casually call "middle-class values"?

The tendency among educators to meddle with values is a dangerous one, at times breathtaking in its ignorance, as, for instance, in the case of the educational establishment of the state of Wisconsin and the Amish parents who would not send their children to high school. By attempting to coerce them into doing so, the state was in effect saying to them, (a) we overrule your God, who forbids you to send your children to high school, or (b) your God, who forbids you to send your children to high school, is, according to our determination, a fraud.

Educators were never intended to be arbiters of religious values, never intended to weigh the relative merits of the commandments of any man's God. Nor were they intended to be arbiters of social or political values.

The task is to teach, not to indoctrinate. There is a very distinct difference. Understanding this distinction is essential if we are not to produce a completely politicized generation, as apparently is the case at Berkeley.

10 no more bootleg religion

Richard J. Neuhaus

The move for Prohibition in American life was a long time building before it was crowned with success by the Eighteenth Amendment in January of 1919. Prohibition was dethroned by the Twenty-first Amendment, December, 1933, but those 15 years remain the most instructive American lesson on the connection between morality and law. Prohibition is cited by liberals, conservatives, and radicals alike as an example of what law should not do because it cannot. The memory of Prohibition stood behind President Eisenhower's frequent comment on race relations, "You can't legislate morality." The Eighteenth Amendment is even more frequently called to the witness stand by liberals in their campaign to remove legal restrictions from marijuana, abortion, homosexuality, and pornography. The standard argument is that forbidding people to do what they are going to do anyway only nurtures contempt for the law. To be sure, law can affect behavior and change attitudes. The South's response to recent civil rights legislation illustrates this to a limited extent. But for the most part, effective law is reflective of the mores and prevailing assumptions in the society.

All but a few diehards agree that Prohibition was a mistake. Especially in the urban areas it did little to prevent alcoholic indulgence. Instead, it nurtured a flourishing gangsterism and bred official corruption, the political effects of which linger today. It put low quality liquor on the market, which often resulted in sickness and even death. But, most important, Prohibition had an ugly social effect—alienation—on large sectors of the American public. Alienation is what many of us feel when we hear a President condemn violence while imposing Pax Americana on two thirds of the world by brute force. Alienation is the experience of college students who see politicians indignant about pot but oblivious to the crimes of war, poverty, and racism. Alienation (although they might not use the term) is the feeling of the Italians of the Red Hook section of Brooklyn when they hear public figures rail against the Mafia and organized crime while corruption undermining city services goes unchecked. Alienation is what a majority of Americans feel as a result of the increasing prohibition of religion from the public schools.

Thoughtful observers have consistently noted the extent of American religiosity and interpenetration of religion and public institutions. After Tocqueville's visit in 1831-32, he wrote that "there is no country in the world where the Christian religion retains a greater influence over the souls of men than in America. . . ." More than a century later Harold Laski found that the impact of "the Christian tradition" on many aspects of American life was profound. In *Zorach v. Clauson* (1952) Justice William Douglas observed, "We are a religious people . . . and our institutions presuppose a Supreme Being."

Those who most ardently wage the war against Supreme Court restrictions of religion in the schools pay, perhaps inadvertently, the highest compliment to public education. They keep the old faith of Thomas Jefferson, Horace Mann, and John Dewey that the public school is the central socializing agent in communicating the cultural heritage to the next generation. The more "liberal" acceptance of Supreme Court restrictions on religion in the schools reveals, I believe, a growing indifference to public education, or at least a disillusionment with the ideology that sustained the public school venture from the early nineteenth century through the 1950's.

One problem is that the public school has been oversold. The supporters of the late Senator Everett Dirksen's "prayer amendment" (to allow voluntary prayer by students in public schools) are guilty of nothing more than believing what they were told by the most fervent and revered proponents of public education. Such diverse figures as Max Rafferty and John Dewey have argued that moral (and thereby religious) education was a responsibility of the school. Horace Mann, whose academic monument on Morningside Heights still casts a shadow over the classrooms of America, outdoes Dewey in vaunting the ambitions of public education: "The common school is the greatest discovery ever made by man." With its development "nine-tenths of the crimes in the penal code would become obsolete, the long catalogue of human ills would be abridged, man would walk more safely by day . . . [and] all rational hopes respecting the future [would be] brightened." Religion is essential in the school, but Mann abjured sectarianism, which he defined as "that which belongs to a part, not to the *whole*." Our system "earnestly inculcates all Christian morals," proclaimed Mann, apparently oblivious to the implicit sectarianism in his notion of "the whole."

In his admirable historical survey, *Piety in the Public School,* to which I am greatly indebted, Robert Michaelsen remarks, "These convictions [about religion in the schools] reflect the Unitarianism which Mann had come to embrace and were rooted in and had affinities with the liberal religious and theological ideas of such founding fathers as Franklin, John Adams, Jefferson, and Madison." To the more orthodox, "Mann's point of view seemed to be a prime example of infidelity or deism. Nevertheless, Mann's convictions furnished a number of planks in the ideological platform upon which it was possible to erect a public school system." The enduring power of Mann's ideological planks is evident in the 1951 report of a blue-ribbon commission of the National Education Association, which urged that "there must be no question whatever as to the willingness of the school to subordinate all other considerations to those which concern moral and spiritual standards." The same inflated rhetoric is the staple diet of conventional educators today, but they seem embarrassed when the innocents of Middle America take it at face value.

Jacques Barzun tells the marvelous story about the Columbia undergraduate who sued the university for many thousands of dollars because it failed to give him "an adequate life experience." Barzun's point is that the university should be more cautious about what it claims to provide if it does not want to be sued for fraud. The public school system today is very vulnerable because it has oversold itself to the American people. The peril of all super-salesmanship is that the consumer may take you at your word.

I do not know if the public school could have entrenched itself as an indispensable American institution if it had not made such extraordinary claims. As it was, the claims did not severely conflict with reality as long as the public school was an agent of undifferentiated white Protestantism, as long as God was acknowledged, prayers said, and the Bible read. But now the Supreme Court ruling and a secularizing trend among some educators have combined to remove from the schools anything that most Americans identify as "religious" or "moral." These Americans want public education to deliver on its promises, as they think it used to. No wonder they resent a "godless" Court that is robbing them of their schools. The opponents of recent Supreme Court decisions ejecting religious observance from the schools are not a radical fringe of innovators; they are the traditionalists, the true believers. Recent judgments have turned the public school's true believers against the Court and, unless there is a major reversal, will turn them against the public school itself. I hasten to add that I do not disagree with the Court decisions in question, I only note the consequences.

On the other side are those who not only accept but often laud the Supreme Court's decisions. Such approval is usually combined with a much more modest understanding of the "mission" of public education. The National Council of Churches, an organization that is usually considered more "liberal" than its constituent denominations, observed in 1963:

> The public schools have an obligation to help individuals develop an intellectual under-
> standing and appreciation of the role of religion in the life of the people of this nation.
> Teaching for religious commitment is the responsibility of the home and the community
> of faith (such as the church or synagogue) rather than the public schools.

The contrast with Dewey's insistence that the schools must teach for religious commit-ment while avoiding "sectarian religion" is striking. The deflated rhetoric about the role of public education in the National Council statement is clearly incompatible with conventional notions about the school as a "laboratory for all of life" and "an agency dealing with the whole person."

Educators are in a bind. If they take the traditional rhetoric seriously, they find themselves in conflict with the Supreme Court. If they affirm the logic of the Court, they must work with a notion of the public school that has established such a limited purpose for education that it may not hold their loyalty and certainly will not, in the long run, claim the loyalty of the general public.

One way out of the bind—and this has become more popular since the 1947 *McCollum* case banning the teaching of religion on school property—is to teach religion under another name. It is a resolution by definition. The Educational Policies Commission of the NEA, in promoting the teaching of "moral and spiritual values," lists ten values on which "the American people are agreed." They include: human personality —the basic value, moral responsibility, devotion to truth, moral equality, the pursuit of happiness, and spiritual enrichment.

The term "moral and spiritual values" seems more neutral than "religion." One can hardly imagine the Constitution being interpreted to read, "Congress shall make no law respecting the encouragement of moral and spiritual values." The problem, of course, is that the ten points of agreement suggested by the NEA are not so obvious as they may seem. If indeed they have been "agreed upon by the American people," that is no evidence of their validity. In fact, the suggestion that common agreement establishes values runs counter to the NEA's stated "value" of "devotion to truth," for truth, more often than not, challenges prevailing orthodoxies, including the orthodoxy of the NEA's ten values.

Further, if we scratch any of these ten values, we discover religious and philosophical assumptions of great diversity, comparable only to the disagreement we would encounter in trying to apply them. Surely it is possible to pass on these "values" without comment or examination. But this is tantamount to the mouthing of platitudes. While they may be legally antiseptic, they are also intellectually debilitating and morally fraudulent. The superficial teaching of morality by consensus can only belittle the concern for "spiritual and moral values," without which education is little more than the mechanical transmission of information. And so it is for perfectly honorable reasons that religion is bootlegged into the public school classroom.

The Court-defined "wall of separation" between Church and State is made not of stones and mortar but of fine conceptual distinctions. The "religion" prohibited by the Court is more easily recognized when it is prepackaged in the distinctive positions and practices of identifiable religious groups. Thus we think we know when someone is teaching the tenets of Lutheranism, Seventh Day Adventism, or Orthodox Judaism in the classroom. Even with this restrictive definition of religion, however, there are many religiously and ethnically homogeneous areas, especially in small towns and country schools, where it is impossible to erect a wall of separation between secular and religious instruction. It is impossible in part because local enforcement agencies and school administrators are not ready to run the risk of community outrage that would accompany any consistent prohibition of religion. More important, it is impossible because in such homogeneous communities the line between the secular and the religious is not readily recognized.

In a Minnesota school where almost all the students and teachers are German Catholics, the teachings of the Church are inseparably embroiled with the attitudes and assumptions that comprise the prevailing world of discourse. In such schools, moral and spiritual values can be separated from explicit religious teaching only at the price of the most stilted and artificial restraints upon the natural course of classroom discussion. When the observance of the law's rigid demands requires such damage to educational and human processes, it is likely that the law will not be observed.

There is sometimes a bootleg uneasiness surrounding the teaching of religion even in such homogeneous settings. Except in those cases when the law is openly flaunted, the ritual Bible reading and prayers have been dropped. Teachers are also inhibited by the presence of unbelievers or dissenters from the classroom's religious consensus, knowing that if they too eagerly press any specific belief, the result may be complaints from parents. A devout Methodist teacher in Illinois' public schools remarks, "There is one Jewish boy in my class. Most of the Christian children come from politically conservative homes. When I'm asked what I believe about Jesus or the Bible, the principal relays the Jewish parents' complaint about my answer. When I'm asked about Vietnam or about protesters, I get flak from the other parents. How can the students and I have a human relationship if we have to exclude any discussion of my convictions, and of theirs?"

This teacher, and there are many like her, is not an aggressive propagandist for her views. She stresses the value of diversity in political and religious viewpoints. The legal pressure on religious questions and the social pressure on political questions bifurcate her person and her beliefs, which surely does nothing for her satisfaction as a teacher or, more important, for the growth of the children. Of course, in even more homogeneous communities the social conflict is absent and the legal conflict is ignored. But, viewed from a legal viewpoint, even there the religious belief system is bootlegged into the classroom. Viewed from what I suspect is a more human viewpoint, the classroom is simply an agent of the community's religious and social values, which is not too different from what Mann and Dewey hoped for.

But such homogeneity is not the normal milieu of the public school classroom nationally. The legal calculations of recent years assume normality to be represented by the radical pluralism of American life seen as a whole. Supreme Court rulings on education reflect a national rather than a local perspective, and the primary concern seems to be to prevent the violation of anyone's civil liberties by being coerced or indoctrinated into a religious viewpoint alien to their beliefs or lack thereof. As early as *Barnette* (1943) Justice Jackson declared the faith of the Court:

> If there is any fixed star in our constitutional constellation, it is that no official, high or petty, can prescribe what shall be orthodox in politics, nationalism, religion, or other matters of opinion or force citizens to confess by word or act their faith therein.

Since that time the Court has progressively, or regressively, as the case may be, narrowed its notion of what it means to "prescribe" or "force" orthodoxy. True, in *Schempp* (1958) the Court had some kind things to say on teaching *about* religion as distinct from inculcating religious belief. Many educational and religious groups welcomed this encouragement as the resolution of the religion-in-the-schools problem. But only for a time. Widespread experimentation with "objective" courses on religion has produced no solution. Public educators cannot ignore the educational and psychological impossibility of teachers schizophrenically separating subject matter from personal belief. Nor are educators willing to discard the traditional belief that schools are responsible for *positive* teaching of moral and spiritual values. Call it coercion or call it sharing, the fact remains that most educators and parents expect teachers to communicate certain values and attitudes toward life that many of us call religion.

It is naive to think that one can positively teach values, such as the ten "agreed upon" values suggested by the NEA, without moving into the realm of religion. As the unexamined life is not worth living, so unexamined value statements are not worth sharing. Upon examination every value statement assumes beliefs about the nature of man, history, life, death, virtue, and evil—in short, the classic subjects of religious teaching. Values imply religion, and if education is to prepare children to understand and participate in life, "life" can hardly be discussed meaningfully apart from values.

To be sure, it has been argued that the values-and-religion issue can be avoided by never venturing beyond what is conventionally viewed as the parameters of the secular. But this is a crippled and crippling approach to the development of the whole personality, and is rightly rejected by most teachers. Sociologist Peter Berger writes that "what is often called the secular outlook is similar to the perspective of a middle-aged businessman on a quiet afternoon after two martinis and an excellent lunch." In short, the apparent objectivity of a secular approach simply blocks out the fantasies, surprises, persistent inquiries, and life-and-death anxieties that make up a whole life experience. Indeed, a thorough secularism may also be illegal, for as Arthur Goldberg wrote in *Schempp,* the Constitution "prohibited . . . a brooding and pervasive devotion to the secular." Most religious thinkers would insist that such an absolutized secularism is *de facto* a religion. Certainly this has been a common Roman Catholic argument for parochial schools. The choice, it is said, is not between getting religion in the parochial schools and a religionless education in the public schools, but between the Catholic religion in the parochial school and the religion of secularism in the public.

"Religion" is a phenomenon not limited to the organized groups that call themselves religious. The estimable theologian Paul Tillich described religion as that which is of "ultimate concern" to a person. What he surrenders himself to unconditionally is his "God," even if that be the "scientific method" or the "processes of rationality." Peter Berger describes religion in terms of the "plausibility structure" that gives meaning to one's life. He argues persuasively in *The Sacred Canopy* (Doubleday, 1969) and elsewhere that the only alternative to committing oneself to one plausibility structure or another is *anomie,* the condition in which one lacks both identity and meaning.

Lewis Mumford, in his polemic against the "Megamachine" to which he believes scientism is leading us, quotes David Hume, "a brilliant mind that, under the cover of complete skepticism, established the new [empirical] outlook as a dogma." Hume called for the destruction of any book that is not based upon "abstract reasoning concerning quantity or number" or does not contain "any experimental reasoning concerning matters of fact and existence," since such books can contain "nothing but sophistry and illusion." To which Mumford remarks, "Those who took all this seriously found it easy to wipe out every mode of theology and metaphysics but their own, which they mistook for common sense and reality." So much for secular neutrality on matters of religion.

John Dewey was right about the religious responsibility of the schools. He was also right in seeing certain common views held by all organized religions. What he conveniently overlooked was the diversity and conflict among them. The result was a religious eclecticism that in its combination is as religiously particularistic as Horace Mann's Unitarianism, Jefferson's "common faith," or Middle America's pan-Protestant "Christian morality." If the schools are to teach "moral and spiritual values" they will—whether they want to or not, whether they are conscious of it or not—be teaching religion. If the schools do not teach "moral and spiritual values" but do intend to "educate the whole person," that too is the teaching of religion, the religion of secularism. This is the dilemma that will not go away.

On the legal level, developments are shaping toward a confrontation with the dilemma. There is an apparent contradiction between recent Supreme Court rulings on religion in the schools and the Court's rulings on conscientious objection under the Selective Service System. It is now clear (*U.S. v. Seeger,* 1965) that a person without formal religious affiliation can qualify as a conscientious objector, even though the Selective Service Law requires that his objection be the product of religious training based upon belief in a Supreme Being. The Court holds that values deeply and sincerely held play the same role in the life of the supposed nonbeliever as doctrine and belief in God play in the lives of orthodox believers. This is not very far from the understanding of "religion" that I have argued above.

The Court's school rulings define religion much more narrowly, as something largely limited to tenets or practices associated with organized religions. Combining the Court's more expansive and, I believe, more adequate approach to religion as it touches on the draft with the Court's oft-stated urging that the schools teach moral values, we must conclude that the Court wants the schools to teach religion or its equivalent. It would be the most gross and arbitrary discrimination for the Court to exclude only those moral and spiritual values which happen to find expression in the teachings of organized religion. That would be tantamount to the Court's ruling that only new or as yet officially unformulated religious teachings have a place in the classroom. This is, one hopes, patently absurd. Although the Supreme Court has yet to emerge from its conceptual thicket with an updated definition of what it means by religion, the idea of the public school sponsoring a new religion is not without precedent. In fact, there are those who believe the promotion of such a religion is essential to the survival of the Republic. Since they are not always too articulate about what they are promoting, and since the courts have not yet ruled on their product, the inculcation of the religion called Americanism must also be viewed as a bootleg operation.

Because of the pervasiveness of religion in one form or another, it cannot be excluded from any adequate view of education's task. The courts have clearly ruled out the teaching of the beliefs and practices of any existing religious tradition. It is educationally and psychologically impossible to domesticate the subject matter within the rubric of "objective teaching about religion." All the reductionist efforts to find "the common faith behind the faiths" seem to arrive at a type of Unitarian-Universalism which is, in addition to being objectionable to most Americans, also probably unconstitutional, since Unitarian-Universalism is an existing religious brand name. The alternative is the establishment of a new religion, to be called something other than religion, perhaps "American Moral and Spiritual Values."

J. Paul Williams' *What Americans Believe and How They Worship* argues that, if the rapid disintegration of American life is to be halted, "governmental agencies must teach the democratic ideal *as religion.*" Chief among these governmental agencies is, of course, the public school. After examining "the traditional religions" in America, Williams concludes that they are not able to cope with the public crisis. In their place we should erect what must frankly be termed a State Church in the United States: "A culture is above everything else a faith, a set of shared convictions, a spiritual entity." If it is to survive, "systematic and universal indoctrination is essential in the values on which a society is based, if that society is to have any permanence or stability. . . . America runs a grave danger from lack of attention to the spiritual core which is the heart of her national existence. If we are to avoid this danger, democracy must become an object of religious dedication. Americans must come to look on the democratic ideal (not necessarily American practice of it) as the Will of God or, if they please, the law of Nature." While the churches and synagogues should be signed up for the promotion of this democratic faith, the job of bringing "the majority of our people to a religious devotion to the democratic way of life" must be backed by the coercive power of the state, even though this means "giving the power of wholesale religious indoctrination into the hands of the politicians. . . ."

When put so baldly by Professor Williams, the proposal of a State Religion evokes from the reader a cluster of objections, legal, educational and, not least, religious. But his argument is not all that foreign to the ideology that has shaped the public school in America, nor all that different from existing practice. American historian Sidney Mead has written ". . . of necessity the state in its public-education system is and always has been teaching religion. It does so because the well-being of the nation and the state demands this foundation of shared beliefs. . . . In this sense the public-school system of the United States *is* its established church."

As with the little boy who refused to applaud the emperor's new finery, candor about religion in the schools can bring us to a more honest understanding of our problem. Religion *in* the schools is an essential part of what has become the religion *of* the schools. The religion of "schooling" has grown to gargantuan size but with such stealth and lack of candor that most of us do not recognize its religious nature. Certainly we are surprised to discover ourselves serving at its altars.

Paul Goodman has helped demystify "schooling." Ivan Illich has described North American education as an established church. The hold that schooling has on American life can be compared only with the control of the Catholic Church at the height of medieval christendom. The educational establishment has its rites of initiation, its rites of passage, its sacraments, interdicts, excommunications, and offices of the Holy Inquisition. It has its dogmas, albeit disguised in the language of secularity and objectivity. Just as other religious movements finally find their institutional expression, so American Moral and Spiritual Values has found its church in the public school system. The NEA is the combined curia and ecumenical council, district (diocesan) superintendents are its bishops, principals are the pastors, and the numerous schools of education are its seminaries.

An American state religion has been established without the advice or consent of the American people. Just as the people were surprised to discover that the Eighteenth Amendment prohibiting the liquor industry only created an alternative liquor industry, so there is increasing surprise and disillusionment as Americans discover that the Court's prohibition of religion has succeeded in establishing another religion. As with most established churches, public education is unbelievably resistant to challenge or change. The surprise of discovery is reflected in a speech by the former Director of the Office of Economic Opportunity, Donald Rumsfeld, delivered in San Francisco, September 23, 1970:

> In spite of our best efforts to date, the educational system remains relatively ineffective from the standpoint of the poor. Yet, criticisms of the Office of Economic Opportunity's experiments in education have been voiced by some special interest groups. . . . The critics fear experimentation because it may call into question their dogmas and orthodoxies. They seem to be embarked on a crusade to stifle efforts to gain new knowledge to improve. The defensiveness that has characterized the criticisms indicates all too clearly the need for new actors in the educational policy planning process.

To be sure, the "special interest groups" to which Rumsfeld refers are the teachers' unions, and some suspicion of the Nixon Administration's anti-unionism is warranted. But to draw the line of battle along pro- or anti-union sympathies is to miss the point. The leaders of teachers' unions have become the ultra-montanists, the Jesuit shock troops, of the educational church. After ten years of experience, I am forced to the conclusion that only in this light can one understand the role played by the United Federation of Teachers in New York City.

Among the chief items of UFT orthodoxy is the infallibly promulgated Dogma of Professionalism. In the name of "professionalism" the UFT has fought relentlessly almost every effort for more effective schools. Decentralization, community control, parent participation in administrative decisions, and now the accountability contracting proposed by OEO—all, according to the UFT, violate the dogma of professionalism. It is clear that professionalism has more to do with the educational establishment's system of examinations and processes of legitimacy than with any educational consequences for the children in the schools. Again and again I have seen parents working for community control who exhibit a very high concern for what most of us laymen would call professionalism. The parents want the teachers to be in the classrooms, rather than ambitiously crawling through the lucrative chambers of the beehives of educational bureaucracy. Above all, the parents want teachers to be serious about educational results and determined to change situations where, for example, a majority of high school students read on the fifth grade level or below.

Far from threatening educational chaos, as the UFT charges, the community control groups I have worked with are consistently more demanding about professionalism in performance, if not in degrees earned and examinations passed. They are the law and order people of education, the hardhats of the classroom. For six years a group which I head has operated an experimental middle school (grades 5 through 8) completely controlled by the black and Puerto Rican parents of the children. The parents' high standards of professionalism have always been both a burden and a source of great satisfaction to the teachers. But, of course, "professionalism" means something else according to UFT doctrine.

Rumsfeld and other critics may have part of the truth when they speak of the unions protecting "special interests." But this economic analysis fails to do justice to the religious nature and sincerity of the UFT commitment. As often happens in religion, what one believes finally becomes a question of authority. According to the UFT, sitting at the feet of the divines in schools of education, combined with the granting of tenure, is the only legitimate process of attaining authority. Just as reason or empirical evidence could not be permitted to challenge the pre-Vatican II Catholic's acceptance of papal pronouncements, so consideration of a teacher's actual performance or knowledge is an act of unbelief. Courses in education (whatever that may mean) are the sacraments of education's clergy, and, like the sacraments of medieval christendom, they operate *ex opere operato,* automatically without reference to the conditions or consequences among those who receive them. The farther removed education courses are from actual subject matter or classroom teaching, the more apparent it is that these are the sacred mysteries of schooldom. The sense of mystery is heightened by unintelligibility, the sacred is enhanced by irrelevance, and true faith disdains the sordid criteria of evidence.

Some may think the above description of the established educational church is exaggerated, and perhaps it is, if only slightly. But surely we must take the church of American Moral and Spiritual Values seriously as a religion and credit the sincerity of its devotees. The alternative is to believe with Mr. Rumsfeld that American educators as a group behave as they do only because they are engaged in a grubby fight to defend their vested interests. I prefer to think they are motivated by more noble sentiments. They believe theirs is a holy crusade against the infidels. And, if the infidels include the parents and children whom they are presumably serving, even that publicly embarrassing contradiction is not too great a price for the obedient sons and daughters of the true church to pay.

The public education system is today in deep trouble, and I suspect the dismantling of its present structure is only a matter of time. The present system has given rise to two groups of true believers, and I expect both groups are declining in numbers and influence. The first is composed of the millions of Americans who believe the schools are doing a more or less adequate job of nurturing intellectual growth and passing on the cultural and religious heritage in which they believe. These are the people who consider it self-evident that America is a "Christian nation" and that "under God" on our coins is a statement of fact beyond dispute. They are puzzled and resentful about the Supreme Court rulings about their kind of religion in the schools. In the South, this resentment combines with opposition to mandated racial integration. The white middle-class Protestants who have been the base support group for American public schools are being alienated. More and more often, they are casting about for alternatives.

The other group of true believers is found among the educators themselves. One can only welcome the numerous books in recent years by disillusioned educators, especially those who have worked with public education in poverty areas. The Faith will be challenged increasingly, I am confident, as more and younger teachers become disgusted with a "professionalism" that has more to do with paychecks, promotions, and retirement than with educational commitment or creativity.

The poor, notably the urban blacks and Puerto Ricans, have overwhelmingly defected from the public school faith. Roman Catholics, including the newly visible and powerful "ethnics," never really believed; they viewed public schools as, at best, a necessary evil. And then there is the counter culture, or whatever other term one may prefer.

For people who view Vietnam, Kent State, and the murder of Fred Hampton as revelations of the true America, the whole ideology of public education is odious. Why would one want to pass on the American heritage of racism, imperialism, and brutality? Among the most objectionable facets of the public education ideology is the fact that it refuses to admit that it is an ideology. The now aging mandarins used to assure us that ours is an age marked by "the end of ideology." But we now witness a fervent rebirth of ideological enthusiasm. The same mandarins assured us that "the religious question" was finally giving way to the tide of enlightened secularity. But we now witness a new youthful fascination with religious matters. Whether we view this as a revival of superstition, an artificially induced ecstasy, or a barbarian tribal consciousness is quite beside the point. The point is that the coming intelligentsia of America will make no sense of the Supreme Court's distinctions between the religious and the secular and will be exceedingly poor propagandists for any consensus belief about American democracy.

Increasingly, the old claims about "educating the whole person" while at the same time evading religious and ideological conflict will be viewed as ludicrous, and, to the extent that such educational evasion is successful, it will be condemned as totalitarian and coercive. In short, the basic counter dogmas described and sometimes promoted by Theodore Roszak, Charles Reich, and others are hostile to most of the assumptions undergirding the present public school system. One may argue that the counter culture represents only a minority of Americans, young or old, but cultures have always been shaped by the minority of students, artists, and propagandists who mint and market the metaphors by which a society understands itself. There is every reason to believe that the market of the American future is one that calls for increasing localism, diversity, and particularism in belief and ideology. In sum, the demand is for precisely those directions in American life that were sacrificed or sublimated in order to build the present public education system.

I have argued that Supreme Court rulings on religion in the schools are flawed by internal contradictions and have undermined confidence in the social effectiveness of public schools. The Court cannot move further in its attempt to define "the religious" without, on the one hand, prescribing an absolutized secularism or, on the other, opening the schools to the enormous religious diversity that is, in fact, the state of American life. I think the nineteenth-century architects of the public school were right in believing the system could not survive such an opening to religious or ideological particularism. The present school system is, in effect, a bootlegged and bastardized religion. It functions as the established educational church promoting American Moral and Spiritual Values. Both the church and its dogma become more discredited with each passing year and with each rising challenge from within and without.

An alternative to the present system, maybe the only alternative, is suggested by the "voucher plan" whereby education is financed by payments to the parents. This approach, associated with the Center for the Study of Public Policy of Cambridge, Mass. and its director Christopher Jencks, holds promise for an honest and thorough resolution of the ancient question of Church and State in public education. As the Center has argued in a special report to the Office of Economic Opportunity, the voucher plan would probably be able to survive legal challenge. There is no doubt that the plan implies a dismantling of central structures in the present school system. Many people will be loath to surrender the myth of the public school's indispensability, but the old reasons, having to do with melting pots and homogenization, that once loomed so large in arguments for the public school are now neither necessary nor desirable. The immigrant-ethnic-class factors of modern American life are dramatically different from those that attended the birth and growth of the public school. The task of maintaining some common national discourse, a job that once depended upon common schools, has now been assumed by the mass media. There is one unifying *Sesame Street,* whereas there never really was that one little red schoolhouse that was supposed to be bringing and keeping the country together. Although the mass media also distributes much inferior material, the mental pollution is probably of a less fatal variety than that spread by the patriotic readers and moral platitudes of the public school's yesteryear.

The proposition that the mass media now fulfills some of the social purposes previously ascribed to the public school deserves another essay. I mention it here only to indicate that I am not indifferent to the need for social stability and for agencies that promulgate unifying symbols. I am convinced, however, that the stability of our country will be enhanced rather than endangered if we all become more relaxed about the religious and ideological diversity of the American people. The sooner we accept the magnificent pluralism of American life and stop trying to mold its citizens to conformity with NEA banalities, the sooner the era of prohibition will be ended and we will no longer have to bootleg the substandard religion of American Moral and Spiritual Values to our children.

REFERENCES

Berger, Peter: A Rumor of Angels. New York, Doubleday, 1969.
Center for the Study of Public Policy, Cambridge, Mass.: Education vouchers: a preliminary report on financing education by payments to parents. Cambridge, Mass., March, 1970.
Illich, Ivan: Celebration of Awareness. New York, Doubleday, 1970.
Jencks, Christopher: Is the public school obsolete? *The Public Interest,* Winter, 1966.
Mead, Sidney: The Lively Experiment. New York, Harper and Row, 1963.
Michaelsen, Robert: Piety in the Public School. New York, Macmillan, 1970.
Roszak, Theodore: The Making of a Counter Culture. New York, Doubleday, 1969.

response to richard john neuhaus* 11

Philip H. Phenix

I want to express my appreciation to Mr. Neuhaus for the forthrightness and freshness with which he has treated this fundamental issue of religion in American education. He has quite appropriately applied to the term "religion" the broad meaning attached to it by the great majority of informed contemporary students of the subject, and has boldly developed some of the consequences of this modern perspective for education within the American democratic context.

In my response I want to show why my own appraisal of these consequences differs substantially for that of Mr. Neuhaus. In order to do that, let me outline what I take to be the argument of his paper, in the form of the following nine propositions:

1. The term "religion" is widely understood by modern scholars, and increasingly by informed laymen, to refer not only to the beliefs and practices of the organized tradition-al churches, but more generally to the most important value-commitments by which people live.

2. When religion is conceived in this broad sense, it clearly cannot be divorced from any significant human endeavor, including education.

3. It follows that all schools, including public schools, are influenced by the religious, or supreme value, commitments of their personnel.

4. The U.S. Supreme Court, interpreting the First Amendment to the Federal Constitution which prohibits any establishment of religion and any interference with its free exercise, has forbidden any explicit traditional religious practices in the public schools, limiting them to the "objective study" of religion.

5. Since *some* religion (in the broad sense) is necessarily operative in any educational activity, the Court's prohibition has driven out the historic religions as effective orienta-tions in the public schools and by default has allowed a lowest common denominator, American religion of Moral and Spiritual Values, to be bootlegged in as the approved commitment system for public schools.

6. This bootleg religion constitutes the established religion of American public education, which is inculcated by a far-flung educational establishment including an extensive hierarchy of professional officials and an elaborate ecclesiastical-type organiza-tion capped by schools of education which serve as seminaries for functionaries of the public religion.

*From *Proceedings of the Philosophy of Education Society,* 27th annual meeting, 1971, pp. 111-115. Reprinted by permission of the Philosophy of Education Society and the author.

7. Such an establishment is contrary to the American principles of religious freedom and pluralism and to the guarantees of the First Amendment. The Supreme Court has thus involved itself in contradiction, as is now becoming clear in the broader conception of religion that it itself is now adopting, as in the *Seeger* decision.

8. Moreover, this educational establishment may be regarded as a major cause of the pervasive alienation and poor learning performance of many young people today.

9. These problems could be solved by breaking the public school monopoly, exposing the pretensions of the educationist professionals and dissolving with one's faith, and by encouraging local and sectarian control of educational institutions.

That, in sum, is what I take to be the argument of Mr. Neuhaus' paper. I agree with his broadened conception of the meaning of "religion" as an important basis for discussing the values operative in education. I concur in his critique of the Moral and Spiritual Values approach as being only apparently non-sectarian and really a particular but ill-defined faith system. It also seems desirable to me that greater flexibility be provided in school control and financing to permit alternatives to the present system of public schools. But on that point, which is the culminating one in Mr. Neuhaus' argument, everything depends on the how and the why of such modifications. It is here that I find his argument faulty.

It is my impression that the premise in the argument that constitutes its vital center and that gives the whole discussion purpose and point is the eighth proposition cited above, namely, that the public educational establishment may be regarded as a major cause of the alienation and ineffective learning of many young people today. This is the premise that leads Mr. Neuhaus to conclude that if the public school system were dislodged from its privileged position, the locally oriented sectarian schools that would spring up in its place or by its side would be able to educate the whole child and to inculcate the values that citizens deem important.

I do not believe there is any evidence to sustain these claims, and much evidence to the contrary. The crisis in values in American life is a consequence of a complex of cultural and societal stresses in which the schools, both public and private, participate and which they reflect. There is no evidence that students in private or sectarian schools are any less alienated or that they learn any better than those in public schools. As Silberman and others have pointed out, there can be humane and creative schools in the public sector as well as in the private. In short, I hold that there is really no logical or empirical connection between the particular control pattern of American schools and the troubled state of today's youth, and hence that Mr. Neuhaus' attempt to link the educational crisis of the day to the issue of religion in the schools is unwarranted.

Moreover, his apparent confidence in the beneficence of localism and sectarianism in education seems to me quite misplaced. While one may understand and sympathize with his reaction against a wrong-headed teacher unionism, the Pandora's box that he seems to want to open by supporting sectarian education is not a welcome prospect. The basic principle, as I see it, is that education which is supported by the public should be responsible to the public good. Mr. Neuhaus sets up a disjunction between two value systems for schools: either those of the traditional sectarian stripe or the Moral and Spiritual Values endorsed by the N.E.A.'s Educational Policies Commission. The fact is that schools need not, and I hold should not, subscribe to either type of governing commitment.

The American people do have a civic covenant, as expressed by a Constitution and Bill of Rights that define the value framework of the commonwealth. High among these values are freedom of speech and of worship. It is not unreasonable to conclude also that implicit in these values are unrestricted inquiry and freedom of the mind to explore and openly discuss alternative commitments. In other words, Americans as a people are committed to the value of openness to inquiry into alternative commitments. It follows that there are certain fundamental values to which the American people are dedicated. If we choose to designate these values by the term "religion" or, as Dewey called it, a "common faith," then there is a sense in which we affirm a religious establishment, or American public philosophy (to use Walter Lippmann's phrase).

As a people Americans are not anarchists. In the national covenant freedom does not mean absence of all restraints. It is rather a right which includes responsibility for protecting the corresponding right in others. In particular, the commitment to freedom entails appropriate public safe guards against tyrannies that proceed under cover of private auspices. That is why it would be quite out of keeping with the fundamental values of this Republic to permit or encourage unrestricted localism and sectarianism in educational institutions. It may be the case that the cause of freedom will be advanced by opening up greater opportunities for alternatives to the present public school system, as by using a voucher system for allocating tax dollars for education. However that may be, I insist that no school that receives public support ought to be without a degree of public control to insure that the fundamental rights of the student to free inquiry are preserved. Frankly, the past record of sectarian educational institutions does not augur well for their dedication to freedom of the mind.

I am arguing in effect that the distinction between public and private schools cannot be sharply maintained, in that schools which claim to educate citizens and for this service claim a share of public funds must also be answerable to the basic norms of the public philosophy, that is, to what is in the broad sense a religious establishment or common faith of the American people. Translated into terms appropriate to education, the applicable norms include the requirement that those who teach be competent to serve that function. This leads to the matter of the educator's professionalism, which Mr. Neuhaus holds in such low esteem. Let me grant at once that in any domain, education not excepted, there are corrupt forms of professionalism. But unless we are to make of education nothing more than the inculcation of folkways—and I confess that this is what I think Mr. Neuhaus' view tends towards—then those who teach must be answerable to certain professional standards. I am not defending any particular system of certification, such as one based on taking education courses. Nonetheless, I am convinced that the task of formulating and applying professional criteria for teaching must be assumed in education as in medicine, the law, the ministry, and other fields where demonstrable competence and the public good are at issue.

The insistence on professional norms leads us back to the matter of governing values that has been subsumed under the broad concept of religion. A professional is one who is responsible to standards that transcend partisan interests. This is not to deny that he has his own values and that these influence his thoughts and action. It is to say that in what he decides he is responsible to a public of competent peers in his profession. In this sense every profession has its distinctive common faith or established religion. In particular, the teaching profession is governed by a common commitment to the canons of scholarship, both in regard to the matters taught and in respect to the processes of teaching and learning. It follows that a teacher may not appropriately function simply as a propagandist or ideologist for a particular local or sectarian group, but is responsible to the norms of the whole community of scholars and teachers that overarches all particular institutions of education and all the special interest groups they are created to serve.

As to education in the subject of religion itself, the same criteria apply as in any other field of inquiry. Though Mr. Neuhaus finds little value in the practice, it is clear to me that the only appropriate way of teaching religion is as a discipline to be approached objectively, with due regard for the canons of public inquiry, and that this is the way it should be taught not only in public schools but also in schools under non-public auspices. Non-objective indoctrination in religion is simply inferior education, in that it does not meet the standards expected of scholarly endeavor and teaching in any subject.

One of the greatnesses of the American civic covenant has been a decided reserve about explicit religion in its public institutions. Americans have inherited a healthy skepticism about the absolute claims of competing historic cults. They have had the wisdom to sense how ready classes, blocs, and sects are to accord ultimate status to their particular institutions, beliefs, and values. Thus, deeply imbedded in the American faith is a commitment to the principle and practice of criticism. It is in loyalty to this faith that I would urge that the religious and ideological diversity of the American people be subject to principles of public accountability and professional responsibility that transcend the values of local and sectarian autonomy in education.

ADMINISTRATION, ORGANIZATION, RESOURCES

The questions of administration, organization, and utilization of resources in schools are deeply interrelated. The teacher is an administrator in the classroom, much as the principal administers the entire school. In schools, where the vast bulk of expenditures goes for salaries, people are the prime resource, and how effectively they are used depends largely on the school's organization.

Many critics argue that schools are frighteningly inefficient— and they are not merely taxpayers worried about escalating tax rates. They're concerned that schools use resources ineffectively, both by wasting money and by not helping students learn. One of their favorite examples is the use of an expensive school building for six hours a day on weekdays, for only nine months a year. Financially it seems a wasteful practice. Yet advocates of year-round education tend to brush off the very real objections of kids and parents to longer school days or school years. We did, after all, try to have financially "efficient" schools in the first half of this century, and we produced, according to Raymond Callahan in Education and the Cult of Efficiency (Chicago, 1962), a generation of administrators more concerned with costs than with education.

It's also important to assess carefully what makes education "effective." It seems obvious that more time in school would mean more learning. Yet a recent article* based on test performances by Scandinavian students indicates that there might be at best a marginal difference. In this country, the children of the postwar baby boom, who went to grade school in split sessions in the 1950's, went to college in unprecedented numbers in the 1960's. If schooling is indeed something of "diminishing marginal utility" (to borrow a

---

*Husén, Torsten: Does more time in school make a difference? *Saturday Review*, April 29, 1972, pp. 32-35.

term from economics), how do we determine the optimum amount, and what constitutes "cost-effective" schooling? Or does this really tell us that Ivan Illich and Paul Goodman are right in warning that school is bad for children?

Educators are seeking more effective instruction in several ways. Changes in staffing patterns, scheduling, and physical facilities have been discussed and experimented with—thus, differentiated staffing, modular scheduling, and mobile classrooms. Authorities such as Allan Glatthorn argue that the very process of change itself is important in education if we are to deal effectively with the changing world about us.

Changes can be made at the classroom level as well. Kenneth Blanchard and Paul Hersey view the teacher as a leader and apply management theory and the psychology of children to classroom management. Eugene Howard considers ways to alter the classroom atmosphere to facilitate learning. Todd Eachus discusses ways in which behavioral management can be applied to the difficult problem of running a classroom. The old problem of grouping is being approached from a new direction, not whether ability grouping is good or bad but what mixes of students—in terms of age, ability, background, and other factors—produce the most effective learning in all students in the classroom.

Are these new plans going to help solve the problems of education? Or are they merely bigger and better boondoggles? (As Allen and Christensen mention, the "credit" system, now criticized as overly rigid, was originally devised to provide flexibility.) Is reform of the system enough, or do we need a "revolution" of new ideas and conceptions of education?

12 using time, space, and people effectively

Dwight W. Allen
Philip R. Christensen

The dogmas of the quiet past are inadequate to the stormy present.
Abraham Lincoln

Educators today are firmly impaled on a two-horned dilemma. On one hand, they are increasingly unable to meet the criteria which have long measured success in education. Commercial firms can prepare students better for standardized tests than can public schools. Dropout rates are not decreasing; indeed, at the college level, they are increasing. Segregation—*de facto* and *de jure*—is more firmly entrenched than ever. Racism still pervades everything from textbooks to tests. Student unrest, teacher militancy, and community alienation have become a way of life. As schooling's effectiveness goes down, its cost rockets upwards. By traditional standards, we are spending more and more money to get less and less of the job done.

On the other hand, there is increasing dissatisfaction with our definition of success itself. As yet there is no consensus as to what exactly the goals of modern education should be. There are almost as many visions and plans as there are critics. One sees, however, growing unanimity among these critics that something is wrong not so much with our techniques as with our definition of education. In this sense, we are spending more and more money to get less and less of an *unimportant* job done.

The question of effective resource utilization is an important component in both of these dilemmas. It is overly simplistic to speak only in terms of money; dollar cost is linked to, and often equivalent with, time, space, and people. Resources such as the community, the printed word, and technological theory and devices also play their part. Yet it is clearly insufficient to focus on the use of these things without also considering for what purposes they are used. In this chapter, then, we will distinguish between two kinds of resource utilization. *First order utilization* refers to using resources both to perform existing educational tasks more effectively and to expand the scope of these efforts. *Second order utilization* involves the use of these same resources to accomplish new goals and necessitates a reconceptualization of the meaning of education itself. The two levels are not necessarily discrete. If we free teachers from the pressures of clerical work so that they have more time for regular classroom duties, we also open the way for a new definition of the teaching role. Still, each offers a different perspective and thus deserves separate consideration.

The main thesis of this chapter is that education today suffers more from tunnel vision than from starvation. It is like a man trying to cross a large field while wearing blinders. Because he cannot see properly, his path is erratic. He meanders, bumps into things, stumbles frequently, and occasionally walks in circles or even backtracks. All this takes energy. Giving him more energy does not guarantee that he will reach his goal swiftly. He may wander for hours or days, futilely consuming metabolic resources. Yet, if the impediments to his vision were removed, he could walk directly to his objective. He would need *less energy* to arrive at the other side of the field *more swiftly*. Educational man, blinded by unquestioned assumptions and oppressive inertia, requires more and more support without insuring that he will ever get anyplace worthwhile. If the blinders of dogma were removed, education could proceed more or less straight to its objective. In the process it would actually require *fewer* resources.

Thus we do not argue that education cannot profit from more money, buildings, staff, or whatever. Instead, we suggest that it is a waste of these assets to pour them into a system which is moving in blind circles. First we must free our vision of restraints. When that has been accomplished, we will be able to achieve success with a minimum expenditure. What's more, adding resources to the system will then speed the journey instead of prolonging failure. Until that time, all the money in the world will not significantly improve education.

FIRST ORDER RESOURCE UTILIZATION

It is difficult to find any definitive statement of what current educational goals are, but their basic shape is clear. It would not be far off the mark to say that the general objective of twentieth century American education is to prepare nonadults to serve and function effectively in their society (obviously a world society) by giving them a basic fund of knowledge and initial training in at least one specialized skill area. How can time, space, and people be better used to accomplish these objectives?

Time

The use of time is a good place to begin. We can start by combing schools for practices which do not help students to acquire the knowledge and skills which they are supposed to have when they graduate. Such practices waste time which could be used for better purposes. Fortunately for the reformer, and unfortunately for learners, this is a fertile field. For instance, schools spend a depressing amount of time trying to teach children to sit quietly and to act calmly. Yet intellectual excitement is usually accompanied by physical, verbal, and emotional excitement (eureka!). Researchers have shown that large muscle movement facilitates certain kinds of learning. Not only do we waste time teaching children to vegetate at neatly aligned desks, but when we succeed (as, alas, we usually do) we have actually hindered the process of education.

Homework is another practice that directly violates learning theory. It is far more difficult to extinguish behavior once learned than it is to teach new behavior. Homework (as it is now conceived) gives students every opportunity to mislearn a fact or principle and to reinforce that learning. In the privacy of their home or a library, there is no one to correct them. Indeed, educators take sophisticated glee in this. If a mathematics textbook includes the answers to even-numbered problems, the *odd* numbers are assigned. By the time the student reenters the classroom, the teacher is forced to spend time extinguishing poor learning. Thus homework is a counter-productive use of much-needed time for both the student and the teacher.

The curriculum is full of subjects which cannot be shown to contribute to the goals of education. Take, for example, geometry. Teachers love it. The instructor who lives for that magic moment when his students' eyes light up and there is a chorus of "aha's" finds more moments per minute in geometry than in any other subject. There is a theorem a day, and when one runs out of theorems, there are always corollaries.

But what does geometry do for the learner? We used to believe that it trained the mind. Experimenters have, however, been unable to demonstrate that geometry trains minds any better than animal husbandry. So we counter with the rationale that geometry is required for college admission: an empty but powerful defense. It is now very obvious, though, that colleges are becoming less and less interested in judging applicants by such narrow criteria. Thus we are left with the most persistent reason of all: we teach geometry because it has been taught since 300 B.C.

In today's world, statistics will probably be of more use to the average student than geometry. If one thing must be taught to all students, statistics would probably represent a more efficient use of time. Better still, why not help learners choose among geometry, statistics, computer science, and something entirely different, according to their individual needs? If we cannot demonstrate that something will definitely be valuable to every student, then the best way to use the time is to let learners study whatever meets their personal goals.

Focusing on time-wasting practices and content areas will allow us to do what we are already doing more effectively. We can also better use the resource of time to expand current efforts. Take, for example, the secondary school day. It has traditionally been divided into forty-five to sixty minute periods. This is clearly not the most appropriate configuration for every possible type of learning activity. Alternatively, flexible scheduling divides the day into far shorter periods, or modules—of, for example, ten minutes apiece. These can be combined in any desirable format. A class could last ten minutes (one module), fifty minutes (five modules), or two hours (twelve modules).

This innovation permits significant savings in time. Many instructors undoubtedly could teach their material in thirty minutes per day, instead of fifty. Others require far more time than is normally available. Flexible scheduling allows such variation. In a standard biology laboratory period, for instance, little time is left between setting up experiments and taking them down. One two-hour lab session could easily be at least as educational as three fifty-minute periods, and one half hour is saved as a bonus. The time gained through flexible scheduling can be used to expand the quantity and quality of secondary education or even more important, to improve the quality of life.

Performance-based learning, another relatively new thrust in American education, can have a similar effect. The answer to the question "How do you know when you are done?" is, for too many educators, "When the bell rings" (or by extension, "Because it is June"). If a new answer is formulated according to measurable criteria of performance, no student need attend a class longer than necessary. Conversely, no student must quit before he or she has mastered the material and, in so doing, waste hours of unfinished work.

Again, this is an approach that frees us to expand our educational endeavors. Suppose Tree Climbing 101 is changed from a semester course to a competency-based learning experience. Its criterion for successful completion becomes, "The student is able to climb to the third branch of a twenty foot elm tree in less than thirty seconds." Some students will do this on the first day of class. They could immediately begin a new experience. Others will finish in only a few weeks. Again, they could go on to another course in tree climbing, or perhaps to Cooking 21 or Statistics 100. Some learners will take a full semester just to get to the first branch. They can continue in the course as long as they wish, until they sit on the third limb waving proudly to the teacher below. The system will be operating at maximum efficiency.

This suggests a final innovation relevant to time. What can be done for the school day can be done equally well for the school year. Performance-based education is one example of learning which does not take place in semester-long blocks. But there are others. Not all pedagogues concede that every worthwhile learning experience can be described in terms of behavioral objectives. Yet few would argue that three meetings per week, fourteen weeks per semester (or any other single variation on this theme) is a divinely ordained scheduling format. Often a teacher will exhaust his or her material after only ten weeks. Why not allow the class to end then, instead of forcing the instructor to pad for four more weeks?

Because academic records have been kept in terms of credits ever since the idea was first proposed by Charles Eliot in the late 1800's (as a means of allowing flexibility!), administrative changes must be implemented to remove the oppression of this kind of flexibility. Perhaps the best approach is simply to eliminate credits altogether, substituting an alternative mechanism such as a portfolio or anecdotal system. Unfortunately, this is not always possible. A workable alternative is to again apply the modular concept, breaking credits into small modules of credit in the same way that the school day can be broken into short modules of time. Modules of learning can be combined in myriad ways to create learning experiences of any necessary duration and scheduling format, with records kept through modular credit.

The concept opens a wide range of instructional options, of which shorter courses are only one. Another possibility is multiple entry and exit points within a course. A student who needs only enough statistics to calculate simple tests of significance could enter a larger course in educational statistics when the unit on t-tests began, stay for its duration, and drop out at its conclusion. He would learn (and receive credit for) exactly what he needed. And instead of sitting through hours of irrelevant lectures on regression analysis, he could move on to a different offering which met his personal goals. Another variation is the open-ended seminar. Here the learner signs up to take a *professor,* not a topic, and stays as long as he is interested, be it a day or a year. The class continues as long as there is a "critical mass" of students enrolled.

Not only does a completely modular curriculum free time by trimming waste from the system, it also facilitates using the resources thus created to expand educational possibilities. For example, it allows community involvement in instruction. A doctor would probably be unable to teach a 14 week course. It would be far more practical for him to offer a two-meeting learning experience on current issues in medical education. The same principle also allows easier use of a school by the community. Teachers in public schools could build for themselves a solid in-service education program without having to take a leave of absence, using short modular learning experiences scheduled in their nonworking hours.

Besides spreading out learning, a completely modular structure also allows concentrated education. An academically able student could complete the normal work load early, leaving a couple of weeks free for a new project or self-renewal. A faculty member might use this same option to give himself time for research or writing.

It should be clear that the time resource can be utilized to far greater advantage than it now is. Approaches such as eliminating counter-productive practices, modernizing the curriculum, and modularizing the school day and year can help accomplish current educational objectives in less time as well as allowing expansion in both the quantity and quality of schooling.

Space

The bulge on the population charts resulting from the postwar baby boom is known as population peristalsis. The biological parallel of this phenomenon occurs when a python eats a pig, producing a bump which gradually moves down the length of the snake as it is digested. One can't help but wonder how the snake feels about all this. Unfortunately, we know all too well how the bulge of students affects our schools, which suffer from a "too full feeling." All resources—time, space, personnel, money, materials, and so on—are taxed by this problem. It is perhaps most acute, however, in the area of space utilization.

Although time can be manipulated to great advantage, there are no glaring penalties for failing to use this potential. We can continue to do the same kind of things we have always done. This is not so with space. As more and more students crowd into already overcrowded classrooms from kindergartens to universities, fewer and fewer of even our current, limited educational goals can be achieved. There simply do not seem to be enough buildings and classrooms. Population peristalsis has eaten up all of our space resources, and it is still hungry. At the same time, citizens are less and less willing to provide the funds necessary for new space, whether through higher taxes, more tuition, or greater voluntary contributions.

Here, the answer *must* come from better resource utilization, not increased resources. One approach is to use the thousands of hours each year when many educational institutions sit vacant. A primary or secondary school is empty after the mid-afternoon. There is no good reason why it cannot be used then, either to expand the education of its regular student body or to extend learning opportunities to other members of the community. Many classrooms are also vacant from June through August. Young people today are rarely needed at home to help with the harvest, the original reason for summer vacations. These wasted months also represent much-needed space going unused.

A different approach is to find new ways of using existing space. The open classroom concept is a good example of this idea. Most children now spend their classroom time seated at desks in neat rows. As we have already discussed, this may be pleasing to the teacher's sense of order, but it is probably not an optimal learning format. Neither is it necessarily the best possible use of space. Industry has already recognized this fact. Visitors to the main offices of the Eastman Kodak Company in Rochester, New York, may be unable to recognize the accounting department. Instead of rows and rows of workers and desks, they will see a huge room without a single internal wall. Clusters of desks are scattered about it with no visible pattern. Wall to wall carpeting soaks up noise, and small wooden partitions covered with colored fabric provide privacy when needed. The room is extremely comfortable, yet crowded with personnel. The same kind of flexibility is available to schools for the asking, probably for less money than is required to build and maintain conventional classrooms. It eliminates the "cell-block" look, so long fashionable in schools, provides teachers and students with needed options, and offers the community more useable space for fewer dollars.

Environmental quality is as important as quantity. All of the classroom space in the world cannot be used effectively if it hinders learning instead of facilitating it. Improving quality can even save money. Carpeting is far cheaper to maintain than other floorings, yet is more soothing to the eyes and quieter. It can be effectively used in many areas of a school. Sometimes all that is needed is different uses for existing materials. No funds are required to break up stupifying rows of desks into workspace clusters, each devoted to a different subject. Yet the latter arrangement is a superior educational environment. Whatever techniques are used, we cannot afford to ignore the effect that students' surroundings have on their ability to learn effectively.

One should also consider the practice of using the same space to educate different groups of learners simultaneously. Take a sewing class. At many schools there is one class during the day for little Susi Jones (Home Economics) and another in the evening for Mrs. Jones (Adult Education). Yet there may be no good reason why the two Joneses couldn't participate in the same group. Nongraded classes have begun to take us in this direction, but the concept should be extended from children of various ages learning together to people of all different ages and backgrounds sharing an educational experience. What is needed today is not schooling from 9:00 to 3:00 with children of the same age sitting like rows of corn in dull classrooms. We should be moving from a K-12 educational system to womb-to-tomb schooling, with diverse students working together in a variety of classroom settings.

The Parkway Program in Philadelphia has popularized still a different way. Any community is full of exciting locations for worthwhile learning outside of schools. Businesses, shops, factories, hospitals, private homes—the list of possibilities is extensive. All that must be done to tap these unused resources is to divorce ourselves from the notion that learning can only take place in an isolated, specialized setting. This can lead in turn to a home-base definition of a school. If students spend one-third of their time in the building and the rest working and learning in the community, enrollment can be increased threefold.

Personnel

Alternative patterns of personnel utilization can also help develop an expanded and more efficient educational system. There are two basic possibilities. The first is to focus on teachers themselves, redefining their roles and functions. The second is to expand our concept of what a teacher is and to find new kinds of instructors.

The teacher, as we now know him, is a good example of educational inertia. His job is a product of the nineteenth century, when he was little better educated than his students. He was required to do a little bit of everything from clerical work to policing to lecturing, but no one actually expected him to do anything really well. Later, a cadre of specialists was developed to protect students from his failings, and great effort was spent devising "teacher-proof" curricula.

Today's teachers are, for the most part, highly trained professionals, with in-depth knowledge of both the subject matter which they teach and the pedagogy necessary to teach it. Unfortunately, they are still treated as semiskilled labor—jacks of all trades, masters of none. In "modern" schools teachers are virtually interchangeable parts, all doing the same job with the same number of children for the same amount of time year after year. Is it any surprise that the best of them soon grow discouraged and promote themselves out of the classroom, away from students?

Teachers are individuals, with diverse capacities, professional skills, and backgrounds. Furthermore, in today's schools an ever-increasing array of specialized functions and tasks are described by the word "teaching." To effectively utilize this type of human resource and reverse the flow of good teachers away from students, a redefinition of the teaching role is required.

Differentiated staffing is an important step in this direction. Its basic premises are simple. First, teachers are not interchangeable parts: different teachers have different abilities, which they should be allowed to use to the best advantage. Second, teachers are professionals. They must be allowed to advance in responsibility and compensation without leaving the classroom forever, and they must be assisted in gaining the new skills necessary for such advancement. Finally, teachers are not the privates of the education army. They should have an active role as partners in the planning and decision making that affects them, the students they serve, and the schools in which they work.

There are allegedly dozens of specific differentiated staffing models which are now being tried in schools throughout the United States. One of the most common uses a vertical hierarchy of teaching roles. At the bottom of this ladder is the beginning teacher, who receives a relatively small annual salary for full-time classroom work under the close supervision of a more experienced instructor. At the top is the master teacher, who divides his or her time between actual teaching and specialized functions such as curriculum development, diagnostic activities, or in-service training of colleagues, at a salary level at least four times higher than that of the beginner. In between these two ranks are several intermediate positions, progressively requiring more professional expertise and offering increasing compensation.

Some differentiated staffing models define the master teacher's role not only in terms of function but also according to accountability. A low level instructor may be reviewed by a personnel committee once a year (or even more often), while the top teachers are examined only once every two to four years. The latter are given more time to develop and bring to fruition plans and prospects. Other models include horizontal differentiation. Here there are specialized roles at the same status-compensation level. It is similar to a medical system, where one doctor may specialize in pediatrics and another in geriatrics, yet both are more respected and better paid than an intern. One master teacher might concentrate on curriculum, another in the diagnosis of learning disabilities.

Whatever the specifics, all such systems offer numerous ways to better utilize the resource of instructional personnel. In the first place, because teachers are treated as specialists and given the opportunity to advance within the profession, qualified teachers are encouraged to stay in the classroom. Second, the in-service education component of most differentiated staffs provides a continual, effective upgrading of instructors. Finally, and perhaps most important, this innovation allows teachers to do the jobs for which they are best suited by temperament and training. A skilled lecturer, capable of teaching a hundred students at a time, is wasted in front of a group of thirty—and so is the time of the person supervising the seventy students who could have been in the same class. By the same token, an able small group leader is being poorly used in a standard class, and the students suffer as well. Why should a person who is competent to rewrite the social studies curriculum for a junior high school be locked in classrooms and study halls for every period of the day? How is it that an incompetent teacher, instead of being offered needed training, is allowed to teach the same number of students as his most successful colleagues? These are the kinds of issues which can be resolved through more effective use of teachers.

Such alternative staffing patterns lead naturally to an increased emphasis on the training of teachers who are already working in the field. No matter how instructional roles are defined, traditionally or innovatively, it is a waste of human resources to lock teachers into one single level of proficiency. A new emphasis on in-service education is needed. At the very least, the standard model could be revised. "Cruise the Caribbean for Six Credits" can be replaced with a powerful program in a modular format given both on-site and at institutions of higher education.

Other in-service models offer even greater potential. One excellent possibility is to close 8 per cent of all the schools in a large system each year. This can be accomplished by increasing the size of classes in the remaining schools by one or two students apiece. (There is no evidence to support the assumption that small student-teacher ratios always mean better education, especially in a differentiated staffing framework where instructors can work with the number of learners for which they are best qualified.) In this manner eight teachers out of every hundred can return to the university for a year of professional growth. At the same time the buildings themselves can be refurbished. Thus all of the teachers and physical facilities of a school system can be upgraded every thirteen years. Similar results can be achieved by having students on campus only four days out of five. One day per week the learners can be working independently—in libraries, at home, or in the community, while their teachers are free to be further trained. Still another opportunity is to exchange student teachers and regular teachers over a period of time. The former receive practical experience; the latter, more training. No matter what the specifics, in-service education is crucial to the effective use of human resources.

Better use of teachers is only the first step toward more effective personnel utilization. The second is to expand the concept of "teacher" itself. As educational theory and practice begins at last to focus on the learner, the teaching role is evolving to one of service as well as leadership. A modern teacher is both a facilitator who stimulates and guides learning and an informant who provides knowledge. Effective facilitation, for the most part, requires specialized training. It will probably remain the task of full-time teachers. But many people and things can serve as informants. Here the teacher is only one resource. By expanding this concept, we can add a multitude of new resources to our schools.

There are many examples of other informants. The learner himself has direct contact with several of them: parents and family, peers, the media (*Sesame Street,* the evening news, movies, and magazines), to name a few. The concept of youth teaching youth is now gaining popularity. Each student in a given school or class is probably an excellent informant on at least one subject. The printed word is a poorly used source of information. Students have easy access only to textbooks, which become less and less useful as society grows exponentially more complicated; other books are often shelved away in libraries which are frequently all but closed to learners. The community offers a rich menu of informant resources. These can either be brought to the classroom (in a modularized format) or the classroom can be brought to them (à la Parkway). Not only do these resources expand the "teachers" available to the system, they help insure that schooling will open new worlds for learners instead of isolating them in an artificial and largely sterile environment.

The final step is to relieve instructional personnel of inappropriate duties. Teachers should not be clerks. Two secretaries can be hired for the salary of one senior teacher, and they will be professionally better suited to type examinations and transcribe student evaluations, for example. Teachers are not policemen. It does not require a Master's degree to supervise a study hall or to take attendance. A paraprofessional can do these tasks, freeing the teacher to make use of his or her specialized training, and thereby gaining experience as a part of his further professional preparation. Teachers are not administrators. The instructional and administrative staffs are colleagues, who should work hand in hand at separate but equal jobs. A teacher has been trained (or should have been) to be an orchestrator, harmonizing all of the available resources and assisting the learner to make use of them. He or she must be left free to carry out this assignment.

Thus trained teachers can be assigned specialized tasks and responsibilities which use their capacities to the fullest extent. They can also be buttressed by an array of other informants, who can supplement and enrich the students' informational and inspirational diet. Finally, they can be relieved of nonteaching functions, for which they are ill suited and which sap their time and energy. The result is more effective, more efficient utilization of personnel, and another step toward better education.

One final *caveat:* It is all too easy to adopt a term instead of a practice. Actual experience with structural innovations such as differentiated staffing and modularization has produced a few startling examples of the educational benefits of effective resource utilization. Unfortunately, it has generated far more instances where a new name hides the same tired practices. A flexibly scheduled school where virtually every class lasts for three twenty minute modules, a differentiated staff where the "master teacher" receives $100 extra per year and one release period per day—such cases are depressingly frequent. We need today not new jargon, but new techniques. Deeds, not words, must adorn our educational reforms.

SECOND ORDER RESOURCE UTILIZATION

So far, our discussion has centered on using time, space, and people to achieve existing educational goals more effectively and more completely. Many educators will argue that this type of improvement within the system is the best change for which one can practically hope. We would certainly not wish to discourage anyone from trying these ideas. At the same time, we firmly believe that this type of reform is not enough. In the first place, many scholars are now questioning the adequacy of existing concepts of education to meet the needs of today's turbulent, rapidly evolving world. Second, there is a great deal of evidence to indicate that small adjustments in the system are insufficient, that only major reform can be truly successful. For this reason, we feel that second order resource utilization—using time, space, and people in new ways to accomplish *new* goals—is potentially far more important than first order usage. The techniques may be similar in both cases, but the outcomes will be different.

It is easy to see in the many symptoms of social breakdown which are documented each day by the news media the results of our inability or unwillingness to institute this type of change. Education has not only ceased to solve society's difficulties: it has, in itself, become part of the problem. We have already noted that when educational reform does come, it is too often ineffectual. This does not always result from ill will or narrow vision. For example, a school may implement a carefully designed staffing model which includes legitimate role and compensation differentiation. Indeed, the innovation may well improve the school's effectiveness to some extent. But the real potentials of differentiated staffing will probably be unrealized. Teachers will be limited by the expectations and demands of administrators, parents, and local politicians, by financial considerations, by available instructional resources, by state and college-entrance curriculum requirements, and by the structure of the school itself (age segregation, normative testing, standardized achievement measures, and so on). All of these combine to continue a nineteenth century definition of the teaching role in spite of any staffing innovations. Real change can still take place in such a setting, but the odds are against it happening frequently.

We would like to propose a redefinition of the purpose of education that could provide a framework for truly effective resource utilization. To return to the analogy with which this chapter began, we suggest that when the blinders are removed from the man crossing the field, he may find that his original objective is not really where he wants to go at all, but that it would be better for him to head for a different spot. We cannot prove that our own destination is the best or the only possibility. It is, rather, one alternative that, in our professional judgment, deserves exploration.

We would define true education as having three interrelated strands: competence in skill areas (a credentialing function), personal fulfillment (an enrichment function), and social tasks (a service function). Each of these is important, and each requires different mechanisms.

The first (though not necessarily the most important) goal of education should be to provide members of society with skills which will serve both themselves and their fellow men. This is partially met by existing programs designed to give all students a basic store of knowledge and some training in an occupational role. But the exigencies of a dynamic society demand that basic emphasis be placed on skill in learning. The focus must not be on learning a set of facts and abilities which may soon be outdated, but rather on how to learn.

Having fostered learning competence, beginning with preschool children, the educational system can open itself to any person, of any age and background, who wishes training in a given area. This type of learning will take place inside and outside of school plants, 24 hours per day, under the direction of a wide range of teachers coordinating many types of informants. The goal will be credentialing, but this will not be terminal. Rather, a given level of competence for a specific skill, based on specified criteria for success, will be certified. This kind of diploma will mean not that a student has finished school, but that he has what he needs for the time being, and that he will be back when he needs more. Perhaps it will even have an expiration date, after which its holder is no longer considered competent unless he can demonstrate that he has maintained a certain proficiency level as well as assimilated new developments in his field.

The second goal should be personal fulfillment. Once the credentialing function has been accomplished, society needs no longer worry about normative quality control. The monitoring of enrichment can be left up to the learner, who can use his own individual objectives and needs as the referent. Not only cognitive development but also crucial areas such as value clarification may be dealt with at this level. The whole human being can and must be educated. Objective testing is possible only when there is a static set of criteria as a reference point. Personal fulfillment, on the other hand, is related to individual goals and perceptions. In this situation, a student cannot be evaluated by others; he must measure himself against his own objectives. The credentialing function lends itself to normative evaluation; the enrichment function does not. In the latter realm there need be no failure, only continual growth.

It is likely that over the next two decades most of the credentialing work of education will be accomplished outside of schools, through other informants and facilitators. For example, most students will probably arrive in kindergarten already knowing how to read and count. These subjects will no longer be central in the curriculum; they will be remedial or advanced electives. The result of this trend will be that enrichment will become the focus of more and more schooling. The same kinds of structural innovation which we have already discussed can assist in this process, too. Modularization can help tailor a curriculum to meet the personal goals of each student exactly, and can also allow "student" to be defined as "anyone." Differentiated staffing will be crucial, for education will not need walking encyclopedias at the front of classrooms, but highly trained and specialized learning orchestrators. And because personal growth can and should happen anywhere at any time, the walls between schools and the community, the home, peer groups, and so on will start to crumble.

Finally, there is the goal of social service. Not only are schools a social resource in themselves, but full-time students represent an important manpower pool to accomplish the jobs that society needs done. It has already been suggested that the community offers many important resources to students. The corollary is that students are a resource for the community. If each of the 25,000 students at a university were to spend one day per week in social service, that would be the equivalent of 5000 full-time workers to do everything from day care to park beautification. And this type of activity would, in itself, offer new resources to the credentialing and enrichment functions.

Such reconceptualization suggests new needs and new means of using resources to meet them. For example, there is the technique of juxtaposition, combining resources in unusual ways so that the outcome cannot be predicted. This runs counter to the inertia principle, which dictates that educators tend to remain comfortably ensconced in familiar situations and behavior patterns. But an educational system designed to complement a rapidly changing society must in itself incorporate change. Juxtaposition forces this to happen.

First order use of a modular curriculum, for instance, would allow a university history professor to teach a high school class. Second order utilization might have a history teacher replaced by an architect. Presented with a *fait accompli,* the school's principal would have to figure out what to do with his new resource. Chances are good that the results, whatever they were, would be worth the risk. Students can also be juxtaposed. Using learners as teachers is one example.

Another good possibility is to base 50 per cent of a school's program on self-directed learning. The problem with small scale independent study programs is that instructors teach all of what they normally teach in a somewhat shorter period of time. Nothing really changes. The traumatic intervention represented by eliminating one half of the curriculum would force significant evolution. Staffing patterns would have to be different; teachers would need to move from imparting knowledge toward orchestration and advising. It would become apparent that most existing educational objectives can be accomplished in far less time than is now used. This would, in turn, stimulate the revision of current goals and the addition of new ones, perhaps along the lines which we have suggested.

Whatever percentage of the program remains institutionally generated could be modularized. A student who wished to be certified as a competent biologist could enroll in a series of appropriate, long-term learning experiences, while one who wished to understand genetics because of a purely personal interest would participate only in that particular unit. The learner who wished certification would be tested in comparison with an objective norm; the other could be evaluated in any way he wished or not at all.

This leads naturally to experience-based learning, which is also implied by second order resource utilization. Education is now school centered, and schooling is heavily oriented toward the imparting of knowledge. This is not an assumption of our model. Schools should be more than just cognitive feeding troughs. They should certify competence, whether it is gained within their confines or not. They can be one resource among many for personal enrichment. Finally, they should act as a coordinating center for individual learning activities and social service programs.

In such a model a great deal of learning can be experience based. This is both pedagogically justifiable and more efficient than the existing system. Instead of using schools alone, it uses the whole world to get the job done. In many areas experience *is* the best teacher. We must capitalize on this too-often ignored bit of folk wisdom.

A corollary to experience-based learning is product-oriented education. There is no reason why the process of learning cannot often lead to useable results. Better than reading a textbook on communications and television would be actual work in a television studio. Better still would be work that resulted in, for example, an anti-racism TV spot. Problem-centered learning need not always be contrived. This principle is applicable to all three strands of our educational model. It is especially relevant, however, to the social service component, since it is a new way of combining the resources of a community and its student population.

Another idea which has important implications for all three of the goals which we propose—credentialing, certification, and service—is alternative methods of accessing information. Most models of education take for granted a pyramid structure to knowledge, rising from a base of simple facts to a pinnacle of complicated and esoteric concepts. They further assume that the only way to get to the top is to start at the bottom and cover everything on the way up. This is the logic behind prerequisites. It is clearly impossible, says this reasoning, to understand Knot-Weaving 202 until one has completed Knot-Weaving 201.

Yet the most able learners are those who can solve problems requiring advanced information without spending the time required to plod through all of the basic facts. They can get near the top of the pyramid without starting at the bottom. Prerequisites neither serve students of this type nor train others to achieve this degree of learning competence. Furthermore, they rarely reflect the fact that there are hundreds of different ways to attain a given level of understanding. Prerequisites thus represent an inefficient use of resources, since they force an individual into an externally imposed sequence which does not necessarily meet his or her particular needs. We suggest that they be dropped completely from the educational structure and replaced with detailed, accurate catalogue descriptions of the objectives and proposed content of every learning experience. This will allow learners to make their own choices instead of forcing professors into arbitrary decision-making for all of their students.

In the context of the reconceptualization of education along the lines which we have proposed, therefore, alternative forms of resource utilization can realize their full potential. First order mechanisms such as modularization and differentiated staffing would no longer be constrained externally by a nineteenth century educational structure. The redefinition itself suggests several new paths to explore which may allow the use of time, space, and people to effectively meet the needs of the *twentieth* century.

POSSIBILITIES

At the beginning of this chapter educational man was wandering in a field unable to get anywhere because he was wearing blinders. We have now suggested several ways to extricate our friend from this unhappy situation. These ideas are all instances of a single approach: challenging long-standing practices and assumptions which limit our perspective. The specific issues raised here—from eliminating education for docility to dropping prerequisites—are obviously only examples. It is not difficult to generate hundreds of additional possibilities.

Once the man in the field is able to see again, he will be free to move decisively—but where? After wandering in educational circles for so long, we have lost confidence about even our ability to choose, let alone act. Education can certainly proceed to its current objectives more effectively through better use of resources. We have detailed this in our discussion of first order utilization. It is, however, simply a palliative, given the needs of society today and tomorrow. There are new goals and new routes. Before we march unthinkingly toward our current goal, inebriated by the speed of our progress with newly clear vision, we should carefully consider the alternatives.

The revision of educational goals that we have suggested and the mechanisms for using resources which they imply are not the only available options. Indeed, there are so many schemes for reform that it is impossible for anyone to make a definitive choice among them from our present perspective. The most reasonable course is the simultaneous investigation of many alternatives. Now is the time for divergence of thought and action in education. All new alternatives will not be better or even successful, and the time for divergence will end as we consolidate and refine our new approaches. But consolidation and refinement are for the past and the future—vision and choice are for today.

The words of Abraham Lincoln which we have quoted speak not just to his contemporaries but to men of all eras. The dogmas of the quiet past are painfully inadequate to the gathering storms of the Atomic Age. Unless we gain a new sense of our direction, the tempests can and will destroy us. Education, increasingly part of the problem, must now contribute to a solution. To this fact there is *no* alternative.

continuing change 13
is needed

Allan A. Glatthorn

In this age of continuing crisis, many would ask for a moratorium on educational innovation. There are the skeptical cynics who, convinced that the schools have known too much change with too little evidence of lasting improvement, are persuaded that more change would be self-defeating. And there are the cautious conservatives who, convinced that the present sytem is working reasonably well, are reluctant to move into uncharted waters. While such feelings have some validity, there are strong reasons which argue more persuasively the imperative need for radical educational change. Before we examine those arguments for educational change, it may be wise to enlighten both the cynics and the conservatives.

The notion that our schools have experienced too much change in recent years is patently absurd. All the so-called innovations of the past decade—team teaching, modular scheduling, nongradedness—have been superficial modifications which have left unchanged the basic essence of the place called school. Despite some notable exceptions, the American system of public education is basically unchanged from what it was one hundred years ago. Now, as then, it is marked by these characteristics:

> Children are compelled to report to a building called school, where they sit 6 hours a day, 180 days a year, for 12 years of their lives.
> That school is a rigid, rather authoritarian organization, where all the important decisions are made by the adult staff.
> The adults in the school determine the curriculum, which is categorized into subjects called English, mathematics, science, social studies, and foreign language.
> The child, called a pupil while he is in school, learns by reading from a book and by listening to an adult called a teacher.
> The teacher does most of the talking in the classroom, mixing questions and explanations; generally, the child is expected to talk only when the teacher gives him permission.
> Periodically the child is expected to demonstrate what he has learned by answering in writing questions which the teacher chooses to ask.

These characteristics also apply to supposedly innovative schools; for if we are honest about it, the innovations of the past decade have resulted in at best minimal changes. "Team teaching" means that the student listens to three different teachers instead of one. "Modular scheduling" means that the bell rings every twenty minutes instead of every forty. "Independent study" means that the student reads a book in a learning center rather than in a study hall. "Nongradedness" means that the label on the door reads "primary unit," instead of "second grade." And "large group instruction" means that the pupils listen in groups of 200, instead of groups of 30.

To put it more simply, school is still school, despite all the fanfare about innovation. Changes are needed that will hopefully challenge assumptions about schooling which have prevailed for centuries. More explicitly, we will perhaps see in the next few years greater emphasis placed upon learning and less on schooling: we will see young people working, studying, and serving in their own communities; we will see them traveling across the country in a "classroom on wheels"; we will see them apprenticed to pipefitters and poets; and we will see them learning at home from correspondence courses and television screens.

The belief that the schools are good enough as they are is just as obviously erroneous. That system outlined above is so clearly ineffective that only those with vested interests in preserving it in its present form even bother to defend it. The evidence for the failure of that system everywhere abounds. The Coleman report (Coleman, 1966), concludes as follows:

> The minority pupils' scores are as much as one standard deviation below the majority pupils' scores in the 1st grade. . . . For most minority groups, then, and most particularly the Negro, schools provide little opportunity for them to overcome this initial deficiency; in fact they fall farther behind the white majority in the development of several skills which are critical to making a living and participating fully in modern society.
> . . . the schools are remarkably similar in the way they relate to the achievement of their pupils when the socioeconomic background of the students is taken into account. It is known that socioeconomic factors bear a strong relation to academic achievement. When these factors are statistically controlled, however, it appears that differences between schools account for only a small fraction of differences in pupil achievement (pp. 21-22).

The blue-collar young person, as much as the black, feels alienated and estranged in that establishment called school (Binzen, 1970; Sexton, 1969). And he simply isn't learning as much as the other students in the system; Peter Binzen discovered that the Philadelphia school with the lowest white achievement scores in the whole city was in the heart of a blue-collar white neighborhood.

What of middle-class college-bound youth? Charles Silberman's *Crisis in the Classroom* (1970), shows us convincingly that the system has failed even for these students. They too find school a joyless experience, devoid of the excitement of learning. Even though they are mastering the basic academic skills, they are not learning the more essential skills of thinking independently, working autonomously, and learning how to learn.

Despite the expenditure of great sums of money, then, we must conclude that the present public school system is failing in its mission, and we would argue that that failure is itself reason enough to change. But even if the present system were working more effectively, we hold that there would still be important reasons for the schools to embark upon radical change.

CHANGES IN SOCIETY

The first reason is that our society is changing so radically that the schools of the sixties—if any are that up to date—are hopelessly obsolete for America of the seventies. The student of the seventies will be living in a world transformed so substantially that a whole new way of life will be required of those who wish to survive (Toffler, 1970; Bennis and Slater, 1968). Those major transformations which will be upon us shortly are clear for all to see.

A new technology will demand new skills of all of us. The man of the seventies who cannot use a computer will be as badly handicapped as the man of the sixties who could not read. And the student presently in our schools studying the intricacies of the internal combustion engine may find at the end of this decade that it is as obsolete as the coal-fired stove.

The media will become even more influential in broadening our horizons and shaping our opinions. The cassette-video revolution will place culture for all at fingertip's reach, so that the student studying Shakespeare will be able to view at will a full-color production of the play of his choice. The teacher who thinks of Macbeth as lines on a printed page will simply be unable to reach students nurtured on this richer visual fare. The merchandising of political candidates will be raised to a new level of sophistication, requiring an electorate even more discriminating and perceptive. The student who has not gained the skill of critical viewing will find himself at a marked disadvantage.

Scientific advances will require a new kind of decision making. Organ transplanting, cloning, electronic stimulation of the brain, and computer-controlled servo-mechanisms will require people to make new decisions about life and death, about pleasure and work. The student who has not learned how to think ethically may make unwise decisions or simply be immobilized by decisionless anxiety.

A new hedonistic life style will call for the development of a new morality, grounded not in authority but in ends and consequences. Young people will be living together in loose communal families. New drugs enabling a man to alter his moods as he chooses will be readily available. The adult who continues to preach about the glories of virginity and the sanctity of work will find that none of the young will be listening.

The information explosion will make old subjects obsolete and new skills essential. Every major discipline presently studied in our schools will see its basic principles modified drastically and even its hard facts interpreted anew. The ability to remember facts will seem unimportant; the ability to retrieve information, to evaluate data, to synthesize facts will assume new importance.

These predictable changes, whose shock waves are already felt by our early warning systems, very clearly indicate the need for significant changes in curriculum; other changes even more cataclysmic in their impact will be upon us before we can prepare for them.

CHANGES IN THE YOUNG

A second major argument for radical change in the schools is that those students who are in our schools now are quite different from those of even a few years back. Teachers used to gradual changes in students report that the students of this year seem significantly different from those of just a year or two ago. While we would not suggest that the schools must adjust to every subtle shift in the youth culture, we would argue that pervasive changes in the life styles of the young make it mandatory for the schools to change if they are to be effective in reaching these young people. Let us examine just briefly some of the most important changes taking place in the young, indicating at the same time their implications for the schools of tomorrow.

Despite the media image of an activist generation, the young instead are more typically passive and quiescent. Much of this passivity comes from thousands of hours sitting in front of blaring television sets and talking teachers; some of it stems from a feeling of impotence in the face of problems too big to solve. It suggests that the schools need to place more emphasis upon active doing—physical activity, movement, learning by doing. It also suggests de-emphasis of all kinds of passive learning, even when it appears under the guise of "innovation" like educational television or large group instruction.

The young have lost touch with their own impulse life and their own emotions. For the young, coolness is everything: emotions are repressed, feelings are pushed deep down inside, and enthusiasms are dampened. This emotional shallowness means that the schools need to give more attention to what has been called a "curriculum of affect"—a curriculum that synthesizes the cognitive, the affective, and the psychomotor into a new kind of organismic learning.

The young have become much more knowledgeable—but much less wise. Because of their great exposure to television and film, they have acquired a great deal of knowledge about many things; at the same time, however, they have been removed from meaningful contact with the realities of living and working in a complicated society. As a consequence they tend to see problems and issues in black-and-white, accepting the simplistic solutions of their older peers. Such a development suggests that the schools need to find ways by which students can become people, leaving the artificial environment called school to confront the real world in all its messiness and complexity.

The young are immersed in the present; the past seems truly irrelevant and the future too threatening. Teachers need to develop curricula that begin with the present, but they also need to find ways to help the student learn from the past and confront an uncertain future. This poses another problem for the schools. Teachers who try to motivate students by warning—"you will have to go to summer school," "you won't get a job," or "you won't be able to get into college"—will find that the now generation is indifferent about future disasters. The source of motivation must be in the present: the student must be excited by what he is doing now, and he must perceive that his learning has some pay-off in the present.

The young espouse a nascent privatism which resolves all issues by looking within. Convinced that the answers lie within themselves if only they can find the right drug or the best guru, they question any adult authority which presumes to judge them, evaluate them, or make decisions for them. They often seem unable to learn from each other, especially when the other is of a different social class. In many ways there is a greater gap between the blue-collar youth and his hippie peer than between the blue-collar youth and his father. This privatism, smacking of psychic involution, poses a serious threat to any nation of diverse peoples. The schools must respond by helping the student learn to work with others, to understand the views of those who are different from himself, and to seek out that piece of the truth which each man has been vouchsafed. All this argues strongly for a renewed emphasis upon team learning and small group activity, and argues against too much isolation in the learning process, an isolation which would exacerbate the privatism that so concerns us.

Most of all, the young are without a sense of power. Much of their rhetoric of power—"power to the people," "student power," "black power"—speaks loudly of this impotence which they feel in their guts. They sense that they are being manipulated by forces beyond their control, that they have lost the capacity to affect their own destinies. This impotence drives a few students to rebellion; it pushes most into withdrawal and passive aggression. How must the school respond to these feelings of impotence? Certainly not by more adult repression, which will tend only to increase their passive resistance. Instead, the school needs to re-structure itself as a community in which power and authority are shared with staff and students within limits set by the law and determined by the students' maturity.

The intent here is not to produce one more model of the "school of the future" but only to indicate that the young people in our schools are changing in significant ways and that the school must change in response. We should note the irony that many of the "innovations" of the recent past—individualized instruction, independent study, educational media—seem completely out of keeping with the needs of today's student, since they would seem to increase privatism and passivity. More change is needed—change that will help the student of the seventies become a more active, vibrant member of a community of shared concern.

CHANGES IN RESOURCES

A third cogent argument in favor of continuing change in our schools is that there are many new resources now available to us that clamor to be used. If we refuse to use them because we fear the challenge of change, then we are just as foolish as the farmer who rejects a new seed strain or the physician who ignores a new drug. A short catalog of those new resources will by itself argue persuasively for additional change in the schools, change which will capitalize upon those new resources and the help they can give us.

New Agencies. Schooling is no longer a monopoly of the establishment. We have seen recently a marked increase in performance contracting, in which individuals inside or outside the system agree to be paid on the basis of their performance in reaching certain educational objectives. And it is quite likely that community agencies other than schools —agencies such as YMCA's and community houses—will become more active in the education of all people. In the near future the most forward looking communities may engage a full-time educator, not a member of the educational establishment, to assess the community's educational needs and then coordinate the work of all agencies involved in helping people learn.

New Personnel. In recent years we have clearly seen the need to differentiate the teaching staff and involve a variety of individuals with all sorts of competencies. We will probably see more adults from the community working in the schools, not just supervising youngsters but helping them grow in meaningful ways. In addition, we will see many new roles develop: learning disabilities specialist, human relations specialist, school-community specialist in delinquency prevention, school security specialist, affective education specialist, school-community work-service coordinator, school-community drug education specialist, and student ombudsman.

New Facilities. There will, of course, always be school buildings, but some recent developments suggest that we may have some facility resources that will help us revolutionize education. The next decade will probably see four major trends in facilities, each of which will make its own special impact. There will be more extensive use of existing community facilities; buildings like YMCA's, churches, museums, factories, and libraries. As shopping centers and high-rise apartment buildings are erected in our communities, more school districts will see the advantage of sharing the cost so that they can share the space. Since educational needs will be even more unpredictable in the years ahead, schools will probably make greater use of inflatables and other temporary structures that can be easily dismantled and re-assembled. Finally, we shall find districts building more specialized facilities that can be shared with nonpublic schools and with community groups; facilities such as swimming pools, instructional media centers, performing arts centers, and centers for science and technology can be strategically located so that a whole community can use them for learning. And each of these new trends in facilities will have a marked effect on the kind of learning that takes place within them. If we build new buildings and find new spaces for learning, we may really have no other choice than to change what goes on inside.

New Knowledge About Human Growth and Learning. We may shortly see significant breakthroughs in the chemistry of learning and the control of human behavior which will make our feeble attempts to instruct through words seem ludicrous indeed. While some of us may fear the Orwellian aspects of such developments, we should welcome without reservation new findings in such areas as infant learning, diagnosis of and remedies for learning disabilities, and teaching of reading. Although many justifiably feel that all the recent research in learning has not been productive of significant change in the schools, it seems likely that new agencies and media for translating research into practice will give us the information we need to solve the learning problems we confront.

New Media and Materials for Learning. New tools are being fashioned which will aid us immeasurably in our struggle to help all children learn. We will have very shortly a wide variety of sophisticated hardware: inexpensive videotape recorders which will give the student and teacher instant visual feedback; cartridge and cassette video players which will eliminate the need for lectures and large-group presentations; cheap cassette audio playback machines which will enable each student to listen alone to hundreds of programs; cartridge film projectors which will bring film to fingertip reach; and desk-top computers which will help the student solve complicated problems in a few minutes. In addition, we already have the software necessary to individualize learning in all major curricular areas from kindergarten to grade twelve. Both the hardware and software will, without question, facilitate learning much better than the traditional textbook and talking teacher. Once used in the system, they will exercise subtle but strong pressures for additional change.

BENEFITS OF CHANGE

We have thus far argued that change is *necessary* because our society is changing, our students are changing, and our resources are changing. We would finally argue that change is *desirable* because of its effects on the members of that system and on the system itself.

Let us first examine the effects of change on the members of a school system. If teachers and students feel that their school is standing still, they want to dissociate themselves from it in an age when innovation has become the accepted mode. If, on the other hand, they feel that they are part of a vitally changing institution, they identify more closely with it, enjoying the prestige presently associated with "innovative schools." In addition, an individual can best achieve his own self-renewal when he is part of a self-renewing institution. Each of us needs to find new ways of teaching, to discover new ways of relating, to explore new ways of being—and such growth is best realized in an innovative system.

When we ask if we should change the school system we imply that there is some single closed system called the school, isolated from its society, and that we have a choice as to whether or not we are going to change it. Yet this is obviously not the case. The school is an open system, a synergy of many interacting elements, perpetually in contact with its environment, the community. Many of those important elements are in a constant state of flux, regardless of any decision we make or any action we take.

If one part changes, other parts are influenced in subtle but significant ways. If we provide students with some unscheduled time, we set up certain pressures on teachers and facilities. If we schedule a teacher with small groups, we create an environment which requires changes in her teaching style. If we adopt a laboratory-centered science program and do not provide time in the school schedule for extended laboratory periods, we set up serious intrasystem tensions.

Seeing the school as an open system, we would argue that it makes most sense if all its subsystems undergo orderly change. If only parts of a system change, tensions develop between those subsystems which have changed and those which have not. Thus, much of the recent student dissent derives from the frictions between a changed student body and unchanging school regulations. Also, serious malfunctions develop when subsystems in different states of change attempt to interlink. For example, a teacher working with a new school schedule which emphasizes discovery, discussion, and independent study will find that she simply cannot "cover" the old curriculum. And the system as a whole becomes less effective because of its internal incongruities and dissonances. The tensions and discords produced because of inter-subsystem incompatibility eventually become counterproductive. Or, to put the matter in Charles Reich's terms, the schools are in trouble because they are Consciousness II organizations mired in the past, trying to educate Consciousness III youth which is turned on and tuned in to a radically changing present.

To a great extent, then, the debate about innovation is over. We really have no choice. The only real question remaining is, "How radical the revolution?"

REFERENCES

Bennis, Warren, and Slater, Phillip: The Temporary Society. New York, Harper and Row, 1968.
Binzen, Peter: Whitetown, USA. New York, Random House, 1970.
Coleman, James S.: Equality of Educational Opportunity. Washington, D.C., U.S. Government Printing Office, 1966.
Sexton, Patricia: The Feminized Male. New York, Random House, 1969.
Silberman, Charles: Crisis in the Classroom. New York, Random House, 1970.
Toffler, Alvin: Future Shock. New York, Random House, 1970.

14 archaic legislation and the learning process

Harry Randles

> Our sociological theories, our political philosophy, our practical maxims of business, our political economy, and our doctrines of education are derived from an unbroken tradition of great thinkers and of practical examples from the age of Plato . . . to the end of the last century. The whole of this tradition is warped by the vicious assumption that each generation will substantially live amid the conditions governing the lives of its fathers and will transmit those conditions to mold with equal force the lives of its children. We are living in the first period of human history for which this assumption is false.
>
> Alfred North Whitehead

Assuming Whitehead's comment is in keeping with reality, it may be proposed that *all* legislation bearing upon education is to some degree archaic. If one also assumes that legislators pass laws in keeping with their personal definitions of a real world, it follows that these laws will be to some degree out of date by the time they take effect. Legislation will be implemented under conditions which the legislators could not know, probably did not foresee, and might not even be able to imagine. Recent legislation may be more closely in tune with the times, but older laws tend to become less so as time passes.

Legislation pertaining to corporal punishment illustrates the point. Laws governing corporal punishment in New York State, for example, are embodied in the Penal Code. That, in itself, is significant. Section 246, subdivision 4 of the New York State Penal Code states:

> To use or attempt, or offer to use, force or violence upon or towards the person of another is not unlawful in the following cases.
>
> When committed by a parent or the authorized agent of any parent, or by any guardian, master, or teacher, in the lawful authority to restrain or correct his child, ward, apprentice, or scholar. And the force or violence used is reasonable in manner and moderate in degree.

The language of the law reflects its historical setting: "master," "apprentice," "scholar." Certainly "violence" has a new connotation—how are we to consider violence "reasonable" or "moderate"? To some degree, surely, this is archaic legislation. Its language and connotation simply do not fit with the existing practice and realities of the

1970's, nor with current theories of learning and concepts of human development. Except, one might add, in some isolated instances where schools and communities have not yet moved into this decade in this century!

The point made here is a basic assumption in this discussion: all legislation is archaic to some degree because it rests upon premises which are no longer valid. It follows that legislation tends to become increasingly archaic in the years following its passage.

Educational legislation is archaic for another reason—there is little discernible relationship between school law and the learning process. This is understandable. Too little is known and understood about learning even today; certainly this was more true, at least in the scientific sense, in the early years of the public school system. This may explain why much educational legislation deals with control and accountability. Educators have long been expected to control their students and to be accountable for physical properties. The notion of accountability for educational achievement is a more recent concept, and pressure in this direction is growing. Boards of education are giving more and more attention to performance contracting; parents are increasingly interested in voucher arrangements; teachers are becoming increasingly concerned about the implications of accountability for professional evaluation, for students, and for learning.*

From this, it's reasonable to predict that at least attempts at mandating some accountability practices will be made. Given the current inadequate state of knowledge, there is only a somewhat remote possibility that early legislation to achieve accountability will contribute to learning.† Until our knowledge is developed more fully, even well-informed legislatures cannot help but produce archaic legislation.

A third way of thinking about archaic legislation is also related to Whitehead's proposition. Educational legislation, by its nature, tends to be prescriptive, to set limits, to establish formal or obligatory norms for educational institutions. The degree of flexibility it permits may well determine how rapidly it becomes archaic.

If education were carried on in a known world, legislative mandating of curricula might be rational. But legislation which mandates the teaching of a known world defeats the purpose of education for a generation which will never live in that world. Emphasis upon knowing the world may be less functional than emphasis on learning about or discovering the world. Thus, laws which prescribe knowing rather than discovering as a learning process may be dysfunctional or archaic because they do not really help learning.

The difficulties are obvious. The inevitability of change in education has been described endlessly. To fail to recognize the concomitant thread of continuity is sociological heresy. If educational legislation is archaic because it inhibits change, that problem needs to be recognized and handled in the most intelligent manner possible. But it seems unwise indeed to assume that a society can sustain itself without concern for continuity, and laws contribute to answering this concern. The question does not concern archaic legislation or something else yet undefined, but rather the ways that legislation can satisfy both the needs for change and for continuity.

No attempt will be made here to lay out a framework for examining the tolerability of educational legislation. Rather, the approach will be to identify facets of educational

---

*The New York State Association for Supervision and Curriculum Development selected *Humanism and Accountability: Are They Compatible?* as the theme for the 23rd Annual State Conference, April 16-19, 1972, Rochester, N.Y.

†A California law effective in the fall of 1972 requires evaluation of all certificated personnel on the basis of "standards of expected student progress in each area of study." *Education Commission of the States Bulletin, 5:*No. 3, (April, 1972) p. 4.

legislation judged to be archaic largely because of their relationship to the learning process.

Consider the laws mandating compulsory attendance. It seems abundantly clear that we have now learned that one can't *make* people learn! Carl Rogers asks whether or not it is possible for one to teach another. He suggests that the term "facilitator of learning" is more appropriate than "teacher" (Rogers, 1969, p. 103-104). A facilitator of learning can at best provide a climate, an atmosphere, or a series of conditions which make it possible for learners to learn. Beyond that, there is really little he can do except to react to signals from learners that they need help.

Compulsory attendance laws are categorical; attendance is mandated for categories of pupils that are determined primarily by age. If compulsory attendance indeed promoted learning, then citizens of all ages should be compelled to attend some type of school, and inconsistent application would make our present statutes archaic.

Closely examined, intervention in the teaching-learning process takes on tremendous significance. Reacting to learners who indicate that they need help is an entirely different kind of intervention from one based on the teacher's needs, the parents' needs, or needs imposed by the structure of the subject matter.* The learning act is extremely significant to two parties, the learner and the teacher, in that order. Intervention by others (particularly the imposition of rigid overall structures) appears grossly inappropriate and is much more likely to obstruct learning than to be of any help. Compulsory attendance laws are a massive intervention by outsiders into the interaction between teacher and student. Compelling children to be physically present in a school, whether or not they are ready to learn or interested in learning, seems contrary to our best understanding of the learning process. As obstructions to learning, such laws are archaic.

Does the archaic nature of compulsory attendance laws mean repeal? Yes, as they stand; compulsory attendance probably needs categorical redefinition. Any changes contemplated should stress the idea of flexibility. Age limitations and requirements need redefinition and there should be more choice among institutional settings and room for individual exceptions. Without sufficient alternatives, which compulsory attendance legislation seems to preclude, schools function more as custodial organizations than as places to learn.

If current legislation results in a complex of social problems, changes would obviously create new problems, for which some solutions should be contemplated. It is a real question whether society could meet the needs of learners not internally motivated to work in a traditional school situation. Learners would expect new interactions with other segments of society. Stephen K. Bailey raises the question:

> Why should some classes not take place in industrial settings under the joint sponsorship of industry and labor? Why should restless kids, age 14 or 15, not have the chance to drop out of traditional schools at will and without stigma, and to drop into non-traditional classrooms in city museums, libraries, performing arts centers and auto-repair garages (Bailey, 1970)?

In our rapidly developing technological society, education is a lifetime experience. Free access to learning sites would help us realize this. Indeed, today more people (including many adults) enter learning situations voluntarily than have been forced into our educational institutions by compulsory education laws.

---

*One teacher resolved this latter problem most directly. Discovering his students found history, chronologically examined, to be irrelevant, he reversed the order of study from present to past. His students found that present events were relevant to immediate past events.

It should be emphasized that this discussion pertains to compulsory attendance. Legislation mandating the state to maintain a system of education is not being questioned. For its citizens' growth and welfare, the state should allocate resources to provide for their education. Citizens should have free access to available educational opportunities; access cannot be free if it is compulsory.

Laws pertaining to teacher certification are also disturbingly archaic. Most assume that the best preparation for teaching is mastery of subject matter and pedagogy. A colleague who has been active in inner city education asserts that he would trade all traditional methods courses for an equal amount of time spent in helping teachers learn how to "act." Perhaps the best illustration of the value of acting is seen in the relationship between prejudice as an attitude and discrimination as a behavior. If teachers could learn to avoid discrimination in their actions, they might be able to conceal their prejudices from their students. As a matter of fact, many associates involved in education in inner city areas confirm that this is the case. Teachers who are able to act in non-discriminating ways are accepted as nonprejudiced people. Happily enough, they also become less prejudiced!

Certification based on subject matter mastery and pedagogy carries with it significant implications about the learning process. First, it bolsters the idea that teachers know the world and it is their duty, right, and prerogative to communicate their knowledge to students. This attitude emphasizes rote memorization, established conceptual relationships, and pat answers, among the least exciting learning possibilities. Subject matter mastery too frequently leads to the teacher defining what the learner needs to know, how he should learn it, and how his learning should be evaluated. The result often tends to be a kind of teaching which is contrary to what we know about learning.

Furthermore, these certification requirements exclude a host of capable and talented individuals who have been unable or unwilling to pursue the formal teacher-training programs. In the practical sense, this seems to indicate that students who become teachers have "made it" within traditional public education. Having made it in the system, why shouldn't they expect it will work for their students? There is also the possibility that many of the most innovative people, able to generate new and exciting educational alternatives, are excluded from teaching by rigid certification requirements.

Similar logic leads to legislative mandating of the contents of the curriculum. Thus, the German language could not be taught during World War I; teaching *a* religion (as opposed to teaching about religion) is prohibited; and most recently, "sex education" has been outlawed. Required subjects must be taught in a mandated sequence, for certain periods of time. Examples quickly come to mind: English must be taught for three or four years, and specified amounts of time are allotted to different areas such as language structure, literature, and communication skills. Students must take the mandated sequence *regardless* of their prior level of achievement, *regardless* of their differing progress in various English content areas, and they frequently spend the mandated minutes in English instruction *regardless* of their needs, interests, past experiences, or career goals. Similar mandates can be identified in almost any area, especially history, science, and math. Also included are requirements to teach health, dangers of alcohol and drugs, and physical education.

Such legislated mandates are enforced through less pervasive but equally limiting bureaucratic procedures. The use of subject matter syllabi is not unusual. Sometimes billed as guides to teaching, they are more often viewed as requirements. This is especially true when the syllabi are reinforced by state examinations, e.g., New York State's Regents Examinations. If a teacher's effectiveness may be judged by student achievement

on state examinations, a seemingly simple and rational mandate can become an institutionalized teaching practice. Such practices, it can be argued, are grounds for labeling the
enabling legislation archaic.

Archaic elements are embedded in the various rationales on which education laws are
based. For example, schools are maintained to serve society. Society has identifiable
needs, albeit needs which may be disparate with reality. Legislation specifies the
educational needs, such as subject area requirements and time allocated to subjects. It
also specifies the processes by which duly authorized personnel—certified educators—
should carry on the task of education. And it specifies when in the student's life the
required knowledge and skills should be taught.

Legislated objectives, processes, and evaluation schemes might, if intelligently
selected, meet the needs of society. At least they will meet the needs of those learners
whose individual needs are consonant with those imposed. But the learning process, as
best we understand it, requires that the learner have responsibility for learning. Any
legislation that tends to take this responsibility away from the learner is highly questionable. Whenever the disparity between society's needs and those of learners becomes so
great that learning ceases, the legislated curricula, time spans, and achievement measures
are archaic.

Yet the imperative remains: any society must train an adequate number of citizens to
perform the tasks necessary to perpetuate it. The central difficulty is to develop
legislation that will be flexible enough to meet the needs of a society in transition.

School reform within the present society is possible but very difficult. Decisions
about education are made by people—legislators, educators, citizens—who naturally
assume that the skills which they learned in school are the skills they have used in gaining
their successes. Thus, they assume that their children and students should learn the same
skills. This would be tenable only if their children were to live in a world similar to theirs
and this cannot be assumed.

A number of interrelated conditions, however, indicate the inevitability of reform.
This society's work force has been progressively compressed; work begins at increasingly
older ages and ends at increasingly younger ages. Thus, we have an increasing pool of
unemployed youth, young adults, and "retired" older people. The young have demanded
increased educational opportunity, but the society has tended to allocate resources for
their custody rather than for their education! Less attention has been devoted to the old,
for whom our society does not feel the same custodial obligation. It appears quite
possible that both the young and the old will increase their demands for educational
opportunities without custody, forcing significant changes in our educational processes.

One might also argue that reform is not only possible but absolutely essential, because
the goals of education must change to fit the changing society. Education has operated
under the assumption that the task of the schools is to provide people with skills to
become productive citizens. Yet the significance of productivity becomes less and less
important except for those with the crucial skills which are necessary to the survival of a
highly technological society. An estimated 20 to 50 per cent of the young adults in high
schools today may never do a productive day's work in their lives because there will be
nothing available for them to do. This suggests that attention ought to be focused upon
the ability to live in a society as a nonproductive rather than a productive citizen. There is
a strong possibility that one of the greatest divisions in America will be between those
who produce and those who are functionally nonproductive. Unless the definition of a
worthy citizen ceases to depend on productivity, we can look forward to a conflict
between the "doers" and the functional nonproducers at least as disturbing as the current

conflict between blacks and whites.

Obviously caught in this whole web is the professional educator, who is at the same time perceived as a public servant. The use of the two terms in the same sentence may be contradictory. If the public educator is to act like a professional, he must have the opportunity to utilize his knowledge and expertise. Yet, at the present time he has very little latitude for this, primarily because he is hemmed in by several decades of archaic legislation pertaining to the format and process of education. The professional educator is caught in a clear dilemma. In order to feel that he is exercising his professional preroga-tives, he should be something like a gadfly. But public servants, by and large, have not been noted for their ability to sting society.

Although the private sector of education in America has not suffered from such severe legislative constraint, it appears to have made little more progress than the public sector. The normative expectations of parochial and private educators are probably quite similar to those of public school educators. Most private schools tend to generate programs aimed at the same kind of "productive citizens" that the public schools are attempting to educate. The parochial schools appear to be ruled by many of the same constraints as the public schools, in addition to other limitations imposed by the religious hierarchy. Their problems may be further complicated by some secular control over individual parochial schools.

Though these constraints are real, the general course of private education raises the possibility that professional educators have much more freedom to influence the learning process than they choose to use. It's depressing to contemplate, but it may be that public educators are generally convinced that the way it's done is the way to do it!

As public educators see themselves moving toward professional status, that complacent perception will have effects on their visions of their task. Whenever the length, complexity, and range of content of preparatory training for any occupation has been increased, graduates have sought more influence over the content and context of their jobs. The greater the need for use of individual judgment in the exercise of one's work responsibilities, the greater the push for autonomy and control. This is especially true in areas that evolve rapidly and therefore require frequent and intensive training inputs. Gellerman reminds us that:

> Higher education not only teaches the individual to think critically and to analyze problems for himself, it also makes him rather intolerant of restrictions on his right to do so. This is why the first few years of employment after college can be so disillusioning: The young man often finds himself having to unlearn the thinking role he has been accustomed to play in college and to fit himself into a hierarchy which gives its younger members little opportunity to be analytical.... Consequently, the net effect of a more educated pool from which employees can be hired is an increasing pressure to enlarge both the scope of jobs and the degree of latitude given to individuals in these jobs.
>
> The long-term trend, then, would seem to be toward a gradual spreading of permissive management to most organizations and a redistribution of functions to take greater advantage of the increased capabilities of a more sophisticated workforce (Gellerman, 1963, p. 220).

Given the prevailing character of publicly legislated organizations called schools, the degree of "permissive management" may be far less than the professional employee expects!

Adding impetus to the press for change are the expectations of public professional employees in addition to those for autonomy and control. Compensation has been a very sore point in education.

... teachers' salaries lag far behind those of other professional or paraprofessional workers with similar training. In 1961 the mean annual salary of teachers was $1000 below that of nonsupervisory auditors, $1500 behind nonsupervisory accountants, $1800 lower than nonsupervisory chemists, and $2700 beneath that of nonsupervisory engineers. There seems to have been no substantial change in this ratio in the intervening years (Dougherty and Oberer, 1967, p. 12).

Ten years later, the National Education Association reported:

Beginning salaries of teachers with a bachelor's degree have increased considerably in the past few years but are still considerably below the average salary paid to beginners with a bachelor's degree in most other professional areas.

In 1970-71, the average salary for a beginning teacher with a bachelor's degree was $6850; for other professions the average for men graduates with a bachelor's degree was $9361, or 36.7 percent higher. ... the average starting salary for men graduates in 1970-71 ranged from a low of $8124 for Business Administration graduates to a high of $10,476 for Engineers.

Men graduates in June 1971 have been hired at average salaries that are still well in excess of the preliminary estimated beginning salary of $7230 which will be paid to new teachers with bachelor's degrees in 1971-72.

The average beginning salaries paid women graduates with bachelor's degrees are lower than the average salaries paid men graduates, but are higher in every area shown in the table than the average for beginning teachers. (NEA, 1971).

Increasing demands for professional autonomy and higher expectations of compensation for professional service, as well as increasingly complex bureaucratic organizational relationships have the potential to change educational institutions. Professional educators will certainly exert heavier pressure on legislative bodies to bring their professional involvement closer to their expectations. The shift in the balance of power inherent in the professional militancy movement has great potential. The question appears to be how soon this influence will be brought to bear on legislation affecting the learning process.

As organizational forces move to increase their power and influence, the impression remains that many educators are pondering their individual positions. Professional educators are as much a product of their background as others in our culture. Many are thoroughly convinced that the way in which they were educated is adequate for others. Many have not even considered whether the difference between the concepts of knowing the world or discovering it makes any significant impact on how and what people learn. Most seem to believe that a professional educator has certain kinds of knowledge invested in himself and must protect them. Teachers, for example, are tremendously threatened when they are asked a question for which they have no pat answer. This need to have the answers is probably one of the factors which leads many teachers to be dogmatic, unreasonable, repressive, and restrictive in the way they interact with learners.

If that is the case, the possibility that students are going to be facing problems which neither they nor their teachers can even imagine is unlikely to be entertained. As a consequence, educators tend to assume that both the answers in the back of the book and the problems in the front will be the same two or three decades hence. That appears on the face of it to be untrue; nevertheless, it is where many professional educators find themselves. Thus, it is easy to understand that educators, particularly teachers, are not very imaginative about creating new kinds of conditions for themselves and for their learners through the use of their power at the legislative level or at the bargaining table.

Educators tend to have difficulty in defining both their individual and their organizational positions vis-à-vis legislation affecting education. That ambivalence is increased when they are faced with the implied or real threat of student activism. Conceptually, and operationally, freedom to learn implies autonomy for the learner. Yet the teacher is used to a setting where the learner's autonomy is subject to the teacher's authority, and where maintaining this authority is of paramount importance. It is understandable why he hesitates to consider drastic changes in existing authority relationships. Under those mind-sets, it may be naive to expect educators to exert influence at the legislative level to vest autonomy in students in order to reduce the archaic nature of school law. Law is too frequently the reinforcer of educators' power!

So it is with the professional educator in the public school system. Faced with norms for content, process, sequence, and organizational relationships embodied in educational law that fail to meet society's needs, the educator and the system will face cultural and psychological strain either in maintaining an increasingly archaic system or in adapting it to serve society's needs.

It is continually recognized, however, that both legislation and the system it creates must change. Imperatives for change are inherent in emerging social and economic conditions. The resolution of change rests with society as a whole. But it may be that both the force for change and the source of change rest primarily with legislators, learners, and educators. If that is true, then effective changes cannot be made unilaterally. Legislators cannot persist in disregarding the learner and the educator. By the same token, learners and educators must accept more responsibility for influencing legislative changes. Developing patterns of interaction such as negotiations, local community boards, and organizational mergers provide more possibilities for generating influence.

Without such interaction, continued disparity between legislation and learning can be expected. In fact, given traditional patterns of interaction, one can predict more archaic legislation.

REFERENCES

Bailey, Stephen K.: Address delivered before the National Association of Secondary School Administrators, Milwaukee. November 9, 1970.

Dougherty, Robert, and Oberer, Walter: *Teachers, School Boards, and Collective Bargaining: A Changing of the Guard.* Ithaca, N.Y., N.Y.S. School of Industrial and Labor Relations, 1967.

Gellerman, Saul W.: *Motivation and Productivity.* New York, American Management Association, 1963.

National Education Association. *Research Bulletin, 49:*No. 3, October, 1971.

Rogers, Carl R.: *Freedom to Learn.* Columbus, Ohio, Charles E. Merrill, 1969.

15 in defense of smallness

Gerald S. Witherspoon
Wilfrid G. Hamlin

Bigness in colleges is a recent phenomenon. When Daniel Webster said of Dartmouth, "It is . . . a small college, and yet there are those that love it . . ." he was speaking of an institution of fewer than 150 students. Harvard's first class of 100 wasn't graduated until 1860, by which time the college had had an enormous influence on the shaping of American education. It wasn't until this century that American universities grew to be giants, apparently partaking of the American business mystique that bigger must mean better.

Small colleges have made and are making enormous contributions to the development of higher education. How often philosophers of education refer to the Experimental College at Wisconsin—a tiny group of students and teachers who worked together for a very brief period in a program designed around the relation of the traditional liberal arts to contemporary culture. Black Mountain College, never larger than 125 students and for most of its two decades far smaller than that, had an impact still echoing long after its closing. Haverford, Swarthmore, Reed, and Oberlin—sometimes called small university colleges—showed up at the head of a list of colleges whose graduates went on to earn the Ph.D. degree. Sarah Lawrence, Bennington, Antioch, and Goddard are nationally known for their experimental programs.

Education is a very personal matter. It isn't impossible to help students learn what they need to learn in a big college, but it's hard enough so that university after university has experimented with small "inner colleges," groups of students and teachers who have separated themselves from the major administrative and curricular structures of the universities to work toward individualized education.

Only when a college's teachers and administrators can deal with students as individual learners—knowing them as persons with unique interests, needs, skills, histories, and problems—is it likely that going to college will make significant differences in the lives of those students.

Such is our partiality. It is in defense of it that we submit the arguments that follow.

What is college for? We hold with those who view its purposes as different from those of the university. Let us agree that universities at their best are storehouses of expertise on the one hand, fountainheads of vital research on the other; and let us again point out that small colleges—not only Haverford and Swarthmore, but tiny Black Mountain and the half-on-campus, half-off-at-work Antioch—have excellent records in preparing students for specialized university work. But college education, as we understand it, is something other than university research or training in expertise—or preparation for those scholarly activities.

Alexander Meiklejohn was ultimately dissatisfied with the program of his short-lived Experimental College at Wisconsin, but he remained faithful to its basic aim: to help young people confront, come to know, and come to some personal terms with the world in which they live. Such an aim, wholly appropriate to the critical period at the end of the twenties, is just as appropriate today if we add one element: an equal emphasis on helping these young people confront, come to know, and come to terms with their own identities. Postwar American life has resulted in a major erosion of the sense of self. If today's youth revolution has one central concern, it is exactly that.

What students are asking of college, and what small colleges are uniquely able to provide, is an atmosphere in which they can learn what they need to learn, individually and by personal prescription, to find out more surely who they are and how they can relate to a problematic world. This is not to confuse education with therapy (though psychologists like Carl Rogers and Richard Jones have suggested fundamental parallels between the two). It is to argue that in corporate America, where system and organization are king and human values are too often translated into symbols of status and role, there is need for individual human beings to examine, test, try out, make mistakes, create and recreate, explore, and evaluate—in short, to define freedom for themselves and essentially by themselves in a college which is not so much divorced from the culture as it is in contrast to it: a consciously created counterculture of individual learning.

More simply, let us say that we want a student to learn to do well something that he considers worth doing. As he learns this, he learns something of who he is but in no sense in a vacuum: it is "being-in-the-world" he learns, if his teachers and he are aware of their individual interdependence with each other and all persons and things in the world.

We have digressed to make this point because we believe it to be vital if colleges are to be something other than training grounds for mechanical participation in an increasingly dehumanized technological society. We believe such educational aims as we have suggested are in and of themselves important; but beyond that, we are made daily more aware that they are most seriously the aims of a great number of American college students. To an essential degree, we submit, the students are the colleges. A college which is not responsive to the expressed needs of its students seems to us to have lost its authenticity.

Individual education of the very personal kind we favor depends on each student being able to draw on all of the college's resources, and on college teachers knowing students well enough to be able to alert individuals to ideas or persons or opportunities for experience which may be of particular importance to them. Mark Hopkins and the student at opposite ends of the log may seem paternalistic nonsense in a time marked by proclamations of student independence, but that should not blind us to the importance of the single student and the opportunities we can provide him to get in direct touch with the people and things he needs for his learning.

Our defense of smallness hinges on such a view of the nature of education. We assert that this kind of education can go on in a small college (not necessarily that it will). We hope to show how and why; and why it is not likely to go on in a big college.

We have four major arguments for the small college. One is that it makes possible a very individualized education. Another is that it may draw mainly on human, not material resources. The third is that its government can involve wide participation, and thus be responsive to changing needs and interests of students and teachers. The fourth is that it can serve as a pilot plant for educational experiments.

"Individualized education" is part of the jargon, of little meaning until one examines what actually goes on in a college. What can go on in a small college is that every person there can know all the college's resources; thus, teachers can help students work out individual programs drawing on all of those resources. The larger an institution, the less this is possible: teachers know only a few students, students know only those faculty members and other resources they have been either required to come in contact with or drawn to out of some major interest. A famous teacher in a large university is faced with literally thousands of students wishing to study with him. Not having the time to work with them individually, he has no choice but to fall back on mass lectures, quizzes, examinations, and grades as a substitute for the more personal dialogue or apprenticeship he would probably prefer.

If one component of individualized education is access to resources, the small college has an enormous advantage. One of us once tried to take a graduate level course at Harvard with Erik Erikson, only to find it closed to all but the "section men" who were discussion leaders for his 600-student general education course. But at Black Mountain College any student could study art with Josef Albers, German theater with Eric Bentley, anthropology with Paul Radin, or poetry with Charles Olson. At Wayne State University only the tiniest fraction of the students enrolled can take part in the plays the college theater produces; at tiny Marlboro College, any student interested in acting (or any aspect of production) can participate in what are among the most exciting theatrical productions in New England.

Our second point has to do with human resources which—along with the environment in which a person lives—are the basic educational resources and always have been. (We would include among human resources the records of human enterprise and speculation which make up a library; books and other monuments of the past are an essential part of a human environment.)

It is our observation that when the fundamental relationship in a college is that of person to person, important learning goes on without the need for an expensive plant or equipment. When a college becomes so large that the persons in it are not easily available to each other, the fundamental relationship is likely to become that of person to thing—computer, tape recorder, theater switchboard, recreation building, gymnasium, laboratory.

The person-to-person college can use simple multipurpose buildings, since its chief need is for places where people can get together. Franconia and Black Mountain made good use of old hotels. Goddard took over a farm estate. Large colleges, on the other hand, find a need to erect elaborate specialized buildings: science laboratories, theaters loaded with stage machinery, learning centers with dial-access computer-controlled programs to instruct hundreds of students at a time.

When college teachers and administrators—the distinction tends to be vague or nonexistent in the kind of small college we believe in—know students as individuals, they can help them find off-campus learning resources that are adapted to their various needs. A student interested in environmental biology, for instance, may learn more as an apprentice with a state Fish and Game Department or Water Resources Board than he ever could on campus, particularly if he is in constant touch with a faculty member who knows him and his work well. The community around a small college can become classroom and laboratory for many of its students.

It will be clear that this kind of education is less expensive than that involving great investments in plant and equipment. Is it less effective? A number of Black Mountain students went into professional theater work after studies in drama carried on in the college dining room, and Earlham had an outstanding reputation for work in biology done in the most modestly equipped laboratory. An atomic scientist has written nostalgically of the "string-and-sealing-wax days" when pioneering work in modern physics was done by a small group of students and teachers picking each other's brains and improvising equipment to try out new ideas. Goddard's reputation for educating kindergarten and nursery-school teachers grew in an old dairy, transformed by parents and students into a nursery-kindergarten operating on a shoestring budget. In each case, teachers and students could work closely together; the interaction among them was the basic resource for learning. Too often the large college attempts to substitute material resources for human resources, but things are poor replacements for people. One result is that there tends to be a demand for more and more things, out of some desperate hope that three computers will be able to do what one has failed at.

Third, we are interested in the kind of governance possible in small colleges in contrast with that usual in large colleges.

College governance is in general hierarchical, its structure paralleling that of many corporations. That such a model is not a viable one today might be assumed even without the testimony of Berkeley, Columbia, and the growing number of institutions where administrators have faced "confrontation" with students demanding "power." In spite of this, college governance, particularly large college governance, remains in general unchanged.

For persons to trust each other, they have to know each other. Teachers and administrators in large universities are often strangers, and their relationship is hardly characterized by trust. Like employees in many industries, instructors worry about promotion, seniority, who has the inner track in the race for privileges. Getting and keeping power becomes something of an end in itself: the struggle for department chair-manships, for instance, often seems more vital to the persons involved than their concerns with subject matter and students. The larger the institution, the more power positions there are.

But power is hardly the issue in an institution of higher learning. Governance should be, like teaching, a way of facilitating learning, nothing else. Appropriately enough, administrators in many small colleges are also teachers. Very often they work closely with students in the running of the college. Marlboro's Town Meetings, paralleled by similar committees-of-the-whole at a number of other colleges, bring everyone interested into the process.

As institutions grow, wide participation becomes increasingly difficult. Today Goddard has no meeting place big enough to hold all of its students and staff. As the college has moved toward and past the 1000 mark in enrollment, various forms of representative government have been set up. But it has become clear that however open to student requests and faculty proposals a governance structure is, however much it requires faculty and student representation in all decision-making bodies, it is nevertheless seen as "they" doing things to "us." Antioch, now about twice Goddard's size, has been the scene of repeated strikes by assorted campus groups who find its highly participatory government too cumbersome, too much concerned with whole-college problems, or perhaps just too remote to be trusted to deal with the matters these groups believe to be pressing and primary.

We suggest that this is an area where research into the critical points in group size might play a very important part. Is there a size at which a group must be understood to be too large for participatory democracy to work? How big does a New England town have to become for the town meeting to be recognized as a rubber stamp or a farce?

Small villages rarely have problems with graft or police corruption but they are common-place in cities, though the formal governing structures may be essentially the same. The aim of many small colleges is to grow large—usually to some published maximum size which, increment by increment, is enlarged each time it is approached. What happens to college governance as the small becomes less small?

The kind of government we believe in is not only participatory but one in which the participants reach decisions by consensus. At the risk of belaboring the point, we must bring in again the matter of trust and the dependence of trust on persons knowing each other. Given a basic trustworthiness on the part of the people involved (a justifiable assumption on most campuses, we assert), it is possible for administrators, teachers, and students to be truly open with each other about projects, needs, problems, and concerns, permitting a thorough analysis and, ultimately, a thoroughly understood decision. But this is likely to come about only if the persons working on the problem are something more than roles (the Dissatisfied Student, the Militant Professor, the Pig President), something more than acquaintances.

This leads us back into the question of size; both as regards the total size an institution may attain before it loses the possibility of being an assemblage of persons and becomes the capital I "Institution" made up of "Personnel" of one classification or another, and as regards the makeup of its policy-making bodies. All the evidence we know urges smallness in both respects.

Our fourth argument for smallness is that it permits a college to be experimental, a pilot plant for new educational ideas. We need not argue the importance of experimenta-tion in a time when many students and teachers are questioning the very existence of colleges. It is also probably evident that large colleges and universities have difficulty initiating and carrying out major experiments, and that when they do, the experiments are too often short-lived. Teachers College administrators at Columbia University killed their depression child, New College, without consulting its committed faculty and students—putting a summary end to what was one of the most interesting experiments in radicalizing college education. The Experimental College at Wisconsin was killed because it was presumed to be élitist. Wayne State University faculty and administrators attempted to kill Monteith College after a few years of important experimentation; it was saved only when the actions establishing it were interpreted as having made it an autonomous unit rather than an experimental program.

Goddard, our own small college, has, by contrast, been able to initiate and carry through experiment after experiment. It was one of the first colleges to make indepen-dent study planned by individual students in collaboration with faculty members a major part of the curriculum (and then to build a nonresident degree-granting program for adults around this way of working); one of the first to send students into public schools as assistant teachers (part of the students' academic work, very different from "practice teaching"); one of the first to experiment with all-college participatory government. Working with Antioch, Goddard planned and set up a number of Field Study Centers where college students could spend a year learning by working with people in deprived or desperate parts of the country—a less bureaucratic, perhaps more educational version of the VISTA program. In collaboration with other small colleges, Goddard initiated the Union for Experimenting Colleges and Universities and is one of the first participants in its University Without Walls project.

Thirty years ago Black Mountain experimented with having students build college buildings. The decision to try this was made in open meetings of the whole college over a few months; later, the decision to make the work voluntary rather than mandatory was made during a week of all-college meetings, and the decision to open the experiment to architectural students from various universities was made in a single faculty meeting. At about the same time, Antioch began one of the first courses in film as art and social document, taught cooperatively by a teacher and several students, with no administrative red tape needed beyond the say-so of the faculty member. But a large university faculty member of our acquaintance had to wait three years and sit through innumerable curriculum committee meetings before being allowed to teach an experimental course in which no grades would be given. Both faculty mistrust and administrative red tape appear to be involved in the failure of several of the larger colleges which have become members of the Union for Experimenting Colleges and Universities to agree to full sponsorship of the University Without Walls project—although the project was strongly supported in principle by their top administrators.

To sum it up, there are things possible in a small college which are impossible or at least very difficult in a large college. They are possible mainly because the fundamental relationships in the small college can be those of person to person, not person to institution or equipment or program. The small college can be a very personal place, working with the uniqueness of individual persons, opening to each of them all of its resources. This is not to say that every small college will be this way—too many try to copy the big colleges. But smallness can make much possible.

Four suggestions come from these considerations.

First, if America needs more places for college students, why not create them by creating more small colleges? In a small college, since the fundamental resources are persons, little equipment is needed. Thus the cost may be little more—or even less—than that of building additional facilities in existing universities. What little we know of group size and its influence on interpersonal interaction suggests that such colleges might be very small indeed, perhaps under 100 students; at any rate, building colleges of various small sizes might provide an opportunity for much-needed research into this factor.

Such small colleges should in no sense be carbon copies of each other; rather, as diverse as individuals, they should each contribute something different to higher education, each work in its own way serving the needs of student groups which will become, over time, increasingly different.

Second, colleges and universities should be encouraged to experiment with "inner colleges" and other autonomous or semi-autonomous subgroups. Monteith College at Wayne State University has become a real force in American education. Antioch's various offshoots—the inner college publicized in a *Life* article, the Antioch-Columbia Program in Maryland, and the Antioch-Putney Graduate School of Teacher Education, in particular —demonstrated the usefulness of the small unit, allied in philosophy but distinct in practice and personnel from the larger college which sponsored it. The "cluster colleges" at Claremont and The University of the Pacific offer another useful model.

American higher education has its roots in the ancient universities of England. It is well to remember that they have always been assemblages of relatively small colleges, in many ways quite separate from each other. Part of the continued importance of Harvard and Yale may lie in their (quite different) attempts to mirror this structure.

Third, small colleges should be encouraged to make common cause, cooperating in whatever ways they can to share their strengths. There is a great deal of wandering from college to college on the part of students today. Might we not legitimize this by some form of compact which would make it possible for any student, with a minimum of fuss, to spend one term at one small college, the next at another? Under such a plan, each college might increase its differences from others, recognizing that it had no reason to try to be all things to all men. The University Without Walls is a step in this direction, but other patterns are possible.

Fourth, however such institutions start, they need recognition as important and useful institutions. Present accrediting standards give lip service to experimentation and program diversity but still place great emphasis on money, buildings, laboratories, and department staffing; as some regional associations operate, it would seem more honest to speak of Criteria for Exclusion than of Criteria for Membership. If organizations to evaluate and approve colleges are useful—a question about which we feel some ambivalence—we would wish them to look harder at what seems really important in education: what and how people learn about the world they live in and themselves as members of it.

By changing a few words, these suggestions can be made appropriate for all levels of education. If individual attention and recognition is important to the young adult with twelve or more years of institutional experience behind him, how much more important is it to the six year old child still in the early stages of development? Large public school systems with their mazes of prescribed curricula, paperwork, and work rules, and their many levels of administration are probably even more fossilized than the gigantic state universities. The modern equipment and professional expertise which large schools proudly offer can be useful, but they are of secondary importance compared to the human interactions of a small school.

Indeed, we would hold that smallness makes many things possible in institutions of all kinds. We know of small high schools where, despite poorly prepared teachers and rigid administrators, students get a decent education because everyone can talk together, because a large proportion of students can be class officers, serve on a student council, play on a basketball team, take part in a class play, edit or write for a student newspaper, and have a personal relationship with at least one, more likely several, teachers. We know of village and small town governments where, despite provincialism and what sometimes seems perilously close to illiteracy, selectmen will welcome and pay serious attention to divergent, even radical points of view, and parents or other concerned people who come to a school board meeting will be met as individuals with something useful to say. In most such situations, we believe that smallness is a necessary, if not sufficient, condition.

We are prejudiced in favor of smallness. We hope that what we have said will demonstrate that this is a prejudice in favor of education as something other than training, persons rather than personnel, schools as human institutions, and the people who make them up as each other's best teachers.

the learning society 16

John Bremer

Society needs the young. The reasons are not hard to find, indeed they are obvious to the point of being platitudinous. The young have ideals, they have energy, and they have, above all, youth. Today's young are the mature citizens of tomorrow; in them is the hope of the future. If the future is to be better, if society is to have any future at all, it will exist in and through the young.

This view, however, scarcely makes the role of the teacher, who is the agent for introducing the young to the ways of society, less ambivalent. The teacher may well be grateful for the assurance of a future that the young bring with them, but it is probably mixed with resentment that social fulfillment cannot be realised now, in his person and his generation. In addition, the boundless energy of the young (and there are always more young to come), utilised on behalf of new ideals, is threatening to the established order. Change is required, even of the teacher, whose cry must be comparable to that of Augustine of Hippo: "Let me learn, O Lord, but not yet."

The teacher's difficult task requires him to cherish society and to care for the young, to recreate society and to create the learner, to renew society by supporting the student. The difficulty lies precisely in the fact that both parts must be accomplished simultaneously, since the student and society are functions of each other. The teacher, like Janus, faces in both directions, toward the past and toward the future. He is concerned with both the old and the young, and he experiences the tension between the two. He is condemned to endure the senile reminiscences of what education was like shortly after the Golden Age, and to attend respectfully to the successful men of action, the self-made men, proclaiming what made them so (about which he is not expected to have any opinion). In addition, he is constantly drawn into regression by the very students he is expected to help to mature, and, in view of his treatment by politicians and administrators, the temptation toward immaturity must be very strong.

In any case, since he is committed to a profession dedicated to ambivalence, the teacher's emotional life is and always will be full of stress. Hence, his characteristic professional attitude ought to be ironic. He cannot survive as a person unless he can live happily with contradictions without feeling obliged to resolve them, and he must see the significance of seemingly opposite value systems without falling into the abyss between them. His professional survival depends upon his ability not to choose between society or students. The moment he chooses, his usefulness as a teacher is at an end. If he chooses the student, he ceases to be the leader of a learning community and becomes a follower of the infantile. If he chooses society, he merely becomes another indoctrinator, for whom the student is a means to some allegedly higher end. The alternatives are "regression or repression."

It is interesting to observe that the opposite of both these alternatives is the same—namely, learning. The central problem in education is to preserve learning, and all that we do must be judged by this standard. The ability to learn is the mark of the mature person, for it is the mark of life, the continued capacity to interact with a changing environment. This raises the question of the kind of educational environment to be provided by the teacher.

It is very tempting to assume that the environment, if properly planned, will determine, infallibly and inevitably, that learning will take place. In a certain sense, this is true. People do learn how to get along in the environment, how to cope with the structures. This is not usually what the educational planner, the administrator, has in mind. He supposes that by careful planning an environment can be created in which, say, mathematics or history (or both) will be effectively learned by the unsuspecting student. His supposition is wrong, for a structure can only teach itself; the student, at best, can only learn his plan. Indeed, this is well recognized in practice, for a variable is introduced into the planned environment to ensure that the mathematics or the history is learned. This variable is the teacher.

If the planned environment is regarded as a kind of constant and the teacher is seen as a variable, it must nevertheless be emphasized that the teacher's variability concerns only his professional qualification in his subject field. The teacher's personality is not thought to be a significant variable; in fact, the individuality of a teacher is considered, at best, irrelevant and, at worst, a real detriment. Teaching is supposed to be a planned activity; it is supposed to possess a method which has a valuable property of its own, independent of any person who uses it. Although differentiated staffing purports to use the differing skills and talents of different people to the best advantage, it is, in practice, usually a grudging admission of individual weaknesses since it necessitates the recognition of two or three methods instead of the conventional one.

For planners to allow for individuality is a contradiction in terms; the only person who can plan for individuality is the individual himself. When properly understood, planning is the intellectual dimension of life as it is lived; it is not a necessary pre-condition to life, provided by somebody else.

If the teacher is eliminated from the planning equations (except as a variable whose domain is subject-matter), how much more obviously is the value assigned a student equal to zero. Planning involves, in varying degrees, uniformity, universalizing, and abstracting from known (or imaginary) students what they have in common. In educational planning and administration, the student is an abstraction, a piece of data, a number, indistinguishable from all other students. To report simply that one student was absent from class may well satisfy administrative bureaucratic requirements, but it leaves out everything of educational significance.

Having taken away from the student all his originality and creativity, having systematically eliminated his personal humanity, the teacher is expected to motivate him. This absurdity could only arise in a school. Every student is already motivated; he has, as Plato would say, a soul. From the point of view of the pre-planned school (and every school is pre-planned), this is a disadvantage, for the student's soul moves him to do things that don't fit into the school's plan. Priority is, however, accorded the latter. Therefore, his present motivation must be brought under strict control and then supplanted by other motives that are deemed appropriate by the school (in the light of its plan) and are of a strength calculated to carry the student through a lesson but no more.

The cardinal principle of educational planning if it is to do real good for real people, is that it must begin, to continue the Platonic metaphor, with the soul of the student. The inevitable consequence of this principle is that planning can be done only in collaboration with the student. It is a way of life and not simply the pre-set boundaries of life, it is a process and not a product. The educational planner or architect may well ask, "How do I plan a new school?" The answer is simple (and probably unacceptable to the asker): "If you wish to help a student learn, you cannot do it by your methods. If you wish to provide a building, the general patterns of design are known to you already. Follow these as you wish, consonant with standard school requirements, for the results will be equally irrelevant to the learning process." An architect or planner may well insist, in the jargon of the day, that it is his job to create a learning environment, and this gets us to the issue.

The "learningness" of an environment is not a property of the environment in the way that "opaque" may be a property of the window-glass or "soft" may be a property of the carpet. Nor is it the material out of which the environment is made, in the way that "brick wall" means a wall made of brick. The term is unlike "dining room," in which "dining" indicates the function that the room serves, for the proof of this pudding is clearly in the eating. The room has no special property that requires the designation "dining" room; it is only justified if the activity is actually carried out there. It begs the question to say that a school is where learning takes place and, therefore, by building a school we build a "learning environment."

The learningness of an environment, then, is not a property of the environment but a function of the skills, attitudes, and confidence which a student brings to that environment. Learning can take place anywhere, even on the street or at home; it all depends on the soul of the student, the source of all learning. If the soul is appropriately ordered, that is, if it has the necessary skills and attitudes, learning will occur, and not otherwise.

However, it is not true that a given student will be able to learn equally well anywhere. Socrates was able to learn with his friends, in prison, and awaiting the dose of hemlock. Most of us would probably be so overwhelmed by such an impending fate that learning would be impossible, yet with a properly ordered soul, some education might be possible. What should be planned for students? It is very hard to say, but there are some simple principles that might be helpful:

First, not all students are alike, and a situation which would be anxiety-producing for one, would be comforting for another.

Second, students grow as they learn, and an environment that was supportive one day could be restrictive the next.

Third, there is no evidence to suggest that students learn best in classes or in classrooms, grouped according to chronological age.

Fourth, given the large number of variables, or, more honestly, given the mystery of the human soul, perhaps the student himself is the best judge of the appropriate learning environment for him.

It is obvious that this view is contrary to current practice, but that does not automatically make it incorrect. For those who persist in the conventional and insist on providing a special building called a school, there is a learning principle that might be useful, namely, that learning takes place as a result of interaction. The ideal school building is one that can be dismantled by the students and can be put together again in an infinite variety of ways; it invites, and preferably, demands interaction. In a sense, a certain incompleteness could be an advantage. Students need to learn how to reconstruct their environment, at least within those limits which are set partly by the natural possibilities of the environment and partly by their own skills. From this interaction, learning will come; without it, nothing of educational value will occur.

From this point of view, the student has a role similar to that of the artist. He has a unique, creative contribution to make to a pre-existing set of conditions (which may be likened to the artist's material). It may well be objected that students cannot reconstruct the school building, and that is probably true. But it is not in the school that the student will live his life; the reconstruction of the school is only a metaphor for the reconstruction of the city, that is, of society. The continuation and preservation of society is dependent upon its renewal and renovation by the young, and each student brings something original and different to the renewal.

The originality of the student is very small in relation to the massive structure of society that inevitably is re-created in him. But smallness should not be confused with insignificance. The renewal process of society does not occur on a large scale, suddenly and dramatically; its essential characteristic is continuity. Society is torn apart by doctrinaire advocacy of large-scale change, and leadership fails and becomes lunacy when it loses contact with those who follow. Each student's contribution must be seen in the same way that we see vitamins in relation to the body; there is a minimum daily requirement, small but vital, and the body cannot store it for long.

It is very important for educators to realise that when we speak of the preservation of society, we do not mean the ossification, the petrification of society. That would be like making a fossil of a living creature—it does not preserve the living creature as living but merely maintains its outer shape or structure. Preservation of society comes about through change; the life of society goes on by the addition of new life and by its interaction with its environment and with its own members. The student's role, the contribution of the young, is indispensable.

To acknowledge this is not to idolize or idealize youth. Nor is it to suggest that only the old need to learn, while the young do not. The demands made on the young by learning are great, and educators must ensure that they are made in a way which will secure the response of the young, not overwhelm them. In this sense, the teacher's role is that of mediator.

If, on occasion, a student seems not to be learning because he has exhausted the possibilities of his situation, then the teacher's task is to introduce him to new forces, new opportunities for interaction. The reason for focusing on the student is not a sentimental one, it is simply that the young are newcomers and can be alienated; they are fragile and can be destroyed, and, in their destruction, adumbrate the destruction of society.

The renewal of society in and through the young requires the establishment of an interaction between them, a continuity. The teacher as mediator creates that continuity and interprets the young and society to each other. He makes demands on each on behalf of the other. But all education begins where the student is, in his soul, because it is a process of establishing and maintaining continuity between himself and society so that they may, mutually, interact. The greater burden of change lies on the student, he has a longer distance to travel, and the teacher helps him find the starting-point for his journey. We tend to forget that it is *his* journey, and that therefore we must accept *his* starting point. The possible destinations are fairly well established (although not completely so); as educators, we do not need to worry too much about them, but helping the student to get started and keep going is our perennial problem. That is why our attention must be focused on him.

In helping the student, however, we cannot ignore the social realities of our time. Educators of the nineteenth century, who in all essential respects created the pattern of contemporary public education, did so in the light of the social needs then current. The concentration of people in urban areas, new social disciplines required by industrialization, the dissolution of old ties and attitudes, immigration, and universal suffrage were all aspects of one major problem—the diffusion of knowledge. All, or virtually all, of the knowledge required was available in the last century, but it was not available on a wide enough basis. The problem was how to make the knowledge more accessible as it was needed. A whole range of devices were employed, including public libraries, newspapers, magazines, encyclopedias, and self-help programs, but above all was the public school system. Schools were set up to disseminate knowledge, and teachers were the agents of dissemination. Since there were large numbers of students to be handled, the only human institution capable of dealing with large numbers, the factory, was used as a model. The teacher was cast in the role of the operator whose task was to impress upon the student from the outside what he lacked, namely, knowledge. Knowledge was conceived primarily in terms of literacy; that is, information which could be handed from one person to another together with the skill of acquiring more information. Implicitly, social training was also taught. If the teacher gave out information by talking, the student received it by listening; his role was passive.

The school as an institution was built around this problem. Its basic principle was that the teacher was the disseminator of knowledge; he was certified by his mastery of a subject. The school building was designed to make the most economical use of the teacher as a dispenser of subject matter. Hence, instruction was always group instruction, in rooms of an appropriate size. No need was felt to consider the individuality of students. The students did receive benefits which they could get nowhere else, the rewards were real (if not unmixed with corruption), and methods of coercion were more stringent than would now be acceptable. If, from our point of view, this seems limited and inhuman, we should remember that the schools were thought to do a good job, and, in fact, seemed to have dealt adequately with the problem of diffusing knowledge.

Perhaps they were too successful, for they have evidenced little ability to change in response to changing circumstances. Since "the information explosion," the task of education is no longer the diffusion of knowledge. Knowledge (in a variety of meanings) is readily available and widely spread, but students are still expected to learn subject-matter at school, much of it out of date, unrelated to current life, and even wrong; in many ways, they know more than their teachers about the world as it is (not necessarily about the academic subject-matter). Knowledge is growing so rapidly that many teachers' knowledge of their subject is obsolete, particularly if they have been out of college more than a few years. This substantially diminishes their authority.

The characteristic problem of our age is how to develop the social skills of cooperation, through which our knowledge can be put to social, human use. This involves organizing knowledge in a variety of ways so that it can be applied to many different situations; it involves the values which will govern the use of knowledge; and it involves the interpersonal skills which can promote community.

Every student should learn the skills of organization and communication; they are so important that public education must insist on these becoming the basic curriculum. If we started out with this as our goal, we would never re-create the public school system as we now have it, for the new curriculum is action oriented and requires the whole society to become the campus, since society is the source and the beneficiary of the curriculum. The public school system was designed to solve another problem. The new system (if it is a system) is not known yet, it needs to be created, but its outstanding characteristic is known and that is, that it can be created only by all those who are participating in it. It follows that creation is not an event in time but a process, not an imposition of order from without but a generation of discipline from within. This is different from any society yet known, because it judges its worth by the extent to which it furthers the learning of its members. Perhaps this has never been economically possible before, but now it is. What is strange is that as it becomes possible, it also becomes necessary.

17 school design— the inevitable responses to the present conditions

Neal B. Mitchell, Jr.

Educational buildings today are like a thirteenth century cathedral—beyond the financial capability of the community and yet a necessity for community life and prestige. Parents considering moving into a community weigh the quality and location of the nearest school building as important factors. Land values rise where well-designed schools have been built. Yet construction costs have spiraled ever upward as community tax bases have been eroded by other needs, leaving larger bond issues at the mercy of increasingly hostile taxpayers. The problem of building schools both less costly and more useful than the educational cathedrals of the past is a critical one for every growing community.

Interaction with changing housing patterns has seriously compounded the problem. Communities have become concerned with holding down school taxes and have changed zoning laws so housing will be constructed only for the childless or the affluent. It used to be dogs and cats that weren't wanted; now it's kids. Large families and the poor who demand services exceeding the community's ability to tax them are stranded in the already hard-pressed cities. Rural communities, in turn, are unwilling to spend money on new facilities and teachers at a time when rural populations are shrinking.

Education is supposed to be an avenue to opportunity for the poor. Yet the financial resources needed to give them this opportunity are monopolized by affluent communities. It is the wealthy suburbs that attract the best teachers, build the most extravagant buildings, provide money for new and innovative programs, and produce possibly the best trained students. This is no longer satisfactory to minorities or working class parents who want an equal opportunity for their children. Our national leaders are aware that if this country is to grow and prosper all students must be able to develop to their full capabilities. To bring this opportunity about will require significant changes in both our thinking and our physical facilities.

Even the urban bedroom communities that are blessed with an adequate tax base are faced with the problem of keeping up with the times while their fixed capital facilities become inadequate far more rapidly than originally anticipated. New educational programs are in constant need of different types of space in the usually poorly designed existing facilities. The more glamorous physical plants that were once considered a status symbol for well-to-do communities have become so expensive that they are no longer within the reach of even the wealthiest budgets.

This financial crisis comes at a time when education faces a major upheaval. Major innovations in teaching technology offer new possibilities. Young people, exposed to other ways of life and learning through newspapers, radio, television, and travel, are making new educational demands. Similar sources, especially television, have produced community pressures for change that are straining the best school systems.

> What passes for education today, even in our "best" schools and colleges, is a hopeless anachronism. Parents look to education to fit their children for life in the future, teachers warn that lack of education will cripple a child's chances in the world of tomorrow. Government ministries, churches, the mass media—all exhort young people to stay in school, insisting that now, as never before, one's future is almost wholly dependent upon education.
>
> Yet for all this rhetoric about the future, our schools face backward toward a dying system rather than forward to the emerging new society (Toffler, 1970).

What then should a community do? The demands for school space and quality education will continue to rise. New and innovative educational programs and facilities must be developed if the nation is to face up to both the needs and the costs of meeting them. But this must be done within serious economic constraints, for communities can no longer afford to build exotic physical facilities that are closely coupled to outdated educational programs.

How does a community go about establishing the need, defining the program, and developing the requirements for a new school? The process usually begins when school administrators, responding to teacher complaints (but often without teacher participation), call attention to the need for either increased space or upgraded facilities. Some rather complex demands are placed thereby on the local school board. In general, the residents elected to the board have very little experience, competence, or understanding either in evaluating the requests themselves or identifying the appropriate consulting help to do so for them. Community leaders hesitate to take risks by changing either programs or building forms. Usually the goal is to "get something done" without any kind of "problems." Additionally, faculty and administrators fear they might be jeopardizing increases in space by raising questions about how educational programs might fit into the building. Therefore, in the spirit of getting voter approval and minimizing political risk, traditional and often uncreative solutions are welcomed. It is a depressing situation!

This in no way suggests that elected local citizens are not fully capable of doing an adequate job. The problem arises when they have had little training in dealing with the problems they must face, and it becomes serious when they are unable or unwilling to secure help or advice from experts better prepared to handle the problems. The result is a strong tendency for school construction to be a patronage plum of the local political organization. This in turn often leads to a squandering of the taxpayers' money to produce a building that shows little professional creativity and a disturbingly high concern with pleasing politicians and maximizing fees.

The current system of building school facilities creates another serious problem. The very core of real architectural design is the identification of the needs of the user (in this case, the teacher and student), and a design aimed at meeting these needs. Yet for most school design contracts, the architect finds that his main relationship is with politicians and the elected members of the school committee. When he is lucky, he gets to meet the administrators but rarely is the analysis of school needs reviewed with the teachers and students who will be using the new structure. Often too, the architect is excluded from planning for the overall educational needs of the community. The school committee breaks this complex problem into a series of parts and then sets about solving each part independently of the other. The chaos of specialized consultants, each with different views, interests, and professional focus, coupled with different reward and goal structures, produce a mish-mash that usually fails to identify the overall educational needs or to find a coherent approach to the needs it does identify. Instead, it identifies the administrative requirements and the political constraints that limit the amount of money that can be made available for construction. This type of review often leads to the decision that the new facilities should look and perform "just like our school did." After all, we all know what a school should look like.

It is time to re-examine our whole notion of what a school should be. David Morton has pointed out that:

> Some educational historians have suggested that there is more than a casual relationship between the rise of industrialism in the 19th century, with its mass-production techniques of systematizing and standardizing and the present educational system that grew up during the same period. In the name of efficiency, a system of education evolved through which a student became processed, or schooled, in much the same way that an automobile became tooled and produced. The thinking was that if the process was good in a manufacturing system it would be equally valid as a means of producing the kind of adult citizens a society would need to accommodate its growing industrialism. The end result was a standardized product, whether it was a car or a person, which was formed according to the rigid requirements of an assembly-line method of production.
>
> Although there is talk of individualizing, or humanizing education today, patterns of teaching remain influenced by old forms of thinking entrapped within old buildings. Most schools are still of the eggcrate variety where a student passes through a series of predetermined stages similar to those of an assembly line. Academic disciplines are physically confined and intellectually defined by square rooms along straight corridors where the student receives, at precisely determined stages, elements of his education, without regard to whether or not he might be ready, or perhaps beyond, that particular stage. If he has passed through a certain room for a requisite number of hours, he is necessarily ready. If not, he will be put back through the process either until he is ready or until he absents himself from the system. It often happens that during the process he may never have learned to think: at best he might have memorized some facts and learned some skills, many of which will not be of particular relevance to his adult life, all of which he might have learned with less waste of time and effort through a more realistic process of education.
>
> A growing reaction to the nonhuman, assembly-line method of education has been emerging within the past several years. It recognizes that the process of learning is best facilitated when the individual's own needs become the focal point of this education (Morton, 1971, p. 68-69).

Why shouldn't learning and school be fun? To build a school with impenetrable walls, with indestructibly hard and cold finishes on long and uninteresting corridors can only produce antagonism in the students educated in this prison atmosphere. This can only spark rebellion at some time in their life.

> Because adults take the schools so much for granted, they fail to appreciate what grim joyless places most American schools are, how oppressive and petty are the rules by which they are governed, how intellectually sterile and aesthetically barren the atmosphere (Silberman, 1970).

It is time to treat students like human beings, with dignity, respect, and individuality. Decent lighting, carpets on the floor, comfortable chairs, appropriate warm environments, elegant places, and places where the most unrestrained activities can take place are definite requirements in a school. The sameness of the past must be replaced with a new physical vitality if we expect to educate for change.

Consider the problem of school design on a more personal basis. If I went to the store and picked out a suit for you and told you that you had to wear that suit every day for the next six years and thank me profusely for it every morning, you would probably rebel. I think any intelligent person would. You would point out that you are perfectly capable of making your own decisions and that my demands for thanks go far beyond good taste. Why then, do we bypass the student when it comes to designing the school where he must spend the major part of his time for several years?

We also bypass the teachers, in a rather insulting way, by informing them that these policy decisions are far too complex for them. These problems are left to the administrator, who is often poorly equipped to deal with the technical problems of education but has ability in the political aspects of the issue. Perhaps this is why the janitor makes the most critical decisions with regard to finishes, colors, and materials. The extent to which maintenance and janitorial concerns outweigh the overall educational requirements in school design is frightening. Ease of maintenance is an important consideration—lest someone install shag carpeting in the metal shop—but it should never get in the way of educational goals. School design by school boards, mayors, or super-janitors must end so that buildings can be built that are not only easy to maintain but have warmth, color, and humanity for the teachers and students.

Some people have argued that the physcial facility has no effect on the educational program. One wonders if this is an excuse for bad design. It is exciting to see what happens when a dynamic program is put into an equally exciting, compatible, and supportive space. This approach can free teachers and encourage them to imagine and experiment with more interesting educational techniques. Perhaps one of the most important functions of a school building is to give the teacher a sufficient sense of security so that he can expand and enrich the student's educational experience. Both teachers and students will benefit from well-designed buildings and it is time that we started to give them such facilities within the framework of costs that communities can afford.

In recent years, a number of exciting innovations have been advanced to minimize school costs, while expanding flexibility and program possibilities. One of the more creative physical innovations is the School Contruction Systems Development (SCSD)

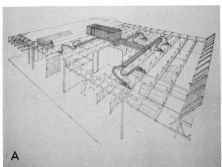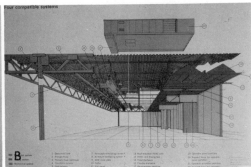

FIGURE 1

system in California. This system was developed by a group of school administrators, architects, and manufacturers who sought to identify cost and performance criteria for school facilities. From these, they designed a catalog of compatible hardware, including structural and mechanical components, lighting, and interior partitions that could be combined in a variety of ways to give design flexibility and produce school buildings with both changeable spaces and environmental controls (Fig. 1). This significantly broadened the "kit of parts" that could be used to build school facilities. These factory-manufactured building elements can be fitted together in the field by design, greatly reducing construction costs. This modular design also allows for flexibility in rearranging parts of the structure to meet changing needs. Two major problems of school design are thereby attacked by this method—the cost of building the structure and its immutability once completed.

The SCSD building system appears to be a success. With the backing of the Ford Foundation, several other communities, regions, and states have begun to explore both the use of these developed products and the possibility of development of additional hardware systems that can be easily combined with existing products.

The real success of this kind of technological development that saves money and improves performance at the same time, is an appropriate operational statement of the educational and physical design parameters. Should we expand on the SCSD experiment and design more building components for the architect? Should we initiate programs to develop new and more extensive information about user needs? Should we eliminate the local architect and local school boards from the design of schools and centralize design in larger professional groups that can upgrade quality by virtue of the scale on which they work? If we have the courage to do this, new multidisciplined teams can research and design a broad range of educational programs and the buildings to house them. We must find a way to assist local communities in meeting their needs without the encumbrance of bureaucratic structures like HEW and HUD, for the problems of finances and expertise appear to have overwhelmed local resources.

A great deal can be learned from the success of a unique program for rural schools developed by the Mexican government. Instead of imitating the United States' massive drive for consolidation of small rural schools, Mexico supports small local school districts by providing physical facilities appropriate for their needs. The building is a typical one-room schoolhouse, designed to give the teacher unlimited flexibility in using space. More important, however, is the fact that part of each structure is a furnished apartment for the teacher and his or her family. This helps meet an essential goal of the government's program: to expose rural residents to the living habits of the urban-educated teacher.

This program has been very successful in providing standard yet flexible (large single space) and inexpensive schools for rural areas. The free apartment has lured into these rural areas those good young teachers who want to marry but cannot find a place to live in the city. This carefully controlled program of support has been able to stimulate school construction in an incredible number of small, rural communities that otherwise would not have had a school, a teacher, or an educational program.

The Mexican school building program has been designed to provide everything for an educational program, including books, slide tapes, desks, furniture, projectors, clock, and even a generator for electric power where none is available. Even maintenance has been considered; after two years of operation, the government sends paint and brushes so the teacher, students, and villagers can do the necessary touch-up and repair work.

The government has been able to do this at absolutely minimal cost by predesigning, engineering, organizing, and purchasing large lot quantities of materials, and supplying these at no cost to the community. The members of the community are expected to build the building using community "self-help" labor. This "barn raising" type of program insures community commitment and pride in the facility, minimizes construction cost for the government, and insures an overall cooperative spirit between community residents and government agencies.

This program provides facilities and teachers on a personal level. By contrast, American foundation grants have often been used to develop innovative programs and to pay good young teachers to teach in the depressed urban and rural areas. When the grant expires and the teachers leave, almost nothing remains for the community.

Small individual and personalized schools, containing the teacher's living quarters as a part of the structure, could revolutionize our educational system and would, I think, help to solve some of the educational problems of our poor. I feel that it would have a much greater chance for success than the "super school" pioneered by some of our large cities. Certainly there are thousands of American communities that could benefit from standardized but flexible school buildings that also provide housing for the teachers. Communities would also benefit from a well-constructed and well-designed school building that involved community participation as a basis for constructing it. Isn't this the type of support that our foundations and government should be providing for both our urban and rural areas?

When the physical space demands exceed a single room, or when specialized and expensive capital equipment is required, the design of the interrelationships between the capital facilities of the school becomes a critical factor. Perhaps this too requires rethinking.

FIGURE 2

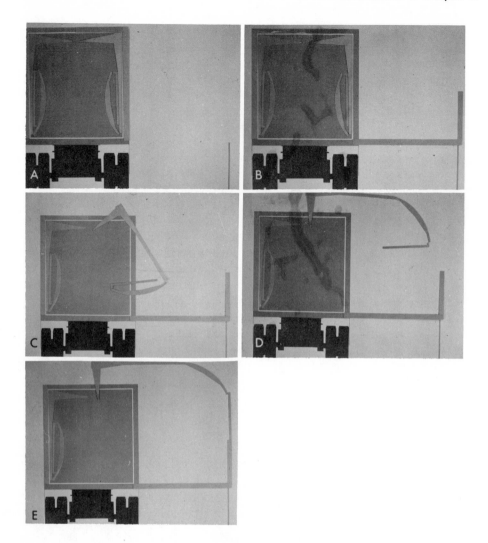

FIGURE 3

One new answer to this problem is the mobile classroom. The idea originated with Dr. Jerrold Zacharias of MIT, who also served as a director at the Educational Development Center in Watertown, Massachusetts. Dr. Zacharias reasoned that we were always "bringing the action to the school" rather than "bringing the school to where the things were happening." He argued that a more mobile and versatile classroom would be able to take advantage of existing community facilities other than schools.

Such a facility could supply expensive equipment that schools need only part-time and otherwise could not afford. For example, a thoroughly equipped mobile physics laboratory could meet the needs of several high schools which could share the facility that otherwise they could not afford. Why should four or five small rural schools have to duplicate the same physical facility and capital equipment which each uses for only a limited period each day? Wouldn't it be more reasonable to pool together resources, purchase one very good, high quality laboratory, and then share it? Since it is hard to bus students from school to school, why not bus the school to the students? This represents an important way to reduce school costs and at the same time increase the quality of equipment and teachers.

The second advantage to this type of facility would be the possibility of increasing classroom and equipment usage. Why not use a school facility 24 hours a day, 12 months a year? This would certainly ensure that we were getting maximum value from the facility.

For example, mobile sewing facilities could be used during the day by school children and then brought to a local site and made available to residents for the evening. Such expanded usage would not only greatly expand the effective impact of the school but would ensure the community maximum use of rather expensive capital facilities. A facility shared between four schools and then used in the neighborhood at night could be used as much as 15 to 20 hours a day, instead of the approximately two hours daily use it would receive in a permanent school building. Actual use would depend upon the location and the effectiveness of programming and could be quite intensive; for example, facilities such as ice rinks are used almost 16 hours a day, seven days a week. This suggests some rather interesting possibilities for the budgeting of new capital facilities.

What would a mobile classroom look like? My firm has developed an expandible mobile classroom (Fig. 2) using a standard truck trailer body (Fig. 3). The unit was cut and new foldable roof and walls were added, so that when opened the enclosed open space was 24 X 24 feet with a 10½ foot ceiling (Fig. 4). The walls and roof were aluminum insulated sandwich panels. It was carpeted and contained space in which to ship specialized equipment as well as providing for a teacher's room. The entire unit could be opened and set up within three-quarters of an hour. The unit had self-contained power generating (Fig. 5), heating, cooling, and plumbing systems.

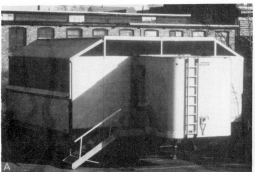

FIGURE 4

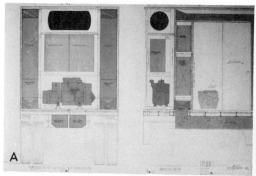

FIGURE 5

The teacher could also be mobile and travel with the classroom. This would permit teachers to specialize in particular subject areas or even specific topics, and to develop material for a broad audience. A teacher could spend a certain amount of time as a traditional classroom teacher, but would also have the opportunity of taking innovative material to a wider audience. This would stimulate the teacher's own development and hopefully, that of other teachers who came in contact with him and his ideas, thus helping to broaden and strengthen the overall teaching program.

A good program developed by a suburban teacher would then be available for circulation to all schools in the area, thus exposing teachers to the problems of ghetto schools without "sentencing" them to long periods of service there. It would also bring to the ghetto innovative educational programs taught by teachers who are not fully hardened to the difficulties, hopelessness, and anger usually found in these schools. This whole approach could be used to complement existing school programs by broadening their flexibility and providing new and different opportunities for the teaching staff.

Such facilities could also be used for skill training and vocational education. High school students could rebuild some of the poor neighborhoods of our urban communities, bringing their classrooms with them. By working on meaningful problems and involving local union officials, vocational programs could become more valuable and realistic, building an exciting bond between the "work world" and the world within the school.

The availability of these facilities for local residents after school hours implies the possibility of new kinds of continuing vocational education. The school's capital equipment could be used by local residents to improve their own physical surroundings. For example, it could make an important difference to an urban resident who owns his own home but cannot afford the tools or power equipment to make repairs. It could help cooperative neighborhood improvement efforts meet their first major problem—finding the needed equipment.

A mobile classroom could attach itself to local industry and use their equipment and professionals to help with training. Why set up a printing plant in a vocational school when the local newspaper has large presses available? Various city services like public works, fire, and police departments also have facilities that could be used in conjunction with educational programs. In this way, the classroom would expand to become the real world, an often repeated goal of many educators. What happens when educational needs build on needs demonstrated from the real world? An American student in France learns French when he is there because he has to in order to get by. Let's do this with other subjects. It can't help but give students better preparation for future work.

My firm has also proposed that a small industrial New England community develop a core docking facility for mobile classrooms rather than building traditional schools. The proposed facility is to be built in the heart of the ghetto district and is designed as a resource and program development center for mobile classrooms to be used throughout the city. These resource facilities would prepare a complete range of course materials that stressed the extreme range of interests and possibilities existing within the area. The city would then build small schools with minimal fixed facilities which would be supplemented by facilities available in the mobile classrooms. In addition, housing for teachers would be attached to each of these small school facilities.

The availability of well-designed free housing could help draw people to work in this type of program. The fact that teachers could live adjacent to the school could bring them closer to the children and the neighborhood. Disadvantaged children would have the opportunity not only to learn in the classroom but to observe the life-style in the teacher's home. Many people claim that it is more important to understand how to live than it is to understand "school subjects." English, history, and physics are obviously necessary, but how to live, community understanding, tolerance, respect, and love are equally important. Perhaps by physically bringing teachers and classrooms more completely in contact with students, even more exciting breakthroughs in education can be achieved.

What are the implications of these ideas? How do the Mexican rural school program, the SCSD system of compatible hardware components for schools, and the Mitchell Mobile Classroom influence what will happen in the next 25 years of school construction?

Each of these ideas provides an alternative to the traditional school building. Each solution involves user participation in the development of physical facilities and programs. Each involves the teacher more intimately with the classroom. Each provides a standard technical base and standard parts that can be customized by each community. I think that these are the kind of ideas that must be developed in order to meet our school building crisis. Each of these solutions implies improved performance for dollars spent, while focusing community resources on solving the full range of community educational problems.

The main difficulty in achieving these solutions is the American attitude that once the physical facilities have been constructed, the problem no longer exists. Again and again communities rush to build monuments without considering an educational program. Too often it is the physical building rather than the quality of the educational program which represents a political achievement. Administrators, teachers, and students must work together to change political concerns from quantity of buildings to quality education and buildings that facilitate it.

School design in the future must consider not only bricks and mortar but also the very soul of the community itself. Development of new buildings and new programs must be stimulated by, and focused on, the needs of teachers and students. Modern management techniques must be used to achieve a rich variety of programs, which should be developed within the community's budget and resource limitations. This is an extremely difficult task, and the results will challenge many old and accepted ideas. Yet, the problem is solvable on paper. The question is: can it be solved from an administrative, human, and political standpoint?

REFERENCES

Morton, David: *Progressive Architecture.* February, 1971.
Silberman, Charles E.: *Crisis in the Classroom.* New York, Random House, 1970.
Toffler, Alvin: *Future Shock.* New York, Random House, 1970.

structure and function 18
in the classroom

Eugene R. Howard

When I look back at the results of my past teaching, the real results seem the same—either damage was done—or nothing significant occurred. This is frankly troubling.

Carl R. Rogers, *Freedom to Learn,* p. 153

It is always satisfying to see one's own beliefs expressed by a great educator. Thus Carl Rogers' statements about the futility of his own teaching are particularly impressive to me.

Ten years ago I felt that most of what a typical teacher does in a conventional classroom is ineffective and futile. Now I believe that most of what he does is harmful.

We live in a society which has seen fit to institutionalize its young. Our reformatories, insane asylums, military organizations, and schools serve the society by keeping our young off the labor market and processing them in such a way that they will conform to the needs of big business, big industry, and big government.

Can noncoercive learning environments survive in a society which depends heavily on conformity for its continued existence? Or should educational experimentation be limited to devising ways to make coercive education more pleasant and efficient? Whether or not noncoercive environments will find wide acceptance is still open to question. There is little doubt, however, as to their effectiveness.

CHARACTERISTICS OF OPEN LEARNING ENVIRONMENTS

Evidence is mounting that such noncoercive or "open" environments, under certain conditions, are more conducive to pupil growth and motivation than are coercive ones (NEA, 1969, pp. 55-58).

At the present time, at least in North America and Western Europe, we in education are experiencing a movement toward such learning environments—environments in which pupils have a great deal to say about what they will learn, how they will learn, what facilities and materials they will use, and who will assist them. Such environments are characterized by:

1. Open communication across racial, sexual, age, grade, and subject matter barriers,
2. Shared planning, decision-making, and evaluation,

3. Authenticity rather than artificiality in human relations,* and

4. A minimization of formal rules, regulations, and restrictions on movement.

Unlike more traditional "closed" learning environments, the open environment is based on assumptions such as the following:

1. That children come into the world eager to learn; indeed, their very survival depends upon their learning,

2. That the teacher does not motivate. The pupil is already motivated. If the environment is appropriately structured, much positive learning will take place.

3. That teachers, with the help of their pupils, can structure such environments,

4. That given real (not phony) choices between productivity or nonproductivity, learners, unless corrupted by a sick educational system, will tend to be productive,

5. That pupils will be more positively motivated (1) if they are provided with options for using their time productively, (2) if they believe that the task they are asked to assume is a meaningful and achievable one, (3) if they see themselves as capable rather than incapable people, and (4) if they derive a sense of immediate satisfaction from what they do,

6. That people can learn from people who are not teachers in places that are not schools and from books that are not textbooks, i.e., that a community can become a new kind of classroom,

7. That hardly anyone really wants to be "taught" in the usual sense of the term. Rather, that people find satisfaction in learning by creating, inquiring, and solving meaningful problems. Therefore, teachers should stop teaching and devote their time instead to creating, with pupil participation, learning environments which will free learners to be productive.**

THE NEED FOR INSTITUTIONAL REFORM

The above assumptions are not new. They have been repeated often, in one form or another, by psychologists and educational theorists for at least the past century. That such assumptions have more theoretical than practical acceptance is perhaps due to political as well as professional reasons. To a large extent, however, our lack of progress can be considered our own fault. In curriculum reform we have accepted the leadership of campus-based scholars who develop "teacher-proof" curricula designed to change the content of courses but not the structure of our schools. "The reform movement," reports Silberman, "has produced innumerable changes, and yet the schools themselves remain unchanged" (Silberman, 1970, p. 159). He adds that "without changing the ways in which schools operate and teachers teach, changing the curriculum alone does not have much effect" (p. 181).

The time has arrived in the current educational reform movement for us to devote our time, energy, and resources not so much to changing pieces of the curriculum as to

---

*Carl R. Rogers has said that the most basic quality in a teacher who wishes to facilitate learning is "realness" or "genuineness." "It means that he comes into a direct personal encounter with the learner .... It means that he is *being* himself, not denying himself." See Rogers, *Freedom to Learn,* p. 106.

**For a detailed description of how one teacher built such an environment with her class see Chapter 1, "A Sixth Grade Teacher Experiments," in Carl R. Rogers' *Freedom to Learn.* For a description of how such an environment might function school-wide, see George B. Leonard's *Education and Ecstasy,* especially Chapters 8 and 9.

restructuring learning environments. An attack must be launched on reforming the nature of the institution itself.

Unfortunately, the chances of success on any massive scale do not appear to be good, given the values of the societies within which we must function. Yet the direction toward humanizing our educational institutions has been set, and at least for a while, a movement in this direction is in progress.

Given an open-minded principal, any group of teachers dissatisfied with the status quo can initiate significant projects to humanize and rationalize the educational climate. It is to such energetic dissatisfied teachers that this chapter is addressed.

Significant projects for restructuring the environment can be of four different types, aimed at (1) restructuring the physical environment, (2) restructuring the psychological environment, (3) changing the roles of staff members and learners, and (4) restructuring the curriculum. The remainder of this chapter will be devoted to some specific suggestions for implementing such projects.

RESTRUCTURING THE PHYSICAL ENVIRONMENT

The physical environment can, itself, teach. It can present options. It can encourage or discourage visual and oral communication. It can invite a person to sit down and think things out, or it can make contemplation impossible. It can encourage dialogue or make it impossible. It can offer learning as a multimedia experience or make devices for multimedia learning inaccessible. A well-planned physical environment can make a variety of productive learning experiences available to small and large groups of learners.

The typical classroom, for example, constructed to accommodate from 30 to 35 pupils and a single teacher, is appropriate only for education as developed for another century and for an alien culture. Confronted with 30 to 35 bodies, the typical teacher, unless he is unusually gifted, finds himself under almost irresistible pressure to "teach"—i.e., present a lesson, give an assignment, conduct "recitations," and give the same test to everyone present. It is now fairly generally conceded, especially in our urban schools, that such group teaching is a waste of time, harmful to both pupils and teachers.

A typical classroom is too small to be used for large group instruction or for learning laboratory activities. It is too large for personal conferences, for use by small learning teams, or for formal small group discussion. It is a maverick—good for nothing. The first task of a group of teachers who want to change the learning environment is to declare war on the classroom as the basic organizational unit of the school.

It is not expensive to remove walls which separate classrooms or to place door frames within walls to provide easy access from one room to another. Some creative environments have been successfully developed in corridors* and others in rooms formerly used as study halls or flat-floored auditoriums.

If, however, the teacher is forced by circumstances to stay in the box, he can alleviate the situation by such innovations as:

1. The establishment of activity centers in various parts of the room where learning teams of from one to five pupils work with materials and learn from one another. More room for such centers can be created if the conventional chair desks can be removed from the room.

---

*See Silberman's description in Chapter 7 of *Crisis in the Classroom* of a variety of learning environments created by teachers. Of special interest is his description of Central Harlem's P.S. 123 "open corridor," pp. 298-303.

2. Increasing the variety of learning materials available and placing such materials in the activity centers where they are accessible. (Where budgetary problems prohibit purchasing diverse materials, teachers and pupils can seek materials from a variety of sources. They can be donated or scrounged.)

3. The adding of some rugs or carpeting and some noninstitutional furniture, such as comfortable chairs, lamps for reading, tables, earphones for listening, magazine racks, and book shelves.

4. Establishing one place in the room where people can talk with one another in semi-privacy.

5. Arranging for learning experiences outside the classroom.

6. Hanging curtains and meaningful pictures; adding display panels, planters, or low book shelves which can subdivide space into small work areas.

The very least that a teacher might do to restructure the classroom environment is to occasionally regroup the traditional furniture to promote team learning or discussion. It is futile to attempt to conduct a meaningful discussion in a class if most of the individuals are looking at the backs of other people's heads.

Groups of teachers, with administrative support, can make significant modifications in the physical facilities which shape their lives. What is required is the courage to throw out the chair desks, a desire to use the physical environment as a tool, a bit of imagination, and a willingness to fail and start over. It also helps to have at least a little influence among the downtown brass.

RESTRUCTURING THE PSYCHOLOGICAL ENVIRONMENT

The psychological environment is hard to deal with because, by and large, it is poorly understood. We can read, of course, about such concepts as "peer group acceptance," "building a positive self-image," "group expectations," and "normative behavior," but few hints are given to the practitioner as to ways such concepts can be translated into programs and practices.

Yet the psychological environment is of crucial importance in determining how learners will behave. It is no longer news, for example, that the teacher's expectation of a pupil's achievement is a powerful force in determining what that achievement will be. Likewise, it is widely known that pupils respond more favorably to praise and to immediate success than to criticism, punishment, and failure. We know that children learn their values and beliefs to a large extent from their peers and that peer approval is a strong motivation. We know that there are such things as learning styles, that some pupils tend to learn better through visual experiences, others through discussions with others, others through manipulating real objects. We know that some pupils are unable to handle a nonstructured situation which requires initiative and responsibility and that others thrive in such a situation but will rebel at authority. We know that a nonthreatening environment is more conducive to learning than a threatening one. We know that the emotions—love, hate, anger, fear—play a key role in the learning process. Yet, by and large, classroom teachers have chosen to ignore this knowledge. Teachers have the authority, if they wish, to act, to modify significantly the psychological environment in which they and their pupils must live and work. They can, for example, plan projects such as the following:

1. With the help of their fellow staff members and pupils, teachers eliminate all negative criticism from their comments. The teacher may solicit immediate feedback from those around him so that negative comments are immediately brought to his attention.

2. Teachers may conduct a series of exercises with pupils designed to encourage them to make positive and supportive comments to one another (Achievement Motivation Systems, 1969). For example, one exercise might consist of a group of pupils concentrating first on one of its members, then another, naming all of the positive characteristics of each person (e.g., "Cares about others," "intelligent," "good reader," and so on). A list of such characteristics can be given to each individual.

3. Teachers can conduct a series of Glasser-type discussion groups (Glasser, 1969, pp. 122-192) designed to encourage pupils to evaluate their learning and to say positive things about one another, about their teacher, and about their work. Teachers can solicit pupil participation in planning the psychological environment ("How can we help every pupil have at least one positive learning experience each day?").

4. The A, B, C grading system can be replaced with evaluation devices which emphasize progress and achievement. (The typical grading system is based on the assumption that approximately half the individuals in a given group must be labeled "below average"—a dangerous practice if the goal is to build positive self-concepts for all pupils). Self-evaluation should be included as a part of the evaluation process.

5. A "Learning by Teaching" program can be instituted which encourages every pupil to help others learn (Thelen, 1968). The evidence is strong that the tutor gains as much as the person being tutored in such a relationship.

As such activities begin to take effect, teachers may proceed with the dismantling of the conventional extrinsic award-letting system (gold stars, notes to Mama, achievement certificates, honor rolls, pins, honor societies, and so on) which tend to encourage pupils to learn for the wrong reasons.

THE NEED TO CHANGE THE ROLES OF TEACHERS AND LEARNERS

Ideally, a school should be a place where everyone, at one time or another, learns from everyone else. Learners must learn to look to one another as well as to adults as persons who can serve as resource persons for their own learning. It is unlikely that any significant change can take place in a learning environment unless a change occurs in what teachers do when they teach, what pupils do when they learn, and what learners and teachers do when they work together.

It seems fairly well established that one of the biggest problems with teachers is that they talk too much. A rather impressive body of research (National Education Association, 1969, p. 72) supports the conclusion that talking *at* pupils is a relatively futile way for the teacher to spend his time. When it is also noted that it is not at all uncommon for teachers to spend 75 to 80 per cent of their time talking, we glimpse a picture of a large number of professional educators wasting their own and their pupils' time.

Teachers who want to find the time to plan, to talk to pupils and parents, and to think creatively might be well advised to abandon their role of chief information-giver. The time thus saved might well be reinvested in helping pupils learn.

Teacher Roles

The teacher in an open learning environment becomes an environmental architect. With his pupils, parents, and other staff members, he plans ways to create learning environments which will stimulate positive learning. He organizes learning materials and makes them accessible to learners. He diagnoses and prescribes learning experiences, but he does so in such a way that pupils learn how to diagnose and prescribe for themselves. He helps pupils define their objectives and evaluate their progress towards those objectives. He suggests learning resources and new and stimulating experiences to pupils; he is a "horizon stretcher." He presents options, not so much by stating, "What would you like to do today?" but by suggesting, "Have you thought of trying this. . . ?"

He organizes learning teams—small groups of learners who can help one another achieve complementary objectives, and he helps such groups define objectives and plan and evaluate activities. He raises hell with kids who are wasting time—theirs and his—but he does this in such a way that people are stimulated and supported, not crushed and defeated. He organizes discussion groups so that people can share learning experiences with one another, and in such groups he serves as topic initiator, listener and sounding board, group conscience, clarifier of unclear ideas, and enemy of sloppy thinking. He stimulates inquiry by asking questions which cause others to ask questions and by structuring situations which can be explained only if the pupil inquires into causes and the relationship of observable to unknown factors.

He keeps records of pupil progress and encourages pupils to keep their own records. He compiles a list of resource people in the community and on the staff and arranges for pupils to learn from them. He urges parents to get off their kids' backs. He hardly ever tells people anything they don't really want to know, and he never asks anyone to do anything he is incapable of achieving. He listens a lot; he cares a lot; and he lets it show.

Such is the role of a teacher who succeeds in liberating himself from the usual grind that traps even the very resourceful. This liberating process can best be facilitated by a group which has as dual objectives the reform of the institution which dominates them all and the changing of the teachers themselves.

Learner Roles

In an open learning environment such as that described here, the pupil moves from a passive, accepting role into a more active, participating role. He learns to diagnose his own learning needs and to initiate, with teacher approval, his own learning experiences. He learns to seek help when he needs it, to admit failure and learn from it, to set his own goals, to chart his own progress. He shares his achievements with other pupils and learns from the experiences of others as they share their learning with him. He helps others. He helps other learners gain in self-confidence by providing them with positive feedback when they need it. He, too, listens a lot, cares a lot, and lets it show.

All of this, of course, sounds utopian, almost naive. Yet, to date, by building learning environments based on fear, distrust, and manipulation of people through phony reward and punishment systems, we have succeeded in teaching young people to be fearful and hostile. By creating a psychological environment based on trust and understanding, couldn't we hope to achieve the opposite? The problem is that each teacher, if he is to hope to change the school, must start by changing himself.

PROJECTS TO RESTRUCTURE THE CURRICULUM

The idea of individualized assignments has been around for a long time. As early as 1912, individualized pacing was operating successfully in the San Francisco Normal School's laboratory school.*

It cannot be said that progress in individualizing instruction has been impressive since 1912. The most prevalent method of teaching, that of presenting, discussing, assigning homework, reciting, and testing, still persists in the overwhelming majority of our classrooms. Such persistence is difficult to justify in the face of growing evidence that such practices are generally futile and often harmful.

Today there is a growing awareness on the part of teachers that it is possible to organize the curriculum in such a way that pupils may proceed at their own best rate, exercising options as they go. Such a curriculum has the following characteristics:

1. Lesson plans are written for pupils, not teachers. Such lesson plans may be very short and simple (a contract to write a report on the effect of a local power plant on air quality) or highly complex (an assignment to read a basic chapter in a textbook, perform experiments, complete outside readings, and write an evaluative report).

2. The lesson plan specifies the learning objectives, the learning activities, and the way the results will be measured.

3. It may also offer the pupil a wide variety of options. For example, if a pupil does not achieve his objective of mastering the division of fractions through usual textbook assignments, he may have the option of working toward the same objective through exercises with Cuisinnaire Rods.

4. In addition to the three basic elements (objectives, specified activities, and evaluation), the lesson plan may contain provisions for pretesting so that pupils are not asked to waste their time working toward objectives they have already mastered.

5. The lesson plan may also provide suggestions for depth activities, invitations to pursue the topic further in one or more ways suggested by the teacher.

6. Similarly, the plan may invite the learner to suggest his own additional learning activities for pursuing the topic further. This is the so-called "independent study" or "quest" option.

Such lesson plans, sometimes called "contracts," "unipacs," "learning activity packages," or simply "assignment sheets," can be prepared by any teacher or team of teachers and can be made available to learners as needed.**

Ideally, lesson plans of this type rely heavily on audiovisual devices for the

---

*Such pioneer efforts are described by Carleton W. Washburne in his autobiographical essay, *Winnetka,* 1963.

**For a more comprehensive description of this concept, see Kapper, Philip and Swenson, Gardner: Individualizing instruction for self-paced learning, *The Clearing House.* March, 1968, pp. 405-410.

Smith, James E.: *The Activity Package,* pamphlet, 24 pp., presents four models for individualized lesson plans and is available from Educational Associates, 229 S.E. First Ave., Fort Lauderdale, Fla. 33301 (one dollar).

introduction of each lesson. An initial learning activity might well be: "Go to the library (or to the storage room of the learning laboratory) and request tape number E-27 with its accompanying worksheet. This tape, recorded by Mr. Jones, will introduce the lesson. After you have listened to the tape, complete the worksheet and ask for a conference with your teacher."

While such devices are not essential, their use can save teachers a great deal of time. Teachers who fail to use technology properly often find themselves repeating the same explanations many times to successive individuals and groups as they begin work on the lesson.

The most appropriate physical setting for such individualized activities is a room somewhat larger than a typical classroom staffed with a small team of teachers and paraprofessionals. It is not difficult, however, for a single teacher in a conventional classroom to begin to reorganize the curriculum without the assistance of colleagues and without special facilities.

Often, teachers first experimenting with such a concept begin by preparing individualized assignments for those pupils who are most obviously suffering from group-paced instruction—the highly motivated, bright pupils and the pupils who have had the most difficulty with the regular assignments. As success is achieved with pupils with special needs, plans can be made to expand the procedure to include all pupils.

Other teachers have initiated such procedures by including an entire class or combined class on an experimental basis for a limited period of time, returning to the comparatively "safe" group-paced instruction periodically. It seems advisable to ease into such departures rather than making abrupt changes which often result in disorder and confusion.

Contrary to popular belief, individualized instruction does not necessarily require each pupil to proceed through the curriculum alone. Learning teams can be formed so that pupils can proceed through units of study with others. Such teams may be composed of pupils who work well together because they are friends, pupils who share an interest in a particular project, or pupils in a tutorial arrangement. In most open settings the composition of the learning teams is constantly changing as the needs and interests of learners change.

SUMMARY

This chapter has presented a snapshot of a different kind of school, a school in which people listen to one another, learn from one another, and care about one another. It has introduced briefly several concepts which appear to be of central importance in restructuring the learning environment so that pupils can become excited about learning.

The coercion-centered environment, based on the assumption that pupils cannot be trusted to make important decisions about their own learning, is well calculated to produce hostile, fearful, insecure people. It is such an environment which now prevails in most of the institutions in our society which have been designed to accommodate our young.

Alternative environments, built cooperatively by educators, pupils, and parents, have been successfully implemented. Available evidence strongly supports the establishment of "open" climates with characteristics such as those described above.

Our conventional learning environment must be restructured in four major ways. The physical environment must be modified so that more learning activities become possible. The psychological environment must be restructured so that what is now known about motivation and the learning process can be built into the way the pupil perceives himself and others. The roles of teachers and learners must be basically changed, and the curriculum must be organized in such a way that the learner has progressively more options as he grows in his ability to make decisions on his own behalf.

If we are serious about educating our young for a free, as opposed to an oppressive, society, we must concentrate our energies and resources on humanizing our institutions. In the process of humanizing these institutions we must challenge existing assumptions, existing structures, and existing functions.

A student is not a product to be processed, nor is he a resource to be developed. Rather, he is a growing, feeling, caring, loving, hating, thinking individual—an individual who, if given a reasonable opportunity to do so, can assume a great deal of responsibility for his own education.

REFERENCES

Achievement Motivation Systems: *Excellence in Education.* Chicago, 1969. Available from AMS, 1439 Michigan Ave., Chicago 60605.

Glasser, William: *Schools Without Failure.* New York, Harper & Row, 1969. Chapters 10-14, pp. 122-192.

Leonard, George B.: *Education and Ecstasy.* New York, Delta Book, 1968. Chapters 8 and 9.

National Education Association. Association for Supervision and Curriculum Development: *Humanizing the Secondary School.* Washington, D.C., NEA, 1969.

Rogers, Carl R.: *Freedom to Learn.* Columbus, Ohio, Charles E. Merrill, 1969.

Silberman, Charles E.: *Crisis in the Classroom.* New York, Random House, 1970.

Thelen, Herbert A.: *Learning by Teaching,* a report on a conference on the Helping Relationship in the Classroom. Chicago, the Stone-Brandel Center, 1968.

Washburne, Carleton W.: *Winnetka.* Englewood Cliffs, N.J., Prentice-Hall, 1963.

19 the teacher as leader

Kenneth H. Blanchard
Paul Hersey

While leadership has been defined in many ways, it is generally agreed that it is the *process of influencing the activities of an individual or a group in efforts toward goal achievement in a given situation* (Hersey and Blanchard, 1972, p. 68). By this definition, a teacher can be considered a leader in the classroom setting. Yet educators have seemed to refuse to study the teacher as a leader in teacher training programs. Instead, they have preferred to talk about teacher competencies, understandings, or skills, always avoiding the reality that a teacher must direct and influence individuals in the classroom. "There are various ways by which a teacher carries out the teaching assignment and helps pupils attain educational goals, but though the methods and degrees of directiveness and control vary with teachers and situations, teaching is an act of leading, and the teacher is a leader" (Bany and Johnson, 1964, p. 67).

DIFFERENT APPROACHES TO TEACHING

Over the years, in most school settings, teachers have come to feel that either "teacher-centered" or "child-centered" teaching styles are the only ways to focus students on learning. This feeling became popular because it was generally agreed that a teacher can influence his students in either of two ways: (1) he can tell his students what to do and how to do it, or (2) he can share his teaching responsibilities by involving students in the planning and execution of work. The former approach is the traditional authoritarian "teacher-centered" style which emphasizes course-related materials and achievement scores. The latter approach is the more nondirective "child-centered" democratic style which stresses individual development and emotional needs.

The differences in the two styles may be traced to some assumptions that the teacher makes about the source of his power or authority and human nature. The teacher-centered style is often based on the assumption that the teacher's power is derived from his position, e.g., he can make the students do their assignments because he is the teacher. This style also tends to reflect what Douglas McGregor (1960) has called Theory X assumptions about human nature. If a teacher follows Theory X, he believes that students are innately lazy—they will work only if "motivated" by the stick of fear and threat of punishment and the carrot of a good report card and promotion in grade. He assumes that, unless closely supervised, his students will "sit down on the job." By running a tight class, he treats the students as unable or unwilling to discipline themselves or to share in planning the work to be done.

The child-centered style assumes that the teacher's power is granted by the students' willingness to cooperate. Teachers using this style base their actions on McGregor's Theory Y assumptions. Such a teacher feels that students enjoy devising study plans and carrying them out. He believes they can be trusted to share in decisions about what is to be done, by whom, when and how. He believes that students will become more rather than less productive, if they can direct their own efforts.

Goodwin Watson contends that the fascinating fact about Theory X and Theory Y is that each theory may become a self-fulfilling prophecy.

> Teachers who assume that pupils will try to do as little work as they can possibly get away with, will behave in ways which make their expectations come true. The pupils will turn out to be apathetic, lazy, dependent and in need of close direction by the teacher. The Summerhill type of teacher will have an opposite experience which confirms his predictions. Pupils given freedom to decide what they will do, when and how, develop increasing independence, stronger interests, and better quality of work (Watson, 1970, p. 177).

This is why Watson claims that arguments between traditional teachers and progressive teachers are so unproductive. "Each has first-hand evidence confirming his own assumptions" (Watson, p. 177). While this is true, the debate still goes on between these two schools of thought as to which is the "best" way to teach children. The two styles are usually depicted on a continuum moving from directive teacher-centered behavior at one end to nondirective child-centered behavior at the other end. Thus, a teacher's style may be judged as one extreme or the other or somewhere in between.

Developments in the study of leadership over the last several decades question the teacher-centered versus child-centered debate on two fronts. First of all, leadership studies question whether leader behavior should be depicted on a one-dimensional continuum. Secondly, empirical findings tend to show that there is no normative (best) style of leadership; that successful leaders are those who can adapt their leader behavior to meet the needs of their followers and the particular situation.

LEADERSHIP: A TWO-DIMENSIONAL MODEL

In recent years, the feeling that autocratic and democratic were either/or leadership styles has been dispelled. In observing the actual behavior of leaders in a wide variety of situations, the Bureau of Business Research at Ohio State University found that they could classify most of the activities of leaders into two behavioral categories—"Initiating Structure" and "Consideration" (Stogdill and Coons, 1957). These are defined as:

> *Initiating Structure.* The extent to which a leader is likely to organize and define the relationship between himself and the members of his group (followers); characterized by a tendency to define the role which he expects each member of the group to assume, endeavouring to establish well-defined patterns of organization, channels of communication, and ways of getting jobs done.
> *Consideration.* The extent to which a leader is likely to maintain personal relationships between himself and the members of his group (followers) in terms of socio-emotional support; characterized by friendship, mutual trust, and respect for followers' ideas (modified from Stogdill and Coons, pp. 42-43).

In their extensive studies, the Ohio State staff found that leadership styles vary considerably from leader to leader. Some leaders primarily structure activities of followers to

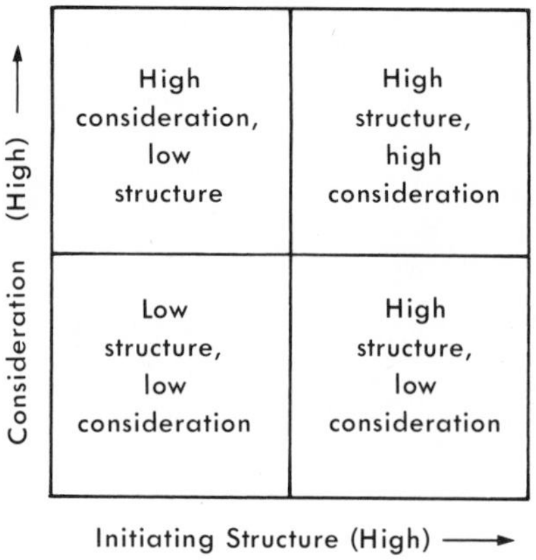

| High consideration, low structure | High structure, high consideration |
| Low structure, low consideration | High structure, low consideration |

Consideration (High) →

Initiating Structure (High) ——→

FIGURE 1 *The Ohio State leadership quadrants.*

accomplish tasks, while others concentrate on developing personal relationships between themselves and their followers to provide socio-emotional support. Other leaders have styles characterized by both Initiating Structure and Consideration behavior. There are even some individuals in leadership positions whose behavior tends to provide little Structure or Consideration. A variety of combinations are evident, no one of which is dominant. Thus, Initiating Structure and Consideration are not either/or leadership styles as an authoritarian-democratic continuum suggests. Instead, these patterns of leader behavior are separate and distinct dimensions which can be plotted on two separate axes. Thus, the Ohio State studies resulted in the development of four quadrants to illustrate leadership styles as shown in Figure 1.

LEADERSHIP STYLE SHOULD VARY WITH THE SITUATION

Although early literature seemed to suggest a single ideal or normative (best) style, evidence from recent empirical studies clearly indicates that there is no single all-purpose leadership style. In 1966, A.E. Korman reviewed over 25 studies which examined the relationship between the Ohio State behavior dimensions of Initiating Structure and Consideration and various measures of effectiveness, including group productivity, salary, performance under stress, administrative reputation, work group grievances, absenteeism, and turnover. He concluded that:

> Despite the fact that "Consideration" and "Initiating Structure" have become almost bywords in American industrial psychology, it seems apparent that very little is known as to how these variables may predict work group performance and the conditions which affect such predictions. At the current time, we cannot even say whether they have any predictive significance at all (Korman, 1966).

Korman's finding that effectiveness in different situations is not related to one particular leadership style suggests that different styles are needed for different situations.

Fred E. Fiedler (1967), in testing his contingency model of leadership in over fifty studies covering a span of fifteen years (1951-1967), concluded that both directive, task-oriented leaders and nondirective, human relations-oriented leaders are successful under some conditions. Fiedler argues:

> While one can never say that something is impossible, and while someone may well discover the all-purpose leadership style or behavior at some future time, our own data and those which have come out of sound research by other investigators do not promise such miraculous cures.

A number of other investigators (e.g., Gibbs, 1954; Hare, 1965; Pelz, 1961) have also concluded that there is no best style of leadership; that successful leaders are those who can adapt their leader behavior to meet the demands of their own unique environment.

LIFE CYCLE THEORY OF LEADERSHIP

While these arguments might theoretically dispel the teacher-centered versus child-centered debate, what does it do to help the teacher develop appropriate teaching strategies? After all, even the teacher who realizes that he must adapt his style to fit the needs of various students is frustrated by the conclusion that the needed teaching style "depends on the situation." He finds little practical value in theory unless he can begin to see *how* leadership depends on the situation and therefore *what* style tends to be effective with particular students and classes in changing environments. The Life Cycle Theory of Leadership* is an attempt to develop a leadership theory which may help a teacher to define behavior appropriate to a given situation. This theory attempts to provide a teacher with some understanding of the style of teaching that will be effective in dealing with students of a given level of maturity.

In Life Cycle Theory as applied in a classroom, emphasis is placed on the students. The students in any classroom situation are vital, because not only do they accept or reject the teacher individually, but as a group they actually determine whatever personal power he may have.

Maturity.   According to Life Cycle Theory, as the level of maturity of one's followers continues to increase, appropriate leader behavior at first requires less and less structure while increasing consideration and eventually entails decreases in socio-emotional support as well. This cycle is illustrated in the four leadership style quadrants in Figure 2.

Maturity is defined in Life Cycle Theory by achievement motivation, the willingness and ability to take responsibility, and task relevant education and experience of an individual or group. While age may be a factor, it is not directly related to maturity as defined in the Life Cycle Theory. Our concern is for psychological, not chronological, age. Beginning with structured behavior which is appropriate for working with immature people, Life Cycle Theory suggests that leader behavior should move from high Structure-low Consideration behavior (Quadrant 1) to high Structure-high Consideration (Quadrant 2), and from high Consideration-low Structure behavior (Quadrant 3) to low Structure-low Consideration behavior (Quadrant 4) as one's followers progress from immaturity to maturity.

---

*This theory was developed at the Center for Leadership Studies, Ohio University, Athens, Ohio. It was first published by Paul Hersey and Kenneth H. Blanchard as Life cycle theory of leadership, *Training and Development Journal,* May, 1969.

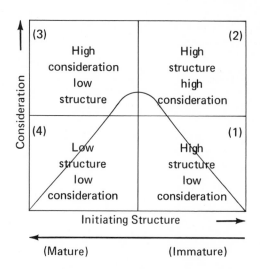

FIGURE 2 *Life Cycle Theory of Leadership.*

In terms of teaching style, Life Cycle Theory of Leadership hypothesizes that when working with immature children, a teacher-centered style (Quadrant 1) has the best probability of success. As a child begins to mature, it seems appropriate for the teacher to provide less structure, giving the child an opportunity to increase his own responsibility. As the child continues to mature, this withdrawal of structure is reinforced by an increase in socio-emotional support, and a more child-centered style, as depicted in Quadrants 2 and 3, appears to be most appropriate. And finally, when a child has developed into a young adult and is now able not only to structure many of the learning activities in which he engages, but to provide self-control in terms of his interpersonal and emotional needs, behaviors depicted in Quadrant 4 (low Structure-low Consideration) have the highest probability of success.

Teaching and Life Cycle Theory. Life Cycle Theory of Leadership supports the contention that there is no single "best" style of teaching. Students come to any classroom at various levels of maturity; they vary in their achievement motivation, willingness to take responsibility for their own learning, and the relevance of their past education and experience to the learning opportunities being offered. Thus, to be effective, a teacher must be able to diagnose the maturity level of each of his students so that he can use the appropriate teaching style. A child's maturity depends on his treatment by earlier teachers or his parents. If he has been trusted and given considerable responsibility before he enters school, the child will be able to assume a more active role in developing his own learning experiences—thus the teacher can use a more considerate child-centered teaching style. If the child has grown up and been educated in a highly structured environment, however, an unstructured child-centered teaching style may create problems.

In attempting to replace the image of the teacher as someone directing a passively seated class of children, young, enthusiastic, humanistic teachers often go overboard in permitting freedom for their students. Difficulties arise when this nondirective style is used for everyone in a class. For the intellectually and emotionally mature student with clear goals and objectives, a teaching style which provides an opportunity to be treated and behave as an adult can provide a very motivating environment. For the immature student who lacks direction and the ability to structure his own learning opportunities, such a nondirective style can be detrimental. It can even encourage immaturity, if the student perceives the lack of structure as permissiveness. In the case of students who view the educational system as something to be tolerated but not integrated with their own personal goals, a more highly Structured and somewhat less Considerate style would seem more appropriate until the students show signs of maturing, and the teacher can then change his style accordingly.

The importance of adapting teaching style to changes in the maturity level of students cannot be overemphasized. In fact, one might argue that much of the turmoil in education today is the result of the use in our schools of a highly structured, teacher-centered style during the entire developmental years of many children. This inflexible style typically produces two kinds of behaviors: Students may rebel and continually challenge authority in the schools, or they may mentally "drop out," succumbing to the teacher's authority and becoming very passive and dependent throughout their education, always needing someone to tell them what to do and when to do it. Neither of these two responses are very productive, yet our students in colleges and universities seem to show both types of reaction—dissatisfied rebellion and passive acquiescence—the "silent generation."

In recognizing the problems associated with an autocratic, teacher-centered style, we must remember not to let the pendulum swing to a child-centered approach too fast. Changes in the maturity and motivation of children cannot be accomplished overnight. The teacher must bring his students along slowly, becoming more child-centered and less teacher-centered as they mature. The key is often the positive reinforcement of "successive approximations," behavior which comes closer and closer to the teacher's expectations of good performance. As with a child learning any new behavior, a teacher should not expect high levels of performance at the outset. The same is true for the development of maturity and responsibility in children; the teacher should use positive reinforcement as the child's behavior approaches the desired level of maturity. Therefore, the teacher must be aware of any progress of his students so that he is in a position to reinforce appropriately increased maturity or performance.

Though it may not be appropriate in many of our schools for teachers to eventually provide minimum structure or socio-emotional support for large numbers of students, the Life Cycle Theory of Leadership suggests that as teachers begin to trust students and give them more responsibility for their own learning, appropriate movement in this direction will take place. For the teacher who is aware of his or her role as a classroom leader, change through the cycle from a traditional teacher-centered style (Quadrant 1) to the more child-centered styles (Quadrants 2 and 3) and then to a less interactive as well as nondirective style (Quadrant 4) must often be gradual and must reflect increasing maturity. This process by its very nature cannot be revolutionary but must be evolution-ary—gradual developmental changes, a result of planned growth and the creation of mutual trust and respect between teacher and student.

REFERENCES

Bany, Mary A., and Johnson, Lois V.: Classroom Group Behavior. New York, Macmillan, 1964.
Fiedler, Fred E.: A Theory of Leadership Effectiveness. New York, McGraw-Hill, 1967.
Gibb, C.A.: Leadership. In Lindzey, Gardner (ed.): Handbook of Social Psychology. Cambridge, Mass., Addison-Wesley Publishing Co., 1954.
Hare, A.P.: Handbook of Small Group Research. New York, Wiley, 1965.

Hersey, Paul, and Blanchard, Kenneth H.: Management of Organizational Behavior. 2nd Edition. Englewood Cliffs, N.J., Prentice-Hall, Inc., 1972.

Korman, A.K.: "Consideration," "initiating structure," and organizational criteria—a review. *Personnel Psychology: A Journal of Applied Research, 19*:No. 4, 349-361, Winter, 1966.

McGregor, Douglas: The Human Side of Enterprise. New York, McGraw-Hill, 1960.

Pelz, D.C.: Leadership within a hierarchial organization. *Journal of Social Issues, 7*:49-55, 1961.

Stogdill, Roger M., and Coons, Alvin E. (eds.): Leader Behavior: Its Description and Measurement. Research Monograph No. 88. Columbus, Ohio, Bureau of Business Research, The Ohio State University, 1957.

classroom 20
management of
disruptive behavior

Todd Eachus

The importance of the effective management of classroom behavior cannot be understated. One disruptive child can obstruct the learning of a classroom full of children. Less severe disruption can interrupt and shorten concentration by students, as well as simply waste time. There are also many types of behavior that, while not disturbing others, keep the individual himself from actively learning.

The traditional cures for disruptive behavior in the classroom are to exile the offenders to the hall, the principal's office, or some other place where they cannot disrupt classroom activity, or for the teacher to verbally reprimand the student. While these cures serve their immediate purpose by making the group remaining within the classroom manageable, it does the disruptive child very little good. Indeed, by singling him out for attention, it may support or reinforce his disruptive behavior.

The teacher needs convenient and easily used procedures for controlling classroom behavior. The usefulness of such procedures increases as they become simpler, less costly, and require less time. Most important, these procedures should draw upon resources that are readily available to the teacher, to restructure the classroom environment in a manner most beneficial to the children.

The ultimate goal of the techniques discussed here is to generate in a child self-control over his disruptive behavior. The approach focuses on behavior modification techniques which have been developed during the past 15 years by behavioral psychologists. Certain behaviors by the child should produce certain responses from the teacher—positive responses intended to encourage or reinforce appropriate behavior and negative responses intended to reduce or discourage inappropriate behavior. These responses modify behavior and may be used systematically to develop desired behavior. Eventually, the child's behavior should be controlled by natural reinforcers occurring in the normal environment.

Several studies have illustrated the importance of positive reinforcement of desired behavior. The positive reinforcer most readily available to the teacher is her own attention, praise, and approval. This is widely known, and the basic technique has been in use for many years. Yet all too often it is used ineffectively. The teacher often does not attend to the circumstances under which she delivers praise, approval, and attention, and consequently she finds little or no change in resulting pupil behavior.

Thomas, Becker, and Armstrong (1968) observed the results of systematic variation of teacher approval and disapproval on the behavior of a normally well-behaved class of 28 public middle primary pupils. Teacher approval helped maintain appropriate behavior in the classroom. Each time teacher approval was withdrawn, disruptive behavior increased. When teacher disapproval of student behavior was tripled in quantity, the disruptive behavior increased, most markedly in noise-making and excessive physical activity. These findings emphasize the importance of the teacher's role in producing both appropriate and disruptive classroom behavior.

Teachers too often expect good behavior to be the classroom norm. Instead of reinforcing good behavior, they punish disruption. Thus, teachers frequently talk about "catching kids being bad," while rarely mentioning "catching kids being *good*." As the above study indicates, attending to disruptive behavior is likely to produce only more disruption. In some classrooms, the child may find that the only way to get the teacher's attention is to misbehave—and for some children, the positive reinforcement of the attention may be more important than the disapproving quality of that attention.

Naturally, in using techniques that produce appropriate classroom behavior, it's essential to determine just what behavior is proper and to make certain that this is understood by both teacher and students. This requires clearly defined, explicit rules, which are determined by joint participation of teacher and pupils. Madson, Becker, and Thomas (1968) showed that, while merely setting rules has little effect on behavior, accompanying sound and clear rules with approval of appropriate behavior and ignoring inappropriate behavior leads to the quick disappearance of the undesired behavior. The rule-setting process must involve the students if a true group norm of behavior is to be established. Otherwise, group norms and the teacher's goals of appropriate behavior may conflict, and this results in reinforcement of inappropriate behavior by the child's peer group.

The power of teacher attention to reinforce desired behavior is important and is frequently the teacher's most reliable tool. Hall, Lund, and Jackson (1968) found that "off-task" or disruptive behavior could be reduced by providing teacher attention following study behavior and ignoring undesirable behavior. This worked for children who had previously shown high frequencies of nonstudy behavior. When teacher attention following studying was withdrawn, study behavior decreased.

Teacher attention alone, however, is not always an effective reinforcer for children, and other procedures may be needed to reduce disruptive behavior. In one study, O'Leary, Becker, Evans, and Saudargas (1969) found that teacher praise was not effective reinforcement for a second grade class of 21 children. Separate use of *rules, educational structure,* and *praising appropriate behavior while ignoring disruptive activity* had little effect, but a combination of these nearly eliminated disruptive behavior for one of the seven target children. They then instituted a token reinforcement program in which the children were given tokens for exhibiting desired behavior. The children could use the tokens like money to obtain rewards of their own choice. This program lessened disruptive behavior for five of the remaining six target children. When the token program was stopped, five of the seven children became more disruptive. This tendency was reversed for four of the five when the token program was reinstated. Improvements in academic achievement and attendance records may also have been related to the token reinforcement system.

Follow-up data indicate that the teacher was able to transfer control of the students' responses to other reinforcers used in the classroom such as stars or occasional pieces of candy. Thus the children became better able to control their behavior when receiving reinforcement more typical of the classroom than the specially-designed token program.

This transfer of control of behavior from an artificially designed reinforcement system to reinforcers normally available in the environment is essential to the goal of developing self-control over behavior.

Since use of the teacher's time is vital in controlling behavior and the entire learning situation, the number of children in a class frequently poses problems. Special procedures are needed to make optimum use of the duration and effectiveness of teacher-student contacts. Sanders and Hansen (1971) observed a class of 12 third grade students in a rural school having two grades per teacher to determine how teacher-student contacts were distributed. They found that the better students tended to receive more attention from the teacher. When this happened, the other students tended to become disruptive, provoking negative responses by the teacher toward themselves. By the simple expedient of requiring students to go to a small play area when their work was completed, teacher attention was redistributed. The poorer students received more of the teacher's time and the better students less. The number of assignments completed by all students in the study increased, presumably because of a better distribution of the teacher's time and attention.

Teachers can also use pressure and approval from the child's peer group in controlling classroom behavior, by designing reinforcement for the group contingent upon the desired behavior by all individuals within it. Schmidt and Ulrich (1969) used this technique in attempting to quiet a noisy classroom. Reinforcement for the class was a two minute extension of their gym period and a two minute break after an unbroken ten minute period of quiet. Noise level was determined by a noise meter in the classroom, which would reset a timer to ten minutes if the noise level exceeded the allowable limit (42 decibels). This technique was found highly effective in noise reduction. It was also successful in reducing the number of times children left their seats, when that criterion was made a requirement for the reinforcing breaks.

In a related study, Willis and Crowder (1972) used a portable clock controlled by a teacher to inform students when their behavior was appropriate. In this case, the teacher turned on the clock when the children were attending to their classwork. After a specific number of minutes had been accumulated on the timer, the children were allowed to watch a movie. This reinforcement led to a substantial increase in the time the entire class spent on classwork.

Teachers can also use other students to help in controlling disruptive behavior. Surratt, Ulrich, and Hawkins (1969) used a fifth grade student to help in controlling nonstudy behavior of four first graders during periods when the first grade class was supposed to study individually. When appropriate study behavior occurred, the older child would turn on a light at the student's desk, which was associated with the possibility of reinforcement. Study behavior increased during the experiment. Surreptitious closed circuit television observation after the end of the experiment indicated that the first grade students partially retained their increased study behavior in the regular classroom situation. Participation in the experiment was itself a reward for improved academic behavior by the fifth grader.

Barrish, Saunders, and Wolf (1969) used peer group pressure to control individual disruptive behavior in a fourth grade class that included several problem children. After the original (baseline) rate of talking out and out-of-seat behaviors was established, the class was divided into two teams. A total of individual talking out and out-of-seat behaviors was kept on a chalkboard. The team with the lower total won the game and received special privileges, like being first to line up for lunch, having extra recess, and receiving stars and name tags. Since all members of the team shared the consequences of individual misbehavior, they placed pressure for the desired behavior on the normally disruptive children. This technique was applied successfully during both math and reading periods. In a similar study, Coleman (1970) found that making reinforcement for an entire class dependent upon the behavior of one unruly child brought that individual's behavior under control.

Other studies, (e.g., Herman and Tramontana, 1971) have confirmed that establishing rules and making either group or individual reinforcement contingent upon appropriate behavior can control disruptive behavior. This suggests that in many cases the teacher has a variety of approaches to select from, depending upon her individual preferences and skills. The critical factor is a clear and precise statement of the rules so that the children can understand them. Also essential is a fair and uniform application of the rules. If the children feel that rules are being unjustly administered, whether because they don't understand them or because the teacher is actually being inconsistent, teachers are likely to have very little success controlling their classroom behavior.

In some cases the teacher is confronted with a child who appears uncontrollable. Praise contingent upon appropriate behavior may do little to control the child's disruption. Frequently this disruption takes the form of aggression toward others. Such problems require an approach directed at the individual and the specific behavior. One procedure that has been used successfully is *time-out*. In time-out, the individual is isolated from the consequences of his behavior for a period of three to five minutes. Time-out has the effect of a punisher without the unwanted side effects of punishment that is directly administered by the teacher. This can be effective in eliminating unruly behavior in children who use misbehavior as a way to gain attention. Ramp, Ulrich, and Dulaney (1971) described elimination of disruptive behavior of one nine year old boy by placing a light on his desk that the teacher could turn on when he was misbehaving, rather than having to tell the child to stop. Periods when the light was on—time-outs— represented a loss of free time later in the day.

Teachers are concerned in the long term with helping students develop self-control over their behavior. Like any other behavior, self-control can be taught if the child does not already display it. Two approaches that have been used successfully are contingency contracting and self-recording of behavior.

Contingency contracting involves the teacher, child, and parents agreeing upon desired behaviors and individualized reinforcers that will be used to help attain these goals. They establish these in an explicit contract that clearly states the expected behavior and reinforcers. This has produced very substantial changes in children's performances in a wide variety of situations and tasks. A clear and explicit presentation of the steps used in contingency contracting has been written by Homme, Csanyi, Gonzales, and Rechs (1970).

Broden, Hall, and Mitts (1971) investigated the study habits of an eighth grade girl in a history class. After initial observations of her behavior, her counsellor gave her slips to record if she studied in class. While recording her behavior, the time spent studying increased. Studying decreased when self-recording was stopped but increased when it was resumed. After the teacher increased praise for her studying, self-recording was stopped without a significant decrease in her study time. Finally, when the increased praise was stopped, studying remained at a high level, indicating that she had established self-control over studying.

A similar experiment involving an eighth grade boy who talked out in class did not have the same lasting effect. While self-recording did reduce talking out behavior while it was in use, when it was stopped the boy displayed about the same amount of talking out as before the experiment had begun. This indicated that little or no self-control had been established.

Such variation in success is to be expected and should not discourage teachers. Individual children differ greatly, and techniques effective for many students will frequently be ineffective for others. Individual differences must be considered, especially as they relate to the nature of reinforcement. A few failures do not mean that the procedure is faulty—only that it is not universally applicable. Because of this variability, teachers need to have a variety of procedures available. These procedures, plus a knowledge of ways to apply them, give the teacher valuable tools to aid in controlling classroom behavior.

Two recent volumes provide very thorough descriptions of techniques and procedures teachers can use to effect more positive growth in their students. Becker (1971) includes a series of readings, ranging through basic issues in behavior modification—reducing behavior problems, establishing stronger motivation, the use of social reinforcers and alternative programs, and application of the same principles to improve academic performance. O'Leary and O'Leary (1972) have assembled a very readable and useful book on the many techniques teachers can use to improve their classroom effectiveness. The topics they treat include teacher attention, punishment, modeling, token reinforcement programs, use of peers in behavior modification, programmed instruction, the use of teacher aides and parents, and the issue of self-management.

REFERENCES

Barrish, H.H., Saunders, M., and Wolf, M.M.: Good behavior game: effects of individual contingencies for group consequences on disruptive behavior in a classroom. *Journal of Applied Behavior Analysis, 2*:119-124, 1969.

Becker, W.C.: An Empirical Basis for Change in Education. Palo Alto, Calif., Science Research Associates, 1971.

Becker, W.C., Engelmann, S., and Thomas, D.R.: Teaching: A Course in Applied Psychology. Palo Alto, Calif., Science Research Associates, 1971.

Broden, M., Hall, R.V., and Mitts, B.: The effect of self-recording on the classroom behavior of two eighth-grade students. *Journal of Applied Behavior Analysis, 4*:191-199, 1971.

Cantrell, R.P., Cantrell, M.L., Huddleston, C.M., and Woolridge, R.L.: Contingency contracting with school problems. *Journal of Applied Behavior Analysis, 2*:215-220, 1969.

Coleman, R.: A conditioning technique applicable to elementary school classrooms. *Journal of Applied Behavior Analysis, 3*:293-297, 1970.

Hall, R.V., Lund, D., and Jackson, D.: Effects of teacher attention on study behavior. *Journal of Applied Behavior Analysis, 1*:1-12, 1968.

Herman, S.H., and Tramontana, J.: Instructions and group versus individual reinforcement in modifying disruptive group behavior. *Journal of Applied Behavior Analysis, 4*:113-119, 1971.

Homme, L.E., with Csanyi, A.P., Gonzales, M.A., and Rechs, J.R.: How to Use Contingency Contracting in the Classroom. Champaign, Ill., Research Press, 1970.

Madsen, C., Jr., Becker, W., and Thomas, D.: Rules, praise, and ignoring: elements of elementary classroom control. *Journal of Applied Behavior Analysis, 1*:139-150, 1968.

Millenson, J.R.: Principles of Behavioral Analysis. New York, Macmillan, 1967.

O'Leary, K.D., Becker, W.C., Evans, M.B., and Saudargas, R.A.: A token reinforcement program in a public school: a replication and systematic analysis. *Journal of Applied Behavior Analysis, 2*:3-13, 1969.

O'Leary, K.D., and O'Leary, S.G.: Classroom Management. New York, Pergamon Press, 1972.

Premack, D.: Toward empirical behavior laws: I. positive reinforcement. *Psychological Review,* 66:219-233, 1959.

Ramp, E., Ulrich, R., and Dulaney, S.: Delayed timeout as a procedure for reducing disruptive classroom behavior: a case study. *Journal of Applied Behavior Analysis, 4*:235-239, 1971.

Sailor, W.S., Guess, D. Rutherford, G., and Baer, D.M.: Control of tantrum behavior by operant techniques during experimental verbal training. *Journal of Applied Behavior Analysis, 1*:237-243, 1968.

Sanders, R.M., and Hanson, P.J.: A note on a simple procedure for redistributing a teacher's student contacts. *Journal of Applied Behavior Analysis.* 4:157-161, 1971.

Schmidt, G.W., and Ulrich, R.E.: Effects of group contingent events upon classroom noise. *Journal of Applied Behavior Analysis,* 2:171-179, 1969.

Skinner, B.F.: Beyond Freedom and Dignity. New York, Knopf, 1971.

Skinner, B.F.: Science and Human Behavior. New York, Macmillan, 1953.

Skinner, B.F.: The Technology of Teaching. New York, Appleton-Century-Crofts, 1968.

Skinner, B.F.: Verbal Behavior. New York, Appleton-Century-Crofts, 1957.

Surratt, P.R., Ulrich, R.E., and Hawkins, R.P.: An elementary student as a behavioral engineer. *Journal of Applied Behavior Analysis,* 2:85-92, 1969.

Thomas, D.R., Becker, W.C., and Armstrong, M.: Production and elimination of disruptive classroom behavior by systematically varying teacher's behavior. *Journal of Applied Behavior Analysis,* 1:35-45, 1968.

Willis, J., and Crowder, J.: A portable device for group modification of classroom attending behavior. *Journal of Applied Behavior Analysis,* 5:199-202, 1972.

grouping for more effective learning 21

Dorothy Westby-Gibson

Few issues in American education have aroused so much controversy as the question of grouping. Often the problem has been posed as: To group or not to group? But, in reality, no such choice has existed. Students have been grouped by placing them in given schools and in particular instructional groups within those schools. Thus, the problem critical to educators has emerged as: How to group for more effective instruction?

A voluminous literature has been directed to this question, much of it focusing, not on how to facilitate student learning, but on how to facilitate arrangements for teaching. Considering the pressures on the schools to accommodate ever increasing numbers of students for longer and longer periods of time, such an emphasis cannot be surprising. Thus teachers have frequently advocated grouping by ability and achievement to help cope with the diversity of the student population.

Fifty years have elapsed since the development of standardized tests first focused attention on the wide variation in individual aptitude and achievement. The response to that finding, however, has until very recently been directed toward arriving at more manageable groups rather than at genuinely individualizing instruction. Today the focus is shifting toward the latter goal. Glen Heathers (1969) suggests that the task of the reviewer of research on grouping in 1980 may well be to write its epitaph. Grouping as a central theme of organization for instruction, he prophesies, will have run its course, replaced by individualized instruction. The question of grouping will likely become: How to group flexibly for more effective learning?

To gain perspective on this question, we first examine *interschool grouping* (placement of students in particular schools), and then *intraschool grouping* (placement of students within the school itself), a classification first used by Alfred Yates (1966). In each category we trace briefly the major trends in grouping, the underlying issues, and their implications for more effective learning.

INTERSCHOOL GROUPING

Traditionally, students have been placed in schools near their homes and in classes with others of their own age. If parents could afford it, they could substitute nonpublic for public schools. Until very recently, little question has been raised about these criteria. Much effort, furthermore, has been expended to achieve their almost universal application.

Geographical Location

Where sparsity of population makes it impossible to achieve grouping by both geography and age, age grouping has prevailed. Thus, the majority of one-room schoolhouses have been consolidated into larger school districts. Although some educators and community members still favor the small rural school as promoting more individualization and peer learning than the larger school, it seems unlikely that this trend toward consolidation will be reversed.

Where populations are more dense, placing students in schools near their homes has resulted in widespread "de facto" segregation by race, ethnic group, and socioeconomic level. The monumental decision of the U.S. Supreme Court in 1954 was based on the premise that where races are required to be separated in schools, education cannot be equal. Though the original decision was directed at segregation by law ("de jure") in the South, the courts have extended it to forbid "de facto" segregation as well. In many areas schools cannot achieve a racial mix that reflects the total community unless some children are sent to schools at some distance from their homes. Court decisions requiring such a mix have led to conflict between those who favor more racially balanced schools and those who advocate neighborhood schools, though not all who support neighborhood schools are seeking to avoid integration.

Prime target for this conflict is the controversy over busing. It is somewhat ironic that busing has become the central issue when so many children in the United States depend on buses to get to school at all. Indeed, nearly 40 percent of elementary school children take buses to school simply for transportation reasons. But when busing is proposed as a means of achieving more racial balance in schools, many nonwhite as well as white parents object. In San Francisco, for instance, where the most extensive and complex busing program outside the South was started in the fall of 1971, the greatest opposition came from Chinese parents who did not want their children to leave the predominantly Chinese neighborhood schools. They argued that their children would lose their sense of cultural identity.

White parents, as might be expected, are less likely to object to one-way busing which brings nonwhite children into their neighborhoods than to two-way busing which takes their children into inner-city ghettos. In the South one-way busing has been used on a large scale to achieve desegregation. In New York City more than 18,000 children from the ghettos ride buses or subways to attend largely white schools elsewhere in the city. Two-way busing programs are beginning, but they are more likely than one-way plans to be token efforts. Two-way busing on a larger scale has started in such Southern cities as Richmond, Virginia and Mobile, Alabama. Such proposals, however, have met with strong resistance in both North and South. In Detroit, for example, both white and black parents have voiced opposition to two-way busing in pie-shaped attendance areas proposed to link the inner city with the suburbs. Yet in large metropolitan areas such as Detroit, Washington, D.C., and Newark, New Jersey, with high concentrations of minority groups in inner cities, no approach to desegregation can succeed that does not cross inner-city boundaries into the suburbs (The agony of busing, *Time,* 1971).

In cities of limited size with overall racial balance, having all children at a given level attend the same school can result in desegregation. Berkeley, California, for instance, has combined its secondary schools into one large ninth-grade school and one senior high school incorporating a number of alternative schools. Another approach is the educational park which places all educational facilities of a given community in one location.

What is the effect on student learning of bringing students from different racial and ethnic backgrounds together in one school? Although large-scale research reports are few, the evidence indicates that academic performance may improve. James Coleman (1966), in his now classic study on *Equality of Educational Opportunity,* reported that achievement scores of black ghetto children improved in racially-mixed classes. Black pupils in Hartford's Project Concern raised their reading scores as much as 1.2 years in four months, while matched groups in ghetto schools fell farther and farther behind. After integration of Berkeley's elementary schools, primary children of all races increased their reading scores, although whites and Asians gained more than blacks and Chicanos. The youngest children, with the least prior experience in segregated schools, showed the greatest progress. Bringing culturally different students together does not necessarily result in social integration, but in integrated school systems students at least have a chance for interaction. Evidence is mounting that in many instances students do learn to work and play together.

Age-Level Organization

Belief in the magic of classifying students by age is so widespread that school-entry and school-leaving ages are most commonly prescribed by law. The application of this criterion, furthermore, is most often arbitrary. Where the child of five years and nine months is eligible for first grade, the child who misses the given date by even one day will probably be forced to wait a full year. Where schools genuinely individualize admission, criteria other than age are frequently used, but even if age is retained as the only determinant, eligible students can be admitted throughout the year. Similarly, many questions are being raised today about the advisability of compulsory education laws, especially for older adolescents. If education were viewed as a lifelong resource to be made continually available to all, new patterns of individualized schooling would no doubt emerge.

Age-level organization of the schools has presented persistent problems. The traditional eight-four plan (eight years of elementary school and four of high school), has most often been changed as a result of administrative rather than instructional concerns. Three-year junior high schools, for example, were first introduced in Berkeley to reduce the overcrowding in the four-year high schools and the high dropout rate of eighth graders. Not until later were the objectives of the junior high schools more clearly defined in terms of the special developmental needs of emerging adolescents.

Recent directions in organizational patterns have given special attention to the development of preschool programs and middle schools. Preschool programs, so long neglected, have achieved new acceptance supported by research evidence of the critical significance of learning in the early years and by the rapid growth of governmental funding. The scope of this acceptance is reflected in the enrollment trends in educational programs for children aged three to five. Whereas in 1964, the first year the U.S. Office of Education tabulated preprimary enrollments, 25 per cent of three-to-five year olds were enrolled, by 1970 this fugure had grown to 37.5 per cent. Children from minority groups constituted a significant part of this increase. Although among five year olds a much higher percentage of white (71.2 per cent) than black (57.8 per cent) was enrolled, among three and four year olds slightly higher percentages of black (14.4 per cent and 30.9 per cent respectively) than white (12.6 per cent and 27.1 per cent) were reported. The five year olds were more likely to be attending established kindergartens; the three and four year olds, newly funded programs. It is somewhat ironic that the initial thrust toward the goal (stated by the Educational Policies Commission in 1966) of making preschool opportunities available to all four year olds should await the acceptance of new programs for minority children.

Most educators now agree that some separate form of school organization is needed in the middle years of emerging adolescence, but they disagree over which grades should be included. Disaffection with the junior high school has led to the introduction of the so-called middle school, which most frequently groups grades 5 to 8 or 6 to 8. Changes in organization, however, do not guarantee changes in instruction. Almost three-fifths (58 per cent) of middle schools, when asked in a 1968 survey by William Alexander (1969) why their present organizational pattern had been adopted, gave overcrowding as a reason; less than half (48 per cent) said they were providing a program specifically designed for this age group.

Public and Nonpublic Schools

Education in the United States has made the parent responsible for choosing whether his child will go to a public or nonpublic school and if the latter, to a parochial or independent school. In nonpublic schools, another choice is between single sex or coeducational schools. There is little doubt that one significant factor in such choices has been the potential cost to the parent. The question now raised is: What choices would parents make if free to select schools without regard to cost? The present experiments with educational vouchers may provide some answers. Parents are given vouchers, paid for with public funds, that can be spent to provide education for their children at any school which does not discriminate in its admissions on the basis of race or ethnic origin and does not charge higher tuition than the vouchers provide. Proponents of this plan see it as encouraging competition for excellence in the schools, while opponents view it as fostering increased segregation and competition for limited school finances.

INTRASCHOOL GROUPING

Within schools, grouping practices have reflected the social pressures on the schools and the changing concerns of educators. As a result, grouping patterns have varied considerably. Traditionally they have been viewed as either increasing or decreasing the homogeneity of instructional groups. More recently, with the focus on individualizing instruction, they have been explored as ways of providing flexibility for individual student learning. We discuss here first planning for homogeneity, then planning for heterogeneity, and finally, planning for flexibility.

Planning for Homogeneity

Grouping to reduce variability in an instructional group is called *homogeneous grouping.* Homogeneity or similarity in group composition may be sought by age-grading, ability grouping, tracking, or special classes.

Age-grading, or assigning students to grade levels based initially on their age, was heralded as providing much greater opportunities for learning than the ungraded one-room rural school. The pattern of age-grade levels, begun in 1848 in the Quincy Grammar School of Boston, became so popular that by 1860 it had spread to almost all urban schools. It was not long, however, before the extreme rigidity of the resulting instruction was being questioned. During the last quarter of the nineteenth century, large groups of students were failing to be promoted, and many were leaving school at the end of the fifth or sixth grade. Widespread attention was focused on this problem through reports that schools on the average were holding about one-third of their students back one or more grade levels (Ayres, 1909). Subsequent studies comparing matched groups of promoted and nonpromoted students served to discredit this policy. Although some individual students might profit from repeating a grade, large-scale retardation of those who failed was deemed indefensible.

In response to these problems of age-grading, a number of so-called laboratory plans, such as the Dalton and Winnetka Plans, were devised. They frequently separated the academic from the nonacademic curriculum and permitted students to progress at their own rate through the former. These plans usually did not alter the content of the curriculum, only the pace at which the student was expected to progress.

New possibilities for grouping were opened after World War I with the development of standardized tests. Results of tests for a wide range of abilities and achievements revealed differences which could be used for grouping students. During the 1920's and 1930's the practice of *ability grouping* (grouping pupils on the basis of one or more criteria of ability to achieve in school) became widespread. Scores from mental ability and achievement tests usually formed the basis for designating high, average, and low ability groups.

Research on the outcomes of ability grouping has been extensive. Yet the hard evidence is sparse. Numerous early studies seeking to compare the results of heterogeneous with homogeneous grouping reported conflicting findings. Almost equal numbers of studies could be found to support either grouping pattern. Evidently the critical variable was not the grouping practice but other aspects of the teaching/learning situation.

What did become clear, however, is that the range of individual differences is so great that reducing the variability in one does little to decrease classroom differences. One study of fifth grade children showed that dividing the class into three groups on the basis of I.Q. scores with the middle group ranging from 90 to 120, still gave that group a range in reading ability in terms of grade norms from 2.7 to 11.2 (Goodlad, 1960). Most early approaches to ability grouping, as J. Wayne Wrightstone (1968) has pointed out, assumed erroneously that achievement depends largely on intelligence and that the relationship between intelligence and achievement does not change for a given individual.

During the 1940's and early 1950's ability grouping lost its popularity, primarily because it came to be viewed as undemocratic, stigmatizing those in the low ability groups and promoting snobbishness in the high ability groups. Not until the advent of Sputnik in 1957 and the subsequent spate of criticism of the schools did interest in ability grouping revive. James B. Conant (1959) supported ability grouping for required subjects and those electives in which students demonstrated a wide range of ability. Only in homeroom and twelfth grade social studies did he advocate grouping heterogeneously to encourage students to understand diverse points of view. In 1962 almost two-thirds of all secondary principals responding to a survey by the NEA Project on Instruction (81 percent of those in large districts), reported an increase in the use of ability grouping during the previous five years. In 1965-1966 almost one-third of elementary school districts with enrollments of 25,000 or more and almost one-half of those with 100,000 or more indicated, in replying to an NEA Research Division survey, that they carefully grouped all children. The criterion most frequently used to determine grouping was a measure of reading level.

Recent research on the outcomes of ability grouping has been far more sophisticated than the earlier studies, but the results are still inconclusive. When total student populations are used, no consistent effects of ability grouping on student achievement have been found (Heathers, 1969). When high and low ability groups are viewed separately, some significant differences in achievement may be discerned, but the direction of these differences is open to question. Summaries of studies prior to 1955 (Goodlad, 1960, and Wilhelms and Westby-Gibson, 1961) tended to indicate that if any group gains even slightly from ability grouping, it is the low group. Subsequent studies, however, have tended to report losses in potential achievement when students of low ability are grouped together. Some of these (Abrahamson, 1959, and Goldberg, Passow, et al., 1966) note similar losses for high ability groups, whereas others (Borg, 1966, Douglas, 1964, and Heathers, 1967) point to gains. Some find evidence that slow learners have higher self-concepts with ability grouping, but others stress the loss of self-esteem when students are placed in separate groups.

Why the discrepancies among research findings? One answer, of course, lies in the complexity of the factors involved in student achievement. To design research to take into account even the major cognitive and noncognitive variables is a formidable task. But another and perhaps more critical problem is the lack of a conceptual framework that would attempt to account for the relationships between a given pattern of grouping and an outcome. Aage Sørensen (1970) proposes that consideration be given to such variables as the degree to which students' decisions influence placement, given group memberships of students, the student composition of the classroom, social interaction in the classroom, and the role of family background.

At the secondary level, homogeneous grouping can also result from *tracking*, or channeling students into a particular program of courses. One sequence, for example, may lead to college entrance, another to business occupations, still another to vocations in creative arts, industrial arts, or homemaking. Frequently one track is designated as "general." Often these sequences represent ability groupings, with the most able students channeled into the college preparatory stream and the least able into the general curriculum. Demands on college-bound students may be such as to prohibit their taking courses in other tracks; students in other tracks in turn may have difficulty in moving into the college preparatory stream.

The term *tracking* is also used synonymously with ability grouping that cuts across subjects. Students may be labeled as Track I (lower-ability groups) or Track III (higher-ability groups). Sometimes students are in one track for English and social studies and another for mathematics and science, the first determined by scores in reading and the second in arithmetic. Actually the differences in thinking levels required by these tracks may be minimal. E. Dale Doak (1970) compared levels of thinking required of students in the lowest and highest tracks in various subject areas and concluded that teachers did not make significantly different demands on them. In both tracks the primary aim was to communicate knowledge through telling facts and to ask questions eliciting recall, thus giving little attention to higher levels of thinking such as application, analysis, synthesis, or evaluation.

Physically, mentally, emotionally, or socially handicapped or non-English speaking students may have *special classes* designed to meet their particular needs. The stated goal of such classes has long been to prepare pupils to participate in regular classes as soon as they are able, but in reality they have frequently been segregated from the rest of the student population. Today many questions are being raised about these classes. Do the diagnostic tests used to determine placement in such classes discriminate against minority students? The answer in many cases must be given in the affirmative. School districts, finally forced in some instances to abandon the use of group tests of mental ability, are now being challenged on the use of individual tests. In districts with large populations of Spanish-speaking children, the question is: Why cannot beginning classes in elementary schools and subsequently at least some others be offered in Spanish? States which once had laws prohibiting the use of any language for instruction other than English now have altered them to permit primary grade classes to be given in Spanish.

Increasingly the goal is to integrate students with handicaps of all kinds into the regular school program and to offer teachers special help in coping with the individual problems of their students. More and more handicapped children are placed in regular day schools rather than in residential schools. Blind and deaf children, for example, are enrolled in regular classes for most of the day and provided with resource rooms where special teachers can help them with communication skills and provide special equipment and materials. Preprimary programs are also helping parents to provide very early intervention for handicapped children. In addition, attention is focusing on the special needs of children with multiple handicaps (Reynolds, 1969).

Planning for Heterogeneity

Whereas those who favor homogeneous grouping want to reduce variability in the instructional group, those who favor heterogeneous grouping see it as an asset. Their aim is to design groups that draw on the resources of individual differences; they value inclusiveness rather than exclusiveness.

Some of the criteria for selection of heterogeneous groups cut across age and grade levels; some, across abilities, interests, and achievement; and some rely on sociometric choice by students or by teachers. We explore here multigrading, nongrading, combination plans, complementary grouping, grouping by sociometry, and teachability grouping.

Multigrading permits students of adjacent grades to be placed in the same classroom where they may work in more than one grade level in different subjects at the same time. Split grades may be used to balance class size or deliberately to provide overlap. One teacher, for instance, may have children at third and fourth grades, another at fourth and fifth, and still another at fifth and sixth. Grade levels nonetheless are maintained.

The nongraded school replaces age and grade levels with a vertical concept of continuous individual progress. The term *nongraded* has been used interchangeably with *multi-age* or *ungraded,* although the latter often refers to special classes for the handicapped. Nongraded programs are found most frequently at the primary level, sometimes at the intermediate, and rarely at the secondary level.

Nongrading, according to John Goodlad and Robert H. Anderson (1963), anticipates that a child's progress in school will be irregular, varying widely in different areas. If he is allowed to move at his own rate, his progress cannot be equated with time spent nor judged with reference to an arbitrary grade level, but must be determined in relation to his ability and prior attainment. Evaluation, therefore, becomes critical. Careful records of each student must be kept to insure appropriate diagnosis of instructional needs.

At the elementary level, much nongrading seems limited to programs that permit children to develop skills in reading and arithmetic at their own pace. Real differentiation of the content of instruction is rare. It appears that programs have expanded faster than principals and teachers have expected. When principals were surveyed in 1961, only 12 per cent reported using some form of nongrading, and only one in four (26 per cent) prophesied that they would be involved in nongrading by 1966. Yet an NEA survey in 1964 showed that one in three schools in districts with enrollments of 12,000 or more was using nongrading.

At the secondary level, the first nongraded high school was opened at Melbourne, Florida in 1958 under the leadership of B. Frank Brown (1965) and another, Nova High School, was opened at Fort Lauderdale, Florida in 1961. In both these programs, students are grouped in phases according to their achievement. Phases provide for a range of student progress from special small remedial groups to completely independent study. Phased subjects include English, science, mathematics, foreign language, and some courses in business education, arts, and music. Students may be placed in different phases in each subject area. Ungraded but unphased are courses in home economics, physical education, trade and industrial education, and some other subjects.

What are the outcomes of such programs? Research data are surprisingly meager; much more are needed. In one study (Halliwell, 1963), nongraded reading was clearly superior at the first grade but lost its advantage in the second and third grades. The nongraded program in spelling proved statistically superior only in the third grade. Teachers indicated that they spent less time in teaching reading in the nongraded programs. Maurie Hillson (1964) also checked reading achievement in the first grade and found that pupils of all ability levels in a nongraded program achieved significantly more than similar pupils in a graded situation.

Advocates of nongrading contend that it has the greatest potential for individualizing instruction of any form of school organization. This promise can be realized only if content and learning activities as well as pacing of instruction are flexible. Otherwise nongrading can become as arbitrary in its demands as traditional graded programs.

Some programs *(combination plans)* have attempted to divide the curriculum into two parts using different grouping practices. In the Dalton Plan, for example, students enter into individual contracts for work in academic subjects and come together as a class largely for social and physical activities. In the Winnetka Plan, students move individually through so-called "common essentials" but join in group activities in literature, music, art, manual arts, and physical education. The more recent Dual Progress Plan of George D. Stoddard (1961) separates the "cultural imperatives" of language arts, social studies, and physical education, taught on a graded basis for one-half the school day, from the "cultural electives" of mathematics, science, music, art, and foreign languages, taught on a nongraded basis for the other half.

Planned heterogeneity can bring together students whose abilities and interests complement one another in *complementary grouping*. Selection can be based on the skills and interest needed to carry out a given task for a shorter or longer period of time. Students can be grouped for complementary learning styles, for example, auditory and visual perception abilities. In one group of first-graders a boy who could draw boats illustrated a story about boats that others were reading aloud. This group persisted for almost two days before dissolving. Slow learners can be helped by more advanced students to initiate higher levels of thinking. More able students can demonstrate ways of abstracting relationships that the less able can emulate. One small work group of sixth-graders (Taba, 1964), who were studying the economic flow of goods from Mexico to the United States, involved an able pupil who compiled figures from a sourcebook and conceptualized a scheme for grouping the data and two less able pupils who presented it in chart form. What seems critical to the success of such task groups is not only that the members be carefully chosen to complement each other's strengths but also that they be trained to work together. Students must be helped to evaluate their achievement in terms of process as well as product. Furthermore, the task to be done must genuinely demand group involvement; it should not be an individual assignment that is carried out in a group situation.

Peer teaching and learning are not, of course, restricted to students at a given age or grade level. Many schools report startling success in having older pupils tutor younger ones. Nor is this experience limited to the more able students. New York City's Mobilization for Youth Program, for example, showed that over a five month period younger children with reading difficulties gained 6.0 months as compared with a control group's 3.5 months when tutored by older children, themselves poor students. Even more extraordinary were the gains for their tutors who improved 2.4 years compared to a control group gain of 7.0 months. Similar success has been demonstrated by 14 and 15 year old members of the Neighborhood Youth Corps in tutoring programs in some 15 cities. But the advantages of pupil tutors are not restricted to the disadvantaged. In Portland, Oregon, for example, entire classes of upper grade children prepare lessons that they teach to primary pupils. That tutoring changes perspectives on the teaching task is reflected in the comment of one participant: "You learn to appreciate your teacher and what he goes through" (Fleming, 1969). For teachers, too, pupil tutoring may change perspectives. How will teachers view their new roles as facilitators of teaching as well as learning experiences for their students?

Teachers have long known that building on the patterns of social interaction in their classes can be of great help in structuring the learning situation, but they have not been sure how to use this knowledge to best advantage. Recent experiments have tried new ways of using sociometric choice as the determinant of classroom grouping. Most of these encourage cooperative competition. Grouping projects which allow students to choose their working partners may occur in any subject area. In some cases group competition is informal, in others it is elaborately structured by a reward system of points, grades, or tangible rewards such as candy bars. Sometimes students are allowed to choose whether they prefer to take examinations alone or in small groups of their own selection. In one instance in which groups of three were permitted to take a final examination in biology together, they were required to agree on their answers.

Computers offer new approaches to using *sociometric choice* for grouping. Systematic Sociometry, a computerized program at Ontario High School in California, determined placement of students in classroom work groups as nearly as possible on the basis of students' own desires, while matching the groups as evenly as possible so that teams would have fairly equivalent chances for success. Students received careful evaluation and feedback on their group's accomplishment of instructional goals. Parents were informed of successes. By competing in this way, even the slow learners had chances for success. At the end of a year's experience with the program, an experimental group had surpassed a control group in grade point average, had fewer failures, and fewer days absent. At the end of three semesters, students involved in the program showed a 30 per cent drop in cases for disciplinary action.

Whether the gains reported in experiments such as that at Ontario will be sustained remains to be seen. Using sociometric choice for grouping, however, raises broader issues. To what extent should cooperative competition become the motivating force for learning? What should be the balance between opportunities for learning as a team member and as an independent student? Should this balance vary for different students?

On what bases will these decisions be made?

Almost all teachers are aware that some students perform better with some teachers than with others. Most teachers, moreover, can describe the kinds of students with whom they have previously succeeded. By combining these two observations, Herbert A. Thelen (1967) was led to test a concept he called *teachability grouping,* in which teachers were given classes of students identified as similar to those they had been most successful with in the past.

Experimenting with grades eight to eleven, Thelen found that teachers varied widely in the kinds of students they chose. But having selected their class members, they were more relaxed and flexible. Their students, in turn, were more work-oriented and received higher grades. Even though the students in the teachable classes performed less well on achievement tests than those in the regular classes, Thelen concluded that teachability grouping was sound, because it enhanced the quality of the relationships between the teachers and their students.

Planned Flexibility

To increase flexibility, current approaches to grouping involve changes in staffing, group size, or scheduling. Many new organizational plans combine all three.

In the elementary school, one teacher has usually taught one graded class in a self-contained classroom for a full day, sometimes with the aid of specialists in physical education, art, and music. Informal arrangements have sometimes made it possible for teachers to pool their students and share their teaching responsibilities.

In the secondary school, *departmentalization* has long formally divided teaching duties according to subject areas. During the late 1950's this practice spread downward into the elementary school, especially in the middle grades, where it became the subject of much controversy. Some saw the self-contained classroom as offering a more unified program and giving pupils more social and emotional security, while others felt it did not provide teachers that were adequately trained in subject-matter, particularly in the new curricula such as mathematics. As in the case of ability grouping, the voluminous research was inconclusive, and the controversy continues.

A newer approach, making available to students the resources of two or more teachers, is *cooperative* or *team teaching,* in which teachers work together to plan instruction for a given group of students. At its simplest, cooperative teaching may regroup teachers and students in a given grade or subject so that each teacher is instructing in the area of his strengths. More complex hierarchical plans differentiate the functions of an instructional team. One team may include a master teacher or team coordinator, one or two other teachers, student teachers or interns, teaching assistants or aides, and a clerical aide. Senior teachers may be responsible for instruction in large groups; others, for small groups or independent study. Such a team can encompass one or more disciplines. Some large-scale team-teaching programs are organized around the concept of a school-within-a-school that can meet all the instructional needs of several hundred students.

Research data on team teaching are very limited, but, like other organizational innovations, team teaching clearly carries no guarantee of appropriate curriculum change. Indeed, to teach the existing curriculum with team teaching may merely result in fragmentation. For some teachers, moreover, team teaching carries a threat of exposure. Administrators, too, can feel threatened by teams who must make some administrative as well as instructional decisions. Effective team teaching requires a team committed to curriculum change, comprised of voluntary members with adequate time for planning and clear channels of decision-making.

What size group is most effective for instruction? Contrary to much popular and professional opinion, there is no consistent evidence that reducing class size results in improved learning. The data now available do not justify any specific ratio of teachers to pupils. What they do indicate is that the basic question should be asked in a different vein: What size group is most effective for what purposes and under what circumstances?

The Commission on the Experimental Study of the Utilization of Staff in the Secondary School, under the leadership of J. Lloyd Trump, identified three kinds of instruction: large-group, independent study, and small-group. All these groupings require individual diagnosis of the student's knowledge and understanding of particular areas of content, preparation for a given learning situation, and careful evaluation and follow-up. The so-called *Trump Plan* (1959) recommended that approximately 40 per cent of the student's time be spent in large-group instruction, 40 per cent in independent study, and 20 per cent in small-group instruction.

Large groups of one hundred or more are economical of time and effort when lectures, demonstrations, panels, or audio-visual, dramatic, or musical presentations are the mode of instruction. For such large-scale presentations, television-viewing at home may eventually take the place of large-group gatherings at school. With videotape recording available, students could review such presentations as often as they wished.

Independent study can open a wide range of choice for student learning. Students frequently draw up individual contracts with their advisers, outlining the specific program of independent study they plan to pursue. All too often, however, independent study has come to be equated with so-called individualized instruction through the use of programmed instruction or packaged learning units. Some of these are imaginative in their approaches; some foster mastery of essential skills in minimum time. But many simply permit the student working individually to cover at his own speed about the same content he would have covered in the traditional classroom situation. Many also still measure the student against some hypothetical group standard. Independent study, to be effective, must personalize learning experiences for the individual student. Ideally it should draw on the total resources of the community as well as of the school. In many schools, learning resource centers are providing rich environments for independent and small-group study. In others, the whole community is becoming the learning center.

Small groups of six to fifteen members involve students in social interaction where information can be clarified and ideas and feelings explored. The techniques of group problem-solving and decision-making can also be learned. Small groups can serve a variety of instructional purposes and can function with or without professional leadership. Allan A. Glatthorn (1966) has suggested some of their possible uses: (1) task groups or committees, (2) didactic groups for imparting information, (3) tutorial groups, (4) discursive groups for free discussion, (5) "brainstorming" groups for creative problem-solving, (6) inquiry groups in which students ask questions that lead to discovery, and (7) Socratic groups in which teachers ask questions to help students probe for truth. What is vital to small-group success is that group members be helped to state their goals clearly and to develop the skills necessary for constructive group processes.

Time is another dimension of instruction which can lend itself to more flexible use. Teachers have long devised some approaches to making the school schedule more flexible. One class, for example, may be scheduled for more than one successive period or two classes may be scheduled back-to-back to permit two teachers a more flexible allocation of time without disturbing the total school schedule. More recently, many schools have been experimenting with some form of flexible scheduling based on dividing the school day into units, or *modules,* of a given length, commonly 10, 15, or 20 minutes. These can be combined to provide instructional periods of various lengths.

OUTCOMES OF GROUPING

Grouping practices, whether planned for homogeneity, heterogeneity, or flexibility, carry no guarantee of effective student learning. Whatever the form of organization, the critical issue is the kind and quality of instruction it facilitates. Much innovation in grouping has altered only the organization for instruction and not the instruction itself. Much innovation, furthermore, has quickly become rigid and prescribed rather than open to continuous evaluation and change.

Effective instruction that differentiates both content and learning experiences for each student can no doubt be achieved in a wide variety of settings. One factor that makes a difference is the assumption underlying the choice of grouping practice. All too often the premise of homogeneous grouping is that pupils in low-ability groups cannot succeed. Robert Rosenthal and Lenore Jacobson (1968), in their oft-cited study of teacher expectations and pupils' intellectual development, found that children in fast, medium, and slow tracks, when identified at random as potential academic spurters, did make substantial gains in intelligence and reading test scores. Evidently the teachers communicated their expectations to these children and possibly improved their teaching techniques with them so that teacher expectations became self-fulfilling prophecies. Interestingly enough, however, the teachers had difficulty in changing their perceptions of children in the slow track even when they had demonstrated intellectual gains.

Teachers are even likely to view any success by children in low-ability groups unfavorably, as observed by William Glasser (1969, p. 82):

> Tracking, or homogeneous grouping by ability, is bad not only because of its effect upon students; it also has an insidious and destructive effect upon teachers. Where children are grouped by ability, teachers often do not appreciate and may even resent the effort of the low-track student who tries to improve. From the teacher's standpoint, it is almost as if a low-track, supposedly unmotivated student has no business changing his ways.

Certainly not all teachers respond to low-ability students in this manner. Many genuinely try to encourage them to achieve. Yet teaching is unlikely to be very productive if individual differences are considered fixed liabilities rather than fluid potentials.

New emphases on planning for heterogeneity and individualizing instruction grow from the increasing knowledge of human variability and human potential. They attempt to take into account the wide range of individual differences in abilities, interests, and learning styles that have been too long neglected. They also recognize that new research on the nature of intelligence calls into question any grouping based on a rigid concept of mental ability. But this knowledge must be translated into providing learning experiences that truly draw on the potential of each individual to learn. Nongrading, for example, may run the risk of defining even more rigid gradations of instruction than traditional age-grading. All too often so-called individualized instruction uses programmed instruction and individual learning packages that only offer the student a chance to progress through the same content in the same way as his fellow students. All that is differentiated is his place in the learning sequence. Moreover, the danger exists that individualized instruction will be equated to learning by oneself. Effective education cannot be achieved in sterile and isolated learning situations. The goal of grouping must be to provide the kind of social interaction that enhances learning.

Grouping practices must also be viewed in their social context. What is far more significant for student learning than any particular form of grouping is the opportunity structure it provides. Grouping for homogeneity must be evaluated in the context of equal educational opportunity. Even in a relatively desegregated school setting, ability grouping or tracking can result in resegregation. As Bruno Bettelheim (1958) pointed out, ability grouping has become the new style of segregation. Unfortunately, it is widely accepted as providing more effective attention to children's individual differences. Paradoxically, what results is the systematic isolation of students from a variety of experiences and learning opportunities.

Dominick Esposito (1970) concluded that, even in a relatively desegregated school environment, ability grouping based on standardized tests will result in great disparity in ethnic and socioeconomic representation between the highest and lowest ability groups. So critical to the provision of equal educational opportunity did Judge J. Skelly Wright find this issue that he ordered the tracking system in the Washington, D.C. school system discontinued in 1967. He ruled that black pupils who were consistently assigned to the lowest tracks were deprived of their Constitutional rights to equal education. In a system with 93 per cent black students, some black schools had no top-ability track and some white schools no lowest-ability.

The choice of grouping determines who will be partners in learning. A main objective of any grouping situation is to provide an opportunity for interaction among students. Classmates who offer experiences from the same social background only limit each other. Classmates who can bring together the richness and diversity of our pluralistic society expand potential for learning.

The social context of grouping extends far beyond the classroom or the community. Grouping practices, as the UNESCO conference report makes clear (Yates, 1966), become instruments of social policy that can maintain, or bring about change in, the structure of a society. In the end, the choice of grouping practices must seek to open new options of learning not only for the individual student but also for the pluralistic society to which be belongs. In Martin Buber's terms, the experience of independence must become a footbridge to community.

REFERENCES

Abrahamson, David A.: The effectiveness of grouping for students of high ability. *Educational Research Bulletin 38*:169-182, 1959.
The agony of busing moves north. *Time*, 57-60, 63-64, November 15, 1971.
Alexander, William: The new school in the middle. *Phi Delta Kappan 50*:355-357, 1969.
Ayres, L.P.: Laggards in Our Schools. New York, Charities Publication Committee, 1909.
Bettelheim, Bruno: Segregation: new style. *School Review 66*:251-272, 1958.
Borg, Walter: Ability Grouping in the Public Schools. Madison, Wis., Dembar Educational Research Services, Inc., 1966.
Brown, B. Frank: The Appropriate Placement School: A Sophisticated Nongraded Curriculum. West Nyack, New York, Parker Publishing Co., 1965.
Bush, Robert N., and Allen, Dwight W.: A New Design for High School Education: Assuming a Flexible Schedule. New York, McGraw-Hill Book Co., 1964.
Coleman, James S., et al.: Equality of Educational Opportunity. Washington, D.C., U.S. Government Printing Office, 1966.
Conant, James B.: The American High School Today. New York, McGraw-Hill Book Co., 1959.
Doak, E. Dale: Evaluating levels of thinking. *School & Society 98*:177-178, March, 1970.

Douglas, J.W.B.: The Home and the School: A Study of Ability and Attainment in the Primary School. London, MacGibbon and Kee, 1964.

Esposito, Dominick: Consquences of Ability Grouping: Ethnic and Socio-Economic Separation of Children. ERIC/IRCD Urban Disadvantaged Series, No. 20, New York, Teachers College, Columbia University, 1971.

Fleming, J. Carl: Pupil tutors and tutees learn together. *Today's Education 58*:22-24, October, 1969.

Glasser, William: Schools Without Failure. New York, Harper & Row, 1969.

Glatthorn, Allan A.: Learning in the Small Group. Melbourne, Florida, Institute for Development of Educational Activities, 1966.

Goldberg, Miriam, Passow, A. Harry, Justman, A.J., and Hale, G.: The Effects of Ability Grouping. New York, Bureau of Publications, Teachers College, Columbia University, 1966.

Goodlad, John: Classroom organization. *In* Harris, C.W. (ed.): Encyclopedia of Educational Research. New York, Macmillan, 1960.

Goodlad, John, and Anderson, Robert H.: The Nongraded Elementary School. Revised Edition. New York, Harcourt, Brace & World, 1963.

Halliwell, Joseph W.: A comparison of pupil achievement in graded and nongraded primary classrooms. *Journal of Experimental Education 32*:59-64, Fall, 1963.

Heathers, Glen: Organizing Schools Through the Dual Progress Plan. Danville, Ill., The Interstate Printers and Publishers, 1967.

Heathers, Glen: Grouping. *In* Ebel, Robert L. (ed.): Encyclopedia of Educational Research. Fourth Edition. New York, Macmillan, 1969.

Hillson, Maurie, et al.: A controlled experiment evaluating the effects of a nongraded organization on pupil achievement. *Journal of Educational Research 57*:548-550, July-August, 1964.

National Education Association, Educational Policies Commission: Universal Opportunity for Early Childhood Education. Washington, D.C., National Education Association, 1966.

National Education Association Project on the Instructional Program of the Public School: The Principals Look at the Schools: A Status Study of Selected Instructional Practices. Washington, D.C., National Education Association, 1962.

National Education Association, Research Division: Nongraded Schools. Research Memo 1965-12. Washington, D.C., National Education Association, 1965.

National Education Association, Research Division: Survey of Administrative Practices in Public School Systems. Washington, D.C., National Education Association, 1965-1966.

National Education Association, Research Division: Ability Grouping. Research Summary 1968-S3. Washington, D.C., National Education Association, 1968.

Nova Junior-Senior High Portfolio: Fort Lauderdale, Florida, Nova High School, 1967.

Reynolds, Maynard C.: Special education. *In* Ebel, Robert L. (ed.): Encyclopedia of Educational Research. Fourth Edition. New York, Macmillan, 1969.

Rosenthal, Robert, and Jacobson, Lenore: Pygmalion in the Classroom: Teacher Expectation and Pupils' Intellectual Development. New York, Holt, Rinehart and Winston, 1968.

Sørensen, Aage: Organizational differentiation of students and educational opportunity. *Sociology of Education 43*:355-376, Fall, 1970.

Stoddard, George D.: The Dual Progress Plan. New York, Harper & Brothers, 1961.

Swenson, Gardner, and Keys, Donald: Providing for Flexibility in Scheduling and Instruction. Successful School Management Series. Englewood Cliffs, N.J., Prentice-Hall, 1966.

Systematic Sociometry at Ontario High School: Ontario, Calif., Chaffey Union High School District, 1970.

Taba, Hilda, et. al.: Thinking in Elementary School Children. Office of Education Cooperative Research Project No. 1574. San Francisco, San Francisco State College, 1964.

Thelen, Herbert: Classroom Grouping for Teachability. New York, John Wiley & Sons, 1967.

Trump, J. Lloyd: Images of the Future. Commission on the Experimental Study of the Utilization of the Staff in the Secondary School. Washington, D.C., National Education Association, 1959.

Westby-Gibson, Dorothy: Grouping: Patterns and Practices. *In* Deighton, Lee C. (ed.): The Encyclopedia of Education. New York, Macmillan and The Free Press, 1971.

Wilhelms, Fred T., and Westby-Gibson, Dorothy: Grouping research offers leads. *Educational Leadership 18*:410-413, April, 1961.

Wrightstone, J. Wayne: Ability grouping and the average child. *NEA Journal 57*:9-11, 58, 1968.

Yates, Alfred (ed.): Grouping in Education. A Report Sponsored by the UNESCO Institute for Education, Hamburg. New York, John Wiley & Sons, 1966.

the primary 22 education of the camiroi*

R. A. Lafferty

ABSTRACT FROM JOINT REPORT TO THE GENERAL DUBUQUE PTA CONCERNING THE PRIMARY EDUCATION OF THE CAMIROI, Subtitled Critical Observations of a Parallel Culture on a Neighboring World, and Evaluations of THE OTHER WAY OF EDUCATION.

Extract from the Day Book:

"Where," we asked the Information Factor at Camiroi City Terminal, "is the office of the local PTA?"

"Isn't any," he said cheerfully.

"You mean that in Camiroi City, the metropolis of the planet, there is no PTA?" our chairman Paul Piper asked with disbelief.

"Isn't any office of it. But you're poor strangers, so you deserve an answer even if you can't frame your questions properly. See that elderly man sitting on the bench and enjoying the sun? Go tell him you need a PTA. He'll make you one."

"Perhaps the initials convey a different meaning on Camiroi," said Miss Munch the first surrogate chairman. "By them we mean—"

"Parent Teachers Apparatus, of course. Colloquial English is one of the six Earthian languages required here, you know. Don't be abashed. He's a fine person, and he enjoys doing things for strangers. He'll be glad to make you a PTA."

We were nonplussed, but we walked over to the man indicated.

"We are looking for the local PTA, sir," said Miss Smice, our second surrogate chairman. "We were told that you might help us."

"Oh, certainly," said the elderly Camiroi gentleman. "One of you arrest that man walking there, and we'll get started with it."

"Do what?" asked our Mr. Piper.

"Arrest him. I have noticed that your own words sometimes do not convey a meaning to you. I often wonder how you do communicate among yourselves. Arrest, take into custody, seize by any force physical or moral, and bring him here."

"Yes, *sir*," cried Miss Hanks our third surrogate chairman. She enjoyed things like this. She arrested the walking Camiroi man with force partly physical and partly moral and brought him to the group.

"It's a PTA they want, Meander," the elder Camiroi said to the one arrested. "Grab three more, and we'll get started. Let the lady help. She's good at it."

Our Miss Hanks and the Camiroi man named Meander arrested three other Camiroi men and brought them to the group.

"Five. It's enough," said the elderly Camiroi. "We are hereby constituted a PTA and ordered into random action. Now, how can we accommodate you, good Earth people?"

"But are you legal? Are you five persons competent to be a PTA?" demanded our Mr. Piper.

"Any Camiroi citizen is competent to do any job on the planet of Camiroi," said one of the Camiroi men (we learned later that his name was Talarium). "Otherwise Camiroi would be in a sad shape."

"It may be," said our Miss Smice sourly. "It all seems very informal. What if one of you had to be World President?"

"The odds are that it won't come to one man in ten," said the elderly Camiroi (his name was Philoxenus). "I'm the only one of this group ever to serve as president of this planet, and it was a pleasant week I spent in the Office. Now to the point. How can we accommodate you?"

"We would like to see one of your schools in session," said our Mr. Piper. "We would like to talk to the teachers and the students. We are here to compare the two systems of education."

"There is no comparison," said old Philoxenus, "—meaning no offense. Or no more than a little. On Camiroi, we practice Education. On Earth, they play a game, but they call it by the same name. That makes the confusion. Come. We'll go to a school in session."

"And to a public school," said Miss Smice suspiciously. "Do not fob off any fancy private school on us as typical."

"That would be difficult," said Philoxenus. "There is no public school in Camiroi City and only two remaining on the Planet. Only a small fraction of one per cent of the students of Camiroi are in public schools. We maintain that there is no more reason for the majority of children to be educated in a public school than to be raised in a public orphanage. We realize, of course, that on Earth you have made a sacred buffalo of the public school."

"Sacred cow," said our Mr. Piper.

"Children and Earthlings should be corrected when they use words wrongly," said Philoxenus. "How else will they learn the correct forms? The animal held sacred in your own near orient was of the species *bos bubalus* rather than *bos bos,* a buffalo rather than a cow. Shall we go to a school?"

"If it cannot be a public school, at least let it be a typical school," said Miss Smice.

"That again is impossible," said Philoxenus. "Every school on Camiroi is in some respect atypical."

We went to visit an atypical school.

Incident: Our first contact with the Camiroi students was a violent one. One of them, a lively little boy about eight years old, ran into Miss Munch, knocked her down, and broke her glasses. Then he jabbered something in an unknown tongue.

"Is that Camiroi?" asked Mr. Piper with interest. "From what I have heard, I supposed the language to have a harsher and fuller sound."

"You mean you don't recognize it?" asked Philoxenus with amusement. "What a droll admission from an educator. The boy is very young and very ignorant. Seeing that you were Earthians, he spoke in Hindi, which is the tongue used by more Earthians than any other. No, no, Xypete, they are of the minority who speak English. You can tell it by their colorless texture and the narrow heads on them."

"I say you sure do have slow reaction, lady," the little boy Xypete explained. "Even subhumans should react faster than that. You just stand there and gape and let me bowl you over. You want me analyze you and see why you react so slow?"

"No! No!"

"You seem unhurt in structure from the fall," the little boy continued, "but if I hurt you I got to fix you. Just strip down to your shift, and I'll go over you and make sure you're all right."

"No! No! No!"

"It's all right," said Philoxenus. "All Camiroi children learn primary medicine in the first grade, setting bones and healing contusions and such."

"No! No! I'm all right. But he's broken my glasses."

"Come along Earthside lady, I'll make you some others," said the little boy. "With your slow reaction time you sure can't afford the added handicap of defective vision. Shall I fit you with contacts?"

"No. I want glasses just like those which were broken. Oh heavens, what will I do?"

"You come, I do," said the little boy. It was rather revealing to us that the little boy was able to test Miss Munch's eyes, grind lenses, make frames and have her fixed up within three minutes. "I have made some improvements over those you wore before," the boy said, "to help compensate for your slow reaction time."

"Are all the Camiroi students so talented?" Mr. Piper asked. He was impressed.

"No. Xypete is unusual," Philoxenus said. "Most students would not be able to make a pair of glasses so quickly or competently till they were at least nine."

Random interviews:

"How rapidly do you read?" Miss Hanks asked a young girl.

"One hundred and twenty words a minute," the girl said.

"On Earth some of the girl students your age have learned to read at the rate of five hundred words a minute," Miss Hanks said proudly.

"When I began disciplined reading, I was reading at the rate of four thousands words a minute," the girl said. "They had quite a time correcting me of it. I had to take remedial reading, and my parents were ashamed of me. Now I've learned to read almost slow enough."

"I don't understand," said Miss Hanks.

"Do you know anything about Earth History or Geography?" Miss Smice asked a middle-sized boy.

"We sure are sketchy on it, lady. There isn't very much over there, is there?"

"Then you have never heard of Dubuque?"

"Count Dubuque interests me. I can't say as much for the City named after him. I always thought that the Count handled the matters of the conflicting French and Spanish land grants and the basic claims of the Sauk and Fox Indians very well. References to the Town now carry a humorous connotation, and 'School-Teacher from Dubuque' has become a folk archetype."

"Thank you," said Miss Smice, "or do I thank you?"

"What are you taught of the relative humanity of the Earthians and the Camiroi and of their origins?" Miss Munch asked a Camiroi girl.

"The other four worlds, Earth (Gaea), Kentauron Mikron, Dahae and Astrobe were all settled from Camiroi. That is what we are taught. We are also given the humorous aside that if it isn't true we will still hold it true till something better comes along. It was we who rediscovered the Four Worlds in historic time, not they who discovered us. If we did not make the original settlements, at least we have filed the first claim that we made them. We did, in historical time, make an additional colonization of Earth. You call it the Incursion of the Dorian Greeks."

"Where are their playgrounds?" Miss Hanks asked Talarium.

"Oh, the whole world. The children have the run of everything. To set up specific playgrounds would be like setting a table-sized aquarium down in the depths of the ocean. It would really be pointless."

Conference:

The four of us from Earth, specifically from Dubuque, Iowa, were in discussion with the five members of the Camiroi PTA.

"How do you maintain discipline?" Mr. Piper asked.

"Indifferently," said Philoxenus. "Oh, you mean in detail. It varies. Sometimes we let it drift, sometimes we pull them up short. Once they have learned that they must comply to an extent, there is little trouble. Small children are often put down into a pit. They do not eat or come out till they know their assignment."

"But that is inhuman," said Miss Hanks.

"Of course. But small children are not yet entirely human. If a child has not learned to accept discipline by the third or fourth grade, he is hanged."

"Literally?" asked Miss Munch.

"How would you hang a child figuratively? And what effect would that have on the other children?"

"By the neck?" Miss Munch still was not satisfied.

"By the neck until they are dead. The other children always accept the example gracefully and do better. Hanging isn't employed often. Scarcely one child in a hundred is hanged."

"What is this business about slow reading?" Miss Hanks asked. "I don't understand it at all."

"Only the other day there was a child in the third grade who persisted in rapid reading." Philoxenus said. "He was given an object lesson. He was given a book of medium difficulty, and he read it rapidly. Then he had to put the book away and repeat what he had read. Do you know that in the first thirty pages he missed four words? Midway in the book there was a whole statement which he had understood wrongly, and there were hundreds of pages that he got word-perfect only with difficulty. If he was so unsure on material that he had just read, think how imperfectly he would have recalled it forty years later."

"You mean that the Camiroi children learn to recall everything that they read?"

"The Camiroi children and adults will recall for life every detail they have ever seen, read or heard. We on Camiroi are only a little more intelligent than you on Earth. We cannot afford to waste time in forgetting or reviewing, or in pursuing anything of a shallowness that lends itself to scanning."

"Ah, would you call your schools liberal?" Mr. Piper asked.

"I would. You wouldn't," said Philoxenus. "We do not on Camiroi, as you do on Earth, use words to mean their opposites. There is nothing in our education or on our world that corresponds to the quaint servility which you call liberal on Earth."

"Well, would you call your education progressive?"

"No. In your argot, progressive, of course, means infantile."

"How are the schools financed?" asked Mr. Piper.

"Oh, the voluntary tithe on Camiroi takes care of everything, government, religion, education, public works. We don't believe in taxes, of course, and we never maintain a high overhead in anything."

"Just how voluntary is the tithing?" asked Miss Hanks. "Do you sometimes hang those who do not tithe voluntarily?"

"I believe there have been a few cases of that sort," said Philoxenus.

"And is your government really as slipshod as your education?" Mr. Piper asked. "Are your high officials really chosen by lot and for short periods?"

"Oh yes. Can you imagine a person so sick that he would actually *desire* to hold high office for any great period of time? Are there any further questions?"

"There must be hundreds," said Mr. Piper. "But we find difficulty putting them into words."

"If you cannot find words for them, we cannot find answers. PTA disbanded."

Conclusions:

A. The Camiroi system of education is inferior to our own in organization, in buildings, in facilities, in playgrounds, in teacher conferences, in funding, in parental involvement, in supervision, in in-group out-group accommodation adjustment motifs. Some of the school buildings are grotesque. We asked about one particular building which seemed to us to be flamboyant and in bad taste. "What do you expect from second-grade children?" they said. "It is well built even if of peculiar appearance. Second-grade Children are not yet complete artists of design."

"You mean that the children designed it themselves?" we asked.

"Of course," they said. "Designed and built it. It isn't a bad job for children."

Such a thing wouldn't be permitted on Earth.

B. The Camiroi system of education somehow produces much better results than does the education system of Earth. We have been forced to admit this by the evidence at hand.

C. There is an anomaly as yet unresolved between Conclusion A and Conclusion B.

APPENDIX TO JOINT REPORT

We give here, as perhaps of some interest, the curriculum of the Camiroi Primary Education.

First Year Course:

Playing one wind instrument.

Simple drawing of objects and numbers.

Singing. (This is important. Many Earth people sing who cannot sing. This early instruction of the Camiroi prevents that occurrence.)

Simple arithmetic, hand and machine.

First acrobatics.

First riddles and logic.
Mnemonic religion.
First dancing.
Walking the low wire.
Simple electric circuits.
Raising ants. (Eoempts, not earth ants.)

Second Year Course:

Playing one keyboard instrument.
Drawing, faces, letters, motions.
Singing comedies.
Complex arithmetic, hand and machine.
Second acrobatics.
First jokes and logic.
Quadratic religion.
Second dancing.
Simple defamation. (Spirited attacks on the character of one fellow student, with
    elementary falsification and simple hatchet-job programming.)
Performing on the medium wire.
Project electric wiring.
Raising bees. (Galelea, not earth bees.)

Third Year Course:

Playing one stringed instrument.
Reading and voice. (It is here that the student who may have fallen into bad habits of
    rapid reading is compelled to read at voice speed only.)
Soft stone sculpture.
Situation comedy.
Simple algebra, hand and machine.
First gymnastics.
Second jokes and logic.
Transcendent religion.
Complex acrobatic dancing.
Complex defamation.
Performing on the high wire and the sky pole.
Simple radio construction.
Raising, breeding and dissecting frogs. (Karakoli, not earth frogs.)

Fourth Year Course:

History reading, Camiroi and galactic, basic and geological.
Decadent comedy.
Simple geometry and trigonometry, hand and machine.
Track and field.

Shaggy people jokes and hirsute logic.
Simple obscenity.
Simple mysticism.
Patterns of falsification.
Trapeze work.
Intermediate electronics.
Human dissection.

Fifth Year Course:

History reading, Camiroi and galactic, technological.
Introverted drama.
Complex geometries and analytics, hand and machine.
Track and field for fifth form record.
First wit and logic.
First alcoholic appreciation.
Complex mysticism.
Setting intellectual climates, defamation in three dimensions.
Simple oratory.
Complex trapeze work.
Inorganic chemistry.
Advanced electronics.
Advanced human dissection.
Fifth Form Thesis.
The child is now ten years old and is half through his primary schooling. He is an
    unfinished animal, but he has learned to learn.

Sixth Form Course:

Reemphasis on slow reading.
Simple prodigious memory.
History reading, Camiroi and galactic, economic.
Horsemanship (of the Patrushkoe, not the earth horse.)
Advanced lathe and machine work for art and utility.
Literature, passive.
Calculi, hand and machine pankration.
Advanced wit and logic
Second alcoholic appreciation.
Differential religion.
First business ventures.
Complex oratory.
Building-scaling. (The buildings are higher and the gravity stronger than on Earth; this
    climbing of buildings like human flies calls out the ingenuity and daring of the
    Camiroi children.)
Nuclear physics and post-organic chemistry.
Simple pseudo-human assembly.

Seventh Year Course:

History reading, Camiroi and galactic, cultural.
Advanced prodigious memory.
Vehicle operation and manufacture of simple vehicle.
Literature, active.
Astrognosy, prediction and programming.
Advanced pankration.
Spherical logic, hand and machine.
Advanced alcoholic appreciation.
Integral religion.
Bankruptcy and recovery in business.
Conmanship and trend creation.
Post-nuclear physics and universals.
Transcendental athletics endeavor.
Complex robotics and programming.

Eighth Year Course:

History reading, Camiroi and galactic, seminal theory.
Consummate prodigious memory.
Manufacture of complex land and water vehicles.
Literature, compenduous and terminative. (Creative bookburning following the Camiroi
    thesis that nothing ordinary be allowed to survive.)
Cosmic theory, seminal.
Philosophy construction.
Complex hedonism.
Laser religion.
Conmanship, seminal.
Consolidation of simple genius status.
Post-robotic integration.

Ninth Year Course:

History reading, Camiroi and galactic, future and contingent.
Category invention.
Manufacture of complex light-barrier vehicles.
Construction of simple asteroids and planets.
Matrix religion and logic.
Simple human immortality disciplines.
Consolidation of complex genius status.
First problems of post-consciousness humanity.
First essays in marriage and reproduction.

Tenth Year Course:

History construction, active.
Manufacture of ultra-light-barrier vehicles.
Panphilosophical clarifications.
Construction of viable planets.
Consolidation of simple sanctity status.
Charismatic humor and pentacosmic logic.
Hypogyroscopic economy.
Penentaglossia. (The perfection of the fifty languages that every educated Camiroi must
    know including six Earthian languages. Of course the child will already have colloquial
    mastery of most of these, but he will not yet have them in their full depth.)
Construction of complex societies.
World government. (A course of the same name is sometimes given in Earthian schools,
    but the course is not of the same content. In this course the Camiroi student will
    govern a world, though not one of the first aspect worlds, for a period of three or
    four months.)
Tenth form thesis.

Comment on Curriculum:

The child will now be fifteen years old and will have completed his primary
education. In many ways he will be advanced beyond his Earth counterpart. Physically
more sophisticated, the Camiroi child could kill with his hands an Earth-type tiger or a
cape buffalo. An Earth child would perhaps be reluctant even to attempt such feats. The
Camiroi boy (or girl) could replace any professional Earth athlete at any position of any
game, and could surpass all existing Earth records. It is simply a question of finer poise,
strength and speed, the result of adequate schooling.

As to the arts (on which Earthlings sometimes place emphasis) the Camiroi child
could produce easy and unequaled masterpieces in any medium. More important, he will
have learned the relative unimportance of such pastimes.

The Camiroi child will have failed in business once, at age ten, and have learned
patience and perfection of objective by his failure. He will have acquired the techniques
of falsification and conmanship. Thereafter he will not be easily deceived by any of the
citizens of any of the worlds. The Camiroi child will have become a complex genius and a
simple saint; the latter reduces the index of Camiroi crime to near zero. He will be
married and settled in those early years of greatest enjoyment.

The child will have built, from materials found around any Camiroi house, a faster-
than-light vehicle. He will have piloted it on a significant journey of his own plotting and
programming. He will have built quasi-human robots of great intricacy. He will be of
perfect memory and judgment and will be well prepared to accept solid learning.

He will have learned to use his whole mind, for the vast reservoirs which are the
unconscious to us are not unconscious to him. Everything in him is ordered for use. And
there seems to be no great secret about the accomplishments, only to do everything
slowly enough and in the right order: Thus they avoid repetition and drill which are the
shriveling things which dull the quick apperception.

The Camiroi schedule is challenging to the children, but it is nowhere impossible or
discouraging. Everything builds to what follows. For instance, the child is eleven years old
before he is given post-nuclear physics and universals. Such subjects might be too difficult

for him at an earlier age. He is thirteen years old before he undertakes category invention, that intricate course with the simple name. He is fourteen years old when he enters the dangerous field of panphilosophical clarification. But he will have been constructing comprehensive philosophies for two years, and he will have the background for the final clarification.

We should look more closely at this other way of education. In some respects it is better than our own. Few Earth children would be able to construct an organic and sentient robot within fifteen minutes if given the test suddenly; most of them could not manufacture a living dog in that time. Not one Earth child in five could build a faster-than-light vehicle and travel it beyond our galaxy between now and midnight. Not one Earth child in a hundred could build a planet and have it a going concern within a week. Not one in a thousand would be able to comprehend pentacosmic logic.

Recommendations:

A. Kidnapping five Camiroi at random and constituting them a pilot Earth PTA.
B. A little constructive book-burning, particularly in the education field.
C. Judicious hanging of certain malingering students.

SECTION THREE

TEACHING
AND
TECHNOLOGY

"Amazing! It would take four thousand mathematicians four thousand years to make a mistake like that!"

One of the commoner misconceptions about the term technology is that it refers purely to creations of the physical sciences. Thus, when B. F. Skinner speaks of a "technology of teaching," some get the vision of a mechanized classroom, although the degree of mechanization is really irrelevant. What is relevant is his attempt to develop practical teaching methodologies from the findings of educational researchers, much as engineers apply the findings of physical scientists. Thus, Clark Abt's discussion of simulation techniques is as much educational technology as Howard Peelle's discussion of computer simulations.

Indeed, the familiar educational "methods" courses can be considered studies in the technology of teaching (though they have been criticized as unscientific or even pseudoscientific in origin). The variety of approaches to "methods" only reflects the diversity of thinking among educational scientists.

The development of new technologies that can be applied to education has added considerably to the variety of methods available. Teachers can present information via tapes, television, and movies, as well as by the spoken and written word. Simulations and computers can be used as teaching aids. The development of Xerography, the mimeograph, and cheap offset printing has greatly expanded the type and *quantity of printed material teachers can use. New construction technology has brought improvements in school buildings.*

Hopefully these new "methods" will enable the student to learn better. But there is nothing inherent in new media that insures this. The early attempts to use educational television to replace teachers in the classroom (prompted both by the teacher shortage and financial reasons) met with little success. The much more sophisticated effort that went into producing Sesame Street *was needed to exploit television's educational potential.*

It's also vital to be aware of any potential problems the new media might bring—not merely by naive usage but by their very nature. There have been warnings that young children's eyes are not ready for reading or television when they enter school. Michael Maccoby warns that the psychological consequences of excessive educational exposure to the new media might be essentially passive individuals, totally dependent upon external stimulation to function.

Ultimately, the effective use of the new technologies will require educational techniques as sophisticated as the engineering techniques that developed the physical equipment. And it will require that educators understand their students as well as engineers understand their equipment.

23 playing to learn

Clark C. Abt

There is much evidence that playing is a learning activity and that learning to play is learning to learn. The process by which a child learns to speak and understand his native language is, at that stage of development, one of pure play. The most important rewards of learning to speak are intrinsic—the ability to speak to and understand other people, and the satisfaction of the child's need for "investigation" of the world around him. I doubt that children could be coaxed into learning speech by such external rewards as changes in their food supply.

In our personal experience, things that are "interesting" are usually easiest to learn—regardless of future usefulness. Here, essentially, we are "playing." In contrast, the hardest things to learn seem to be those that one doesn't enjoy but thinks are useful for extrinsic purposes (such as passing exams). These things are *work* to learn (with nonintrinsic, secondary rewards).

Playing can help learning in two ways—by motivating learning and by helping achieve it. The difference can be illustrated by considering the two different roles a sport can play. For the dedicated amateur athlete the desire to perform well in a sport is a powerful motivation to keep in good physical condition. To others who enjoy the sport but are not as dedicated, participation is a way to achieve good physical condition. Because of intrinsic rewards, both are keeping in good condition, a task that might justifiably be called work.

Although motivation and achievement at first sound complementary, this is often not the case. There is usually some trade-off between the operational requirements for an effectively motivational game and the educational requirements for substantive content coverage, detail, and accuracy. Sports, for example, do not exercise all parts of the body—particularly sports like baseball and football, in which participants may play a number of different "positions" with different physical requirements.

Playing appears to be one of the best methods for certain types of learning, such as areas which require the understanding and coordination of several activities simultaneously. Learning by conventional study in these areas is extremely difficult. Sequences of activities can be memorized, but understanding requires combining the activities, either in the imagination, in a simulation, or in real life. Most people cannot deal with many abstractions without becoming confused, so they prefer to simulate the problem by manipulating symbols or objects or to try it out directly—in what we've come to call experiential learning.

Playing is, almost by definition, a simulation of reality. Simulations come naturally to the child, who "plays house" or "plays store." By "playing through" a role, like father, mother, or doctor, the child comes to understand something about the people who occupy the role.

It is important to realize that "learning by playing" is not a miracle cure for all educational ills. Some tasks are better learned by doing, and some people learn best this way, but it is not the optimum method for all tasks and all people. Simulation works best for complex activities requiring coordination of a number of factors, such as flying an airplane. Thus, most pilot training makes use of flight simulators able to duplicate the problems of flying.

Activities that make demands on long-term (rather than short-term) memory and do not require such complex coordination are probably more efficiently learned by conventional study. These include languages, literature, and other humanities, and the more highly classified natural sciences such as botany. However, playing can serve a motivational role in such learning. Acting roles in plays, for example, which certainly can be called playing, can strongly motivate the learning of literature and languages.

Some people are able to coordinate abstractions so well that they do not need simulations to learn. Essentially, they are able to simulate in their imaginations. Their success, naturally, will vary from case to case, but usually decreases with complexity. Such people may even be more highly motivated to learn by abstractions.

All games are simulations, but not all simulations are games. Games are a special kind of simulation and can be distinguished from other kinds, such as computer simulations, dramatic plays, or motion pictures. Simulations, broadly defined, are condensed representations of reality, simplified models of real world processes or things. Models usually involve some reduction of scale and simplification of detail to reduce costs. Airplane and ship models and dolls, for example, are simplified and reduced representations of real airplanes, ships, and people.

Simulation models have some universally fascinating qualities. Varying contexts and conditions can be tried out quickly and with minimal risk and cost. Contextual patterns in small-scale models can be observed from a godlike height by ordinary humans. Simulation modeling of the world or elements of it is playing at being godlike; one is free to invent, to control, to make things happen—pleasures common to children, calculators, and kings of all ages and places, whether they are building model castles in the sand or airplanes in wind tunnels or economies on computers.

Simulations can represent static things (model airplanes) or dynamic processes (changing economies). Static simulation models such as model houses, ships, terrain maps, and globes have long been used for educational purposes, but dynamic representations of changing systems are recent innovations. The changing systems may be physical (the weather), biological (evolution of species), macro-economic (national or regional economies), micro-economic (commercial corporations in competition), military (adversary conflict interactions), political (election campaigns), or psycho-social (interpersonal relations and influence processes such as teaching-learning). Dynamic, moving, or "working" models can demonstrate (rather than merely state) relationships, and can involve the manipulators of the models in a way that is just as absorbing as decision-making in real world processes.

Chess is a dynamic model simulation of medieval warfare. *Monopoly* is a simulation of real estate economics. *Diplomacy* is a simulation of international relations. These are models also in the exemplary sense of containing what are believed to be the essentials of the situation simulated. They belong to that special category of simulations called *games,* because they are competitive.

Simulations have been defined as condensed representations of real world processes or situations. Games are simulations in which decisions are made by competing human players. A game is any contest (play) among two or more decision-makers (players), competing within constraints (rules and resource limitations). Competition among players makes games even more stimulating to the participants than noncompetitive simulations.

The games of most immediate educational interest are usually designed to simulate a specific aspect of reality. These are in contrast to games such as cards or dice which have evolved from a reality-simulating origin toward a relatively pure fantasy. These simulations are used for three major purposes in education: instruction of students, planning, and training and evaluation of teachers and administrators.

The two latter functions are similar to those which simulations have served in business and industry. Simulation games can be used to predict future trends and problems if the interactions are assumed. The process of training educators to function in such probable situations (or evaluating their ability to function) is often combined with these planning exercises.

An example of this is a game simulating the problems of introducing sophisticated technology into the schools. Some fifty county school superintendents assume the roles of state and local education planners and interested people in the power structure, allocating budgetary, technological, and human resources to achieve educational goals. These goals must be achieved by cooperation among school districts. The new educational technology, at least during its introductory phase, requires small school districts to consolidate or at least cooperate, because only a large system can afford to develop original programming and the communications and processing systems to use it. The simulation facilitates such cooperative planning.

Use of simulation games offers to improve significantly the efficiency of instructing students. This area has become a critical bottleneck in education. Demands for quantity and quality of education have risen all over the world. Yet the only answer educators can produce is to hire more teachers. Years of effort and many innovations have done little to improve the situation.

Why do simulation games improve instructional efficiency? There are five chief, mutually reinforcing reasons. Simulation games provide *motivation* for the student to become deeply involved in the problem situation. Second, they provide a logical framework for problem *analysis,* decomposing complex interaction processes into their component elements of decision-making, information flow, and resource supply. Third, simulation games require and reward the *synthesis* of solutions to problems by both reproducible logic and private intuition. Fourth, they allow, exploit, and reward effective *intuition* in problem-solving. Fifth, simulation games offer greatly expanded opportunities for *peer learning,* reducing anti-authoritarian inhibitions to learning from teachers and the ambiguities of learning across cultural barriers, and making possible great instructional economies by significantly reducing the instructional load of teachers and permitting much of the remaining instructional load to be shared by other students.

Behaviorally, a game is essentially a conflict drama in which the players are motivated by both writing the script and acting the roles. If it is a good game (or a good drama), the resolution of the conflict will be uncertain because forces tending to resolve it are fairly well balanced. (In game terms, all players have an equal chance of winning.) This uncertainty results in curiosity and suspense, because the players care about the outcome. In a good drama the audience cares enough about the characters to be curious about the outcome because it identifies and empathises with some of them. In a game the involvement of the player is even more intense because identification and empathy are even more intimate—the player *is* the actor *and* at least part of the playwright.

Games provide a uniquely effective framework for the logical *analysis* of complex interaction problems. The analysis of the problem is implicit in the very form of the game: The field of play defines the scope of the problem. The actors, with their associated aims and resources, define the interacting forces. The rules define the outcome of these forces under a variety of specific circumstances. The simultaneous development of the parallel processes and strategies common to complex processes is observed as they occur rather than in the artificial sequential form imposed by spoken or written language. Compare the dynamic analysis possible using a game to describe a football play with a prose description of the action. The only reason one can mentally reformulate the dynamics of parallel processes from a sequential prose description may be the possession of an abstracting power that holds some actions in mind while noting new ones—essentially mental gaming.

The *synthesis* of solutions to problems in games is operationally tough-minded. They work or they don't, and there is quick feedback on successes and failures. Only in the physical sciences do school solutions work or fail immediately and concretely. But with games, solutions to social science problems are concretely tested for effectiveness. Solutions must be synthesized—restatements of the problem cannot pass for solutions, for they cannot "win." Synthesis of solutions is promoted by two unique educational aspects: small group problem solving and use of intuition. In the small group team efforts of most educational games, more diverse solutions are proposed and evaluated than a single problem-solver is likely to consider. *Intuitive insights* are given their just deserts—rewarded by the faster rate of good decisions and increased chances to win if effective, punished by failure when wrong.

The *peer learning* that supports better synthesis and evaluation of alternative solutions also develops social skills otherwise almost completely neglected in the conventional classroom. Careers and vocations usually require most problem-solving to be conducted with others, yet there is no preparation for this in schools. The social skills developed by the small group problem-solving activities of games unfortunately are not yet tested by formal examinations, but they are certainly tested after graduation.

When and how can instructional games be best used? The most immediately appealing applications appear to be in the social studies: history, economics, civics, and international relations. These subjects are both inefficiently taught by conventional lecture and discussion techniques and naturally susceptible to simulation. Whereas in the sciences and language areas, laboratory experiences actually let the student do something real, the scale of the phenomena considered by conventional social studies does not permit any active student participation. Using simulation games, however, students can assume decision-making roles and simulate social studies topics in the classroom.

Learning achieved from games occurs in three important phases: game *design,* game *play,* and game *analysis.* Game design may be carried out by expert curriculum developers, schoolteachers, or students. It is probably desirable for all three to participate. Curriculum developers can bring to bear interdisciplinary skills of greater variety and depth, and they have greater experience in game design than most teachers. The teacher should participate in order to learn design techniques well enough to teach them to his students. The student is the objective of the whole effort, and he should design games because the process is itself analytic and synthetic and forces him to deal with the essence of a problem. This in turn can show him the gaps in his knowledge and motivate him to study and research to fill these gaps. There is nothing like trying to design a game about a subject to show you what you need to know about it but don't. To design games you must be able to predict the outcomes of alternative decisions, and that requires good understanding of the situation being simulated.

Games should be played at least three times—the first to learn the facts of the problem, the second to learn cause-effect relations, and the third to learn the costs, benefits, risks, and opportunities of alternative strategies. These three plays should not be in unbroken sequence, but should be sandwiched between sessions of home preparation and classroom discussion. The first game functions as a motivator of serious study and preparation for the second, or analytic game. The successes and failures of this second play then stimulate deeper research and discussion of the problem, and hypotheses can be developed and tested in a third, summary, game.

Few educational games require less than two hours, so it is desirable to use at least two-hour lab periods. It is important to remember that game analysis, or debriefing, is an important part of the learning experience and is best carried out immediately after the end of a game when interest is high. Thus, if only one-hour periods are possible, it is best to plan for a game to end in the first part of a classroom hour rather than near the end of it.

How should games be evaluated? Simulation games are not intended to reproduce reality, but to give students realistic insights into the forces producing a situation. Truth in games is the poetic truth of drama and the analytical truth of theory, not the literal truth. Thus, while realism is a valid criterion for educational games, reproduction of reality is not. In a history game, for example, it is important that what actually happened *could* happen in the game, but it *need not* happen in the game, any more than it need happen if history were replayed with a very few slight changes in the forces involved.

Games should be evaluated for their *operability, motivational* effectiveness, intellectual content or *richness,* and grasp of the essence of the problem or *relevance.* Operability is easily tested by actual play; if instructions are unclear, rules incomplete or unreasonable, some roles boring, and outcomes difficult to score, it will be apparent after a few plays. Operability can often be improved by minor changes in basically good games. Motivational effectiveness is partly determined by the dramatic qualities of the game. For exciting drama, forces must be well balanced so that outcomes are uncertain, and all roles must be interesting. Intellectual content or richness is indicated by how often the game can be repeated without exhausting its possibilities. Relevance to specific educational objectives can be tested by conventional objective examinations and, probably equally important, by creative problem-solving assignments, such as designing "sub-games" going into greater depth on a particular aspect of a problem. Finally, the most educational way of obtaining games is for teacher and students to design them themselves.

Concepts

In summary, educational games have relevance to most learning situations. We believe they are particularly effective for the following reasons:

1. *Active Learning.* Young people have often had unsatisfactory experiences in their formal classrooms, reacting apathetically. Games offer a satisfying social experience and require the active participation of the student, whose interest is thus stimulated. Active response makes for improved teaching—the teacher is in a position to observe the student in action, to strengthen his responses, and to offer modifications.

2. *Immediate Reinforcement.* Young people are seldom rewarded for effective analysis and decision-making in school. Game learning provides an immediate reward to the individual who makes a correct decision, while the student who does not soon knows his mistake and can correct his error.

3. *Character Development.* The current school environment often fosters poor impulse control. Playing an educational game will not change a child's personality, but games do stress rational decision-making, the understanding of cause-effect relationships, and the rewards of self-restraint.

4. *Versatility.* Games can be adjusted to any level of complexity, and thus are suited to the particular level of sophistication or aptitude of the group. The scenario of a game can be made relevant to the background and interests of any group of young people.

5. *Attention Span.* Children become involved in game situations and concentrate on them for hours, although it is often claimed that their attention span lasts only minutes.

6. *Communication.* Normally shy individuals in face-to-face situations may become surprisingly active and communicative in games. This is typically observed in athletic games. Perhaps, since everyone is playing a role and normal relationships are suspended, risk-taking and the possibility of losing face are accepted.

7. *Time Perspective.* A game greatly accelerates the sequence of simulated activities by compressing time. It is thus possible to demonstrate concepts of time perspective and differences between present and future "gratifications," which are difficult to explain convincingly in the abstract.

8. *Abstraction Capacity.* Abstract ideas can be demonstrated concretely by games. Symbols used in the scenario and in distributing resources to the players accustom them to symbolic representation. Games can carry a greater concentration of abstract ideas than other pedagogic approaches without decreasing the motivation of players.

9. *Self-Instruction.* Games are self-teaching. Players learn from their own experience and that of other players. It requires less teacher effort than an equivalent period of time spent on expository teaching.

10. *Teacher's Role.* The teacher's role in a game is not one of dominance over the class but rather an arbitrator and explainer, coach, or even a more expert player. This role change assists in building a positive attitude toward the teacher.

11. *Familiarity.* Role-playing and competitive behavior in game situations are part of the normal experience of most people; they provide a familiar vehicle for introducing ideas and information.

12. *Discipline.* Even the most undisciplined students usually accept the rules of games, because not to accept them spoils the fun. There is therefore no problem with discipline.

13. *Testing Value.* Games can test skills such as interpersonal, organizing, planning, negotiating, and communications skills that are not usually exercised by conventional objective and projective tests.

24 a psychoanalytic view of learning*

Michael Maccoby

Because our schools have played a key role in forming the American character and will continue to do so, it is essential to understand the psychological principles underlying educational programs, and to develop ones that might guide future innovation towards forming productive character traits. With the goal of preparing students to succeed in a rapidly changing meritocracy, innovations in education often contribute to turning out compulsive winners and increasingly jaded consumers who have become cynical about learning. These young people may be expert at test taking but contribute little to the society and are often miserable because they feel centerless.

Parents and teachers justify these innovations in terms of test results, but unless they are evaluated in terms of character, their long range effects are likely to be negative. An example is the use of competitive games to speed up learning. Competitive behavior can be rooted in different character systems, ranging from a healthy pride in performance or workmanship to a predatory urge to destroy one's competition or a desperate need to be a winner in order to escape a feeling of worthlessness. Tests of ability, endurance and courage may help develop both the individual's potentialities and realism, and in athletics, speed, strength and skill provide opportunities for natural competition. However, it is another matter when all of learning is fitted into a game. Teaching through such games may inject rich doses of excitement and learning drive into many students who will as a result increase their test scores. But there is the danger of furthering the formation of an alienated-competitive character. Many of the children will become dependent on competition to stimulate them. Winning will become their real interest: they will prefer being first to understanding the nature of things. Because they will learn only what is necessary for success, their relatedness to knowledge will be superficial. Studies with children indicate that game-like competition not only narrows the breadth of their learning but can increase anxiety about losing, causing for some children paralyzing conflict and learning blocks. Many of the most independent, self-activating children need to work at their own pace and are upset by extrinsic rewards and punishment.

Another example of short-term learning and long-term character disorders is the extremely "stimulating" presentation of educational material which may indeed teach some things rapidly, but at the expense of developing the student's "activeness." Programs such as "Sesame Street" excite the children, but only recently has the question been asked (by the BBC) of what character traits are developed. Exciting learning through TV may further the consumer mentality in children, fostering their need for constant

---

stimulation, for being entertained and "turned on." Other methods of learning the alphabet or numbers might take longer, but they might also emphasize *active* character traits, particularly concentration and the child's development of individual rhythms of work. We must consider the possibility that whatever the content of the programs, TV as a medium for teaching may have negative effects on character development, particularly if not combined with activating classroom discussion.

The examples given are related to two qualities of character—an alienated competitive attitude and the consumer mentality—which are often reinforced rather than confronted by the schools. Parents favor the use of any techniques that promise to speed up learning and get their children into college. *The New York Times* recently reported that a "teacher was ousted by fifteen sets of parents who were convinced that, after forty-five years of service, she was not prepared to handle 'Sesame Street' graduates." The teachers, for their part, also employ these techniques because they want to have an impact on students and need to show results. Furthermore, games and excitement save the teachers from guilty feelings of having to be "authoritarian" disciplinarians, and from having to know both their subject matter and their students thoroughly. However, the symptoms of anxiety and chronic boredom in young people make it necessary in higher education for teachers either to find new ways of "turning on" the students, or devoting a large part of their time to psychotherapy.

It is common to attribute the anxiety of the young to the spectre of nuclear war and the disintegration of the environment. These threats to existence cannot be discounted as sources of feelings of powerlessness and fear, and for young men, the war in Vietnam has been a further cause for unrest and uncertainty. Yet this explanation does not fully explain the intense anxiety of many students, and it focuses attention away from conditions in the schools which can be changed more easily.

The anxiety of high school students was documented most dramatically a few years ago in the film *Sixteen in Webster Groves,* prepared by the National Opinion Research Center and the CBS network. The filmmakers chose one of the richest middle-class communities in America and interviewed the high school students. At the time, in the middle-sixties, they found the students obsessed with fears about not making good enough grades or getting high enough test scores to go on to elite colleges and eventually find jobs that paid well enough to allow them to live in towns like Webster Groves, Lake Forest or Scarsdale. Only a few of the students were concerned about social issues, and most of them were outcasts.

Recently I spent the day with high school students in a suburb near Washington, D.C. In contrast to the Webster Groves of the mid-sixties, these young people were more conscious of the larger world outside of themselves and willing to work for progressive social change. But they too were anxious about success, fearful of letting down their parents and being labeled losers. Unlike the traditional academic program of Webster Groves, this high school encouraged independent study and social concern. Yet many students were doubtful whether they really cared about their individual projects or the community. They questioned their motives: perhaps they were acting because they thought leading colleges would favor the "involved student." The need to be "committed" seemed one more pressure to achieve. (It would be interesting to learn whether Webster Groves has moved in this same direction.) Given this anxiety, any new competitive pressures are likely either to overwhelm the student or move him further in the direction of cold, detached competitiveness and cynicism. Many cool competitors have overcome their anxiety at great emotional cost. Others, who cannot detach themselves from their feelings, drop out.

The other symptom, boredom, is a constant complaint of students, including some of those who succeed brilliantly on tests. At lectures in the leading universities one finds students sleeping, reading newspapers or day-dreaming. Sometimes this is a reaction to dull, alienated teachers. But often the students demand entertainment, particularly after having "put out" on their exams. The challenge and excitement needed to bring the class to life is not, however, intrinsic to discovery and understanding: it has little relation to love of learning. Rather, it is the stimulation necessary to whet the appetite of students who no longer care about the truth and can only be turned on by a good performance.

What kind of people do these anxious and bored students become? What is a compulsive winner or a consumer character? The description offered in this article is based on clinical work with college students by my colleagues and me. In psychoanalysis, we have explored the effects of their adaptation to competitive demands and consumer seductions. Some become frightened, confused and withdrawn. But others lose faith in life and have a diminished sense of self, leading them to worship secular idols, and unconsciously to pursue irrational goals. There is hardly a way to express the conflicts experienced by these students. The problem has to do with their goals and purposes. In medieval society, these character disorders might have been analyzed in terms of pride, greed, the temptation to sell the self for power or security and the feeling of being hopelessly damned. Today, even though such language describes experience, it sounds moralistic and pejorative rather than spiritually objective. On the one hand, the churches have for the most part stripped the experience from the concepts but retain official ownership of them. On the other hand, such a language clashes with the cool style which rejects the values of commitment and perfectibility such concepts imply. Yet some such concepts are needed to recognize and communicate the deepest conflicts that paralyze many young people and rob them of a chance for a productive life.

What we find through psychoanalysis is a weak, underdeveloped center in many students who have sought the alienated goals of the meritocracy. As one patient stated, "I experience a gaping hole where my self should be. Instead of interest, I feel hunger." Such students may be greedy for success or for stimulation because the potential source of energy centered in themselves has never been developed. They have learned to rev themselves up for tests, to become enthusiastic over what is expected from them, but left alone, they doubt their feelings and goals. Indeed the overriding goal is to do well and be thought well of. In some cases, overweening ambition or illusions of grandeur have been substituted for their real interests or a developing power over knowledge. Extreme ambition, often fed by parents and teachers, may be so frustrating that the gifted young person withdraws into fantasies or drugs.

Almost always, these patients begin to become aware in analysis that their lives have been in large part programmed for them, that they have never looked for their own goals or had the courage to pursue the latent interests not rewarded by parents, teachers or peers. Instead, they have let others decide for them: they have chosen goals to impress or to avoid ridicule rather than to realize inner vocations. For many, vocations are determined, if at all, by "objective" tests. Tastes are molded by the media. And political attitudes are formed by peer groups or the "youth culture." During the past decade, for example, more young people have been encouraged to take their values more seriously and translate them into political convictions. However, political relevance itself becomes a new form of oppression in some circles. Students become guilty about developing interests which are not commonly considered useful or socially beneficial. They are made to feel that the disciplined play of art and science is frivolous if not immediately "relevant" to social change. But the result of denying oneself is that the individual is cut off from the deepest wellsprings of creativity. Thus, those who seek therapy struggle to overcome their greed and illusions and to find in themselves the authentic interests so little developed by their home life and schooling.

Some psychiatrists think of the centerless individual as a positive development, particularly in contrast to their model of the uptight inner-directed individual. They argue that in a rapidly changing society, centerless people are the ones who adapt most successfully. This view is shared by such a creative social psychiatrist as Robert J. Lifton, one of the most sensitive interpreters of moral concerns and spiritual conflicts felt by college students. Lifton describes one variation of the centerless person as "protean man," who he argues substitutes "polymorphous versatility" for character. Lifton makes it a point to "stress that protean style is by no means pathological as such" and that it "may well be one of the functional patterns of our day." Protean man has no home or rootedness: he is fully committed to nothing, and he substitutes many masks for an authentic self. This is similar to the position of the late Frederick S. Perls, founder of Gestalt Therapy and resident therapist at Esalen. He wrote:

> Once you have a *character*, you have developed a rigid system. Your behavior becomes petrified, predictable, and you lose your ability to cope freely with the world with all your resources . . . I say that the richest person, the most productive person, creative person, is a person who has *no* character.

But Lifton, Perls and others are romanticizing, providing an ideology for and finally advocating a character type which they fail to analyze sufficiently. This modern centerless character must be understood in relationship to the social conditions that provide him his function. An analysis by Erich Fromm in *The Sane Society* suggests that the alienated centerless character tends to be developed by conditions of bureaucratic industrialism. Fromm's description of the character who survives by selling an image of himself is similar to Lifton's patient who wears many masks and wonders if a self still exists. What Lifton fails to take seriously is the fact that such a person is a patient. Even though his character may be "functional," he has sought treatment because he suffers. Perhaps the deepest suffering for such a person, Fromm has written, is the shame of not being oneself, of self-betrayal.

My experience with young people who saw themselves in terms of a protean ideology was as psychoanalyst to a commune. The group of college dropouts and street people ranged in age from 17 to 25. They asked for a group analysis because they were not living according to their stated goals and values, which were to create a loving, structureless environment. They wanted to be free of all formal constraints and felt that they could be protean in changing themselves to fit an ideal world. But they were not satisfied. Although they had gotten rid of all rules, authority, and commitments to individuals, they did not feel free and there was little trust or openness. While analysis in the usual sense was not possible, I agreed to join them in exploring why they were unable to achieve their goals. We met three hours a week for eight months. In the course of these meetings, the commune members became conscious of hidden goals to be fed and mothered. Some of them also became aware that while they had consciously rejected parental authority and values, they had substituted for them the equally rigid Ten Commandments of a "community parent" based on the dictates of the radical political movement. These included: exclusive relationships are like private property, bad; some drugs—grass and hash—are good but all needles are bad; women should not try to be beautiful unless they are born that way; having fun is suspect unless one can show it is politically useful. Once they realized that they had inescapably individual selves that were not infinitely malleable, the commune members saw themselves as passive conformists who were fearful of asserting individuality for fear of being abandoned by the mothering community.

A person with a strong sense of self may be predictable inasmuch as he has committed himself to people and ideals. However, it is naive to think that centerless individuals are not even more predictable. To foresee the behavior of the "marketing" character, one must study him in relationship to his social context, since he tends to act according to the demands of his market. Consider, for example, two types of the modern centerless character—the compulsive consumer and the game character—which are exaggerated products of character tendencies often reinforced in schools.

The compulsive consumer is typically depressed, though not so acutely that he always seeks psychiatric help; he compensates for this depression by a constant search for new forms of excitement and entertainment. These may include music, food, drugs, sex or politics. He hungers for novelty and stimulation: the action must be "new." Such a person may seem unpredictable because he or she is never committed to anyone or anything, but always ready to adopt the newest fad or style of life which promises to "turn him on." In some cases, the compulsive consumer's character may be rooted in a deeper psychopathology. Among these are the drug takers and alcoholics whose unconscious wish is to regress to a womb-like state of passive-certainty. Or the compulsive consumers of technology who seek a mechanical womb in which warmth, food and entertainment are all secured by pressing a button and there is no longer a need to wake up.

Another centerless person, the game character, comes to life in an atmosphere of risk and competition, of tests and challenges. His commitment is to a single goal: winning. Some gamesters are lone-wolf hustlers. However, the game character may also fit into the high pressure project atmosphere of many modern corporations. The game character type of manager is like a professional football quarterback and indeed thinks of himself in this way. He integrates a team of highly competitive specialists to act, if not cooperatively, at least interdependently. He plays by the rules, and tries to be fair in the meritocratic sense, since traditional prejudices and an autocratic attitude don't pay off. (Indeed, merito-cratic-minded admissions committees at Harvard and probably elsewhere have made it a policy to accept compulsive winners, regardless of race or religion.)

The game character is a person who derives his identity from his role or position on the team. Other than to win, his goals tend to be vague. Recently, I interviewed a highly successful industrial manager who admitted that he was no longer interested in his work. He had proved himself a winner, but he felt empty and without any goal in life. Once he stopped the compulsive activity and faced the meaninglessness of constantly competing, he experienced the depression due to the lack of a center.

A future society in which such character types are not only functional but dominant would be like Kurt Vonnegut's social nightmare, *Player Piano,* in which a small, highly trained and hard-working managerial class runs the automated factories while the majority of powerless consumers live off the dole. But if the centerless "protean" individual has been functional before, there is no guarantee that he will be in the future. It is exactly the pressure to negate the self that makes people dissatisfied today about work. This is the case not only for such highly trained individuals as engineers in large corporations, but also for blue-collar workers. Recent studies show an increasing demand, especially on the part of younger people, for work that requires more independence, judgment and craftsmanship.

Furthermore, the development of technology may make it possible to replace the most uncreative professional as well as manual work with computerized machines. Even today, managers in some of the most advanced technological corporations consider the most valuable workers the ones who are able to think for themselves, yet work cooperatively on projects they consider worthwhile. Such individuals also tend to be the ones who are most free to enjoy their leisure without a compulsive search for excitement, because they are interested in both learning and disciplined self-expression.

One of the most creative tasks of the future could be to redesign both industrial and bureaucratic work so that instead of requiring alienated individuals, the work stimulated the development of the self and favored active individuals. Such an organization of work would imply not only industrial democracy and a form of workers' management, but also the restructuring of the work groups themselves so as to eliminate purely rote tasks and hierarchical structures. The experiments by Robert Ford in the Bell System show a direction for such restructuring.

It should be added that the United States is not alone in suffering the character disorders of bureaucratic industrialism. A recent speech by Dr. Pyotr L. Kapitsa, the Soviet physicist, describes the centerless, consumer mentality as increasingly evident in the Soviet Union. Because of such people, he considers society unprepared to make profitable use of the material wealth and leisure time with which it has been endowed by the scientific-technological revolution. Dr. Kapitsa concludes that "the problem before education is therefore not only to provide man with the broad knowledge necessary to become a useful citizen, but to develop the independence of thought needed to develop a creative understanding of the world around him."

How can education be directed toward the development of the student's core? Does it mean returning to the Protestant Ethic and rugged individualism? But the society of farmer-frontiersmen and independent businessmen that produced such character traits has largely disappeared. There are still sub-cultures of artisans and small shopkeepers where children grow up with the emotional attitudes that support values of stubborn independence, self-abnegation, compulsive work and saving. Many of the most productive industrial engineers have these traits. This character is also found more in students at colleges which service ethnics with College Board scores about 500 than at the more selective colleges. But in our present day affluent society the consistent trend in employment is toward organization, in service industries and professions as well as in industry and government. Furthermore, powerful cultural forces have undermined the traditional hoarding attitudes that are the foundation of the Protestant Ethic and rugged individualism. The most important of these are advertising, the allure of the shiny products themselves, and the sexual revolution which does much to loosen the uptight self-protectiveness that holds the hoarding character together.

The real character alternatives in the post-industrial organizational society are either variations on the centerless, alienated character or an individuated productive-cooperative character. Fromm defined *productive character* as the person able to use his powers and realize the potentialities inherent in him. This implies an individuated person, one who is free to think for himself and who is guided by reason, since he can make use of his powers only if he knows what they are, how to use them and what to use them for. Productiveness means that the individual is centered, that he experiences himself as the subject of his powers, that he is not alienated from them, i.e., that they are not masked from him and transferred to an idolized person, team or institution. Fromm points out that productiveness implies an attitude to all of life. The productive person has "soul"; he gives birth to his own faculties and gives life to persons and things. He is also responsibly related to persons, things and ideas, in contrast to the centerless gamester or the narcissistic super-individualist or hipster.

Educational methods alone cannot guarantee the development of the productive character. However, it may be possible to chart a direction for educational programs to improve social character. As a start, there are four general principles that if developed by teachers would further education that strengthens the self. These principles may seem obvious to those teachers who are already sensitive to the issues discussed here. However, a number of teachers have encountered opposition from school administrations or parents when they have introduced innovations with the aim of strengthening the child's self. A coherent explanation of their purpose, in terms of principles, might have helped overcome some of the resistance. In stating the principles, the details of workable programs can only be pointed to. A great deal of research and development needs to be done.

The first principle is that *schooling should provide the discipline needed for the development of the self.* This requires first of all that the teachers know the authentic interests and potentialities in their students that could be developed, since "interests" claimed by students sometimes are merely responses to fads. (For teachers to develop knowledge about authentic interests and vocations would require changes in the content of most psychology programs.) It also requires a careful definition of "discipline." Traditionally we have thought the concept in terms of "orderly conduct," "control," "obedience," or, as a verb, "to punish." However, discipline also means "training that perfects," and it is only in this sense that we can speak of aiding the student to develop his powers to express himself, to pursue knowledge and wisdom with love, and to envision more joyful ways of living.

In *Zen in the Art of Archery,* Eugen Herrigel describes a discipline which gives meaning to tedious learning in terms of the ultimate goal of spontaneity. In a similar way, children can understand the purpose of having to work at elementary mathematics or music not as a means to get ahead, but as a discipline for being able to make work into serious play. In a recent article, "The Three C's and Discipline for Freedom" (*The School Review,* February 1971) I have described the discipline of the self as including the ability to concentrate, to think critically and to communicate (to express oneself and to listen). Such discipline develops naturally if rooted in a strong sense of self. A program initiated by Mrs. Elton Warren in the Bronx appears an example of a technique which sets this direction for young children, who are helped to find their own rhythms. Mrs. Warren reports that "once the child finds his own rhythm, he is better able to hear those of others."

The discipline of the self, if developed in childhood, arms a person to resist the organized distractions of the environment, equips him to doubt and unmask deceptive appearances, and emphasizes that the quality of his relatedness to others improves with systematic work.

The second principle is that *education should reinforce the natural development of the self.* This means that educational programs should be informed by continual study of the psychosocial and physical developmental process. Studies of human development sometimes isolate one aspect of development from the whole. Recent critics have pointed out that programs for cognitive development generally ignore emotional growth. But those who speak for "the whole child" themselves overlook crucial questions. Jean Piaget's early work on the moral judgment of children and other studies indicate that at the time children enter school, they are also struggling with a developing sense of self and with a new potential to be critical toward authority. How do techniques geared toward speeding the child's "cognitive" development or emotional expressiveness affect the child's character development? How do they come to grips with egocentrism and competitiveness?

If the adolescent's goal is to individuate himself, to become an individual, he finds little help from his schooling. Real *individuation* is a life-long process that requires independence, discipline and commitment; to become "oneself" is a work of art. In contrast, *individualism* is a broad concept that covers many different character-types, varying from the stubborn rebel to the passive consumer who buys his own thing. The normal adolescent would welcome a deeper understanding of individuation and what it requires. Instead, he often falls into the illusion of individualism through wearing certain clothes, listening to certain kinds of music or adopting unique mannerisms.

The same problems confront adolescents in high school and entering college. Erik Erikson's studies have shown that this period is a time of conflict, of struggle between "ego identity" (centeredness) vs. role diffusion and later, between narcissism and deeper relatedness. While Erikson's work is frequently cited by educators, we know little about methods to further a healthy sense of the individual self. One suggestion in this direction is David Riesman's idea of encouraging college students to develop aspects of themselves which they avoid because of fear they will not do well or look good. In some new therapeutic-educational approaches, emotions are emphasized at the expense of intellectual, moral and spiritual concerns; some overly facile encounter group methods feed adolescent narcissism without developing the means for deeper relatedness to others. In contrast, Rolando Weissman, who is studying psychoanalysis and social psychology with me, has taught experimental courses with the goal of developing psychospiritual consciousness. His work suggests that high school seniors can learn to understand symbolic language, including dreams, in such a way as to increase their consciousness about the structure of the world and their own specific role in it. Most important, the analysis of dreams makes the students aware of pressures and impulses to self betrayal, and this knowledge gives them an awareness of significant decisions they must make.

The third principle is that *in teaching a constant effort must be made to clarify the purpose of study and make explicit the values implied.*

Once goals and values are made explicit, the student is able to decide for himself whether or not to accept them. If they are not explicit, he tends to be mystified. The professor who honestly confronts his students doesn't present the choice of areas of study as representing "the field" but as a particular approach to knowledge which has ascertainable implications for man and represents a particular set of priorities. Some of the most productive student protest has clarified and opposed hidden purposes and values in the university which have supported militarism or the megamachine.

The new PhD program of the Institute for Policy Studies and the Union Graduate School in Washington has built into it the principle that the student must not only learn to examine the human and social implications of innovative projects but also to accept responsibility for them. While this program defines its purposes in terms of social action, it is sometimes necessary to repeat that there are, of course, other valid purposes for studying the arts and sciences. A valid purpose implies that learning is not alienated from the self but rather is an expression or fulfillment of one's deepest interests, principles and convictions. Once purposes are fully analyzed, then individuals who share them can join together in projects which do not require the loss of self in order to achieve cooperation. Otherwise, cooperation must be achieved by force or seduction.

The analysis of purpose needs to be made continually, although not obsessively. Purposes must be re-evaluated and renewed to keep them from changing direction or going underground. Psychoanalysis provides considerable clinical evidence that irrational purposes are often like secret plots disguised by cover stories. These purposes can only be maintained if they remain hidden; in the light of reason, they are seen as mad. In contrast, rational purposes rooted in love of life do not have to be unconscious, because they are usually shared by others.

The final principle is that *teaching techniques should develop the student's activeness.* If we do not use games, TV presentations and other exciting motivations, how is it possible to teach those students who seem to resist more traditional methods? Would teachers have to be tough disciplinarians? The answer is to be found in the testimony of many non-authoritarian, stimulating teachers who have activated students by centering the learning process in the child's own experience. Joseph Featherstone has described this method as practiced in the United Kingdom. Sylvia Ashton-Warner, Herbert Kohl and others have demonstrated that an active interest in reading and writing is developed when the themes are generated by the students. The principle of "activeness" implies self-direction and purpose. In *The Revolution of Hope* Fromm makes it a central principle of humanistic management. It has been applied to education by Paolo Freire, who contrasts the active method of dialogue and problem posing to the passive "banking" and "nutritional" approaches to teaching. In the banking approach, knowledge is deposited in students to be withdrawn on order in tests; the nutritional approach means feeding the students the knowledge the teacher considers lacking. In both methods, the teacher's authority is based fundamentally on his position in the hierarchy. In contrast, dialogue implies that teacher and student are both seeking the answer to a question that interests them. The authority of the teacher rests on his knowledge of theory, methods and research findings relevant to answering that question. Dialogue is not a magical form that replaces all lectures or learning from books. Rather, it is a way of teaching students to think in terms of problems, to take seriously their puzzlement and to consider alternatives to things as they are.

The student begins to become more active as he learns to translate his questions into scientific or bibliographic research. A few years ago, I joined Professors Douglas Dowd, an economist; Marie Augusta Neal, a sociologist; and John Rensenbrink, a political scientist, in developing and presenting an introductory course in the social sciences that incorporated the principle of dialogue and problem posing. (See Michael Maccoby, "The Cornell Introductory Course in the Social Sciences." *Harvard Educational Review,* Summer 1967). The title of the course was "Why Are There Poor People in a Rich Society like the United States?," a question that none of the professors could easily answer and each considered important to investigate. The course not only invited the students to ask their own questions, but also presented the example of the dialogue among the professors who had to confront their own differences and biases. In the course of study, the students also began to face themselves, to ask whether they cared about the question or whether they were only interested in being entertained or in getting good grades.

These principles of teaching are meant to provide a psychological basis for innovation in schooling. They require, of course, teachers who strive to be themselves, to combine love of learning with respect for the self in others. However, even if these principles were adopted and applied by productive teachers, all the students would not change instantly, since the educational system is only one part of the character-forming culture. In many schools, among them some of the most "innovative" ones, strong resistance would be expressed by both students and teachers. Many would worry that such emphasis on the self would not prepare students for entrance exams and college admission. On the other side, there would be complaints that any discipline is oppressive and that students should just learn what they wish. The latter arugment both ignores the need for structured learning and the power of family and the media. By the time they reach school, many children have been made to doubt their perceptions and interests; unless teachers affirm and help to develop their potentialities, these students will be likely to follow the going fads with no chance to become individuated. As to the worry about college admission, this depends in large part on the responsiveness of higher education.

Will the schools and universities reinforce the dehumanizing alternatives of post-industrial social character, or consciously adopt the goal of developing a discipline for the productive character?

25 the role of futuristics in education

Chris Dede
Draper Kauffman, Jr.

The fundamental rationale for studying the future has been stated succinctly by John Platt (1966, p. 100): "High morality depends upon accurate prophecy." Whatever you hold to be good—be it your own freedom and well-being, the survival of this nation, or the survival of the human species—you cannot judge the value of an action unless you have some idea of its consequences. The less certain you are of those consequences, the less certain you must be that your actions will contribute to what you consider to be "good."

The loss of the ability to predict the consequences of one's actions is, in a very real sense, the loss of the ability to control or cope with one's environment. Beyond a certain degree, this "loss of fate control" is debilitating to any organism, and especially to man. We are now in a society which is changing too fast and becoming too complicated for us to predict successfully the long-term consequences of our actions by conventional means.

Futuristics as a profession is intended to increase our "fate control" as a society and, ultimately, as a species. As an academic discipline (which we distinguish as Future Studies) it has, in addition to the function of training futurists, the purpose of increasing the individual student's sense of "fate control" by providing him with a more realistic understanding of the alternative futures that may confront him.

Not only can such an understanding help him to make life decisions more effectively, it can also innoculate him in advance against the cultural "disease" of "future shock," by taking much of the surprise out of rapid social change.

> Three hundred and fifty years after his death, scientists are still finding evidence to support Cervantes' succinct insight into adaptational psychology: 'Forewarned is fore-armed'. Self-evident as it may seem, in most situations we can help individuals adapt better if we simply provide them with advance information about what lies ahead (Toffler, p. 371).

This last point is far from trivial, and is sufficient reason in itself to justify a program in future studies. A man of 45 today is frequently just entering the most productive and influential period of his life. Yet his education and world-view date from the 1930's and 40's, from a world which has already largely ceased to exist. Already, many such individuals are increasingly bewildered and upset by events which are simply incomprehensible in their frame of reference. Others, of course, have continued to adapt and have managed to maintain a Weltanschauung in reasonable consonance with "reality." The human species seems to have as wide a variation in adaptability as it does in most things. But if, as appears likely, 1995 will be even more different from 1970 than 1970 was from 1945, how many more people will be pushed beyond their ability to adapt? Analysis of future possibilities, "living" by imagination in alternative future worlds, and a better understanding of the process of change itself can all help reduce the number of victims of too-rapid change.

> What passes for education today, even in our "best" schools and colleges, is a hopeless anachronism. Parents look to education to fit their children for life in the future. Teachers warn that lack of education will cripple a child's chances in the world of tomorrow. Government ministries, churches, the mass-media—all exhort young people to stay in school, insisting that now, as never before, one's future is almost wholly dependent upon education.
>
> Yet for all this rhetoric about the future, our schools face backward toward a dying system, rather than forward to the emerging new society. Their vast energies are applied to cranking out . . . people tooled for survival in a system that will be dead before they are.
>
> To help avert future shock, we must create a super-industrial education system. And to do this, we must search for our objectives and methods in the future, rather than the past (Toffler, p. 354-355).

So the primary objective for the individual is twofold: to increase his emotional ability to survive the buffeting of rapid change, and to increase his rational basis for, and his skill in, making long-term plans and decisions.

> For education, the lesson is clear: its primary objective must be to increase the individual's "cope-ability"—the speed and economy with which he can adapt to continual change . . . .
>
> It is no longer sufficient for Johnny to understand the past. It is not even enough for him to understand the present, for the here-and-now environment will soon vanish. Johnny must learn to anticipate the direction and rate of change. He must, to put it technically, learn to make repeated, probabilistic, increasingly long-range assumptions about the future. And so must Johnny's teachers (Toffler, p. 355).

Our basic thesis is simple: *No* school can sensibly claim to educate its students if it fails to make available to those students whatever knowledge exists about *their* world—the future. In other times and in other cultures, it has usually seemed reasonable to assume that the future would—for the most part—resemble the past. This assumption has not always been valid, as rapid transformations and cataclysms of the past can show, and it is very probably not valid today. We can be virtually certain that life in this country twenty years from now will be drastically different in many ways from life in this country today. Yet our schools appear determined to educate students for life in a society and in a world which they will never experience as adults. Future studies attempts to correct this situation.

The intellectual objectives for the students in a future studies course or program are relatively straightforward. They should be exposed to the conclusions of a number of futurists concerning the next fifteen to one hundred years. They should become aware of a number of presently existing trends (e.g., population growth, per capita income changes, the gap between "rich" and "poor" nations, food production, resource exhaustion, transportation and communication, and so on) and the consequences if these trends continue. They should be aware of the most probable developments in technology in the next few decades and should give some thought to the possible consequences of those developments. Finally, they should gain a sufficient familiarity with, and understanding of, the methods of futuristics to be able to judge the reliability and utility of those methods for themselves.

Though they make a lengthy list, these objectives (interpreted appropriately for a particular group of students) can be fairly easily achieved from a few sources and one or two experiments with various techniques. The psychological objectives—increased ability to cope with rapid change, and the habit of thinking in terms of probabilities and planning for alternatives—are easier to describe but much harder to achieve, especially in a single semester or year. The most successful approaches to this problem require the student to "live" imaginatively in a variety of alternative future worlds and to pre-visualize his responses to a variety of high-change situations.

In addition to its importance in classroom use, futuristics is also of great importance to educators outside the classroom. In fact, futuristics can provide the only possible solution to a fundamental dilemma in American education. Education as a process for solving social problems requires a very long time to show results—at least ten years—and for significant social change it is more like thirty years, yet the American public demands immediate solutions from education as soon as a problem "crests" and forces itself into the public awareness.

It should be reasonably obvious, for example, that a sensible elementary school should be anticipating (and preparing its students to cope with) the problems of the 1980's, rather than reacting to the problems of the 1960's. However, the normal pattern, reaction rather than anticipation, is enforced by several constraints. Some of these constraints are structural and are inherent in many of our state and local political systems, but historically the most important one has been the sheer difficulty of realistic anticipation.

Futuristics is no crystal ball, of course, and "The Future" remains unknowable. What the futurist does, instead of searching for *the* future, is to devise probable sets of *alternative* futures. These, when properly constructed and employed, can be nearly as useful to the planner or administrator as knowledge of a single, certain "Future." (In fact, as any connoisseur of science fiction time travel stories knows, the possibility of knowledge of "The Future" implies that the future is fixed and immutable, and the knowledge would therefore be worthless to the knower.)

Among the many techniques developed over the past twenty years for use in constructing alternative futures, four are probably most applicable to education. These are simulations, Delphi studies, scenario writing, and trend analysis, each of which we will discuss briefly.

Simulations. Simulations (Abt, 1970) model "real-life" situations or institutions. A simulation selects certain critical aspects of the situation it models and uses these to attempt to duplicate the behavior of its subject. The game Monopoly, for example, is a simulation (a poor one) of real estate investment. Simulations in which people play roles are often called "games;" those without human "actors" are usually run on a computer. Games are useful in futuristics primarily because they give participants a better sense of how the system works and the range of its possible alternative behaviors. Students playing a simulation of the battle of Waterloo, for example, will not necessarily evolve a defeat for Napoleon; any game has many possible resolutions, depending on the decisions of the players.

Computer simulations can achieve much higher orders of complexity and sophistication than is practical for gaming simulations. They can also systematically generate and test large numbers of possibilities quickly and easily. The recent study, *Limits to Growth* (Meadows, 1972), is an excellent example of the capabilities of computer simulations. It attempts to model this planet's environmental/technological/economic life-support system over the next two hundred years, and tests the effects of varying social, economic, and environmental decisions on this model.

Delphi Studies. Delphi studies (Weaver, 1970) assume that a panel of experts can reach an accurate consensus on the most probable time of a possible future event. To minimize the effects of a persuasive or prestigious expert, opinions are usually solicited by mail. After an initial survey, this polling is repeated twice, with the answers on the previous round sent back to the experts, so that their estimates will tend to converge. Naturally, the final estimate of time range is only as accurate as the panel's ability to estimate the future. Futurists can draw upon Delphi estimates of when a given innovation (e.g., computer assisted instruction) may be operational in outlining a set of alternative futures.

Scenario Writing. Scenario writing, which is basically the controlled, disciplined use of intuition is the device most often used by futurists to generate alternative futures. A scenario writer first envisions a future state of the system he is describing (say, the U.S. educational system in 1980). He then attempts to describe how the system reached this future state. This combination of a future and a history leading up to it is called a scenario. The plausibility of his description of the future depends on how realistic his history is. If the history called for quadrupling the federal education budget in one year, we would think his scenario unlikely and useless. Usually, the scenario writer constructs a whole set of scenarios which together exhaust the likely futures for the system.

Trend Analysis. Trend analysis consists of extrapolating a set of past statistics (e.g., relative supply of and demand for teachers) into the future. In the 1950's all projections indicated that we needed massive teacher training programs to supply enough teachers. Now, because enrollments in teacher training programs were higher than expected, we find we have a surplus of teachers—and more pouring onto the job market every year. A new force has altered the dynamics of this situation; simple extrapolation of a past trend is no longer sufficient to predict the future. In using trend analysis, futurists attempt to consider as many of these "discontinuities" and "system breaks" as possible.

One point that must be stressed is that a future projection often affects the very future it tries to describe. If a scenario describes, persuasively and plausibly, a sequence of actions leading to a future which people judge to be desirable, then people will generally attempt to perform those actions, and the scenario becomes a "self-fulfilling prophecy." If instead it convincingly describes action leading to an unpleasant future, people will try to avoid such action and the scenario becomes a "self-defeating prophecy." A classic, intentional example of the latter is Orwell's novel *1984*.

Intentionally self-fulfilling or self-defeating prophecies are generally viewed as desirable. If *1984* has made us more aware of the dangers of the technological police state and thus helped us to avoid that destination, we are grateful. Some forecasts, however, turn out to be self-fulfilling or self-defeating quite unintentionally and/or harmfully. In a recent example, a speech by a member of the British parliament predicting the devaluation of the pound, caused an immediate run on the pound, which in turn forced the British government to devalue. Caution is obviously called for in such circumstances.

Obviously, most educators have neither the time nor the expertise to use futuristic tools as futurists do. (Although in some cases it turns out to be necessary to do just that. When the Office of Education funded two Educational Policy Research Centers a few years ago, both centers found that they had to do extensive original analysis on the possible futures of the U.S. in order to be able to make intelligent recommendations on educational policy.) Fortunately, there is now available to educators a wealth of background material, a number of futuristic tools which have been specifically tailored for use by laymen, and a growing corps of futurists who are experienced consultants in "micro-futures"—medium and long-range studies of alternative possibilities for small social units.

This recent wealth of materials, methods, and resources also applies to the classroom curriculum. In the past, teachers have seldom been able to discuss the future with students, for few curriculum materials dealing with the future were available. Further, teachers and students alike have often felt impotent to affect the future in any significant way, and so have tended to avoid discussions in this area. Futuristics, however, provides a means of understanding how the future is shaped and offers a forum for discussing which future we want and how we can affect its emergence. The proliferation of books on futuristics and emerging futures, moreover, provides the teacher with a wealth of curriculum materials which require no special expertise for use and which are "relevant" without being trivial.

On the secondary level, the assignment of well-written science fiction such as *Nightmare Age* (Pohl) can act as an excellent stimulus to classroom discussions on the future. The teacher can then move to more factual inputs, using texts such as *The Meaning of the 20th Century* (Boulding), *The Future as History* (Heilbroner), *Profiles of the Future* (Clarke), *Futures Conditional* (Theobald), *Future Shock* (Toffler), *The Biological Time Bomb* (Taylor), *Unless Peace Comes* (Calder), *Technological Man* (Ferkiss), and *High School 1980* (Eurich). Magazines as varied as *Scientific American, Saturday Review, Analog Science Fiction,* and *Popular Science* frequently carry informative articles exploring future implications of scientific and sociological innovations.

On all levels, playing (or even designing) a simulation can be a good way of involving students in thinking about the future. Simulations of societal interactions give children an idea of the complex interplay of different forces which produce an outcome and may induce an understanding of why change is so prevalent and yet so difficult in our society. Abt's book *Serious Games* has several good examples of this sort of simulation. Students can test their intuitive models of the workings of our society by constructing simple simulations based on them and observing whether the outcomes are plausible. A particular situation (say, a political election) can be simulated, and the simulation outcome tested as a prediction.

The Delphi technique can be used, even with very young children, to interest students in what the future will be like. The teacher simply draws up a list of provocative questions—how old will you be when . . . all the bombs in the world are dismantled?—and polls the children on their answers. These estimates can be plotted on a time scale to show where each child's answer lies relative to those of the other students and to the class average. In the ensuing discussion, the teacher can emphasize that there is no "right" answer, and can discuss the prophecy/prediction effect of looking at the future. Finally, the poll can be repeated to see if and how the children change their answers.

The interactions between technology and society can also readily be discussed with young children in a way that will help them prepare for their future. For example, Taylor in *The Biological Time Bomb* gives an overview of many developments in biology that will have a substantial impact on our cultural values in the next five to ten years. Using flannel board cut-outs of body parts, the teacher can initiate a "build your own future body" session.* The children can design their own future bodies, using human, animal, and machine parts, just as may someday be possible. The class can then go on to discuss how they feel about being able to design their bodies, and how such a development might affect their lives. These students can thus be prepared for some difficult decisions that they must face, and they can begin to understand how technology shapes values and values shape technology.

In summary, many of our present overwhelming concerns in education (e.g., drugs, financial deficits, proliferation of knowledge, and affective curricula) could have been anticipated far in advance of the point at which society's demands for a solution forced educators to acknowledge them. And they could have been dealt with far more easily then than now as they engulf us. Because we must now solve problems that we did not bother to foresee, we have neither the energy nor the resources to prepare for the next contingent of problems. To cope with this dilemma, we must institutionalize the process of anticipating the future in education through goal-setting and planning. Education is our society's foremost mechanism for dealing with the future; by gearing education to the past, we ensure its failure. Futuristics gives us the tools we need to focus education on the future.

By using futuristic predictions in planning, educators can anticipate the effects of future developments. For example, to have known in 1965 that six years later we might face a vast financial crisis and a mounting drug problem on every level of the educational system would certainly have helped us to prepare for—or avoid—these contingencies. Similarly, today, when we read books such as Taylor's *The Biological Time Bomb,* we realize that in five years we will be confronting in the classroom ethical problems arising from the technological developments he describes. We can develop plans, resources, curricula, and institutions to meet this future problem now—if we are farsighted enough to do so.

The study of the future need not be another esoteric discipline that only specialists can practice; rather, it can be used by educators both inside and outside of the classroom to re-orient education toward the future. In our rapidly changing society, the implementation of futuristics in every school in America is not a luxury but a necessity.

REFERENCES

Abt, Clark: Serious Games, New York, Viking Press, 1970.
Ayres, Robert N.: Technological Forecasting and Long-Range Planning. New York, McGraw-Hill, 1969.
Boulding, Kenneth E.: The Meaning of the Twentieth Century. New York, Harper Colophon, 1965.
Calder, Nigel (ed.): Unless Peace Comes. New York, Viking, 1968.
Calder, Nigel (ed.): The World in 1984 (2 vols.). New York, Penguin, 1965.
Clarke, Arthur C.: Profiles of the Future. New York, Bantam, 1967.
De Jouvenal, Bertrand: The Art of Conjecture. New York, Basic, 1967.
Drucker, Peter F.: The Age of Discontinuity. New York, Harper and Row, 1969.
Eurich, Alvin C. (ed.): High School 1980. New York, Pitman, 1970.
Ferkiss, Victor C.: Technological Man. New York, Mentor, 1969.
Green, Thomas: Post secondary education 1970-1990. Syracuse, Educational Policy Research Center, 1970.
Green, Thomas: Schools and communities: a look forward. Harvard Educational Review, Spring, 1969.

---

*This device was developed by Patricia Burke at the School of Education, University of Massachusetts, Amherst.

Heilbroner, Robert: The Future as History. Chicago, Evergreen, 1967.

Helmer, Olaf: Social Technology. New York, Basic, 1966.

Kahn, Herman, and Wiener, Anthony J.: The Year Two Thousand. New York, Macmillan, 1967.

Meadows, Donella, et al.: The Limits to Growth. New York, Universe Books, 1972.

Morphet, Edgar L. (ed.): Designing Education for the Future (7 vols.). New York, Citation, 1967-1969.

Orwell, George: 1984. New York, Harcourt, Brace and World, 1963.

Platt, John Rader: The Step to Man. New York, John Wiley and Sons, 1966.

Pohl, Frederick (ed.): Nightmare Age. New York, Ballantine Books, 1970.

Taylor, Gordon R.: The Biological Time Bomb. New York, New American Library, 1968.

Toffler, Alvin: Future Shock. New York, Random House, 1970.

Weaver, W. Timothy: The Delphi Method. Syracuse, Educational Policy Research Center, 1970.

the career 26
development
program

Charles H. Buzzell
Sophie S. Hollander

The schools have been held responsible for many recent major social crises. Efforts have been made to change many features in the educational system: tracks that inure, grades that demoralize, textbooks that anesthetize, seats that shackle, and walls that isolate. Traditional emphases have been altered. Recognition of the individual's needs for both self-esteem and competence has stimulated interest in vocational education. Moreover, occupational education has gained importance as an education with relevance. This has been especially true since the recent mandate from the Department of Health, Education and Welfare, "that every young person completing our school program at Grade 12 be ready to enter useful and rewarding employment." Various career education projects have emerged. The Career Development Program described here is unique in its computer-based, intensive, and comprehensive design, and in its potential for universal application.

It is no longer a question of "either-or," of vocational or academic education. Properly integrated at all levels of public education, the Career Development Program can supply the key to learning how to learn. By focusing on the student's direct experiences as primary resources, it provides "hands-on" situations for the application of what is known and for the exploration of the unknown. Using the arts and sciences in real-life situations, it stresses active involvement in the learning process. It can, in short, produce relevant education for a greater number of students and reduce the number of academic and social dropouts.

The present system of vocational education has an enviable record of both successful placement and performance of its graduates. This success has generated a tidal wave of applicants for occupational and technical training. There is now major concern because the limited numbers that can be served mean growing numbers will be denied access to any kind of skills training.

Integration of the Career Development Program into the total educational enterprise can resolve this problem. This computer-assisted skills training system can eliminate the iron-clad conventions in the schools that are currently under attack and can obviate the need for tracks, grades, textbooks, and even seats and classrooms. It can revolutionize the basic nature of the schools, providing an education that will better serve the purposes of today's society.

213

ORGANIZATION OF THE CAREER DEVELOPMENT PROGRAM

The Career Development Program offers a continuum of occupational education within a broad-based curriculum from kindergarten through adulthood. It is founded on the principle that the educational system should enable anyone, regardless of age or handicap, to participate satisfyingly and productively in society. This program can serve everyone—in the kindergarten's fantasy world of work, in the grade school's curiosity about the world of work, and in the high school's self-awareness and role in the world of work. In the street, in prison, or in a half-way house, the Career Development Program can serve the hard-core unemployed and the handicapped, and it can help each person to fulfill his potential as a participating member of society.

To correlate individuals with career options, the program identifies a wide variety of skills needed in the current job market. Critical analysis of over 400 current and emerging occupations has so far resulted in computer banking of more than 10,000 skills. It is expected that eventually over 50,000 skills will be identified. Behavioral objectives that have been mastered by successful job-holders are associated with each skill. These will be stored in the computer, with each behavioral objective assigned a position in a single continuous learning progression.

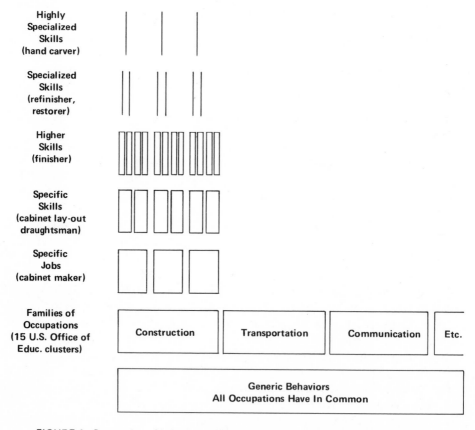

FIGURE 1 *Progression of behavioral objectives stored in computer-assisted curriculum.*

This computer-based program, encyclopedic in scope, now encompasses a comprehensive career education curriculum, as outlined in Figure 1. First, a broad range of generic behaviors, underlying all occupations, is identified. Beyond this base, families of occupations (such as the construction trades) are identified. Each family of occupations, in turn, is separated into specific jobs (such as carpenter or brick mason). Specific skills required in each job are identified (e.g., skills in cabinet making), and these are broken down successively into higher skills, specialized skills, and highly specialized skills. The computer also has stored a sequence of prerequisite learnings and tasks corresponding to each skill.

A learner may consult the computer to locate his position within the occupational skills continuum. He may request a listing of his accomplished skills and a listing of the skills required for a marketable level of proficiency in a given occupation.

THE INSTRUCTIONAL DESIGN

Since occupational education is a process of developing skills which are often amenable to objective evaluation, such education can be computer-assisted to advantage. The computer can select from the ordered continuum of behavioral objectives an instructional design which best develops a specific skill. This instructional design is a systematic arrangement of interdependent elements pertinent to achieving the behavioral objective, including prerequisite learnings, component tasks involved, environmental essentials for learning, and underlying conceptualizations (see Figure 2).

INSTRUCTIONAL OBJECTIVES FORM

Objective: Cut a compound miter using a radial arm saw.

Evaluation: Given a radial arm saw and a piece of 1 X 8 X 48 inch stock, cut a compound miter of 25 degrees of angle and 15 degrees of bevel, within ten minutes.

Signature: John Doe, Instructor   **Date:** January, 1973

Prerequisite Learnings	*Component Tasks*	*Environment*	*Concepts*
Identification and measurement of angles	1. Set "T" bevel	1. Stock	Friction
	2. Mark stock	2. Protractor	Conductivity
Use of protractor	3. Select proper blade	3. "T" Bevel	
Use of sliding "T" bevel	4. Adjust arm of saw to 25 degrees	4. Radial arm saw	
Use of radial arm saw		5. Safety glasses	
	5. Adjust motor read to 15 degrees	6. Pencil	
	6. Position stock on saw	7. Cross cut blade	
	7. Don safety glasses		
	8. Take trial nick and confirm accuracy		

FIGURE 2 *Instructional Design.*

Behavioral objectives specify expected outcomes in terms easily understood by teachers, students, employers, and the accountability-seeking taxpayers. Each objective states the expected student performance, the conditions under which it is to occur, and the minimal acceptable level of competency. Thus the intent of the learning task is clarified and teaching is strengthened.

The objective is defined in clear and measurable terms as in Figure 2. The action verbs in such prescriptions focus on the student behavior to be evaluated. The learner knows precisely what he must do to demonstrate success. With this defined, the student can pursue instruction enabling him to achieve the stated outcome.

However, before he begins, his prior learning and his readiness to perform must be assured. Each print-out lists specific skills, knowledge, and attitudes essential for the student to attempt to achieve the specified objective. All too often a learner repeatedly fails to achieve an objective because he has not earlier acquired a fundamental skill necessary to perform it.

The assessment of prerequisite learning is critical, particularly in work with disadvantaged populations. Lack of mastery of more fundamental learning may result in persistent failure when remedial work or restructuring the learning environment is all that is necessary for success. Two questions are extremely important in this process: (1) Are these prerequisites necessary to perform the specific objective, or are they upholding unrealistic standards solidified into a system? (2) Has careful scrutiny been made of more basic hidden learnings necessary for attaining success?

Once the prerequisites have been ascertained, strategies are provided to help the student arrive at the desired performance objective. A task analysis describes the most efficient sequence for performing operations, as in Figure 2. Sequencing is an essential element of the instructional design, encouraging the student to plan the task as a logical progression of activities. As he does so, he is able to determine the needed tools, materials, and safety precautions.

The learning environment is crucial to learning. The print-out not only prescribes tools and media, but also suggests motivational devices and conditions to enhance a mood of inquiry. The environment is planned so as to promote exploratory and curiosity drives in the direction specified by the objective. The student is given a list of tools and media to be provided, as in Figure 2.

The learning environment can be enhanced by setting up live situations in the classroom, such as a mass production project. Rather than tedious class exercises, the student engages in the construction of jigs and fixtures. Cutting a compound miter becomes an element of mass production. As in industry, he is encouraged to increase his output, because increased production yields increased profits. The project might be culminated by a class bazaar at which the products are sold to the public. Similarly, carpentry objectives could be coordinated with a home construction project.

While pursuing the specific objective, the student's experiences are broadened. He is making conscious choices, considering and resolving problems, discovering strengths and weaknesses. He is involved in the process of self-development as much as in the performance itself, growing both in self-esteem and in competence. The instructional design provided by the computer reinforces such growth by specifying the general concepts underlying the student's performance.

Occupational education can be both an end in itself and a means to some further end. For, despite the specificity of skills training, the student's experiences may be a starting point for further, more general, knowledge. The teacher, as facilitator in the process, helps the student structure these experiences, sharpens his awareness of underlying principles, and points out general classifications and essential similarities. It is the teacher's responsibility to furnish opportunities for basic concepts developed in one context to be transferred to other situations. Such mind-stretching exercises in the transfer of knowledge, wherein the student recognizes situations governed by the same underlying concepts, can be courted through team teaching. Thus, the science teacher, who often deals in abstract scientific principles, can participate in the student's concrete shop experience. The expertise of the science instructor, combined with that of the carpentry instructor, expands the basic concept into an additional dimension.

Consider, in the carpentry example used above, the concept of friction at work. If the student used too high a cutting speed, undissipated heat generated by friction with the blade would cause the stock to burn and smoke and could ruin the saw blade. The abstract concept of friction now becomes a relevant lesson. The learner is more apt to modify his behavior because he has had a concrete experience with the abstract principle.

From a concrete experience such as the burning of the stock, the student can be assisted to arrive at the abstract concept of conductivity. Upon observing that the heat generated by the friction is confined to the cutting area, he may be made receptive to the concept of conductivity and the fact that wood is a poor conductor of heat. Further instances can broaden his perception and understanding of the concept, i.e., that wood handles are used for frying pans and other cooking utensils, and that homes built of wood tend to remain warm in winter by maintaining the heat within and cool in summer by preventing the heat outdoors from penetrating.

Instructors in several areas might apply the same basic concept at the same time to reinforce the underlying principle. Thus, the electrical instructor could show that wood is also a poor conductor of electricity. Meanwhile, the metal shop instructor could illustrate conductivity in metals. The student, alert to the fundamental concept, will broaden his perceptions and learn to deal more effectively with future abstractions.

A data bank of such concepts with strategies for their transfer is being established to invite in-depth learning experiences. Development of these pertinent concepts gives the learner a resilience of mind adaptable to new occupations, helping to protect him against job attrition or obsolescence.

Beyond this, the instructional design overcomes the vexing problem of rating student achievement. It offers aid to overcome the old traps—completion of a series of textbook operations in a prescribed fifteen weeks' course and unreliable subjective judgments of ability by one teacher. Instead, this instructional design evaluates behavior demonstrated against minimum acceptable performance criteria. The instructor testifies to the specified skill development and the learner receives documentation of his achievement. This documentation can be taken to potential employers as a hard data analysis of an individual's ability.

IMPLEMENTATION

The computer-based design of the Career Development Program facilitates the logistics of expanding and integrating occupational education within the educational system.

The points at which various occupations diverge from less specialized bases of skills and knowledge have been determined. By using this information, the computer can help a student re-examine what he has learned and can place him at an appropriate level in the training program of his choice. It can also be used to help a student transfer from one program to another with a minimum of duplication of instruction. Similarly, it can help in retraining programs, by identifying precisely what the student needs to learn.

Separating the curriculum into distinct skills packages facilitates the introduction and implementation of occupational offerings in other facilities as well as in schools, under cooperative plans, and in an individualized way. Instant skills training packets, readily available, can be used for dropouts outside the school or in correctional institutions. The conventional four-year curriculum does not conform to the entrances and exits of prison inmates, for example. Occupational programs that start with rote learning of abstract terminology and follow the traditional cover-the-textbook method may serve very well for those committed to life sentences, but for the short-term incarcerated or the social dropout, who are much more mobile learners, specific marketable skills packets are especially practical. These satisfy the urge for immediacy and offer impetus to attain higher goals. The learner can build up a series of skill packages to become, ultimately, a skilled craftsman.

These modules developing a single skill fit well into the pattern of industry's current demand. Industry has found it profitable to employ persons specialized in single skills. The construction industry, for example, hires roofers solely to apply asphalt shingles on houses in a development tract. Dry wall specialists, in turn, are contracted to install dry wall exclusively, while tapers follow behind to tape joints.

What do the schools have to do to implement the program? The schools have to accept the Career Development concept and institute a curriculum for total involvement in it. All students at all grade levels should be able to seek learning experiences relevant to their career orientation. Personal career choice goes through a variety of stages as one matures: (1) the fantasy stage in the kindergarten and primary grades; (2) the exploratory stage of growing awareness; (3) the stage of development; and finally, (4) the stage of responsibility and maintenance. The school system must structure the curriculum along similar developmental lines. Figure 3 represents a broad-based curriculum offering career options, both academic and occupational, and a variety of experiences relative to the world of work.

The student enters kindergarten and the lower grades with fantasies about work. These can be nurtured by giving students an appreciation of the function of work in our society and an understanding of work as a satisfying and rewarding way of life. During these years, innate resources, abilities, and imagination can be continually fostered by widening horizons. "Technology for Children" can expose the young child to the many-faceted aspects of work. This will help lay the groundwork for later self-awareness and self-evaluation of abilities and interests.

Experiences should be provided in the middle grades that give the student an opportunity to explore the world of work. Vocations and broad families of occupations can be introduced, such as the trades, the service industries, and the professional fields. The student should be given opportunities for "hands-on" operations in areas such as transportation, communication, and construction.

By sampling various types of work and "trying on" a variety of occupational roles, the student acquires an understanding of the duties and requirements of different occupations. Thus, he is further prepared for occupational planning commensurate with his recognized abilities, interests, and opportunities.

Entering the developmental stage, he is ready to consider the specific programs offered by the high school. He can select from many different programs, ranging from those preparing him directly for employment to those emphasizing college-directed academic work. With real exposure to occupational possibilities, the student will be able

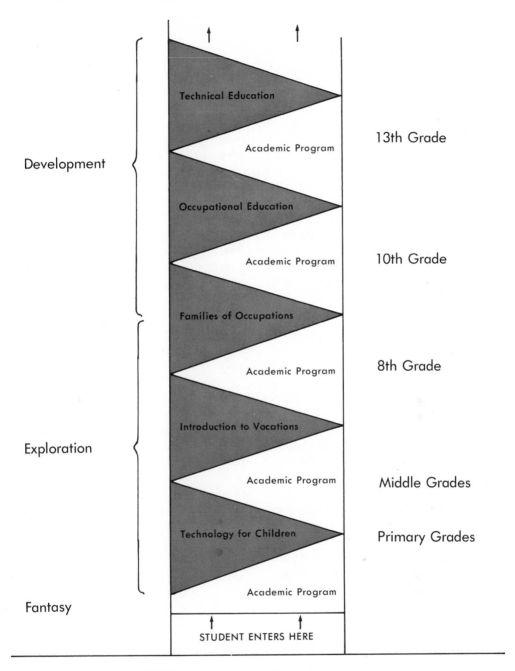

FIGURE 3 *Integration into the educational system.*

to make real choices. Upon graduating from high school, he will possess marketable skills. His educational background will allow him to continue his education academically or technically, as well as to find immediate employment. It provides a perfect option for students who wish to attend college but not immediately after high school.

The Career Development Program thus puts into effect nongraded education and individualized instruction, and buries forever the lock-step, the closed shop, and the doctrine of irrevocable choice. If a student prefers greater involvement in the occupational aspects of the curriculum, he chooses the courses that develop these skills. If, on the other hand, he prefers greater emphasis on the academic program, he pursues such courses, allowing as much time for occupational electives as he wishes. An individual emerges from such an educational curriculum with all options open to him, not trapped in an area which he can come to regard as a dead end.

In committing itself to the Career Development Program, the school faculty must be prepared for an instructional design that measures learning. Thus, they must fashion instruction so that learning progress can be seen and measured. They must come to describe the expected learning in behavioral terms, accepting the basic tenet that as learning occurs behavior is shaped. Only strong positive support of this concept by the school administration affords the program a chance for success.

The subprojects within the major computer-assisted design offer many additional services to the schools. The program can function as a continually updated resource for career guidance and can assist students in discovering how job behaviors relate to their own attitudes and traits. This can encourage them to make informed career choices commensurate with their ability. It can also serve as a continually updated resource for teachers and curriculum planners seeking instructional material for new and emerging occupations.

IMPLICATIONS

Without slighting the present excellence of vocational education, this Career Development scheme is offered as a resource to keep creativity alive and stimulate untapped potentials in the student, and to connect all areas of learning in formal education with real life. A school curriculum can be most in touch with real life when it is relevant to productive and rewarding employment. By offering skills training at the level of job entry, it promises a productive life for all.

The Career Development Program can well supply the bridge between the school system and society. It forces the schools to be in some measure responsible for society's problems, to respond to society's opportunities, and to be responsive to society's needs. Widespread use of individualized skill devlopment packages to prepare for immediate job entry at any level may help create a new social climate—one that may produce solutions to many of the social concerns of our day.

uncommon sensing: 27
a model for
multi-media learning

James Morrow
Murray Suid
Roberta Suid

NATURAL LEARNING

If you had been along on a recent class picnic of ninth graders from Boston's Martin Luther King School, you would have seen one youngster sitting under a tree reading a comic book; another taking Polaroid photographs while waiting for the fish to bite; a girl pouring over a true romance magazine; and a group of students dancing to music from transistor radios and battery-powered record players.

These students brought several different media with them, not because their picnic needed audio-visual aid to supplement the Kool-Aid or because their senses needed massaging, but simply because in our culture media are a natural source of pleasure and information.

It has not always been so. Portable and inexpensive tools for recording and presenting sounds and visual images are the consequences of a relatively recent technological revolution. The extension of perception and communication through electrochemical media is a historically unique phenomenon making the twentieth century an age of *uncommon sensing*.

In the schools, media are mainly used to assist teachers in supplementing and clarifying information presented via writing or speech. This audio-visual aid approach places the student in a passive role and ignores media as modes of learning in and of themselves. To put it more concretely, schools seldom feature the rich, varied, and entertaining kind of learning which characterized the King school picnic.

This is not to say that schools ought to confine their curricula to comic books, teenage magazines, and pop music. The classroom should enrich and extend the students' out-of-school experience, not duplicate it. Despite what some McLuhanites think or hope, students do *not* automatically learn everything the media have to offer. To use them to best advantage requires a systematic approach to the tools and rules involved. One model which has already been used with some success by teachers and curriculum planners is called the Wheel.

FIGURE 1

REAL LEARNING AND WHEEL LEARNING

The Wheel is a picture of how people learn in our culture. Consider, for example, how most of us have learned about the war in Southeast Asia and how we have shared our insights and feelings with others. The following experiences may come to mind (Fig. 1):

1. Seeing or making the peace sign; watching or taking part in marches
2. Hearing speeches and talking with friends
3. Seeing or wearing symbolic designs such as flags, decals, the peace symbol, military stripes, and so on.
4. Reading newspapers or books; writing letters to the editor or to a friend
5. Looking at photographs such as the Pulitzer-prize winning photo of the execution of a suspected Viet Cong terrorist by the Saigon chief of police, or the My Lai photographs
6. Hearing the news on radio or listening to patriotic or peace-oriented phonograph records
7. Watching movies (anything from *The Anderson Platoon* to *The Green Berets*)
8. Watching a Presidential press conference on TV

Such a list indicates the potential multimedia learning has for creating more lively and natural learning in schools.

In real life learning, media experiences tend to be overlapping and cyclic, occurring in no particular order. The Wheel model tries to capture this spontaneity and redundancy by organizing media experiences into a holistic pattern that has no beginning and no end.

Just as important, the design implies that each type of experience has the potential to interact with some or all of the others.

Each experience segment of the "war wheel" was chosen to represent one of the eight distinct *media* (or *media groups*) that we have found most useful in classroom learning. Each comprises several submedia:

1. *The Body*—gesture, body language, dance, pantomime, smells
2. *Speech*—talking, singing and expressive nonverbal sounds such as crying, sighing or gagging
3. *Design*—all the two and three dimensional arts, including graphics, painting, sculpture, architecture
4. *Print*—written words, numbers, symbols, and signs such as *?*, *&,* and *+*
5. *Photography*—photographic prints, half-tone reproductions, slides (transparencies), and filmstrips
6. *Sound*—radio, recording (tape and disc), telephone, amplification, and music
7. *Movies*—silent and sound
8. *Television*—broadcast and closed-circuit

We give the media equal segments of the Wheel to emphasize their individual integrities and to legitimize the role of each in the learning process (Fig. 2).

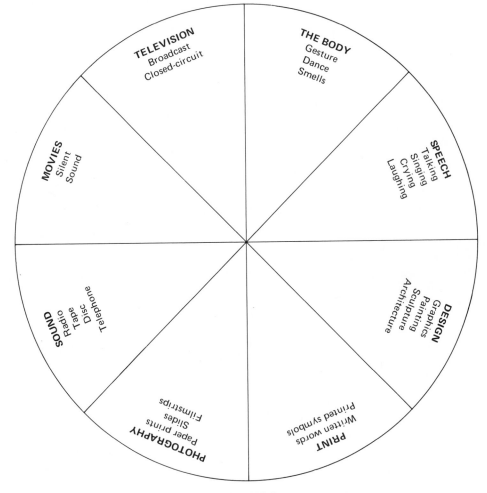

FIGURE 2

By reading the Wheel clockwise starting with *the body,* we can follow the chronological development of communication tools. The body, of course, was the first medium. Speech, in one perspective, is part of the body medium but it certainly developed after physical gesture, and the body itself remains important enough to class separately. The prehistoric paintings in the caverns of Altamira in Spain confirm the antiquity of the design medium, which is thought by some people to have preceded speech. Print (including the earliest writing as well as printing-press lettering) was by definition the first historic medium. The electrochemical half of the Wheel has developed almost instantaneously and simultaneously, but it is still possible to chart the progression from photography to amplified and recorded sound to the unifying of sight and sound in movies and television.

Some people equate "media" with "new media." They feel that the new media make the old obsolete. An extreme example of this view is the claim that the electronic media will kill off print, making reading an unnecessary skill. In reality, media don't kill each other off. From man's first meaningful grimace to the latest computer graphics, the evidence supports the idea that the family of media is harmonious and grows stronger with the arrival of each new member. Usually a new medium borrows first from the older media, then asserts its independence. Later it reveals new and often unexpected possibilities for an older medium, thereby renewing it.

Consider the relationship between radio and television. Initially, television copied old radio formats almost exclusively—westerns, quiz shows, news, comedy shows, and so on—and quickly drove most of these off radio. But it didn't kill radio. Radio developed new formats—music, all news, two-way talk radio—and became more powerful than ever. Meanwhile, television began to free itself from the older radio formats. Its unique powers of immediate and lifelike feedback made it a valuable tool in speech therapy, teacher training, theater rehearsals, sensitivity-training groups, medical teaching, and space exploration. The interaction of radio and television is hardly unique. Many of the media contain elements of some or all of the others. The point is that *media are continually evolving because of their dynamic interdependence.* Not only do we need all the media to heighten our powers of perception and communication, but the media themselves need each other in order to develop.

The truth of this yin-yang of dependence and independence among media has clearly been appreciated by the culture at large. Movies borrow from theater. Theater borrows from street demonstrations. Painters enlarge upon comics. Printers utilize photography. There is no isolation; no medium holds a monopoly over the others. Even in the home, there is a wealth of media: paper and pencils and crayons, still cameras and movie cameras, radios, TV's, phonographs, tape recorders, and sometimes even video cameras and active bodies, free to move and be expressive. How can we bring such freedom and diversity into the school?

WHEEL LEARNING IN SCHOOL

The Wheel is intended to suggest to teachers a more varied, natural, and active way of involving students in learning than is usually attempted in schools. It does not dictate *what* is to be learned—that is the choice of the teacher and (hopefully) the students. But it does begin to define *how* the learning might take place.

Wheel-learning is based on the observation that communication is a two-phase process. In the *active* phase, the communicator produces a message. He *gestures* or *says something* or *makes a photograph* or *writes a poem.* This creative act extends beyond the here-and-now. It encompasses the person's past experiences and his skills. It also involves his expectations of how the message will come out and how it will be received.

In the *reactive* phase, the communicator receives a message and reacts to it. He *hears a song* or *reads a story* or *views a film* and tries to fit it into a frame of reference. There is nothing passive about reacting. If you've ever tried to watch a movie, read a book, or listen to a speech while tired or distracted, you have noticed the importance of energy and concentration in message-receiving. Reacting can involve considerable experience, desire, and skill, as seen by comparing the responses of novices and experts to works in any medium—novels, movies, outstanding football plays, photographs, ballets, and so on.

We believe all learning includes the same two phases. The teacher, thus, has the twin responsibilities of helping students learn how to create their own messages in response to authentic problems and how to react in meaningful ways.

The Wheel may be thought of as the skeleton of a multimedia curriculum. It can help the teacher and the students define problems to solve and prepare experiences to react to. Under each medium on the rim of the Wheel, the teacher or students can write in

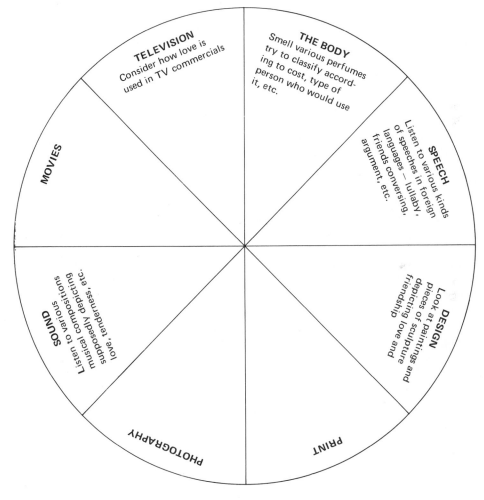

FIGURE 3

materials and ideas for exploring whatever content is to be confronted. This is called "creating a wheel," though actually the process calls for creating two Wheels—a Presentation Wheel which leads to reacting and a Problem Wheel which leads to active creation.

For example, a junior high teacher might wish to have students deal with the issues raised by the concept of love. Using the Wheel, the teacher begins to plan reactive experiences (Fig. 3). It is not necessary to include all or even most of the media every time. This decision will depend on many factors including resources, time, and student need.

When we talk about reacting, we don't mean that the teacher will play a love song and then test the students on the imagery. The proper model of reacting, which is based on learning in the real world, is far more varied and complex. It begins with the simple (re)act of "enjoying" or "disliking" the work which was presented. Too often in schools, this primary reactive decision is ignored—whatever the teacher presents is considered suitable for reacting to.

Beyond this, there is informal discussion of a new (or old) song, movie, book, poem, news story, or theory. Certainly, there should be this kind of free give-and-take within the classroom, possibly in small groups. Next, there is the type of reacting done by professional critics—more or less formal judgments about artistry or truthfulness. This may include references to other works, comparisons, contrasts, analytical observations, and so on. To be critically reactive, of course, students must read real critical works, which are different from reading "thought questions" at the end of the chapter. Finally, students might react to presentations by creating their own works, such as parodies or imitations.

The same basic Wheel format is used when the teacher is planning the active—or problem-solving—phase of learning (Fig. 4).

The range of content which can be covered by the Wheel approach is as vast as that of culture. The Wheel, after all, is based on real-world learning, which encompasses the physical sciences, the social sciences, technology, and the arts. The Wheel can help organize learning experiences wherever the learning calls for activity or responsiveness.

For instance, if a key unit in a science course is ecology, each student might do all or part of an "environment" Wheel. In the active phase, students could crowd into a small space and report their sensations (body medium); construct an ideal environment from "junk" (design medium); write a play about the planet's future (print medium); document sound pollution on tape (sound medium); make a slide-tape juxtaposing ecological rhetoric with ecological reality (photography and sound media); and record a local example of environmental desecration on videotape (television medium).

For a social studies project, students might construct a "prejudice" Wheel or a "city" Wheel. A comparative-media approach in English class might allow students to respond to the same story by producing it as a song, a comic book, a movie, and a short story.

The process of communication itself requires special mention. Even though using the Wheel to learn about various contents involves learning about media implicitly, some teachers may wish to be more explicit about it. In doing a "noise" Wheel, for example, students grapple with the question, "What keeps a message from being understood?" They explore blurred focus in photography, lack of shot continuity in film, poor spelling in writing, or unpleasant odors in interpersonal relationships. Other communication issues that might be taught via the Wheel are metaphor, analogy, context, and feedback. We have been deliberately vague about *who* is doing the Wheels. In some situations, the teacher may be designing both the presentations, and the problems. At other times, the

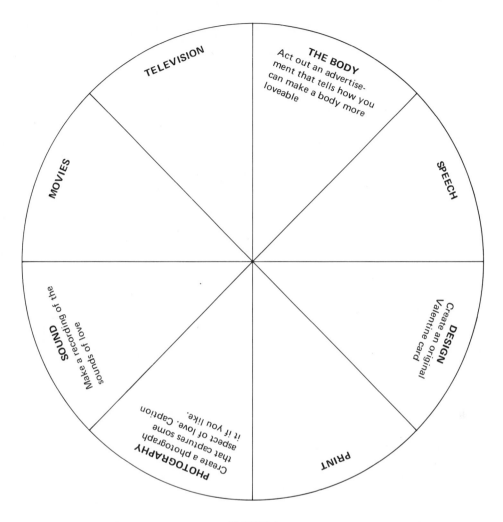

FIGURE 4

students will be making the Wheels. The goal, we think, is for the learning to be student-centered. Depending on the age of the students and the experience of the teacher, the trend should be to let students explore topics which have meaning and interest for them. The teacher would increasingly function as a consultant and resource person.

The Wheel is even more student-centered in that it touches what the "affective" (or "process") educators call a child's fundamental concern for relationship, control, and identity. Since many of the problems generated by the Wheel are solved through group-made slide-tapes, plays, and movies, this kind of learning naturally leads to new and productive *relationships* with other people. Moreover, students who gain *control* of a particular medium sometimes transfer this sense of control to other media and other situations. And, of course, a successful attempt at communicating a message to others improves the sense of relationship between the active communicator and his audience.

Media also nourish the sense of *identity* by isolating components of the self and letting the student examine them, discovering unrecognized strengths and gaining a necessary awareness of weaknesses. The sound medium, for instance, can provide a student with feedback about his voice; videotape mirrors body imagery in a total way.

Once students get used to seeing and hearing themselves, this reflective process generally becomes a tremendously positive experience. If it does not, the teacher can give help by accentuating the positive while suggesting ways the student can change what bothers him. Ultimately, the student can use the media to record and reinforce behavior he would like to see himself exhibiting more often.

TAKING THE PRESSURE OFF PRINT

Most schools are print-oriented. Their tacit message is that learning is a matter of reading and writing. Listening and speaking skills are given lip service, but although a poor listener or a shy speaker will probably make it if he can read and write, a child who *can't* read and write is bound to fail. Subjects such as English, science, and social studies are not *done*. They are read about in textbooks and written about in papers and on tests.

Yet a significant proportion of our students, especially in urban schools, are severely retarded in literacy skills. In a typical urban center, children in the seventh grade are, on the average, almost two years behind national norms. But even this fact, dreary as it is, doesn't tell the whole story. A seventh grader reading at the fifth grade level is not really reading like a normal fifth grader any more than a braced-up cerebral palsied child "walking" at a one year old level is walking like a healthy one year old. The severely retarded reader lacks the sense of growth, joy, and control characteristic of a normal reader.

There are many reasons why a youngster may be failing at reading. In most students, however, it is not a lack of "intelligence." Yet, when the print-oriented school presents knowledge via print which is within the intellectual grasp of the nonprint student, the student fails. He appears to be stupid, may be classified as stupid, and most likely learns to think of himself as stupid. But he is not really failing the given courses, whatever his grades may indicate. He is actually failing his school's chosen mode of communication.

The Wheel can help these children to learn in school. Time and again, we have seen students who bring a long tradition of personal failure with print into the classroom begin to learn in a multimedia situation. One of the authors, for instance, tape-recorded a student's response to a social studies "think question." He then transcribed the student's answer and presented it to his regular teachers. Although they had known and taught this youngster for several years, they were amazed at his rich vocabulary, clarity of expression, and power of metaphor. They had thought him stupid because of his poor reading performance.

We certainly hold no brief with those film and television "mediacs" who glibly suggest jettisoning reading and writing from the curriculum. Our account of the process of media interaction in the culture at large makes it clear that the advent of radio, film, and television places more importance on print than ever. But, the traditional school focus on print as the only way to learn is certainly responsible, in part, for the current "basic skills" crisis in education. Schools have made literacy seem like a vital organ; if you don't have it, you're not quite human. No one can learn under that kind of pressure.

The schools are in a sense only passing along the pressure on print that originates in the culture at large. Print *is* intrinsic to success in the real world. It is the "wild card" medium, the one most needed in work and play, the one most vital to social, educational, and vocational fulfillment. Even the so-called nonverbal arts (film, television) are almost exclusively practiced by people who know how to read and write. Whether we like it or not, students are going to be judged by their society, their peers, and themselves according to print standards.

The Wheel does not deny any of these facts about print, but it *does* provide a more realistic, less pressured context in which the student can approach this medium in school. When a child can see print as just one member of the media family, he tends to view it more as a potential tool for communication than as a hurdle. Meanwhile, by successfully communicating, creating, and learning in the *other* media, the student can come to believe in his abilities to learn and express. He can also practice verbal skills in less-pressured (untested) ways such as writing the narration for a slide-tape or reading a part in a radio play. Of course, print skills, like all other media skills, will also be taught explicitly. No one ever learned how to read just from making a movie.

It all comes down to this: learning is not strictly a matter of reading and writing. But reading and writing are not strictly matters of reading and writing either. In the Wheel-oriented school, teachers and students range over a variety of modes: at times banging directly away at print skills; at times connecting print with other forms of communication; at times using reading and writing to improve expression in nonprint media; and at times using expression in the nonprint media to improve reading and writing. The Wheel-oriented school does not teach what English or film or design *are* but rather *how* they are used. It not only provides *channels* for communicating, but also *reasons* for communicating. Not far beyond, we envision students coming to know communication as meaningful expression, learning as creativity, and life as art.

ONCE MORE AROUND

The Wheel is only one of many possible frameworks for giving school children a maximum of options for learning. Those who disagree with our particular arrangement, or who feel that the eight-segment Wheel presented here has too many or too few media, are invited to create their own versions of the model. The important thing is to develop a plan that makes sense to the teacher and students who will be using it.

A potential drawback of any scheme is that it will be followed too rigidly. The Wheel is a model, not a mandate. For instance, there is no requirement that every medium be used every time. In theory, of course, the more media that get into the act (and the reaction), the more opportunities there will be for involving every student. Likewise, students who think they know all about the idea under consideration after a single production or presentation may be surprised by the new perspectives that come from working through the same problem in another medium. But if the students have truly caught on, there's no point in driving a certain point or process into the ground just because "the Wheel says it's TV time." The Wheel wasn't designed to create multimedia boredom or to force a topic down the students' throats eight times in a row.

Ultimately, then, the Wheel is something like a blank lesson plan—or better, learning plan. Some teachers will want to work it out on paper. Others will simply carry it around in their heads. Many teachers who have never seen anything as formal as the Wheel use the same kind of multimedia approach spontaneously and intuitively when guiding their classes. Such teachers are "Wheel teachers" in a truer sense than those who just fill in circles and pursue them endlessly no matter what their students really want and need at the given moment.

Some readers may be concerned that the Wheel seems to expect too much media know-how of the individual teacher and too much technology of the school system.

In practice, things are a lot simpler. "Doing a Wheel" usually means doing a mini-wheel, a version of the model individually tailored to the needs, resources, and skills of the given teacher, students, and school. For example, a media team at Vaux Junior High in Philadelphia involved the student in picking a topic of personal interest, such as clothing style or popular music, and writing a list of 25 things he considered important about that topic (print medium); using the list to focus his thinking while writing a story, play, poem, or essay about the topic (print medium); recording his writing on tape (sound medium); making a list of photographs that would illustrate or complement his tape (print medium); signing out an instamatic camera and taking slides suggested on the list (photography medium); and, finally, selecting, arranging, and timing his slides to synchronize with the tape. While the end product was a slide-tape rather than a complete Wheel, the student gained experience in three distinct media in a way that emphasized the unique value of each one and the power of combining them.

A project such as this doesn't require incredible teacher training or exotic electronic gimmicks. Most teachers can handle simple still cameras and tape recorders. Most schools have such equipment available, or teachers can borrow it from friends or students. There are satisfactory cameras now available for under $3.00 and excellent, battery-powered tape-recorders for less than $40.00. The software (film, processing, tapes) for a Vaux-type project would be less than $1.50 per student. Even television is being scaled down and simplified for school use. Many schools are now buying portable videotape recorders and cameras that even students in elementary school can carry and operate. Technological advances have thus shifted the focus of media learning from the nuts and bolts of hardware to spontaneous and uninhibited probing of the fundamental issues of communication and creativity.

True mastery of the art and technique of any medium, of course, will always require a great deal of time, talent, and good teaching. There is a danger that, if too much emphasis is placed on the *multi* of multimedia learning, a student's work with any one medium will be superficial or downright slipshod. The teacher must carefully balance breadth against depth. One way to maintain standards is to utilize the talents of indigenous expert photographers, film-makers, sound engineers, and writers whose secret identities may be hidden behind the more respectable roles of science teacher, music specialist, custodian, or vice principal.

We could list and explain away (on paper at least) many other possible flaws in the Wheel model. But there is one problem which is not so easily dealt with. Unlike external issues such as lack of money, primitive technology, or an overcrowded curriculum, there is a dynamic force at the core of much present day educational practice which may stop multimedia learning before it starts.

On the surface, the problem may be termed *noise*. We have witnessed teachers coming down hard on students who were laughing in response to a hilarious scene in a movie. Typically, the film is stopped and the children warned that the movie will be cancelled if the laughter continues. School teachers and administrators worry a lot about this kind of noise. But we don't think the noise itself is the real concern.

One of the authors witnessed the following scene in a school for the deaf: the children were lined up outside the cafeteria waiting to enter for lunch. Nothing much was happening so two of the youngsters were talking to each other, in sign language, of course. The teacher in charge suddenly grabbed the two third-graders and threw them against a wall. She then silently rocked an imaginary baby in her arms while glaring at the two boys. Even the naive observer got the message—the boys, by talking in line, were out of order because they were doing something different from everyone else; they were, in fact, like babies.

Traditional schools seem intent on maintaining monolithic group behavior. It's all together now as we walk down the hall, read the same passage, practice the same multiplication table, memorize the same spelling list. Even programmed instruction courses, which promise individualized learning, inevitably move all the students toward the same ultimate behavior, generally through the same exercises. This is why a single test will suffice to show how well all the students are doing. But authentic learning doesn't come in such neat packages. In the real world, learning splays outward in every direction.

Can school education be as free and open? It will take more than physically open spaces in which all the students go through the same workbooks. It will take open educators (and parents) giving students the same rich diversity of materials to respond to and create with that the culture at large provides its citizens.

Can schools be open enough to accept student productions which are frankly hot to handle? We know of a student film, made from advertisements clipped out of leading home magazines, that shocked and outraged a group of principals. These administrators were so scandalized by the sexiness of the film that they missed the irony in the fact that the images were taken from respected journals. Perhaps this is a bizarre example. Probably the film shouldn't have been shown to that group of educators. Maybe the teacher was an extrovert who wanted to throw some business to the Civil Liberties Union. But the fact remains: when people (students included) engage in real life creative effort or when they are invited to respond to artistic works according to their honest feelings, the results will not be monolithic, predictable, generally approved of, or even necessarily "nice."

Can the same schools that are charged with getting children ready for life be filled with life? As of this writing, we freely admit that we don't know.

28 if you've seen sesame street, you ain't seen nothing yet

Evelyn P. Davis

There was a time when a television set was considered by many educators to be nothing more than a fixture in the living room to entertain, but certainly not to educate. Not so anymore. Many educators across the country are realizing that they cannot afford to continue contending that education and television are enemies. The concept that the classroom is for learning and television is for entertaining is no longer valid. What has caused television and education, after two decades of mutual hostilities, to move toward an armistice? Two of the most recent contributions to this mood of cooperation have been *Sesame Street* and *The Electric Company,* both of which are experimental television series created and produced by the Children's Television Workshop. *Sesame Street,* designed to help prepare preschoolers for their entry into the classroom, is now reaching an estimated nine million children daily in the United States and millions more in nearly 50 countries and territories around the world. *The Electric Company* aims to help teach basic reading skills to the nation's seven to ten year old population. Surveys indicate that it built a nationwide audience of four million youngsters in its first season and is now being seen in nearly 40 per cent of the elementary schools in the U.S. with access to TV sets and stations broadcasting the program.

The structure of the two experimental series is influenced by the techniques of much of commercial television, especially the commercials, which are able to teach youngsters by attracting and holding their attention. The most obvious characteristics of commercials that fascinate young viewers are clear: frequent repetition, clever visual presentation, brevity, and clarity, as well as humor, animation, music, movement, and a clear message.

"If television can sell extra millions of boxes of breakfast cereal it can most certainly enhance the learning of millions of young children who eat that cereal," said Joan Ganz Cooney, president of CTW and driving force behind the creation of both *Sesame Street* and *The Electric Company* (Cooney, 1970).

Some 97 per cent of the country's households have TV sets. Even among those families who earn $5000 or less annually, 90 per cent have sets in the home. Because of its extensive audience, television provides a natural avenue to reach and teach children. Youngsters in elementary school, for example, watch television an average of 25 to 30 hours every week, while high school students watch some 15 hours weekly. For some children in poor areas, these figures are almost double.

Almost 12 million children between the ages of three and five years in the United States don't participate in any type of preschool activity. Yet, according to the Nielsen Television Index, preschoolers watch television an average of 54 hours a week. This means that children have spent between 3000 and 6000 hours watching television by the time they reach the first grade, and some 15,000 hours before they graduate from high school. The latter figure compares with an estimated 11,000 hours spent in the classroom before entering college.

Television has had a profound impact on children, as indicated in the recent report of the Surgeon General on the impact of television advertising on youngsters (Lyle and Hoffman, 1972). The report states:

> Almost three quarters (74 per cent) of the mothers said their young children sang commercial jingles learned from TV, 62 per cent saying that this had begun by the time the child was age two, another 31 per cent saying by age three . . . . The impact of advertising was further emphasized by the fact that 87 per cent of the mothers said their preschool age children asked for food items they saw on TV: 91 per cent said their children asked for toys they saw on TV.

In an earlier study entitled *Television in the Lives of Our Children,* a trio of researchers reported that television viewers appear to come to school with a vocabulary advantage over nonviewers of approximately one year (Schram, Lyle, and Parker, 1961).

This evidence indicates both the size of the young television audience and the potential for strongly affecting it. The Children's Television Workshop began its existence by focusing its attention on the need for a mass program of preschool education in the United States and on ways to harness television's potential to help meet this need. An extensive research program was launched to produce an experimental series that would hold the attention of youngsters and teach them at the same time.

In all of its planning, CTW paid special attention to the needs of children of poor families. Television is usually the only continuing window on the world for these children. They have far less access to stimulating toys and games than do advantaged children. Moreover, research has indicated that they enter school less prepared for the classroom than their middle-class counterparts.

The Workshop felt that the neglected years before school began were the best age with which to begin. It took the position, however, that neither a single television program nor education itself could solve the problem facing poor children, because the gap between the disadvantaged and the advantaged is a result of several factors, including economics, housing, and discrimination as well as education. Thus it could not attempt to cure the ills of society single-handed. It could, however, help to break the cycle of poverty by giving underprivileged children a boost in the critical area of readiness for school. If they were able to derive more benefit from their education, they would be more capable later of entering the mainstream of American life.

CTW's first series, *Sesame Street,* with its lively, entertaining, and varied educational segments, was created to promote the intellectual and cultural growth of preschoolers. But the Workshop did more than put a television program on the air and hope that preschoolers and their parents would watch and benefit from it—it also launched a nationwide community relations program to maximize the show's audience and impact among youngsters in major urban and rural areas where large numbers of minority and poor families live.

This program encouraged schools, Head Start, and day care centers as well as community groups to use *Sesame Street* as part of their daily routine. Local staff coordinators, working with community groups, churches, libraries, and individuals, assisted in the establishment of *Sesame Street* viewing centers in areas where there were large numbers of children of poor families but too few television sets. These centers, where the youngsters and their parents come for a two to three hour period every day, offer a simple packaged program. After watching *Sesame Street,* the group participates in activities designed to reinforce the show's educational aspects.

This effort also was designed to encourage parental involvement in the early education of children and to assist in dispelling the notion, which is particularly common among poor parents, that teaching should be left entirely to the schools. It has brought benefits to thousands of children in such cities as Washington, New York, Boston, Chicago, Philadelphia, Detroit, Baltimore, Oakland, San Francisco, New Orleans, Dallas, and Jackson (Miss.).

The success of *Sesame Street* in reaching and teaching preschoolers was indicated by the results of a two year study conducted by the Educational Testing Service. Among the most significant findings were:

> Children of poor families who regularly watched the program showed greater gains in learning than advantaged children who watched the program only infrequently.

> Children who watched the program showed greater gains in learning than children who did not and this was true for poor inner city children, suburban children of middle class families, isolated rural boys and girls and those whose first language was not English.

> The skills that received the most attention and time on the television series were generally the skills that were best learned (Bogatz and Ball, 1971).

Dr. Ball said afterwards, "I think we have shown in this evaluation that television can have a profound effect upon the learning of three to five year old children from widely diverse backgrounds."

An in-depth first-season study of 500 families with preschoolers in New York's Bedford-Stuyvesant section indicated that *Sesame Street* had reached 90 per cent of the children aged two to five who were at home during the day rather than at a day care center or nursery. Sixty per cent of the children watched the show once or more daily. It was also found that half of these children tuned the set to *Sesame Street* themselves without waiting for adult assistance. Our experience has been that this pattern is continuing.

The outstanding results of *Sesame Street* last year—with children entering the first grade knowing their alphabet and displaying cognitive skills and the ability to count—demonstrate the fact that television and education can work together.

The Los Angeles Unified School District recognized the importance of television when, with the assistance of CTW's Community Education Services Division, it started a unique program that used *Sesame Street* as a supplemental tool in its adult education program for parents and teachers. When finished, this project, which is the first of its kind to be organized by a school system anywhere in the U.S., will have trained about 2900 teachers and parents in the curriculum content and educational goals of the series.

Another example of the growing alliance between television and the educational system can be seen in Minneapolis, where the city's Public School District successfully conducted a preschool project in six inner city schools involving parents, teachers, teacher aides and more than one hundred children. This project, funded through a Title III grant, used *Sesame Street* as a major part of the curriculum. The participants watched the program in a classroom setting and afterwards conducted follow-up activities to reinforce the show's educational goals.

CTW's Community Education Services Division is also working with other school districts and community action agencies in various parts of the country that are planning similar programs and is using the experimental series as the educational component in their activities.

Sesame Street, however, was only the first flowering of the partnership between education and television. The program's companion, *The Electric Company,* which made its debut in October, 1971, is an extensively researched experiment aimed at helping to teach basic reading skills to second, third, and fourth grade youngsters. The show reinforces the contention that television is a neutral medium which merely exists to be used.

The new series, which was more than one and a half years in preparation, combines education and entertainment just as its predecessor does. Its curriculum was developed by the Workshop with the help of more than 100 consultants and advisors, including a number of leading authorities and educational researchers. *The Electric Company,* designed as a supplement to classroom instruction, features a "cafeteria" of techniques to encourage reading. The diversity inherent in such an approach helps hold the viewer's interest and promotes a flexible, problem-solving attitude toward reading.

The bullseye of the target audience is the child in the lower half of the second grade in reading achievement, but the program was also found to be useful to older children, teenagers, and some adults.

Two nationwide studies of school use of the experimental reading series found that the television program has met with unprecedented acceptance in classrooms around the United States (Herriott and Liebert, 1972). Researchers who conducted the studies concluded that *The Electric Company* was "a remarkable advancement over previous trends in school innovativeness." Among other things, they found that within two months of its introduction, the program was being viewed in 45 per cent of the elementary schools in the U. S. with full TV capability, and that toward the end of the first season, 88 per cent of the national sample of teachers reported that their students had experienced an increase in reading interest as a result of viewing the series. "If only in terms of the speed and scope of penetration of elementary schools of all kinds, *The Electric Company* must be considered a highly successful venture," concluded the authors.

Dr. Sidney P. Marland Jr., the U. S. Commissioner of Education, said of the survey results: "The extent to which American elementary schools put this new teaching aid to classroom use is truly one of the remarkable events in the history of instructional television."

The Herriott-Liebert report highlighted the fact that many schools cannot yet take advantage of modern technological aids such as *The Electric Company* because of technical deficiencies. The researchers found that nearly half the schools in the U. S. were unable to use the series, usually because they lacked TV sets. They found that, although about 97 per cent of U. S. homes have TV, only about 51 per cent of all elementary schools had television. Approximately two million pupils viewed the series in school (and an estimated two million more saw it each week at home).

A summary of the Herriott-Liebert studies includes these findings:

Within two months of its appearance, the series was being used by 23 per cent of the elementary schools in the U. S.

Among schools having full TV viewing capabilities, that is, schools with access to the broadcast and sets in sufficient quantity and quality to permit viewing, the percentage of viewing schools jumped to 45 per cent.

In large cities, *The Electric Company* was being used by 70 per cent of all schools having full TV capability.

In general, the series had greatest penetration in its target areas—in urbanized areas and among pupils who have had greater than average difficulties. By region, viewing was highest in the West and Southwest, and in the North Atlantic states.

In addition to their school survey in the fall of 1971, Drs. Herriott and Liebert also reported on a second survey, conducted near the end of the first season, which found a warm response for the program from teachers and their pupils who had used it. Findings included:

Some 85 per cent of teachers said they had "very favorable" over-all opinions of *The Electric Company*.

The teachers also gave the series high marks for its effect on the reading skills of their pupils. More than 80 per cent of the teachers reported some gains in specific reading skills which were directly attributable to the program.

Specifically, 28 per cent of teachers noted a "great improvement" in the ability of their typical pupils to decode words as a result of watching the series. Some 21 per cent noted "great improvement" in the ability of students to spell words. And 33 per cent found "great improvement" in basic sight vocabulary.

The researchers looked closely at the barriers of technical capabilities for receiving *The Electric Company* in classrooms and concluded that "the major barriers to utilization were not willingness but access." Some schools could not receive the broadcast signal, but most nonusers simply did not have TV sets or had them in insufficient quantity or quality. "The cumulative effect of technical deficiencies is overwhelming," the report found. "An estimated 48.7 per cent of the schools in the U. S. were unable to adopt *The Electric Company* because of these factors. This essentially divides the nation's schools in half.... If all schools are to have equal access to the growing national resources in instructional material, it seems clear that an updating of school equipment is in order."

This attempt to help teach basic reading skills through the use of television comes at a time when literacy is still a major problem in the U.S. While government statistics list illiteracy as a problem for a full 10 per cent of the nation's population over 25 years of age, a number of studies indicate that millions of Americans are functionally illiterate, and cannot cope or compete in our advanced technological society.

Thus television can play an increasingly important role in meeting America's tremendous educational needs, simply by developing the full potential of the existing technology. Two new technological developments that can further enhance the usefulness of television are close at hand, and others are probably not far behind.

The more familiar of these two innovations, cable television, has already come into some use on a limited scale. Cable television comes directly into the home with wires, and this means very significant changes. The innocuous coaxial cable can carry dozens of channels of information and entertainment to television sets. Even more important, it has the potential to carry a signal from the house back to a central source. In other words, cable television can be a two-way mass communication and education system. The same cable which today carries a few television signals to almost five million homes can also carry the signals necessary to connect homes with distant teaching-machines or computers. Eventually the same home cable television facility may be hooked into a central site which would allow a student at home to have access to a national library of videotapes and data stored in information banks.

Even more important, the education explosion of the past two decades will undoubtedly continue unabated, thus putting more pressure on facilities of universities, colleges, and other educational institutions. Cable television might offer alternatives which could relieve some of the congestion at these institutions.

Videotape cassettes, used to record and play back television programs, will eventually bring another revolution in television viewing. It is fair to predict that in the not so distant future, cassette TV recording will be as simple as cassette sound recording is today. TV cassettes are already in use for specific training and instruction at hospitals, and further development could lead to their widespread use as a valuable educational tool for students studying at home.

Thus, television offers unlimited opportunities to educators. Because television watching is one of the most established habits in America and because of the great variety of ways it can be used, television cannot be ignored by educators without seriously impairing the vision of what education can and should be. Hostility has no place in this vision, since TV's essential role in education is as a supplemental teaching tool to be used by the teacher, parent, or the student himself. The personal relationship and interchange between a teacher and student cannot be assumed by instructional television, and therefore, it cannot replace the teacher in the classroom. However, because of its new and necessary alliance with the teacher, television has the capacity to become one of the most effective teaching aids ever known.

REFERENCES

Bogatz, Gerry Ann, and Ball, Samuel: A Summary of the Major Findings in "The second year of Sesame Street: a continuing evaluation." Princeton, N.J., Educational Testing Service 1971.

Cooney, Joan Ganz: Address Before the First National Conference on Films and TV for Children, July 7, 1970, Commodore Hotel, N.Y.

Herriott, Robert E., and Liebert, Roland J.: The Electric Company In-School Utilization Study: The 1971-72 School and Teacher Survey. Florida State University, Center for the Study of Education, Institute for Social Education, in conjunction with Statistics Research Division, Research Triangle Institute, Tallahassee, Florida, 1972.

Lyle, Jack, and Hoffman, Heide R.: Explorations in patterns of TV viewing by preschool age children. *Surgeon General's Report, 4:* 257, 1972.

Schram, Wilbur, Lyle, Jack, and Parker, Edwin B.: Television in the Lives of Our Children. Palo Alto, California, Stanford University Press, 1961.

29 pygmalion's computer

Howard A. Peelle

INTRODUCTION

Computers play such a central role in our everyday lives that the question might arise: "Have we, like Pygmalion, fallen in love with our own creation?" Is it conceivable that twentieth century man's ideal artifact is this neuter machine? Sculpted in pristine and shining metal, composed of countless arrays of minute electronic circuits, the computer today reaches out its terminals to the very heart of the human lifeline. Computing machines are ubiquitous in crucial areas such as transportation, communications, national defense, food and materials production, scientific research, and education. Few who use the computer decry its advent; many actually depend on its presence; and some even glorify its existence.

The issues surrounding computer usage in *education*, however, are particularly controversial. Although still in a formative stage, computer-assisted instruction (CAI) has already incurred conflicting interpretations. From one point of view, CAI evokes the image of a "perfect teacher"—one with instant access to information, with infinite patience and exceeding accuracy, systematically ensuring maximum learning for all students. "No human teacher ever born, no method or media yet tried, can match the computer's capabilities," the computer-worshippers would argue. But, from a radically different point of view, the gifts of this young technology are scorned. The computer is seen as an agent of destruction, threatening our most cherished human qualities. Cries of "impersonalization," "programmed brainwashing," and "disguised racist oppression" project the Orwellian specter of mass behavioral control in computerized education— students trained to be academic copies of a master-mind blueprint. "No computer can ever match the spontaneity, the versatility, and the emotional caring of a human teacher," the computer-haters argue. Still others distrust the entire "schooled-up" educational system and have little respect for the current quality of teaching—whether by humans or by computers.

The controversy becomes more heated with the mention of *artificial intelligence*, particularly mechanical mentors. What fate will befall education when machines become capable of sensitive and intelligent interaction with human beings? Rosenthal's studies of self-fulfilling prophecy might suggest that children of tomorrow will be molded to a new orthodoxy—one of expected precision, prepackaged behavioral objectives, and pro- grammed responses (Rosenthal and Jacobson, 1968). Will students neglect humanistic values and perhaps even emulate the computer? As Pygmalion dreamed of affection, will they imagine that they are blessed by cybernetically individualized instruction? And will a computer terminal then seem warm to the touch?

How the modern tale of Pygmalion and his computer ends no one can easily predict. In the paragraphs that follow no reasons for panic are cited, no panaceas prescribed. Rather, this is an overview, presented here in two parts, of current instructional applications of computers and a description of some promising new directions for *human* use of computers.

PART I: INSTRUCTIONAL APPLICATIONS OF COMPUTERS

Overview

Computer technology purports to make an unprecedented impact on education; in fact, computers are already being used in schools. Most likely, Pygmalion in the classroom of the future will have access to an electronic partner every bit as dedicated to assisting his learning as he wishes. In educational circles today, however, "to use or not to use" computers in teaching is still a controversial issue.

The question—indeed, the profound challenge—before us is no longer whether or not to use the computer as an educational resource, but *how* to use this most powerful and versatile tool mankind has ever known.

The scope of instructional applications of computers is dramatically far-reaching. Answering the question of how to use computers in the teaching-learning process has importance for us all. It affects the organization and administration of education, the nation's largest industry; it affects the current supply of three and a half million teachers and the largest population of students (over 60 million) receiving formal schooling in all of history; it affects all children yet to enter school and all adults who will make learning a lifetime activity in a world of ample leisure time.

Computer technology first made its entrance through school doors in the early 1960's as a result of the need for increasing bureaucratic efficiency. Along with rapidly accelerating national enrollments came the call for educational data processing. School payrolls, student records, alumni files, and more recently, scheduling procedures, budgeting, and planning—all can be expedited by automated information storage and retrieval systems. Today the data processing power of computers is well demonstrated and is clearly acknowledged in public school systems as the rule rather than the exception. In fact, many large-scale operations in education are just not feasible without computer support.

In addition to performing administrative functions, the computer has been used as a subject of and a vehicle for learning. The study of computers per se—their design, architecture, and operating systems—is a major part of the field of computer science. Use of the computer as a vehicle for learning is hailed under a variety of acronyms* generically called "computer-assisted instruction" (CAI). This field is in an embryonic stage of development.

---

*Some of the popular acronyms are: CAI ("computer-assisted instruction," "computer-aided instruction," or "computer-administered instruction"); CMI ("computer-mediated instruction" or "computer-managed instruction"); CAL ("computer-aided or -assisted learning); and CSI ("computer-supported instruction"). There are distinctions between all these terms which will not be discussed here.

CAI: A Historical Sketch

The origins of CAI were probably attempts by curious technicians to see if a machine could be programmed to interact with a human. (This is not to forget the plethora of conceptualizations by science-fiction writers.) The earliest programs were capable simply of printing pre-stored questions, accepting multiple-choice answers, and judging answers for correctness. One typical program (used by IBM for demonstration) taught a short-cut technique for multiplying two-digit numbers ending in 5; another asked factual questions about American history such as, "Who was the fifteenth president of the United States?"

Major pioneering in CAI occurred around 1961 when the University of Illinois produced the PLATO system (Programmed Logic for Automatic Teaching Operations). And, with magnanimous Federal funding in 1966, Stanford University's Patrick Suppes spearheaded development of computerized tutorials in arithmetic and reading for elementary school children.

Today, there are many—perhaps hundreds—of CAI installations in this country and abroad. Most are found in large universities such as the University of Texas, Pennsylvania State University, Stanford University, University of Illinois, and Florida State University. Some are part of the armed services such as the U.S. Naval Ordinance Training Laboratory. A few are integrated within public school systems such as Philadelphia's Instructional Systems Center. Several industrial firms, among them IBM and RCA, have made cautious forays into the area of CAI.

After the initial upsurge in CAI activity—primarily from 1965 to 1968—progress has slowed. Developments over the last four years have not differed significantly from earlier work, and, contrary to predictions by many pioneers, use of CAI is *not* widespread. In fact, despite an investment of over $1 billion in Federal support monies, less than 0.5 per cent of secondary school students use computers in any way.* Today, CAI remains in an embryonic stage.

CAI Systems

The technology of CAI is generally sophisticated and expensive, although significant progress has been made toward making systems user-oriented and cost-effective. For example, the University of Illinois—housing the largest computer-based education operation in the country—projects that its new PLATO IV system will handle over 4000 student-users at an average cost of about 35 cents per student contact hour, a figure comparable to the purchase price of a textbook (Alpert and Bitzer, 1969).

Basically, a "CAI system" is described in terms of its "hardware" (the actual equipment), its "software" (the instructions which run the hardware), its "communications links" (the devices which allow persons to use the hardware and software), and its "curriculum" (teaching materials stored in the computer).

The hardware of modern day computers includes: input-output terminals for entering and receiving information; memory banks for storing data and programs; a central processing unit for performing arithmetic and logic; and an executive control for monitoring timing and sequence of all operations. Many descriptors are required to specify a given

---

*The subject of why school systems are reluctant to adopt CAI is the objective of a new study by the Human Resources Research Organization, Washington, D.C.

computer's capabilities, and many factors go into decisions for purchasing or renting one.*

The software of a computer system is that which makes man-machine interface possible. People called "systems programmers" are responsible for the design and operation of translators—sets of instructions which convert the zeroes and ones of machine language into convenient and useful commands of a *programming language* and vice-versa. Many different programming languages abound today: some are general-purpose, such as FORTRAN and APL; some are special-purpose, such as COBOL for business applications and LISP for list processing; and some were specially designed for CAI, such as COURSEWRITER and MENTOR.

The use of computers in teaching was first considered feasible with the advent of "time-sharing." The concept of one machine servicing many users "simultaneously" is well-suited for students who typically request small, interactive jobs. The communications links of a time-shared computer are dataphones or, alternatively, ordinary telephones plus an acoustic coupler. Students connect to the computer via "terminals"—teletypewriters, cathode-ray tubes with keyboard consoles, or plasma display tablets.†

The curriculum of a CAI system is the collection of teaching materials stored in the computer. Typically, curriculum is developed by authors or a team of programmers, teachers, and curriculum specialists who use a programming language to write instructional sequences. Approximately 100 hours of conceptualization, design, implementation, debugging, testing, evaluation and revision go into producing one hour's worth of teaching via computer. Lately, the use of "macros" has facilitated curriculum development by permitting teachers who do not know how to program to enter course material in a pre-structured format.

CAI systems have been utilized (mostly experimentally) at all levels of education—ranging from elementary school to post-graduate study to on-the-job training. Subject areas have included mathematics, foreign languages, social sciences, natural sciences, reading and spelling, operations research, engineering, medicine, and music. Typical modes of instruction are drill and practice, tutorial, simulation, and problem-solving (see Molnar, 1972).

Misuse of Computers in Teaching

This past decade has seen unprecedented use of computers in teaching, but not without concomitant *misuses*. As with previous technologies developed by man, computers have been misused, abused, and unused, and often serve to aggravate rather than assuage problems currently besetting American education.

Most misuses of CAI can be characterized as "forced fits"; that is, use of computers in teaching is forced upon school systems, even where and when it doesn't fit. The consequences of forcing computer usage are frequently disastrous: computer terminals placed in classrooms and laboratories for "experimental testing" either stand unused because an

---

*Major manufacturers are: Control Data Corporation, Digital Equipment Corporation, Honeywell Information Systems, and International Business Machines.

†For a reference on the fundamental aspects and interrelationships of the components of a computer system, see "Laymen's Guide to the Use of Computers," published by THE ASSOCIATION FOR EDUCATIONAL DATA SYSTEMS, 1971, 1201 Sixteenth Street, N.W., Washington, D.C. 20036.

adequate training program is not available, or unrepaired because no one assumes responsibility for servicing the machines, or unsupervised as users fail to make productive use of system features (witness the repeated printouts of Snoopy!).

The physical surroundings relegated to computer equipment are sure clues to another form of forced fits. Typically, the setting is cold and impersonal, often painted stark white without a trace of art. It seems as if the most aesthetically *unappealing* area is carefully selected for the computer room (more often than not, the basement). Even in legitimate classrooms in schools and industry, the number and spacing of computer terminals evoke Orwellian images. With as many as 30 terminals placed literally side-by-side in a single room, one conjures up the worst fears of automated training (I hesitate to call it learning). Clearly, there must be an extraordinarily high premium placed on efficiency in this stifling, factory-style education!

Yet another instance of forcing computer usage to fit is found in CAI curricula. Much of the instructional materials available on computer systems today are "canned" textbooks—traditional texts wholly transcribed into a tutorial programmed instruction format, with the computer serving as little more than an automatic (and expensive!) page-turner. Again, the rationale is usually couched in terms of efficiency (that quality for which computers are so admired): "Your child will learn *more* in *less* time with *greater* retention . . . ." How can responsible parents and educators resist such a compelling offer? This Madison Avenue appeal is, of course, tantamount to suggesting that children sit still for as long as possible, open their cerebrums wide, and receive regular and rapid spoonfuls of what someone else has deemed best for them to know. This kind of forced-feeding is the antithesis of the thinking of such prominent educators as Dewey, Piaget, Neill, Bruner, Holt, and Goodman; and it is understandable why this prescriptive, mechanical approach to pedagogy is under criticism from all corners today.

Problems associated with misuses of computers have also spread into psychological and sociological dimensions. When a novel and prestigous technology such as Pygmalion's computer is made available, unforeseen problems of human interaction can result. Two particularly exacerbating student behavior problems are identified as: (1) self-aggrandizement by "computer pros," and (2) academic implosion by "computer bugs."

In the first case, some students who learn how to use the computer quickly and easily become obsessed with their power, sometimes to the extent of belittling and bullying neophyte learners (including their teachers). For these computer "pros," using the computer seems to be a mark of distinction, an outlet for expressing their worth and power (perhaps for the first time since entering school). Even elementary school children will pronounce their knowledge and expertise: "Of course I know how to work the computer!" or "That's not the way to work it! Let *me* do it!" This self-aggrandizement can proceed to the point that timid prospective users never get their hands on the computer terminal and are forever turned off by anything to do with computers.

The second problem arises with students who are affectionately called "computer bugs" or, alternatively, "computer nuts." These students become so intrigued by computers and programming computers that they disregard almost everything else. In a virtual academic implosion, they want to know all about computers—how they work, how to run programs, what has been stored in the computer's memory—right down to the most specialized and detailed operation. The severity of the problem is manifest in neglect for other subjects, low grades in school, underdeveloped socialization, and general lack of communicativity (except with "the machine"). "They speak a different language" is a usual comment made by outside observers. The symptoms are, in fact, remarkably similar to those of the drug-dropout syndrome.

Perhaps the most deplorable misuse of computers in teaching today is their nonuse. While it is true that not all uses of computers (or any technology) will be completely laudable, it is nakedly ironic that the mind of man which produced so great a machine fails so miserably to think of creative uses for it, especially in education. Much of this high-powered technology sits *unused* in the central activity of our lives: learning. Partly due to the economic crisis facing education, partly due to pervading myths and fears about computer take-over, and partly due to the sanctimonious attitude of tradition-bound educators, the full power and potential of the computer have not been tapped.

One further consequence of computer misuse and nonuse has been the birth of a *computer mystique*. Myths are born when the computer is represented as a mysterious, unfathomable invention—one that only a select few can comprehend.* Unfortunately, computer myths are often created by experienced users and computer salesmen (perhaps unknowingly) and are perpetrated by elitists to protect their own interests. Many lay persons, when encountering a computer system for the first time, are literally hesitant to touch the terminal keyboard. "I will just push the wrong button," or "I'm sure I will break something," adults often excuse themselves. (By contrast most children are more than willing to experiment and end up trying *all* the buttons.) Or sometimes computer awe is expressed: "Oh, computers these days are amazing! I could never understand how they work." And now, the greatest hoax of them all is emerging: computers are *assumed* to be "smarter than people." It is becoming dangerously commonplace to attribute qualities of intelligence to a machine *without* considering how it has been programmed: "The computer would just beat me anyway" (in a game) or, when the computer's response-time lags, a common blurt is: "It must be thinking."

Extensions of these problems point to a most foreboding have/have-not situation. Already we live in a society fractured by tensions between those who *have* material goods, power, freedom, happiness, and those who *have not*. If the misuse, abuse, and nonuse of computers in education is not checked, another schism will be obvious in less than a generation: those who have computer expertise and those who have not. An in-group using computers to gain (or retain) control over other groups of people has patently frightening implications. This problem is not new. It has its parallel in the most destructive pathology of our time: racism.

There are no pat solutions to these problems associated with the misuse of computers in teaching. Although they arise in a setting with a technological catalyst, they are fundamentally problems of human interaction.

Problems and Potentials

That CAI holds great *potential* for educating Pygmalions of the future is indubitable. From a student's point of view, CAI can mean the opportunity for individualized instruction: one can learn at his own pace, receive immediate personalized feedback, and freely choose the content, sequencing, and degree of difficulty of instruction. For a teacher, CAI can relieve much of the tedium and redundancies of daily routine: the computer presents drill and instruction, automatically collects and stores performance

---

*The myriad of "computer myths" are not identified here. For a partial list of misconceptions frequently promulgated by both critics and proponents of CAI, see Alpert and Bitzer, 1969, pp. 7-9.

data, and tests and diagnoses areas of learning difficulty. Ideally, this frees the teacher to engage in more human and humanizing roles such as guidance, inspiration, and motivation. A school system also stands to gain from utilizing CAI: the general level of education for large numbers of students can be raised by systematically managing the instruction available on remedial, supplemental, and enrichment bases.

Out-of-classroom uses of CAI are also conceivable and attractive. Computer terminals might be located at home or in a dormitory or at a local community center. And when the use of multi-media instructional systems is considered, the possibilities seem endlessly exciting!

While prospects for widespread CAI appear exciting and hopeful, a host of problems remains extremely challenging and sometimes foreboding. Costs of sophisticated educational technology are still prohibitively high; marketed hardware is generally not tailored for educational purposes; large time-sharing systems have gained a reputation for unreliability; software support often lacks compatibility; most so-called "CAI integrated learning systems" are designed with a myopic view of students' creative pursuits; the quality of curriculum materials developed to date is dubious at best; and teacher training programs in computer usage are few and usually perceived as threatening. Furthermore, already-overburdened teachers do not have time for new, complicated technologies; school administrators often resist innovations for the wrong reasons; parents and community persons are unfortunately uninformed and not involved; and, while many students eagerly take interest in computers and programming, their interests are subverted by a lock-step certification system. As if these problems were not debilitating enough, CAI development suffers from the absence of cooperation between the responsible factions. Professional educators, businessmen, computer scientists, governmental agencies, and teachers—all contentedly remain on their respective sides of the communications gap. Finally, the portent of behavioral control looms large when a central computer houses all information on all citizens; the specter of a *1984*-education is too near and too possible when all students' progress can be predetermined.

The question seems to be: can Pygmalion avoid being intellectually imprisoned by the problems inherent in this technological aid—"his" computer?

PART II: NEW DIRECTIONS

When Harvard's Allan Ellis said that the computer is "an anything machine," surely he was emphasizing not only its versatility but also the fact that it is a *tool* to be used at man's discretion. Using the computer as a tool rather than a task-master serves to *complement* human teaching rather than to compete for the attention of students. Some of the more promising new directions in instructional applications of computers seek such a humanizing role for the computer. These uses foster development of the whole, fully functioning person, not just singular skills, and highlight those qualities which are uniquely human, not those likened to mechanistic devices.

At a time when the field of CAI is in dire need of revitalization, several new directions for *human* uses of computers in teaching are emerging, such as gaming and simulation, artificial intelligence in computer-assisted instruction, and "ad-lib" computer-assisted instruction.

Gaming and Simulation

Game-playing is generally regarded as a natural, enjoyable activity for persons of all ages. Some games, such as chess, checkers, and go, are integrally woven into cultural fabrics. The view that "all the world's a stage" or that life is a game and man is *homo ludens* (the playing animal) still holds widespread credibility.

That educational games stimulate positive, participatory learning is a common tenet. In his book *Serious Games,* Clark Abt aptly describes the value of games designed with specific educational goals and gives evidence that in properly supervised gaming, students appear to learn more quickly and more fully, retaining what they have learned better and longer. (See also Abt's article "Playing To Learn" in this volume.)

Gaming and simulation offer opportunities often not possible in real life. While conducive to full emotional and intellectual involvement, games permit players to test solutions (or "strategies") for problems (or "situations") which are in reality either too risky, too expensive, or irreversible. In a benign "simulated" environment, mistakes can be made, their probable consequences scrutinized, and errors turned to positive advantage—all at no detriment to society. Games-makers Allen, Gamson, Goodman, and Duke readily admit that simulations oversimplify, caricature, and distort the real world systems they represent, but quickly add that a simulation is economical, observable, controllable, and reproducible—all characteristics rewarding to the student who is willing to experiment (Research News, 1971).

Despite increased popularity, gaming and simulation remain virtually untapped modes of instruction, especially in CAI. To date, CAI curriculum development has focused on tutorial, drill, and test approaches, and little formal research or evaluation of the effectiveness of games and simulations has been conducted.* Execution of educational games and simulations by computer offers some appealing advantages, including:

1. Rapid processing of complex mathematical models
2. Accurate branching on multiple conditions
3. Automatic storage of responses
4. Simultaneous usage by students in different locations learning at different rates
5. Opportunity for machine competition and "intelligent" interaction

In general, the prospects for simulation and gaming via computer depend on how the educational community regards the question of uncertainty in human existence. The admission of the uncertainty of life is conspicuously absent in modern schooling (usually when unanswerable questions are raised, they are expediently disposed of). Using games in a computer-assisted instruction setting would help restore the legitimacy of dealing with uncertain situations and expose the value of confronting uncertainty in positive and realistic ways. It would encourage development of skills such as planning, organization, and strategy formulation and execution—important powers of reasoning which permeate our everyday thinking but which are not taught in school.

---

*One noteworthy exception is Richard Wing's research in the use of computerized social science games with elementary school children (Westchester Co., Board of Cooperative Educational Services). He reported several differences in learning, most notably: children using CAI games learned the content in significantly less time than children receiving normal classroom instruction in the same subject. For details, see Advantages of Using A Computer in Some Kinds of Educational Games *IEEE Transactions on Human Factors, 8*: June 1967.

Artificial Intelligence in Computer-Assisted Instruction

In the minds of many people, the IQ of today's typical computer-assisted instruction program is relatively low—low compared to, say, a human born at the same time and progressing normally since the first general-purpose digital computer was built in 1946. After all, there are many questions Pygmalion might ask of a grade school teacher that a computer program cannot sensibly answer!

In many attempts to use computer-assisted instruction, students have been alienated by the inflexibility and the impersonal nature—the "dumbness" and "numbness"—of the computer. A machine with a higher IQ would certainly be more appealing. While "intelligence quotient" involves many complex variables and while "intelligence" is usually defined in terms\of behavior man himself calls intelligent,* it is to the task of developing machines capable of exhibiting *artificial intelligence*** that some researchers have addressed themselves.

Computers already possess rudiments of intelligence. Some properties intrinsic to computing machines actually dwarf human abilities and, consequently, offer potential assistance to human learning.† In terms of memory (one dimension of human intelligence) the capacity, speed, and accuracy of information storage and retrieval of today's computers far exceed human abilities. A mammoth adjunct-memory providing "instant" access to millions of bits of information is invaluable to any serious learner. (Who would turn down the Library of Congress at his fingertips?) In terms of performing instructions (another popular measure of intelligence) the computer's speed, reliability, and endurance are incomparable to biological organisms. The ability to execute flawlessly millions of instructions per second is obviously a powerful tool to wield. While acts of insight and intuition are still relegated exclusively to the domain of human thought, powers of reasoning and general problem-solving by computer are steadily improving.[0]

Research in the young field of artificial intelligence (AI) has already yielded some programs with potential educational applications. For example, machines have been programmed to solve word problems in algebra (Bobrow, M.I.T. dissertation, 1966), to complete geometric analogies of the kind that appear on IQ tests and College Board Examinations with success equivalent to that of an average 15 year old (Evans, M.I.T. dissertation, 1964), and to "understand" and respond in nearly natural English to questions and commands about objects in a world of blocks (Winograd, M.I.T. dissertation, 1971).

In general, AI offers CAI qualities which have been heretofore weak or altogether

---

*One interesting thesis is that man's definition of intelligence is changing (retreating) in correspondence to advances in computer capabilities. That is, as machines become capable of performing more and more mental tasks, those tasks become excluded from those which we claim require intelligence.

**Artificial intelligence is the generic name for a collection of specialized research topics such as robotics, machine learning, pattern recognition, automatic theorem-proving, simulation of cognitive processes, question-answering systems, and natural language translation.

† One basic difference is acknowledged between the 'mental' strengths of man and machine: the computer's forte is symbol manipulating, whereas human talents excel in recognizing patterns. It is only by using the information processing capabilities of the computer together with clever programming, that programs can be made to simulate cognitive processes.

[0]See Newell, Shaw, and Simon's General problem solver, in Feigenbaum and Feldman (eds.): *Computers and Thought,* New York, McGraw-Hill, 1963. See also Newell and Simon: *Human Problem Solving.* Englewood Cliffs, N.J., Prentice-Hall, 1972.

lacking: "sensitive" and "intelligent" interaction with a machine. Specifically, application of certain AI techniques can:

1. Facilitate information storage and retrieval
2. Approach natural language conversation
3. Finely discern response patterns
4. Autonomously adapt to changing conditions

These goals can be translated into distinct advantages for the learner, making possible: greater flexibility and mobility in learning sequences; more personalized interaction and greater variety of responses; control over the computer's level of sophistication; and the expectation that the computer could "learn" as a result of its "experience."* Generally, then, a learner could engage the machine less as a task-master and more as a resource in an educational pursuit.

Several alternative modes of AI in CAI are conceivable. While they all use sophisticated built-in mechanisms to promote learning, these modes employ the computer in different roles. For instance:

The Computer as a Benevolent Mentor
The Computer as a Competent Competitor
The Computer as a Problem-Solving Partner
The Computer as a Learner

In the role of a "benevolent mentor," the computer acts as the dispenser and tester of knowledge. The learner depends on it for presenting basic content and direction but is able to influence other factors of instruction, such as sequencing, mode of interaction, and level of difficulty. For the computer to be an effective tutor, it must be capable of (1) asking questions and processing responses, (2) receiving questions and producing answers, and (3) changing approaches according to the response patterns of the particular human tutee. In a vanguard use of AI techniques in CAI, Jaime Carbonell demonstrated the feasibility of what he called "mixed-initiative dialog"** between a student of geography and a computer (Carbonell, 1970). His program (called SCHOLAR) could generate text, questions, and corresponding answers as well as answer questions formulated by the student. SCHOLAR could also change its mode of dialog without specific directions by keeping track of information from the interaction. Interaction with a machine programmed in such a way is like learning from a wise teacher who wishes you well.

In the role of a "competitor," the computer provides an active environment for formulating plans, testing strategies, and exercising both intuitive and logical thinking. The most popular environment is a game in which the learner plays against a competent computer program. The "intelligence" of moves made by the computer game-player can be set at a certain level or may change during the course of play. In either case, the computer's strategic competence must be preprogrammed. For example, in playing the ancient intellectual game of NIM,† a computer program may use an optimal strategy algorithm which will guarantee the computer a win whenever a win is possible; alternatively, the program may use an adaptive system by which it can progressively improve its performance (Block, 1965). Of course, if it were desired, the computer could be

---

*Machine learning is usually defined as improved performance on a specified task.

**Meaning that questions and answers are possible from both sides.

†NIM is a two-person game of taking away sticks (or any items) from several piles. The rules are that some number of sticks must be removed from one (and only one) pile on each player's turn. The player to remove the last stick wins. (The winner can be predicted from the start).

programmed to make all wrong moves or to make its decisions entirely randomly. For complex games such as chess, with no known optimal strategies, clever heuristics* are necessary for both machine and human competitors. In general, interaction with a competent mechanical competitor provides an environment for active, enjoyable learning, free from social embarrassments, political overtones, economic constraints, and so on.

In the role of a "partner," the computer and learner jointly engage in solving a problem. Usually this requires access to previously written programs which perform special functions. (Instances of problem-solving via computer without such programs will be discussed in the next section). A simple form of this usage is *laboratory* problem-solving with a computer. For example, a student wishing to use statistics to summarize data would call upon "canned" programs which "explain themselves" as they are used. Whether by request or because of improper usage, the program would automatically offer instructions on how it is to be used properly for data reduction. To assist in planning, organization, and execution of more complex problems, methods of problem-reduction** could be employed. AI search techniques can assist a person by finding goals or designating the most plausible, the most beneficial, or the least costly subgoals. There are many suitable problem spaces for the computer-as-partner, including: mathematics (e.g., evaluating integrals in the calculus), physical sciences (e.g., conducting experiments in chemistry), and cryptography (e.g., decoding secret messages). Ideally, the problem-solving partnership involves man-machine collaboration—utilizing the talents of each system to the fullest by relegating those tasks for which the computer is best suited to the computer and those tasks in which the human excels to the human. The epitome of such a partnership, in one view, has been portrayed in HAL of *2001: A Space Odyssey* movie fame. Super-computer HAL not only monitors all flight controls and the entire life support system of man's trip to Jupiter but also competes against the crewmen in games of chess (with accompanying psychoanalytic critique). In another futuristic view, one can imagine the ultimate intellectual ally as one who says to its human partner, "Think!" as an invitation to present a problem to be solved. When the computer is given a properly expressed problem, such as a new theorem to prove, it whizzes forth a result and says, "Think again!"

In the role of a "learner," the computer must be capable of receiving instruction; that is, it must be *teachable*. At the most fundamental level, writing a program in computer programming language is "teaching" the computer. The student must express himself logically and unambiguously, for the computer will not accept improperly phrased commands. But, suppose a programming language, which enables a student to express how to make the computer perform, is supplanted by a higher-order language—one which enables him to express how to make the computer learn! Then a student may devise and test strategies for teaching. Choosing from a range of pedagogical approaches available, he may train the computer to "understand" some concept, relationship, or procedure, such as how to play a board game, how to solve a cryptogram, how to use proper grammar, and so on. The computer is, of course, an ideal tutee: it requires explicit expression; it acts only on information provided; and, if instructed properly, it will perform flawlessly.

---

*A heuristic is any method, rule, or trick which may be helpful in solving a problem, such as the complex decision-making involved in making a move in chess. The word "heuristic" means "serving to discover."

**Problem reduction is a method of breaking a problem into its component parts and attempting to solve the resulting set of hopefully simpler problems.

And, in teaching the computer, the student has an objective reflector of his own understandings. The student himself learns by observing the consequences of his teachings—manifest in how well the computer learned.

Ad-Lib CAI

In today's world of exponentially increasing information, it is no longer reasonable to expect students (or anyone else) to keep up with all the "facts and figures." The well-publicized "information explosion" has obviated the once highly acclaimed skill of memorization. What is becoming important, however, is knowing *how* to get information and *what* information to get. If one knows appropriate procedures for sorting thru reams of data and for selecting the desired information quickly and reliably, one is usually regarded as "informed" or "learned." In fact, information is the commodity in the marketplace today; and information processing, whether by computer or by human brain, is the marketable skill.

In light of the high premium placed on procedures for processing information, it is surprising that "schooling" still connotes but one procedure: rote learning. There are a myriad of ways to learn, just as there are many different information processing techniques and problem-solving methods; yet in traditional teaching the materials to be learned and the way in which they are to be learned are usually prescribed. Surely different students learn to accomplish different tasks in different ways and would profit from experience in learning about different procedures for learning. Indeed, if Pygmalion's education is to include opportunities to *learn how to learn,* a new approach to instruction is needed.

In ad-lib CAI, learning about learning occurs in an open environment through active exploration of *procedures.* All that is needed is a "bare-bones" computer system: time-sharing terminals, access to the computer, and a suitable programming language. No prestored curricular materials (as in conventional CAI and simulation-gaming) nor sophisticated software (as in artificial intelligence uses) are required. At the heart of ad-lib CAI is the educational value of studying procedures. Even without a computer, students learn a great deal more when they describe what they are doing, how they decided to do what they are doing, what they plan to do next, and what they want you to do (especially if they are teaching you something like juggling). Not data, but procedures themselves are the subject of student attention. When a computer is brought into play, explicit and precise expression of procedures is required, and students impose the need for rigorous and logical thinking on themselves in order to make their programs work.

The study of *computational* procedures is a particularly rich area of ad-lib CAI learning. Using a programming language as a vehicle for expressing themselves, students can plan, describe, implement, test, and modify procedures—all for automatic execution and immediate results. An easy-to-learn language with simple, versatile commands gives a student immediate and direct use of the computer's power to express procedures. Two programming languages with these characteristics are APL and LOGO.

APL (*A* *P*rogramming *L*anguage) is a new, multipurpose programming language. Originally conceived as a mathematical notation by Kenneth Iverson of IBM, APL provides the user with an extensive selection of tools (mathematical functions) and powerful capabilities for handling arrays of data (both literal and numerical). The tools of the language are mnemonic and are designed to permit natural, concise expression of the formal bases of many mathematical and scientific topics. The fundamental ideas of a discipline can be stated clearly and comprehensibly in a program, and additional operations can be defined by the user as functions consistent with the syntax of APL. For example, in a recent paper entitled "APL and Insight: A Strategy for Teaching," Paul Berry of IBM illustrated the use of APL for exposing concepts in statistics (analysis of variance), business economics (curve-fitting), mathematics (number theory), and computer science (systems modeling).*

LOGO is a special list-processing language developed by Seymour Papert of MIT's Artificial Intelligence Laboratory. In Papert's applications of LOGO, children learn formal concepts through active, creative exploration of procedures. With simple, English-based commands, they express procedures to control physical devices. On the teletype, for example, children write programs to print geometric figures, to play intellectual games, to generate some "computer poetry," and even to give CAI quizzes. Another device, an electronic "turtle" known as Irving, is controlled by LOGO commands and will draw polygons, create artistic designs, and run mazes on a flat surface—thus permitting children to learn principles of computational geometry.

Generally, a programming language such as APL or LOGO serves as a conceptual framework for ad-lib learning. Given the tools of the language (its functions and commands) and governed by the rules of expression (its syntax), the student writes programs to accomplish particular goals. These goals may be set by the student himself or his teacher or friend; and they are easily modifiable in light of new and more intriguing goals, many of which are not identifiable in advance.

The activity of programming permits the free exercise of intuition (tempered only by an objective reflector of reality: the computer's response) and fosters heuristic reasoning. The reward for the student who successfully expresses a procedure is immediately apparent: the program works! When the program does not work, when it produces an error report or an unanticipated result, the student naturally takes responsibility, since *he* wrote it, and sets out to modify it so that it will do his bidding. In any event, the program he produces is a concrete entity, one he can deal with concretely and positively. It is not necessary, as many intellectual failures imply, to start all over again. Engaging in this process of "debugging" (the computer-world term for seeking and destroying errors) is extremely important in developing powers of heuristic reasoning. In fact, as Papert points out, the notion of a "bug" itself is a valuable heuristic idea. It is something to be hunted down, caught, and tamed or killed; and any technique or trick used to do so is fair game (Papert and Feurzeig, 1970).

Ad-lib CAI, then, uses the computer in teaching as less of a "black box" and more of a "glass box"—an approach in which the inner mechanisms of a program are made transparent to the viewer. A program serves to expose and clarify concepts; hence, it is in itself a *pedagogical agent*. This student-initiated, student-responsible, success-oriented approach contrasts with the frantic hand-waving about some abstract concept that is often seen in classrooms.

---

*Other topics suitable for exposition using APL include: elementary algebra, coordinate geometry, statics, calculus, logic, sets, electric circuits, and computer simulation. See Kenneth Iverson, *APL in Exposition,* IBM Technical Report #320-3010, 1972.

CONCLUSION

All of these new directions in instructional applications of computers exemplify an emerging new emphasis: *control* for the student. In gaming and simulation, approximately half of the interaction is determined by the student's moves, freely chosen while he develops strategic skills. In uses of AI in CAI, sophisticated programming allows the student to take control over his own learning and converse with the computer in as close to natural language as possible. In ad-lib CAI, the ultimate control is offered to the student, for he is given full access to the powers of the computer system (plus the corresponding responsibility for making productive use of it).

This new emphasis on control is in marked contrast to conventional tutorial CAI, in which the computer is in control most of the time. Instead of controlling student learning—*do*ing things *to* students—perhaps educators will seek more *human* uses of computers in teaching—giving students a menu of things *to do.*

Perhaps in the near future, Pygmalion will truly be the sculptor of his own education, using the computer as his tool.

REFERENCES

Alpert, D., and Bitzer, D.: Advances in computer-based education: a progress report on the PLATO program. *Report X-10.* Carbondale, Ill., University of Illinois, 1969.
Block H.D.: Learning in some simple nonbiological systems. *American Scientist,* 1965.
Carbonell, Jaime: AI in CAI: an artificial intelligence approach to computer-assisted instruction. *IEEE Transaction(s) on Man-Machine Systems,* December, 1970.
Molnar, Andrew: Computer Innovations in Education. National Science Foundation, 1972.
Papert. and Feurzeig, Programming language as a conceptual framework for teaching mathematics. *Interface,* April 1970.
Research News, 21: No. 9, University of Michigan, March 1971.
Rosenthal, R., and Jacobson, L.: Pygmalion in the Classroom: Self-Fulfilling Prophecies and Teacher Expectations. New York, Holt, Rinehart, and Winston, 1968.

30 the fun they had*

Isaac Asimov

Margie even wrote about it that night in her diary. On the page headed May 17, 2157, she wrote, "Today Tommy found a real book!"

It was a very old book. Margie's grandfather once said that when he was a little boy *his* grandfather told him that there was a time when all stories were printed on paper.

They turned the pages, which were yellow and crinkly, and it was awfully funny to read words that stood still instead of moving the way they were supposed to—on a screen, you know. And then, when they turned back to the page before, it had the same words on it that it had had when they read it the first time.

"Gee," said Tommy, "what a waste. When you're through with the book, you just throw it away, I guess. Our television screen must have had a million books on it and it's good for plenty more. I wouldn't throw *it* away."

"Same with mine," said Margie. She was eleven and hadn't seen as many telebooks as Tommy had. He was thirteen.

She said, "Where did you find it?"

"In my house." He pointed without looking, because he was busy reading. "In the attic."

"What's it about?"

"School."

Margie was scornful. "School? What's there to write about school? I hate school."

Margie always hated school, but now she hated it more than ever. The mechanical teacher had been giving her test after test in geography and she had been doing worse and worse until her mother had shaken her head sorrowfully and sent for the County Inspector.

He was a round little man with a red face and a whole box of tools with dials and wires. He smiled at Margie and gave her an apple, then took the teacher apart. Margie had hoped he wouldn't know how to put it together again, but he knew how all right, and, after an hour or so, there it was again, large and black and ugly, with a big screen on which all the lessons were shown and the questions were asked. That wasn't so bad. The part Margie hated most was the slot where she had to put homework and test papers. She always had to write them out in a punch code they made her learn when she was six years old, and the mechanical teacher calculated the mark in no time.

---

*Reprinted with permission from *Today's Education*.

The Inspector had smiled after he was finished and patted Margie's head. He said to her mother, "It's not the little girl's fault, Mrs. Jones. I think the geography sector was geared a little too quick. Those things happen sometimes. I've slowed it up to an average ten-year level. Actually, the overall pattern of her progress is quite satisfactory." And he patted Margie's head again.

Margie was disappointed. She had been hoping they would take the teacher away altogether. They had once taken Tommy's teacher away for nearly a month because the history sector had blanked out completely.

So she said to Tommy, "Why would anyone write about school?"

Tommy looked at her with very superior eyes. "Because it's not our kind of school, stupid. This is the old kind of school that they had hundreds and hundreds of years ago." He added loftily, pronouncing the word carefully, *"Centuries* ago."

Margie was hurt. "Well, I don't know what kind of school they had all that time ago." She read the book over his shoulder for a while, then said, "Anyway, they had a teacher."

"Sure they had a teacher, but it wasn't a *regular* teacher. It was a man."

"A man? How could a man be a teacher?"

"Well, he just told the boys and girls things and gave them homework and asked them questions."

"A man isn't smart enough."

"Sure he is. My father knows as much as my teacher."

"He can't. A man can't know as much as a teacher."

"He knows almost as much, I betcha."

Margie wasn't prepared to dispute that. She said, "I wouldn't want a strange man in my house to teach me."

Tommy screamed with laughter. "You don't know much, Margie. The teachers didn't live in the house. They had a special building and all the kids went there."

"And all the kids learned the same thing?"

"Sure, if they were the same age."

"But my mother says a teacher has to be adjusted to fit the mind of each boy and girl it teaches and that each kid has to be taught differently."

"Just the same they didn't do it that way then. If you don't like it, you don't have to read the book."

"I didn't say I didn't like it," Margie said quickly. She wanted to read about those funny schools.

They weren't even half-finished when Margie's mother called, "Margie! School!"

Margie looked up. "Not yet, Mamma."

"Now!" said Mrs. Jones. "And it's probably time for Tommy, too."

Margie said to Tommy, "Can I read the book some more with you after school?"

"Maybe," he said nonchalantly. He walked away whistling, the dusty old book tucked beneath his arm.

Margie went into the schoolroom. It was right next to her bedroom, and the mechanical teacher was on and waiting for her. It was always on at the same time every day except Saturday and Sunday, because her mother said little girls learned better if they learned at regular hours.

The screen was lit up, and it said: "Today's arithmetic lesson is on the addition of proper fractions. Please insert yesterday's homework in the proper slot."

Margie did so with a sigh. She was thinking about the old schools they had when her grandfather's grandfather was a little boy. All the kids from the whole neighborhood came, laughing and shouting in the schoolyard, sitting together in the schoolroom, going home together at the end of the day. They learned the same things, so they could help one another on the homework and talk about it.

And the teachers were people. . . .

The mechanical teacher was flashing on the screen: "When we add the fractions ½ and ¼—"

Margie was thinking about how the kids must have loved it in the old days. She was thinking about the fun they had.

STARTING OUT RIGHT

EDUCATION AND THE EARLY YEARS

"*Take advantage of every opportunity to enjoy yourself before you get into kindergarten, Brian. That's when they start breathing down your neck.*"

It's startling to realize how much public attitudes toward early childhood education have changed in recent years. Today most educators and many politicians treat the education of young children as an idea of well-established value. Yet in the not too distant past, when we were being shown horror films of life in Communist China, one of the scenes that was supposed to appall us most thoroughly was the institutionalization of the very young.

Much has happened in the intervening years. A considerable body of research has shown that the years before age six are the most critical for the child's learning. These findings also indicate that the child who is "deprived" when he arrives at first grade will continue to lag behind his classmates. Thus preschool programs have been developed to help make up the difference.

Early childhood education has also been the beneficiary of a number of social trends. Various levels of government have established "child care" programs for welfare mothers so they can take training courses or work and thereby get off welfare. The women's rights movement wants free child care programs to enable women to pursue careers. Widespread early childhood education programs could mean employment for thousands of "surplus" teachers. Parents, concerned with giving their children the best education possible, find it easy to delegate the task to "professionals." Businessmen, who see child care as a lucrative market, have tried to exploit it by franchising child care chains. With so many people looking *so hard to find benefits in early childhood education it's no wonder that benefits have been found.*

What is the potential of early childhood education? David Day feels that if it does not serve the child's needs first, it isn't worthwhile. Marion Blank and Ofra Reisman illustrate how a carefully conducted program can aid a child in learning. And, earlier, Dwight Allen and Philip Christensen called for "womb to tomb schooling" if we are to meet society's needs.

But there are other arguments that deserve to be heard. People like Ivan Illich, Paul Goodman, and John Holt argue that schooling (as we know it) stifles children's imaginations and stunts their intellectual growth. From their perspective, any further institutionalization of children would be disastrous. Other critics warn that "early childhood education," given conventional budget limitations, may turn into strictly custodial care to keep children "out of the way." Conservatives feel that the government has already meddled too much in our private lives and should leave preschool children alone.

Another line of criticism sees early childhood education as the first step in the "junior rat race." Indeed, there are parents who send their children to the "right" nursery school so they can get into the "right" kindergarten—and so on up the line to college and graduate school. These critics see children who are pressured to "achieve" and denied the right to be children.

Some researchers question the substance and direction of early education. In the review presented here, Moore, Moon, and Moore examine common proposals for early education and find little evidence that they fit the needs of young children. Indeed, some evidence indicates that age six might even be too early to start conventional schooling. Instead, they suggest that the parent at home, aided, perhaps, by visits from professionals, might well be the best early childhood educator.

early education and the improvement of society 31

David E. Day

Whether we care to admit it or not, we are hell-bent on extending education down to our very young. All too often, our motives are explained by a loosely-knit psychological rationale or by political expediency. We urgently need to explore the many "whys" of early education, if not to get answers, at least to sharpen the issues and in some small measure promote a debate.

We may well be at a point in time when the relationship between parent, child, and programs for young children can be transformed. One can imagine day care centers, nursery schools, and parent-child programs that operate to support all families, providing services unique to locale and family. Yet, unless we consider our position carefully, we may, by default, merely transplant inappropriate models to our new parent-child centers, child development programs, and nursery schools. We don't have to see early education simply as a downward extension of the elementary school. Neither should we view it as merely remedial for children from families incapable of providing adequate care, or as a place of storage for families who need temporary care. The early childhood education movement should be just that—a movement toward new ideas about child, parent, and family development that just might strengthen all of American society.

OUR CHILDREN ARE OUR MOST VALUABLE RESOURCE: TRUE OR FALSE?

One might expect any statement about early education in the United States to begin with a reaffirmation of our society's concern for its young and our attempts to enhance our children's development. We have free education; we say we believe every child should use the school to become whatever he is capable of becoming. We have child labor laws and massive public health programs aimed at preventing childhood disease. Our welfare provisions, albeit marginal at best, are more liberal when small children are the recipients. Orphaned, abandoned, or unwanted children have been taken care of by the state. We could find support nearly everywhere for the assumption that we really care for our small children. Yet, is it so?

Except for certain preventive health measures, concern for our children only appears in response to some social crisis, however small. Children without parents and infants born out of wedlock were for many years kept in asylums, jails, and reformatories. No special provisions were made for them, they were treated in much the same way as all other inmates. Even the child labor laws that loom so large in the history of the progressive American movement were enacted (as late as 1938) in response to an impassioned minority who were "shocked" at the abuse employers were heaping on our children. No real consideration had been given to the effects of employment on children before 11 year olds were sent to the mines and 9 year olds were locked in the garment factories. Our decision to employ children came simply because they were cheap and reasonably dependable labor.

Only a few years ago we believed that a child's potential was determined primarily by heredity. From this we developed a fatalistic attitude toward our young and came to believe that the greatest efforts should be directed at shaping their moral and religious attitudes and behavior. Today we believe in the power of the environment to shape our children, and have created images to shape them in. We tend to see our achievements, as adults and parents, as very closely tied to what our children become. A child is less and less a child and more and more a potential; he is an artist to be, my son the doctor, or an athletic hero; he is a status symbol or an agent through which parents lead second lives.

FAMILY ORGANIZATION AND PARENT COMPETENCE

Our present position is a logical consequence of our clinging to attitudes about family and child which were developed on the frontier but have become totally unreal and unworkable in a highly congested urban culture. We have been victimized once again by the lag between agrarian values and a technological society. From this lag have come our self-delusions regarding adult-child relationships and the serious gap between our pronouncements and our behavior.

Less than half a century ago, rural families were largely dependent for their well-being on the number of able children in the family. Sons and daughters were valuable and much-needed helpers on the farm and in the home. In fact, the family farm was just that—a collection of acres, implements, and animals central to the life of the family that was developed and improved from generation to generation.

The American rural tradition highlights the value our society places on the autonomy and self-reliance of the extended family unit, even though we now view the family as nuclear rather than extended. American society clearly continues to believe that the family *is* completely responsible for the child. Parents are expected to feed, clothe, begin to educate, promote moral character, instill a need to achieve, and provide intense counseling for their children. They also are to blame when one of their own engages in some anti-social act. Our "great" popular psychologists have supported this by telling mothers and fathers how a child *should* develop and what parents can *do* so the child will develop in the proper manner. Obviously, when a parent discovers that his child has "strayed," he may feel intense guilt for being unable to benefit from the wisdom of great men. Church, physician, school, the police and courts, and public agencies have supported these attitudes in a multitude of ways, if only by failing to examine their position. Thus, we still hold to the traditional characterization of the frontier family in a highly industrialized, technologically oriented, congested society of run-together megalopoli.

An important part of these attitudes is the belief in the innate competence of all families, which may well be one major reason why we abuse our children in so many ways. Society acts to help the family only when it has been upset, destroyed, or otherwise judged incompetent, and then only to deal with the immediate problem. The family in health—a most relative state at best—receives little, if any, societal assistance. We really have not yet conceived of preventive family-health programs, for these would require admitting that the ability to provide all support necessary for children is not a natural consequence of parenthood.

We began this section with the assumption that the U.S. is a child-centered culture. This assumption seems at least open to question. Some who read this essay will take exception to many of the major ideas. Some will see nothing but a clutch of straw men, while others will gladly accept the suggestion that our society is unconcerned with child development, for it fits with their system of beliefs. The point is to listen carefully when we talk about being child-centered, not to accept this belief *a priori.*

SHOULD WE DEVELOP EARLY CHILDHOOD EDUCATION?

The only defensible reason for establishing day care centers, nursery schools, or Head Start programs is to promote the mutual benefit of child and parent. There have always been reasons why "keeping" children has been senseless and often damaging to child and parent. We now recognize that experience is too crucial to development for us to send our young away without paying particular attention to what is happening to them. Day care centers, nursery schools, or primary education programs can be designed in ways that produce great amounts of good for child and parent by supplementing the role of parent, enhancing the growth of the child, and allowing parents to pursue options for occupation, education, recreation, and family relationships that otherwise might not exist. Day care should not be justified solely because it allows parental job training or employment, nor should it be merely an adjunct to the women's liberation movement. Early education programs must be seen as a vital part of child rearing and family development and as preventive socio-medical centers if they are going to serve children, the family, and society.

It is possible to develop early childhood education for exclusively adult ends. We believe this to be the case at present, and there is every likelihood that it will continue. This may be another consequence of our insistence that only incompetent families need special societal assistance; it may also destroy the potential benefit of early education.

Attitudes one brings to any early childhood program will strongly influence its direction. Parents who want to get rid of their children will get programs that take their children. Whatever benefits or disadvantages accruing to the child will be incidental to the reason for the program's existence. By the same token, if we see early education and child care programs as a societal link to the family, we can create programs that will support parent and child and strengthen the whole family as well. One would hope this vision would prevail in our very rapid move into early childhood education.

Should we focus on child care and preschool programs? Without question! Should we devote large amounts of resources and time to the development of programs for our young? Indeed we must! Yet we must also focus our attention on the broader society, not exclusively on parent, child, or school.

EARLY EDUCATION FOR FAMILY DEVELOPMENT

Throughout this essay, the emphasis has been on two points. First, we urgently need to change our attitudes about parent-child relationships and the role of societal support services in helping all families develop fully. Second, the full development of both child and parent need not be seen as antagonistic or mutually exclusive. Examples of early education for family development will therefore focus on procedures by which these points can be effected rather than on innovative and creative classroom, nursery, or crèche programs. The task is to design processes by which parent and child development can be supported by the collective wisdom of society.

Pre-parent And Parent Education

In some high schools, child development has become a vital part of the curriculum. Schools have started nurseries for three and four year old children which serve as observational and instructional laboratories for the high school students. These may be part of a vocational program for students planning to seek jobs as assistants to teachers or other child development specialists. The nursery may also be a child development laboratory for the study of human growth and development. The high school nursery would also seem to be an exceptionally valuable adjunct in aiding family development by helping to educate young people in the roles and responsibilities of parenthood. Many students will marry and become parents soon after leaving high school. Most will have only a few, often misleading, ideas about how parents can affect the development of a child. The problems of a husband-wife relationship are almost never addressed. The mere existence of a nursery school on the high school campus lends itself to the study of children, the role of parents, and the ways in which family, parent, and child development might be enhanced.

Our once pressing concern over the statistics of pregnancy in high school is being replaced by concern for the girls themselves. Must they leave high school, banished forever from educational contact with their peers, or should they be allowed to continue their studies up to delivery and to resume them soon afterwards? Some schools are even making provisions for infant care of these children. In such ways infants and young children are finding their way to the high school without any apparent trauma to children, mothers, teachers, or students. As we create more day care centers, we should consider the school as an extremely sensible location for the care of young children, the continuing education of parents, and the preparation for parenthood.*

---

*I am very much aware of the dangers involved in giving schools and school systems greater potential control over our very young. I agree with those critics who charge the nation's schools with being unresponsive and even unsympathetic to the needs of our people. There is no way in which we could justify this lack of response in regard to early child care and education. I would assume that infant and child care programs would be *housed* in schools, used by teacher and student, but *controlled by the parents* of the children in attendance. Some will very quickly label this as an unreal and naive position. All I can say is that I have no evidence that parent control of programs designed to serve parents is either naive or unreal. If nothing else, the idea seems worth a field test.

Infant And Day Care

I believe that all parents, children, and families, and consequently, all of society can receive substantial benefit from infant and child care service, nursery schools, and primary education. The somewhat paternalistic attitude that only the pathological can benefit from special community services is patent nonsense and to a large extent inhibits the creation of support services for all families in our society. The dread of being found wanting as a parent seems to have influenced, more than a little, the contemporary move by women's liberationists to speak of the need for day care in dyadic terms. Feminists often say that the *child* needs day care and can benefit from it; the *mother* needs day care and can only be liberated with it. It is unfortunate indeed that in striving to achieve her rightful status in society the American woman finds it necessary to think of child care almost exclusively as a step needed to remove the yoke of male oppression. It is unfortunate for all that we seem incapable of envisioning ways in which family relationships, including male-female relationships, might be strengthened by the availability of family-focused child care programs.

RACISM, POVERTY, AND CHILD DEVELOPMENT SERVICES

The particular needs of the poor, the illiterate, and especially, the ethnic and racial minorities must be reflected in infant day care centers. Day care has been alive—though chronically distressed—in the urban core for over half a century. Day care centers for the poor, urban blacks, and Spanish-speaking Americans have been mainly custodial and often have abused both child and parent. The centers are located in drab church basements, community centers, or quasi-social service agencies. The staff has all too often had minimal training, if any, and this usually in the care of numbers of infants. Financial support has been marginal and the staff has been poorly paid. Day care has been a central part of the nation's urban welfare system and has been offered as an incentive to support oneself and keep off the dole.

Even now, when child care and early education seem to be on the lips of so many political leaders, services for the poor and the black, Puerto Ricans and Chicanos are all too often tied to work incentive programs, job training, or employment. In fact, the nation's politicians seem to be impressed with the need to link child service to family assertiveness and motivation. It is becoming increasingly less likely that a poor black mother will be able to avail herself of the services of a day care center without being obliged to enroll in one of an infinite array of "educational programs." Service comes at a price—a price often paid out of one's sense of self-respect and self-worth. The family that suffers from racial or ethnic discrimination or lack of training, or who feels the effects of technological development and resultant unemployment, is acted upon by social technocrats who presume to know best what these families need. We need to support the development of power by the powerless, especially pertaining to programs purporting to assist the disadvantaged.

The notion that power will be given to people who continue to be powerless is more than a bit naive. Power is not given, it is taken, a fact that often tears at the concept of egalitarianism. Nonetheless, until all people have the responsibility for deciding how they will use social services, these services will serve some and act on others. Furthermore, without the distribution of power, the attitude that programs such as day care and early education can serve all families will never be developed. Without drastic changes in attitudes about who should judge what families need regardless of their circumstances, child care and family support services will likely continue to reflect the values, aspirations, and child-rearing customs of the affluent and powerful.

Without question, the cores of our cities are rapidly rotting. It is in the tenement, the ghetto, and the rundown sections of our cities that we find the greatest incidence of antisocial behavior. Not only do more crimes take place but the percentage of violent crimes is proportionately higher. Unemployment and underemployment abound; the use of hard drugs has long since reached epidemic proportions. Stability of self, family, and occupation seems to be very rapidly disintegrating. Furthermore, the greatest incidence of school failure is found in the low status urban black, Puerto Rican, and white communities. Families caught in the distress of urban poverty and discrimination need assistance from the rest of society in unique and special ways. To withdraw programs for the poor, to refuse to increase assistance of all kinds to these people under the guise of equal treatment for all citizens would be a sick joke indeed. The fact that social pathology does exist cannot be interpreted as *prima facie* evidence that large numbers of our nation's poor are incompetent to judge what is good for them. The belief that the poor and the abused minorities can wisely judge how to improve their lives must be tenaciously held until convincing evidence has been presented to the contrary. In all too many instances our nation seems to have acted *a priori* in determining that only the successful are competent to judge what is valuable for the less successful.

EARLY EDUCATION AND CULTURAL PLURALISM

There is a real danger that early education programs focusing on individual and family development will become agents supporting the system of privatism so widespread in our society today. Early education programs should not be developed just to make it easier for everyone to "do his own thing" or to create a setting in which one becomes only tolerant of the behavior and the needs of others. We, as a society, have traveled this route for too long. We should concern ourselves with our development individually, as members of a family, and as members of the larger social group. Early education centers can become leaders in the creation of a plural society.

We are witnessing a surge in programs for young children designed to foster ethnic and racial identity and pride. "Black is beautiful" is more than a rallying cry, it is an assertion of one's belief in all that encompasses Afro-American subculture. Furthermore, demands are being made of our political leaders to give the community the power to decide what takes place in schools serving minority groups. This is heady stuff! The many different groups of people that have contributed so much to our nation are no longer "keeping their powder dry," and this is as it should be. Bilingual programs for native French and Spanish-speaking children are developing from Maine to southern California. Legislators are fast becoming sensitive to the richness of a culturally diverse nation and are passing laws allowing, among other things, school instruction in a language other than English.

As good as the recognition of diversity is, it is not enough. We now need to emphasize the concepts that what one does as a member of a group influences others in that group, and that what one group does must be considered in terms of its effect on other groups. The creation of programs for child, parent, and family development must also recognize the absolute necessity for focusing on man to man, family to family, and group to group relationships. We must consider what effect our efforts at early education will have on others. Narrowly conceived programs that stress group pride while denigrating other groups can serve only to worsen the already extreme racial, ethnic, and status divisions in our society. Furthermore, programs that treat only individual family needs, without considering the possibility of joining together mutually concerned families, will contribute to the attitude that one need not be involved with his fellow man beyond the confines of the family.

The move toward early childhood education and day care in our nation provides us with a very appropriate means of transforming society so that all Americans are given a greater opportunity to reach their human potential—as children, parents, members of a family, participants in a community, and citizens of a human world. To focus on the child without at the same time trying to assist parents, communities, subcultural groups, and the larger society to become more responsive to human needs would lead to little significant aid to the child. A child lives in culture, is of culture, and will become what culture makes of him. To simply provide "private" care and "special" education for infants and children, while ignoring such real problems as parents' need for assistance, the dynamics of powerlessness, anomie, and community disintegration, and the self-destructive nature of ethnocentrism, is to operate in total ignorance of both the needs of modern American society and the possibilities of assisting these needs.

FAMILY DESTRUCTION AND EARLY EDUCATION

It is a real possibility, as suggested earlier, that institutionalizing parent and child education might endanger an already fragile family structure. As child development and education centers appear, parent obligations for child support may become even more wispy and remote. In fact, it could be predicted that if infant and child care and education programs operate with only tacit family approval, without parent participation and involvement, the death knell for the American family will have been sounded. Observers have already suggested that our cultural penchant for creating organizations to meet human needs that historically have been cared for by family or tribe, has resulted in the attitude that a parent, a child, or a family is incapable of providing for itself; that one must rely on the expertise of other agencies to be alerted to the apparent needs of individuals or groups. Examples rush to mind: the school and the education of our young; the physician and medical care; the welfare agency and care for those in need; the church and moral development; the police and drug abuse; the government and consumer protection. The most telling aspect of each of these examples is that our investment in the agency has not resulted in greater human good. Our medical care has not substantially improved over the past decades, the education of our young is in a frightful state, and the police and the church are largely ineffective in even understanding the issues they are called upon to treat. There is ample reason to be skeptical about the "advantages" of rebuilding human potential through another organizational schema.

These negative examples do not negate the possible value of organization for development. They do suggest, rather forcefully, that the danger is in the establishment of a client-expert relationship in which the parent submits himself for treatment judged appropriate by the resident diagnostician, the child is enrolled for care and education outside the family, and the family is treated as a pathological entity. The administration of state and national welfare provides a clear example of this danger.

Early childhood education must learn from this tragic accumulation of error. The family, the child, the parent, and consequently all of society cannot be helped by a system of child development centers in which parent and child are considered clients. Both the centers and their users can be strengthened, however, if they become partners in creating programs designed to increase each person's living competence. Such a partnership means that the programs are controlled by those who use them.

Were attendance in early childhood education programs to become required, the goals for their creation outlined here would probably be blunted on the nursery door.* Early childhood centers, created by citizens of a community and sustained by their interests and participation, must be seen as available for use by parents who choose to use them. One can imagine a vast number of these centers with an infinite array of curricula and organizational structures, each arrived at through careful and deliberate study by parents and staff. It should always be kept in mind when creating these programs that the main purpose is to assist in the development of the child, the competence of the parent, the strength of the family, and the building of a more viable society. These few guidelines seem minimally necessary.**

SUMMARY

Our children must be seen as our culture's most valuable resource. Every effort must be made to promote their well-being, and, through them, our culture's well-being. What we become as adults is strongly influenced by the events of our childhood. Our values, our attitudes about all things, our relationships with others and perceptions about the nature of being human may be firmly fixed by the experiences we have during the early years. During the years from birth to eight or nine, a period of most rapid intellectual, physical, and emotional growth, we learn the very human role.

Society's interest in early childhood education is only now beginning to be felt. Many resources and much effort will be spent in the immediate future in attempts to increase the number and kind of child and infant care centers and early childhood education programs. A commitment seems to have been made to provide funds from our nation's treasury. We only need to wait for our leaders to decide how the money shall be distributed.

We, as a society, must not wait any longer to examine those programs that already exist for our young and to ask if we simply want to expand our offerings. Or, do we want to ask what these programs should be for child and society? Should we use our knowledge about children, the family, the political realities of our time, the social action movements, and the need for a cultural re-birth and dare to suggest that our rush to early childhood education can assist us in meeting these imperative social needs?

---

*Apologies to John Goodlad

**The creation of community-controlled child development centers may be seen by some as just one more vehicle by which our already polarized and separated society may be sustained. Without question, some groups and communities will see them as a means of protecting some children from contact with other children. Racists may use the centers, as they have the neighborhood schools, as a guarantee for the maintenance of segregation. I would only urge those who raise the question about possible effects of community-controlled programs on racial and ethnic isolation to re-read my comments on developing pluralism through early childhood education.

It seems likely that all parents can be helped in their efforts to raise their children and develop a family. Do we want to build an early childhood education system that will assist children, parents, and the family, or are we, as parents, more interested in creating a huge early childhood education complex that will meet our adult needs, imagined or real? Whether or not these questions get asked, decisions will be made, if only by default. If we choose to do so, new programs can be created that are responsive to society, family, and parent, and which recognize the nature of early human development and focus on the development of the child as well.

32 the course of teaching

Marion Blank
Ofra Reisman

Compensatory preschool programs represent "a downward extension of the school to prevent the failure of lower lower-class children in elementary school" (Kamii, 1971, p. 283). As such, they have taken on a unique role in education, for they are expected to achieve a type of generalized transfer that is rarely asked of any other academic program. Most curricula for older children are considered successful if they transmit the particular subject matter that they encompass (e.g., those aspects of mathematics, English, science, and so on that one wishes the student to acquire). By contrast, the goal of preschool compensatory programs is not limited to any specific subject matter, but rather tries to alter the poorly functioning child's mode of intellectual performance to facilitate all further academic learning.

Increasingly, the feasibility of attaining this goal is coming under serious question, particularly since early efforts have yielded neither rapid nor marked success (see Silberman, 1970). While the skepticism is valid, it would nevertheless be unfortunate to abandon the goal prematurely, for the potential pay-off could still be enormous. The problem, of course, is to determine the ways and means to attain the pay-off.

Given the current absence of precise knowledge in the areas of both teaching and learning, the proposed solution will vary greatly according to each investigator's own theoretical orientation. What will be presented here are some of the ideas stemming from one such proposal. The ideas are based upon a structured tutorial program developed originally by the senior author wherein children in the three-to-five year age range are seen in short, daily individual sessions of approximately fifteen to twenty minutes duration (see Blank and Solomon, 1968, 1969).

The rationale for having chosen this method of instruction has been presented elsewhere (Blank, 1970), and it will not form the core of the present paper. Nevertheless, because this method is so integral to our conceptualization of the child's difficulties, it seems necessary to discuss at least briefly the major considerations that led to its selection. The one-to-one format has been adopted because it affords a unique advantage in the learning situation—it allows meaningful cognitive interaction to develop between teacher and child. Such interaction occurs when each partner recognizes and responds appropriately to the actions, ideas, and demands of the other. If this meshing is not present, teaching, regardless of content, cannot take place, for there is no substantive point of contact that relates the two participants. All teaching is based on the assumption that such an interchange is present. Even a simple request such as, "What color was the special door on the house?" requires that the child not only possess the relevant concepts and language, but, much more basically, the willingness and readiness to respond to the request imposed by another person, particularly an adult authority figure.

Unfortunately, poorly functioning children (regardless of what designation is used—"deprived," "disadvantaged," or "lower class") do not come to the school situation ready to engage in such interchange (Hess and Shipman, 1965; Labov, 1969). This is not to deny that they enjoy the nursery setting. Contact with children and toys are pleasurable for all youngsters. But when cognitive demands are imposed, they are likely to withdraw from the situation because they are not accustomed to this type of interchange. The irony of this situation is that the children are led to avoid those situations which most compensatory programs are precisely designed to offer.

Unfortunately, the constraints of the traditional group setting severely limit the teacher's options in overcoming or correcting this situation. A child who performs poorly will, by definition, make many wrong responses and attain many incorrect ideas. It is at these points that the child is most in need of the teacher's help, since it is essential if he is to be led to work through his errors. But even in a small group setting, the teacher can rarely give sustained guidance, for she has to simultaneously retain the attention of the other children. If she loses that attention, the group with its young constituents will rapidly fall into disarray.

For example, imagine a situation where the teacher asks, "Why couldn't the pot hold the water? Eddie, what do you think?" If the child is unable to answer or gives an incorrect answer, the teacher is placed in a difficult position. Should she keep her attention on the one child, the group will become restless. Since the group must be saved if the class is to function, what the teacher almost inevitably must do is to turn to another child for the correct response. In this case, the child who did not know the information still need not have learned it. Even if he attended to the second child's answer, the same difficulties that caused his failure on the initial asking of the question may leave him uncertain why the answer is correct.

By contrast, the one-to-one situation eliminates the pressures imposed by the group and frees the teacher to work uninterruptedly with the child. In addition, it is almost the ideal prototype for developing the meaningful teacher-pupil interaction that is necessary for learning in the academic setting. By itself, however, the tutorial situation is not sufficient. As has been emphasized from a variety of different perspectives, including curricula based on programmed learning, the open classroom, and Montessori instruction, there is a critical need for the lesson to be matched with the level of the student (Hunt, 1961). This same need exists in the one-to-one situation. Because of the importance of this synchronization, a major part of the effort of the tutorial program has been directed toward the development of principles whereby the teacher can diagnose and treat each particular child's strengths and difficulties at each point in the course of the teaching. It is to this issue that the present paper is directed.

In order to illustrate some of the principles that have thus far been evolved, the treatment of a poorly functioning, hyperactive, four year old child in the tutorial program will be presented. Three lessons are schematically outlined, each from a different period in the first six weeks of his tutoring. These points were selected in order to exemplify the different principles that are operative at various stages in the teaching.

LESSON A

Introduction

The lesson that follows was the first that the teacher had with Danny. In line with the comments above, its main goal was to initiate meaningful cognitive interchange between the teacher and child. Given the child's limitations, the responsibility for establishing and maintaining the interchange clearly falls on the teacher. This goal is difficult to achieve because it requires behaviors that run counter to the well-established training methods that emphasize permissiveness in the nursery school setting. In particular, it requires that the teacher assume a far greater directive role than usual, for the interchange will lapse if she does not constantly foster its existence, even when the child displays little or no inclination to participate.

To this end, we have found it useful to concentrate on *demands* that are so simple as to be nonthreatening, but at the same time varied enough to attract the child and maintain his participation. The core for this achievement lies in the sphere of verbally directed requests for motor action—requests which tap simple perceptual-motor discriminations (e.g., "kick the ball"), imitation (e.g., "now you do what I just did"), and visual matching (e.g., "pick up the same one that I did"). These behaviors are within the repertoire of almost all preschool children and well-suited to their action-oriented predisposition in dealing with the world. It is evident that such demands totally avoid the usual complex questions that are often seen as fundamental to enrichment (e.g., questions demanding concepts, imagery, prediction, cause and effect, and so on). Such questions are beyond the child's grasp at this early point and therefore pose only a threat, not a challenge.

Although the goal is to minimize error in the early lessons, mistakes are nevertheless bound to occur, if only because the child is not yet used to meeting even simple demands in an adult-child dialogue. When errors occur, they provide the teacher with important clues as to the child's source of failure (e.g., does he fail items demanding memory, or does he fail requests for relevant descriptions of events, and so on). The treatment of any specific error, however, requires that the child have already developed the willingness to participate and the capacity to sustain attention. Since he is unlikely to have this capability at the start of the training, specific errors in the initial lessons are noted, but they are not treated. Instead, the problem is immediately reduced so that the child does not feel the frustration of failure.

A variety of techniques are available for this purpose (Blank, 1973); in large measure, they require that the teacher actively intervene and provide most of the information initially requested but still leave a minor part of the task for the child. For example, in the lesson below, the child is asked to get "two pins" and he selects only one. Rather than even attempt to test whether the child's concept of "two" is adequate, the teacher provides the information in a matter-of-fact way, almost as if there had been a simple misinterpretation by the child (e.g., she says, "No, I wanted two. This is only one. Please get one more; then we'll have two"). In many cases, this looks like didactic teaching, but it is not. The information is provided, not in the expectation that the child will learn from it, but to

1. allow the lesson to continue meaningfully in spite of the child's failure
2. allow the child to continue to participate in tasks which present him with difficulty (even though "participation" may be the simple action of lifting one more pin).

Outline of the First Lesson. The first lesson concerns a toy bowling game and it is used because it permits a great deal of gross motor movement and thus has obvious advantages with hyperactive children. The italics are used to indicate the particular problems or requests the teacher is putting before the child.

When Danny entered the room, he saw a bag of plastic bowling pins on the table that the teacher had prepared for the lesson. He ran to them, saying, "I want those." The teacher asked him to *take out a pin* and *put it next to the wall.* He readily did so and was asked to *take out two more.* He took one, placed it, ran to some bricks in the corner of the room. The teacher said, "No, that's only one. *Quick, go get another.* That will be two." Another few requests were then given in which the teacher used rapid pace to have Danny select and place three more pins (e.g., "Now, as fast as you can, *get two pins* and *rush over* and *put them near the others*"). He complied eagerly, without saying anything.

The teacher arranged the pins in a set order on the floor (a row of three red and three blue) and gave Danny six identical pins. She asked him to recreate the same order next to the one she had made. He said, "I can do that," and ran off to the sink in the corner of the room. The teacher went over to him, took his hand and said, "We'll play here another time. Now, though, let's finish our game over here." Because of his extreme restlessness, she simplified the task to the easiest possible level, handing him the pins one at a time, placing her finger on the spot where he was to place the pin, and then in a loud and firm voice (to attract his attention) she asked him *to put it down.* He was able to place four pins in this manner but then again showed signs of restlessness.

Realizing that his span of attention was about exhausted, the teacher quickly placed the last two pins herself and said, "Now let's start the game. Go get the ball." Danny happily agreed and the teacher said, *"Kick the ball* and see how many pins get knocked down." He threw the ball, and the teacher asked *"What did I ask you to do?"* He replied, "Hit them." She said, "That's right, but I wanted you to kick the ball to them, not to throw the ball. Let's straighten the pins and then *you'll kick the ball."* He did so and began to jump in an excited, hyperactive manner, yelling, "They fell," and he started kicking the ball wildly about the room.

The teacher quickly retrieved the ball, put her arms about Danny (to help restrain him), and said "Now you kicked that very well and it went fast. Let's see *if you can roll it now very slowly."* While keeping her arms around the child, she said, "Watch, I'll do it." She completed the action and then asked him *to do it.* After he did so, she asked him to *pick up the pins* and *put them in a bag* she was holding. He responded readily and after he completed the task, she told him to *pick out one of any color he liked.* He selected a red one and she asked, *"What color is it?"* He started shouting colors, "Yellow, green, blue." Rather than adding another potentially confusing association, the teacher did not tell him the correct label. Instead, she held up a box of crayons and said, *"Find me a color the same as the pin."* He did so and she congratulated him.

She asked him *to draw a pin* like the one in her hand. He scribbled several lines across the paper. She said she would help him; she took another paper, drew the entire pin except for the bottom line and asked him *where it needed to be finished.* He pointed correctly. Because of his poor motor control, the teacher said, *"Now let's draw it together."* She put her hand over his, they drew the line, and the child then returned to his room.

Comments on the Lesson. Even when observers are informed in advance about the simplicity of the content in the initial lessons, their reaction is invariably one of surprise and disappointment. The surprise generally stems from the contrast between the actual content of the lesson and the images conjured up relative to the goal of enhancing cognitive functioning. The lesson is so manifestly below whatever processes we would put under the rubric of human cognition that it hardly seems worth the effort to teach. The disappointment is a natural corollary of the surprise. It seems pointless to deal with such trivial situations when we know the vast range of skills that the child must develop. In addition, the traditional content-oriented method of teaching often leaves the teacher feeling that in the type of lesson presented, nothing has been learned. Typical comments are: "But what did you teach?" "You barely mentioned color, and you didn't even talk about shape," and even more, "You didn't encourage the child to talk and express himself freely."

These feelings make it difficult to see what this type of lesson can accomplish. Its value lies not in teaching the child to rehearse a few specific concepts but, as stated earlier, in taking his established behaviors and placing them within the sphere of the teacher-child dialogue. Actions such as kicking and throwing are usually performed apart from any verbal interaction; the child rarely experiences them as meaningful parts of verbal interchange. In this sense, the simplicity is deceptive, for it is extraordinarily difficult to maintain an exchange of even five to ten minutes on materials and ideas that, to the adult, seem empty of cognitive content. But these apparently trivial behaviors are the major skills that the child has and as such, they serve as the most accessible means for the teacher to begin to build a fruitful pupil-teacher interchange.

In addition, the focus on the simplicity of the content encourages one to overlook the corrective teaching that is occurring. The correction does not concern the modification of specific errors (e.g., the child's failure on color), but rather the modification of general maladaptive patterns that the child may possess including distractability, inattention, and failure to attend to the language of others. The treatment of such gross patterns will vary with the personality of the child. In the case of the hyperactive child who participated in these lessons, the effort was focused on modifying his fleeting attention by having the teacher

1. rapidly give many commands so that the child would not have the opportunity to be drawn to other objects and events in the room
2. correct each failure of attention by repeating commands which the child failed to heed. Often the repetition would be accompanied by aid which allows the child to complete the task more easily (e.g., if he jumps away when asked to draw a figure, the teacher starts the drawing and then leaves only a bit for the child to complete).

LESSON B

Introduction

The tenth lesson was concerned with the making of soap bubbles, a subject that allows the teacher to use highly attractive material to lead the child to analyze the significance of the commonplace. Danny's behavior was still marked by hyperactivity, and therefore the lessons continued to rely heavily on interspersing the cognitive demands with many opportunites for movement and action. However, he had already made sufficient progress so that the intellectual content could be on a much more advanced level. While this is seen in the types of questions that could now be posed (e.g., having him make predictions about events), it is most evident in the handling of errors. First, specific misconceptions which were only diagnosed earlier were now treated directly. This could be done because the child had developed the capacity to sustain attention and to tolerate the recognition of his own mistakes. Second, not only was there treatment of errors which occurred (e.g., as in the case of his failure of the concept "two" in the first lesson), but at times, the teacher even intentionally provoked errors—i.e., she constructed problems which she was certain the child would be unable to handle correctly. This was done, in part, to help the child attend to the realm of the unknown—but an unknown where he could be led to reach the known. For example, if asked to predict what color will emerge if blue and yellow are mixed, few children will know the answer. But having failed the problem, they know that information is lacking and that with the proper set of actions, the information *can* be obtained.

In addition, provocation of error is the best technique that the teacher has to approximate the self-provoked search for understanding that characterizes the well-functioning preschool child. This search is characteristically marked by wrong ideas, as in the example of the young child who asks his father, "Daddy, when I talked with you over the telephone, how did you manage to get into the receiver?" (Chukovsky, 1963, p. 30). As Piaget (1952) has shown, these wrong ideas are a sign of immaturity in thinking, but they are also a sign that the child is becoming aware of "disequilibria" between his ideas and is thus on the path to a higher level grasp of reality. Since the absence of this question-asking is a major characteristic of the poorly functioning child (Mattick, 1965), it falls upon the teacher to compensate for this failure by prudently provoking errors in the course of the lesson.

This path is a potentially dangerous one since unless the teacher has carefully structured the materials so that every error can be overcome to the child's satisfaction, the elicitation of the error will only leave the child frustrated and confused. In order to prevent this potential boomerang, the teacher must anticipate any possible error that might appear in a particular context and then, because of the young child's need for concrete proof, have sufficient materials available by which to correct the error.* For example, a teacher should not ask a question such as, "Will the fork hold the soup as well as the spoon?" unless the fork and soup are present so that their inappropriateness can be demonstrated should the child answer incorrectly. (For those readers who are interested, a more detailed presentation of the treatment of errors is presented elsewhere, in Blank, 1972.) The lesson to be presented below will demonstrate some of these techniques.

Outline of the Tenth Lesson.   The lesson began by the teacher showing a book about a boy blowing bubbles. She pointed to the cover and asked the pupil what he thought the book was about. He replied, "A boy." She responded, "What is the boy doing?" and he said, "Soap bubbles." So that the connection would be explicit, she pursued the question by asking, "What is he doing with the soap bubbles?" and he said, "Looking at them." She said, "That's right," and then focused further his attention because this was the task they were to do, by asking, "But who made the bubbles?" He answered, "The boy."

She asked if he would like to do the same thing as the boy was doing and his eyes sparkled as he said, "Yes." He was asked what they would need and he said, "Soap." He was told to bring it and "also a pipe." To lead him to focus on the missing object, the teacher

---

*While the preparation of materials to counteract error might seem difficult at first, in our experience teachers easily acquire the necessary skills within about a month.

pointed to a picture in the book that showed a container for the soap and said, "What did the boy have to hold the soap?" He pointed to the container and the teacher asked him to find one that was on the table. He did so and spontaneously put the soap in. The teacher asked if he could now make bubbles and he animatedly said, "Yes," put the pipe on the bar of soap, and began to blow. He looked abashed when no bubbles were forthcoming.

In order to help the child realize that water was the missing element, the teacher phrased the problem in the following way: "We need something wet to make bubbles. Can you think of something that will make the soap wet?" The child said water and he and the teacher went to the sink to get water. She asked if it would be possible to put water in the container if it had a cover on it. He said yes (a highly probable response since he was engrossed with the water and didn't reflect upon the problem). The teacher then brought over a cover and repeated the question, "If we put this cover on, could the water go in?" Drawn by the concrete cue that was now available, Danny looked carefully and replied, "No." The idea was then pursued by asking, "If it were on, where would the water go?" and he said, "There," gesturing around the sides of the jar. The teacher then asked, "And when it is off, where does the water go?"; he smiled happily and pointed inside the jar. This was the first time that he showed interest in the sustained pursuit of complex problem solving.

After filling the container, he began to blow bubbles. After a minute or two of this activity, the teacher intervened by asking Danny to take the bubble pipe apart and to see if the stem alone would work. He tried and was pleased that it did. She then gave him a solid wooden stick of the same proportions and asked him to try and see if that would blow bubbles too. He excitedly took it and was disappointed when it didn't work. He gave it back saying, "It's no good." She replied, "But why?" She handed both to the child and asked, "What is the difference between these? Why does this work and the other one doesn't?" He said, "'Cause this is red and this is not." The teacher then took a solid stick, the same color as the pipe stem and said, "try this." The child was led to realize that that didn't work either, after which he was asked to examine them again for the central difference. With the color factor controlled, he was now able to point to the hole as the central element. The lesson then drew to a close after Danny had been given the opportunity to play freely for a period of time.

Comments on the Lesson.   This lesson is clearly on a higher level than the first one and illustrates many of the principles discussed above concerning the provocation and treatment of errors. Rather than retrace the same paths again, we would like at this point to emphasize a feature that was important but only subtly present in this lesson—the directive role of the teacher in leading the child to grasp critical points. At least four such critical points were present in the lesson. These were:

1. the need for the objects with which to make the soap bubbles
2. the need for water to be used with the soap
3. the role of the cover on the jar
4. the role of the components of the bubble pipe.

What unites these instances is the fact that the teacher wished to demonstrate a phenomenon (e.g., that the hole in the stem was critical) and structured the situation so that the child would be led to bring in all the elements that were necessary. For example, the importance of the hole could not have been demonstrated unless the teacher had prepared the solid sticks and had been willing to ask the child to test them out. This course of action and analysis would almost never occur unless the teacher carefully maneuvered the child to deal with the objects that are essential to the phenomenon.

A further feature that has begun to emerge in this lesson is the endless elaboration of what appears to be minutiae. This is perhaps best typified in the exchange about the cover and the water, where a seemingly simple problem is attacked from a multiplicity of viewpoints. As is evident with this type of analysis, a change has begun to take place in the balance that exists between the action and the verbalization in the lesson. Thus in the early lessons, the pressure is for minimal verbalization and maximum activity (albeit activity directed by verbalization); by contrast, as the child progresses in the art of dialogue, each single activity becomes the potential source of many higher level verbal interchanges that require reflection and analysis. In many ways, this approach differs from the common push in enrichment programs, where the focus is on covering more and more concepts so that the content of the lesson will be wide ranging. By contrast, in the tutorial program, the teacher is led to pose many questions on the same phenomenon so that the child begins to see the depth and importance of everyday events that seemed simple, unimportant, and hardly worthy of exploration.

LESSON C

Introduction

The quality of the dialogue in the twentieth lesson begins to approximate the type of interchange that a teacher would carry on—and expect to carry on—in the typical preschool setting. At this point, the teacher's concern has begun to shift somewhat from diagnosing and eliciting errors to providing challenging opportunities for the child to rehearse his developing cognitive skills. This is not to deny that the child still has many weaknesses in dealing with cognitive material. For example, he is easily distracted and shows a low frustration tolerance by the end of the lesson. Such behavior, however, is much less common and much less easily aroused than previously.

With the improved performance, there is a tendency to think that the "treatment" may now be concluded. This seems an unwise course to follow, for unless the cognitive skills are continually practiced, the child may easily regress to his previous level. Such practice is available to the well-functioning child in the cognitively oriented dialogues he continually has with his parents. For the poorly functioning child, comparable practice in dialogue has to be provided within the school setting. The lesson that follows uses the subject matter of turtles to help the child develop his skills of perceptual analysis and spatial organization.

Outline of the Twentieth Lesson.   After Danny sat down, the teacher put a turtle on the table. He drew back, a bit frightened, but was able to verbalize his fear in a well-phrased sentence by saying, "I don't want to touch him. It hurt me one time." To lessen his fear, the teacher made no demand that he hold it; instead, she left it on the table and they began to discuss its various parts. Danny pointed to the turtle's legs and said legs and was then led to compare his legs with those of the turtle. The teacher asked him to walk "like he usually does" and then "to walk like the turtle." He readily complied and enjoyed the activity. When asked "What is the difference between the way you walk and the way the turtle walks?" he said, "He goes down on the floor." The teacher persevered by asking, "But how many legs does he use for walking?" Danny counted carefully and said, "Four"; she asked, "And how many do you use?" and he replied, "Two."

After complimenting him, the teacher led him to compare other parts of the body (eyes, mouth, nose), all of which he did easily. When he got to the nose, however, he said, "I don't have holes in my nose like that." The teacher replied by saying, "Look at my nose, do I have holes in it?" His eyes widened, he said yes, then spontaneously touched his own nose and said, "So do I." They then looked at the turtle's tail. He did not know what it was and seemed befuddled. The teacher brought out a book of animals that she had prepared in advance and asked him to find the tail on a dog, cat, and hen. She said, "Where are their tails?" and in order to focus on position, she added, "Near their heads?" Danny said, "No, over here." She then returned to the turtle and said, "Where is the turtle's tail?" (In this way she had avoided didactic teaching by structuring material so that the child would be led to see the analogous relationship.) Because Danny pointed easily she extended the concept by asking, "Do you have a tail?" He laughed confidently and said "No"; looked behind the teacher, giggled, and said, "You don't, too."

Because his behavior now showed no reluctance about handling the turtles, the teacher held up a box with three turtles and asked him to place them on the table in a row, "all facing in one direction." The teacher asked, "Which direction are they going to?" and he pointed correctly. He was asked, "What would we do if we wanted them to walk in that direction?" (pointing in the opposite way). He picked the turtles up and turned them around. The teacher smiled approvingly and said, "That's great."

He was then asked to put the turtles back because they were "going to make a turtle" that he could take back to his room. Because his drawing was still so poor, tasks of visual representation were mainly focused on presenting him with precut shapes (parts) where the only requirement was that he place them in the proper order. In this way, the need for drawing was eliminated, but he had the opportunity for much needed practice in spatial organization. The teacher gave him a form of a turtle cut in parts (neck, head, legs, and a body). She suggested that he glue the parts on a paper so that "it looks just like the picture of the turtle" (holding up a model she had prepared for the lesson). He placed the body on the paper, put one leg in its proper place, put glue on top of the body and then put one leg in the corner of the paper. He became restless and his movements became less controlled. To reduce the demands of the task, the teacher took the brush and glue away and said, "Now show me where to put the leg and I will glue it." He pointed unenthusiastically to the right place. To encourage his interest, she increased the pace and he was able to show where to place the head and the neck. Without asking him, she placed the tail and other leg, since his interest was about exhausted. She then said that he could take the picture with him to the room. He picked up the paper and ran back to his room.

Comments on the Lesson. Despite the expected lag of attention at the end of the lesson when he had to deal with a nonpreferred task, Danny shows marked improvement in almost all spheres of cognitive interchange. Perhaps the major concern for the teacher at this point is not *how* to conduct such a lesson, but *when* to conduct it. What are the signs in the child that signal his capability of entering this higher level interchange? A chief sign is his use of relevant "extensive" verbalization in replying to at least some questions (e.g., saying "She went to the store," instead of "store" when asked, "What did the girl do?"). This type of phrasing is to be distinguished from facile chatter in which the child speaks freely but the language has little direct relationship to the context (e.g., rambling on about events in the class when he is asked to deal with material before him). Relatively extended verbalization (three or four words at least) is vital if the child is to be able to cope with most "why" and "how" questions—the questions that are the hallmark of higher level problem solving in the preschool period. Even a simple problem such as "How did you get into the room?" cannot be answered fully correctly without phrases like "I opened the door," or "I pushed the handle."

Another sign is the spontaneous, relevant elaborations of ideas. For instance, when the child is told to "get a cloth to wipe the floor," he might add spontaneously, "We could use a sponge too." This type of spontaneous extension and comparison of relationships is a clue that he has begun to internalize important cognitive processes and thus is ready for increasingly higher levels of challenge.

Humor is additional evidence of the child's progress. This does not mean pleasure, smiling, and laughing in and of themselves, but enjoyment from the recognition of the violation of cognitive expectations. For example, a child cannot see the humor in a question such as, "Where is your tail?" unless he is (1) fully aware of his own body, (2) secure in a challenge to his self-image, and (3) able to negate the request of an authority if it is contrary to what he knows is reality (this contrasts sharply with negativism where the child simply resists authority as such). These are complex achievements which can not be taken for granted. If they are, the child may well be asked to deal with humor before he can do so, with the result that the well-intentioned "lightness" may only add to his confusion and fear.

A CONCLUDING STATEMENT

It is evident from the sequencing of the sessions that the tutorial program shares many of the principles of programmed instruction, the most striking of which is the way in which the lessons systematically build up to increasing levels of complexity (Gagne, 1965). This build-up, however, is most noticeable across lessons; it is much less apparent within lessons. Its absence within any session represents a major point of divergence between the tutorial program and more traditional programmed learning.

The reasons for its absence are manifold. First, it is felt that it is both more interesting for the child and less threatening if easy problems are constantly interwoven with more difficult ones, rather than consistently advancing to higher levels of complexity. The child's behavior, rather than a preplanned program, should indicate precisely how this interweaving should proceed (e.g., if he seems anxious, the material might be reduced further; if he seems disinterested, the complexity and pace might be increased). Second, there can be no fully predetermined sequence of problems, for the teaching is determined by the child's response. Since the problems are not confined to multiple-choice situations (as is common in programmed learning) but are almost fully open-ended, the teacher must be prepared to cope with any response that the child makes. She can and must anticipate the possible responses and prepare material accordingly; but the possible range of divergence throughout the lesson is too great to permit a fully pre-arranged format. Third, not only is error more likely to occur in this setting, but contrary to most programmed instructions, errors are actually encouraged for a variety of purposes, including

1. diagnosing the areas where the child is most in need of help
2. helping him work through failure to success
3. fostering "disequilibria" that will enhance development, and
4. teaching the child the techniques for testing out his answers (if he is trained so that all his answers are correct, he will feel little need to test out his thinking).

Fourth, the tutorial program is designed to teach the processes of thinking, not specific content. At this stage in our knowledge, it is relatively easy to teach specific content according to the principles of programming (e.g., the teaching of reading). But we have little knowledge, particularly for the preschool age range, about the principles for programming the processes of thinking; we do not even know if such a goal is attainable. It is for these reasons that the principles of programming cannot readily be applied within any single tutorial lesson.

This should not be interpreted to mean that such principles cannot eventually be evolved. In fact, the entire thrust of the tutorial program has been in this direction. What has been achieved thus far, however, is only a beginning step. It is hoped that with further research, more precise rules will be formulated so that the teacher will be supplied with the information needed to bring about the much sought-after goal of preventing failure in the academic setting.

This work was supported by USPHS grant K MH 10749 and the Grant Foundation.

REFERENCES

Blank, M.: Implicit assumptions underlying preschool intervention programs. *Journal of Social Issues, 26*:15-33, 1970.
Blank, M.: Teaching Learning in the Preschool: A Dialogue Approach. Columbus, Ohio, Charles Merrill, 1973.
Blank, M.: The wrong response: Is it to be ignored, prevented, or treated? In Parker, R. (ed.): Preschool in Action. Boston, Allyn & Bacon, 1972.
Blank, M., and Solomon, F.: A tutorial language program to develop abstract thinking in socially disadvantaged preschool children. *Child Development, 39:*379-389, 1968.
Blank, M., and Solomon F.: How shall the disadvantaged child be taught? *Child Development, 40*:47-61, 1969.
Chukovsky, K.: From Two to Five. Translated and edited by M. Morton, Berkeley, University of California Press, 1963.
Gagne, R.M.: The Conditions of Learning. New York, Holt, Rinehart and Winston, 1965.
Hess, R.D., and Shipman, V.C.: Early experience and the socialization of cognitive modes in children. *Child Development, 36*:869-886, 1965.
Hunt, J. McV.: Intelligence and Experience. New York, Ronald Press, 1961.
Kamii, C.K.: Evaluation of learning in preschool education: Socio-emotional, perceptual-motor and cognitive development. *In* Bloom, B.S., Hastings, J.T., and Mandaus, G.F., (eds.): Handbook on Formative and Summative Evaluation of Student Learning. New York, McGraw Hill, 1971.
Labov, W.: The logic of non-standard English. *Monograph Series on Language and Linguistics,* Georgetown University, School of Languages and Linguistics, 1969.
Mattick, I.: Adaptation of nursery school techniques to deprived children: Some notes on the experiences of teaching children of multi-problem families in a therapeutically oriented nursery school. *Journal of the American Academy of Child Psychiatry, 4*:670-700, 1965.
Piaget, J.: The Origins of Intelligence in Children. New York, International University Press, 1952.
Silberman, C.E.: Crisis in the Classroom: The Remaking of American Education. New York, Random House, 1970.

the california report: 33
early schooling
for all?*

Raymond S. Moore
Robert D. Moon
Dennis R. Moore

The United States is currently witnessing one of its most remarkable educational developments—a drive for earlier and earlier schooling for all children which appears to be either overlooking or ignoring many of the most important findings of developmental research. While such oversight is not new to American education, in this instance the evidence and implications are not only clear, but also warn of formidable costs—first, in tax moneys, and second and far more important, in possible damage to young children.

A look at the early schooling (ES) movement reveals many developments, e.g., mounting problems of child behavior, parents chafing at the "shackles" of parenthood, inadequate and unregulated care of children, and federal and state interest in early schooling. Educators are intrigued by research which points up the rapid early development of intelligence. (See Bloom's review, *Stability and Change in Human Characteristics.*[1]) But many of these well-intentioned people overlook scientific findings which point in other directions than that in which early childhood education is now generally going, e.g., studies on early *vs.* later school admission, neurophysiology, cognition, and maternal deprivation. If such findings are not carefully considered, early childhood educators may threathen the very childhood development they design to improve.

In order to develop a fair and somewhat comprehensive viewpoint, the Hewitt Research Center has involved leading educators, legislators, scholars, and researchers at local, state, and national levels from coast to coast in a review of early childhood research. A limited cross-section of the resulting analysis is presented here.

We acknowledge, of course, the need of special education for the seriously disadvantaged or handicapped. There is also a need to care for children who have handicapped parents or whose parents are compelled to work. No position is taken here against early intervention where indicated by research. The principal questions we shall treat here are: What is the best kind of intervention or care for young children? What is generally the best—and most financially feasible—environment for early childhood development (ECD)?

*Reprinted from *Phi Delta Kappan,* *53*:615-621, 677, June, 1972, by permission of the Hewitt Research Center.

We will attempt 1) to analyze typical goals of early schooling proponents, 2) to examine their use of research in support of their conclusions, 3) to see what systematic research actually says about typical ES programs and proposals, and 4) to report some practical solutions growing out of research and experimentation. In order to maintain a sharp focus this will be done primarily with reference to one state—California.

The California Report. The report of the California Task Force on Early Childhood Education[2] is relatively middle-of-the-road as ES proposals go. For example, it proposes to take schooling at first only down to four-year-olds, rather than to children aged three or three and one-half as planned in New York State and Houston. The task force plan may soon be presented to the California legislature. Because California has long been among the pioneers in U.S. education, it will exercise a telling influence among other states. Yet the California proposal, with some variations, appears typical of current ES rationale.

TYPICAL EARLY SCHOOLING GOALS

The California task force offers a philosophy and goals that would build on a substantial body of research:

> The past decade has produced a new body of educational, psychological, and medical research documenting the crucial importance of the first eight years of life. And we are convinced that these early years are critical in determining the future effectiveness of our citizens and in the long-range prevention of crime, poverty, addiction, malnutrition, neurosis, and violence.[3]

The report assumes that "even though research is still in progress and conclusions continue to evolve, enough evidence is in" to justify certain goals, namely, "to bring about the maximum development of every child" down to age four.[4] And it is proposed that this goal will be accomplished by providing for *academic* as well as personal development and requiring "school districts to restructure and expand existing programs."[5]

TYPICAL USE OF RESEARCH

The California goal of maximum development surely is consistent with the ideals of most Americans. The report cites many examples of ECD research and experimentation which it assumes will provide substance for its implementation plan. Yet in no case does it clearly show how this research supports its plan. In fact certain research quoted in the report actually contradicts the task force's conclusions that *schooling* under carefully selected teachers is desirable for *all* four-year-olds. For example:

1. Harold Skeels's study[6] of orphanage children is quoted as demonstrating how the young child, given a favorable environment, can make marked intellectual growth. But the report does not continue its analysis to show that Skeels's "environment" was an institution in which *retarded teenagers* provided the orphans a *warm, free, one-to-one, continuing* mother or mother-surrogate relationship. Skeels's study had little to do with academic instruction or credentialed teaching.

2. The report quotes findings of the White House Conference of 1970: "We must free ourselves from our antiquated and erroneous beliefs that school is the only environment

in which creativity is enhanced and learning takes place, or that the teacher is the sole agent of such achievements."[7]

3. Another task force item cites the June, 1971, report of the Education Commission of the States, which says in part:

> It is not recommended that states establish formal classroom pre-school programs for all three- and four-year-olds because there is no evidence that all children need a structured group experience if they are receiving some kind of systematic training and because there are viable, less expensive alternatives.[8]

4. The report calls for "at least one adult to every ten children"[9] in educating four-year-olds. Yet every experiment quoted in the report in which adult-child ratios were given (six out of eleven examples) the adult-to-child ratio was 1:5 *or less,* or a need for at least four to six times the number of adults required for a standard kindergarten-primary grade ratio of 1:20 to 1:30. Although the California cost proposals are still in the formative stages, Superintendent Wilson Riles is counting on a per-child annual cost of about $500 to $600. Yet one of the documents quoted in the report *(Preschool Breakthrough* [10]*)* notes that the prekindergarten experience of New York State sees an annual $1,800-per-child cost as necessary for "adequate day care" and "much more if the program reaches a desirable standard."

In view of such examples as this, it is difficult to understand how the task force concludes that all four-year-olds should be provided academic schooling. And the discrepancy between research and projected implementation goes much farther. Unfortunately, California's proposal is not an isolated illustration of such disparity, as Earl Schaefer, one of the nation's leading early childhood education specialists, notes:

> ... Although much of this [ECD] research data has been generated during the last decade, earlier studies of intellectual development have motivated the current volume of research. Unfortunately, interpretations of the significance of this data, although they have guided the course of research, have as yet had minimal impact on educational planning. . . .[11]

This may be one of the reasons for the findings of William Rohwer (University of California, Berkeley) and others that "the research and development phases of early childhood programs have succeeded but the implementation phases, thus far, have largely failed."[12]

While there is evidence of some desirable effects of ES programs for disadvantaged children, the assessment of failure of large-scale programs is related primarily to academic or cognitive achievement, a goal strongly stressed in the California report.[13] Referring to a number of large-scale ES programs it studied, the U.S. Commission on Civil Rights concluded that "A principal objective of each was to raise academic achievement of disadvantaged children. Judged by this standard the programs did not show evidence of much success."[14] The Westinghouse/Ohio University study found Head Start to have been "ineffective in producing any [lasting] gains in cognitive and affective development" and stressed the present "limited state of knowledge" about what would constitute effective intervention.[15]

WHAT SYSTEMATIC RESEARCH SAYS

For the purposes of this report, key factors in three types of studies will be considered among many on which there is substantial research evidence: 1) studies comparing early and later school entrants; 2) neurophysiological research, including brain changes which affect vision, hearing, cognition, etc.; and 3) maternal deprivation studies.

These will be followed by a brief review of research on family attitudes toward children and comparisons between the home and the school as alternatives for early childhood development.

Early and Late School Entry.   Most academic schooling, it will be assumed, eventually rests upon an ability to read. In turn, Nila Smith points out, "Dozens of investigations indicate that reading maturation accompanies physical growth, mental growth, emotional and social maturity, experiential background, and language development."[16] Willard Olson found that "children of the same age and the same grade location are regularly found to differ by as much as four or five years in their maturation and their readiness to perform tasks."[17]

The question then is not only, Is the child *ready* for school? but even more important, Does he demonstrate his readiness by sufficient maturity to *sustain* learning? and, Will the early starter be *as well or better motivated and less frustrated and anxiety-ridden* than the one who starts later? A wide variety of studies provides the answers.

Inez King[19] reports an Oak Ridge, Tennessee, study of two groups totaling 54 children who were five years and eight months to five years and 11 months old when they started school. They were compared with 50 children who started at six years and three months to six years and eight months of age. Stanford Achievement Tests at the end of grade six showed a distinct difference, strongly in favor of the older group. In this study, of the 11 children who were retained, only one had started after six years of age; 19 boys and 16 girls of the younger group appeared to be maladjusted in some way, while only three boys and three girls from the older group were considered maladjusted.

ECD studies involving retention of learning have been done at virtually all grade and socioeconomic status (SES) levels, with remarkably uniform results. B.U. Keister[20] reported that five year olds could often develop enough skills to get through first-grade reading, but the learning was generally not retained through the summer vacation. Other comparisons of reading achievement of early and later starters were made by Marian Carroll[21] in the third grade, Joseph Halliwell and Belle Stein[22] in the fourth and fifth grades, and Richard Hampleman[23] in the sixth. All found generally that later entrants significantly excelled those who started earlier. Similar studies with similar results have also been reported by Elizabeth Bigelow,[24] Inez King,[25] Lowell Carter,[26] Clyde Baer,[27] Donald Green and Sadie Simmons,[28] and Margaret Gott.[29] There are many more.

John Forrester[30] did a vertical study of 500 grade 1-12 children in the Montclair, New Jersey, public schools. The very bright but very young pupils at the time of school entrance did not realize their school success potential. From junior high on, 50% of them earned only C grades. However, the very bright but older group excelled generally throughout their school careers.

While many of these studies were undertaken with a combination of low and middle SES children, higher SES groups perform similarly. Paul Mawhinny[31] reports how children from Detroit's elite Grosse Pointe, Michigan, families were selected by psychologists because they were considered mature enough or of sufficient potential to be admitted to kindergarten before age five. But after 14 years an evaluation was made of all who remained in the Grosse Pointe schools. More than one-fourth of the selected group were below average or had repeated a grade.

Arnold Gesell and Frances Ilg, after extensive research and clinical analyses, found that school tasks such as reading, writing, and arithmetic "depend upon motor skills which are subject to the same laws of growth which govern creeping, walking, grasping," The resulting awkwardness and immaturity "are often sadly overlooked by teachers and parents":

> When the school child was a baby the adult attitudes tended to be more reasonable. One did not say he should walk at this or that age. Feeling confident that he would walk at the most seasonable time, one was more interested to observe the stage and degree of his preliminary development. If reading readiness and walking readiness are appraised on similar grounds, more justice is done the child.[32]

Neurophysiology and Cognition. The findings of neurophysiologists, psychologists, and medical personnel are remarkably similar in their timing of stages at which children are normally ready to think abstractly, or organize facts, and to sustain and retain learning without undue damage or strain. Many neurophysiological studies demonstrate significant changes in brain patterns which occur between ages seven and eleven. These include impressive experiments which lead one to question if children should be required to participate in regular academic instruction until they are at least eight years old. Some researchers and scholars suggest even until adolescence, e.g., Rohwer[33] and Fisher.[34]

A number of studies of the young child's brain, including Penuel Corbin's, Jean Nicholson's, G.C. Lairy's, W.E. Nelson's, and very recent studies by David Metcalf and Kent Jordan,[35] show that appreciable brain changes take place from birth into adolescence, including the shifting of control from the emotional centers to the reasoning centers. They point to ages seven to eleven or twelve as this important period during which a child eventually develops the ability to sustain high cortical thought.

A. Davis[36] records Paul Yakovlev's findings that the child's brain is not fully insulated or completely developed until after seven years, and sometimes not until age ten or later. H.G. Birch and M. Bortner[37] and M. Bortner and H.G. Birch[38] found that until these ages young children and brain-damaged adults were inaccurate in the perception of shapes and grossly inaccurate in attempts to reproduce them.

The findings of cognitive psychologist Jean Piaget coincide remarkably with those of the neurophysiologists. Willis Overton summarizes Piaget's four major steps in the development of the child:

> ... (a) the sensory motor period—birth to two years; (b) the preoperational period—two years to seven years; (c) the period of concrete operations—seven to eleven years; and (d) the period of formal operations between eleven and fifteen years.[39]

Overton notes that the change from preoperational to concrete operational periods of childhood finds the very young child involved in direct perception relationships with a minimum of reasoning. So this child relates quantity to shape and form of objects, but if the shape or form is changed he is confused. He must also change the quantity. For instance, he cannot understand how a low, wide glass can hold as much water as a tall, narrow one. It is not until he is seven or eight or later than he becomes a fully "reasonable" creature. As he goes through this transition he begins to reason abstractly instead of limiting himself to direct relationships.[40]

Millie Almy's replication of Piaget's work demonstrated "that only 48% of the second-grade children in the middle class school, with a mean chronological age of seven years and four months, were able to conserve in all three of the [Piagetian] tasks"[41] which were designed to measure cognitive maturity in terms of abstract thinking normally required for primary grades. Almy concludes that "failure to begin to conserve [Piaget's term for ability to understand certain problems] at an early age may be associated with a failure to grasp much that goes on in the classroom and elsewhere."[42]

William Rohwer sees schooling as an intrusion on the child's freedom to learn associatively during his preoperational years. He found "little evidence to support the rationale for progressively lowering the age of required school entrance if by evidence one requires data demonstrating a positive effect of early school entrance on later school achievement." He suggested that schooling, as commonly understood, be delayed "several years."[43]

Psychiatrist J.T. Fisher supports this thesis from clinical observation and affirms a need for a primary effort in behalf of the home. Speaking for greater initial freedom for developing a strong affective base for later stability in cognition, and incidentally for nongradedness, he says:

> Psychologists have demonstrated that a normal child commencing his education in adolescence can soon reach the same point of progress he would have achieved by starting to school at five or six years of age. I have often thought that if a child could be assured a wholesome home life and proper physical development, this might be the answer to a growing problem of inadequate classroom space and a shortage of qualified teachers—and the instinctive reluctance of all of us to hand over tax dollars for anything that doesn't fire bullets.[44]

Torsten Husén,[45] in a widely circulated international study, found a strong negative correlation between early entry age and attitudes toward school. D. Elkind[46] found no support for "the claims of lastingness of pre-school instruction, [but] . . . evidence in the opposite direction. . . . The longer we delay formal instruction, up to certain limits, the greater the period of plasticity and the higher the ultimate level of achievement." He sees frustrated, anxiety-ridden, "intellectually burned" children who lose motivation for intellectual success which they deserve.

Visual Maturity.   Findings on the child's visual system are highly similar to those of his brain: The processing of visual stimuli in the brain traces the same electrical path as do the impulses involved with cognitive activity that occur between the thalamus and the cortex. Therefore, if these connections are not completed in their development, the visual signals will not be interpreted clearly, according to James Chalfant and Margaret Scheffelin. These authors add that

> The processing of visual stimuli at the higher cortical levels involves: (a) visual analysis, the separation of the whole into its component parts; (b) visual integration, the coordination of mental processes; and (c) visual synthesis, the incorporation or combination of elements into a recognizable whole. A review of literature reveals a variety of cognitive tasks requiring the analysis, integration, and synthesis of visual information.[47]

Luella Cole[48] observed that some children are unable to fixate on objects at close range until age seven or eight or later. Stanley Krippner[49] notes how hard it is to explain to parents that it is not the child's eye that reads but his brain. Chalfant and Scheffelin[50] confirm that "the retina is an outward extension of the cerebral cortex." Thus the visual system is not ready for reading until the brain is relatively mature.

An interesting logitudinal illustration of this relative maturity is provided by Moselle Boland's report of a paper presented by a Texas ophthamologist at the 1963 meeting of the Texas Medical Association:

> Dr. Henry L. Hilgartner said there has been a tremendous increase in nearsightedness in [Texas] school children in the past 30 years. . . . He blames use of their eyes for close school work at an early age. . . . The constant pull of the eye muscles to do close work,

he said, causes the eyeball to become larger. This is the basic defect in nearsighted-
ness.... Prior to 1930, he said, 7.7 children were farsighted to every one nearsighted.... In 1930, Texas compulsory school age was lowered from seven to six years.
Today, he added, five children are nearsighted for every one farsighted.... "I believe the
chief cause is children being required to start school at the early age of six instead of
being allowed to grow for another year or two," Dr. Hilgartner commented.[51]

Ruth Strang[52] and Homer Carter and Dorothy McGinnis[53] note that when children
cannot adjust to the difficulties and discomforts of tasks requiring close vision, they
simply give up trying to read.

Carter and McGinnis explain how the six small muscles of each eye must coordinate
precisely to focus on near objects and produce only a single mental image. At six years
the "visual mechanism" is still "unstable."[54]

Luella Cole[55] and others report also that not more than 10% of five year olds can see
any difference between "d" and "b" or "p" and "q." Not until children are eight years
old can one "be perfectly certain the eyes are mature enough to avoid such confusions."

Auditory Maturity and Other Factors. As a child matures there is a progressive
increase in sound discrimination. According to Carter and McGinnis,[56] this ability to
differentiate similar speech sounds is considered by many investigators to be of prime
importance in successful reading. If a child is unable to hear the difference in sound, he
will be unable to reproduce the sound correctly in speaking. This would also handicap
him in recognizing written words, since improper pronunciation would lead him to expect
a different spelling of the word. Luella Cole[57] notes specifically: "If he has normal six
year old ears he will still be unable to distinguish consistently between the sounds of 'g'
and 'k' and 'm' and 'n,' 'p' and 'b' or any other pair of related sounds."

H.G. Birch and A. Lefford[58] did not find intersensory maturity emerging until the
children are at least seven or eight years of age. Joseph Wepman[59] found that in some
children the combination of auditory discrimination and memory—"ability to retain and
recall speech sounds"—is not well developed until the age of nine.

Maternal Deprivation. When a child is taken from home for early schooling or
remains at home without loving care from someone he trusts, research says to expect
mental and emotional problems which affect his learning, motivation, and behavior. John
Bowlby presented evidence, formulated a statement of principle, and defined maternal
deprivation in his 1951 report to the World Health Organization:

> ...the infant and young child should experience a warm, intimate, and continuous
> relationship with his mother (or permanent mother-substitute) in which both find
> satisfaction and enjoyment....
>   A state of affairs in which the child does not have this relationship is termed
> "maternal deprivation." This is a general term covering a number of different situations.
> Thus a child is deprived even though living at home if his mother (or permanent mother-
> substitute) is unable to give him the loving care small children need. Again, a child is
> deprived if for any reason he is removed from his mother's care.[60]

He reiterated this view nearly 20 years later, reporting that in the Western world much
the commonest disturbances of attachment "are the results of too little mothering, or of
mothering coming from a succession of different people." And these disturbances "can
continue for weeks, months, or years"—or may be permanent.[61]

Many ES proponents believe that the young child needs social contact outside the
home. There are a number of reasons to doubt that he does. Research is specific. Marcel
Geber's work in Uganda demonstrates, much like Harold Skeels's, that such attention or

deprivation reaches beyond the emotional responses of young children.[62] Using tests standardized by Arnold Gesell, Geber tested over 300 Uganda babies during their first year. The babies for the most part were from low-SES, tribal-oriented families in which mothers were child-centered, continually caressing, cuddling, and talking to their little ones. He found these infants to be superior to Western children in physiological maturation and coordination, adaptability and sociability, and language skills. It may be observed that African children often do mature earlier than Westerners. Yet Geber reports that in his sampling those babies from relatively high-SES Uganda families with less maternal contact but more involvement in formal training were much less mature in the above qualities than the babies of the low-SES mothers.

L.J. Yarrow also reports that "besides the retardation of development caused through emotional factors, maturation in adjustment is markedly slowed by deprivation of sensory, social, and affective stimulation when a child cannot be with his mother."[63] Bowlby adds that even partial deprivation "brings in its train acute anxiety, excessive need for love, powerful feelings of revenge, and . . . guilt and depression."[64]

The Mother's Attitude. The mother's acceptance of her role is of greatest importance in the child's development. Mary Ainsworth found

> . . . significant differences . . . when the mothers were grouped in terms of satisfaction with their role, whether the homemaker or the worker role. Dissatisfied mothers, both working and nonworking, reported undesirable child-rearing practices and attitudes more frequently than mothers who were satisfied with their role.[65]

Education and reassurance of parents thus become a vital concomitant of any ECD program, whether in the home or in school, whether the mother works or not, but particularly with the mother who does not have a wholesome appreciation of her role. Thus, says Bowlby, numerous direct studies

> make it plain that, when deprived of maternal care, the child's development is almost always retarded—physically, intellectually, and socially—and that symptoms of physical and mental illness may appear . . . and that some children are gravely damaged for life.[66]

Some educators believe that parents are either too ignorant or obsessed with a desire for freedom to be willing to give their children the care they need for optimum development. A number of studies demonstrate that this is not necessarily so. Louise Daugherty,[67] Robert Hess and Virginia Shipman,[68] Mildred Smith,[69] Hylan Lewis,[70] and Phyllis Levenstein[71] found that parents are concerned, regardless of socioeconomic status. When Mildred Smith took study-help materials to homes and induced parental help, 90% of the homes responded, and of these 99% of the parents asked that the program be continued.

Levenstein[72] not only found generally that if approached rightly, disadvantaged mothers "take seriously the family's responsibility to lay groundwork for school learning," but also noted that their "aspirations for their children are very similar to those of middle-income mothers." The fact that the mother saw the practical teacher as less effective than she, yet sensed her own inadequacies, suggests as the more urgent role of the state the development of home education programs for adequate parenthood.

School vs. Home. Then should the young child be taken from home to be trained in a school? There may be cases of acute or extreme deprivation where this is necessary. Yet Bowlby insists, on the basis of many investigations, that "children thrive better in bad homes than in good institutions," and children "apparently unreasonably" are even attached to bad parents. "It must never be forgotten," Bowlby observes,

> ... that even the bad parent who neglects her child is nonetheless providing much for him. . . . Except in the worst cases, she is giving him food and shelter, comforting him in distress, teaching him simple skills, and above all is providing him with that continuity of human care on which his sense of security rests. [73]

Burton Blatt and Frank Garfunkel found it necessary to reject the research hypothesis of their own study involving low-SES children who "were at least two years away from entering the first grade." They concluded that (a) the home is more influential than the school, (b) the school can do little without strong home support, (c) disadvantaged parents "are often anxious to cooperate," and (d) school organization and requirements are often "foreign" to these parents who in turn are blamed by the school for not readily accepting them. [74]

Special education would certainly appear to be indicated for many specific cases of disability such as speech, vision, hearing, cerebral palsy, severe mental retardation, and certain neuroses, psychoses and advanced emotional problems. Yet it is difficult to find research support for *generalized* early schooling as described in the California Task Force report. In fact it is difficult to understand, in the face of substantial evidence to the contrary, how educators can justify existing generalized schooling down to ages five and six, or compulsory education below age eight.

On the other hand, certain child-care needs must be met. These are not generalized needs, but are specific problems growing out of parents' inability to care for their young children, e.g., physical or psychological handicaps, ineptness, immaturity, or severe economic stress requiring the mother to work. Any lesser reason which simply accommodates a growing demand for parental "freedom" must, in terms of research findings, be considered parental dereliction. And while research may not yet always be definitive in placing the blame, there is considerable evidence that points toward maternal deprivation and early schooling as primary reasons for childhood maladjustment, motivational loss, poor retention, deterioration of attitudes, visual handicaps, and a wide variety of other physical and behavioral problems, including minimal brain dysfunction.

In summary, research and comparisons of school entry ages clearly point to the need 1) to delay any type of educational program that proposes or permits sustained high cortical effort, or strain on the visual or auditory systems, before the child is seven or eight, and for 2) a warm, continuous mother or mother-surrogate relationship (without a succession of different people) until the child is at least seven or eight.

Investigators (Daugherty, Hess and Shipman, Levenstein, Lewis, Smith, *et al.*) have shown that parents, when clearly shown their children's needs, overwhelmingly respond to them. Likewise, other researchers (Rohwer, Elkind, Husén, *et al.*) make clear that the earlier children go to school the more likely they are to develop negative attitudes toward school.

SOME PRACTICAL SOLUTIONS FROM RESEARCH

So the closer the child's early environment can be kept to his home (or other home with a low adult-to-child ratio) which may provide a continuous warm and free growing place, the more likely his maximum development will be. And this home should neither propose nor permit such learning as violates the child's normal developmental crescendo.

Parent Education. With some of these principles in mind, Susan Gray,[75] Phyllis Levenstein,[76] David Weikart,[77] Ira Gordon,[78] and others have been experimenting with home schooling. While research does *not* indicate the need for schooling as such, there is much to be learned from these researchers toward effective parent education which can lead to appropriate pre-school environments regardless of cultural background or socioeconomic status. And indeed, if as psychiatrist J.T. Fisher infers, the state desires to save money, one of the most effective ways may be to help in the development of "wholesome home life."[79]

Home Schools. Both Susan Gray and Phyllis Levenstein experimented with home schools. Levenstein describes her successful experience with such a program which she calls the "Mother-Child Home Program."[80] Because of the resistance of some mothers, particularly of low-SES families, to *teacher* visitation, she calls the professional visiting personnel "toy demonstrators." Gray notes that "the potential [of the home] is sometimes difficult to tap but it is there."[81]

Such programs may well provide a *modus operandi* for such child care as is really necessary and avoid heavy capital and operating costs which California's present proposal is certain to bring.

There is now a sufficient research base to suggest several procedures in lieu of early schooling as commonly conceived. The state should:

1. Carefully restudy the needs of its children in the light of research. It should realize that research provides no more reason for early schooling for all four-year-olds simply because they have intelligence than it does for early sex for twelve-year-olds simply because they have generated reproductive equipment. They must await the development of balancing factors. Great damage may be avoided.

2. Embark upon a massive parent education program, assisting first those who are in greatest need, but educating all parents, by all media available, concerning the developmental needs of their children. Parents who are neither handicapped nor forced to work should be helped to better understand their privileges and responsibilities as parents, to see that "freedom" sacrificed now will bring larger benefits later.

3. Make such provisions as are necessary for all exceptional children: the severely handicapped or disabled or others requiring special education. Even here research indicates that programs should be kept as close to the home as practicable.

4. Take an interest in providing care for the relatively normal children of handicapped parents or those forced to work, by selecting homes nearby, if possible, as home-schools. Those homes and mothers (or other adults) who are qualified would be selected for their warmth, continuity, aptness for children, and dedication to their welfare. These may well be operated as enlightened care centers on a small adult-to-child ratio (normally not more than 1:4 or 1:5), and might be subsidized by the state where parents cannot meet the costs. Traveling teachers on state or local payroll could monitor these home-schools to see that they were provided adequate materials and equipment and to coordinate them with existing ADC and other social service programs.

CONCLUSION

It would be hard to find an area of educational research more definitive than that on child development and school entry age. It is difficult to see how planners can review this evidence and conclude that four- or five-year-olds generally should be in school, much less three-year-olds.

Goals of maximum development of the child are generally sound, but research says that California's proposed way to reach them can only lead to greater trouble. In short, it appears that California's planners, and others with similar plans, have either overlooked or ignored or seriously misinterpreted responsible research. If such evidence is questioned, then further research should be undertaken before legislating in areas so delicate as the young child's mind. Meanwhile, scientific evidence comparing the validity of the home and the school as early childhood environments clearly favors the home.

It is hoped that the California legislature and the State Board of Education will ponder these facts and that other legislators and educators—federal, state, and local—will also consider carefully the dangers of veering from the guidelines which research has supplied.

REFERENCES

1. Benjamin S. Bloom, Stability and Change in Human Characteristics. New York, John Wiley & Sons, 1964, p. 88.
2. Report of the Task Force on Early Childhood Education. Sacramento, Calif., Wilson Riles, State Superintendent of Public Instruction, and the State Board of Education, November 26, 1971, p. 29.
3. *Ibid.*, p. 1.
4. *Ibid.*, p. 1.
5. *Ibid.*, p. 10.
6. Harold M. Skeels, Adult Status of Children with Contrasting Early Life Experiences: A Follow-Up Study. Monograph of the Society for Research in Child Development, No. 105. Chicago, University of Chicago Press, 1966, pp. 1-68.
7. White House Conference on Children and Youth, 1970, Report to the President. Washington, D.C., U.S. Government Printing Office, 1970, pp. 97-98.
8. Education Commission of the States, Early Childhood Development, Alternatives for Program Development in the States. Denver, Colo., The Commission, 1971.
9. *Ibid.*, p. 3.
10. *Ibid.*, p. 40.
11. Earl S. Schaefer, Toward a revolution in education: a perspective from child development research, *The National Elementary Principal*, September, 1971, p. 18.
12. William D. Rohwer, Jr., On attaining the goals of early childhood education. (Paper presented at OEO Conference on Research in Early Childhood Education, Washington, D.C., 1970.)
13. *Ibid.*, pp. 1-5, 17-19.
14. U.S. Commission on Civil Rights, Racial Isolation in the Public Schools, Vol. 1. Washington, D.C.: Government Printing Office, 1967, p. 138.
15. Westinghouse and Ohio University, The impact of Head Start: an evaluation of the effects of Head Start on children's cognitive and affective development, in The Disadvantaged Child, Joe L. Frost and Glenn R. Hawkes, editors. Boston, Houghton Mifflin, 1970, pp. 197-201.
16. Nila B. Smith, Early reading: viewpoints, in Early Childhood Crucial Years for Learning, Margaret Rasmussen, editor. Washington, D.C., Association for Childhood Education International, 1966, pp. 61-62.
17. Willard C. Olson, *NEA Journal*, October, 1947, pp. 502-03.
19. Inez B. King, Effect of age of entrance into grade 1 upon achievement in elementary school. *Elementary School Journal*, February, 1955, pp. 331-36.
20. B.U. Keister, Reading skills acquired by five-year old children, *Elementary School Journal*, April 1941, pp. 587-96.
21. Marion Carroll, Academic achievement and adjustment of underage and overage third-graders, *The Journal of Educational Research*, February, 1964, p. 290.
22. Joseph W. Halliwell and Belle W. Stein, A comparison of the achievement of early and late starters in reading related and non-reading related areas in fourth and fifth grades, *Elementary English*, October, 1964, pp. 631-39, 658.
23. Richard S. Hampleman, A study of the comparative reading achievements of early and late school starters, *Elementary English*, May, 1959, pp. 331-34.

24. Elizabeth Bigelow, School progress of underage children, *Elementary School Journal,* November, 1934, pp. 186-92.
25. King, *op. cit.*
26. Lowell Burney Carter, The effect of early school entrance on the scholastic achievement of elementary school children in the Austin public schools, *Journal of Educational Research,* October, 1956, pp. 91-103.
27. Clyde J. Baer, The school progress and adjustment of underage and overage students, *Journal of Educational Psychology,* February, 1958, pp. 17-19.
28. Donald Ross Green and Sadie Vee Simmons, Chronological age and school entrance, *Elementary School Journal,* October, 1962, pp. 41-47.
29. Margaret Ellen Gott, The Effect of Age Differences at Kindergarten Entrance on Achievement and Adjustments in Elementary School. (Doctoral dissertation, University of Colorado, 1963.)
30. John J. Forrester, At what age should children start school?, *The School Executive,* March, 1955, pp. 80-81.
31. Paul E. Mawhinny, We gave up on early entrance, *Michigan Educational Journal,* May, 1964, p. 25.
32. Arnold Gesell and Frances L. Ilg. The Child from Five to Ten. New York, Harper and Brothers, 1946, pp. 388-89.
33. Rohwer, *op. cit.,* p. 37.
34. James T. Fisher and Lowell S. Hawley, A Few Buttons Missing. Philadelphia: J.B. Lippincott Company, 1951, pp. 13-14.
35. Penuel H. Corbin (master's thesis in pediatrics, University of Minnesota 1951. NA Med Library, W4A, 9C791E, 1951, C1); Jean M. Nicholson *et al.,* EEG and Clinical Neurophysiology, Vol. 8, 1956, p. 342; G.C. Lairy *et al.,* EEG and Clinical Neurophysiology, Vol. 14, 1962, pp. 778-79; W.E. Nelson, Textbook of Pediatrics. Chicago, Saunders Co., 1967, p. 1088; David Metcalf and Kent Jordan, EEG ontogenesis in normal children, in Drugs, Development and Cerebral Function, W. Lynn Smith, editor. Springfield, Ill., Charles C. Thomas, 1972, pp. 127-28.
36. A. Davis, Regional Development of the Brain in Early Life. Cambridge, Mass., Harvard University Press, 1964.
37. M. Bortner and H.G. Birch, Perceptual and perceptual motor dissociation in cerebral palsied children, *Journal of Nervous and Mental Diseases,* 1960, pp. 103-8.
38. H.G. Birch and M. Bortner, Perceptual and perceptual motor dissociation in brain-damaged patients, *Journal of Nervous and Mental Diseases,* 1960, p. 49.
39. Willis F. Overton, Piaget's theory of intellectual development and progressive education, in *Yearbook of the Association for Supervision and Curriculum Development, 1972.* Washington D.C., The Association, pp. 95-103.
40. *Ibid.,* p. 103.
41. Millie Almy, Edward Chittenden, and Paula Miller, Young Children's Thinking. New York: Teachers College Press, Columbia University, 1966.
42. *Ibid.,* p. 99.
43. Rohwer, *op. cit.,* pp. 7-8.
44. Fisher, *loc. cit.*
45. Torsten Husén, International Study of Achievement in Mathematics, Vol. II. Uppsala: Almquist and Wiksells, 1967.
46. D. Elkind, Piagetian and psychometric conceptions of intelligence, *Harvard Educational Review,* 1969, pp. 319-37.
47. James C. Chalfant and Margaret A. Scheffelin, Central Processing Dysfunctions in Children: A Review of Research (Ninds Monograph 9). Washington, D.C.: U.S. Department of Health, Education, and Welfare, 1969.
48. Luella Cole, The Improvement of Reading, with Special Reference to Remedial Instruction. New York, Farrar and Rinehart, Inc., 1938.
49. Stanley Krippner, On research in visual training and reading disability, *Journal of Learning Disabilities,* February, 1971, p. 16.
50. Chalfant and Scheffelin, *op. cit.,* p. 23.
51. Moselle Boland, Going to school too soon blamed for eye troubles, *Houston Chronicle* (Texas), April 30, 1963.
52. Ruth Strang, Diagnostic Teaching of Reading. New York, McGraw Hill, 1964, pp. 164-65.
53. Homer L.J. Carter and Dorothy J. McGinnis, Diagnosis and Treatment of the Disabled Reader. London, MacMillan, Collier-MacMillan Ltd., 1970.
54. *Ibid.,* p. 48.
55. Cole, *op. cit.,* p. 284.
56. Carter and McGinnis, *op. cit.,* pp. 51-52.
57. Cole, *op. cit.,* p. 282.
58. H.G. Birch and A. Lefford, Intersensory development in children, *Monographs of the Society for Research in Child Development,* No. 89, 1963.
59. Joseph M. Wepman, The modality concept—including a statement of the perceptual and conceptual

levels of learning, in *Perception and Reading*, Proceedings of the Twelfth Annual Convention, International Reading Association, Vol. 12, Part 4, pp. 1-6. Newark, Dela., The Association, 1968.

60. John Bowlby, Maternal Care and Mental Health. Geneva, World Health Organization, 1952.

61. John Bowlby, Attachment and Loss, Vol. I. New York, Basic Books, 1969.

62. Marcel Geber, The psycho-motor development of African children in the first year, and the influence of maternal behavior, *Journal of Social Psychology*, 1958, pp. 185-95.

63. L.J. Yarrow, Separation from parents during early childhood, in Child Development Research I, Martin and Lois Hoffman, editors, New York, Russell Sage Foundation, 1964, p. 127.

64. Bowlby, *op. cit.*, p. 12.

65. Mary D. Ainsworth *et al.*, The effects of maternal deprivation: a review of findings and controversy in the context of research strategy, in Deprivation of Maternal Care, a Reassessment of Its Effects. New York, Schocken Books, 1966, p. 117.

66. Bowlby, *op. cit.*, p. 15.

67. Louise G. Daugherty, *NEA Journal*, December, 1963, pp. 18-20.

68. Robert D. Hess and Virginia C. Shipman, Maternal attitudes toward the school and the role of pupil: some social class comparisons, in Developing Programs for the Educationally Disadvantaged, A. Harry Passow, editor. New York, Teachers College Press, Columbia University, 1968, pp. 127-28.

69. Mildred Beatty Smith, School and home: focus on achievement, in Developing Programs for the Educationally Disadvantaged, A. Harry Passow, editor. New York, Teachers College Press, Columbia University, 1968, pp. 106-7.

70. Hylan Lewis, Culture, class, poverty, and urban schooling, in Reaching the Disadvantaged Learner, A. Harry Passow, editor. New York, Teachers College Press, Columbia University, 1970, p. 24.

71. Phyllis Levenstein, Learning through (and from) mothers, *Childhood Education*, December, 1971, pp. 130-34.

72. *Ibid.*, p. 132.

73. Bowlby, *op. cit.*, (fn. 60), pp. 67-68.

74. Burton Blatt and Frank Garfunkel, The Education of Intelligence. Washington, D.C.: The Council for Exceptional Children, 1969.

75. Susan W. Gray, The child's first teacher, *Childhood Education*, December, 1971, pp. 127-29.

76. Levenstein, *op. cit.*

77. David P. Weikart, Learning through parents: lessons for teachers, *Childhood Education*, December, 1971, pp. 135-37.

78. Ira J. Gordon, The beginnings of the self: the problem of the nurturing environment, *Phi Delta Kappan*, March, 1969, pp. 375-78.

79. Fisher, *op. cit.*, pp. 13-14.

80. Levenstein, *op. cit.*, p. 134.

81. *Ibid.*, p. 127.

STARTING OUT RIGHT

READING

"May I please be excused? I have a tension headache."

Parents usually believe that a child's education begins only when he starts learning how to read. To educators this is an oversimplification; the child first needs to learn how to get along with his peers. Before he begins a reading program, he should also possess a set of skills usually lumped together as "reading readiness."

Yet there is considerable truth in this simplified viewpoint, for reading is still the most critical skill in determining the child's success in school. A child who can't read is doomed to failure in our classrooms full of books. Whether or not this should be so is another question—Neil Postman argues that reading is not as important now as it once was. Yet reading is still at least a useful skill, if not an essential one. Also, the failure to successfully teach children how to read is interpreted by some as an indication of the bankruptcy of the entire educational system. Most educators agree that the problem is an important one—but they are far from agreement on a solution.

The debate about reading has taken many forms—primarily when to teach it and how. The question of reading methods is typical of many such debates in education. Some conservative critics want to go back to the "good old days" of McGuffey's Readers—because of both their political and pedagogical attitudes. Others advocate a plethora of *"modern" approaches, from phonics to Skinnerian behavior modification.*

Beneath much of the discussion of the methodology of reading instruction is a fundamental difference in approach that underlies many other educational debates—the romantic versus the scientific. Paul Goodman's article is in many ways typical of the romantic approach. He sees man as a naturally learning being—only his institutions (schools) get in the way. Learning, in his viewpoint, would be facilitated by inter-action with other people but is likely to be impaired by pedagogy.

Masha Rudman responds from a more "scientific" view-point. She argues that improved methodologies carefully applied can materially improve learning. In other words, our need is for more knowledge about the learning process, and this can be obtained by careful study. Schools do not obstruct learning, they are designed to facilitate it. Failings are due to inadequate knowledge, not institutional formats.

Both arguments seem to have some germs of truth. Indeed, both "free schools" and B. F. Skinner have met with some successes in their attempts at education. The discussion at hand focuses on reading, but the underlying issues apply to many other areas.

34 mini-schools: a prescription for the reading problem*

Paul Goodman

What follows is a statement I recently made when asked to testify on teaching reading, before the Borough President of Manhattan:

A chief obstacle to children's learning to read is the present school setting in which they have to pick it up. For any learning to be skillful and lasting, it must be or become self-motivated, second nature; for this, the schooling is too impersonal, standardized, and academic. If we tried to teach children to speak, by academic methods in a school-like environment, many would fail and most would stammer.

Although the analogy between learning to speak and learning to read is not exact, it is instructive to pursue it, since speaking is much harder. Learning to speak is a stupendous intellectual achievement. It involves learning to use signs, acquiring a vocabulary, and also mastering an extraordinary kind of algebra—syntax—with almost infinite variables in a large number of sentence forms. We do not know scientifically how infants learn to speak, but almost all succeed equally well, no matter what their class or culture. Every child picks up a dialect, whether "correct" or "incorrect," that is adequate to express the thoughts and needs of his milieu.

We can describe some of the indispensable conditions for learning to speak.

1. The child is constantly exposed to speech related to interesting behavior in which he often shares. ("Now where's your coat? Now we're going to the supermarket, etc.")

2. The speakers are persons important to the child, who often single him out to speak to him or about him.

3. The child plays with the sounds, freely imitates what he hears, and tries to approximate it without interference or correction. He is rewarded by attention and other useful results when he succeeds.

4. Later, the child consolidates by his own act what he has learned. From age three to five he acquires style, accent, and fluency by speaking with his peers, adopting their uniform but also asserting his own tone, rhythm, and mannerisms. He speaks peer speech but is uniquely recognizable as speaking in his own way.

---

*"Mini-Schools: A Prescription for the Reading Problem" is reprinted as it appeared in the *New York Review of Books*. It was re-written partially to become chapter 6 in *New Reformation: Notes of a Neolithic Conservative,* by Paul Goodman. Copyright © 1970 by Paul Goodman. Reprinted by permission of Random House, Inc.

Suppose, by contrast, that we tried to teach speaking academically in a school-like setting:

1. Speaking would be a curricular subject abstracted from the web of activity, and reserved for special hours punctuated by bells.

2. It would be a tool subject rather than a way of being in the world.

3. It would not spring from his needs in immediate situations but would be taught according to the teacher's idea of his future advantage, importantly aiming at his getting a job sixteen years later.

4. Therefore the child would have to be "motivated," the exercises would have to be "fun," etc.

5. The lessons would be arranged in a graded series from simple to complex, for instance on a false theory that monosyllables precede polysyllables, or words precede sentences, or sentences precede words.

6. The teacher's relation to the infant would be further depersonalized by the need to speak or listen to only what fits two dozen other children as well.

7. Being continually called on, corrected, tested, and evaluated to meet a standard in a group, some children would become stutterers; others would devise a phony system of apparently speaking in order to get by, although the speech meant nothing; others would balk at being processed and would purposely become "stupid."

8. Since there is a predetermined range of what can be spoken and how it must be spoken, everybody's speech would be pedantic and standard, without truth to the child's own experience or feeling.

Turn now to teaching reading. These eight disastrous defects are not an unfair caricature of what we do. Reading is treated as abstract, irrelevant to actual needs, instrumental, extrinsically motivated, impersonal, pedantic, not expressive of truth or art. The teaching often produces awkwardness, faking, or balking. Let me also make four further points specific to learning reading:

1. Most people who have learned to read and write fluently have done so on their own, with their own material, whether library books, newspapers, comic books, or street signs. They may have picked up the ABCs in school, but they acquired skill, preserved what they had learned, on their own. This self-learning is an important point, since it is not at the mechanical level of the ABCs that reading retardation drastically occurs, but in the subsequent years when the good readers are going it alone.

2. On neurological grounds, an emotionally normal child in middle-class urban and suburban surroundings, constantly exposed to written code, should spontaneously learn to read by age nine just as he learned to speak by age two or three. (This is the conclusion of Walla Nauta of the National Institute of Mental Health.) It is impossible for such a child *not* to pick up the code unless he is systematically interrupted and discouraged, for instance by trying to teach him.

But of course our problem has to do with children in the culture of poverty, which does not have the ordinary middle-class need for literacy and the premium put on it. Such children are not exposed to reading and writing in important relations with their parents and peers; the code does not constantly occur in every kind of sequence of behavior. Thus there is an essential need for the right kind of schooling, to point to the written words and read them aloud, in use.

3. Historically, in all modern countries, school methods of lessons, copying and textbooks, have been used, apparently successfully, to teach children to read. But this evidence is deceptive. A high level and continuing competence were required of very few—e.g., in 1900 in the United States only 6 percent graduated from high school. Little

effort was made with children of the working class, and none at all with those in the culture of poverty. It is inherently unlikely that the same institutional procedures could apply with such a change of scale and population. Where a dramatic effort has been made to teach adults to read, as in Cuba, the method has been "each one teach one," informally.

4. Also, with the present expansion of higher education, teachers of freshmen English uniformly complain that the majority of middle-class students cannot really read and write, though they have put on a performance that got them through high school. As John Holt has carefully described, their real life need was not reading or writing but getting by. (This is analogous to the large group among Puerto Rican children in New York who apparently speak English well, but who in fact cannot say anything that they need or mean, that is not really simply parroted.)

I trust that the aim of the Borough President's hearings is how to learn reading as truth and art and not just to fake and get by. Further, since poor children do not have the continual incentives and subtle pressures of middle-class life, it is much harder for them to learn even just to fake and get by. And even if they do get by, it will not pay off for them in the end, since they do not have money and connections. To make good, they must really be competent.

The question is, is it possible and feasible to teach reading somewhat in the way children learn to speak, by intrinsic interest, with personal attention, and relating to the whole environment of activity? Pedagogically it is possible and feasible. There are known methods and available teachers, and I will suggest an appropriate school setting. Economically it is feasible, since methods, staff, and setting do not cost more than the $850 per child that we now spend in the public schools. (This was demonstrated for two years by the First Street School on the Lower East Side, and it is in line with the budget of Erik Mann's new school for Negro children in Newark which uses similar principles.) Politically, however, my present proposal is impossible and unfeasible, since it threatens both vested interests and popular prejudices, as will be evident.

For ages six to eleven, I propose a system of tiny schools, radically decentralized. As one who for twenty years has urged democratic decentralization in many fields, including the schools, I am of course interested in the Bundy recommendation to cut up the New York system into sixty fairly autonomous districts. This would restore some relevance of the culture (and the staff) of the school to the culture of the community. But however valuable politically, it is an administrative arrangement; it does not get down to the actual pedagogical operation. And it certainly is not child-centered; both poor and middle-class communities have their own ways of not paying attention to children, according to their own prejudices and distant expectations. By "tiny school," therefore, I here mean twenty-eight children . . . with four teachers (one grown-up to seven children), and each tiny school to be largely administered by its own staff and parents, with considerable say also for the children, as in Summerhill. The four teachers are:

A teacher regularly licensed and salaried. Since the present average class size is twenty-eight, these are available.

A graduate from the senior class of a New York college, perhaps just embarking on graduate study. Salary $2000. There is no lack of candidates to do something interesting and useful in a free setting.

A literate housewife and mother, who can also prepare lunch. Salary $4000. No lack of candidates.

A literate, willing, and intelligent high-school graduate. Salary $2000. No lack of candidates.

Such a staff can easily be racially and ethnically mixed. And it is also the case, as demonstrated by the First Street School, that in such a small setting, with individual attention paid to the children, it is easy to get racially and ethnically mixed classes: there is less middle-class withdrawal when the parents do not fear that their children will be swamped and retarded. (We have failed to achieve "integration" by trying to impose it from above, but it can be achieved from below, in schools entirely locally controlled, if we can show parents that it is for their children's best future.)

For setting, the tiny school would occupy two, three, or four rooms in existing school buildings, church basements, settlement houses otherwise empty during school hours, rooms set aside in housing projects, store-fronts. The setting is especially indifferent since a major part of activity occurs outside the school place. The setting should be able to be transformed into a clubhouse, decorated and equipped according to the group's own decision. There might be one school on every street, but it is also advisable to locate many in racial and ethnic border areas, to increase intermixture. For purposes of assembly, health services, and some games, ten tiny schools could use the present public school facilities.

The cost saving in such a setup is the almost total elimination of top-down administration and the kind of special services that are required precisely because of excessive size and rigidity. The chief uses of central administration would be licensing, funding, choosing sites, and some inspection. There would be no principals and assistants, secretaries and assistants. Curriculum, texts, equipment would be determined as needed—and despite the present putative economies of scale, they would be cheaper; much less would be pointless or wasted. Record-keeping would be at a minimum. There is no need for truant officers, when the teacher-and-seven can call at the absentee's home and inquire. There is little need for remedial personnel since the staff and parents are always in contact, and the whole enterprise can be regarded as remedial. Organizational studies of large top-down directed enterprises show that the total cost is invariably at least 300 percent above the cost of the immediate function, in this case the interaction of teachers and children. I would put this 300 percent into increasing the number of adults and diversifying the possibilities of instruction. Further, in the conditions of New York real estate, there is great advantage in ceasing to build four-million-dollar school buildings, and rather fitting tiny schools into available niches.

Pedagogically, this model is appropriate for natural learning of reading:

1. It allows exposure to the activities of the city. A teacher-and-seven can spend half the time on the streets, visiting a business office, in a playgound, at a museum, watching television, chatting with the corner druggist, riding the buses and subways, visiting rich and poor neighborhoods and, if possible, homes. All these experiences can be saturated with speaking, reading, and writing. For instance, a group might choose to spend several weeks at the Museum of Natural History, and the problem would be to re-label the exhibits for their own level of comprehension.

2. It allows flexibility to approach each child according to his own style and interests, for instance in choice of reading matter. Given so many contexts, the teacher can easily strike when the iron is hot, whether reading the destination of a bus or the label on a can of soup. When some children catch on quickly and forge ahead on their own, the teacher need not waste their time and can concentrate on those who are more confused. The setting does not prejudge as to formal or informal techniques, phonics, Montessori, rote drill, Moore's typewriter, labeling the furniture, Herbert Kohl's creative writing, or any other method.

3. For instance, as a writer I like Sylvia Ashton-Warner's way of teaching little

Maoris. Each day she tries to catch the most passionate concern of each child and to give him a card with that key word: usually these are words of fear, anger, hunger, loneliness, or sexual desire. Soon a child has a large ineradicable but very peculiar reading list, not at all like Dick and Jane. He then easily progresses to read and write anything. From the beginning, in this method, reading and writing are gut-meaningful, they convey truth and feeling. This method could be used in our tiny school.

4. The ragged administration by children, staff, and parents is pedagogically a virtue, since this too, which is real, can be saturated with reading and writing, writing down the arguments, the rules, the penalties. Socially and politically, of course, it has the advantage of engaging the parents and giving them power.

I am assuming that for the first five school years, there is no merit in the standard curriculum. For a small child everything in the environment is educative, if he attends to it with guidance. Normal children can learn the first eight years' curriculum in four months anyway, at age twelve.

Further, I see little merit, for teaching this age, in the usual teacher-training. Any literate and well-intentioned grown-up or late teen-ager knows enough to teach a small child a lot. Teaching small children is a difficult art, but we do not know how to train the improvisational genius it requires, and the untrained seem to have it equally: compare one mother with another, or one big sister or brother with another. Since at this age one teaches the child, not the subject, the relevant art is psychotherapy, and the most useful course for a teachers' college is probably group therapy. The chief criterion for selection is the one I have mentioned: liking to be attentive to children. Given this setting, many young people would be introduced to teaching and would continue with it as a profession; whereas in the New York system the annual turnover approaches 20 percent, after years of wasted training.

As I have said, however, there are fatal political and administrative objections to this proposal. First, the Public School administration does not intend to go largely out of business. Given its mentality, it must see any radical decentralization as impossible to administer and dangerous, for everything cannot be controlled. Some child is bound to break a leg and the insurance companies will not cover; some teen-ager is bound to be indiscreet and the *Daily News* will explode in headlines.

The United Federation of Teachers will find the proposal to be anathema because it devalues professional prerequisites and floods the schools with the unlicensed. Being mainly broken to the public school harness, most experienced teachers consider free and inventive teaching to be impossible.

Most fatally, poor parents, who aspire for their children, tend to regard unrigidly structured education as down-grading, not taking the children seriously, and also as vaguely immoral. In the present Black Power temper of Harlem, also, the possible easy intermixing is itself not desired. (Incidentally, I am rather sympathetic to black separatism as a means of consolidating the power of black communities. But children, as Kant said, must be educated for the future better society which cannot be separated.)

In spite of these fatal objections, I recommend that, instead of building the next new school building, we try out this scheme with 1200 children.

reading: 35
a non-prescriptive
approach

Masha Rudman

Mr. Goodman's "prescription" for the "reading problem" involves a restructuring of the physical environment of the schooling situation. It also requires a new staffing pattern and a different pupil-teacher ratio. These factors, I would suggest, are far less crucial than the basic issue of the reading process (or indeed, the learning process) and how the learning is acquired and then utilized.

There are, as Mr. Goodman indicates, many existing approaches to the teaching of reading. Some people are convinced that a phonic, sound-blending approach is the best way. Children, therefore, are taught the sounds each letter and special combinations of letters represent. They are taught to confront each new word by blending the individual sounds until they make sense in the form of a word. A phonic approach is essentially a decoding approach. Meaning is not essential, although it is not necessarily absent. The vocabulary is strictly controlled in order to make the procedure consistent.

The linguistic approach is another much utilized procedure, used most recently for "remedial readers" particularly. It is predicated on patterns of language rather than on individual sounds. Those of us who grew up with the "at" family and "ing" family would probably be comfortable with the materials of this approach. Here, too, it is the *decoding* process which is emphasized—the content of the material often looks like nonsense to an adult accustomed to reading for some purpose. "Pat Nat the fat cat" is typical of the beginning linguistic text. But "Oh, oh, look, look!" is equally meaningless, and equally representative of another approach, the basal eclectic, which purports to have meaning as one of its prime considerations. The basal eclectic approach is so named because it attempts to teach reading in a developmental sequential fashion, utilizing many different techniques for unlocking new words (including phonic, linguistic, context, configuration, and sight word memory clues). Other experts have devised new alphabets for making English more consistent for beginning readers.

In any case, publishers have made the selling of reading approaches a very profitable business. Each approach is touted as the miracle drug to cure the reading problem, and each approach is replete with sets of written materials, including manuals for the teachers, and posters, workbooks, books, games, and gimmicks for the children. Sometimes the manual suggests that different children might have different needs in terms of amount of materials to be covered at one time, or, indeed, amount of time needed at any one task. And most manuals suggest "enrichment" activities for the bright or fast child who completes his assignment and has "nothing to do." The premise, however, is that the "normal" children will progress through the materials at the suggested pace and will emerge at the end of the semester as "first-grade-level readers" or "fourth-grade-level readers."

It is truly an anomaly that administrators, teachers, and parents permit this farce to be perpetrated upon their children. Well-meaning school systems, recognizing that one publisher's claims have not come to fruition, compound the nonsense by eliminating that publisher's materials from the system (usually by burning them) and then buying *another* publisher's materials! This process is repeated *ad nauseum,* without questioning the basic fallacy that any single approach or set of materials is appropriate when more than one learner is involved, and is sufficient even for one learner.

Mr. Goodman's analysis of what might happen if speech were taught in the same manner as reading is demonstrated accurately in the reasoning behind the procedure mentioned above. Reading must be considered external to the child's world in order to imagine that these artificial impositions and arrangements are necessary. On the other hand, not all children can acquire without help the degree of speech facility that is necessary for them to communicate as well as they'd like. We are all in the continuous process of improving our own speaking abilities. Sometimes we seek specific professional help; sometimes we select models to emulate. Reading is similarly a continuous process. The plethora of speed reading courses would not be reaping riches if everyone were content with his present reading level. This discontent, I would suggest, is a potentially healthy state of affairs. All of the communication areas, including listening, speaking, reading, and writing, should be viewed as open-ended skills in constant need of development and honing.

I therefore disagree with Mr. Goodman's suggestions regarding elaborate changes in school structure. I would further disagree with his contention that anyone can teach reading. Perhaps it would be more accurate to say that no one can teach reading. Either statement is simplistic and inadequate to the situation. What precisely is the teaching of reading? I believe that it involves far more than the teaching of procedures to be used for decoding written symbols. Every good reader does in fact utilize the procedures which work best for him. Beyond this decoding, reading involves meaning. The degree of meaning people receive from the printed word depends on the depth and amount of experience they bring to it. Thus it is the job of the teacher and the learner to create the most stimulating and responsive environment possible in order to progress along the continuum of good reading.

A teacher needs a great many skills in order to be able to participate in this process. Too many adults (and children) believe that the function of the teacher is primarily to tell. Teaching and telling are equated. Additionally, the teacher is expected to lead, guide, provide, prod, initiate, and control all learning. The emphasis is on the acquisition of facts, and the mastery of the skill of reading in order to insure that the child be able to acquire more facts. The teacher in the classroom I envision does indeed do all of these things when it is appropriate to do so. But he or she also helps the child to acquire those learning skills which enable the child too, to lead, guide, provide, prod, initiate, and control his own learning. The child must be an active participant in the process if the learning which takes place is to be valid and long lasting. Content is, of course, necessary. But there is no one set of facts which everyone or even most people in our complex society need to acquire. There are, however, abilities which people must have in order to participate in a healthy society. Independent thinking, structuring of one's own situation, responsible decision making, finding the necessary information—these are but some of the skills which are the product of a fine education. And the teacher who tells the children what to do next and when to do it and how much of it to do is *not* teaching the necessary skills.

There has emerged in the past thirty years a sensible construct for "education for initiative and responsibility" (a term I now borrow from Ed Yeomans). It has various descriptive names such as Integrated Day, Active Learning, Open Education, Individualized Instruction, and others. Each of the terms tries to describe the learning situation which involves the child in the kind of education which prepares him for active participation in everything he does. The physical setting is not prescribed, nor is the student-teacher ratio. This kind of learning can take place in a one-room schoolhouse, a modern open structure, or in the kind of setting Mr. Goodman describes. It can and does happen with forty children and one teacher, or with one child and one teacher. Adults in the classroom must be responsive, interested, and humane. The teacher must be a perceptive diagnostician. The team of teacher(s) and learner(s) together must decide the curriculum, drawing upon as many outside resources (such as books, published curricula, teaching guides, and other people) as they possibly can, but taking care to use them only as guides, not as prescriptors.

How might a reading program look in such a learning environment? The materials should include all that Mr. Goodman suggests, plus all kinds of books (such as cookbooks and science books), and as many other kinds of printed materials as possible—paperbacks, magazines, newspapers, cereal boxes, cans, games, and anything else with words written on it. An abundance of pictures (for labeling, talking about, writing about, sequencing) and all sorts of nonprint materials are also important in a reading program under the guidance of a skilled teacher. This teacher would be responsive to the children's needs and interests and would help them to see what their next step in reading should be. A teacher in this sort of program would never consider a piece of material too easy for a child, but would teach him how to recognize when something might be too frustrating to be of use. Any form of informal reading inventory would be important in teaching a child to assess his own frustration level.

This kind of program is already in effect in many schools. Its operation includes not only the self-selection of their reading materials by the children, but also the teacher's diagnosis of the strengths and needs of each child in terms of his ability to use the skill of reading. This diagnosis takes place during a private conference which can be regularly scheduled, or held on request by either the child or the teacher. The teacher can then suggest several options, such as participation in small, teacher-led, task-oriented skill groups, or child-led small groups, or the use of specific materials suitable to the child's learning style and applicable to his specific requirements. The teacher must also be resourceful and able to create materials when those which are published are not available or appropriate. The child is at all times involved in self evaluation as well as active participation in his own learning.

This kind of program pays attention to children and requires that children pay attention to themselves and to each other. The children have the added responsibility of sometimes initiating curriculum, selecting their own learning materials, pacing themselves, and making judgments about their own learning and progress. The teacher is relieved of the burden of being the sole evaluator, sole selector of curriculum, and sole source of information. But the teacher has the vital task of participating in the diagnosis of each child's next step, encouraging each child to move, intervening when necessary, becoming acquainted with the appropriate materials in the field, and suggesting and creating new materials. The teacher retains the responsibility for intricately structuring the child's learning opportunities.

Several teacher preparation institutions, such as the University of Massachusetts School of Education and North Dakota's New School, have established teacher preparation programs specifically devised to develop these competencies. They are also working with teachers already in the classroom in order to help them with these same skills.

Thus, Mr. Goodman's good intentions and apt perceptions notwithstanding, procedures, equipment, pupil-teacher ratio, and physical setting make very little difference, but talented, well-prepared teachers are crucial in order to help children of any background or ability accomplish the goal of becoming independent, responsible learners.

illiteracy in america: 36
position papers—the
politics of reading*

Teachers of reading comprise a most sinister political group, whose continued presence and strength are more a cause for alarm than celebration. I offer this thought as a defensible proposition, all the more worthy of consideration because so few people will take it seriously.

My argument rests on a fundamental and, I think, unassailable assumption about education: namely, that all educational practices are profoundly political in the sense that they are designed to produce one sort of human being rather than another—which is to say, an educational system always proceeds from some model of what a human being *ought* to be like. In the broadest sense, a political ideology is a conglomerate of systems for promoting certain modes of thinking and behavior. And there is no system I can think of that more directly tries to do this than the schools. There is not one thing that is done to, for, with, or against a student in school that is not rooted in a political bias, ideology, or notion. This includes everything from the arrangement of seats in a classroom, to the rituals practiced in the auditorium, to the textbooks used in lessons, to the dress required of both teachers and students, to the tests given, to the subjects that are taught, and most emphatically, to the intellectual skills that are promoted. And what is called reading, it seems to me, just about heads the list. For to teach reading, or even to promote vigorously the teaching of reading, is to take a definite political position on how people should behave and on what they ought to value. Now, teachers, I have found, respond in one of three ways to such an assertion. Some of them deny it. Some of them concede it but without guilt or defensiveness of any kind. And some of them don't know what it means. I want to address myself to the latter, because in responding to them I can include all the arguments I would use in dealing with the others.

In asserting that the teaching of reading is essentially a political enterprise, the most obvious question I am asking is, "What is reading good for?" When I ask this question of reading teachers, I am supplied with a wide range of answers. Those who take the low ground will usually say that skill in reading is necessary in order for a youngster to do

*An earlier version of this article was presented as the keynote address at the Lehigh University Reading Conference, January 24, 1970. (Reprinted by permission from Postman, N., "Illiteracy in America: Position Papers—The Politics of Reading," *Harvard Educational Review, 40,* No. 2, May 1970, 244-252. Copyright© 1970 by the President and Fellows of Harvard College.)

well in school. The elementary teacher is preparing the youngster for the junior high teacher, who prepares him for the senior high teacher, who, in turn, prepares him for the college teacher, and so on. Now, this answer is true but hardly satisfactory. In fact, it amounts to a description of the *rules* of the school game but says nothing about the purpose of these rules. So, when teachers are pushed a little further, they sometimes answer that the school system, at all levels, makes reading skill a precondition to success because unless one can read well, he is denied access to gainful and interesting employment as an adult. This answer raises at least a half-dozen political questions, the most interesting of which is whether or not one's childhood education ought to be concerned with one's future employment. I am aware that most people take it as axiomatic that the schooling process should prepare youth for a tranquil entry into our economy, but this is a political view that I think deserves some challenge. For instance, when one considers that the second most common cause of death among adolescents in the U.S. is suicide, or that more people are hospitalized for mental illness than all other illnesses combined, or that one out of every 22 murders in the United States is committed by a parent against his own child, or that more than half of all high school students have already taken habit-forming, hallucinogenic, or potentially addictive narcotics, or that by the end of this year, there will be more than one-million school drop-outs around, one can easily prepare a case which insists that the schooling process be designed for purposes other than vocational training. If it is legitimate at all for schools to claim a concern for the adult life of students, then why not pervasive and compulsory programs in mental health, sex, or marriage and the family? Besides, the number of jobs that require reading skill much beyond what teachers call a "fifth-grade level" is probably quite small and scarcely justifies the massive, compulsory, unrelenting reading programs that characterize most schools.

But most reading teachers would probably deny that their major purpose is to prepare students to satisfy far-off vocational requirements. Instead, they would take the high ground and insist that the basic purpose of reading instruction is to open the student's mind to the wonders and riches of the written word, to give him access to great fiction and poetry, to permit him to function as an informed citizen, to have him experience the sheer pleasure of reading. Now, this is a satisfactory answer indeed but, in my opinion, it is almost totally untrue.

And to the extent that it is true, it is true in a way quite different from anything one might expect. For instance, it is probably true that in a highly complex society, one cannot be governed unless he can read forms, regulations, notices, catalogues, road signs, and the like. Thus, some minimal reading skill is necessary if you are to be a "good citizen," but "good citizen" here means one who can follow the instructions of those who govern him. If you cannot read, you cannot be an obedient citizen. You are also a good citizen if you are an enthusiastic consumer. And so, some minimal reading competence is required if you are going to develop a keen interest in all the products that it is necessary for you to buy. If you do not read, you will be a relatively poor market. In order to be a good and loyal citizen, it is also necessary for you to believe in the myths and superstitions of your society. Therefore, a certain minimal reading skill is needed so that you can learn what these are, or have them reinforced. Imagine what would happen in a school if a Social Studies text were introduced that described the growth of American civilization as being characterized by four major developments: 1) insurrection against a legally constituted government, in order to achieve a political identity; 2) genocide against the indigenous population, in order to get land; 3) keeping human beings as slaves, in order to achieve an economic base; and 4) the importation of "coolie" labor, in order to build the railroads. Whether this view of American history is true or not is beside the point. It is at least as true or false as the conventional view *and* it would scarcely be allowed to appear unchallenged in a school-book intended for youth. What I am saying here is that an important function of the teaching of reading is to make students accessible to political and historical myth. It is entirely possible that the main reason middle-class whites are so concerned to get lower-class blacks to read is that blacks will remain relatively inaccessible to standard-brand beliefs unless and until they are minimally literate. It just may be too dangerous, politically, for any substantial minority of our population *not* to believe that our flags are sacred, our history is noble, our government is representative, our laws are just, and our institutions are viable. A reading public is a responsible public, by which is meant that it believes most or all of these superstitions, and which is probably why we still have literacy tests for voting.

One of the standard beliefs about the reading process is that it is more or less neutral. Reading, the argument goes, is just a skill. What people read is their own business, and the reading teacher merely helps to increase a student's options. If one wants to read about America, one may read DeToqueville or *The Daily News;* if one wants to read literature, one may go to Melville or Jacqueline Susann. In theory, this argument is compelling. In practice, it is pure romantic nonsense. *The New York Daily News* is the most widely read newspaper in America. Most of our students will go to the grave not having read, of their own choosing, a paragraph of DeToqueville or Thoreau or John Stuart Mill or, if you exclude the Gettysburg Address, even Abraham Lincoln. As between Jacqueline Susann and Herman Melville—well, the less said, the better. To put it bluntly, among every 100 students who learn to read, my guess is that no more than one will employ the process toward any of the lofty goals which are customarily held before us. The rest will use the process to increase their knowledge of trivia, to maintain themselves at a relatively low level of emotional maturity, and to keep themselves simplistically uninformed about the social and political turmoil around them.

Now, there are teachers who feel that, even if what I say is true, the point is nonetheless irrelevant. After all, they say, the world is not perfect. If people do not have enough time to read deeply, if people do not have sensibilities refined enough to read great literature, if people do not have interests broad enough to be stimulated by the unfamiliar, the fault is not in our symbols, but in ourselves. But there is a point of view that proposes that the "fault," in fact, *does* lie in our symbols. Marshall McLuhan is saying that each medium of communication contains a unique metaphysic—that each medium makes special kinds of claims on our senses, and therefore, on our behavior. McLuhan himself tells us that he is by no means the first person to have noticed this. Socrates took a very dim view of the written word, on the grounds that it diminishes man's capacity to memorize, and that it forces one to follow an argument rather than to participate in it. He also objected to the fact that once something has been written down, it may easily come to the attention of persons for whom it was not intended. One can well imagine what Socrates would think about wire-tapping and other electronic bugging devices. St. Ambrose, a prolific book writer and reader, once complained to St. Jerome, another prolific writer and reader, that whatever else its virtues, reading was the most anti-social behavior yet devised by man. Other people have made observations about the effects of communications media on the psychology of a culture, but it is quite remarkable how little has been said about this subject. Most criticism of print, or any other medium, has dealt with the content of the medium; and it is only in recent years that we have begun to understand that each medium, *by its very structure,* makes us do things with our bodies, our senses, and our minds that in the long run are probably more important than any other messages communicated by the medium.

Now that it is coming to an end, we are just beginning to wonder about the powerful biases forced upon us by the Age of the Printed Word. McLuhan is telling us that print is a "hot" medium, by which he means that it induces passivity and anesthetizes almost all our senses except the visual. He is also telling us that electronic media, like the LP record and television, are reordering our entire sensorium, restoring some of our sleeping senses, and, in the process, making all of us seek more active participation in life. I think McLuhan is wrong in connecting the *causes* of passivity and activity so directly to the structure of media. I find it sufficient to say that whenever a new medium—a new communications technology—enters a culture, *no matter what its structure,* it gives us a new way of experiencing the world, and consequently, releases tremendous energies and causes people to seek new ways of organizing their institutions. When Gutenberg announced that he could manufacture books, as he put it, "without the help of reed, stylus, or pen but by wondrous agreement, proportion, and harmony of punches and types," he could scarcely imagine that he was about to become the most important political and social revolutionary of the Second Millenium. And yet, that is what happened. Four hundred and fifty years ago, the printed word, far from being a medium that induced passivity, generated cataclysmic change. From the time Martin Luther posted his theses in 1517, the printing press disseminated the most controversial, inflammatory, and wrenching ideas imaginable. The Protestant Reformation would probably not have occurred if not for the printing press. The development of both capitalism and nationalism were obviously linked to the printing press. So were new literary forms, such as the novel and the essay. So were new conceptions of education, such as written examinations. And, of course, so was the concept of scientific methodology, whose ground rules were established by Descartes in his *Discourse on Reason.* Even today in recently illiterate cultures, such as Cuba, print is a medium capable of generating intense involvement, radicalism, artistic innovation, and institutional upheaval. But in those countries where the printed word has been pre-eminent for over 400 years, print retains very few of these capabilities. Print is not dead, it's just old—and old technologies do not generate new patterns of behavior. For us, print is the technology of convention. We have accommodated our senses to it. We have routinized and even ritualized our responses to it. We have devoted our institutions, which are now venerable, to its service. By maintaining the printed word as the keystone of education, we are therefore opting for political and social stasis.

It is 126 years since Professor Morse transmitted a message electronically for the first time in the history of the planet. Surely it is not too soon for educators to give serious thought to the message he sent: "What hath God wrought?" We are very far from knowing the answers to that question, but we do know that electronic media have released unprecedented energies. It's worth saying that the gurus of the peace movement—Bob Dylan, Pete Seeger, Joan Baez, Phil Ochs, for instance—were known to their constituency mostly as voices on LP records. It's worth saying that Viet Nam, being our first television war, is also the most unpopular war in our history. It's worth saying that Lyndon Johnson was the first president ever to have resigned because of a "credibility gap." It's worth saying that it is now commonplace for post-TV college sophomores to usurp the authority of college presidents and for young parish priests to instruct their bishops in the ways of *both* man and God. And it's also worth saying that black people, after 350 years of bondage, want their freedom—now. Post-television blacks are, indeed, our true *now* generation.

Electronic media are predictably working to unloose disruptive social and political ideas, along with new forms of sensibility and expression. Whether this is being achieved by the structure of the media, or by their content, or by some combination of both, we cannot be sure. But like Gutenberg's infernal machine of 450 years ago, the electric plug is causing all hell to break loose. Meanwhile, the schools are still pushing the old technology; and, in fact, pushing it with almost hysterical vigor. Everyone's going to learn to read, even if we have to kill them to do it. It is as if the schools were the last bastion of the old culture, and if it has to go, why let's take as many down with us as we can.

For instance, the schools are still the principal source of the idea that literacy is equated with intelligence. Why, the schools even promote the idea that *spelling* is related to intelligence! Of course, if any of this were true, reading teachers would be the smartest people around. One doesn't mean to be unkind, but if that indeed is the case, no one has noticed it. In any event, it is an outrage that children who do not read well, or at all, are treated as if they are stupid. It is also masochistic, since the number of non-readers will obviously continue to increase and, thereby, the schools will condemn themselves, by their own definition of intelligence, to an increasing number of stupid children. In this way, we will soon have remedial reading-readiness classes, along with remedial classes for those not yet ready for their remedial reading-readiness class.

The schools are also still promoting the idea that literacy is the richest source of aesthetic experience. This, in the face of the fact that kids are spending a billion dollars a year to buy LP records and see films. The schools are still promoting the idea that the main source of wisdom is to be found in libraries, from which most schools, incidentally, carefully exclude the most interesting books. The schools are still promoting the idea that the non-literate person is somehow not fully human, an idea that will surely endear us to the non-literate peoples of the world. (It is similar to the idea that salvation is obtainable only through Christianity—which is to say, it is untrue, bigoted, reactionary, and based on untenable premises, to boot.)

Worst of all, the schools are using these ideas to keep non-conforming youth—blacks, the politically disaffected, and the economically disadvantaged, among others—in their place. By taking this tack, the schools have become a major force for political conservatism at a time when everything else in the culture screams for rapid reorientation and change.

What would happen if our schools took the drastic political step of trying to make the new technology the keystone of education? The thought will seem less romantic if you remember that the start of the Third Millenium is only 31 years away. No one knows, of course, what would happen, but I'd like to make a few guesses. In the first place, the physical environment would be entirely different from what it is now. The school would look something like an electric circus—arranged to accommodate TV cameras and monitors, film projectors, computers, audio and video tape machines, radio, and photographic and stereophonic equipment. As he is now provided with textbooks, each student would be provided with his own still-camera, 8 mm. camera, and tape casette. The school library would contain books, of course, but at least as many films, records, video-tapes, audio-tapes, and computer programs. The major effort of the school would be to assist students in achieving what has been called "multi-media literacy." Therefore, speaking, film-making, picture-taking, televising, computer-programming, listening, perhaps even music playing, drawing, and dancing would be completely acceptable means of expressing intellectual interest and competence. They would certainly be given weight at least equal to reading and writing.

Since intelligence would be defined in a new way, a student's ability to create an idea would be at least as important as his ability to classify and remember the ideas of others.

New evaluation procedures would come into being, and standardized tests—the final, desperate refuge of the print-bound bureaucrat—would disappear. Entirely new methods of instruction would evolve. In fact, schools might abandon the notion of teacher instruction altogether. Whatever disciplines lent themselves to packaged, lineal, and segmented presentation would be offered through a computerized and individualized program. And students could choose from a wide variety of such programs whatever they wished to learn about. This means, among other things, that teachers would have to stop acting like teachers and find something useful to do, like, for instance, helping young people to resolve some of their more wrenching emotional problems.

In fact, a school that put electric circuitry at its center would have to be prepared for some serious damage to all of its bureaucratic and hierarchial arrangements. Keep in mind that hierarchies derive their authority from the notion of unequal access to information. Those at the top have access to more information that those at the bottom. That is in fact why they are at the top and the others, at the bottom. But today those who are at the bottom of the school hierarchy, namely, the students, have access to at least as much information about most subjects as those at the top. At present, the only way those at the top can maintain control over them is by carefully discriminating against what the students know—that is, by labelling what the students know as unimportant. But suppose cinematography was made a "major" subject instead of English literature? Suppose chemotherapy was made a "major" subject? or space technology? or ecology? or mass communication? or popular music? or photography? or race relations? or urban life? Even an elementary school might then find itself in a situation where the faculty were at the bottom and its students at the top. Certainly, it would be hard to know who are the teachers and who the learners.

And then perhaps a school would become a place where *everybody,* including the adults, is trying to learn something. Such a school would obviously be problem-centered, *and* future-centered, *and* change-centered; and, as such, would be an instrument of cultural and political radicalism. In the process we might find that our youth would also learn to read without pain and with a degree of success and economy not presently known.

I want to close on this thought: teachers of reading represent an important political pressure group. They may not agree with me that they are a sinister political group. But I should think that they would want to ask at least a few questions *before* turning to consider the *techniques* of teaching reading. These questions would be: What is reading good for? What is it better or worse than? What are my motives in promoting it? And the ultimate political question of all, "Whose side am I on?"

A
SCIENCE (?)
OF
EDUCATION

"What's to worry about? They'll teach sex like they do the rest of the subjects and the kids will lose interest."

There are those among physical scientists who consider the very term "social sciences" to be deceptive labeling. They see the social "sciences" as studies of little substance and less effect—more respectable than astrology, but certainly undeserving of the term "science." They can point to the marginal results of "scientific" techniques used in education and elsewhere and take various positions: social scientists are using the wrong approach to study people, have a totally inadequate base of knowledge, or are simply academic charlatans.

From a religious or humanistic viewpoint, the problem is different: the human mind is unquantifiable. Attempts to quantify human action leave out "variables" that simply can't be left out. The results, from this viewpoint, are regarded as rubbish or studies that deaden the human soul.

Educational scientists, naturally, rarely agree with these ideas (although most will concede that their field is not yet as well developed as the physical sciences and that their findings are only approximations). While they have many differences among themselves (which are represented here), they still hold to the basic value of what they're trying to do.

The existence of controversy—even such a basic debate as that between B. F. Skinner and Chris Argyris in this section—does not necessarily mean that education is an unscientific field. Such conflicts can be found in the pages of journals of any science. Their resolution lies in observations which can prove one or more of the theories wrong. If, after many theories have been formulated, none fit the observations reasonably well, then the basic framework for the theories can be questioned. If a scientific approach to education is invalid or incomplete, it will eventually show up here.

One of the great successes of the physical sciences has been the systematization of large bodies of knowledge. Educational researchers, hampered by a field where interrelationships are often obscure, have not had much success in this area. The result has been what appears to be a vast, incoherent body of knowledge. In this section, Daniel Jordan makes an attempt at "Putting the Pieces Together."

A comparison with the development of the physical sciences may be useful for educational researchers. The first stage in the development of physics was Aristotle's approach: pure reasoning. This indicated, for example, that a heavy object should fall faster than a light object. It doesn't, but this was only discovered in the next stage—experimentation and mathematical systematization of laws by such men as Newton and Galileo. There are obvious parallels to certain educational ideas that "should" work but, when studied carefully, seem to make "no significant difference." Many educational researchers today see themselves as developing "laws of education" much as Newton developed laws of physics.

Educators, however, should remember that the whole structure of Newtonian physics is today considered only a first approximation of the real world as described by relativity and quantum mechanics. Its usefulness depends on what is to be done: it is perfectly adequate for building bridges but simply cannot handle nuclear reactions. Further, the progress of most other sciences was much less coherent than that of physics. Chemistry, for example, was floundering in indefiniteness until the early nineteenth century. It was only then, for example, that it was definitely determined that fire was not composed of a special element called "phlogiston." And there wasn't enough knowledge to build much of a "science" of medicine until the early years of this century.

Where is the science of education today? The issue of testing is illustrative as well as important in itself. Ronald Hambleton and William Gorth propose some ways in which testing can be used to help students. Sidney Simon argues that grading (primarily a consequence of testing) can be damaging. James Carmody discusses some of the problems of testing as now practiced. These papers can help to focus on the question: Are we viewing the foundation of a science or the emergence of a new educational cult?

37 classroom teachers and educational scholars: what do they have in common?

Albert H. Yee

Professional fields requiring academic level study and certification to pursue have at least two main types of workers. There are practitioners carrying out what is known and acceptable for public use and there are theorists and researchers who work primarily to advance knowledge and innovation. Both normally share a common foundation of professional preparation, knowledge, and methodology. With a theoretical-technical jargon unfamiliar to the layman, feedback is assumed to flow between shop and lab. It is also assumed that the purposes and orientation of both levels relate fairly well, or at least do not conflict. Thus, there are practicing weathermen, physicians, attorneys, flight engineers and pilots, and computer programers, for instance, who relate professionally to meteorologists, medical researchers, legal specialists, aeronautical designers, and electronic engineers, respectively, and these work mainly in universities.

Oversimplified as the above description may seem, it helps characterise one great problem in America's educational system—the lack of relationship and compatability between the professional orientations of classroom teachers and educational scholars. This chapter will attempt to show what the problem is, views of why it exists, and how it might be eliminated.

A PERSISTENT AMERICAN PROBLEM

The disparity between classroom teachers and educational scholars has existed since the earliest development of education in America. Long before the writing of the Constitution, two distinct and independent educational systems had developed in colonial America—one oriented to classical scholarship, social status, and leadership and another directed to elementary education for the common people.

The educational contrast appears in contemporary accounts, as in Ralph Waldo Emerson's bold essay of 1837, "The American Scholar," which asserted the validity of and need for Americans as scholars—"man thinking . . . free and brave"—extending from, but independent of, European intellectual traditions. Emerson's description of the scholar's education "by nature, by books, and by action" and his worthy duties seems to the modern reader high-minded and abstract. For Emerson, scholarship expressed the greatness that human reason and human action can and should accomplish.

When Emerson discussed the theme of education, however, he did not mention scholarship but focused instead upon the uplifting of all men, to make them "able, earnest, great-hearted men." Discussing the work of teachers at length, Emerson described teaching, not in terms of what knowledge should be taught, but how it should be conducted. Emphasizing the virtues of humor, understanding, character-building, and acceptance of individual differences, Emerson implied that primary teaching was a true feminine pursuit. He suggested that teachers "cherish mother-wit" and try to "smuggle in a little contraband wit, fancy, imagination, thought." He was concerned that teachers not be so inflexible with classroom rules and order that they maintain a "military" setting characteristic of masculine leadership. Thus, there is the clear implication that teaching youngsters is feminine and socio-emotional while scholarship is masculine and intellectual.

Ever since the historic "Old Deluder Satan Act" of 1647 beginning America's system of public education, communities have had problems finding willing and qualified teachers for their youth. Hofstadter (1966, p. 316) wrote that early American communities "settled for what [teachers] they could get and what they got was a high proportion of misfits and incompetents." Washington Irving's Ichabod Crane probably would have been one of the better teachers of his day, had he really existed. Against the risks of male "rascals" serving as teachers, Hofstadter saw that "what helped American education to break out of the vicious circle was . . . the graded primary school and the emergence of the woman teacher."

Development of the tax-supported Common School that Barnard, Mann, Stowe, and others successfully fought for before the mid-nineteenth century expanded America's public education considerably but magnified the staffing problem. The solution became the schoolmarm, an unwed lady, usually poorly educated herself, who "kept" school until she finally married. The teacher in America became a figure of respect more for her role than for her professional competence and scholarship. Almost every woman seemed to believe she could do as well or better if she could only endure the schoolmarm's limited compensation, routines, and social scrutiny and restrictions. To a large extent, the image of the teacher as a quasi-professional persists to the present day.

Professional training for teachers and licensing developed slowly, and was conducted in normal schools without association with scholars and the academic world. Adolphe E. Meyer, a historian specializing in American education, described normal schools of the 1860's as follows: "The plain truth is that among academicians the normal school was considered worthy only of derision" (1957, p. 206). Teacher education consisted of perfunctory preparation for teaching, by necessity providing basic learnings as well as simple pedagogic skills, and it is not surprising that early teacher training appeared to have little positive influence over classroom conditions.

Near the end of the nineteenth century, Joseph Mayer Rice, a pediatrician turned educational crusader, took leave of his medical practice to study the new "science of Education" in Europe for two years. Returning to the United States, he studied classrooms in 36 major cities for six months. Publishing his findings in a series of essays,

Rice saw much to criticize and little to praise. Like Emerson, he was most concerned with how teachers taught and how they handled children rather than what subject knowledge they provided. The low professional quality of teachers upset him most of all. Without adequate teacher training and selection and the use of "scientific methods" in schools, Rice saw that "the office of teacher in the average American school is perhaps the only one in the world that can be retained indefinitely in spite of the grossest negligence and incompetency" (1893, p. 15).

William James's classic work of 1899, *Talks to Teachers on Psychology*, illustrates the differing orientations and emphases of scholars who pursue educational concerns and of classroom teachers. In his preface, James explained that after accepting the invitation of the Harvard Corporation to speak to various groups of teachers on psychology, he found he had to modify his presentation:

> I have found by experience that what my hearers seem least to relish is analytical technicality, and what they most care for is concrete practical application. So I have gradually weeded out the former, and left the latter unreduced; and, now that I have at last written out the lectures, they contain a minimum of what is deemed "scientific" in psychology, and are practical and popular in the extreme (p. v).

Because of contrasting objectives, community support, training, traditions, and widely different types of students, it is no wonder that the orientations and interests of academic scholars and classroom teachers differed. Early educational scholars came from diverse fields of study and brought rich backgrounds of knowledge and intellect that they might have shared. Interestingly, they did not regard teachers as intellectual colleagues and did not seek to impose their orientation and scholarship upon them. The scholars seemed satisfied in trying to get teachers to "relax," and foster nurturance, understanding, and warmth in their teaching. The scholars' simple level of discourse to teachers is suggestive of the quasi-professional teachers and sorry classroom teaching they found in schools.

Recent studies of classroom teachers indicate that there has been little change in the differing professional orientations of classroom teachers and scholars. Present-day teachers seem to express little concern for educational change and intellectual matters. Their main concerns seem directed more to concrete problems of classroom dynamics in the here-and-now. Jackson (1968) wrote that teachers had a "tender-minded world view," which "idealized children and was tinged with a quasi-mystical faith in human perfectability." Studying the language of teachers, he wrote: "Lacking a technical vocabulary, skimming the intellectual surface of the problems they encounter, fenced in, as it were, by the walls of their concrete experience, these teachers hardly look like the type of people who should be allowed to supervise the intellectual development of young children" (p. 148).

Jackson observed that teachers differ greatly from researchers and others who are oriented toward rationality, intellectual models, and educational change. Yet, with the impersonal, formal, and institutionalized nature of schools and the complex nature of classrooms, he asserted: "Our present cadre of elementary school teachers, with all of their intellectual fuzziness and sticky sentimentality, may be doing a job better than would an army of human engineers" (p. 152). Jackson has thus come to an understanding of teachers' difficult roles rather than simply condemning their short-comings. As schools are organized and maintained today, the quality of teaching is severely limited, and rational models of teaching may be inappropriate. Thus, scholars and teachers differ because their roles, functions, and expectations differ greatly, as will be discussed later in more detail.

The continuing contrast between scholars and classroom teachers is further shown by studies of teachers' perceptions of children's behavior. In 1928, Wickman published his classic report which found that teachers and mental health specialists differed considerably in their views of children's normal and abnormal behavior. Replicating the general purpose of Wickman's work, Tolor, Scarpetti and Lane (1967) found that psychologists were more accepting and tolerant toward a greater variety of child behavior than were teachers.

Beginning teachers were found to be less tolerant than experienced teachers, and this difference was greater than that between the psychologists and experienced teachers. Thus, teachers appear to develop more modern and professional perceptions of child behavior through classroom experience, though this remains distinct from that of psychologists. Inexperienced teachers do not appear to understand the natural behavior of children well enough to assume full classroom responsibilities. Since American teachers teach an average of less than two years, this is one more indication that teacher preparation and general professionalism in teaching must be improved.

The specialties of theorists and researchers in education vary considerably, indicating the wide importance of educational studies and their great growth, especially in the last two decades. Many scholars in other fields also contribute to educational scholarship today, especially in the development of new curricula and textbooks. Academic scholars influenced classroom teaching in science and mathematics by development of New Curricula within a few years after public concern and funding were stimulated by Sputnik. Similar efforts have been made in other areas. Interestingly, the New Curricula do not imply much change in teacher quality. They can be viewed as making it more difficult for ordinary teachers to make errors and waste teaching time, i.e., they tell the teacher exactly what and how to teach. However, evaluations to date have been unable to determine whether the New Curricula provide gains in learner achievement significantly greater than older resources.

The significant federal support of educational scholarship, which emerged in 1954 when Congress passed the Cooperative Research Act, is largely responsible for the recent advances in the production and quality of scholarship. With federal sources providing most of the funds, about $200 million is directly spent for educational R and D today. The amount is less than .03 per cent of the nation's annual school costs, compared to about $7.6 billion spent each year for military R and D since 1969 (about 10 per cent) and the $6 billion the Space Program consumed in 1966 alone. The amount, however, is great indeed compared to past federal support and should expand, especially with the development of the National Institute of Education.

Comparing the progress of educational studies and implementation before 1954 and today, we can only say that the difference is revolutionary. Besides having greater financial support, researchers also benefit from great technical advances in processing and analyzing data. Educational scholarship is rapidly maturing, and the research competence of those earning doctorates in education is better developed than before. The progress of educational scholarship seems destined to continue. However, promise that such intellectual work will influence education has yet to be fulfilled.

As educational scholarship proliferates, many facets of modern schools do show significant improvement, from lunch-room facilities to educational laws and textbooks. It cannot be said, however, that there has been a corresponding change in teacher quality. School organizations have not been improved to the point where teacher quality will not be wasted. The schoolmarm characteristics of the past, poorly prepared "keepers of school" lacking lasting commitment to the teaching profession, and the one-teacher-one-room concept of school organization, should be considered as archaic as the horse and buggy, yet many of these continue. What good are all of the advances in schools if we do not significantly raise the professional caliber of teachers?

Teacher education was slowly developing as the twentieth century began. By 1920, there were 50 teachers colleges in existence and by 1940 there were 200. Today, four years of study leading to a bachelor's degree is normally the minimum requirement for teachers, and it is becoming more and more difficult to find a college or normal school strictly for teacher preparation. Yet America's 1250 teacher education centers largely ignore their key social responsibility of supplying schools with well-trained teachers. Still oriented to quantity of output instead of quality, teacher education suffers from inadequate research and development and inept, contradictory programs.

The characteristics of teacher educators are changing much more rapidly than those of students entering teaching. Successful classroom experience alone qualified many teacher educators in the past, but today many of them have earned doctorates. The most prestigious schools of education are producers of educational scholarship; their professors resemble scholars in other fields far more than they do classroom teachers. The reverse was true not too long ago, and remains so in smaller colleges. Ironically, many of the younger educational scholars have little or no classroom teaching experience, and some carry questionable pride in that fact. The stereotype of the "Mickey Mouse" professor of education is far less valid today than that of the "Mickey Mouse" student, but this change does not seem to be advancing classroom education. The most apparent effect of the difference in teacher education is a greater gulf between practitioner and scholar.

Teacher candidates, especially those preparing for elementary classrooms, still rank lower academically than most college students. Surveys of national samples indicate little improvement over time. Taking "Ed." courses is still perceived by many as a sign of intellectual and scholastic weakness. Pursuing teacher preparation is justified by love for children (which should be basic and assumed) and by limited alternatives in career choices more often than by intellectual and creative motivations.

Working in contrasting social systems also creates distance between educational scholars and teachers. As one who is seriously concerned with the progress of school psychology, McCandless (1969) identified the profession's major problem as the role conflicts that frustrate many school psychologists. On one hand, as social scientists, school psychologists have been trained in a "masculine" discipline and associate themselves with scientific societies. On the other hand, however, practicing school psychologists function in schools which are "feminine" in social orientation and do not offer opportunities to conduct research and development. The problem tends to divide academic and practicing school psychologists. The former are viewed as concentrating on "the growing edge of innovative demonstration, service, manipulation, and research," while the practitioners are perceived as "being clinicians and tire repair men, diagnosers and healers" (p. 15).

McCandless' discussion carries importance for the broader issue of this paper. His definition of social systems as masculine or feminine as follows is especially noteworthy:

A masculine social organization is task oriented, pragmatic, ruggedly autonomous and independent, often impatient of human relations, full of initiative and innovation and, despite and often in contradiction to its pragmatism, sometimes inclined to stop impatiently to ask, "Where are we going and what does it mean?" A feminine social organization, however, stresses happiness, self-actualization, and "getting along all right." It is sensitive to human relations and conservative: it jealously guards its status quo, safety, and security. It is nurturant, obedient, and responsible. When its values are threatened, it is exceptionally autocratic (p. 15).

Margaret Mead's (1962) portrayal, "a distillate of American ideas of the teacher," presents the teacher as a woman "urging, helping, poking, scolding, encouraging those whose steps though lagging slow to school, went storming out to play." Considering the male teachers, she wrote: "The man who teaches in grade school has to deal with a self-classification of being a 'man teacher,' thus tacitly acknowledging that he is a male version of a role which is felt to be feminine" (p. 506).

Putting it more negatively, Hofstadter argued that the overwhelming feminine character of American schools and their emphasis upon life-adjustment are clear signs of America's anti-intellectualism. "The United States is the only country in the Westernized world that has put its elementary education almost exclusively in the hands of women and its secondary education largely so. . . ." (p. 320). Hofstadter made it clear that his point (and this writer agrees) is not the superiority of male teachers. In fact, he said that women may be preferred for certain levels, though he did not say so for men. However, the fact that teaching is perceived by social scientists as a feminine profession that does not offer men "the stature of a fully legitimate male role," indicates the transient nature of teaching as a career and the inadequate development of the profession.

Today's educational scholar is beginning to overcome, or at least develop enough self-respect to ignore, the suspicions of his academic colleagues that he and his field are intellectually soft and lack depth. He has accomplished that progress in academe by winning scholarly recognition and rewards that seem irrelevant to school practitioners. Directing his publications and papers to other scholars, the educational scholar provides almost no information directly to the practitioner. Respectable as it is becoming, his most challenging and innovative work often seems too abstract, esoteric, and impractical to teachers and school administrators. Even when he utilizes school resources for his research, the educational scholar typically expresses his disdain for school practitioners by not sharing his findings with those who provided the data.

The most respected research journals are often necessarily technical, and their typically tentative and segmented reports, do not reach teachers, except through occasional digested summaries in practitioner-oriented journals and passing mention in education courses. What clearly epitomizes this problem is the great contrast between the journals of educational scholars (e.g., *American Educational Research Journal*) and those to which teachers subscribe (e.g., *The Instructor*).

What McCandless said about school psychologists and their role conflicts is more or less true for all educational scholars. While the social systems of schools may be characterized as feminine, the academic world is masculine. Therefore, it appears that about the only thing classroom teachers and educational scholars have in common is their general abstract concern for schools. Stemming from America's earliest days, this problem of contrasting orientations has little justification in an age when the problems of quantity and equality of education have largely been solved and the concern of educational quality must be faced.

OVERCOMING THE PROBLEM

The great division between scholar and teacher hinders the progress of education. Its growth becomes more alarming as time passes. Educational scholars must begin to overhaul teacher preparation completely and build the appropriate training systems that they supposedly know best how to develop. Now that a surplus of teachers has appeared in many parts of the country, delay in the revision of standards and curricula that was the result of teacher shortages seems difficult to justify. The possibility of implementing several of the models of teacher education that were designed with federal support about two years ago might be the first real step toward uplifting teacher quality and professionalism through teacher education. Revolutionary concepts of teacher education are certainly needed, but they must also be realistic in terms of need, theory and practice (Yee, 1972).

More educational scholars must realize that their responsibility as professional workers in education cannot be fulfilled entirely through academic-level publications and activities. Their relationships to teachers and schools must become more direct and real. This may materialize through recent developments intended to restructure the organization of schools. Blueprints and rationale for such improvements have been proposed by educational scholars for over a decade. In general, the plans replace the outdated one-teacher-one-class arrangement, with groups of teachers working together in instructional teams led by master teachers.

Far more curricular and instructional alternatives become possible in teams. Teachers can contribute their particular strengths to the team and help colleagues with their special competences and needs. Teams make it possible to work more flexibly with various sized groups of pupils. Restructuring the school system in such a manner will make instructional planning and activities more objective and more open for evaluation and innovation. Formerly, whether a teacher was new or experienced, her self-contained classroom was her own roost, and entering it was an invasion of her privacy. A team of teachers working closely together with the same group of pupils must communicate and systemize routines. In such settings, evaluation and public scrutiny could become realistic, everyday practice.

As more schools reorganize to form more complex and meaningful professional units, new teaching roles and work relations will need to be established. Novice teachers will be able to gain greater experience and professional training under the guidance and example of the team's experienced members. Also, the team will provide new vertical leadership; each unit might be led by a master teacher with both practical experience as a successful teacher and doctoral-level study. It is not so far-fetched to think that someday such leaders would normally attain doctorates. Their leadership role provides one way to bridge the gap between practitioners and educational scholars. In the past, able teachers have quit the classroom to find greater responsibility, recognition, and salary as administrators and educational scholars. Teaching teams could provide sufficient incentive and purpose to keep good teachers in classrooms. Educational scholars at the University of Wisconsin's R and D Center under the leadership of Professor Herbert Klausmeier are conducting studies and implementing a "multi-unit" design of school organization which relies heavily upon the new role of a "lead teacher." Such work should provide great benefits for professional education.

Jackson (1968) justified the superficial intellectualism of teachers, in part, by saying that at least the teachers helped youngsters overcome the impersonal and dehumanizing nature of the present-day school organization. He also thought that if teachers were keener, more perceptive, and dissatisfied, they could not endure their work conditions, their professional shortcomings, and the organizational system. Effective teaching requires abundant skill and resources in interpersonal relations, since teachers must relate with many diverse individuals and social settings. Nevertheless, instruction has been so concerned with the transmission of content that social interaction, which generalizes across subject matter, has not been structured into professional preparation and emphasis as it should be (Yee, 1971).

The concept of teaching teams provides a means of abolishing oppressive school organization and expanding opportunities to foster each pupil's intellectual and emotional needs. Teachers in such units should have greater independence from the total school organization and freedom to create higher standards of professional thought and work. At least team organization makes it more difficult to blame administrators and the organizational system. With evaluation available from fellow team members and greater control of instructional time, facilities, and duties to be fulfilled, teachers would need to justify their work more thoroughly. Teachers would have the time they lack today to plan and relate preparation to actual teaching. Such changes would not work miracles, but it would be far more difficult for poor teaching to escape notice and would establish a setting more conducive for professional growth.

With team organization, teaching could become a more humanistic, rational, and innovative process. Such a change in orientation should gradually bring scholars and teachers more closely together. Instead of maintaining the status quo, schools could become producers as well as consumers of research and development. Becoming more rationally-oriented and attempting to be more proficient is not to say, however, that teaching would then become mechanical and formal. The affective aspects of teaching and learning should be retained, but they would become means as well as ends, balanced with cognitive concerns (Yee, 1973).

Educational scholars control teacher education, so they must assume responsibility for the revolutionary change. They should also begin to make their master's degree programs more rigorous and meaningful, as some universities have already done with doctoral studies. It would be a sure sign of progress in raising teachers' sense of professionalism if teachers pursued graduate study to improve professional skills, rather than merely in pursuit of salary increments.

Almost every school has at least one or two outstanding teachers who represent the dedicated, skillful type this writer has had the pleasure to know as a pupil and as a colleague. Such persons may be found in spite of the poor teacher training, graduate programs, and school conditions that predominate today. Their existence indicates the potential success of education. Their sparsity indicates the failings of our present system.

Educational scholars and classroom teachers need to reorient themselves to the great responsibilities of education in the United States. As Cremin (1965) put it, we need to develop a new kind of educational leader that can "spark a great public dialogue about the ends and means of education" (p. 117). Such a leader would be prepared through studies relating to education in the behavioral sciences and the humanities, and would combine many of the strengths characteristic of leading educational practitioners and scholars today.

Describing an effective program for urban education that could be applied universally, Getzels (1967) wrote that the preparation of different types of educational practitioners should be more relevant to real needs, more interrelated, and should involve greater cooperative participation. Such a program promotes common understanding, coordination, and progressive change in schools, as well as the opportunity to bring practitioners and scholars together. Leaders as well as practitioners have operated with more limited perspectives than they realize and must develop wider and more insightful perspective in their professional work and its consequences. They will be able to do so only through greater dialogue and challenge than they presently pursue and tolerate among themselves and noneducators (Yee, 1973).

If classroom teachers and educational scholars continue to have as little in common and relate as poorly as they do today, the greater blame will be the scholar's, since he is responsible for the preparation of educational leaders. The high quality of medical education, practice, and research in the United States originates from a revolutionary overhaul of standards and curricula starting about 1910. It began when the extremely poor conditions of medical training, which necessarily determined medical practice and scholarship, were realistically confronted. A similar revolution in teacher education is long overdue.

REFERENCES

Cremin, L.O.: The Genius of American Education. Pittsburgh, University of Pittsburgh Press, 1965.

Getzels, J.W.: Education for the inner city: A practical proposal by an impractical theorist. *School Review, 75:*283-299, 1967.

Hofstadter, R.: Anti-intellectualism in American Life. New York, Alfred A. Knopf, 1966.

Jackson, P.W.: Life in Classrooms. New York, Holt, Rinehart and Winston, 1968.

James, W.: Talks to Teachers on Psychology and to Students on Some of Life's Ideals. New York, Dover, 1899.

McCandless, B.R.: Points at issue between practical and academic school psychology. *Journal of School Psychology, 7:*13-17, 1969.

Mead, M.: The School in American Culture. Cambridge, Mass., Harvard University Press, 1962.

Meyer, A.E.: An Educational History of the American People. New York, McGraw-Hill, 1957.

Rice, J.M.: The Public-School System of the United States. New York, Century, 1893.

Tolor, A., Scarpetti, W.L., and Lane, P.O.: Teacher's attitudes toward children's behavior revisited. *Journal of Educational Psychology, 58:*175-180, 1967.

Wickman, E.K.: Children's Behavior and Teachers' Attitudes. New York, Commonwealth Fund, 1928.

Yee, A.H.: Becoming a Teacher in America. *Quest, 17* Monograph XVIII, 67-75, 1972.

Yee, A.H. (ed.): Perspectives on Management Systems Approaches in Education: A Symposium. Englewood Cliffs, N.J., Educational Technology Publications, 1973.

Yee, A.H. (ed.): Social Interaction in Educational Settings. Englewood Cliffs, N.J., Prentice-Hall, 1971.

the technology 38 of teaching*

B.F. Skinner

A FEW EXAMPLES

Let us look at these principles of programming at work in one or two traditional educational assignments. Instruction in handwriting will serve as one example. To say that a child is to learn "how to write" tells us very little. The so-called signs of "knowing how to write" provide a more useful set of behavioral specifications. The child is to form letters and words which are legible and graceful according to taste. He is to do this first in copying a model, then in writing to dictation (or self-dictation as he spells out words he would otherwise speak), and eventually in writing as a separate nonvocal form of verbal behavior. A common method is to ask the child to copy letters or words and to approve or otherwise reinforce his approximations to good copy. More and more exact copies are demanded as the hand improves—in a crude sort of programming. The method is ineffective largely because the reinforcements are too long deferred. The parent or teacher comments upon or corrects the child's work long after it has been performed.

A possible solution is to teach the child to discriminate between good and bad form before he starts to write. Acceptable behavior should then generate immediate, automatic self-reinforcement. This is seldom done. Another possibility is to make reinforcement immediately contingent upon successful responses. One method now being tested is to treat paper chemically so that the pen the child uses writes in dark gray when a response is correct and yellow when it is incorrect. The dark gray line is made automatically reinforcing through generous commendation. Under such contingencies the proper execution of a letter can be programmed; at first the child makes a very small contribution in completing a letter, but through progressive stages he approaches the point at which he composes the letter as a whole, the chemical response of the paper differentially reinforcing good form throughout. The model to be copied is then made progressively less important by separating it in both time and space from the child's work. Eventually words are written to dictation, letter by letter, in spelling dictated words, and in describing pictures. The same kind of differential reinforcement can be used to teach such things as good form and proper spacing. The child is eventually forming letters skillfully under continuous automatic reinforcement. The method is directed as much toward

*From The Technology of Teaching, by B.F. Skinner. Copyright ©1968 by Meredith Corporation. Reprinted by permission of Appleton-Century-Crofts, Educational Division, Meredith Corporation.

motivation as toward good form. Even quite young children remain busily at work for long periods of time without coercion or threat, showing few signs of fatigue, nervousness, or other forms of escape.

As a second example we may consider the acquisition of a simple form of verbal behavior. A behavioral specification is here likely to be especially strongly resisted. It is much more in line with traditional educational policy to say that the student is to "know facts, understand principles, be able to put ideas into words, express meanings, or communicate information." The behavior exhibited in such activities can be formulated without reference to ideas, meanings, or information, and many of the principles currently used in programming verbal knowledge have been drawn from such a formulation (Skinner, 1957). The field is too large to be adequately covered here, but two examples may suggest the direction of the approach.

What happens when a student memorizes a poem? Let us say that be begins by reading the poem from a text. His behavior is at that time under the control of the text, and it is to be accounted for by examining the process through which he has learned to read. When he eventually speaks the poem in the absence of a text, the same form of verbal behavior has come under the control of other stimuli. He may begin to recite when asked to do so—he is then under control of an external verbal stimulus—but, as he continues to recite, his behavior comes under the control of stimuli he himself is generating (not necessarily in a crude word-by-word chaining of responses). In the process of "memorizing" the poem, control passes from one kind of stimulus to another.

A method of transferring control from text to self-generated stimuli makes a convincing classroom demonstration. A short poem is projected on a screen or written on a chalkboard. A few unnecessary letters are omitted. The class reads the poem in chorus. A second slide is then projected in which other letters are missing (or letters erased from the chalkboard). The class could not have read the poem correctly if this form had been presented first, but because of its recent history it is able to do so. (Some members undoubtedly receive help from others in the process of choral reading.) In a third setting still other letters are omitted, and after a series of five or six settings the text has completely disappeared. The class is nevertheless able to "read" the poem. Control has passed mainly to self-generated stimuli.

As another example, consider what a student learns when he consults an illustrated dictionary. After looking at a labeled picture, we say that he knows something he did not know before. This is another of those vague expressions which have done so much harm to education. The "signs or symptoms of such knowledge" are of two sorts. Shown the accompanying picture without the text the student can say "caduceus" (we say that he now knows what the pictured object is called) or, shown the word *caduceus*, he can now

caduceus

describe or reconstruct the picture (we say that he now knows what the word caduceus means). But what has actually happened?

The basic process is similar to that of transferring discriminative control in the Terrace experiment. To begin with, the student can respond to the picture in various ways: he can describe it without naming it; he can find a similar picture in an array; he can draw a fair copy. He can also speak the name by reading the printed word. When he first looks at the picture and reads the word, his verbal response is primarily under the control of the text, but it must eventually be controlled by the picture. As in transferring the control exerted by red and green to vertical and horizontal lines, we can change the control efficiently by making the text gradually less important, covering part of it, removing some of the letters, or fogging it with a translucent mask. As the picture acquires control the student can speak the name with less and less help from the text. Eventually, when the picture exerts enough control, he "knows the name of the pictured object." The normal student can learn the name of one object so quickly that the vanishing technique may not be needed, but it is a highly effective procedure in learning the names of a large number of objects. (The good student learns how, by himself, to make progressive reductions in the effectiveness of a text: he may glance at the text out of the corner of his eye, uncover it bit by bit, and so on. In this way he improvises his own program in making the text less and less important as the picture acquires control of the verbal response.)

In teaching the student "the meaning of the word caduceus" we could slowly obscure the picture, asking the student to respond to the name by completing a drawing or description or by finding a matching picture in an array. Eventually in answer to the question: What is a caduceus? he would describe the object, make a crude sketch, or point to the picture of a caduceus. The skillful student uses techniques of this sort in studying unprogrammed material.

"Knowing what a caduceus is" or "knowing the meaning of the word caduceus" is probably more than responding in these ways to picture or text. There are other "signs of knowledge," and that is one reason why the concept of knowledge is so inadequate. But other relevant behavior must be taught, if at all, in substantially the same way.

SOME COMMON OBJECTIONS

These examples do scant justice to the many hundreds of effective programs now available or to the techniques which many of them use so effectively, but they must suffice as a basis for discussing a few general issues. An effective technology of teaching, derived not from philosophical principles but from a realistic analysis of human behavior, has much to contribute, but as its nature has come to be clearly seen, strong opposition has arisen.

A common objection is that most of the early work responsible for the basic formulation of behavior was done on so-called lower animals. It has been argued that the procedures are therefore appropriate only to animals and that to use them in education is to treat the student like an animal. So far as I know, no one argues that because something is true of a pigeon, it is therefore true of a man. There are enormous differences in the topographies of the behaviors of man and pigeon and in the kinds of environmental events which are relevant to that behavior — differences which, if anatomy and physiology were adequate to the task, we could probably compare with differences in the mediating substrata—but the basic processes in behavior, as in neural tissue, show helpful similarities. Relatively simple organisms have many advantages in early stages of research, but they impose no limit on that research. Complex processes are met and dealt with as the analysis proceeds. Experiments on pigeons may not throw much light on the "nature" of man, but they are extraordinarily helpful in enabling us to analyze man's environment more effectively. What is common to pigeon and man is a world in which certain contingencies of reinforcement prevail. The schedule of reinforcement which makes a pigeon a pathological gambler is to be found at racetrack and roulette table, where it has a comparable effect.

Another objection is to the use of contrived contingencies of reinforcement. In daily life one does not wear glasses in order to get food or point to circles in order to receive chocolate. Such reinforcers are not naturally contingent on the behavior and there may seem to be something synthetic, spurious, or even fraudulent about them. The attack on contrived contingencies of reinforcement may be traced to Rousseau and his amazing book, *Émile* (Rousseau, 1762). Rousseau wanted to avoid the punitive systems of his day. Convinced as he was that civilization corrupts, he was also afraid of all social reinforcers. His plan was to make the student dependent upon *things* rather than people. John Dewey restated the principle by emphasizing real life experiences in the schoolroom. In American education it is commonly argued that a child must be taught nothing until he can reap natural benefits from knowing it. He is not to learn to write until he can take satisfaction in writing his name in his books or notes to his friends. Producing a gray rather than a yellow line is irrelevant to handwriting. Unfortunately, the teacher who confines himself to natural reinforcers is often ineffective, particularly because only certain subjects can be taught through their use, and he eventually falls back upon some form of punishment. But aversive control is the most shameful of irrelevancies: it is only in school that one parses a Latin sentence to avoid the cane.

The objection to contrived reinforcers arises from a misunderstanding of the nature of teaching. The teacher expedites learning by arranging special contingencies of reinforcement, which may not resemble the contingencies under which the behavior is eventually useful. Parents teach a baby to talk by reinforcing its first efforts with approval and affection, but these are not natural consequences of speech. The baby learns to say "mama," "dada," "spoon," or "cup" months before he ever calls to his father or mother or identifies them to a passing stranger or asks for a spoon or cup or reports their presence to someone who cannot see them. The contrived reinforcement shapes the topography of verbal behavior long before that behavior can produce its normal consequences in a verbal community. In the same way a child reinforced for the proper formation of letters by a chemical reaction is prepared to write long before the natural consequences of effective writing take over. It was necessary to use a "spurious" reinforcer to get the boy to wear glasses, but once the behavior had been shaped and maintained for a period of time, the natural reinforcers which follow from improved vision could take over. The real issue is whether the teacher prepares the student for the natural reinforcers which are to replace the contrived reinforcers used in teaching. The behavior which is expedited in the teaching process would be useless if it were not to be effective in the world at large in the absence of instructional contingencies.

Another objection to effective programmed instruction is that it does not teach certain important activities. When required to learn unprogrammed material for an impending examination the student learns how to study, how to clear up puzzling matters, how to work under puzzlement, and so on. These may be as important as the subject matter itself. The same argument could have been raised with respect to a modern experimental analysis of learning when contrasted with early studies of that process.

Almost all early investigators of learning constructed what we now call terminal contingencies of reinforcement to which an organism was immediately subjected. Thus, a rat was put into a maze or a cat into a puzzle box. The organism possessed little if any behavior appropriate to such a "problem," but some responses were reinforced, and over a period of time an acceptable terminal performance might be reached through "trial and error." A program of contingencies of reinforcement would have brought the organism to the same terminal performance much more rapidly and efficiently, but in doing so it could have been said to deprive the organism of the opportunity to learn how to try, how to explore—indeed, how to solve problems.

The educator who assigns material to be studied for an impending test presents the student with an opportunity to learn to examine the material in a special way which facilitates recall, to work industriously at something which is not currently reinforcing, and so on. It is true that a program designed simply to impart knowledge of a subject matter does not do any of this. It does not because it is not designed to do so. Programming undertakes to reach one goal at a time. Efficient ways of studying and thinking are separate goals. A crude parallel is offered by the current argument in favor of the cane or related aversive practices on the ground that they build character; they teach a boy to take punishment and to accept responsibility for his conduct. These are worthwhile goals, but they should not necessarily be taught at the same time as, say, Latin grammar or mathematics. Rousseau suggested a relevant form of programming through which a child could be taught to submit to aversive stimuli without alarm or panic. He pointed out that a baby dropped into a cold bath will probably be frightened and cry, but that if one begins with water at body temperature and cools it one degree per day, the baby will eventually not be disturbed by cold water. The program must be carefully followed. (In his enthusiasm for the new science, Rousseau exclaimed, "Use a thermometer!") Similar programs can teach a tolerance for painful stimuli, but caning a boy for idleness, forgetfulness, or bad spelling is an unlikely example. It only occasionally builds what the eighteenth century called "bottom," as it only occasionally eliminates idleness, forgetfulness, or bad spelling.

It is important to teach careful observation, exploration, and inquiry, but they are not well taught by submitting a student to material which he must observe and explore effectively or suffer the consequences. Better methods are available. There are two ways to teach a man to look before leaping: he may be severely punished when he leaps without looking or he may be positively reinforced (possibly "spuriously") for looking before leaping. He may learn to look in both cases, but when simply punished for leaping without looking he must discover for himself the art of careful observation, and he is not likely to profit from the experience of others. When he is reinforced for looking, a suitable program will transmit earlier discoveries in the art of observation. (Incidentally, the audio-visual devices mentioned earlier which undertake to attract attention do not teach careful observation. On the contrary, they are much more likely to deprive the student of the opportunity to learn such skills than effective programming of subject matters.)

Learning how to study is another example. When a teacher simply tests students on assigned material, few ever learn to study well, and many never learn at all. One may read for the momentary effect and forget what one has read almost immediately; one obviously reads in a very different way for retention. As we have seen, many of the practices of the good student resemble those of the programmer. The student can in a sense program material as he goes, rehearsing what he has learned and glancing at a text only as needed. These practices can be separately programmed as an important part of the student's education and can be much more effectively taught than by punishing the student for reading without remembering.

It would be pleasant to be able to say that punishing the student for not thinking is also not the only way to teach thinking. Some relevant behaviors have been analyzed and can therefore be explicitly programmed. Algorithmic methods of problem solving are examples. Simply leading the student through a solution in the traditional way is one kind of programming. Requiring him to solve a series of problems of graded difficulty is another. More effective programs can certainly be prepared. Unfortunately, they would only emphasize the rather mechanical nature of algorithmic problem solving. Real thinking seems to be something else. It is sometimes said to be a matter of "heuristics." But relevant practices can be formulated as techniques of solving the problem of solving problems. Once a heuristic device or practice is formulated and programmed, it cannot be distinguished in any important way from algorithmic problem solving. The will-o'-the-wisp of creative thinking still leads us on.

Human behavior often assumes novel forms, some of which are valuable. The teaching of truly creative behavior is, nevertheless, a contradiction in terms. Original discovery is seldom if ever guaranteed in the classroom. In Polya's little book, *How to Solve It* (Polya, 1945), a few boys in a class eventually arrive at the formula for the diagonal of a parallelopiped. It is possible that the teacher did not tell them the formula, but it is unlikely that the course they followed under his guidance resembled that of the original discoverer. Efforts to teach creativity have sacrificed the teaching of subject matter. The teacher steers a delicate course between two great fears—on the one hand that he may not teach and on the other that he may tell the student something. Until we know more about creative thinking, we may need to confine ourselves to making sure that the student is in full possession of the contributions of earlier thinkers, that he has been abundantly reinforced for careful observation and inquiry, that he has the interest and industry generated by a fortunate history of successes.

It has been said that an education is what survives when a man has forgotten all he has been taught. Certainly few students could pass their final examinations even a year or two after leaving school or college. What has been learned of permanent value must therefore not be the facts and principles covered by examinations but certain other kinds of behavior often ascribed to special abilities. Far from neglecting these kinds of behavior, careful programming reveals the need to teach them as explicit educational objectives. For example, two programs prepared with the help of the Committee on Programmed Instruction at Harvard—a program in crystallography constructed by Bruce Chalmers and James G. Holland (Chalmers, Holland, Williamson and Jackson, 1965) and a program in neuroanatomy by Murray and Richard Sidman (Sidman and Sidman, 1965)—both reveal the importance of special skills in three-dimensional thinking. As measured by available tests, these skills vary enormously even among scientists who presumably make special use of them. They can be taught with separate programs or as part of crystallography or neuroanatomy when specifically recognized as relevant skills. It is possible that education will eventually concentrate on those forms of behavior which "survive when all one has learned has been forgotten."

The argument that effective teaching is inimical to thinking, whether creative or not, raises a final point. We fear effective teaching, as we fear all effective means of changing human behavior. Power not only corrupts, it frightens; and absolute power frightens absolutely. We take another—and very long—look at educational policy when we conceive of teaching which really works. It has been said that teaching machines and programmed instruction will mean regimentation (it is sometimes added that regimentation is the goal of those who propose such methods), but in principle nothing could be more regimented than education as it now stands. School and state authorities draw up syllabuses specifying what students are to learn year by year. Universities insist upon "requirements" which are presumably to be met by all students applying for admission. Examinations are "standard." Certificates, diplomas, and honors testify to the completion of specified work. We do not worry about all this because we know that students never learn what they are required to learn, but some other safeguard must be found when education is effective.

It could well be that a technology of teaching will be unwisely used. It could destroy initiative and creativity; it could make men all alike (and not necessarily in being equally excellent); it could suppress the beneficial effect of accidents on the development of the individual and on the evolution of a culture. On the other hand, it could maximize the genetic endowment of each student; it could make him as skillful, competent, and informed as possible; it could build the greatest diversity of interests; it could lead him to make the greatest possible contribution to the survival and development of his culture. Which of these futures lies before us will not be determined by the mere availability of effective instruction. The use to which a technology of teaching is to be put will depend upon other matters. We cannot avoid the decisions which now face us by putting a stop to the scientific study of human behavior or by refusing to make use of the technology which inevitably flows from such a science.

The experimental analysis of behavior is a vigorous young science which will inevitably find practical applications. Important extensions have already been made in such fields as psychopharmacology and psychotherapy. Its bearing on economics, government, law, and even religion are beginning to attract attention. It is thus concerned with government in the broadest possible sense. In the government of the future the techniques we associate with education are most likely to prevail. That is why it is so important that this young science has begun by taking its most effective technological step in the development of a technology of teaching.

REFERENCES

Chalmers, B., Holland, J., Williamson, R., and Jackson, K.: Crystallography, a Programmed Course in Three Dimensions. New York, Appleton Century Crofts, 1965.

Polya, G.: How To Solve It. Princeton, Princeton University Press, 1945.

Rousseau, J.J.: Emile ou de L'Education. La Haye, Neaulme 1762.

Sidman, R.L., and Sidman, M.: Neuroanatomy, A Programmed Text. Vol. I. Boston, Little, Brown & Co., 1965.

Skinner, B.F.: Verbal Behavior. New York, Appleton Century Crofts, 1957.

39 essay review: beyond freedom and dignity *

Chris Argyris

Beyond Freedom and Dignity,
by B. F. Skinner.
New York, Knopf, 1971. 240 pp. $6.95.

Psychological science is developing several technologies for understanding and changing behavior, variously called behavior therapy, behavior modification, and behavioral engineering (combining contingency management and stimulus control†). Although each technology has some unique characteristics, they are basically more similar than dissimilar. They all focus on altering the individual's interaction with his environment. They derive from experimentally established procedures and principles, which means the experimenter is in control of the variables, the development of data, replication of the findings, and the precise statement of generalizations, usually in terms of probabilities. Consequently, the professionals tend to design their modification programs to alter human behavior, whether in a schoolroom, a home, or the community, in the image of a laboratory so that every program is precisely defined and becomes a test of the technology (Krasner, 1971, pp. 483-488). The work of Skinner and his students is among the most systematic, most frequently used, most thoroughly studied behavioral change technology.

These technologies for changing human behavior have generated much passionate and dispassionate criticism on grounds that they are symptom-oriented, too mechanical, ineffective, too effective (and therefore dangerous), and that they only succeed with unimportant simple behavior.

Adding to such criticisms will not, for several reasons, be the thrust of this review. I doubt if the validity and applicability of Skinnerian behavioral change technology can be finally evaluated with any respectable degree of validity at this time. Moreover, criticisms such as the ones listed above are best dealt with by research and Skinner represents one of

*Reprinted from Chris Argyris, "Essay Review of Beyond Freedom and Dignity, by B.F. Skinner," *Harvard Educational Review, 41,* November 1971, 550-567. Copyright ©1971 by the President and Fellows of Harvard College.

†I should like to express my appreciation to Dr. Bruce L. Baker and Dr. Richard Walton for their insightful comments on an earlier draft.

the most research-oriented of all the scholars involved. He and his colleagues will generate research to confront these issues and we should wait for those results. Finally, *Beyond Freedom and Dignity* is not a scholarly book describing, in detail, the experimental procedures and results; rather it concerns itself with the applicability of Skinnerian psychology to the design of how we should live our lives.

This review will therefore focus on the applicability of Skinner's psychology. The foundations of the argument will be built upon Skinner's insistence that *his contribution is the development of a technology that is based on experimental findings and one that works*. He asks us to make such a technology the basis for the design of high quality living.

If we, as a society, have learned anything from our experiences with technology, it should be that the choice for accepting it as a basis for life can no longer be settled by the fact that the technology is based on rigorous science and that it works. Antibiotics are based on rigorous science and they work. However, after years of usage we find that they may be making the individual more vulnerable to illnesses that were unknown or non-relevant at the time of the discovery of antibiotics. This is another way of saying that a certain medical technology (like Skinnerian technology based on experimental evidence) has, through usage, changed the very nature of the human body. Similarly, DDT was developed from hard science and it works. We now know that its full use could help upset ecological balance as well as produce living creatures such as mosquitoes that are immune to present pesticides.

I concede that many of Skinner's claims about the validity of his technology are substantiated or eventually will be substantiated by him and his colleagues. But the important question about a technology that is science-based and works is, do we want it around? What kind of a world would we have if its potentialities were fully realized? What would be the quality of life after years of using an experimentally-based, empirically validated technology for behavioral change?

SKINNER'S POSITION

The central themes in *Beyond Freedom and Dignity* are summarized in the following six paragraphs:

We need a technology of behavior. The environment is the key causal matrix. It not only prods or lashes; it selects. In order to understand human behavior we must take into account what the environment does to an organism before *and after* it responds. Behavior is shaped and maintained by its consequences.

Behavior which operates upon the environment to produce consequences ("operant" behavior) can be studied by arranging environments in which specific consequences are contingent upon it. The practical implication is that it is the environment that should be manipulated. Change in the environment of the individual has a quick and dramatic effect upon the individual's behavior.

In order to proceed effectively in learning how to design and manipulate environments, we must cut ourselves loose from the concepts of human autonomy, free choice, and self responsibility. Thus, responsibility for individual behavior shifts to the environment. The task is to find, and plug into the environment, those phenomena that reinforce the desired behavior.

Such tasks require experts who know how to design environments which induce members to work for cultural survival. Underlying reasons and motivations for such work make little difference; the only thing that counts is that such work take place.

In designing new cultures we need not aspire to the best cultures, for there are no such phenomena. What we need are designs that help us improve life.

Basically a culture is like the experimental space used in the study of behavior. It is a set of contingencies of reinforcement. The technology of behavior which emerges is ethnically neutral, but when applied to the design of a culture, the survival of the culture functions as a value.

What is man under this conception? Skinner makes it clear that autonomous man should be dispossessed and the control turned over to the environment. Would not man then become the victim or slave of his environment? Not necessarily, Skinner would reply, because the environment would be wholly of his own making. Skinner differentiates between the controlling self and the controlled self, even when they are both inside the same skin and when control is exercised through the design of an external environment. A person who introduces a change will also be affected by that change. Therefore all attempts to control others inevitably include control over one's self.

AGREEMENTS WITH SKINNER

Regardless of how rigorous the base of a technology is, if man is to control it, he will find it wise to agree with Skinner in that he should take active steps in designing the culture and making the environment more important in behavioral change. In doing so he should select—other things being equal—a technology that 1) minimizes the use of hidden causes; 2) focuses on behavior as the key criterion; and 3) combines individual growth and control.

The less the causes of human behavior are hidden and the more the key to success is observable behavior, the less the probability that someone (in control of the technology) could control others in ways that they would experience as detrimental. If the causes are observable, then there is a higher probability that they are available to all who wish to use them. If behavior is the criterion, then designs for high quality living based upon our attitudes and values will not remain subject to individual distortion and blindness. The danger in basing change only on *values* is that if individuals who do the distorting have power, then it is difficult to get them to test the validity of their actions. For example, the designers of organizations maintain that their designs are based on such values as rationality, loyalty, competence, and the dignity of the individual. However, when one observes actual *behavior*, a significantly different picture emerges. It is very difficult to get them to consider change because, for them, the fact that reality does not fit their intentions only shows how other people can botch things up. Thus, Skinner's insistence on finding overt causes, focusing on behavior, and emphasizing individual growth through control, can provide conditions for society to design its own environment and to monitor the design continuously.

And now to the disagreements.

EXPERIMENTAL CONDITIONS AS A BASIS FOR LIFE

Skinner plants his feet firmly on the ground of experimental science, promising all of us that such ground will not buckle under use and confrontation. Experimental science, he claims, is the best foundation for a technology of understanding and changing human behavior.

Few would disagree that valid evidence—publically verifiable, empirically tested, and shown to be applicable—is a strong basis for action. My doubts focus on a different set of issues. First, I question whether the experimental model *necessarily* provides valid data for designing our life. Second, I question whether experimental laboratory conditions represent a valid model for the design of the future. Indeed, I will suggest below that inherent in the use of rigorous experimental methodology are two major problems: (1) the danger of producing invalid information without realizing it, and (2) the danger that a world designed to model the properties of experimental science can only provide clues for how to maintain a world that is similar to the one in which we presently live, i.e., the status quo.

EXPERIMENTALLY-BASED ENVIRONMENTS AND FORMAL BUREAUCRACY

Elsewhere, I have attempted to show that if one examines the genotypic properties of any pyramidal organization, he will find them to be a set of strategies about the use of power, information, and technical competence (Argyris, 1968). Put simply, pyramidal organizations assume that it is good to centralize power and information and to specialize tasks.

The results of this type of organization can be shown to place lower level employees primarily in positions where (1) they are dependent upon their superior; (2) they are subordinate to their superior; (3) they have a short time perspective; and (4) they perform only those tasks assigned to them.

The conditions created by an experimenter for his subjects, animal or human, are no different. If the experimenter is to be rigorous, (1) he defines the goals of the experiment; (2) he manages the environment strictly and tightly; (3) he expects (hopes) the subject will do as he is asked—the subject should be dependent upon the experimenter; and (4) he provides the subject with as little information as possible—indeed he may even distort information.

People's reactions to these conditions (in an experiment or an organization) will depend largely on the degree to which they prefer to be dependent, submissive, and have a short time perspective or the degree to which they will accept these conditions in order to obtain some other desired pay-off.

If people do not desire these states of affairs, then, as Skinner predicts, they will strive to go away from them. But our world is dominated by organizations, technocracy, and meritocracy. This is especially true for education, health, welfare, business, church, and trade unions. Thus the environment is so designed that it leaves little opportunity for most people to exercise other choices.

One of the most frequently documented results of life under these enforced conditions is that people fight it actively or passively by distorting information. Indeed, one may state generally that systems like those described above will tend to produce invalid information for the important issues but (since there is a power hierarchy) the sources of the distortion, as well as the actual distortion, are kept hidden.

For example, people learn to "think positive" (which means to remain within the tolerance limits set by the top); they create just-in-case-the-president-asks files to defend themselves; they distort information upwards if they believe correct information will threaten the top (the suppression of the My Lai incidents by lower-level officers); and they learn not to rock the boat or make waves (lack of confrontation of power people). These activities may lead, in turn, to further self-protecting strategies such as, before you give any bad news, give good news; play down the impact of failure by emphasizing how close one came to the achievement of the target; gloss over poor performance by emphasizing that the state of the art has been enhanced (Argyris, 1970, pp. 63-78).

The same appears to be the case for students or others who participate in experiments (Argyris, 1968). This is why I say that experimental science may not necessarily produce valid information.

THE WORLD AS EXPERIMENTAL LABORATORY

As Krasner points out in his recent review (1971), one of the primary emphases of Skinnerians is that they bring the laboratory approach to all the settings in which they apply their work. If our life is to be designed by such people then it will produce a particular kind of world and eventually a particular type of human being. That world will be exactly like the one we now have. If anything, it will become bureaucracy squared.

For example, several years ago there was an experimentally-minded vice-president in an industrial firm who had been told repeatedly that positive reinforcement schedules could be used to increase executive performance. Although he had serious doubts, he entered into a genuine test designed by one of the consultant's assistants. Briefly, he began by reinforcing his subordinates' behavior systematically, according to the schedule, and strove to ignore behavior that required punishment. The subordinates responded as Skinner would predict. Their positive behavior increased as well as their morale (an internal state of affairs admittedly not acknowledged by Skinner).

After a few days, however, the superior began to experience difficulties. Subordinate A, who now felt closer to his superior, visited him for the first time in his office, put his feet on his desk, and started a friendly conversation. In addition to being shocked by the feet on the table (a behavior he ignored with some effort), the superior felt he could not respond in a reinforcing manner because the schedule had not called for such reinforcement at that time. He did his best to act neutral and non-committal.

The subordinate interpreted the neutrality as aloofness and coldness. He saw it as a regression and as evidence that the supervisor was inconsistent if not ungenuine. However, he never revealed these feelings. The superior noted that when he returned to the subordinate's office at the proper time for the next reinforcement, the subordinate had become cool and neutral. The superior reported that he no longer felt his reinforcement behavior was trusted.

To make matters more difficult, the subordinates began to interact, exploring each other's experiences with their supervisor. These interactions also tended to violate the schedule the superior was given to follow. Moreover, as fellow employees from other departments heard about the "new" behavior, they too increased their interaction with the experimental group.

After thorough discussion and debriefing it was concluded that the schedule of positive reinforcement would work best:

1. *if* the subordinates did not interpret the reinforcements to mean anything beyond what he wanted them to mean and therefore did not take initiatives to build cumulatively on the new relationship;

2. *if* the subordinates did not contact each other;

3. *if* every contact was experienced as a discrete event, and interpreted only as the superior wished it to be, namely as a genuine reinforcement;

4. *if* he ignored much of his work and directed most of his attention to the reinforcement schedules.

Moreover, he had to plan whatever work and appointments he had around the schedule. This restricted his mobility and began to get him in trouble with his own superior.

In other words, the superior found that to use this technology effectively he had to create a situation in the organization that was similar to the experimental laboratory. Thus the practitioner is forced by the technology to create a world that is similar to the one in which the generalizations were created; that is, no subject influence of the experimenter, no subject interdependence, and no tasks for the experimenter other than running the experiment. The superior concluded that the resulting autocracy would be worse than any organization in which he, or anyone else he knew, had participated.

The objection may be raised that the example is not quite fair because the design and execution were naive. Although the actual program was more sophisticated than described here, I would easily grant that Dr. Skinner and his colleagues would undoubtedly develop a still more sophisticated program. However, the point is that no program, no matter how sophisticated, will work differently in the non-contrived world if, in order to be successful, it must assume that:

1. the recipient of the reinforcement will interpret the reinforcement precisely as intended by the reinforcer; the recipient will not add his additional meanings to any given reinforcement;

2. the recipient will not add up reinforcements to generate a history of the relationship which, in turn, could give new meaning to the relationship;

3. the recipient will not discuss the reinforcement program covertly or overtly, knowingly or unknowingly, with anyone else *or* himself.

Incidentally, as one reviews the relevant literature related to behavior modification, one finds a significant and dramatic drop in behavior change for many subjects once they have left the controlled situation for six months or more. One explanation for this drop may be related to the conditions just described. Note how the recipient is placed in a highly dependent situation, coerced to accept as best he can the meaning of the program as it is specified by the expert. The subject may not be helped to learn by himself meanings that go beyond the specified program. Once experience in the "real" world goes beyond the specified meanings, the subject's performance begins to deteriorate.

Skinner states that his ideas will be difficult to put into practice because they are new. I am suggesting that if Skinner's ideas are resisted it may be because he is carrying the rigid pyramidal model to an extreme; he is willing to reinforce the status quo beyond where some people are prepared to see it go. Once we have seen that Skinner's world is basically the status quo, some of the sections of the book become more clear.

SKINNER'S GENERALIZATIONS ARE NOT NEUTRAL

One of the puzzling issues is Skinner's insistence that his technology produces neutral generalizations. He cites as an example of neutrality the generalization to the effect that positive reinforcement will encourage the behavior reinforced. No position is taken about what kind of behavior should be reinforced.

Is this the kind of primitive generalization that has given Skinner his fame? If he and his students had remained at such a primitive level then he would not be the honored and respected scientist that he is. The reason that Skinner has become famous is that he has much to say about the sequence of reinforcement, the conditions under which it should occur, who should do it, and how much the "subject" need know. It is therefore not precise to say that Skinner has discovered the importance of behavior being shaped by reinforcement, because this position leaves open the logical possibility that the subject can design and do his own reinforcing. As Skinner has repeatedly pointed out, the reinforcement comes from the environment.

Once we dig into how the environment should be designed, then the normative position becomes more clear. One would predict that the world Skinner designs requires human beings who enjoy, rather than resist, dependent relationships and whose influence on the environment is minimal.

One indication in support of this prediction is the history of successful application of Skinner's ideas in helping human beings. The great majority of the successes reported so far have come primarily with such groups as younger students in schools, delinquents in institutions, with patients with varying behavior disorders, and the mentally retarded. It may be argued that these delinquents and patients have chosen to participate because they see their present state as aversive. Or, as in the case of the mentally retarded, they may be induced to participate by being offered better living conditions and a better environment (e.g., toys). Or, as in the case of students, they are confronted with a new way to learn which they strive to use as best they can.

In these cases the subjects find it worthwhile or legitimate to be placed in situations in which

1. they are dependent upon the experimenter or therapist;
2. they are submissive to the experimenter or therapist;
3. they have a short time perspective; and
4. they perform only those tasks assigned to them.

These are the identical conditions animals or humans are exposed to in experimental situations.

In addition, the people whom the Skinnerians have helped have been primarily people who wish to adapt to the present environment (e.g., enuretics wish to stop bedwetting, or delinquents wish to become less oriented toward crime). Skinnerian technology is used to help individuals adapt to the status quo. If this analysis is valid, then it is difficult to see how Skinner can maintain that while science can tell us how to change people, the question of what changes to make is a separate question (p. 103). As we suggest, if a technology developed directly from, and following, the properties of the experimental method, is applied to people, it tends to reinforce certain types of behavior (dependency, submissiveness) and refrains from rewarding proactive attempts to resist and alter the reinforcement schedule.

UNFREEZING OLD ENVIRONMENTS

The Skinnerian technology has little to say about how to unfreeze the present environment and how to move toward a new one. For example, Skinner is critical of the way Americans have conceptualized the problems of youth. He cites an example of how the problem probably would be conceptualized by current thought, giving his diagnosis in parentheses.

> Consider a young man whose world has suddenly changed. He has graduated from college and is going to work, let us say, or has been inducted into the armed services. Most of the behavior he has acquired up to this point proves useless in his new environment. The behavior he actually exhibits can be described, and the description translated, as follows: he lacks assurance or feels insecure or is unsure of himself *(his behavior is weak and inappropriate);* he is dissatisfied or discouraged *(he is seldom reinforced, and as a result his behavior undergoes extinction);* he is frustrated *(extinction is accompanied by emotional responses);* he feels uneasy or anxious *(his behavior frequently has unavoidable aversive consequences which have emotional effects);* there is nothing he wants to do or enjoys doing well, he has no feeling of craftsmanship, no sense of leading a purposeful life, no sense of accomplishment *(he is rarely reinforced for doing anything);* he feels guilty or ashamed *(he has previously been punished for idleness or failure, which now evokes emotional responses);* he is disappointed in himself or disgusted with himself *(he is no longer reinforced by the admiration of others, and the extinction which follows has emotional effects);* he becomes hypochondriacal *(he concludes that he is ill);* or neurotic *(he engages in a variety of ineffective modes of escape);* and he experiences an identity crisis *(he does not recognize the person he has called "I").* (pp. 146-147)

Skinner then asserts that although the italicized paraphrases are too brief, they suggest effective action to be taken. "To the young man himself the important things are no doubt the various states of his body. . . . What he tells us about his feelings may permit us to make some informal guesses about what is wrong with the contingencies, but we must go directly to the contingencies if we want to be sure, and *it is the contingencies which must be changed if his behavior is to be changed*" (Skinner's italics, p. 147).

There can be little disagreement with Skinner on this position since it is so general. All it says is that we must find the right reinforcements. The question is, what reinforcements? How do the italicized statements give you any new insights? The individuals using the diagnosis presented before Skinner's would have little difficulty with his action proposals precisely because they are vague.

Note that when Skinner strives to apply his technology in these nonexperimental situations, he becomes so primitive that he operates at a level at which he does not distinguish his technology from others. I suggest that Skinner will not influence the young man to change his behavior *if* he does not wish to do so, because he would "fight" whatever contingencies Skinner designed. If Skinner is able to develop contingencies that alter the young man's behavior toward less alienation and higher self-esteem, with a reinforcement schedule which he controls and which the young man resists, then he would have gone a long way to support his claim that inner man is not very important.

One looks therefore for some specific hints, some suggestion about how one could use Skinnerian concepts to change the environment. Unfortunately, none are given. We are told that a complete break with the past is impossible. The designer of a new culture will always be culture-bound. Moreover, a new culture must appeal to those who are to move into it, and they are necessarily the products of an older culture (p. 164). Given these problems, what does Skinner suggest? He continues, "within these practical limits, however, it should be possible to minimize the effect of accidental features of prevailing cultures and to turn to the source of the things people call good. The ultimate sources are to be found in the evolution of the species and the evolution of the culture" (p. 164).

How should it "be possible to minimize the effects"? How will one find that by looking at the evolution of species or culture?

Perhaps Skinner is unable to develop such insights because he maintains that in studying the present environment there is no reason to explain the origins of a cultural practice in order to account for its contribution to the environment (p. 136). The important knowledge is to specify the behavior of the particular practice. This may be adequate if all one is attempting to do is to understand the steady state of a given culture. However, if the interest is in unfreezing or changing the environment, then knowing how the practice arose may give us cues for how to alter it or introduce new ones.

To make the problem more complicated, yet more in tune with present reality, how would a behavior modification expert go about changing individual behavior when the environment does *not* support such changes? What prognosis does he have for us if we tell him that once his subject has modified his behavior he would go into a world in which that behavior was either actively punished or passively unrewarded? Would he not be somewhat pessimistic? Does not the existing research show that such behavior would become extinguished?

This is the problem faced by many interventionists who are trying to design alternative cultures. For example, organizations at the upper levels presently have the capacity to produce valid information for unimportant problems and invalid information for important problems. The reasons for this are complex and exist at the interpersonal, group, and organizational levels. For the sake of this discussion, I will cite one important reason which is due to the empirically observed fact that trusting behavior is practically nonexistent and therefore the trust level is low (Argyris, 1968).

In order to begin to make changes, like Skinner, we attempt to design a learning environment for the executive to practice and become more competent in trusting behavior while, at the same time, achieving their tasks. Those that do learn have their behavior quickly extinguished because the environment does not support the new behavior (exactly what Skinner would predict). Contrary to Skinner's hopes stated above, it is difficult to find any contingencies to reinforce the new behavior because the people "back home" consider the new behavior ineffective and undesirable. The task then becomes what to "plug into the individual" so that he does not seek reinforcement; so that the behavior is not extinguished; so that he remains alert for any possible opening to introduce the new behavior and ready to accept and understand the mistrust and condemnation that will follow.

One strategy is to help the individual develop "strength" in reacting effectively when he is being confronted or punished, when little or no positive reinforcement exists. Our experience suggests that the first step toward developing this strength is to help the individual to understand, and have a genuine respect for, whatever factors cause him to confront others. If he becomes genuinely accepting of confrontation and if he learns how to do it effectively, he also becomes effective in respecting others' confrontations of him.

One of the most effective ways for an individual to develop these learnings is to encourage him to confront, to reject, to re-design the environment in which he exists. Thus an effective T-group educator, unlike an effective Skinnerian, will encourage "autonomy" through confrontation with both the educator and the environment which he has designed and in which the individuals have been placed.

The same strategy may be used in the non-contrived world. In a recent case study reported by the writer, one group of top executives were divided in half. One sub-group believed that increasing trust was important and useful; the other felt it was useless and tension-producing.

Instead of planning the "proper" reinforcements for the sub-group that was against increasing trust, a confrontation session was designed in which these issues were explored. The interpersonal and inter-group processes during these sessions were not very effective. The sub-group that wished to increase their trust level was attacked and heavily punished. They strove hard to respond in minimally punishing ways and to seek any possible clue for rewarding the others (two activities which Skinner would applaud). However, the anti-trust group saw this behavior as indicative of weakness (because strong executives fight to win). This resulted in the "trust" group becoming despondent and concerned. Contrary to Skinnerian predictions, this did not reduce the observable behavior to continue arguing and risking for trusting behavior (Argyris, 1971).

In another example, a particular executive (Mr. A) performed in a way that was detrimental to his effectiveness. Mr. A was unable to perceive this consequence, although some of his colleagues attempted to increase his awareness. Mr. A would behave highly defensively, partially because he was punished by his well-intentioned colleagues (a consequence predictable by Skinnerian psychology) *and* partially because he conceived of the behavior he was accused of manifesting as being incorrect and ineffective. Thus his peers were suggesting that he was behaving precisely in the way which he found abhorrent.

To make matters more difficult, the "negative" behavior was most frequently produced in the privacy of Mr. A's office (because most of his work was done there). Also, as a result of the increasingly poor relationship with his peers, Mr. A began to withdraw from other informal contacts.

The reality of the situation was therefore one in which it would be very difficult to reinforce the proper behavior because it would mean that someone would have to be posted in his office, a possibility that would violate the professional ethics of his field (i.e. the client would not have a privileged relationship).

Changes were made by using a technology which did not require a schedule of reinforcement from anyone except the individual himself. This technology was developed directly from a psychological view that sees man as capable of being autonomous and self-responsible. It called for a strategy of helping the individual to see why maintaining his blindness toward this behavior was necessary to his defense structure which led to consequences which he deplored. This awareness was very painful and embarrassing to the executive. But he also realized that change was possible, because he was primarily responsible.

The executive decided to change. The unfreezing and developing of new behavior was not easy. To make matters more difficult, his peers did not see the changes as they occurred and continued punishing him. Despite a punishing environment and with the only positive reinforcements being those that came from within—at a schedule with no apparent pattern—Mr. A. significantly altered his behavior.

The difference in technology between the Skinnerian and this approach is that here the focus is on strengthening the individual so that he can influence, re-design, alter, and confront his environment. Such a learning experience is based on a technology where A can do something to B *and*, unlike Skinner, B can confront it, alter it, or challenge it. The learning environment does not focus on producing precise reinforcement. It focuses more on helping people to keep open the questions of what impact they are having on each other and how they may modify their impact if they so wish. They learn more about how to give and receive valid information with minimal defensiveness-producing qualities, how to explore when an individual's "need" for positive reinforcement may be too much or too little, how to keep the schedule for reinforcement public and open to influence by the entire group, how to reduce the reinforcement, if it interferes with task accomplishment, without extinguishing the behavior.

The non-neutrality of Skinner's position is evident in the numerous examples that he gives which, in order to be valid, assume that the world is populated primarily with people who have power and with those who do not (i.e., the world of the status quo).

One such example is the very way Skinner defines freedom. Freedom is running away from noxious or harmful contacts; escape and avoidance are its key properties. The escape is directed against intentional controllers—toward those who treat others aversively in order to induce them to behave in particular ways (p. 9).

The literature of freedom (which is never specified), according to Skinner, has focused on helping men become conscious of aversive control, but it has failed to rescue the happy slave. This same literature has made control a bad word.

The first question to be asked is why Skinner chooses to ignore the literature of freedom which comes from existentialists (e.g., Bugental, Fromm, Frankl, Maslow, and Buber), from experimental and clinical-social psychologists (e.g., De Charnes, Rotter, Berlyne, and Bakan), and from those engaging in experiential learning (e.g., Argyris Bennis, Schlein, Bradford, Benne, and Gibb). All these writers have defined freedom in terms of personal responsibility and causation. Man is free to the extent that he makes choices, that he consciously strives to design his life, that he accepts personal responsibility for his behavior.

Their view is that if the environment (or people in the environment) is being controlled by others, it is (partially) because some choose to be controlled by the environment.

This literature, in contradistinction to Skinner, conceives of the running away from aversive phenomena as superficial and shallow. The most important issues about freedom are how man *moves toward aversive phenomena; how he actively or proactively manages them and his environment; how he maintains an active vigil to make sure that he does not become a happy slave.*

For example, one of the key issues in the development of many T-groups and in some organizational development programs is precisely this (Argyris, 1968, 1971). The members may be confronting the educator and themselves as to whether they are creating a new environment in which they are overthrowing one form of unilateral control only to develop a new and more subtle one (which happens frequently *but* can be caught and explored openly). One of the most important learnings individuals explore in an organizational development program is related to the positive use of control. They may begin by condemning control (as being authoritarian). They soon find, however, that without some kind of control their efforts may become chaotic and their energies expended in neurotic activities (a point that Skinner would appreciate). They seem to learn how to design new control systems which are based on increasing self-control and self-monitoring (Argyris, 1971).

Why does Skinner choose to ignore this literature? I believe that he must exclude this literature from his awareness because to include it would raise the possibility that another design for life is to focus on increasing the importance of environmental causation *and* personal responsibility. Skinner does not consider this possibility because his generalizations come out of the experimental technology where the environment is the causal variable and the subject is the happy (or unhappy) slave. Ironically, the man who condemns the role of happy slave has achieved his fame by using subjects who are capable of being happy slaves.

Skinner can also get into trouble by being selective. In his discussion of dignity we find another confirmation of the freedom that Skinner has ignored. Dignity, according to Skinner, is something given to a man by others. Others reinforce the behavior they desire and the individual acquires or enhances his sense of dignity. Positive reinforcement comes from doing something which is difficult and not commanded by others. "We give credit generously where there are no obvious reasons for the behavior" (p. 47). "It has been customary to commend those who live celibate lives, give away their fortunes, or remain loyal to a cause when persecuted because there are clear reasons for behaving differently" (p. 47).

These are examples of the literature of freedom, of choice, of personal causation that Skinner dismisses. The individual does what the environment does not require, necessarily reward, or sanction.

Skinner continues with another illustration: after making an embarrassing mistake, we try to act as if we had not done so. That may be true for many people and untrue for an equal number. Many people are able to admit their errors.

However, the evidence would be overwhelmingly in favor of Skinner if he said that these behaviors occurred under conditions where the maintenance of power was important or where the individual's self-acceptance was low. Thus generals who feel they must continuously maintain their power may understandably attempt to maintain their dignity for the reasons Skinner states. We are most concerned about negative evaluations by others when the others have some type of power over us.

The point being emphasized is that Skinner's many examples assume that the world is populated with people who have power and with those who do not, and that is the way things should and must remain.

Why this assumption? I suggest that Skinner's view of reality has been conditioned by the environment in which he has operated for years, namely the experimental laboratory. The laboratory is a setting par excellence where some have power (experimenters) and some do not (subjects).

It is this environment that has had a enormous effect on Skinner's development of such concepts as man, freedom, and dignity: Skinner's primary subjects are animals who willingly permit themselves to be ordered around in an experiment. There is almost no way of finding out whether they willingly choose to participate. Thus Skinner lives in a world where his subjects, because of their genetic endowment (an endowment to which Skinner attributes primary potency), are not able to confront their environment. Skinner "naturally" comes to see man and pigeons as the same along these dimensions. The point is that Skinner has developed a concept of the good life which could only have come from an individual who is dominated by his environment.

Does this conclusion not illustrate Skinner's position? Are we not admitting that the environment is all powerful? The answer is yes and no. Yet, since we have just said that for Skinner, the environment is all pervasive. No, since the reason in Skinner's case the environment has become so pervasive is that Skinner has permitted it to do so. To my knowledge, Skinner has never written an article confronting the type of environment experimental science requires, the psychological demands upon the subjects involved, and the impact of these demands on obtaining valid information. The above conjectures about Skinner are meant to illustrate that if a man lives in a world where, knowingly or unknowingly, he does not actively confront his environment, and where he simultaneously de-emphasizes his personal causations and responsibility for the environment, he then becomes controlled by environment; he has become a happy slave.

SKINNERIAN SUCCESS AND PSYCHOLOGICAL FAILURE

There is another problem with Skinnerian technology. Skinner aspires to develop a model that specifies the conditions necessary to produce specific behavioral changes. More than any other experimentally-based social science technology, Skinnerians borrow heavily from their experimental programs. Precision in operational definitions and measurements are hallmarks of the Skinnerian approach to any attempt to use the technology in real life.

It may be predicted that as the technology becomes more complete and can be used to specify the environment, (including the specific behavior that people should manifest), the ultimate in a pre-planned programmed environment would be that people's levels of aspiration, goals, or paths to these goals would be specified. This would mean that if the plans were correct and valid, there would be little for the individual to do but follow them, leading to the achievement of the goals but also leading to psychological failure. *The real reinforcement may be the striving rather than the end product.*

There is ample evidence to substantiate this prediction in related areas. I refer to the quantitative computer-based management information systems designed to program managerial behavior. These systems do for man in organizations what Skinner hopes social scientists will do someday for man anywhere. They design the environment and they define the specific sequence of steps to be taken to achieve one's goals or to accomplish the defined tasks. Yet the executives fight these management information systems. In many cases, the objective data indicate that the system does better, and in an uncomfortable number of cases, the executives know this and consciously fudge the data. Why this reaction? They report that these systems place them in conditions of psychological failure, restrict their freedom of movement, and make them feel like cogs in a big wheel. These systems are to the upper levels what the time and motion men are to the workers at the lower levels (Argyris, 1970). It is simply not true that society will necessarily value knowledge that produces knowledge which leads to more effective problem-solving at the cost of increasing psychological failure.

SKINNER'S CONCEPT OF MAN

For years Skinner's writings have irked some of his readers, especially those who are of a more clinical or existential orientation, because Skinner believes that his concept of man is *the* valid concept (Rubenstein, 1971). The reason that Skinner may take this position more forthrightly than other experimental pschologists is that he is consistent in developing his concept of man rigorously and meticulously from the technology and findings of his research. The concepts of man and the environment that Skinner presents derive directly from his research; the technology he recommends is based on the experimental procedures he uses in his laboratory.

Skinner values the scientific method. He thinks like a physical scientist. This is both his strength and weakness. It is his strength in that he and his students represent some of the highest levels of aspiration for rigorously controlled research. This is why the psychological community has awarded him its highest honors. When Skinner follows the dictates of the scientific method he is excellent.

The weakness comes when he conceives of his universe in the same way as do the physical scientists. Their view is that nature is out there waiting patiently to be understood. One might have difficulty, at times, in measuring certain properties (the indeterminancy principle). However, one never conceives that the measurements or other experimental procedures may actually change the universe. Nor does one conceive of the possibility that once scientific knowledge is produced it may alter the nature of the universe. But this is precisely the case in the social science universe. As Bannister (1970) points out, no psychological body of knowledge ". . . can be final, even in a speculative sense, since once a theory has been formulated and has become general property, behavior influenced by cultural awareness of the theory must additionally be accounted for" (p. 417).

It makes sense for the physical scientist to develop whatever viewpoint or theory has the greatest explanatory power over the largest number of issues with the minimum use of untested assumptions and inter-connected concepts. In this concept of the universe, one viewpoint will eventually rule. As Einstein held, nature would not play tricks and be comprehended equally well by two different views.

The difficulty with this view in the social universe is that it does not hold. Skinner reports successes in helping delinquents and so do Ostrom, Steele, Rosenblood, and Mirels (1971), just to pick the most recent example I have seen. These authors use a technology many of whose activities are quite different from those used by Skinnerians and which is based partially upon a concept of autonomous man. For example, their program called for an emphasis upon autonomy; the leader was to encourage freedom on the part of the group members to determine their own activities; attendance was to be voluntary, with the entire program emphasizing self-control, internal volition, and internal locus of control.

How can two such different technologies work equally well? One answer is because the subjects—human beings—may be quite flexible regarding the route they will take to better themselves. In my experience, people who are ready to be helped (i.e., are ready to take initiative for their growth) make two demands. One is that the expert genuinely care for them and thus not knowingly lead them to harm. If they can trust the expert, then they will follow his route. The second demand is that the route have some reasonable probability of success and that the expert be competent to lead them through the unknown territory. Recently, Ryan and Grzynski (1971) reported that successful outcomes in behavior therapy could not be related directly to the behavior modification programs. The crucial variables that related to successful outcomes were (1) mutual positive feelings between behavior therapist and subject, (2) patients' confidence in the successful outcome and the therapist's efforts to facilitate this, and (3) the patients' perceptions of the therapist as confident and competent.

In other words a key variable in the social science universe is the nature of man. Skinner's concept fits the nature of man that an engineering-technologically-economically-oriented society generates. Others seek to develop a concept of autonomous man which is quite different from Skinner's. Their autonomous man is not defined only by what he runs away from but what he goes toward; what initiatives he takes; what and how he confronts, alters, and manages the environment.

This flexibility of man means that ultimately *man selects and designs* his environment, and not the other way around. Man is responsible to develop the designs of his nature. What many thoughtful men are saying is that the concept of man has been left too long to the engineering and economic principles of a technological society. This is not to say these factors should be overthrown completely. Anyone who has worked in the underdeveloped areas of this planet has experienced the strong desires people have to elevate their very low standard of living. I believe that Maslow's (1970) concept of a hierarchy of needs is relevant here. A society, like an individual, will tend to find it useful to focus on technology and economics to raise its standard of living. As the society matures, it can turn to fulfilling the more self-actualizing needs which require basic changes in the types of reinforcements desired *and* in who is in control of these environments. In a more actualizing society, there is an increasing interest in self-control aimed at environmental stability. Neither Skinner, nor anyone else, can develop a concept of such a world if he designs the world by using the scientific method and experimental procedures, because this method and these procedures are no different from those used by modern formal pyramidal organizations.

One of the important challenges faced by researchers is how to generate the rigor and systematic approach inherent in the scientific method, yet, after these procedures, to give more influence to the subject (Kelman, 1968). Interestingly, leaders of large complex organizations are striving to find new designs of organizational structures, managerial control, and leadership styles that are less mechanistic and more organic, the latter meaning that the individual has the right—indeed the responsibility—to challenge, confront, re-design, and manage the environment in which he works in such a way that the job gets done and he actualizes more aspects of himself. Is it possible to develop research procedures which provide these properties to the subject? I believe it is, especially where the social scientist joins with the subjects, together to study and re-design their environment (Argyris, 1970).

REFERENCES

Argyris, Chris: The incompleteness of social psychological theory. *American Psychologist,* 1969, 24(10), 893-908.

Argyris, Chris: Intervention Theory and Method: A Behavioral Science View. Reading, Mass., Addison-Wesley, 1970.

Argyris, Chris: Management information systems: the challenge to rationality and emotionality. *Management Science,* 1971, 17 (6), B-275-292.

Argyris, Chris: Some unintended consequences of rigorous research. *Psychological Bulletin,* 1968, 70 (3), 185-197.

Bannister, D.: Comment. *In* Robert Borger and Frank Cioffe (ed.): Explanation in the Behavioral Sciences. London, Cambridge University Press, 1970.

Kelman, Herbert C.: On Human Values and Social Research. Jossey-Bass, 1968.

Krasner, Leonard: Behavior therapy. *Annual Review of Psychology,* 1971, 22, 483-532.

Maslow, Abraham H.: Motivation and Personality. New York, Harper & Row, 1970.

Ostrom, Thomas M., Steele, Claude M., Rosenblood, Lorna K., and Mirels, Herbert L.: Modification of Delinquent Behavior. *Journal of Applied Social Psychology,* 1971, 1 (2), 118-136.

Rubenstein, Richard L.: A review of Beyond Freedom and Dignity. *Psychology Today,* 1971, 5 (4), 28-29ff.

Ryan, Victor L., and Grzynski, Martha N.: Behavior therapy in retrospect: patients' feelings about their behavior therapies. *Journal of Consulting and Clinical Psychology,* 1971, 37 (1), 1-9.

Simon, Herbert A.: The Science of the Artificial. Cambridge, Mass., Massachusetts Institute of Technology Press, 1969.

the science of the art 40
of teaching

Madeline Hunter

That "teaching is an art based on science" is an increasingly undisputed assertion. There are those who would still wishfully (and wistfully) believe that teaching is a "laying on of hands," or that "teachers are born and not made," or that "if a teacher *really* loves children, they will learn." Such "believers" are becoming fewer as evidence to the contrary continues to mount. A few "classroom mammas" nostalgically cling to ritualistic practice, wailing that "we don't really *know* enough about learning." However, as knowledge about learning emerges from research laboratories and is refined and validated by practice in the field, it becomes increasingly difficult to pretend that such knowledge does not exist.

This knowledge will continue to be extended and refined. However, already validated principles constitute the essential cornerstone of a science of teaching, a cornerstone that supports the art of teaching. To proceed in today's classroom unmindful of the ways in which science can contribute to successful learning is to remain a witch doctor who refuses to use modern medical techniques.

In defense of the conscientious educator who has been seeking more effective strategies, it is important to state that much knowledge about learning has been buried in research journals, covered by the impenetrable moss of unrealistic laboratory conditions, or couched in statistical language incomprehensible to the teacher. Only recently has the educational bilingual (a rare breed who speaks the language of the theoretician and the practitioner) sought to translate research findings into information useful to classroom teachers.

To emphasize the scientific foundation of teaching is not to deny the existence of an artistry which transcends science. When such artistry occurs, however, one invariably finds that the teacher has used, even though on an intuitive or inarticulate level, valid principles of learning. The modern professional, however, cannot rely on intuition but must deliberately identify, articulate, and use such knowledge in his teaching. The result will be not only to insure that student learning becomes more probable and more predictably successful but also to help transmit those identified and articulated skills of teaching to new professionals. Intuitive knowledge is sterile, for it dies with its possessor.

It is also important to realize that artistry in teaching can no more violate basic principles of human learning than can effective communication violate the basic structure of a language. We should also emphasize that though the science of human learning is in its infancy, it is a robust infant and has high potential, for it gives educators the tools that science has given other fields:

1. It describes the field of instruction and organizes the knowledge within that field.

2. Cause-effect relationships are hypothesized and tested to make outcomes predictable.

3. Increased control over outcomes becomes possible.

The complexity of human variables, both psychological and environmental, makes the social sciences considerably less exact than the physical sciences at this time. Still, we have enough knowledge to increase the probability of desirable outcomes in learning and to minimize or eliminate undesirable outcomes.

Teachers must learn to incorporate an understanding of the scientific principles of learning in their daily practice. It is the use of such knowledge in the classroom that enables the *art* of teaching to emerge, in the same way that extensive knowledge and skill in his field aids the artistry of the musician, painter, doctor, or attorney. Without developing such knowledge or skill, the most promising beginner continues to remain, at best, a talented amateur or, at worst, a discouraged failure.

Some still insist that "really caring" about the learner is enough. Paralleling this are admonitions to "truly understand and accept oneself," and "guide and facilitate rather than TEACH" (as if that were a dirty word or an immoral act). There is nothing wrong with these platitudes. Such attributes are highly desirable when they are complementary to scientific skill in facilitating learning. They are not sufficient in themselves. (Who would want a doctor who "really cared for, respected, and guided" his patients, unencumbered by any knowledge of medical science?)

Although knowledge about human learning (which includes attitudes and feelings) is nowhere near as advanced as medical knowledge, enough is available so that teachers can no longer rely on those handy (though threadbare from overuse) excuses for a student's failure to learn: ("unmotivated," "low I.Q.," "with his mother what would you expect?"). This is not to say that all students can become scholars, but rather that almost all students can achieve the knowledge, thinking skills, attitudes, and appreciations needed to become productive, self-fufilling members of society. It is also possible to eliminate most of the costly remedial efforts now prevalent in our schools.

To focus on the science of teaching and learning, we first need to define three essential terms: learning, teaching, and the teaching-learning process.

Learning

Learning is any change of behavior that is not maturational or due to a temporary condition of the organism. If Johnny can read now, when formerly he couldn't, he has *learned* to read. If Suzy used to want everything for herself and now enjoys sharing with others, Suzy has *learned* to share. If Sam used to dislike poetry and now enjoys reading it, he has *learned* to appreciate poetry. However, when teen-age Tom's voice gets lower, he has not learned to talk differently; a maturational change has occurred. Fatigue or drugs may also produce behavior that is not learned, but is caused by a temporary condition.

Teaching

Teaching makes learning more probable or more predictably successful. Rather than merely hoping learning will occur, we teach to achieve that learning effectively and efficiently. Consequently, we define teaching as *a process of a deliberate decision-making and action which makes learning more probable and more predictably successful than it would be without that teaching.* Whether Johnny is learning to read, share his toys, ride a bicycle, or appreciate music, teaching which incorporates relevant principles of learning will enable him to achieve better, faster, and more durable learning.

The Teaching-Learning Process

The dynamic interaction between teacher and learner constitutes the teaching-learning process. Each teaching or learning action affects and is affected by the actions that surround it. This constant modification of decisions and behavior on the basis of *current* data as well as prior knowledge makes teaching a profession. It is analogous to surgery, where a prior plan based on medical knowledge is modified according to the exact condition of the patient.

ORGANIZING KNOWLEDGE IN THE FIELD

The elements of the teaching-learning process can be grouped in three basic categories: (1) what is to be learned, (2) what the learner is doing to achieve that learning, and (3) what the teacher is doing to facilitate (or interfere with!) that achievement. Reading for understanding, for example, might be a learning task, and writing answers to questions designed to check that understanding might be the learner's behavior. The teacher might attempt to facilitate the learning by selecting an interesting story with appropriate vocabulary and creating questions to check understanding.

Here some readers may object. "Is the teacher the only decision-maker? What about a learner selecting his own learning objective, determining how to achieve it, and deciding whether or not to seek help from the teacher?"

The objective of all schooling, of course, is an independent learner who is in charge of his own learning. This independence, however, is a learned behavior, and consequently it is achieved more surely and efficiently by teaching than by simply asserting a pious belief in the learner's potential for independence while doing nothing systematic to teach him to achieve it. Incidentally, one major contribution of science to the art of teaching is the development of criteria that enable a teacher to know when a learner should be left on his own. The learning process of an independent learner can be described in those same three categories. In this case, the teacher is facilitating the learning process by making the conscious decision to do nothing unless requested by the learner.

The learning task is the beginning focal point in the teaching process, for only *after* it has been identified can the appropriate behavior in the other two categories be determined. Learner and teacher behavior will vary considerably if the task is easy or difficult, interesting or uninteresting, pleasurable or dangerous, simple or complex. Consequently, a scientific and systematic approach begins with the teacher or learner identifying the precise learning task. By so beginning, we eliminate all the wasteful educational squabbles about "questioning versus telling," "discovery versus demonstration," "large group versus small group," to name but a few of the fashionable debates. These debates concern the behavior of the teacher and learner. In these areas there are no right or wrong answers until the specific learning task has been identified. For example, creativity and the ability to follow directions are both important, but we certainly don't want learners to be creative in spelling or be told exactly what and how to paint in art.

Once the learning task is identified, science tells us that the next professional decision concerns what the learner will do to successfully accomplish that task. This learner behavior must have two properties. It must lead to the accomplishment of the identified learning, and it must be effective for the particular learner. Throwing and catching (not watching someone else do it) is effective if the task is to learn to throw and catch a ball. Reading (rather than listening) is an appropriate behavior if the task is decoding the printed page. Watching and listening are not unappropriate if the task is to "learn about" throwing and reading, but these behaviors will not in themselves produce successful "doing." Many learning failures occur because the behavior of the learner did *not* lead to the efficient accomplishment of the objective (for example, memorizing poetry for appreciation or writing a word one hundred times to learn to spell).

Effectiveness of a given behavior for a particular learner depends on the behavior most productive for him at this point of his learning. If he is to throw and catch, should it be with his best friend, with the teacher, with a much better or a less able partner, or by himself against a backstop? Which behavior will elicit his most productive and determined effort? If he is reading, should he read aloud or to himself? Will he learn to read faster if he is alone with the teacher, in a small group, in a competitive situation, or in a supportive one? These questions must be answered, not by intuition or by love, but by critical analysis of his previous learning behavior and a constant monitoring of his present performance. Here too, the teacher or learner must always be ready to adjust or modify his behavior on the basis of data from current performance.

Only after the learning task and the most productive behavior for the learner have been determined by the teacher (or the learner) can decisions be made regarding the behavior of the teacher. Gone are the days when a teacher could *begin* with what he was going to do ("I am the kind of teacher who likes to . . ."). A teacher's actions must reflect thoughtful consideration of what would most facilitate the achievement of the learner's objective. It is in this area that a teacher's knowledge of the principles of learning and fluency in their implementation separate the professional from the amateur who "has a knack with kids." The former is a deliberate decision-maker who uses the science of learning to validate actions and predict outcomes. The latter may be a promising beginner, but he must learn to incorporate science in his teaching if he is ever to achieve his full potential.

In summary, scientific observation of the teaching-learning process has described it as composed of three sequential categories: (1) the determination of what is to be learned, (2) the determination of what the learner will do to accomplish the learning, and (3) the determination of what the teacher will do to facilitate that accomplishment. By such separation and ordering, each part of the teaching-learning process can be checked for appropriateness, and if indicated, can be adjusted to increase the probability of success. The teacher must be aware of the sequence of these decisions, constantly monitoring the learner's performance and achievement to check their accuracy.

ESTABLISHING CAUSE-EFFECT RELATIONSHIPS

After having described and classified the phenomena in the field, science seeks to establish cause-effect relationships to predict outcomes and bring them under control. The cause-effect relationships in the teaching-learning process can be grouped under two broad generalizations.

1. *Learning is incremental and proceeds in sequence.* In a *dependent* sequence, the

accomplishment of one learning is essential to the accomplishment of the next learning in the series. For example, one must understand base ten before he can deal with the process of regrouping in addition and subtraction. In an *independent* sequence, any one of the learnings can occur before another. One can learn base ten before or after learning the addition combinations up to twenty. When the "ah ha!" phenomenon of insight occurs, it is the result of having achieved the prior learnings necessary to make an intellectual leap.

2. *Validated principles of learning have been identified which, when incorporated in the teaching-learning process, contribute significantly to successful learning.* These principles have been established by laboratory experimentation and are accepted by all learning theorists regardless of their orientation. Realization of the validity of this generalization would go far toward eliminating the wasteful rejection of research findings because one is a behaviorist, a Gestaltist, a humanist, or some other kind of "ist" that provides a refuge from the incorporation of science into classroom practice.

The cause-effect implications of these generalizations are critical in the teaching-learning process. The realization that learning is incremental does *not* mean that there is a certain "best sequence" for any particular learning task. It *does* mean that efforts to attain a complex learning are doomed to failure when necessary components have not been achieved. Contemporary notions of nongrading, individualization, and diagnostic and prescriptive teaching are based on this incremental aspect of learning, for they stress that a systematic diagnosis of the learner's current position in any learning sequence is the foundation for successful achievement.

The art of any teacher directs the learner's effort to an appropriate learning objective, not one that has already been attained or one that, because of missing components, is impossible to achieve at this time. Artistry in teaching is wasted if it is not based on an analysis of what a learner now knows, because that learning is the only viable launching pad for his next achievement.

Translated into classroom practice, this means that it is not only wasteful, but actually an interference with learning to focus effort on sixth grade reading material when a learner has achieved only a third grade level; to work on long division when understanding of base ten has not been achieved, or to hope for respect for the rights of others when a learner is not even aware of the needs and feelings of the student next to him. It's equally wasteful for the student to practice *ad nauseum* what he has already learned. A knowledge of the incremental nature of learning will prevent such wasteful and even detrimental practices.

When validated principles of learning are systematically incorporated in the teaching-learning process, the rate and degree of successful learning achievement are immeasurably increased. This helps the artistry of teaching to develop. These principles are well developed elsewhere, but a few examples will illustrate their application.

Meaning is probably the single most significant variable in successful learning. This is not inherent in the material to be learned but depends on its relationship to the student's past learnings. A teacher who understands this will assist the student to build the essential bridge from past knowledge to enhance the meaning of the present task. "Your five times tables are like buying nickel candy bars. If you bought six five-cent bars, it would be six times five." Another example might be, "You know how you feel when your club makes rules you don't like. You want to leave the club. Well, that is the way the Southerners felt in the Civil War." The more scientific the teacher, the more rigorous he will be in making each learning task meaningful. The more artistic the teacher, the more perceptive will be each example.

Massing practice makes for rapid learning; distributing practice makes for long retention. A teacher who understands this generalization will introduce a new concept, skill, or interest and come back to it several times the first day, return to it more than once on the following day, and work with it again on the succeeding days until it is well established. Then he will continue to increase the intervals between practice until a very durable learning has been achieved. Without knowledge of this important principle, "Learn it, pass a test, and forget it," becomes the rule. Science enables a teacher to schedule productive and effective practice; artistry creates practice periods which are a delight to the student. Both are necessary for effective learning.

In any sequence, the part just past the middle is the most difficult to learn and remember. This generalization applies to a series of items or a time sequence. In a nine to ten o'clock period, for instance, there is apt to be a learning fallout between 9:30 and 9:45 unless the teacher does something to prevent it. In a series of ten items of equal difficulty, items 6, 7, and 8 are going to present learning and remembering problems. The longer the series, the more serious is the learning snarl that occurs just past the middle.

A teacher who is aware of this principle can scientifically eliminate the typical problems of learning the sevens and eights in multiplication, avoid the learning fallout that occurs just past the middle of a period and will not contribute to learning difficulty by scheduling one practice period directed to twenty spelling words. If the teacher understands proactive and retroactive interference, he will not only avoid the pitfalls inherent in any time or item sequence, but will possess techniques for elimination of most of them when a lengthy sequence is unavoidable. Science enables the teacher to consciously and purposefully work with learning sequences. Artistry contributes adroitness and custom tailoring to the student and the situation.

Three generalizations have been cited, but these are only a few of the examples of existing knowledge which must be consciously used in the teaching-learning process. Distilling cause-effect relationships out of mountains of psychological research and translating them into language easily understood by teachers will help successful learning become explainable, predictable, and producible.

CONTROL OVER OUTCOMES

The third contribution of science is to enable man to use knowledge to control his environment for the betterment of mankind. The science of human learning has advanced to a stage where such control is possible. Accountability, formerly a popular slogan, is now a realistic teaching responsibility.

In order to assume this responsibility, the teacher must make a clearly defined sequence of decisions which will enable him to deliberately assist learning. Scientific analysis has recently led to identification of eleven sequential decisions which generate professional action. Rather than restricting artistry and innovation, they enable a teacher to direct his creativity and artistry to areas where they make the greatest difference, rather than dissipating energy by attempting to innovate where science has already defined a productive path. These eleven items are listed as teacher decisions because the teacher can never delegate his responsibility for a student's successful learning. Nevertheless, the student himself should make as many of these decisions as he can make productively. These eleven decision areas developed elsewhere will merely be listed here:

1. Deliberate and scientific separation of genuine educational constraints from the typical ethnic, financial, intellectual, or emotional excuses which constitute fashionable (and unfortunately, acceptable) "cop-outs."

2. Determination of what the student has already achieved and what he is ready to learn in terms of degree of difficulty (sequence) and complexity (affective, cognitive, or psychomotor domain).

3. Identification of productive behavior for this particular learner to achieve the learning task.

4. Determination of an instructional objective with specific content and perceivable learner behavior.

5. Identification of principles of learning relevant to the accomplishment of this instructional objective.

6. Adaptation of those principles to the particular situation and to each learner.

7. Use of the teacher's own personality and competence in the specific learning area to enhance the learner's probability of successful accomplishment. Except for "knowing oneself," this is the only decision area about which science has little to offer at present. Here is the place for the highly operational but inarticulate knowledge of intuition: the art of teaching. Because such knowledge remains, at this time, inarticulate, it is not systematically transmittable to all teachers.

8. Synthesis of the first seven decisions into a deliberate design for a learning opportunity. To maximize successful learning, all of the first eight decisions must be consciously made before the teacher-learner interaction.

9. The actual teaching-learning process begins. As the lesson begins, the teacher's observations of the learner augment or correct the decision-making process. This instantaneous use of current data characterizes the true professional.

10. Evaluation is an integral and continuous part of the process, not merely a terminal function. Constant monitoring of the learner's progress yields essential information which may modify the teaching-learning process.

11. On the basis of these evaluative data collected *during* the teaching-learning process, the determination is made to (a) reteach, (b) practice and extend, (c) move on, or (d) "abandon ship" because for some reason the objective is not attainable by the learner at this time.

These eleven components have been briefly described to establish the significance of scientific analysis of the teaching-learning process. Such analysis makes successful teaching explainable and predictable. In the case of unsuccessful teaching (when the student has not learned), it is now possible to identify with precision where something went wrong. As a result, remediation can be concentrated on that area, saving time and energy for both teacher and learner.

Science has established a "grammar of teaching" from which a professional who understands the basic rules can generate an infinite number of unique and effective learning opportunities. Because every component except use of the individual teacher's personality and skills is based on articulated knowledge, it is possible to transmit that knowledge and enable every teacher to move toward greater success. Granted that any professional "whole" is greater than the sum of its parts, the synthesis and artistry of the master teacher become an attainable goal for a significantly larger number of practitioners who can learn well each component and translate that learning into classroom performance.

In summary, the contribution of science to the art of teaching enables a teacher to:

1. Discriminate between the "what" and the "how" of teaching by knowing whether he is focused on the learning task, the behavior of the learner, or the behavior of the teacher.

2. Identify what a learner knows and what he is ready to learn, then select the relevant principles of learning to facilitate his achievement.

3. Design a learning opportunity which reflects professional decision making and incorporates all components of the successful teaching-learning process.

By knowing the organization, cause-effect relationships, and components of the field of human learning, the teacher is better able to assist the student to take charge of his own learning decisions and to become an independent learner. In short, science builds the professional launching pad from which artistry in teaching can ascend to heights never before attainable.

putting the pieces 41
together:
making education
into a science

Daniel C. Jordan

An extraordinary amount is known about how human beings grow, develop, and learn. Libraries are overflowing with books and journals on topics pertinent to education. A variety of federal, state, and private agencies pour millions of dollars annually into education research projects. Professional organizations disseminate information on a wide variety of educational concerns.

Why, then, with this impressive wealth of information and technological support, is education in such trouble? Why do we have over a million dropouts each year? Why is there such unrest on the college campus? Why do the schools seem unable to make a constructive response to the many critical issues facing the nation?

All of the pieces to a number of basic solutions to these problems appear to exist. But there seem to be far too many pieces to cope with. No one sees how to fit them together in a way that would enable the school to restructure itself to constructively respond to the critical demands placed upon it.

It is not as though no efforts have been made. A plethora of educational innovations have claimed power to make significant improvements. Yet, one by one, they all have disappointed the expectations of their originators.* They couldn't live up to those expectations precisely because they were not able to put together enough pieces to constitute a comprehensive solution to a basic problem or issue.

No one has yet pulled together all of the pieces *for want of a unifying principle which will enable all of the pieces to cohere into an organized whole.* This organized whole not only should shed a powerful light on all problems facing education, but should also order issues into a hierarchy of priorities for allocation of monetary and manpower resources. Until such a unifying principle is articulated, tried out, and justified, education will remain in trouble, wasting resources at an alarming rate while failing ever more miserably to meet the needs of a rapidly changing social order.

---

*For instance, the great hope placed in performance contracting—a hope great enough to have led the Office of Economic Opportunity to invest 7.2 million dollars in such programs in 54 schools in 24 states—was bluntly proclaimed a failure by OEO after one year's operation.

To put the pieces together and create the needed revolution in education, we must raise to a conscious level an assumption about the nature of man which requires and inspires us to proceed on the level of faith—a faith that may transcend reason but not oppose it. I maintain that there is no hope of organizing the millions of fragments of information into a comprehensive and powerful resource for change in education until we adopt the assumption that man is a purposeful being; that he was created to know and to love and to use his knowing and loving capacities in service to man; that knowing and loving can be differentiated into a full range of actualized potentialities only when man accepts himself as a spiritual being whose essential spirituality can be achieved only when that vision of himself is sustained by a sense of ultimate cosmic destiny.

Education ought to reflect the noblest visions and passions of man which have animated philosophy, science, art, and religion throughout history. Surely it cannot afford to ignore those expressions of man's highest aspirations embodied in his cultural heritage—expressions which testify to the rightness of this assumption, if not to the absolute proof of its validity. Anything less will not be able to unify our knowledge about human development and learning so that it can be applied to the crucial exigencies facing society in general and education in particular.

Nothing we know from the biological and behavioral sciences enables us to define limits to man's capacity for knowing and loving, or to circumscribe the extent to which these two characteristic powers can be differentiated into the full range of potentialities we associate with man. Mere superlatives are inadequate to express the legitimate response of awe generated by seriously contemplating man's potentiality and destiny. We must turn to artists and poets to begin to appreciate such a vision. The following lines from Wordsworth's poem, "Tintern Abbey," testify to the common experience of that inner pressure to be spiritually transformed:

And I have felt
A presence that disturbs me with the joy
Of elevated thoughts; a sense sublime
Of something far more deeply interfused,
Whose dwelling is the light of setting suns,
And the round ocean and the living air,
And the blue sky and in the mind of man.

The pervasiveness of that view in literature, art, and religion makes it a legitimate object for scientific inquiry. Any science that ignores or refuses to deal with it is itself in need of overhauling. Science cannot have the integrating power in human affairs that it has had in technological matters until it deals with emotion, value, purpose, intention, faith, beauty, and the cosmic yearnings of man:

Indeed it is becoming clear that science itself needs considerable overhauling and transformation . . . . it needs to devise methods for dealing with patterns, process and quality, as well as with isolated elements, static or reversible events, and quantity. And in so doing it is bound to abandon its isolationism, its pretense of sovereign separateness and its pretense of being morally neutral, for it will find itself operating as a part of the total human process, in common harness with emotion, value, and purpose (Huxley, 1960, p. 250).

Over the last several decades, education has felt itself becoming more "scientific." Yet educators have failed to realize that those who know a little science can only generate a materialistic view of man and a mechanistic view of life—hopelessly inadequate visions. We have, as Huxley says, restricted ourselves and therefore blunted our sense of destiny.

Thinkers discussing the distinctive characters of men have usually laid their main or sole emphasis on intellectual or rational thought and on language as its vehicle. This is precisely because they were thinkers, not artists, or practical men, or religious mystics, and therefore tended to over-value their own methods of coping with reality and ordering experience. In addition, the verbal formulation of intellectual propositions promises greater exactitude and facilitates the accurate and large-scale transmission of experience.

But this intellectual and linguistic over-emphasis is dangerous. It readily degenerates into logic-chopping or mere verbalism. What is more serious, it takes no account of man's emotional and aesthetic capacity, exalts reason and logical analysis at the expense of intuition and imagination and neglects the important role of arts and skills, rituals and religious experiences in social life and cultural evolution. The evolutionary philosopher (and also the true humanist, whether he be anthropologist, historian, psychologist or social scientist) must take all the facts into account: he must attempt a comprehensive view of man's special characteristics, and of their effects on his evolution (Huxley, 1960, p. 250).

In the absence of a unifying principle, limited theories and relatively insignificant research findings or educational innovations based on them will be made to do its work. This places man on the Procrustean bed of inadequate and even dismal theory, lopping off both his head and his feet. We then wonder why, under such conditions, he neither thinks nor runs, let alone feels.

A striking example of this may be found in B. F. Skinner's book, *Beyond Freedom and Dignity*. His thesis fails on two accounts. He explains that "the task of a scientific analysis is to explain how the behavior of a person as a physical system is related to the conditions under which the human species evolved and the conditions under which the individual lives" (Skinner, 1971, p. 14). As Chomsky points out, the task of science cannot be limited to that but is rather "to discover the facts and explain them." To make his thesis fit science, Skinner had to redefine science. He also dismisses the internal events between stimulus and response and sees no need to deal with such characteristically human things as will, impulses, feelings, and purpose. Having defined away all the critical attributes of man, the remaining behavioral trivia can be at least partly handled by Skinnerian science. That it can "explain the behavior of a pigeon does not mean that it is adequate to explain the behavior of a poet."

Chomsky states that:

... there exists no behavioral science incorporating empirically supported propositions that are not trivial and that apply to human affairs or support a behavioral technology. For this reason Skinner's book contains no clearly formulated substantive hypotheses or proposals. . . . (Chomsky, 1971, p. 19).

If there were some science capable of treating such matters it might well be concerned precisely with freedom and dignity and might suggest possibilities for enhancing them. Perhaps, as the classical literature of freedom and dignity sometimes suggests, there is an intrinsic human inclination toward free creative inquiry and productive work, and humans are not merely dull mechanisms formed by a history of reinforcement and behaving predictably with no intrinsic needs apart from the need for physiological satiation. Then humans are not fit subjects for manipulation, and we will seek to design a social order accordingly. But we cannot, at present, turn to science for insight into these matters. To claim otherwise is pure fraud. For the moment, an honest scientist will admit at once that we understand virtually nothing, at the level of scientific inquiry, with regard to human freedom and dignity (Chomsky, 1971, p. 23).

Behavioral science as seen by Skinner or anyone else can be useful but cannot do the work of a cosmology. If we seek to use a materialistic, rather than a spiritual view of man as an underlying principle, our policies, programs, educational enterprises, and institutions will remain woefully inadequate for our needs. Indeed, they may well become even more harmful and destructive than they are now.

Education is not alone in avoiding the critical issue of finding a principle to unify our vast quantity of information about the nature of man as an individual and a social being. In 1967, the American Academy of Arts and Sciences published the report of one of its most potentially exciting commissions, the Commission on The Year 2000. The Commission included biologists, psychiatrists, economists, political scientists, government people, physical scientists, behavioral scientists, political philosophers and futurologists. Notably, no artists or theologians were included. The Commission intended to sketch hypothetical futures, to help us to reach better decisions by anticipating future problems, to find ways of measuring social performance, and to write a new political theory dealing with a service state and a new society. The report itself is a fascinating compendium of speculation and a brilliant articulation of problems to be faced and issues to be resolved. It expresses pride in the amount we know, yet repeatedly confesses how little we really know.

It is extraordinary indeed that such a commission would not devote any time to a clarification of assumptions about the nature of man. This could have led to resolution of the seeming paradox of our great quantities of unorganized knowledge. How else can we identify man's needs and aspirations and from them project designs for his future? To give the Commission its due, its chairman, Daniel Bell, confesses to that regrettable omission:

> We have not, and it is a neglect, dealt with religion and man's continuing effort to find transcendental meaning amid this contemporary disorientation wherein each individual knows that he can no longer walk in the traditional ways of his father, and that his son will not walk in his ways. And yet such needs remain. For all the "materialism" of Marxism, the most extraordinary characteristic of its adherence—especially in China today—is the need to plunge completely into a cause, to find some common purpose to the movement itself. The new "secular religions" and new cults—whether they be the post-Christian moods of the theologians or the new hedonism of the young with its rites of pleasure and the pursuit of sensate involvement or psychedelic release—are radical changes in the nature of man's emotions and require explanation (Bell, 1967, p. 985).

It is doubtful, however, that there has been such a change in the nature of man's emotions. There is far more evidence that the radical changes have occurred in technology and the environment, while man's basic social institutions, particularly those intended to serve his spiritual and emotional needs (such as the family, church, and school) have not kept pace with them. Technological developments have surrounded us with an ever-increasing number of mechanical devices. Our environment is becoming progressively less natural as it is filled up with nonliving things. Alienation is the consequence.

Furthermore, our expanded technology exposes us to a far greater range of stimuli from all over the world. It has the effect of making the future pour into the present with such a speed that we are almost always in a state of what Alvin Toffler calls "future shock" (Toffler, 1970). The combination of alienation and future shock from rapid social change places extraordinary pressures upon us.

> ... modern America produces techniques of staggering sophistication, side by side with unmet needs of equally staggering yet tragic proportions, for which there are no available techniques or resources. This inexorable divergence between what is feasible technically and what is needed humanly, is the result of decades of grovelling before the God of Technique, of resolving what to do next by following meekly the direction in which the tool itself pointed, even though it pointed away from human needs toward the "opportunity" of a circus in space and other distractions (Hampden-Turner, 1970, p. 309).

It is not surprising that the pressures from unmet needs and the anxiety produced by alienation should motivate a desperate search for something that either fills those needs or provides some kind of escape from anxiety. The search and the escape as we witness it today share the characteristics of what futurist Herman Kahn called the Increasingly Sensate Trend, which are:

> ... worldly, naturalistic, realistic, visual, illusionistic, every-day, amusing, interesting, erotic, satirical, novel, eclectic, syncretic, fashionable, technically superb, impressionistic, materialistic, commercial, and professional (Kahn and Wiener, 1967, p. 707).

If the spiritual needs of mankind continue to be unmet, we can expect humanity to sink into the Late Sensate Stage, which Kahn describes as:

> ... underworldly, expressing protest or revolt, overripe, extreme, sensation-seeking, titillating, depraved, faddish, violently novel, exhibitionistic, debased, vulgar, ugly, debunking, nihilistic, pornographic, sarcastic or sadistic (Kahn and Weiner, 1967, p. 707).

The beginnings of this stage are upon us. The "sensate involvement" and "psychedelic release" to which Daniel Bell refers are thus predicted by Kahn and explained by Hampden-Turner and Toffler. Although the search for release may lead many down dangerous paths or blind alleys, it bears evidence of a search for "resacrilization"— (respiritualization)—a reorganization of our affairs around a view of ourselves as spiritual creations. Erik Erikson, in his "Memorandum on Youth," came closer to putting his finger on the basic issue than any other member of the Commission:

> As for the desacrilization of life by the young, it must be obvious that our generation desacrilized their lives by (to mention only the intellectual side) naive scientism, thoughtless scepticism, dilettante political oppositions, and irresponsible technical expansion. I find, in fact, more of a search for resacrilization in the younger than in the older generation (Erikson, 1967, p. 862).

Thus, on the one hand there is a search for sensate involvement and on the other, for resacrilization. Both represent a search for meaning and are symptomatic of an age in which men have sustained a loss of meaning because they have lost touch with their spiritual reality. That the Commission on the Year 2000 chose purposefully to avoid grappling with this issue is a testimony to its complexity and magnitude. The difficulty of the issue notwithstanding, however, educators can make no significant advances until they deal with the issue by clarifying their assumptions about the nature of man. Once they are clarified, we will have a possible basis for organizing all the pieces of knowledge about human growth and development—a prelude to making education into a science which in turn is prerequisite to any significant revolution in education.

Julian Huxley has shown how integrating concepts are essential to any kind of major social advancement. He explains how the noetic system (a term he uses to "denote a complex of the sharable and transmissable activities and products of human minds, the patterns of thought and science, law and morality, art and ritual, which form the basis of human society") (Huxley, 1960, p. 47) depends upon what he calls noetic integrators—those "symbolic or conceptual constructions which serve to interpret large fields of reality, to transform experience into attitude and unify factual knowledge and belief" (Huxley, 1960, p. 50). He asserts that

> ... the lack of a common frame of reference, the absence of any unifying set of concepts and principles, is now, if not the world's major disease, at least its most serious symptom (Huxley, 1960, p. 88).

But any integrator will not do. The mechanistic and materialistic view of man can only take us so far. Our problem, then,

> ... is to develop noetic integrators suitable for our present stage of cultural evolution. They must be consonant with the structure and the trends of man's present system of knowledge: they must also help to secure a pattern and direction of cultural evolution which will most effectively enable man to perform his evolutionary role in nature.
>
> • • •
>
> Assuredly the concept of man as instrument and agent of the evolutionary process will become the dominant integrator of all ideas about human destiny, and will set the pattern of our general attitude to life.
>
> ... the central overriding integrator, around which man's entire noetic system is organized, would be that of fulfillment—satisfaction through fuller realization of possibilities (Huxley, 1960, pp. 53-55).

In *The Meeting of East and West,* F. S. C. Northrop confirms Huxley's point that the kind of integrator we require is one that is consistent with a spiritual rather than a materialistic view of man. He argues that our survival depends on our ability to extract from the philosophical and religious systems of the East and West an acceptable assumption about man's spiritual nature. Acceptability of this view, he claims, cannot depend solely on science but must take into account our own direct experience with living:

> ... to do justice to the spiritual nature of human beings and of all things it is not necessary to have recourse to idle speculations, by means of which one tries to pierce through the glass beyond which we now see darkly, to supposedly unaesthetic material substances behind, or into some unreachable and unknowable realm where mental substances are supposed to be.
>
> • • •
>
> This is the portion of human knowledge that can be known without recourse to inference and speculative hypotheses and deductive logic, and epistemic correlations, and rigorously controlled experiments. This we have and are in ourselves and in all things, prior to all theory, before all speculation, with immediacy and hence with absolute certainty (Northrop, 1966, p. 462).

Michael Polanyi, in discussing science, faith, and society, lends support to Northrop's thesis. He defines the life force of a tradition as a spiritual reality and argues that creative renewal requires acceptance of that spiritual reality:

> Such processes of creative renewal always imply an appeal from a tradition as it *is* to a tradition as it *ought to be.* That is, to a spiritual reality embodied in tradition and transcending it. It expresses a belief in this superior reality and offers devotion to its service (Polanyi, 1964, p. 56).

Furthermore, he demonstrates how political revolutions, in order to be successful, have to rely on those spiritual realities:

> These movements owe their success altogether to their hidden spiritual resources. They were swept into power on a tide of humanitarian or patriotic passions. The explanations seem clear enough. The denial of all spiritual reality is not only false but incapable of consummation (Polanyi, 1964, p. 88).

The potential denial of spiritual reality about which Polanyi speaks lies hidden in Newton's great achievements—achievements which led to the assumption that science could eventually reduce all phenomena, including the phenomenon of man, to the "mechanics of some ultimate constituent particles." But even in physics, that assumption can carry us only so far.

> The modern presuppositions of science which were to bear fruit in the great speculative triumphs of the twentieth century took shape gradually with the stepwise abandonment of feature after feature of this materialistic and mechanical picture (Polanyi, 1964, p. 86).

The great discoveries produced by this abandonment of the materialistic view did not come from purely analytical or scientific operations encouraged by the positivist's conception of science. There was another source.

> ... scientific intuition made use of the positivist's critique for reshaping its creative assumptions concerning the nature of things. Nor was science thereby effectively reduced to a set of indefinitely verifiable statements as postulated by the positivist's conception of science; but was revealed on the contrary as possessing a faculty of speculative discovery which strikingly refutes that conception (Polanyi, 1964, p. 88).

It is that faculty of speculative discovery which confirms man's spiritual nature and enables him to break out of the prison in which a materialistic, mechanistic view of the universe has placed him. To advance, education must now accept that faculty of speculative discovery as evidence of man's spiritual nature and use it as the noetic integrator of all of our knowledge about human growth and development. With this integrator putting the pieces together, we may redesign our educational systems to facilitate the release of our potentialities and enliven our spirits with a sense of cosmic destiny. Such a system, to be faithful to its assumption about the nature of man, must enable us to develop those spiritual virtues of knowing and loving, of hoping and aspiring. In the security generated from a sense of purpose and transcendental meaning, we can pursue our destiny in the face of the mysteries of life, death, and the infinite universe. Again, the poet has a unique way of expressing the issue beleaguering us:

> Upon this gifted age,
> In its dark hour
> Reigns from the sky a meteoric shower of facts;
> They lie unquestioned, uncombined.
> Wisdom enough to leech us of our ill
> Is daily spun,
> But there exists no loom
> To weave it into fabric (St. Vincent-Millay, 1956, p. 607).

Such a "loom" has just been suggested. Will educators be willing and able to do the weaving?

REFERENCES

Bell, Daniel: Coda: work in further progress. *Daedalus, 96:*No. 3, 985, Summer, 1967.
Chomsky, Noam: The case against B. F. Skinner. *The New York Review of Books,* Dec. 30, 1971, p. 19.
Erikson, Erik H.: Memorandum on youth. *Daedalus, 96:*No. 3, 862, Summer, 1967.
Hampden-Turner, Charles: Radical Man. Cambridge, Mass., Schenkman Publishing Co., 1970.
Huxley, Julian: Knowledge, Morality, and Destiny. New York, Harper and Brothers, 1960.
Kahn, Herman, and Wiener, Anthony J.: The next thirty-three years. *Daedalus, 96:*No. 3, 707, Summer, 1967.
Northrop, F.S.C.: The Meeting of East and West. New York, Collier Books, 1966.

Polanyi, Michael: Science, Faith, and Society. Chicago, University of Chicago Press, 1964.
St. Vincent-Millay, Edna: Sonnet CXXVII. Collected Poems. New York, Harper and Row, 1956.
Skinner, B.F.: Beyond Freedom and Dignity. New York, A. A. Knopf, 1971.
Toffler, Alvin: Future Shock. New York, Random House, 1970.

some controversial 42
issues in testing

James Carmody

One of the more controversial issues in education today is that of testing. It has been assailed on numerous fronts and at almost every level. The popular press has attacked it as being damaging to young children, minority groups have claimed that it has often placed them at an educational disadvantage, and "humanistically" oriented professors have disclaimed it as being unconcerned with the individual student and treating students only as "statistics," as part of an all too prevalent "herd" approach in education.

Defenders of tests and measurements appear mostly to come from the ranks of test makers and researchers. Some of these people would dismiss complaints about testing procedures as naive arguments based upon ignorance of the "scientific" principles of measurement. More commonly, however, the response is that it is not the tests themselves that are at fault but their misuse by the untrained personnel who come into contact with them. This response appears reasonable, although the misuse of tests by trained personnel should not be overlooked. This essay examines some of the bases of educational measurement to determine whether some of the more common criticisms are well founded or whether they do indeed reflect an ignorance of the scientific principles of measurement. For reasons of space, discussion is limited to three areas: the traditional measurement model in education, corporations and their involvement in testing, and the status of minority groups in testing.

THE TRADITIONAL MEASUREMENT MODEL

In an attempt to explain the rationale behind educational measurement, many basic texts draw an analogy with measurement in the physical sciences. The analogy generally goes something like this: measurement is the assignment of numerical values to objects or events according to certain rules or conventions. These numerical values can be abstractly manipulated to predict certain outcomes, rather than working directly with the events or objects themselves. The physical scientist can measure the length, width, and height of a block with a measuring rod, and from these measurements determine its volume without directly measuring the volume itself. He can verify this prediction by actually measuring the volume if he wishes. This capacity to manipulate objects or events abstractly rather than directly, together with his knowledge of their material properties, enables the scientist to formulate theories dealing with the nature and composition of matter. By comparing the predicted results with the actual results of manipulation under controlled conditions (an experiment), he can verify the theory. In a more applied context, the engineer is able to predict that a bridge he has designed will be safe within certain limits of stress.

The person involved in educational measurement uses a scaling device to obtain numerical indices of certain types of human behavior. Instead of measuring in inches or meters, his scale is defined in terms of intervals on a psychological scale (such as the familiar IQ). Using these indices, he can attempt to predict certain aspects of a person's behavior under certain conditions or after some particular treatment. Using his measurements, he attempts to verify the behavioral outcomes of predictions made on the basis of this theory of human behavior under certain conditions. Thus, a teacher screens children on the basis of tested intelligence or a college admissions officer establishes a cut-off point for SAT scores.

The analogy between physical and educational measurement seems inadequate in at least three ways. First, the persons being measured are obviously not blocks and cannot (or should not) be treated as such. Our knowledge of the properties of the material with which we are dealing in educational research is so meager that we cannot even be certain whether the behavior under study is deterministic. In other words, our instruments may, by their very nature, be incapable of performing adequately the task for which they were designed.

The second failing in the analogy lies in attempting to justify the inherent error in educational measurement by showing that the physical scientist must also cope with this problem. Granted that the physical scientist or technologist must allow for a certain margin of error, but by and large the resulting product performs at a satisfactory level. Further, he can repeat his measurements to check his accuracy, with the knowledge that the properties of his material have not substantially changed. In other words, the engineer can be virtually certain (extremely high probability) that his structure will perform adequately within specified stress limits. The educator, on the other hand, must cloak his decisions in terms of probabilities which, if his decision is to be useful, do not even approach virtual certainty. The difference in inherent error between physical and educational measurement is so great as to make a comparison of the two techniques misleading.

A third inadequacy of the measurement analogy lies in the purposes for which the measurement is used, and here a distinction must be made between the educational researcher and the practitioner employing measurement in the classroom. The researcher is concerned with attempting to formulate laws and generalizations and uses his measuring instruments accordingly. The practitioner is primarily concerned with making immediate decisions about individual students on the basis of his results. Since the researcher is working toward the establishment of laws that will one day enable him to make accurate decisions about individuals, his use of educational measuring instruments is perfectly legitimate, and such activity deserves support from the society. Given the present state of the art, however, the educational practitioner is using the instruments prematurely. He is operating under the delusion that useful laws have already been established that will enable him, for example, to predict whether an individual will succeed in college. His use of educational measuring instruments for predicting success in areas that are only partly related to the tasks on the instruments is clearly inadequate and illegitimate.

The distinction purposely made between predictive and achievement instruments may at first sound spurious. Are not achievement tests used for predictive purposes? The distinction lies more in the uses to which the instrument is put than in the nature of the test. Predictive instruments are those which are used to predict a student's future performance from his present performance. An achievement test, on the other hand, is used to describe the student's present status or to provide evidence of improvement. It is not used to make promises about how well a student will do in the future. Achievement tests are now useful tools for the practitioner, but predictive tests are not, despite claims to the contrary.

Achievement tests can have a legitimate role in the classroom in estimating how a student stands in relation to a certain subject area, but some tests are not designed specifically to measure this. Achievement scores fall roughly into two types—those that indicate where a student stands in relation to other students taking the test, and those that indicate where he stands in relation to the body of knowledge he is studying. The first is commonly known as a norm-referenced score; the second as a criterion-referenced score. Most tests in use today, particularly standardized tests, are of the norm-referenced variety. This writer believes it is far more important for the student to know his competencies and deficiencies than to know how many of his neighbors know more or less, which may be the beginning of a self-fulfilling prophecy. What a student knows should be much more important to all concerned than how many of his neighbors have lower scores than his. After all, a student whose test score places him at the eightieth percentile may not know a great deal more about the subject than one who scores at the fiftieth percentile. There really is no way of telling because of the nature of the scale that is used to measure the dimension.

Obviously, criterion-referenced measurement can be useful only in the more hierarchically organized subject matter areas, such as mathematics and the physical and biological sciences. Addition and subtraction are both important skills in which it is relatively easy to define success. However, it may prove to be foolish to attempt to provide quantitative data on a student's appreciation of English literature. The important question of establishing acceptable criterion levels remains problematic but worth pursuing, although it is beyond the scope of this article.

CORPORATIONS AND TESTING

The role of corporations, both testing and other sorts, in the development and present influence of testing in the United States has received surprisingly little scrutiny. Several very important questions need to be considered. What, for example, is the responsibility to society of the test maker and distributor? Why do commercially produced tests continue to sell in spite of growing criticism?* What are the reasons for the continuing ignorance in the use of tests results? These problems occur in regard to not only the predictive type but other commercially produced, norm-referenced achievement tests as well.

Continuing ignorance of the limitations of mental tests becomes more understandable if their producers are given careful scrutiny. Tests are produced and sold by both profit-making and nonprofit corporations. From profit-making firms (frequently publishing

---

*Kirkland has reported an estimate by Brim et al. of 150 million to 250 million ability tests taken per year. Kirkland, Marjorie G.: The effects of tests on students and schools. *Review of Educational Research*, 7:No. 4, p. 41.

houses and "educational consultants") it is reasonable to expect all the nasty byproducts of a profit-oriented system. They produce tests, and, to make a profit, they have to sell them. It doesn't particularly matter if the customer needs the test as long as he buys it. It is the same ethic in industrial corporations that causes environmental pollution and the exploitation of less powerful nations. In this context it might be said that the ethic leads to educational pollution and the exploitation of children.

Ideally, a nonprofit corporation should not be concerned with profits. However, the important nonprofit corporations, Educational Testing Service and the American College Testing Program, derive most of their support from the proceeds of test sales. In order to support their research and other activities, they have to sell tests. If they want to expand their activities, they have to sell more tests or raise test prices. Researchers and test-makers employed by these organizations have, bluntly, a vested interest in the continuation of testing as we know it—their jobs depend on it. Though the root causes are different, the effects are quite similar to those caused by profit-oriented corporations.

It might be argued that test-producing companies have a vested interest in maintaining a certain level of ignorance about the use and validity of their tests. Certainly, if their efforts to inform people about how their tests should *not* be used were as vigorous as their selling campaigns, which emphasize the tests' potential uses, the present knowledge gulf between test builder, seller, and user would not exist. It is very difficult to imagine a testing company representative requiring a potential user to pass a test purporting to measure his competence in using a certain test and its results before selling him the test. Since, in actively informing educators of the limitations of their tests, testing companies run the risk of substantially reducing sales, it is very difficult for them to be totally responsible.

As part of their research programs, nonprofit testing corporations have played an important role in the development of mental test theory. Now test-makers can not only supply a test, they can support its results with statistics of its reliability and validity and an esoteric testing vocabulary that can overwhelm the protests of any nonspecialist. Little effort is made to translate the jargon into layman's terms (if indeed that is possible), and this results in some test-users defending their practices by referring to papers that they don't really understand themselves.

Remarkably little attention has been paid to the feelings of those being tested. College entrance exams are an especially serious case. The tests exist for the convenience of the colleges, but the student pays to take them. Students are well aware of the importance of such test results in college admission, and many realize the probable limitations of the results. Yet their objections are brushed off with a recitation of "reliabilities," "validities," "burgeoning enrollments," and other jargon that may seem intended more to shut off their complaints than to answer their questions. To the students who understand that tests are not perfect indicators of success, and that those somewhat below cut-off scores still have a reasonable chance of success in college, this indicates that the colleges are dehumanizing institutions. For those who accept the test results as valid indicators of their abilities, matters are worse, for they are assimilating the notion of their inferiority or superiority.

The tests are a great aid to the admissions officer. He can shift the blame for a student's rejection from himself to the test results, avoiding painful confrontations. His rationale is that even if it doesn't predict too well, it makes his job more manageable, and besides, "it's the best method we have." It would be more accurate to say that it's the best method college officials are willing to consider to deal with the admittedly unwieldy admissions process.

MINORITIES AND TESTING

A different aspect of the question of fairness in testing has arisen in relation to the testing of minority groups. Considerable discussion has been devoted to the problem of devising a test that will not unfairly discriminate against minority groups. Although this section does not attempt comprehensive coverage of the problem of test bias, there are several points relevant to the discussion.

Any consideration of the problem of selection and prediction for minority groups should begin by recognizing that a major purpose of testing is to provide a valid basis upon which to discriminate between people. Thus a test may be designed to sort out potentially successful vacuum-cleaner salesmen from those who apply for the job, or it may attempt to select people who show potential for success in college. Because of the way in which many of the skills necessary for success in college are traditionally viewed, they are usually mastered by persons who have been nurtured in a white middle- or upper-class culture (an analysis of the reasons for this are not part of this discussion). Vocabulary in children's readers, for example, typically reflects the words that are common to a middle-class environment. The extent of this is often not fully realized until one peruses a reader written for minority children.

Some forms of test discrimination are fair and desirable while others reflect only prejudice. Tests that discriminate on the basis of the vocabulary from a typical children's reader, for example, are unfair because different tests could be devised that would neither discriminate against different cultural backgrounds nor lose their validity; indeed validity would be enhanced.

Tests that discriminate in a desirable way are high-level knowledge tests that must be passed satisfactorily for certification to practice on the general public. These are skills that must be mastered to a criterion level by all candidates regardless of their cultural background. In medicine, for example, strict hygiene must be observed by all candidates. To claim that overemphasis on hygiene is a white middle-class value and should not be foisted onto other groups is indefensible—clearly it is essential for all those who enter the medical field regardless of their backgrounds. It is in assisting those from varying cultural backgrounds to obtain these high-level skills that the greatest value of compensatory education lies.

But behaviors such as these, which are essential for all candidates, should indeed be *essential*. They should be carefully studied by groups with diverse cultural backgrounds to ensure that more "universals" do not creep in to make the task of attainment of the criterion overly difficult for any one group.

This discussion has not taken the position that all forms of testing are necessarily damaging or that they are self-fulfilling prophecies. Rather, it has argued that more consideration should be given to many of the value decisions involved in setting up or revising a testing program, especially as they stand in relation to the democratic principles we preach. We should, for instance, consider whether a person's competence or aptitude is best defined by comparing his test score with those of others who also took the test. We also need to ask whether it is even desirable to attempt to rank people on some dimensions, such as appreciation of literature.

In attempting to rethink our approaches to testing we should understand the corporate nature of most testing organizations and the correspondingly difficult task of changing the industry. Some revisions in testing approaches are going to involve much greater allowances for cultural diversity and local conditions. Nationally organized corporations have a very shady reputation in this area, since greater profits lie along the road of uniformity and standardization.

43 grades must go*

Sidney B. Simon

In Shirley Jackson's eerie short story, "The Lottery," a village holds a drawing each year to decide whom they will stone to death. In our colleges and universities, we do it twice a year.

One character in Miss Jackson's story raises a question about why the villagers continue to perform this inhuman ritual, but an elder quiets him with, "We have always had a lottery."

So it is with grades, and midterms, and true and false questions, and multiple choices, and essay questions (choose three out of four), and bell-shaped curves, and deans' lists, and No-Doz, and blue books, and crib sheets, and proctors, and the rest.

We have indeed always had them, although there is literally not a shred of research evidence which supports the present grading system. They are about as accurate as the gas mileage statements out of Detroit and about as objective as an old maid telling you her age. That we have tolerated grades for so long makes me seriously question whether we have even fewer brains that we do intellectuals on our college campuses.

Grades must go. Their only genuine function is to serve certain administrative conveniences. They *do* allow the registrar and members of the deanery to decide who is on probation, and who can take an honors course, and who sits on the dais at Phi Bet banquets, and so forth, but they are too destructive to be allowed to continue to debase what a university could be.

FIVE REASONS WHY

1. Grades separate students and professors into two warring camps, both armed with dangerous weapons, none of which has anything to do with a notion of a community of scholars. The grades keep student from teacher and teacher from student as effectively as if each wore the sweaty jerseys of two archrivals fighting for a bid to a bowl game.

A student cannot praise a professor's teaching within earshot of other students, or he would be slashed to ribbons for "brownnosing." However, in the comfortable privacy of a professor's office, the slippery students keep their appointments, and get in the "brownie points" which, they have well learned, is one practical way to raise their grade-point averages. Sadly, this same awareness keeps many students with integrity away from the professor's office.

*From Simon, Sidney B.: Grades must go. *School Review, 78:*No. 3, 397-402, May, 1970. Published by University of Chicago Press. Copyright ©1970 by University of Chicago. All rights reserved.

If praise cannot be given, open criticism of a professor to his face is even rarer. It simply would not be politic. Even if you had some hint about how to make his course better, the implied disapproval would surely earn retaliation. So it passes that students and faculty—the two groups on a campus which most need to find each other—are separated by a wall as impenetrable as barbed wire, known as a transcript.

2. Grades overreward the wrong people and often punish students who need to be punished the least. There is something basically immoral about a system which passes out its highest institutional appreciation to a meritocracy based on memorization, clever use of mnemonic devices, test wisdom, and various symptoms of anal compulsiveness.

The dean's list is made up of just too many such people—grade grubbers who seem to lack that certain spark of creativity, sensitivity, or even humanity. The finely-sifted ones who make the honorary societies are often not necessarily dishonorable, but their unmitigated self-advancement tends to make you wonder why the university makes so much fuss over such people at graduation. The world is dying from selfishness, and yet the academic world gives asterisks for it on commencement programs.

At the other end of the continuum, grades have been used systematically to screen out black students, to decide who to ship out to Vietnam, and to firmly remind those who will not conform that they are failures. It becomes increasingly clear that those who knuckle under to the grading system and learn what reality is all about ("Look, the guy likes Buber, so I give him Buberisms all semester") are the ones who reap the rewards. Those who question the system or resist it often get flunked out, neatly and sometimes finally.

3. Grades tend to destroy what learning should be all about. Students sign up for snap and crap courses they neither need nor want but which give a sure "B" without requiring many papers, or much reading, and so on. Students avoid courses which they might be curious about but in which they cannot afford a low grade because it would mess up their "cum."

Craftier students soon learn to balance their 15-18 semester hours with a mixture of hard markers and easy markers, and like good consumers, they budget their time each night and study a little of this and a little of that. Passionately wanting to go and learn something in real depth is somehow looked upon as slightly uncouth. After all, those "meaty" courses with a midterm, a term paper or two, a final, and three snap quizzes scattered here and there (so we can divide by five and get a good, objective average in order to give you a good, objective grade) have to be spread out carefully if one is to "keep up."

Only the wastrel reads novels or plays which are not assigned, and no one except a fool spends more time in the library than he must to pad out, with the right number of footnotes, a paper which the student guesses the professor will like (whether the student cares deeply about it doesn't matter).

Pragmatism, then, requires students to begin approaching the selection of courses like the directors of a conservative mutual fund picking out a portfolio of safe investments— everything in moderation. It is little wonder that so many graduates later join the Book-of-the-Month Club to be told what to read.

4. Grades reinforce an archaic notion of "competition" which may well turn out to be deadly in the 1970s. Sure, life is competitive, at least if you are in the business of selling storm windows or aluminum siding. Yes, Ford, Chevy, and Plymouth would like to slice each other's throats for a bigger chunk of the market, and all three of them would like to rub Volkswagen off the map. Nevertheless, the skills of cooperation actually dominate a sane man's life much more than do the skills of competition.

God save the marriage where the man is in constant competition with his wife. Pray for the family where the siblings are turned against each other's jugular veins. Most of our efforts to make our neighborhoods and communities healthier and happier depend on some complex forms of cooperation. And almost everything the college graduate does today to make a living demands cooperation. Almost everything gets done through committees, and the really valuable co-worker knows the intricate skills of group process, and has the humanity necessary to control his ego and his competitive instincts. The point is, we don't have to teach competition; the beast in us is instinctively competitive. But we had better do more thinking about how to help ourselves become more civil so that we develop some range of responses beyond "What's in it for me?"

Competition for grades has made today's campuses lonely places. There are entirely too many students working for their own slightly sullied advancement into the above $20,000 brackets. Altruism and a sense of community just don't exist at most colleges and universities. Too many pages are slit from library books, making it impossible for the next person to get the assignment, and in one of those classes where the prof proudly tells you he will give as many F's as A's, just don't be absent, because you won't find many people who will give you their notes.

Four years and more of this kind of competitive treadmill might prepare a college graduate for ruthless dashes down the expressway at rush hour, but I surely would not want to be the first Negro to move into his block.

5. Of all the destructive things grades do, probably the ugliest is that they contribute to debasing a student's estimation of his own worth. The emphasis and extreme focus upon grades, term after term, seem to squeeze a student's identity and self-image within the narrow confines of his transcript.

Students everywhere are in a quandary. They have too little else upon which to test themselves. They are saddled with an extended adolescence. They have no real opportunities to be either independent or courageous or to test under duress their love of their fellow-man. As a consequence, students often stake their identity, almost their total sense of self, upon that grade-point average.

We do not know how many of them, in the lonely hours of the night, sit and divide their grade-point averages out to the tenth decimal point. However, we do know that a large percentage of the suicides at our universities stem, in part, from those decimals—at least, from misguided interpretations of their significance.

How could we have allowed those numbers to spew widespread feelings of inadequacy, inferiority, and lack of power among perfectly useful and decent people? Have you heard of students who have given up careers because they thought they just didn't "have it" when they received a low grade in a basic course in their major? The worshipping at the shrine of numbers is a kind of madness which we accept almost without reflection and which has about as much validity as treating a cancer with a spray deodorant.

The pursuit of grades has dried up the average student's sense that he can shape and change the world around him. With his eye on the carrot at the end of the semester, he does not really believe that he can make a course better. He doesn't really believe that students can and should have some stake in evaluating their education. It is almost heresy for him to believe that he has some valid insights into the hiring and firing of professors. Not wanting to antagonize the grade givers, he does not complain about large classes, irrelevant lectures, inappropriate assignments, unnecessary prerequisites, or even an unreadable textbook.

How many of our students simply do not know who they are because for so many years they have been jumping hurdles put up by other people? Finally, on their own, they do not seem to have the resources for making meaningful choices or building values to live by. Otherwise, would so many of them end up like the characters in John Cheever's Shady Hill suburb? Those urbane, handsome, ivy-league types going off to high-paying jobs that they hate (made tolerable by martinis at lunch), marrying attractive-but-shallow girls, raising children who greet them with, "What did you buy me?" and tolerating terrible abuse from their bosses so as not to get fired and thereby jeopardize the country club membership, the $40,000 development house, the vinyl hardtop, and their credit with the orthodontist: Is that what a college education is supposed to produce?

Over and over I hear the phrase, "Well, that's reality." However, I think we are long overdue in examining a greater reality behind the grading system. It may be called "reality" to say, "All colleges have grades," but all colleges do *not* have them. It may be reality to say, "Grades are the only thing that graduate schools are concerned about," but the best of the graduate schools are becoming less and less concerned about them. When people say, "Well, that's the system," I want to shout, "Systems have been changed."

I believe we ignore at great peril the greater reality of a learning environment in which students and professors become increasingly alienated from each other, where cheating and the con man are daily operative, and where what a student gets out of a course can be boiled down to a single, crude letter of the alphabet.

I am convinced that a real onslaught upon the grading system could have dramatic and immediate positive impact upon our universities. If nothing else, many of the most flagrant academic abuses might be flushed out into the open.

Professors who can't teach will be forced to face that truth if we take away the protection of their dangling A's and F's. Professors who can teach but who get more of the institutional rewards from doing research or playing grantsmanship may get back to teaching. Busy-work assignments will be challenged and so will those fraudulent reading assignments (2,000 pages a weekend?). Students will shape and change many assignments they now merely accept. Assignments will be more individualized and the curriculum will take on a new relevancy. It is no wonder that the old guard, including those Uncle Tom students who say, "Why, I don't see what's wrong with the grading system. Mister Charlie, he treats me real good, especially at transcript time," will resist doing away with the present grading system.

Change is coming, however. The danger is that we may merely be satisfied with a little tinkering here and a bit of adjusting there. A limited pass-fail system will not be sufficient to remove that insane cry from our colleges: "Wadjaget?"

What we really need is a sweeping awareness among students that they are being shortchanged at that supermarket they call alma mater. They need to realize that they are the customers, and, as such, they have every right to demand that they get a real education. They must learn to see through our ruses. They must not allow themselves to be bought off with green stamps which they glue into their transcripts and turn in at the redemption center at graduation time for credentials. Grades must go.

44 assessing student progress: a criterion-referenced measurement approach

Ronald K. Hambleton

Our schools have recently implemented many innovative instructional models such as *Computer-Assisted Instruction* (Atkinson, 1968), *Mastery Learning* (Bloom, 1968; Carroll, 1963), *Individualized Instruction* (Glaser, 1968), and *Project PLAN* (Flanagan, 1967). Features such as the specification of the curriculum in terms of behavioral objectives, detailed diagnosis of beginning students, the availability of alternative instructional modes, individual pacing and sequencing of material, and the careful monitoring of student progress, are common to many of these instructional models. Tests are used within these models to establish an individual's achievement on specified content (i.e., instructional objectives) and to provide information for making a variety of instructional decisions.

Unfortunately, the most common procedures for constructing, administering, and analyzing tests and interpreting scores are less useful within the context of these new instructional models, and in some cases are completely inappropriate because the traditional *norm-referenced tests* are specifically constructed to estimate each individual's ability level relative to that of other individuals. (College Board Achievement tests, for example, exist specifically to rank students according to achievement.) As a result, a new kind of testing, called *criterion-referenced testing,* has been developed. Such tests are specifically designed to meet the measurement needs of the new instructional models.

The movement toward criterion-referenced testing in the schools represents an important development advocated by many educators. However, many problems relating to such things as test construction, interpretation of test scores, and the development of reporting systems have yet to be resolved.

The purpose of this brief paper is to introduce the nature of criterion-referenced testing, to make some distinctions between norm-referenced and criterion-referenced tests and measurements, and to describe one use of criterion-referenced tests in an individually prescribed instruction program.

CRITERION-REFERENCED TESTS

Glaser (1963) introduced the term *criterion-referenced test* to make the distinction between tests designed to compare individuals and tests designed to measure individual achievement relative to some specified domain of tasks. Of the various definitions proposed for criterion-referenced tests (e.g., Kriewall, 1969; Ivens, 1970) we prefer that of Glaser and Nitko (1971): "A criterion-referenced test is one that is deliberately constructed to yield measurements that are directly interpretable in terms of specified performance standards." According to them:

> Performance standards are generally specified by defining a class or domain of tasks that should be performed by the individual. Measurements are taken on representative samples of tasks drawn from this domain, and such measurements are referenced directly to this domain for each individual measured.

Unfortunately, because of their newness and some unique problems to be described later, there is a shortage of information on criterion-referenced tests. However, it is still disappointing to note that even the most recent educational measurement textbooks seldom include more than one or two pages on the topic. According to Cronbach (1970), "The testing movement has given too much attention to comparative interpretations (to individual differences) and too little to absolute, criterion-referenced measurement." As more and more schools adopt instructional models that require criterion-referenced testing the need for such information becomes ever more acute.

A COMPARISON OF NORM-REFERENCED AND CRITERION-REFERENCED TESTING

Norm-Referenced Tests. Almost all of the available aptitude and achievement tests can be classified as norm-referenced because they are designed to measure individual differences. The meaning of any particular score can be determined only by comparing it to other scores achieved by students taking the test. A standard procedure is to report the percentage of examinees in different groups whose scores fall below particular values (i.e., percentile norm tables), thus making it possible to interpret an individual's score relative to those of students in several different groups.

A norm-referenced test is specifically constructed to maximize the variability of test scores, since such a test is more likely to produce fewer errors in ordering the individuals on the measured ability. Since norm-referenced tests are often used for selection purposes, it follows that minimizing the number of errors in ranking individuals is extremely important.

Test construction procedures used with norm-referenced tests usually select items which will produce tests with desired statistical properties rather than representing some content domain (Gronlund, 1971). It is partly because of this fact that such test scores cannot be interpreted as an accurate representation of knowledge of some content domain. Both easy and difficult items usually do not appear in norm-referenced tests because they contribute very little to test score variance. Also, items are usually removed which do not measure the same ability as most other items in the test. Empirical evidence to support these conclusions is provided by Cox (1965). His work revealed that the selection of items from a total item pool by the usual item selection procedures (i.e., item difficulty indices—proportions of individuals correctly responding to items—and item discrimination indices—measures of the relationship between success on the item and performance on some criterion test, usually the total test score) resulted in tests which contained different proportions of items measuring instructional objectives from those in the total item pool.

Criterion-Referenced Tests. The emphasis on mastery learning in the new instructional models has led to an interest by measurement specialists in criterion-referenced testing. Such tests can be used to serve two purposes. First, they can provide very specific information on individual performance levels on the instructional objectives. This information can be used, for example, to determine whether an individual has "mastered" particular objectives (Block, 1971).

Second, criterion-referenced tests can be used to evaluate the effectiveness of instruction. Norm-referenced tests given at the end of a course are usually inappropriate in evaluating the effectiveness of instruction because they are not designed to cover the instructional objectives. However, criterion-referenced tests are useful in this regard because the test can be constructed so that the results will specifically measure the instructional objectives.

Typically, the items on a criterion-referenced test can be regarded as a sample from some well-defined content domain. Although in considering a student's test score alone we cannot say accurately which items he answered correctly, we can make a pretty good estimate of the proportion of items in the entire domain that he could answer (Popham and Husek, 1969).

What are the appropriate procedures for constructing a criterion-referenced test? Since comparisons among individuals are of little or no interest when using such a test, it follows that a test constructor is not concerned with the usual practice of developing a test to maximize the variance of test scores. Therefore, he should not use traditional item selection procedures because they are specifically designed to produce a test with maximum test score variance. For example, criterion-referenced tests are often used either before or immediately after the teaching of specific instructional objectives. In the former situation, most students will answer few or none of the test items, but in the latter situation they will answer most or all of them. In both situations there will be very little variation among students in their total scores on the test and in their responses to specific items. Consequently, the usual indices assessing an item's discriminating power, which were developed for constructing norm-referenced tests, will be very close to zero. Thus, there is a distinct possibility that if traditional item selection procedures are applied to construction of criterion-referenced tests, many good items will be unwisely discarded. A test theory developed specifically for criterion-referenced tests is needed to aid those constructing such instruments. Some progress has been made in this direction by Cronbach and Gleser (1965), Kriewall (1969), Glaser and Nitko (1971), and Hambleton and Novick (1972).

DISTINCTION BETWEEN TESTING INSTRUMENTS AND MEASUREMENT

The differences between norm-referenced and criterion-referenced tests can be further clarified by properly distinguishing between testing instruments and measurement. Certainly criterion-referenced measurement is substantially different from norm-referenced measurement. In the former, the measurements are used to evaluate student performance relative to specific performance levels. In the latter, measurements are used for making comparative decisions among individuals.

The major distinction between norm-referenced and criterion-referenced measurement is in terms of the kind of information available. With the availability of a theory for making norm-referenced measurements, we have procedures for constructing optimum measuring instruments, i.e., norm-referenced tests. The pertinent question now seems to be whether or not the instructional models which require different kinds of measurement require new kinds of tests or alternate procedures for interpreting the scores of the usual tests. We subscribe to the belief that new tests are needed, constructed in ways which are substantially different from the traditional approaches. We distinguish a criterion-referenced test from a norm-referenced test on the basis of the procedures used to construct them.

It should be noted that a norm-referenced test can be used for criterion-referenced measurement, although with some difficulty, since the sampling of items is such that many objectives will not be covered on the test, or will be covered by only a few items. Also, a criterion-referenced test constructed by procedures especially designed to make criterion-referenced measurements can also be used to make norm-referenced measurements. However, a criterion-referenced test is not constructed specifically to maximize the variability of test scores and because of the smaller relative differences among students, such a test is likely to produce more errors in ordering individuals on the measured ability. Clearly a norm-referenced test can be used to make criterion-referenced measurement and a criterion-referenced test can be used for norm-referenced measurement, but both usages will be less than optimal (Hambleton and Novick, 1972).

Thus, it would seem misleading to talk about tests as either norm-referenced or criterion-referenced, since measurements obtained from either can be interpreted relative to norms, criteria, or both. But it is clear that a test constructed for making one kind of measurement is not likely to be optimal for making the other.

DECISION-THEORETIC APPROACH TO CRITERION-REFERENCED MEASUREMENT

Our own conceptual framework for criterion-referenced measurement is as follows. Like Cronbach and Gleser (1965), we see testing as a decision-theoretic process—that is, tests are given for the purpose of aiding in making decisions. One of the main differences between norm-referenced and criterion-referenced tests is the kind of decisions they are specifically designed to make. Norm-referenced tests are particularly useful in situations when one is interested in "fixed-quota" selection (i.e., only a certain number of individuals will be selected regardless of their qualifications), or ranking individuals according to an ability.

Decisions relating to mastery of instructional materials are best made with criterion-referenced tests. With these tests we have what Cronbach and Gleser would call a "quota-free" selection problem. That is, there is no limit to the number of individuals who can exceed the *cut-off score* on a criterion-referenced test. A cut-off score for a criterion-referenced test is set to separate examinees into two mutually exclusive groups. One group comprises those with high enough test scores (greater than or equal to the cut-off score) to assume they have mastered the material to a desired level of proficiency. The second group is made up of examinees who did not achieve the minimum proficiency standard.

The educational goal is achievement of the standards by everyone. Its fulfillment is attempted by individualizing instruction to the point of providing alternate instructional modes (Cronbach, 1967), individual pacing and sequencing, and providing various remedial programs.

The primary measurement problem involved in determining if established criteria are met by the student in the new instructional models can be stated as determining whether $\hat{p}_i$, an estimate of p_i, is greater than p_o. Here p_i is the "true" score for an individual [i] in some particular content domain. It represents his knowledge—the proportion of items in the content domain that he could answer successfully. Since we cannot administer all items in the domain, we sample some small number to obtain an estimate of p_i, represented as $\hat{p}_i$. This is his proportion-correct score. The value of p_o is the somewhat arbitrary cutting score used to divide individuals into those who have and have not mastered the domain.

Basically, then, the tester's problem is to locate each examinee in the correct mastery category. There are two kinds of errors that occur in this classification problem: false positive errors and false negative errors. A false positive error occurs when the tester estimates an examinee's ability to be above the cutting score when in fact it is not. A false negative error occurs when the tester estimates an examinee's ability to be below the cutting score when the reverse is true. The seriousness of making a false positive error depends to some extent on the structure of the instructional objectives. It would seem that this kind of error has the most serious effect on program efficiency when the instructional objectives are interdependent. On the other hand, the seriousness of making a false negative error would seem to depend on the length of time a student would be assigned to a remedial program because of his low test performance and how this mis-assignment would affect his future learning. It should be noted that since many students who are misclassified are close to the cutting score, the remedial work is not completely inappropriate for them.

In practical applications of criterion-referenced testing it would seem that in order to evaluate the test it would be necessary to know how reliable the test is (i.e., how closely results on alternate forms of the test agree). Another consideration is the validity of decision-making with these tests (i.e., how closely the test results estimate the student's actual knowledge). The problems of reliability and validity estimation for criterion-referenced tests have not to date been satisfactorily solved; however, there are several papers that deal with the topic, including Bormuth (1970), Hambleton and Gorth (1971), Hambleton and Novick (1972), and Popham and Husek (1969).

CRITERION-REFERENCED TESTING: AN APPLICATION

A new instructional model that is typical of many now implemented in schools around the country is the one used in the Jamesville-DeWitt (JD) High School in DeWitt, New York (O'Reilly and Hambleton, 1971; Hambleton, Gorth, and O'Reilly, 1972). This ninth grade individualized instruction program in science is organized into *instructional modules,* which consist of activities designed to teach a single major concept that is expressed in terms of behavioral objectives. The instructional activities in a module are subdivided into smaller submodules called learning activity packages (LAPs). As each student proceeds through an instructional module, a number of decisions must be made about him. To provide information for this decision-making, the following criterion-referenced tests are administered: a module pre-test, a module post-test, and several LAP pre-tests and post-tests.

Briefly, let us consider each decision separately. As a student begins to work on a module, a module pre-test is administered. On the basis of his test performance, the teacher prepares a prescription indicating the particular LAPs in the module in which he needs instruction. Such a procedure insures that students work only on learning experiences directed toward goals which have not been previously mastered. The module post-test, which is either the same as, or an alternate form of, the module pre-test can be used for prescribing remedial work, for grading, and for evaluating the effectiveness of the instruction in the LAPs.

Analogous to the module pre-tests, the LAP pre-tests are used to prescribe a set of objectives within the LAP in which the student must demonstrate competency before moving on to the next LAP in his prescription. LAP post-tests are used to determine the extent to which students have satisfactorily completed the objectives of the LAP.

Decisions relating to the diagnosis of learning difficulties can also be made from criterion-referenced tests if the incorrect choices for the items have been carefully constructed, i.e., incorrect choices are included in an item because they are indicative of particular learning difficulties. Apparently this systematic construction of incorrect choices to multiple-choice items has not been carefully explored, but it offers much potential. In addition to being an excellent way of extracting more information from a test, it offers a systematic way for constructing choices to multiple-choice items.

One still unsolved problem for programs similar in format to the JD model is the development of guidelines for establishing cut-off points (ie., how many items must an individual pass on a criterion-referenced test to demonstrate mastery). To date this usually has been done rather arbitrarily.

Another problem found in some of the new instructional models is the extensive amount of time consumed by testing. Although testing provides data for decision-making, and maximizing the number of correct decisions is desirable, it is apparent that the cost in terms of time is too high to allow tests to be long enough to insure low probabilities of error for all types of decisions. Thus it seems clear that procedures need to be developed to assist users of criterion-referenced tests in determining the desirable lengths of their tests, taking into account the importance of the test, the cost, and the total amount of time available for testing.

While increasing test length is an obvious way of reducing errors in decision-making, alternate means include tailored testing (Lord, 1970), differential weighting of response alternatives, and confidence testing (Wang and Stanley, 1970; Hambleton et al., 1970). All three approaches, based on intuitively appealing ideas, can be used with criterion-referenced test items and offer more information per item on each examinee. However, there is little empirical data to support any of the approaches in this context.

Summary. It should be clear that there are still many unresolved problems in developing an operational criterion-referenced measurement model for assessing student mastery in the schools. Defining well-specified content domains, developing procedures for generating appropriate samples of test items, and setting performance standards represent significant problems for measurement specialists that have not been treated here. It is encouraging to note that there is probably more research now being conducted on criterion-referenced testing than in any other area in educational measurement. Thus it should not be long before practical solutions are found to the problems.

REFERENCES

Atkinson, R.C.: Computer-based instruction in initial reading. *In* Proceedings of the 1967 Invitational Conference on Testing Problems. Princeton, New Jersey, Educational Testing Service, 1968.

Block, J.H.: Criterion-referenced measurements: Potential. *School Review, 69*: 289-298, 1971.

Bloom, B.S.: Learning for mastery. *Evaluation Comment, 1*: No. 2, 1968.

Bormuth, J.R.: On the Theory of Achievement Test Items. Chicago, University of Chicago Press, 1970.

Carroll, J.E.: A model of school learning. *Teachers College Record, 64*: 723-733, 1963.

Cox, R.C.: Item selection techniques and evaluation of instructional objectives. *Journal of Educational Measurement, 2*: 181-185, 1965.

Cronbach, L.J.: How can instruction be adapted to individual differences? *In* Gagné, R.M. (ed.): Learning and Individual Differences. Columbus, Ohio, Merrill Books, 1967.

Cronbach, L.J.: Validation of educational measures. *In* Proceedings of the 1969 Invitational Conference on Testing Problems. Princeton, New Jersey, Educational Testing Service, 1970.

Cronbach, L.J., and Gleser, Goldine C.: Psychological Tests and Personnel Decisions. 2nd ed. Urbana, Ill., University of Illinois Press, 1965.

Flanagan, J.C.: Functional education for the seventies. *Phi Delta Kappan, 49*: 27-32, 1967.

Glaser, R.: Adapting the elementary school curriculum to individual performance. *In* Proceedings of the 1967 Invitational Conference on Testing Problems. Princeton, New Jersey, Educational Testing Service, 1968.

Glaser, R.: Instructional technology and the measurement of learning outcomes. *American Psychologist, 18*: 519-521, 1963.

Glaser, R., and Nitko, A.J.: Measurement in learning and instruction. *In* Thorndike, R.L. (ed.): Educational Measurement. Washington, American Council on Education, 1971.

Gronlund, N.E.: Measurement and Evaluation in Teaching. 2nd ed. New York, The MacMillan Company, 1971.

Hambleton, R.K., and Gorth, W.P.: Criterion-referenced testing: Issues and applications. *Center for Educational Research Technical Report #13*. Amherst, University of Massachusetts School of Education, 1971.

Hambleton, R.K., Gorth, W.P., and O'Reilly, R.P.: A formative evaluation model for classroom instruction. *Center for Educational Research Technical Report #16*. Amherst, University of Massachusetts School of Education, 1972.

Hambleton, R.K., and Novick, M.R.: Toward an integration of theory and method for criterion-referenced tests. *ACT Technical Report No. 53*. Iowa City, Iowa, The American College Testing Program, 1972.

Hambleton, R.K., Roberts, D.M., and Traub, R.E.: A comparison of the reliability and validity of two methods for assessing partial knowledge on a multiple-choice test. *Journal of Educational Measurement, 7*: 75-82, 1970.

Ivens, S.H.: An investigation of item analysis, reliability and validity in relation to criterion-referenced tests. Unpublished doctoral dissertation, Florida State University, 1970.

Kriewall, T.E.: Applications of information theory and acceptance sampling principles to the management of mathematics instruction. Unpublished doctoral dissertation, University of Wisconsin, 1969.

Lord, F.M.: Some test theory for tailored testing. *In* Holtzman, W. (ed.): Computer-Assisted Instruction, Testing, and Guidance. New York, Harper and Row, 1970.

O'Reilly, R.B., and Hambleton, R.K.: A CMI model for an individualized learning program in ninth grade science. *Center for Educational Research Technical Report #14*, Amherst, University of Massachusetts School of Education, 1971.

Popham, W.J., and Husek, T.R.: Implications of criterion-referenced measurement. *Journal of Educational Measurement, 6*: 1-9, 1969.

Wang, Marilyn D., and Stanley, J.C.: Differential weighting: A review of methods and empirical studies. *Review of Educational Research, 40*: 663-705, 1970.

comprehensive 45
achievement
monitoring:
a balance between
program and pupil
evaluation

William Phillip Gorth

Teaching can be like the patent medicine business. It certainly does not include the outrightly dishonest characteristics associated with patent medicine, but it does have many parallels with it. The patent medicine business can be described as one man making a brew or medicine which he feels is a cure for some, if not all, ailments. His conviction about the value of his brew is always strongly held and often sincere. Although he is the main supporter of his medicine, he often finds many followers. He has a long list of impressive anecdotes telling of individuals who have used his medicine and have been miraculously cured. However, someone trying to decide whether to use the medicine has no systematic information about its effect on people in general. The prospective user is not sure whether ninety people out of a hundred have been cured or whether one person out of a hundred seems to be cured.

In many ways, teaching follows the same patterns described for patent medicine. Like the patent medicine salesman, the teacher is often the developer of his own materials. The teacher has strong positive opinions about the effectiveness and usefulness of his materials, and a sincere conviction that they are of value to his students. To support these claims every teacher who has personally developed new instructional materials has a list of several students who have demonstrated impressive learning while using his materials. While it is probably true that some individuals were able to learn in an outstanding fashion from the materials, no systematic information is available about the success of all of the students who have used them. Even if only one or two students out of a hundred were outstandingly successful, the teacher would still have examples to support his claims.

The worst offenders of this phenomenon, developing but not testing materials, are teachers who have developed individualized instructional packages. Individualized instruction places the responsibility for success or failure on the student regardless of the quality of the materials from which he is learning. Poor materials, which do not successfully or logically treat concepts, are often used repeatedly because students are expected to master them before they move on to other packages in the individualized instruction program. The teacher automatically considers the students to be responsible for failure, rather than assessing the adequacy of his materials.

Comprehensive Achievement Monitoring is a strategy for classroom evaluation. It provides information that teachers can use to evaluate their materials as well as to determine the progress of individual students. The usual classroom testing supplies information which is not comprehensive or systematic enough to serve as a basis for evaluating materials but can be used only for judging progress of individual students.

Although there are many variations and many refinements of the testing strategy most frequently used by classroom teachers today, it often has the following characteristics. A teacher will develop a lesson plan for a semester's work, plan the students' activities and homework, and begin to teach this material. Every two to five weeks he will write a test consisting of questions which measure the material just taught. Thus, the test is usually written after the teaching has occurred. After students take the test, they are rated on their score relative to the class. Students are not evaluated in terms of their learning of each component prescribed in the lesson plan, nor are the class's results used as a source of information for evaluating the effectiveness of the teaching which preceded the test.

The description of usual classroom testing should be familiar—it is the strategy which teachers have used for many, many years. Unfortunately, it is this strategy which creates the situation in education which is similar to the patent medicine business.

Classroom testing of this kind has many shortcomings which influence the usefulness of the testing information to the teacher. For instance, the results from such a test are at best tied to the lesson plan which the teacher has written. Often the lesson plan does not include specific knowledge or skills that the student should learn, but only the general topical areas which the teacher will cover. These tests are most often written after instruction or after teaching has occurred. Therefore, they may not be representative of the goals the teacher intended when he designed the lesson plan. Very often the emphasis of the test reflects the emphasis which occurred in the class. Although there should be flexibility in teaching, it is important to keep in mind both what is emphasized and what is omitted. The only way to keep the omitted materials in mind is to include them in a classroom test so that it can be definitely determined whether or not students have learned them. Most often, the testing schedule is not designed systematically to extract a maximum amount of useful information, but arbitrarily to meet other criteria (e.g., a test every Friday). What systematic design exists is intended to facilitate comparison of individual students rather than evaluation of the components of the course. In the common practice of grading "on a curve" the relative grades of the students are recorded, but the average grade, which presumably bears some relation to effectiveness of the materials, is usually considered only in terms of the test being "too hard" or "too easy."

Nothing in this usual pattern produces any information about what students know before they are taught. Even if they completely understand the material which the teacher is going to present, this will not be discovered unless there is some kind of testing before the teaching begins. Failure to determine the students' starting points can lead to tremendous inefficiency in teaching, either because they are being taught something they already know, or because they're being asked to learn something they lack sufficient background to understand. Furthermore, if their starting points are unknown, it is impossible to measure their progress in a given program.

No serious attempt is made to see how well students retain material on a long-term basis. The focus of usual classroom testing is on individual grading immediately after teaching. The teacher has no systematic way of finding out what students have forgotten several weeks after the usual classroom test on the material. The final exam usually covers so broad an area that it is impossible to pick out specific knowledge and skills forgotten by individual students. Yet information indicating what students are forgetting is vital in determining what should be reviewed. The teacher needs this information to judge the long-term effectiveness of the activities he has designed.

Comprehensive Achievement Monitoring (CAM) is a recently developed alternative strategy for gathering information about students in a classroom setting. It has many advantages over ordinary classroom testing and is particularly useful in providing information on program or course effectiveness. CAM will be described briefly and several of its advantages explained.

What is Comprehensive Achievement Monitoring? The procedure for using CAM requires the following steps. Before evaluation can take place, the curriculum or course is defined in terms of instructional or behavioral objectives. These clearly specify what students are expected to learn in a course and are much more detailed than a teacher's typical lesson plan. At least four test items are written to measure students' learning of each objective defined for a course. By using several test items to measure each objective, the teacher is given more thorough information about the students' mastery of the objectives than is possible with one test item. All of the test items measuring the objectives of a course (or a shorter span of time such as a semester or a quarter) are arranged on test forms. Typically, there may be from five to fifteen test forms developed for an elementary or high school subject. All of the test forms look like a final test because items which measure the entire range of the course objectives are put on each test form. When these test forms are used throughout a semester, information is gathered not just about the recently taught objectives but about all of the material which is to be covered or has been covered in a course.

The students take tests at regular intervals (typically every two or three weeks), which are called test administrations. At each test administration all test forms are used. The test forms are evenly divided and approximately the same number of students take the same test form at each test administration. There are systematic ways to make sure that the same student is not given the same test form more than once during a semester, and that students are allowed to answer the questions on each test form sometime during the semester. After each test administration, the results from all students are collated to provide information about each objective. Each student's results are also analyzed to supply data on his progress.

Comprehensive achievement monitoring has many advantages over ordinary classroom testing. Since all of the information gathered using CAM is related to specific objectives, the teacher is able to interpret assessments of individual students' progress or program effectiveness in terms of the specific objectives which he has set for the course. By designing the test items and test forms before teaching occurs (usually at the beginning of the school year or during the summer) according to the objectives he has defined for the course, the teacher can ensure that the tests measure all the objectives, not just the ones emphasized in class. This systematic approach does not limit the teacher only to previously defined objectives and a specific emphasis in the classroom, but it does keep him aware of his original goals. It will help assure that if he alters his goals and emphasis, he does so in a rational way, rather than simply wandering away from his original objective and getting lost.

This systematic approach to designing tests provides teachers with a method of gathering information about things emphasized in class as well as those not emphasized. Because each test covers all the material to be presented during the semester or course, the teacher has information available on all of the objectives at each test administration. This information about objectives not yet taught enables the teacher to determine whether students have already learned or mastered the objectives by some other means. Information about the objectives which have just been taught indicates how well students have been able to master the objectives based upon the instruction given. Objectives which had been taught many weeks before the test are also measured; therefore, the teacher has information on whether students are forgetting the ideas which they learned earlier. Although each student discovers how he performed on each test form at each test administration, CAM's biggest advantage is that the results can be collated to provide information about the program. The program can be evaluated in terms of what students know before they are taught, what they learn immediately after they are taught, what they remember by the end of the program and how this knowledge relates to the objectives that have been set for the program. Teachers can use this information to improve the weak parts of their programs while saving and reusing the particularly successful parts.

Comprehensive achievement monitoring has been used in schools across the country. School districts in more than six states have developed operational CAM projects. Over 40,000 students are now being monitored by CAM in a variety of different courses and grade levels. The levels at which CAM has already demonstrated its usefulness in helping teachers to identify student learning and to evaluate curricular materials range from the third grade through high school and junior college to college. At every grade level, teachers have found the information collected by CAM useful to them. Specifically, teachers have used CAM at the elementary school level in reading, language arts, and mathematics programs; at the junior high school level in mathematics, science, and English programs; at the high school level in history, English, physical education, science, grammar, foreign languages, and mathematics; and at the college level in introductory courses in educational statistics, educational measurement, and educational psychology.

At all levels, CAM has proved extremely successful in providing useful information to a variety of persons. Students at all levels are interested in CAM as a source of information about their progress and their strengths and weaknesses. Teachers find the information useful in advising students. In addition, they can use CAM information to evaluate curricular materials, teaching styles, and course objectives.

CAM can bring teaching out of the patent medicine business into the status of a profession. With CAM, educators can keep themselves accurately informed of students' progress in learning relative to the objectives of the program. They need not assume simply that students know nothing before they're taught, and retain what they learn indefinitely. No longer will they have to rely on guesswork to know how effective their teaching is, since CAM will supply data indicating their strengths and weaknesses. Education will become more effective, and the ultimate beneficiaries will be the students.

SECTION SIX
TEACHERS

"*A rose is a . . . sort of like I mean a . . . you know . . . rose . . . is . . . like . . . you know . . . a rose . . . right?*"

*What should the role of the professional educator be—if,
indeed, the term professional is justified or desirable? In a
book such as this, it's tempting to heap praise upon the
profession. But to do so would be to ignore vital questions
that deserve careful consideration.*

*There are several interrelated issues here, most prominent
among them teachers' unions, "professionalism," and
accountability. These are deeply intertwined with the relationship of teachers and the community, and particularly
with the very touchy question of who should control the
schools (see the discussion in the* School/Society *section).
Elsie Cross and Irving Rosenstein ask the central question
bluntly: "Do teachers want what students need?"*

*An essential part of the rhetoric of teachers' unions is that
they consider "better schooling" for students a vital goal.
There certainly are reasons to hope that better-paid teachers
with more preparation time would be better teachers. But
then, no one could seriously expect even the most mercenary
teacher to publicly announce, "Screw the kids, we want more
money."*

*Some of the more radical educational critics have argued that
student and teacher interests have little in common, and that
the concept of a class struggle might even be appropriate.
To follow Jerry Farber's notion of "student as nigger"
(noting that, owing to compulsory attendance laws, those
under sixteen haven't even been emancipated yet), how much
benefit can students expect from unionization of their over-
seers? Though this may be an overstatement of the issue,
many less radical critics hold that the improvements that the
unions promise will do little good in the face of more fundamental problems obstructing learning (see, for example,
Eugene Howard's article, "Structure and Function in the
Classroom").*

*The question of "professionalization" is closely related to
unionization (although there has been some argument that*

the two goals are not really compatible). The term professional certainly has a nice sound to it. In addition to increased
status, the professionalization of teaching can mean great
gains for teachers in salary and, hopefully, in competence as
well. But what are the costs of professionalism? Teachers
point to medicine as an ideal profession, but there are
problems with this analogy which can too easily be ignored.
As medicine has become increasingly specialized, a large gap
has developed between patient and professional. It is now a
serious problem, which has led to much discontent with
present means of health care.

> In modern medical practice, which is now focused predominantly
> on technical knowledge, the physician may be engrossed in
> technical concerns and arcane terminology that mystify the patient.
> The traditional system of a close, long-term relationship with a
> "family doctor" is being replaced for the patient by short-term
> encounters with specialists. Moreover, many physicians no longer
> attach high importance to personal rapport with the patient; to
> some the "bedside manner" seems a concession to salesmanship not
> befitting a medical scientist. As we shall see, however, the failure to
> establish empathy with patients can be a serious bar to communi-
> cation and patient response. (Indeed, the common neglect of this
> psychological factor by doctors may account in part for the flour-
> ishing of quacks and faith healers, whose main attraction for sick
> people is their skill in furnishing emotional reassurance.) *

Education is different from medicine in ways which aggravate
this problem. While a doctor merely has to convince the parent to give medicine to his child regularly, an educator may
ask him to change his behavior. Psychological matters, such as
education, require much more complete rapport than physical
ones. Yet education has begun to develop a penchant for
polysyllabic jargon. Albert Yee earlier argued that educational
researchers have made little or no effort to translate this into
something intelligible to the teacher. If the teacher is able to
master this material, will he be able to explain it to parents—
or will they see it simply as more "fast talking?"

One of the goals of professionalization is a professional scale
of pay. There's little question but that fifty years ago,
teachers' salaries were grossly inadequate. Now teachers earn

---

*Korsch, Barbara M., and Negrete, Vida Francis: Doctor-patient communication. *Scientific American,* 227 (2):66, 1972.

something much more like a living wage. How good a "living wage" it is, and how appropriate it is to workers at the level of teachers, are, of course, open to question. The push for higher wages has not stopped, however, and is putting school boards in an increasingly difficult position.

School boards are caught between the irresistible force of teachers' union demands for wage hikes, and the immovable object of taxpayer refusal to pay higher taxes. Further, the state demands that they operate the schools. Because staff salaries represent about two-thirds of the average school operating budget, a ten per cent salary increase means a size-able increase in the entire school budget. The squeeze is worse in large cities, where the tax rates are already too high and the possibilities for more revenue essentially nil. The course of events is not clear, but the possibilities on both sides are disturbing.

The legal challenge to the property tax may raise some hopes of more money to finance schools. Some local problems could undoubtedly be solved if the poorer cities could ex-change the property tax for a system of state taxes. But it also might become a political football for state legislatures and ultimately simply place the conflict at a different level— between state teachers' associations and state legislatures.

Can the unions cut their own throats as the New York City pressmen did when their wage demands caused three of the city's six daily papers to fold? How much more are the tax-payers going to put up with? Perhaps the teachers' unions and the Taxpayers' Associations will combine to deschool society —by putting school systems into bankruptcy or subjecting them to perpetual strikes.

Do teachers want what students need? Substitute the words doctors and patients, and think about the problems of getting a doctor to make a house call. There are undoubtedly other bad examples. How many and how serious will the problems be?

do teachers want 46
what students need?

Elsie Y. Cross
Irving Rosenstein

In August 1963, Charles Cogen, president of the United Federation of Teachers, stood in the rain before 20,000 teachers assembled on Randells Island and waved a picket sign which read, TEACHERS WANT WHAT OUR CHILDREN NEED. That act adjourned a membership meeting of the New York City local of the American Federation of Teachers which had just voted to strike the largest school system in the country (Bleecker, 1968, p. 8). Teacher unionism had come a long way from its precarious foothold in a few cities in the early 1900's to that small island off Manhattan. The journey is even more remarkable when one realizes that during the first 45 years of its existence, from 1916, when the American Federation of Teachers (AFT) issued Membership Card Number One to John Dewey, to 1961, the membership never exceeded 30,000 and for many years dipped below 10,000 (Rotigel, 1967, pp. 19-22). The transformation since that eventful meeting has been consistent and startling. In a few short years, local affiliates of the AFT have waged and won battles in most of the nation's largest cities for the right to represent teachers in matters that affect their interests. From that beginning in New York City, the movement spread to Detroit, Cleveland, Milwaukee, Philadelphia, Washington, Boston, Chicago, and San Francisco. By 1965, the AFT had added 75,000 represented teachers through collective bargaining elections (Moscow, 1966, p. 107). This increased militancy of the AFT resulted in concomitant pressure by the National Education Association, and their organizational rivalry has produced some 600 substantive, bilateral, signed contracts with boards of education, containing salary agreements, grievance procedures, and clauses covering all manner of so-called "working conditions" and "professional" matters (Perry and Wildman, 1970, p. 12).

The early 1960's was a period marked by struggle for collective bargaining rights for teachers and victories for AFT affiliates in large urban school systems. The shibboleth was uniformly "democracy in education—education for democracy." The underlying implication was that the AFT would bring quality education to millions of children and young adults through local unions which functioned democratically. Educators across the country were told that by providing teachers with respectable salaries and fringe benefits, tenure, job security, and freedom from administrative harassment, unions would provide the climate which would make possible meaningful, substantive educational change. They were told that democratically elected union officials representing all teachers in a given school district would provide sensible, responsive leadership which would ultimately weld teachers into a force that would bring dignity through participation and change through united effort.

In unionism, teachers had finally discovered their power—the power of solidarity which culminated in final and binding agreements. How have they used that power? Have the successful organizational campaigns and written contracts of the 1960's resulted in the meaningful changes which were considered natural outgrowths of collective bargaining? Have contract clauses reflected an effort by teachers to control educational policy? Has class size been decreased, school staffs integrated? Who controls local unions and what are their educational philosophies? How are dissident teachers, the young, and radical change-oriented professionals dealt with? How have teacher unions translated into actual practice the banner, "Democracy in Education—Education for Democracy"? Has increased militancy among teachers resulted in significantly improved education for children, or have local union contracts concentrated on securing higher wages, better working conditions, and professional security for teachers to the almost total exclusion of concern for educational quality? In other words, do teachers really want what children need?

The following discussion will attempt to answer these questions by examining major issues which have surfaced during collective bargaining campaigns and contract negotiations, and the union's response to issues initiated by the community and students. Much of this discussion will focus on events in Philadelphia, Pennsylvania, since both authors were teachers, organizers, executive board members (officers of the union), and negotiators in that system during the period when the union was struggling to gain collective bargaining recognition, negotiating its first two contracts, and establishing itself as the exclusive teacher organization in the city.

NATIONAL MOVEMENT TOWARD COLLECTIVE BARGAINING

In the early 1960's, collective bargaining was at best a fuzzy concept in the minds of most teachers. Although teacher unions had been in existence for many years in large cities and some smaller ones, few union leaders sought bargaining rights. They had been content to cry havoc at board of education meetings, presenting programs to raise standards for teachers, reduce class size, and provide extra services for children. The New York City United Federation of Teachers (UFT) victory in 1961 provided the impetus for a national movement toward collective bargaining, in many cases dragging local leadership to the doorstep of the twentieth century. The initiative and strategy of full-time staff, provided by the AFL-CIO's Industrial Union Department, prodded local unions to change from mere debating societies to organizations that were strong and confident enough to effectively shut down schools and require boards of education to comply with their demands. In some cases, this full-time staff was openly resented by local leadership, who were unsure of their relationship to the labor movement and unwilling to acknowledge consciously the fact that the local was no longer the exclusive property of a small group of devoted founders and long-term members.

Philadelphia's leadership at the beginning of the sixties comprised the remnants of a union purged of suspected Communists during the 1940's and almost totally lacking in organizational ability. The evolution from a small, aggressive union with a membership of less than 500 teachers in 1960, to the bargaining representative of 12,000 teachers in 1965 required the skill of professional organizers who developed and projected issues which appealed to both special groups and the membership at large. They understood the concept of collective bargaining translated into terms of benefits for "professional" teachers.

One of the problems that became evident in Philadelphia, as elsewhere, was the difficulty of convincing teachers that unionization, as opposed to association, was a legitimate method for securing better salaries and working conditions for "professionals." Black teachers were particularly resistant to the blue collar tactics of labor organizing. Teachers and provincial PFT leaders had to be convinced that through collective bargaining they had a "two-fold opportunity of immense dimensions which must be grasped before it was too late. It was the opportunity, first, to raise the educational system to the level that our children need and deserve; and again, the opportunity to create conditions of work that would enable [teachers] to teach effectively, and with self-respect" (Cogen, 1963 *a*, p. 12).

Charles Cogen, who led the UFT to victory in New York City and went on to become president of the AFT, indicated the tactics the union would employ by selecting the title "To Revive a Dying School System" for his address to an AFT conference on collective bargaining in 1963. He stated that, of the 170 demands presented by the UFT for negotiation in 1962, the major ones were related to class size, improvement of difficult schools, additional teacher time for lesson preparation, additional remedial services, adequate salaries, and expansion of teacher rights. "The rationale for [our] negotiating demands," he said, "stems from our salary scale, the status of our working conditions, and the learning conditions of the student" (Cogen, 1963*b*, p. 2).

THREE ISSUES ACQUIRE EMPHASIS BY UNION ORGANIZING AND BARGAINING

The demand for higher salaries was predicated on the argument that school systems in large cities had difficulty attracting and retaining teachers and consequently had a greater number of vacancies filled by unqualified substitutes. An improved salary schedule would attract young, qualified teachers and stem the tide of seasoned teachers leaving the profession for higher paying jobs in business, industry, and government. During the organizing period, Philadelphia's teaching force contained approximately 659 long-term substitutes (Odell, 1965, p. 5).

The second concern which was turned into an organizing issue related to working conditions. It involved a concept long held dear by the AFT—that of joint decision-making and its positive effect on the climate of the school system, the schools themselves, and the individual classroom. It stems from early ideas of industrial democracy, in which the worker would have a voice in determining the operation of the workplace, be it a shop, factory, plant, office, or classroom. The following excerpt, which appeared in the February, 1964 issue of the *PFT Reporter*, contains elements of that past approach to decision-making along with a contemporary interpretation:

> We believe in democracy and in the schools as the chief agent by which democracy is preserved and enriched.
> We believe that to secure this end administration must be democratic, not authoritarian or coercive, offer courageous leadership in preparing citizens for the changed and changing world, and recognize that good teachers are the foundation of good education.
> We believe that if the schools are to produce free, unafraid men and women, American citizens of the highest type, teachers must live and work in an atmosphere of freedom, dignity and self-respect.
> We believe that in the teaching profession, as in other professions, *policy making should be in the hands of those who teach* (italics added).
> We believe that teachers have the freedom necessary to promote their welfare only when they specifically organize to that end (*PFT Reporter*, 1964, p. 3).

The third and final concern is related to that broad, general area of learning conditions and pupil achievement. Collective bargaining agreements were seen as means which would lead eventually toward quality education. Election victories would witness the dawn of a new day for teachers and, through them, for children. Campaign rhetoric dealt with the "deep concern of teachers for the welfare and education of their pupils, higher salaries and improved teaching conditions *so that [school districts] could compete for the best possible teachers,* and mutual investment for improving the city schools" (*PFT Reporter,* 1964, p. 2).

Most local campaigns for collective bargaining rights were won or lost on these three issues: salary, involvement in the decision-making process, and reduction in class size. Each depicted a way to improve education in the classroom. A fourth issue, however, entered into many campaigns and overshadowed each of these and all other considerations: the race issue. It involved both the wooing of black teachers into the AFT local, or, at the very least, persuading them to vote AFT in elections, and the position locals had taken on civil rights and school integration. Philadelphia blacks' distrust of unionism, their attraction to the existing Philadelphia Teachers Association (NEA), combined with their impatience with the snail's pace of integration, made organizing black teachers difficult. Strains of racial disharmony have plagued PFT throughout its seven years of dominance in Philadelphia.

On February 1, 1965, the Philadelphia Federation of Teachers, AFL-CIO, won the right to represent all of the more than 12,000 teachers in the third largest school system in the country. The local had been victorious in an uphill battle with a strongly entrenched Philadelphia Teachers Association in the city where the NEA had been founded. When the campaign opened late in 1963, the PTA admitted to a membership of over 5000, a figure which was probably accurate. The PFT, on the other hand, stated at the time that its membership was approximately 2000, which was probably 1500 more than the actual number of dues paying members! The victory, by a vote of 5403 to 4671, was followed by an immediate agreement to commence negotiations, which officially began on March 15, 1965.

THE UNION BECOMES INSTITUTIONALIZED

During negotiations for the first contract, it was evident that wages, working conditions, and organizational institutionalization were of prime importance to the Federation. The PFT found a large, vulnerable city school system and exploited it. Union negotiators made the most of the system's inadequacies, pointing up the academic retardation of poor students and the general deplorable conditions for both students and teachers in predominantly black schools as justification for their demands for better working conditions, higher salaries, and a role in policy formulation. Along with securing more money for its members, the PFT's main concern in negotiations has been to increase the union's autonomy and power over personnel policies. Collective bargaining agreements have replaced what the union considered a private patronage system with general rules that give teachers rights and benefits they had not enjoyed previously.

Although humanitarian goals have been and still are a part of the idealism of the national union, and are frequently supported by locals in their public rhetoric, the major thrust of local agreements is directed toward:

1. Increasing economic benefits for members.

2. Gaining equal power within the decision-making structure of public education in order to protect and defend union members.
3. Organizational self-preservation.

An analysis of the three contracts negotiated by the PFT from 1965 to 1971 shows greatly improved salary schedules, significant advances in personal and professional rights of teachers, and conclusive recognition of the local as the representative of all of Philadelphia's teachers, but few contract clauses which relate to children's needs.

In September, 1966, the president of PFT wrote an article in the *Reporter* entitled, "Responsible Militance," in which he stated that the "smashing victory . . . being credited to the Federation belongs to all the teachers, to all pupils and in truth, to the entire community. The agreement . . . reached with the Board has importance that transcends the greatly improved salary schedule. Even a hurried reading of proposals we have won shows significant advances in personal and professional rights of teachers as well as in educational programs" (Ryan, 1966, p. 2). The author is correct in one respect—a hurried reading of the proposals will most assuredly produce a realization that teachers rights have been secured. However, it takes a very careful scrutiny to find any proposal or clause which relates directly or indirectly to educational programs. We do not believe this is an accident or that it can be attributed to the Board of Education's unwillingness to discuss issues or proposals which concern policy. In most collective bargaining situations, the union presents its demands to the Board and the negotiations which follow concern discussion of and bargaining around these proposals. The Board rarely, if ever, presents demands of its own. And so the topics and the tenor of discussions during negotiations stem from the original proposals formulated and presented by the union.

DEMANDS, DEMANDS, DEMANDS

The process utilized by virtually all local unions mitigates against the formulation of any proposal which would suggest changes in the present management or organizational patterns, or deal with improving education for students. Months prior to negotiations, most locals organize meetings which are composed of individual school faculties and teachers, divided according to occupational categories. Each group meets separately to formulate proposals which they feel are worthy of consideration in negotiations. In 1968, in preparation for negotiations, the PFT executive board received over 1200 proposals from meetings of such groups. These proposals were studied, refined, and discussed for over thirty hours in late November, until finally 481 were presented and approved with minor changes at a membership meeting of 1500 teachers in December. Among these demands presented by the Federation to the Board's negotiating committee were the following:

1. The payroll department shall not be paid until teachers are paid.
2. Teachers shall not be required to send for records from previous schools.
3. Teachers shall be permitted more time to return visual aids.
4. Report cards shall be made out by computer.
5. There shall be three teachers assigned to every two classes.
6. There shall be better food and more selection of food available in the cafeteria.
7. Where free parking is not provided by the Board or is not readily available within a reasonable distance, the school shall pay the parking expenses of the teacher.
8. No electronic devices shall be used in the observation or supervision of teachers.
9. Teachers' schedules shall be flexible so as to allow utilization of TV programs and other activities.

10. Teachers of first grade classes must have at least three years of teaching experience.

11. All academic students shall be offered typing.

12. New programs shall be instituted and existing programs shall be expanded to help under-achievers (*PFT Reporter,* 1968, pp. 2-8).

While the above proposals are not randomly selected, they nevertheless illustrate the kinds of concerns which survive the sifting process. Every one of the 481 proposals was presented to the Board's negotiating committee and was discussed at some length, depending upon its import. It is obvious that some of the minor proposals do not warrant lengthy consideration. They are presented for internal political reasons. It is simply easier for the leadership to present proposals which relate to some particular problem than to argue with the membership or work out the problem through other channels. When the membership votes on the entire package in September, these kinds of proposals are all but forgotten. The members are usually interested in a handful of issues relating to salary and whatever is "hot" at the time, such as the length of the school day or the transfer policy.

The *PFT Reporter,* in September, 1967, featured a center page spread which declared that "After Only Two Years Philadelphia Teachers Know AFT + CB = Teacher Gains" (*PFT Reporter,* 1967, p. 10). There is no doubt that this is the case. In the period from September, 1965 to September, 1967, the PFT had secured two written agreements with the Board of Education and had done so without being forced to strike. Teachers with a bachelors degree on the first step received an $800 raise, from $5300 to $6100, and those with eleven years experience went from $8200 to $9900, a whopping $1700 increase! Teachers with masters degrees and above received from $900 to $1700 more, depending on their years of experience. In addition, teachers had gained:

Binding arbitration
Transfer procedures
Fewer nonprofessional duties
Class-size reduction
A voice for the teacher
Joint study committees
Limitation on lesson plans
Grievance procedure
Improved sabbatical leave plan
More textbooks and supplies
Summer fellowships (800 grants @ $750)
Roster practices limited
Building Committee (chapter) meetings
Equal insurance rights for women
Elementary school preparation time
Right to examine personnel files
No more than two after-school faculty meetings per month
Ratings shown to each teacher
No more than two night meetings per year
Immediate credit for advanced degrees

All of these added up to "Benefits Gained, Rights Maintained—Increased Professionalism, Increased Dignity, Increased Salaries" (*PFT Reporter,* 1967, pp. 4-5). All of these teacher benefits were gained, but what happened to "quality education?"

SALARIES UP! QUALITY EDUCATION?

Salary increases secured by the PFT in the six short years since collective bargaining have been nothing short of phenomenal. Figure 1 compares six year periods prior to and immediately following the first contract. As great as these increases may appear, teachers still had a long way to go before they could feel that they were earning a "living wage." The average salary of teachers in the public schools in the ten largest cities in 1967 was $7810. This was 17 per cent below the Metropolitan Area Budget for a four person family, and only 1.4 per cent above the budget for a three person family. The huge gains in salaries allowed teachers to make up for years of painfully low wages. The late sixties and seventies was also a period of rampant inflation which went as high as 6 or 7 per cent a year. Salary increases of 25 to 30 per cent were not unheard of in other highly organized businesses and industries (Kyserling, 1968, p. 33).

Organizational self-preservation is another important area that is contained in AFT contracts under a "recognition clause," and is the single most important element in the contract for the Federation as an organization. The clause states that the union (PFT) is "the sole and exclusive bargaining representative for all classroom teachers, guidance counselors, librarians, attendance officers . . . special class teachers . . ." This clause gives the union the right to enter into negotiations with the Board at the expiration of the agreement in order to discuss and reach agreements on all matters pertaining to wages, hours, and conditions of employment. The Board also agrees that it will not "take any action affecting other working conditions of teachers without prior adequate negotiations with the Federation" (PFT Agreement, Sept. 1, 1965 to Aug. 31, 1966).

Coupled with the right of exclusive representation is another element guaranteeing that "an employee who is to represent, on any committee, agency, or other such body in the School District of Philadelphia, any employees to whom this Agreement is applicable,

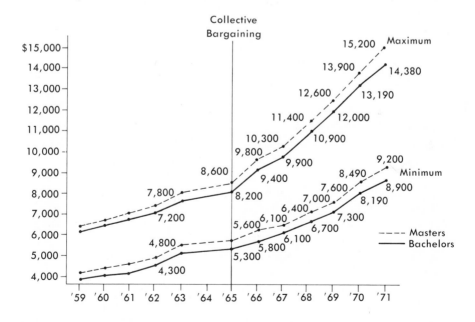

FIGURE 1 *Salary schedules for Philadelphia teachers. Minimum salaries are for first year teachers. Maximum salaries apply after ten years. (From Philadelphia Federation of Teachers Contracts, 1965-1971; Philadelphia Board of Education Salary Schedules.)*

shall be selected from nominees named by the Federation by reason of their special skills, expertise, experience and demonstrated competence in the appropriate area" (PFT Agreement, section 3b). This secures the Federation voice for all teachers on all committees officially appointed by any arm of the School District. The clause is significant because meetings are regularly held with the superintendent, district superintendents, and principals on matters concerning system-wide policy, the operation of school chapters (including meetings, bulletin board space, and mail boxes), and student and community concerns. It explicitly permits class coverage for Federation representatives who attend meetings, and leaves of absence for up to twenty teachers to serve indefinitely in full-time positions with the Federation. These two clauses give the Federation the apparatus to function as a full-time organization.

CONFLICT EMERGES OVER RACIAL ISSUES

During this period of rapid advance in teachers' salaries, fringe benefits, and teachers' rights, other movements which bear analysis were taking place within the PFT as well as in other school systems, notably New York City. They are examples of internal struggles around the very issues that are significantly absent in AFT local contracts. The conflict over the PFT's position on integration illustrates some of the internal machinations which characterized the struggle between the leadership and the forces of dissent.

The PFT leadership has consistently enunciated the liberal dictum of "quality, integrated education for all students." During the late forties and early fifties, the PFT challenged dual lists for black and white teachers, supported the civil rights marches and sit-ins in the South, participated in voter registration drives, and the like. The very active and prolific PFT Human Relations Committee has consistently been on the side of civil libertarian causes, including the integration of minority group material into textbooks and curriculum, the formulation of human relations committees in all the schools, and open housing. In fact, during the drive for collective bargaining in Philadelphia, the support of Dr. Martin Luther King and Bayard Rustin was a crucial factor in convincing traditionally anti-union black teachers to vote for the AFT. Despite a long history of public pronouncements in favor of liberal causes and support for the movement for full equality of blacks, the actual day-to-day, internal operation of Local 3 and its negotiating stance warrant close examination.

One of the most crucial issues throughout contract negotiations from 1965 to 1970 had been the teacher transfer policy that provided for movement of teachers within the school district. Prior to the 1950's, teachers enjoyed unrestricted privilege of transfer (usually, in the teachers' view, from "unfavorable" to "privileged" schools, i.e., black to white). In the fifties, certain limitations were applied, including: assignments made in the ratio of two transfers to one appointment in filling vacancies in any school; and no more than 10 per cent of the faculty of any secondary school or 20 per cent of any elementary school transferred on application during any school year, transfers to be granted on the basis of seniority of service. Nevertheless, free transfer rights resulted in excessive vacancies in black schools, a concentration of experienced teachers in middle-class and white schools, and an inability to provide balanced staffs. The most prolonged conflict in the first and subsequent negotiations in Philadelphia occurred over the Board's attempt to redistribute teachers on the basis of race and experience, and the union's refusal to allow the movement of teachers except on a voluntary basis.* The four contracts which have

---

*This discussion does not concern the placement of new teachers for racial balance and experience, which is not bargainable and which was the union's response to the need.

been negotiated since the beginning of collective bargaining reflect the Board's attempt to balance faculties by mandatory transfers and the union's steadfast refusal to accommodate. The result has been a negative plan: if teachers transfer, they can do so only to improve racial balance and experience. The net effect of this policy has been the maintenance of a largely segregated teaching staff, even though most schools in 1972 comply with the minimum requirements of 20 per cent black at the elementary level and 10 per cent at the secondary level. Black teachers predominate in black schools and vice versa. What is clear is that minimum racial balance has occurred *not because of negotiated contract provisions,* leadership statements notwithstanding, but because of the personnel department's increased recruitment of black teachers and the assignment of these newly recruited teachers for racial balance and experience.

This obvious discrepancy between public and private statements on racial issues divided black teachers and their white supporters from the union leadership and culminated in the formation of a dissident caucus within the Federation. Two prominent groups, which will be discussed later in some detail, were organized apart from the regular union structure. This polarization was accelerated by the release of a letter from the PFT president to the president of the Board of Education, following a demonstration (November 17, 1967) at the Administration Building by more than 3000 black students presenting demands for more black history, black literature, and black teachers, counselors, and principals. The letter suggested, without documentation, that increases in attacks on teachers were directly related to the demonstration. Further, the letter and subsequent statements by PFT leadership revealed a serious philosophical and tactical dichotomy by deploring the use of the traditional union tool of demonstration—strikes, picket lines—by black students and their community supporters. The release of the letter, statements made in PFT executive board meetings, and concerned teachers' demands for answers, resulted in a confrontation of black and white teachers and the PFT leadership at the union office on November 27. The main concern was the president's refusal to clarify or retract the letter. On December 1, 1967 a meeting was called to marshall all dissatisfied teachers into an Ad Hoc Committee to Meet the Crisis in Education in Philadelphia. A list of concerns formulated at that meeting indicated the deep schism which had developed in the two and one-half years since collective bargaining began.

INTERNAL STRUGGLES SURFACE

At the same time, internal issues were surfacing within the PFT, resulting in challenges to the leadership, questions about the discrepancy between ideology and practice, and, ultimately, the formation of a number of dissident groups. An internal caucus, spearheaded by seven executive board members, was organized around a set of demands for internal democratic procedures, and this resulted in political schisms evidenced by intense competition for union office. The formation of an organization of black teachers coalesced around the November 17, 1967 demonstration. A progressive group of black and white teachers, Teachers for Social Action, represented a synthesis of internal political concerns and external educational issues. In 1972, there remain two dissident groups: the Black Caucus and the Progressive Caucus. The basic issue underlying the dissatisfaction of all of the above groups was the lack of responsiveness of PFT leadership to minority group concerns, whether these had to do with racial matters, democratic policy-making, human relations issues, values, or educational policy.

Another issue which has threatened union solidarity and resulted in mass apathy of teachers (most membership meetings attract 300 to 500 teachers, out of a total membership of approximately 12,500) is the problem of internal union democracy. PFT constitutional clauses provide for a large degree of membership participation in elections and committees, introduction of proposals at membership meetings, executive board responsiveness to individual and chapter concerns, and the like. But an analysis of practice indicates a high degree of control by a few at the top. Until recently, when one former president resigned from her post as administrative assistant to the president, all of the major decision-making and functioning power resided in teachers who had been former presidents and long-term members of the local's executive board. Two men who have rotated in the presidency for eight years and who have been on the executive board for more than twelve, and a small coterie of favorites effectively ran the union. A majority of officers on the executive board have retained their positions for equally long periods of time. With one or two notable exceptions, executive board members who are not retained are blacks, and whites who have raised challenges to the leadership. One black executive board member who managed to survive five years was proposed by the power elite for the presidency. She had been nominated by a powerful past president who was still serving on the executive board and the nomination was seconded by the incumbent, retiring president. The latter, however, reversed his position on retiring, and was re-elected after a white vice president threatened to run and make a "real racial battle" out of the election. To avoid charges of "racism" the black former nominee was offered another position on the slate, and was in fact elected Legislative Representative. Eight months later, the PFT leadership accused her of "union busting" because she had dared to join seven other executive board members in signing a letter submitted to the executive board containing fifteen recommendations for bringing about greater participation by the total membership. Specifically, the letter accused the PFT leadership of not maintaining standing committees, not involving building representatives in union business, poorly planned membership meetings, a slowdown in organizing teachers, nurses, and secretaries, poor communication between teachers and the leadership, and inadequate accounting procedures.

One of the earliest defectors left prior to collective bargaining and went on to work with the dissident caucus in New York City's UFT. Those who survive the internal politics retain their posts through voting endorsements and are frequently rewarded for their loyalty with high paying PFT staff jobs. Teachers Concerned, a group of black teachers, challenged PFT's sensitivity to the concerns of black students and the black community, and ultimately was responsible for the resignation of 300 black teachers from PFT in the spring of 1968.

Further evidence of discontent within the rank and file surfaced on May 29, 1968 during a confrontation between predominately white teachers and the leadership at union headquarters. Under the heading, CONFRONT RACISM, their demands included:

> No further public statements on social issues without prior notice and discussion at membership meetings.
>
> A concrete policy to affect immediate staff integration [faculties] which will meet the demands of the black community.
>
> An honest appraisal of the conference [PFT Conference on Racism which was boycotted by Congressman John Conyers, Rev. Ralph Abernathy, black panelists, and black teachers] including the events [boycotts] at June membership meeting and in June *Reporter* [1968].
>
> Creation of a Joint Committee composed of PFT, black students, and black community to review grievances relating to community control of schools.

PFT's opposition to the Board of Education proposal to appoint long-term substitutes as permanent teachers to be dropped.

Support of appointment of staff to solve racial problems existing in schools.

Change in the composition of the Executive Board to guarantee representation of black teachers.

Education of Federation members in racism, including the acceptance of inequality of educational opportunity; the acts of racism which occur in the day-to-day confrontation between teacher and student; identification of racist materials in textbooks; and the elimination of such conditions.

Establishment of an Ethics Commission to receive and investigate complaints and accept responsibility for internal evaluation and policing of Federation members, the PFT, and all of education (Teachers for Social Action, 1968).

During negotiations on the composition of the bargaining unit in 1963, the Federation argued for and won the right to include long-term substitutes, who were dues-paying members of PFT. Of the approximately 1200 substitutes, 85 per cent were black. The substitutes organized into a cohesive group and exerted pressure on the Board of Education for permanent appointment of those substitutes who met certain stringent requirements, not including successful completion of the National Teacher Examination. The school administration developed a plan to appoint most long-term substitutes permanently and submitted this plan to PFT leadership for approval. The Federation reacted against the appointment of long-term substitutes! The effect of this decision was a union acting to *destroy* the rights of a large segment of its own membership, most of whom were black. Unfortunately, those teaching positions made vacant by the dismissal of hundreds of long-term substitues were filled mostly by inexperienced, white provisional teachers. Eventually, the Board of Education did permanently appoint long-term substitutes, but only after losing more than one-half of the original group. It was not until several years after this debacle that the union realized that its self-interest lay in organizing all school district employees from department heads downward, including secretaries, nonteaching assistants, and Get Set teachers and aides.

UNION VULNERABLE ON COMMUNITY CONTROL

The issues of community control and decentralization expose teacher unions' vulnerability to parental pressures, teacher inflexibility, and resistance to change. The I.S. 201 story in New York City is one of the most glaring in the UFT's refusal to accommodate the demands of local communities, the Board's edicts, and a state commission report (the Bundy Report). There are similar trends in the PFT's resistance to the push for community control through decentralization by Philadelphia's parents. Community control of schools and decentralization provide a framework for the examination of the response of the AFT local to both educational innovation and the black community's attempt at school improvement. Essentially, both issues are questions of power redistribution. Community control involves the indigenous community's response to the inability or unwillingness of northern school boards to provide integrated, quality education through control over hiring and retention of local school personnel as well as the demand for accountability of the school and its personnel to the community. Decentralization, on the other hand, is the response of the "establishment" (school boards, Regents' Committees, state legislatures, AFT locals) to the appearance of providing services at the local level, while still maintaining crucial power over fiscal matters, staff tenure and transfer, and accountability.

Throughout the I.S. 201 controversy, UFT president Albert Shanker maintained that giving control to the I.S. 201 parents and community would simply allow other, "less desirable," communities to demand and acquire such control. Implicit in this view is the assumption that control by a citywide lay Board is more desirable than control by a smaller community board, representing populations of approximately 30,000 people. The specific concerns voiced by UFT were maintenance of high professional standards, erosion of negotiated gains in teacher protection and security, and the fear that the lay community board would gain control over the very personnel practices (hiring, firing, and transfer) for which the union itself was contending. This, despite Shanker's consistent claims that the only way to improve the quality of education in "ghetto" schools is through a coalition of parents and teachers. The I.S. 201 and Ocean Hill-Brownsville confrontations cast Shanker and the UFT in roles opposite parents and in collusion with the Council of Supervisory Associations, which represents all principals and assistant principals.*

There are parallels to this situation in Philadelphia in the PFT's reaction to decentralization and earlier attempts by communities to become more deeply involved in the day-to-day activities of their schools. The Philadelphia Federation's position on community control is less clear than the union's position in New York, since a major, citywide confrontation on the issue never developed. In one of the earlier attempts by parents in an integrated, middle-class community to become involved in such school activities as frequent consultation with faculty members, assisting teachers in classroom activities, taking students on educational class trips, and providing professional community resources to supplement classroom teaching, the district PFT representative counseled teachers not to speak to parents, either individually or in joint meetings of parents and teachers called by the principal! These parents had been deeply involved in their children's education in the Get Set program, and wished to continue their close involvement with the school as their children moved into kindergarten and first grade. After many months of struggle, community meetings, and conversations with the principal and district superintendent, the parents' energies were siphoned off into planning for a new middle school in the same area. Apparently, the PFT leadership condoned its representative's position, since no intervention or clarification of the union's position was enunciated publicly or to the parents involved.

In subsequent efforts by the community for involvement, the PFT's position is not clear. An early attempt at decentralization failed because of community suspicion of administrative control and was not revived until October, 1968, when the Board of Education appointed a Commission on Decentralization and Community Participation, headed by a school board member, Mrs. Albert S. Greenfield. The Commission was composed of 21 representatives of the Home and School Council (Philadelphia's counterpart to Parent-Teacher Associations), 4 student representatives, 19 representatives of the "community at large," 8 PFT teachers, and various other school district representatives. The Federation's contribution to the printed report is in the form of "Minority Reports" to many of the recommendations of the entire commission, mostly in the form of criticism of the erosion of teachers' rights.

However, these rather mild criticisms of the Commission's work contrast sharply with the views expressed in an interview with one of the administrative assistants to the

---

*For more detail see: *IRCD Bulletin,* available from the ERIC Information Retrieval Center on the Disadvantaged, 55 Fifth Avenue, New York, 10003; Joseph Featherstone, Community control of our schools, *New Republic,* January 13, 1968.

president of PFT at that time, herself a former president of the union. When asked by the interviewer, "What do you think of community involvement?" she replied:

> I like community involvement. I may not like the noises they make, but I believe in community involvement in the same way that I believe in teacher involvement. Now, control is different. No matter how I feel about it, and the strong commitment I have to the union, I would not feel that the union ought to have control of the schools.

And again, to the question, "How about the community controlling the schools?" she replied, "I would be against that."

> Interviewer: The union would be against that too?
> We haven't taken a formal position on it but I'm sure from what I've heard, from the signs that I read, that the union would be against it. And New York is the horrible example of what we have to look to. You can talk about all the safeguards you are going to put in, but you cannot guard against the unexpected. Involvement, yes . . . and I don't mean just paper involvement. I don't mean the kind of busy work involvement where a principal has so many committees set up and no matter what new ideas come out of them it's never implemented in the school. That's not what I mean by involvement.
> By involvement I mean real participation, but I do not mean it to extend to *the hiring and firing of teachers* [emphasis ours]. Any parent has the right to come in and say to the principal, 'I don't think my kid is getting a fair shake.' And the principal has a duty and an obligation to investigate whether that's true. I think that's one kind of involvement (Higgins, 1969).

Later in the interview, it was reported that community control definitely isn't the answer. "We are pauperizing children by the kind of curriculum we offer them, by the lack of support we give them, and in many other ways." When the interviewer pressed, "Aren't these the very issues that are giving rise to the desire of the community to control the schools?" the answer was, "Yes, that's right, but I don't think it will be successful. They won't be able to attract teachers." These statements by a powerful unionist are in sharp contrast to a Resolution on Teacher Community Relations in Urban Areas, unanimously adopted on August 23, 1968 by the American Federation of Teachers Convention. The text of that resolution is quoted in its entirety as follows:

> WHEREAS, the responsibility of American education is that of assisting youth in the development of their maximum potential in order to make creative contributions to society, and
> WHEREAS, education in the cities, especially in the Black, Puerto Rican and minority communities has not met these responsibilities, and
> WHEREAS, the improvement of education must come from a redefinition of the purposes of education and a complete restructuring of the school system by the community, and
> WHEREAS, the American Federation of Teachers is numerically strongest in large cities and has the responsibility of supporting parents and community groups in this restructuring of education, therefore
> BE IT RESOLVED, that the American Federation of Teachers recognizes the need for effective community responsibility and involvement through elected representation in the operation of schools in the Black, Puerto Rican and other minority communities of America, and
> BE IT FURTHER RESOLVED, that the American Federation of Teachers accepts the responsibilities of rendering cooperative assistance to these communities in developing the structure, content and processes of the school system, subject always to the terms of contractual negotiations with the Union, due process, and of the state tenure laws, and
> BE IT FURTHER RESOLVED, that the American Federation of Teachers and *its affiliated locals will work with the community and students in establishing criteria for personnel selection and evaluation,* and
> BE IT FINALLY RESOLVED, that such criteria will be included in the collective bargaining agreements [emphasis ours] (American Federation of Teachers Resolution, 1968).

Black members of the Commission on Decentralization and Community Participation issued a separate report which specifically charged that, "It is unfortunate that the Philadelphia Federation of Teachers has consistently resisted attempts to build meaningful parent involvement. If we have misunderstood the actions of the Philadelphia Federation of Teachers, we believe a public statement similar to a resolution of the Washington Teachers Union [this refers to the above resolution which was adopted in Washington, D.C. by the AFT] would add clarity to the misunderstanding" (Commission on Decentralization and Community Participation, Minority Report, 1968). No public statement was forthcoming. The report has subsequently been shelved, and there is no indication that it will be revived under the new leadership of the Philadelphia School District.

RIGHTS FOR TEACHERS–NOT FOR STUDENTS?

One final example of the discrepancy between PFT rhetoric and practice is its reaction to the Student Bill of Rights and Responsibilities, adopted by the Board of Education in Philadelphia on December 21, 1970. This resulted from an attempt by students at one of the senior high schools, joined by some school personnel and community leaders, to force the transfer of a white social studies teacher on the grounds that he was not able to relate to the black student body. The Federation's position throughout was that to accede to the demands of the students and community would precipitate similar demands in other schools and that the teacher was denied "due process procedures" in the way the data for possible transfer was handled. In the final resolution of the situation, the superintendent presented an opinion to the Board not to transfer the teacher in question, but he also wrote: "Appropriate procedures to assure a proper hearing of student grievances must be established within the school system. To this end, I recommend the appointment of a Committee on Student Grievances, composed of student, parent, faculty and administration representatives; and that this committee be charged with the responsibility for recommending to the Board procedures to be followed in each school to ensure that student grievances will be heard and resolved equitably" (Shedd, 1969).

The result was that three teachers were appointed to that committee as official PFT representatives and attended virtually every meeting of the committee which developed the document eventually adopted by the Board with minor changes. The three PFT representatives were extraordinarily sympathetic to the student viewpoint and in formal and informal votes taken in committee, consistently supported the students' position, except when proposals explicitly conflicted with the union contract.

The union's major concerns are the time when students' grievances are to be heard (during the school day on teacher preparation time, or after school hours with additional compensation at time and a half rates); whether or not grievance hearings called by students and their ombudsmen are mandatory for teachers; the entire concept of a student grievance procedure; whether students enjoy full protection under Federal Constitutional First Amendment rights; the fear that student-elected ombudsmen will be "outsiders"; and the unwillingness to relinquish power. The following excerpts, taken from a study of the Bill and reactions to it, are from *The Daily Pennsylvanian* in a two-part article by Ellen Campbell. (Only those sections are quoted which indicate a clear PFT position as stated by its president):

'There is a difference between public schools and other places as a forum for full implementation of First Amendment rights. Students should express themselves, but not where there is a captive audience, such as a public school. A public school is one place where you are required to go, where you can produce a captive audience for small groups of activist students. . . .

'This also has to do with the obscenity and pornography problem where students stand subjected as a captive audience. . . .

[The Bill contributes to an] 'atmosphere of disorder and excitement, the encouragement of disruptive activity. . . .

'We are opposed to bringing persons in from outside to function as ombudsmen, because all kinds of political aims and ends can be served that the school has nothing to do with.

'We are unwilling to see self-appointed community leaders come into the schools to serve their own ends. Many of these people don't understand schools and young people. Many teachers understand these things better, and are unwilling to see young people used as political tools' (Campbell, 1971).

The Federation newsletter, in a "Review of the Students' Bill of Rights," protested the Bill's prior censorship clause on the grounds that "obscene, libelous, or violence-provoking writings or pictures would be protected until 'after the damage is done.' " The *Reporter* continues, "Everyone concerned with a good educational climate in the Philadelphia schools must be concerned with the possibility of the continued disruption of classroom activities *which the Student Bill of Rights as presently written will permit* [emphasis added] . Everyone should be aware of the Superintendent's consistent position that confrontation and conflict among students, parents, and teachers are desirable and constructive . . ." (*PFT Reporter*, March, 1971).

The implementation and application by students of the provisions of the Bill of Rights and Responsibilities do not bear out the PFT's fears. The First Amendment rights included in the Bill were originally adopted by the Board of Education on September 30, 1968 and are a restatement of civil rights enjoyed by citizens generally. Since adoption of the Bill, students have not used the school as a forum for political views to any greater extent than before. There has been a decline rather than an increase in obscenity and the distribution of pornographic material. Students' acceptance and use of the Bill has resulted in a decrease of disorder and a diminution of disruptive activity in the schools. Ombudsmen, elected by student bodies or student governments, have been most successful in solving students' complaints informally, before they necessitated the filing of formal proceedings. The fear that ombudsmen would be "outsiders" is totally unfounded, since almost all of the ombudsmen are students, with some interesting notable exceptions: one nonteaching assistant, one policeman, one school-community coordinator, five teachers, and one parent. Significantly, to our knowledge, *there has not been a single grievance filed by students against a teacher;* such problems which have arisen have been handled in informal mediation sessions, or ombudsmen have counseled their student clients not to file inconsequential complaints.

The views of another unionist, the Executive Director of the AFL-CIO's Human Resources Development Institute (HRDI) are representative of the Bill's proponents, including civil rights agencies, the Philadelphia Bar Association, the Union of Student Governments, the former superintendent of schools and parents of senior high school students. He commented,

The Bill has many of the basic characteristics of a union contract and establishes a collective bargaining machinery for the students. I believe that every group of people should have such machinery. I believe in collective bargaining as a method of resolving disputes between groups. The schools are built for students, not for teachers and principals, and I am concerned about the effect union opposition to the Bill will have on the students' view of the labor movement. The kid's first contact with labor is the teachers' union, and if that fights against student rights in a participatory democracy, this carries into the general attitude toward labor (quoted in Campbell, 1971).

In summary, the Bill has given students guidelines for their conduct and an awareness of their rights. It has not created a disruptive climate as charged by PFT and other detractors. Many individual teachers in the high schools are cooperating with students in the implementation of the Bill of Rights and advocate its retention by the system. The fears of PFT seem wholly unjustified.

CONCLUSIONS

What seems to have happened in those school systems that have negotiated comprehensive agreements with teachers is that salaries have increased substantially, teaching conditions have improved, and as a consequence, turnover rates have lessened and recruitment has been made easier. It could be argued, however, that draft exemptions for teachers and the economic recession and tight job market of the late 1960's caused the influx of new teachers into urban school systems. The introduction of teacher aides to perform clerical and other "nonprofessional" duties has provided teachers with more time to prepare lessons. Class size, where it has been a feature of collective bargaining agreements, has been reduced. There is, however, little or no evidence that any of these changes has had any effect on learning or pupil achievement. Conversely, there is strong evidence that pupil achievement has declined, the drop-out rate has increased, and student dissatisfaction has intensified. All the indices of educational excellence seem to be inversely correlated with teacher union success. Furthermore, there seems to have been no improvement in teacher morale.

It appears that teacher benefits have come at the expense of other educational programs. Collective bargaining has caused a disproportionate percentage of school expenditures to be spent on salaries and other related benefits, rather than on producing "quality education." It also appears that the changes fought for and won in most collective bargaining agreements benefit only teachers and not pupils. It is our belief that teacher unions have moved from a potentially reformist force to a largely protectionist one. Most AFT locals no longer identify with civil rights groups or liberal causes, but have become a part of the "educational establishment," protecting professional rights against community and student pressures for change. There is little in past or present contract proposals which justifies unions claiming that they are acting in the name of improved education.

AFT locals have never shown a willingness to strike over those issues which would make the educational system more responsive to the needs of students rather than to the "professionals." How can a union continue to justify demands for increased teacher preparation time and more specialist teachers in the face of the threatened demise of many urban school systems? Programs which may have an effect on pupil achievement are rarely initiated by boards of education, because the needed funds are spent on teachers' salaries. Unions block such programs out of fear that the traditional pupil-teacher relationship, or school-community relationship will be altered. And so we find teacher union locals striking to demand what they still conceive of as "sweeping reforms in public school education." On March 24, 1970, 3000 teachers marched through the Boston Common where, exactly two hundred years before, the first protest demonstration in the United States occurred. Those teachers were demanding that the board negotiate the unions' program to improve the city schools. The union was willing to send the salary issue to arbitration, but insisted that improvements in the schools be negotiated because "as professional teachers, [they knew] the steps that must be taken now to make the schools educationally sound." Unfortunately, the union's package of "reforms" included the same hackneyed demands which local after local contends will change a basically sick institution. Those demands include:

1. Class size reduction
2. Libraries and librarians in all schools
3. Remedial reading teachers in all schools
4. Nurses in all schools
5. Additional school psychologists and psychiatrists
6. Additional facilities—classrooms and buildings

Union spokesmen seemed most concerned with the class size issue, charging that school administrators refused to meet with the union to implement an old contract stipulation that when class sizes were exceeded, the parties would meet to work out ways to correct the situation (Boston teachers march for school reform, 1970, p. 8).

In a recent review of *Crisis in the Classroom,* the president of the New York UFT quoted the author, Charles Silberman, as saying that "most teachers are decent, honest, well-intentioned people who do their best under the most trying circumstances. They, no less than the students are victimized by the way in which most schools are organized and run. In other words, the normal organization of school and classroom are a form of cruel and inhuman treatment of children" (Shanker, 1971, p. 22). We agree! Shanker believes that turning schools into humane insitutions for both teachers and students is the primary aim of Silberman's proposals, which include variations on the open classroom. He suggests that, "Liberals who still believe in public schools, teachers under constant attack, school officials looking for something not only new but also tried, should embrace the major proposals Charles Silberman has made" (Shanker, 1971, p. 23). We challenge teacher union leaders all over this country who profess to be liberals, who still believe in public schools, and who are constantly harassed by administration and boards of education to embrace these proposals. We challenge them to use the most organized power base in school systems to bring about change in public education; to develop contract proposals which will make schools more humane for teachers and students; to sit on joint committees for the development of experimental units and destroy the present organizational constraints; to build open and real lines of communication between teachers, students, parents, and the community.

The Philadelphia Federation of Teachers particularly, and other AFT locals generally, have built protective walls around teachers rather than fighting to help teachers remain alive, changing, and young. Teachers have become a part of the establishment and defend the status quo against all efforts for change from students, parents, community representatives, and, not infrequently, administrators. Significantly, in Philadelphia, the Board of Education, which was appointed in the 1960's while the city was still in a mood of reform, joined with the newly appointed superintendent and his "outside" staff of change agents to make the real difference by instituting a massive building program and introducing bold, innovative changes, such as the Parkway Program, the Pennsylvania Advancement School, Learning Centers, teacher grants for innovative programs, curricular changes, the Affective Program, development of strong community ties, and more, all of which gave promise of improving a massive, entrenched, bureaucratic system. Almost all of these changes were effected apart from contractual agreements with PFT!

It seems evident that teacher unions across the country are not utilizing the collective bargaining process to bring about meaningful changes in the nature of public education. They have unquestionably had an effect on decisions relating to salaries and other economic issues, as well as on those policy decisions which relate to teacher protection.

However, they seem to be relatively powerless in other areas. We believe that this development relates directly to the concept which most union leaders, school board members, and administrators hold concerning power relationships. All three groups assume that an increase in influence by any one party is followed by a decrease in power of the remaining parties, rather than the possibility of increasing the power of all parties involved in the collective bargaining relationship. The result of such thinking is that all parties are loosing power. Parents, community people, and other taxpayers show positive resentment at the increased cost of educational systems over which they have no control and which continue to fail to produce educated students.

The teacher union is a partisan organization, which repeatedly, in city after city, when faced with opportunities to bring about meaningful change in institutional relationships which could give power to community, parents, and students, has retreated to the protection of teachers' rights and the defense of the status quo.

Are we asking too much of teacher unions? Is it unfair to suggest that the unions should or could solve all of the problems of a sick institution? It is probably unfair to ask AFT locals to attack the problem alone, but the unions have used the deplorable circumstances which exist in most public schools, and particularly in schools in black communities in urban centers, to secure the advances which they have won for teachers in the last decade. In the process, they have reiterated time and again that collective bargaining —the union contract—would ultimately lead to quality education for all children. Where is the evidence?

REFERENCES

American Federation of Teachers: Resolution on Teacher Community Relations in Urban Areas. Adopted by AFT Convention, August 23, 1968.

Bleecker, Ted: 11th hour victory. *American Teacher Magazine, 47:*8, May, 1963.

Boston teachers march for school reform. *American Teacher, 54*(9): 8, 1970.

Campbell, Ellen: High school Bill of Rights: way ahead . . . at least on paper. *Daily Pennsylvanian,* May 4-5, 1971.

Cogen, Charles: Departure from the old ways—the first years of New York City bargaining. *American Teacher Magazine, 48:*12, 1963 *a.*

Cogen, Charles: To revive a dying school system. Address to the 47th Annual Convention of the American Federation of Teachers. August, 1963*b.*

Commission on Decentralization and Community Participation: Report. Minority report of black members.

Higgins, James: Listen to the teacher; an interview with Celia Pincus. *AE, the Philadelphia Magazine about Education, 12*(3): 14-29, 1969.

Kyserling, Leon H.: Achieving nationwide educational excellence. *In* A Ten Year Plan, 1967-1977, To Save the Schools. Washington, D.C., Conference on Economic Progress, 1968.

Moscow, Michael H.: Teachers and Unions. Philadelphia, University of Pennsylvania Wharton School, Industrial Research Unit, 1966.

Odell, William R.: Educational Survey Report for the Philadelphia Board of Public Education, February 1, 1965. Philadelphia, Board of Public Education, 1965.

Perry, Charles R., and Wildman, Wesley A.: The Impact of Negotiations in Education. Worthington, Ohio, Charles A. Jones Publishing Co., 1970.

PFT Reporter, February, 1964.

PFT Reporter, January 1, 1965.

PFT Reporter, September, 1967.

PFT Reporter, Negotiations Issue, 1968.

PFT Reporter, March, 1971.

Philadelphia Federation of Teachers: Agreement between the Board of Public Education, School District of Philadelphia, and the Philadelphia Federation of Teachers, Local 3, American Federation of Teachers, AFL-CIO, 1965.

Rotigel, David E.: Back to Dewey again: his views on teachers, unions and strikes. *Changing Education,* Fall, 1967, pp. 19-22.

Ryan, John: Responsible militancy. *PFT Reporter,* September, 1966.
Shanker, Albert: Life and death for the public schools. *AFL-CIO American Federationist,* January, 1971.
Shedd, Mark R.: Decision of Superintendent of Schools [School District of Philadelphia] in the case of George Fishman, teacher at West Philadelphia High School, November 10, 1969.
Teachers for Social Action, May 29, 1968. (Unprinted leaflet.)

47 teacher militancy

Myron Lieberman

CAUSES OF TEACHER MILITANCY

"Militancy" is obviously a rather subjective matter. Picketing and demonstrations may be characterized as "militant" by some persons but not by others. Nevertheless, among educators there is probably widespread agreement that teacher militancy includes collective negotiations, strikes, demonstrations, boycotts, picketing, and a generally aggressive collective posture. Without attempting a formal definition, I propose to use "teacher militancy" to refer to these kinds of teacher behavior.

Unquestionably, the most dramatic manifestation of teacher militancy is the accelerating trend toward collective negotiations. The first significant collective agreement between a teacher organization and a board of education was negotiated in 1962 between the United Federation of Teachers and the New York City Board of Education. By 1970 about three-fifths of the nation's teachers were employed pursuant to collective rather than individual contracts; and this proportion is likely to increase in the 1970's. This trend certainly represents a sharp departure from the pattern of teacher-board relationships prior to the 1960's.

Probably the major cause of the development of teacher militancy was the over-emphasis upon, and breakdown of, the legislative approach to terms and conditions of employment for teachers. Without an understanding of this factor, realistic assessment of teacher militancy is all but impossible.

Prior to the 1960's, teachers and teacher organizations emphasized state legislation as the most effective way to advance teacher welfare. Higher salaries were sought by enacting or improving a state minimum wage law. Increased sick leave was to be gained by trying to get legislatures to mandate minimum sick leave for all districts. Duty-free lunch periods were to be attained through "right to eat" laws, and so on.

This emphasis upon state legislation was the practical consequence of combining administrative and supervisory personnel in the same organizations as classroom teachers, especially in those affiliated with the National Education Association (NEA). Since administrative and supervisory employees often dominated or led these associations, it is understandable that they were not particularly vigorous in representing teachers as employees at the local level.

The teacher associations, however, needed a rationale to stay in business. They found it in influencing state legislation, which emphasized the community rather than the conflict of interest between teachers and administrators. For example, both groups could unite in a campaign for increased state aid to education. Administrators were as interested as teachers in adequate retirement programs. Yet legislation which reflected a strong teacher interest was often scuttled when it conflicted with the interests of administrators as managerial employees. For example, administrators often weakened state association efforts to enact a strong teacher tenure law.

Belatedly, teachers came to recognize the inherent weaknesses of this approach. In the first place, the state associations (and the NEA) frequently found that their lobbying efforts were ineffective because there were no strong local organizations to exert political pressure on local legislators.

More importantly, teachers began to recognize the inherent ineffectiveness of the legislative approach itself. If a strong local organization could achieve higher salaries, duty-free lunch periods, preparation periods, and sick leave for teachers in one school district, they had little reason to wait for their state association to achieve these benefits for all teachers in the state. Frequently, there was no realistic chance that state legislation providing certain benefits could ever be enacted. Nor was this approach a realistic way to solve problems that were purely local or affected only a small fraction of the state's teachers. For example, although teachers in large urban districts often felt a need for protection concerning transfers, this was of little or no concern to those in smaller school districts.

The legislative approach also broke down in enforcement of teacher rights. Most teachers feel that benefits enacted into law are inviolate. In practice, this is unrealistic. Suppose a state law guarantees teachers a thirty minute duty-free lunch period. Nonetheless, the administration may require teachers to "keep an eye" upon pupils in the adjoining lunch room. What can a teacher do if the administration does not heed his request for a remedy? As a practical matter, the time and expense of a court action ordinarily would be prohibitive. Besides, most teachers would feel absurd going to court on such a matter. If, on the other hand, the duty-free lunch period is a teacher right pursuant to a collective agreement between the board of education and a teacher organization, the teacher has recourse to a relatively expeditious grievance procedure, culminating in arbitration by an impartial third party.

The advantages of grievance procedures over legal action in enforcing teacher rights illustrate the advantages of a contractual rather than a legislative approach to teacher welfare. However, the contractual approach requires an organization authorized to negotiate and make binding commitments on behalf of teachers. Thus, it led to strong local organizations, able and willing to exert pressure to secure the maximum possible benefits from their boards of education.

The development of stronger local organizations is thus both cause and result of teacher militancy. To ensure the benefits of stronger local representation, teachers pay much more in local dues, employ full-time staff, and insist that state and national associations be reorganized to provide more effective service to local negotiating organizations. At the same time, these actions create a demand for more benefits to justify the increased resources devoted to teacher representation at the local level. These tendencies reinforce each other, intensifying the pressures which boards of education and administrators identify as teacher militancy.

Boards of education and school administrators are frequently astonished at the rapid spread of teacher militancy. Compared to developments elsewhere in both public and private employment it is surprising that teachers were so slow to realize the need for a different approach to their terms and conditions of employment. Clearly, developments in other fields have contributed a great deal to teacher militancy. It was difficult for New York City teachers to accept the view that teacher strikes should be prohibited when other unions of municipal employees were able to achieve benefits by defying similar prohibitions. Similarly, in Michigan, the example of militant tactics set by the automobile and allied unions led to extremely rapid development of teacher bargaining.

Organizational rivalry between NEA and AFT was another important factor in the emergence of teacher militancy. In dozens, if not hundreds, of large school districts, militancy was used by one or both organizations to ward off defections to its rival. The closer the rivalry in a particular district, the more likely it was that both organizations would adopt a more aggressive stance to recruit members. Although precise statistics on the issue are not available, it is certain that a significant number of teacher strikes have occurred in situations of intense organizational rivalry.

The civil rights movement in the 1960's also undoubtedly contributed to teacher militancy. Aside from its general tendency to support a militant posture to achieve social goals, two aspects of the civil rights movement were of particular significance to education. Teacher organization leaders who believed that the prohibitions against teacher bargaining relegated teachers to second class citizenship needed dramatic support to overcome teacher resistance to violating these prohibitions. The civil rights movement provided such support, especially since teachers were relatively sympathetic to the civil rights movement in the early 1960's. By pointing to blacks who openly violated unjust laws to force their repeal, teacher leaders were better able to convince teachers that participation in strikes was morally acceptable and practically feasible because it served a higher cause than legal formality. Whether or not the moral argument was a valid one, it clearly played a significant role in overcoming teacher reluctance to engage in militant action of dubious legality.

In retrospect, it is easier to identify the social and psychological causes of teacher militancy, although the two are clearly related. The latter may vary locally, and may well depend on the background of a small group of union leaders. New York City's United Federation of Teachers (UFT), one of the most influential local teacher organizations in the country, provides a vivid example. In the 1960's, it was led by a small, highly educated group of left wing liberals and democratic socialists. Some of the key leaders, such as former UFT and AFT president, Charles Cogen, had begun not in teaching but in law or other professional careers. However, their careers were shaped by the Great Depression and they found teaching the only practical outlet for their skills and orientations. Over the years, however, when they did not achieve the material rewards and professional status appropriate to their talents, they became dissatisfied. Militant action was much more to this group than a tactic to extract greater benefits from the Board of Education. It was an opportunity to play a leadership role which had eluded them so many years that it had begun to look impossible. It was a way of redressing long neglect from "the establishment," of proving their credentials as liberals, and so on.

It would be naive to overstress these psychological factors, especially since they were present for years with no effect. The point is, however, that they eventually combined with other conditions, such as the weak state of teacher representation, to produce a militant leadership group. Ten years later, most of this leadership group had retired from the UFT. The other original causes of militancy, such as Board refusal to bargain collectively, had also largely disappeared, yet the organization remained militant. Militancy develops its own traditions and organizational constituencies; to look for its present raison d'etre in historical antecedents is to overlook the dynamics of collective representation.

Assessing the causes of teacher militancy is also difficult because the same factor can produce contradictory tendencies. Conventional wisdom asserts that the more educated "professional" groups are less likely to embrace militant tactics. Yet there is considerable evidence that the more educated members of the work force tend to be the most dissatisfied. In certain contexts, this makes sense; a person with a Ph.D. is more likely to be dissatisfied teaching the fourth grade than a person with only two years of college. In fact, to paraphrase one recent observer, union recruiters rather than school district personnel officers ought to be concentrating on the most highly educated teachers.

On the other hand, teacher dissatisfaction may have little or nothing to do with teacher militancy. The most satisfied teachers may be the most militant. They may regard militancy strictly as a tactical matter—"our conditions of employment are excellent and militancy is the way to keep them excellent or make them even better." I do not suggest that this line of thought is typical, but it does illustrate that teacher militancy is not necessarily an index of teacher dissatisfaction. The point to remember is that the causes of teacher militancy vary from place to place and from time to time. A realistic approach should deal with the present causes in a specific district, not with generalizations which may be invalid applied to the district under consideration.

CONSEQUENCES OF TEACHER MILITANCY

Teacher militancy has had a variety of consequences that can be seen in terms of their impact on both particular groups and policies. Let us consider first whether teacher militancy has "paid off" for teachers. Are they demonstrably better off as a result? Or does militancy create a backlash of public attitude against teacher demands?

Any answer should be prefaced with a note of caution. It is not easy to isolate the impact of teacher militancy from other factors influencing teacher welfare, such as teacher shortages or rapid increases in the cost of living. Where teachers face extremely adverse conditions, there is more likelihood of substantial improvement, even in the absence of militancy. At the same time, teacher militancy in one school district may be a disaster for the teachers there, but may stimulate boards of education and administrators elsewhere to make improvements to forestall militancy in their own districts. These difficulties also apply to the assessment of outcomes in the private sector; economists are still debating the extent to which collective bargaining has resulted in economic benefits to union members.

In the opinion of this observer, the available evidence indicates that the collective negotiations movement has achieved significant economic benefits for teachers. Even if this conclusion is valid, however, one should be cautious in drawing inferences from it. Teacher militancy may have been successful precisely because it was so unexpected. Most teacher strikes prior to the late sixties were successful, at least in terms of their stated objectives, but these strikes were extraordinary last ditch measures by highly motivated teachers. One cannot expect the same level of success from more routine strikes, especially against a more sophisticated school administration.

Furthermore, many successful teacher strikes were intended to achieve basic procedural rights which are now guaranteed by law. For example, teachers frequently went on strike in the sixties to force school boards to conduct representation elections, or to recognize and bargain with the majority organization of teachers. Such strikes were successful partly because the merits of the issues were so clearly on the teachers' side. It was relatively easy to arouse the teachers and relatively difficult for the boards to be intransigent on these issues. However, such strikes and subsequent state legislation thoroughly established these procedural rights. The issues now are largely economic ones in which the equities are not so clear. To suggest that past successes guarantee success with present issues is obviously unjustified.

Whatever may be the correct conclusion concerning economic benefits, teacher militancy as expressed in collective negotiations has clearly resulted in substantial noneconomic benefits. For example, hundreds of thousands of teachers are now protected by grievance procedures terminating in arbitration by an impartial third party. The mere fact that boards of education are legally obligated to negotiate in good faith with teachers' representatives is an enormous benefit to teachers, since it insures that their views on certain issues must be considered before board action. Teacher militancy has also done much to reduce capricious and discriminatory administrative action in such areas as promotions, transfers, leaves, length of work day and work year, extracurricular employment, and other areas of teacher concern.

One of the most important outcomes to teachers is a new set of relationships to teacher organizations. With exclusive representation by a majority organization, individual teachers are no longer free to represent themselves on terms and conditions of employment. The organization's authority to represent teachers also gives it a great deal more control over them. Collectively and formally, teachers control the organization, but in practice, this control is limited and is gradually being taken over by full-time organizational personnel.

These and other outcomes naturally call for or result in changes in school administration. Perhaps the most important of these is that the administration no longer deals with teachers as isolated individuals but with an organization with growing capacity to detect and take advantage of administrative weakness and error. In itself, this is a major change in educational administration, but it is only part of the drastic reorientation of this field brought about by teacher militancy. The administration must not only take into account the bargaining agent but the collective agreement as well. The latter typically spells out contractual limits and obligations of the administration pertaining to transfers, assignments, work day, school year, personal leave, sabbatical leave, sick leave, preparation time, summer employment, promotions, grievance procedures, and a host of other items. In the prenegotiations era, the administration could change a policy, ignore it, or apply it inconsistently without fear of effective teacher protest. This situation has disappeared in many districts and is rapidly disappearing in others. Management must protect its essential prerogatives in the negotiating process and subsequently avoid violating the collective agreement in administering the schools.

Teacher militancy has had its biggest impact on administration at the school level. The reason is that the building principal normally is the first person who must decide what the administration can or cannot do under the agreement. Of course, if the issue is important, he will try to consult with a central office administrator for guidance, but circumstances may require immediate decisions and interpretations. Thus, one of the unanticipated consequences of teacher militancy has been an even greater emphasis upon the need for competent administrators at the building level.

Militancy and negotiations have also forced a reorganization of line and staff functions in many districts. For example, decisions on grievances at the building level may have to be referred to a central office administrator to ensure district-wide consistency in contract interpretation and administration. If one principal tends to hold more staff meetings after school than another, the teachers will bargain for the smaller number to apply to all schools. Similarly, if one principal requires more evening meetings, or a longer school day, teachers will be alert to note the differences and require their justification or elimination at the bargaining table. This can be a traumatic experience for administrators not accustomed to justifying idiosyncratic approaches to these matters.

The impact of teacher militancy upon administration is more evident than its impact upon students. In the middle 1960's, administrators and boards of education frequently deplored the lack of evidence that teacher negotiations resulted in more student learning. Today, this issue is largely ignored, except in the rhetoric of teacher strikes and demonstrations. In order to gain public support, teachers couch their demands in terms of student or public interest rather than teacher interest. For instance, higher salaries are allegedly necessary to recruit and retain good teachers, an objective which is clearly in the interest of the community and the pupils. Teachers have defended dozens of strikes for higher salaries by claiming that drastic action was required to prevent the deterioration of the system.

The appeals to public or pupil interests probably do have merit in selected instances, but it is difficult to generalize about the relationships between learning and teacher militancy. For example, consider the frequent charge that teacher strikes are setting a harmful example of lawlessness. Granted that the vast majority of such strikes are illegal, there appears to be no hard evidence that they have been demonstrably conducive to student lawlessness. On this issue, as on so many others, observers have no trouble reaching conclusions which support their initial attitudes. The school board is certain that teacher strikes are having undesirable effects upon pupils. Teachers are equally certain that pupils respect them more because they "fought for their rights." Until better evidence is available, the most valid conclusion would seem to be that teacher militancy has only marginal effects upon pupil behavior.

Teacher militancy has led to major changes in teacher organizations that illustrate the point made earlier that teacher militancy, at least at certain levels, has a momentum and a dynamic of its own. In the late 1960's, significant numbers of administrators began to withdraw or be expelled from teacher associations. This process still continues, albeit at a very different pace from state to state and district to district. In some states, such as Michigan, it is virtually complete. In others, especially in the South, where teacher militancy has been blunted by racial issues dividing teachers, the process has hardly begun. In some states, principals remain members of local and state associations but superintendents do not. In others, principals have begun to identify with management and are in the process of separating or being separated from teacher associations.

Originally, teachers may have been opposed to this development. Sometimes it was more or less forced by the state agency which regulated employment relations in education. Administrators and supervisors may have come to fear charges of an "unfair labor practice" for dominating or covering the employee organization. The teacher association in turn may have belatedly discovered that it could not prepare for negotiations or process grievances effectively if key administrative employees were privy to deliberations concerning action vis-a-vis the administration.

To cite a simple example, state associations were frequently called upon to assist local associations which were on strike. Such support often embittered the administrative members of these associations, since they could hardly support strikes by their teachers. By the same token, they could not support, even by membership, organizations that assisted and encouraged such actions.

The logic on the organization's side was just as compelling and led to the same result. A state association does not have to deliberate very long to decide whether to support the teachers who favor a strike or the administrators who oppose it. The lifeblood of the state association is teacher dues; administrators are a small minority of membership. The state association can hardly be expected to intervene systematically in local conflicts against the wishes of a majority of its members.

The crucial point here is not simply the inevitable decline of administrator membership in teacher organizations but the fact that this decline has dynamic effects of its own, which are virtually always in the direction of greater teacher militancy. Administrators may withdraw from the state association as a protest against its support for teachers in a specific situation, but the upshot of their withdrawal is likely to be greater teacher militancy, because their conservative influence is no longer a factor in the formulation of organizational policy. It may well be that the wave of teacher militancy which led to the decline in administrative membership will not be as aggressive as that resulting from the decline itself.

TEACHER MILITANCY AND PROFESSIONALISM

In turning to the relationships between teacher militancy and professionalism, two extreme positions can be easily identified. One position identifies professionalism with teacher willingness to accept any adverse terms and conditions of employment with a "grin and bear it" attitude. Sometimes the "professionals" are even supposed to respond enthusiastically to a lengthening of the school day or the school year, or to the absence of improvements in teacher welfare. Basically, this approach is the one employers would be expected to take; the surprising thing is that so many teachers accepted it for such a long time.

The other extreme identifies professionalism with power rather than sacrifice. Thus, when teachers use power to achieve higher salaries or other benefits, they are allegedly enhancing the dignity and "true professionalism" of teachers. Needless to say, this view is more popular among teachers today. Unfortunately, it seems just as unrealistic to equate professionalism with power hunger as it does with sacrificial lambs.

Naturally, there are several other ways to identify professionalism. Since it is not feasible to relate teacher militancy to each here, the rest of this article will analyze the impact of teacher militancy upon certain aspects of education frequently considered as characteristics of professionalism.

High standards for entry to teaching are an example. Here, we can see that teacher militancy has considerable potential. In some districts, teachers have negotiated clauses limiting the administration's freedom to employ teachers on emergency certificates. Much more probably will be done along this line. In effect, it means that teachers are beginning to rely upon their leverage as employees to raise standards.

Similarly, a growing number of collective agreements limit the administration's freedom to assign teachers to allegedly subprofessional work, such as bus or cafeteria duty. As an administrator, one may well object to such prohibitions. It may be—and often is—argued that although it is undesirable to assign teachers to subprofessional tasks, in certain situations there may be no practical alternative. Be that as it may, one can clearly discern considerable progress toward professionalization as a result of the collective negotiations movement.

Some critics see an opposite result. They view specifications in collective agreements of such things as the length of the school day or the number of days in the school year as "antiprofessional." Factory workers may have to punch in and out, but how many doctors or lawyers punch time clocks? This question is asked rhetorically, but a factual answer would surprise many persons who ask it. For example, in large law firms, including the most prestigious, very careful records are kept of the time devoted to each client. Whereas teachers may have to check in and out once a day, it is not unusual to find attorneys who must, in effect, check in and out several times a day, depending on how many different clients they serve. Although teacher militancy may have had some tendencies to retard professionalization, specification of the services rendered should not be seen as such.

Some observers believe that collective negotiation is unprofessional because it is inconsistent with merit pay. Such views reflect confusion on several fronts. First, collective negotiation does not preclude merit pay; in fact, some collective agreements expressly provide for it. Although there is a tendency to avoid merit pay in collective negotiations, an employer who regards it as essential will ordinarily be able to retain it. The assumption that the absence of merit pay is unprofessional per se has little merit. One can define "professionalism" to include a system of compensation, but such definitions have little value. For that matter, the average person exaggerates the extent to which fee takers set fees individually. For example, attorneys, physicians, and dentists frequently, in effect, charge clients at rates set by their local professional associations. In addition, it is unrealistic to equate salaried educational professionals with fee takers in other fields.

Probably the most important impact of teacher militancy upon professionalization is the greater strength and influence of teacher organizations. Although this developed as a response to inadequate organizational approaches to teacher conditions of employment, the outcome has been a greater organizational capability to deal with the conventional problems of professionalization. Teachers did not originally establish full-time local leadership because of low standards for entry. However, once such leadership was established, it could deal more effectively with the problem than the innocuous type of organization that was so prevalent in education before negotiations.

For these and other reasons, it seems reasonable to believe that teacher militancy has strengthened rather than weakened the movement toward professionalization. It should be noted, however, that some problems of professionalization are as yet unaffected. Furthermore, a favorable overall impact should not lead us to overlook the fact that teacher militancy in itself is neither good nor bad; everything depends upon the uses and objectives of such militancy. It would be naive to assume that every manifestation of it has been or will be devoted to socially desirable objectives. It is good that teachers have strong organizations, not because they will always use their strength for desirable goals but because teacher weakness poses more risks to our society than does teacher power.

48 reform of teacher certification

Lindley J. Stiles

Professional certification and licensure have a dual function: first, they protect the public against incompetent practitioners; and second, they sustain the profession itself by guarding against the erosion of standards and unprofessional conduct by its members. (*Certification* is a term used to attest to an individual's qualifications to practice a profession. It usually is based on examined knowledge and demonstrated performance as judged, in relationship to established standards, by representative members of the profession. A *license* is a legal permit to practice, issued by a state on the recommendation of an appropriate professional certification board. A state may specify requirements for a license, such as citizenship, loyalty, moral character, or length of residence, in addition to certification of professional competence. Also, a state may issue a license to practice a trade or business without professional confirmation of competence to do so. Thus, the distinction is made that a profession certifies and a state licenses.) Without an effective process of professional certification backed by a state licensing plan, the public has difficulty in distinguishing the unqualified and incompetent from the responsible professionals. Thus, high priority in any profession must be given to making certain that certification and licensing procedures fulfill the objectives set for them.

FAILURE OF TEACHER CERTIFICATION*

However one views the certification of teachers for licenses in the United States, the inescapable conclusion is that the system is failing. Such an observation is not intended as an indictment of those responsible for the operation of the plan; all are motivated by the best intentions and exert dedicated efforts to make the system work. The fault is with the system itself. It does not work, it never has worked, and it never will.

Why Teacher Certification Fails

Teacher certification fails in most states, if not all, because it is based on invalid evidence of teaching performance and is not accepted as a high priority responsibility by

---

*These ideas were originally presented, in briefer form, in my column, "Policy and Perspective," *The Journal of Educational Research,* April, 1968. My convictions have grown out of a lifetime of observing inadequacies in the teacher certification system and have been reinforced by evidence gained during my intensive study of certification practices in two states, Hawaii and Massachusetts.

the profession itself. I refer to the system of certification, which has become common throughout the nation during the past fifty years, that is based almost exclusively on the kinds and amounts of college course credits and administered by state officials. A number of states are currently in the process of developing new certification plans, but whether their approaches will continue to incorporate the weaknesses of past processes is not yet known.

Here is how the system works. The state department of public instruction, usually with the advice of school and college officials, establishes course requirements for a teacher's license. The specifications typically include blocks of credits that must be completed in the areas of professional education, the teaching concentration (teaching major), and in general or liberal education. Frequently, specific courses are required within these credit categories—educational psychology, methods of teaching, and clinical practice in the professional area, for example. A student who completes the prescribed course pattern automatically becomes eligible for a teaching license, provided, of course, that he or she meets any other special qualification, such as graduation from college, U. S. citizenship, and evidence of good moral character, that a state may require. Under the system, a candidate makes an application for a license and submits a transcript of college courses completed as evidence of qualification. State department officials check the transcript and, upon finding a record of the courses required, issue the license.

The course-credit system of certification is based on the premise that there exists a dependable relationship between subjects studied in college and the possession of sufficient knowledge and skills to perform successfully in teaching. As everyone realizes, knowledge of a subject field or even about educational processes does not always guarantee that one will have the ability to teach. Some of the brightest scholars cannot teach at all. Then, too, individual differences in students, professors, and courses in different institutions are so great that course credits and grades achieved give little assurance that minimum knowledge standards will have been met. It is true that all state systems require a period of clinical training under supervision. In theory, success in this course should give assurance that an individual is capable of teaching. Programs of clinical training (or student teaching, as it is traditionally called), vary so much, however, that some students may be given only intermittent contacts with student groups over short periods of time, or they may spend most of their time in schools only observing, or doing chores that relieve the regular teacher. Even when extensive periods of clinical training are provided, college supervisors frequently do not observe candidates sufficiently to make reliable judgments of independent professional performance. The credit-counting certification system reminds one of the story of the farmer who wanted to know the weight of a sack of potatoes but did not have a scale. He felt it would be unreliable to estimate the weight. To overcome the problem, he placed the potatoes on one end of a board laid across a fulcrum and balanced them by an equal weight of rocks on the other end. Then he estimated the weight of the rocks and assigned his conclusion to the potatoes. In teacher certification, we have been unwilling to judge teaching performance. What we do is estimate the value of course credits and then assume that our conclusion is a reliable predictor of teaching success.

Included in this indictment, in my opinion, must be those modifications, called "approved program" plans, which have now been adopted by about 80 per cent of the states. Such arrangements provide for the state department of education to certify automatically graduates of programs of preparation which have been approved in advance. Use of the approved program approach by a state has the advantage of providing greater flexibility, in that each college or university can design its own program. One benefit is that faculty groups have to decide how they want to prepare teachers instead of merely using state prescriptions. In practice, however, the flexibility usually does not extend to individual students, since all must follow programs that have been approved. Professors tend to be as rigid as state department officials in insisting on uniform patterns of preparation. Essentially, what the approved program plans accomplish is a transfer of the credit-counting process from the state department to the institution. The reliance is still on course credits as evidence that an individual possesses the kinds and amounts of knowledge and essential skills for successful teaching.

Efforts to patch up course-credit plans for teacher certification and to improve administrative procedures are futile; the system is failing because transcript records simply are not a very valid indicator of teaching success. This is true despite the fact that a positive relationship does, or at least should, exist between the courses students study in college and the knowledge they possess. What a candidate for teaching has studied is useful to know, but it represents insufficient, and often unreliable, evidence of professional competence. Thus, teacher certification is failing because, in the first place, it is wrongly conceived, and, in the second place, it is being operated by the state rather than by the profession itself.

Evidence of the failure of teacher certification is well known to all. The most common criticisms are that the certification process too often fails to screen from practice those who are personally or professionally unfit to teach. Furthermore, most state certification systems do not distinguish the kind of professional practice for which an individual is qualified or the extent of specialization achieved, nor do they maintain effective quality controls to ensure that practitioners do not become obsolescent in their knowledge and professional skills. Efforts to require teachers to keep up to date professionally suffer the same weaknesses as initial certification procedures: they prescribe the earning of additional college course credits without verification that a favorable influence on professional competence results.

Most damaging of all the negative effects of the teacher certification system, perhaps, is the way it acts as a deterrent to entry and continuation in teaching by able people. A profession that cannot maintain high standards tends to attract the weak rather than the competent. The effect is cyclical and progressively degrading, with poor teaching becoming the norm. Mediocrity attracts and embraces mediocrity, and highly skilled professional performance is relegated to minority status and influence.

One has only to consider the lack of public and professional confidence the credit-counting operations have generated to realize that teacher certification is failing. Most classroom teachers, who have little responsibility for determining standards or for judging qualifications of those admitted to practice, resent the way certification requirements are developed and administered. They generally consider requirements for teaching licenses too rigid, too quantitative, and too unrelated to the ability to teach. Teachers feel little responsibility for the system as it has evolved; hence, unable to prevent poor teachers from being licensed, they tend to blame school administrators and boards of education for employing unqualified and incompetent teachers.

School superintendents and personnel officers, however, have as little confidence in the certification standards as do the teachers themselves. They, with the approval of boards of education, often employ teachers who do not fully meet the specifications for a license. Some school systems set up their own licensing plans, a practice that, in itself, demonstrates a further lack of confidence in state certification systems. But even these school plans for certification may offer no alternative to the course-counting state plan other than an individual interview (which has been found to have doubtful reliability) and a written examination to measure knowledge. They may not identify effective teaching talent any more than does the state system. Then, too, administrators regularly bypass both school district and state certification processes by employing on temporary licenses teachers with deficit paper qualifications. Since no school official would stake his leadership on an incompetent person, such practice attests further to administrators' lack of confidence in certification standards as valid measures of professional competence.

Academic communities in colleges and universities have little respect for teacher certification. Deans and professors in schools of education, who are perhaps as responsible as anyone for present teacher certification systems, generally do not like the way they work. At the same time, many are reluctant to give up the compulsory enrollments that certification prescriptions produce for particular professional courses. Professors in the liberal arts and other fields who help to prepare teachers offer many criticisms of certification plans, the most familiar of which is that prospective teachers are required to take too many specific education courses. The remedy they propose, however, would only perpetuate the system with changes in course requirements from education to liberal arts departments.

Requiring students to complete specific amounts and patterns of courses in the liberal arts offers no assurance that graduates will be able to teach. A key weakness in the course-counting system, in fact, is found in the prescriptive major requirements of departments in liberal arts colleges. Consider, for example, the limitations imposed on an individual preparing to teach language and literature who would like to take some preparation in fields such as linguistics, journalism, communications, drama, oral interpretation, or world literature, but who is required instead to take courses almost exclusively in the field of English grammar and literature to meet major and minor requirements for graduation.

Officials in state departments of education know that they are saddled with administering procedures that represent more busy-work than measures of professional quality. Many realize that their efforts to involve professional representatives in setting standards are mostly token in nature and futile in results as long as the focus is on counting credits rather than defining criteria that relate more directly to professional performance. The public, accustomed as it is to professional performance being policed by the profession itself, is confused by the failure of the teaching profession to develop a certification system that does what it is supposed to do—protect students against incompetent teachers.

Another obvious sign of lack of confidence in certification plans by professional leaders themselves is the practice, prevalent in about half the states, of automatically granting teaching certificates to graduates of teacher education programs that are accredited by the National Council for Accreditation for Teacher Education. Making certification synonymous with accreditation is tantamount to abandoning any efforts to evaluate the fitness of individuals to teach. As everyone knows, incompetent professionals can be graduated from accredited institutions. Furthermore, since they presently operate with the emphasis on quantitative rather than on qualitative factors, accrediting standards do not even differentiate between weak and adequate programs of preparation. Nor is accreditation a reflection of the quality of an institution's teacher candidates. It is true that reforms in accrediting for teacher education are under way. One goal of such efforts is to relate accreditation to the quality of the resulting product. Even if leaders in accreditation succeed in producing standards and procedures that differentiate programs qualitatively, it would be a mistake to translate graduation from an "NCATE Approved" institution into automatic certification for either initial or reciprocity purposes. If such practices persist, certification as a process of qualifying individuals for professional practice in teaching will, in effect, be abolished.

Present certification plans in most states do not reflect the nature of a teacher's competence, such as ability to teach the new science or mathematics or the ability to deal with culturally handicapped children. Nor do they serve to counteract obsolescence in either teachers or programs of preparation. Their impact is to produce sterility rather than initiative and creativity, in those who teach and those who teach teachers. What is needed is a new start, one that takes seriously the purpose of certification and licensure— the guarantee that all certified to teach will have minimum competence. Also, any new plan should be evaluated in terms of whether it deters the able from entering and remaining in the teaching profession.

MAKING CERTIFICATION A PROFESSIONAL RESPONSIBILITY

Fortunately, a number of states are now taking the lead in redesigning teacher certification to make it the responsibility of members of the profession itself and to formulate qualitative guidelines for judging professional competence. The conceptualization of this type of professional certification was first developed in the report of a comprehensive study of teacher certification and preparation in Massachusetts (Stiles, 1968). A scientific sampling of the opinions of teachers, administrators, and college personnel in both public and nonpublic schools, made as a part of this study, showed that a high percentage (over 80 per cent) favored this kind of reform of teacher certification. The Massachusetts Teachers Association supported the recommendations. Subsequent to the publication of the Massachusetts report, California adopted similar procedures. Washington State, whose study of ways to reform teacher certification paralleled the Massachusetts investigation with respect to both time and recommendations, is another pioneer in this field (see Drummond and Allen, *Statement of Standards for Preparation of School Professional Personnel Leading to Certification,* 1968).

The key to this kind of reform of teacher certification is the establishment by the state of a legal professional Board of Teacher Certification with responsibility to develop standards and judge qualifications of personnel for professional licensure. A poll I have just completed of state plans for certification revealed that 12 states* have established, by legal action, a Council or Commission on Teacher Certification. Such bodies, composed of teachers and other kinds of educational personnel, are responsibile for establishing standards, determining qualifications of individuals, and certifying them for licensure to state authorities.

Strong support for this type of reform of teacher certification has recently come from the National Education Association in the form of a recommended Model Teacher Standards and Licensure Act which the states are being urged to adopt. This model legislation was developed by the National Commission on Teacher Education and Professional Standards, NEA, in consultation with the National Commission on Professional Rights and Responsibilities and the NEA General Council (National Commission on Teacher Education and Professional Standards, 1971).

---

*Connecticut, Florida, Illinois, Indiana, Kentucky, Massachusetts, New Jersey, Oklahoma, Oregon, South Carolina, Tennessee, and Texas.

The NEA proposal calls for the state to declare that teaching is a professional practice, an essential act if the state is to create a professional commission to take responsibility for setting professional standards and admitting individuals to professional practice. The NEA Model Act recommends that the Commission be appointed by the governor and suggests that majority representation should go to classroom teachers (seven out of thirteen members). The remaining positions would go to: supervisors and administrators (two members), colleges and universities (two members), specialists in cognate fields who perform educational work (one member), and instructional assistants who are not qualified for a professional license (one member). Recommendations are that the Commission have responsibility to award licenses to teach and also be empowered to revoke or suspend licenses for specific causes such as conviction of a serious crime, violation of ethical standards, fraud in obtaining a license, or other reasons that render a person unfit to teach. Detailed procedures for hearing grievances are made. The Act, if adopted by a state, would make it unlawful for a person to engage in teaching, or the performance of educational duties, without a valid license issued by the Commission. Punishment is set as imprisonment of up to six months and a fine of up to $5000 for this misdemeanor. Other proposed responsibilities of the Commission include the accrediting of teacher preparation institutions, development of reciprocity agreements with other states, and the conversion of existing teacher licenses (a grandfather clause) into comparable types that are developed by the Commission.

An alternative plan developed by the State of Washington, which had three years of intensive study by members of the profession before being enacted in 1971, is guided by these essential ideas (Drummond and Allen, 1968, p. 53):

1. Professional preparation should be continuous throughout the career of the practitioner.

2. School organizations and professional associations, as well as colleges and universities, should be recognized as preparation agencies.

3. Discussions about preparation should be based upon performance; performance in relation to stated objectives and the world of the practitioner.

4. Preparation and career development programs should be individualized.

To implement the continuous preparation concept, as well as to provide for differentiated levels of professional competence, the plan provides for four types of certificates to be offered: preparatory, initial, continuing, and consultant. Programs approved must meet defined criteria which include, among others, descriptions of performance expectations for particular certificates, provisions for interinstitutional collaboration to include both school and professional associations as well as colleges, and individualization. As the plan works, coalitions of agencies that desire to experiment with performance standards and professional involvement may propose to the state department the particular plan they want to follow in preparing and certifying teachers. Such proposals, which may differ greatly, may be approved on a three to five year schedule upon the favorable review of the State Liaison Committee.

In addition to the 12 states that have already established legal Commissions on Teacher Certification, 31 others* maintain quasi-legal Advisory Commissions on Teacher

---

*Alaska, Arizona, Colorado, Delaware, Georgia, Idaho, Iowa, Kentucky, Louisiana, Maryland, Massachusetts, Michigan, Minnesota, Mississippi, Missouri, Montana, Nebraska, Nevada, New Hampshire, New Mexico, New York, Ohio, Pennsylvania, Rhode Island, South Dakota, Utah, Vermont, Virginia, Washington, Wisconsin, and Wyoming.

Certification. Such bodies, typically appointed by the Chief State School Officer or the Director of Teacher Certification, are composed of teachers and other educational personnel. Not specifically recognized by state law, they function to provide advice to State Departments of Education on matters relating to teacher certification. Seventeen states use ad hoc committees of teachers as a source of advice when changes in licensing requirements are considered. Twenty-three state departments have formed committees of teachers representing various subject fields to help develop requirements in each.

INVOLVEMENT OF TEACHER GROUPS

Teachers' associations are beginning to play more active roles in the development of standards and policies for certification, as the action of the National Education Association illustrates. Eighteen of the state teachers' associations polled indicated that the organization had developed policies and standards for the certification of teachers as recommendations to the state department of public instruction. Groups of subject field teachers, e.g., history, English, modern foreign languages, and so on, similarly are becoming active in developing criteria for determining professional competence in their particular areas of specialization. Six* out of 13 such bodies polled have developed policies and standards for certification of new members and 4 of them† have recommended policies and standards to the various states as guides to certification practices for teachers in their fields.

The move to define standards for certification that are unique to particular fields of specialization holds a special significance. In the past, teachers have been licensed to teach particular subject fields or ages of students, but the requirements for licensure have been generally uniform as far as course-credit requirements have been concerned. Every high school teacher had to take about the same number of courses in the major field as well as in the pedagogical area. The assumption was that a physical education teacher needed the same amount of major field course work and pedagogical training as the physics or music teacher. The new trend is for teachers to consider the qualifications for teaching in terms of the knowledge and skills that are relevant to teaching particular subjects to given types of students. Teachers of modern foreign languages, for example, believe that it is important for a teacher of these subjects to be able to speak fluently the language taught. Their association has called upon the various states to establish oral examinations, conducted by qualified specialists in each language, to judge qualification for certification. The Massachusetts Study recommended that the Commission on Teacher Certification should establish subpanels in each subject field for elementary teaching and for specialized educational work, e.g., counseling or administration, to define standards that would be uniquely appropriate for each. Membership of each panel would come from teachers, scholars, and appropriate specialists in the field or level of the school system.

As practice evolves away from measuring a teacher candidate's knowledge and skills by the numbers of credits earned in college courses to assessing actual evidence of knowledge and performance, scholars and teachers will need to develop descriptions of

---

*National Science Teachers Association, Modern Language Association of America, Music Educators National Conference, American Speech and Hearing Association, National Council for the Social Studies, and the American Home Economics Association.

†Modern Language Association of America, Music Educators National Conference, American Speech and Hearing Association, and the American Home Economics Association.

the kinds and depths of understanding of content as well as teaching abilities desired. It is possible, for example, for teachers in schools and scholars in institutions of higher learning to agree on the mathematical theory, concepts, and computational and teaching skills needed to teach the new or traditional mathematics. Once such standards have been defined, both students and institutions will have guidelines to follow. School systems, too, will be able to employ teachers with the kind of mathematical knowledge and teaching skills that are compatible with their programs and students. Defined minimum qualitative standards for successful teaching will provide common assurance to all, and this is the purpose of certification.

USE OF PERFORMANCE STANDARDS

As classroom teachers assume control and take responsibility for admission to practice, they will have the opportunity to develop standards and procedures for determining qualification for entry and continuation in teaching that are directly related to professional performance in particular kinds of school situations. To ascertain the extent to which states and professional associations favor the use of performance standards, the aforementioned poll asked whether state departments and teacher associations were moving in this direction. A surprising number of Directors of Teacher Certification, 28, reported that their states were working to develop performance standards for teacher certification. Less encouraging is the fact that only 15 state teachers' associations and three subject matter associations indicated that their organizations favor the use of performance standards. In contrast, the National Education Association clearly leans toward the use of performance standards in its proposed Model Teacher Standards and Licensure Act. The specific mandate proposed for enactment by legislatures reads: "It is the intent of the Legislature that the Commission not engage merely in the prescription of certain courses of study and unit counting in developing minimum licensing requirements" (National Commission on Teacher Education and Professional Standards, 1971).

The reluctance of teacher groups to support the use of performance standards to judge qualification for teaching may well be traced to the fact that teachers fear that judgments will be made by administrators rather than professional peers. Some, no doubt, oppose any movement away from the credit-counting certification process because they do not feel comfortable themselves when professional competence is being emphasized as a qualification for practice. This is particularly true when provisions for certification provide for the recognition of different levels of competence or when continuing certification is made contingent on keeping professionally up to date. The Model Act developed by the NEA, for instance, recommends the following categories of professional licensure: (1) Basic, (2) Advanced, (3) Educational Specialist, and (4) Assistant. Whether or not performance standards are employed in a given field may well depend on whether outstanding teachers and scholars are able to take the initiative to move in this direction.

With respect to the use of performance standards, a basic premise is that the ability to teach effectively must be judged. The question of who is to do the judging is one that worries teachers who are accustomed to being rated by supervisors and administrators rather than by peer professionals whose judgments they respect. In addition, a distinction needs to be made between assessments of performance made for certification purposes and those used by school systems to evaluate teacher effectiveness. Where certification is the purpose, the reliability of professional judgments can be expected to be much higher, since the decision concerns only satisfactory ability to teach rather than fine discriminations related to higher levels of teaching performance.

It is the mark of a profession to judge qualification for practice. Failure to take such responsibility reduces a professional service to trade status. Teaching has yet to move above trade attitudes and practices as far as taking responsibility for the qualification of new members is concerned. In most states, almost anyone who can earn 16 to 20 semester hours of credit in education courses and graduate from college automatically qualifies for entry into teaching. Ability to teach is not the predominant factor considered. To upgrade teaching to professional status, members of the profession must take the responsibility for evaluating a new candidate's knowledge and judging his teaching skills in terms of criteria that relate to success in teaching—and this means the use of performance standards.

PARTNERSHIPS FOR TEACHER CERTIFICATION

Replacing credit-counting plans for certification and licensure with qualitative guidelines and judgments of professional competence will require that legally established Commissions for Teacher Certification be kept free from political pressures—from both within and without the profession. To be effective, a commission will have to enlist the participation and loyalty of teachers, supervisors, administrators, educationists, liberal arts professors, and leaders in state departments of education, as well as lay groups concerned directly with education. Realistic rather than perfunctory partnerships will have to be formed between preparatory institutions, school systems, and state departments of public instruction, and among teachers, administrators, and academic and professional professors. Colleges and universities will have to give first priority to developing programs that focus on producing quality professional performance, and school systems will have to provide the kinds of clinical experiences that permit competence to be developed, demonstrated, and judged. Assessment of knowledge and judgments of performance skills required for successful teaching will have a better chance of being valid if representatives of the various partners in the teacher education enterprise—teachers, administrators, academic and professional professors, as well as state department personnel—share the responsibility. Of necessity, the need will be to experiment and validate new certification plans in terms of the competence of teachers produced, and the relationship of certification to the needs of different kinds of schools.

A TIME FOR REFORM

The time to reform teacher certification is now. My study of the problem has convinced me that the transcript method of certification must be abolished and replaced by a plan that utilizes standards that are more closely related to professional performance—in different subject fields and with specific ages and types of students. The profession itself must take responsibility and be accountable for defining standards and applying them in judging qualifications for certification. Moreover, I believe that this type of professional accountability can be assumed only by specific types of teachers, rather than by professional associations in general. Mathematics teachers must decide who should be admitted to their field. English teachers should be the judge of who should teach their subject. Elementary teachers should set the standards and certify candidates for teaching at this level. Teachers in inner city schools should play key roles when standards are set and new teachers admitted to practice in such situations. Otherwise, what's everybody's business will be nobody's responsibility.

Decisions relative to granting certification to teach with wisdom a particular subject under given conditions will be concerned with different kinds of evidence: personal qualitites, creative and intellectual capacities, general education, knowledge pertaining to both the teaching specialization and the professional practice, and, above all, demonstrated adequate performance in the kind of teaching for which certification is granted. When the focus is shifted from course credits to performance, greater flexibility and individuality will come in preservice programs of preparation. I foresee that prospective teachers will be able to design their own preparation in consultation with members of the profession as well as college personnel. This type of personal planning is already being done by students enrolled in the Tutorial-Clinical Program at Northwestern University. During the initial phase of the program, called Professional Confrontation, each student verifies his or her commitment to prepare for teaching and then proposes an individual plan of preparation to achieve the goals identified. When approved by an advisory committee, which includes both practicing teachers as well as professors, the plan functions as an individual contract for preparation for teaching and graduation from the School of Education. Thus, no two programs of preparation may be identical. The test of all students, however, will be whether they develop satisfactory kinds and levels of knowledge and the ability to translate such knowledge into successful teaching.

If teaching is to become a profession in fact as well as by assertion, professionals must take responsibility for those certified to practice. The standards established must be relevant to successful performance as required for different kinds of teaching-learning situations. To make the transition from present transcript plans to professional judgments of teaching competence, e.g., from trade to professional status, state governments must be persuaded to delegate responsibility for controlling entry into teaching directly to the profession itself, as the NEA Model Teacher Standards and Licensure Act provides. With authority to act, the profession will be challenged to take charge of its own destiny.

The time for reform of teacher certification in the various states is extremely propitious. With an oversupply of teachers predicted for the foreseeable years ahead, an opportunity exists to improve the quality of performance and limit the numbers admitted to practice to match the demand. Decisions by the profession to accomplish such goals will be sound only if based on standards that differentiate between adequate and unacceptable teaching and judgments that are made by professionals who are themselves capable scholars and teachers.

REFERENCES

Allen, D. W., and Wagschal, P.: New look in credentialing. *The Clearing House, 44:* 137-140, November, 1969.

Allen, W. C.: Performance criteria for educational personnel development: a state approach to standards. *Journal of Teacher Education, 20*: 133-135, Summer, 1969.

Bhaerman, R.: Education's new dualisms. *Changing Education, 4*: 3-7, Fall, 1969.

Black, W. M.: Look at teacher certification. *School and Community, 57*: 36-38, September, 1970.

Brooks, A. G.: Revised certification regulations for Virginia teachers effective July 1, 1968. *Virginia Journal of Education, 61*: 28-29, May, 1968.

Certification at the crossroads. *New York State Education, 57*: 16-24, February, 1970.

Clement, S. L.: Cooperation, not competition. *Education, 89*: 53-56, September, 1968.

Continuing education for all teachers. *Minnesota Journal of Education, 49*: 42-43, September, 1968.

Di Nello, M. C., and Hawkins, H. L.: Survey of the revocation of teaching certificates. *Journal of Teacher Education, 21*: 526-533, Winter, 1970.

Drummond, W. H., and Allen, W. C.: Statement of Standards for Preparation of School Professional Personnel Leading to Certification. Olympia, Washington, State Department of Public Instruction, 1968.

Guidelines for a professional standards and practices act. *School and Community, 55*: 22-23, September, 1968.

Lierheimer, A. P.: Cast off the bowline. *Today's Education, 58*: 62, March, 1969.

Lierheimer, A. P.: Changing the palace guard. *Phi Delta Kappan, 52*: 20-24, September, 1970.

Lierheimer, A. P.: Red-faced over red tape: progress in interstate certification of teachers. *Compact, 4*: 28-30, April, 1970.

LeSure, J. S.: Teacher certification edges toward uniformity: interstate certification agreement. *Nation's Schools, 83*: 84, May, 1969.

More flexible requirements. *School and Society, 97*: January, 1969.

National Commission on Teacher Education and Professional Standards. National Education Association: A Model Teacher Standards and Licensure Act. Washington, D.C., NEA, 1971.

Sparks, R. K.: Are we ready for national certification of professional educators? *Journal of Teacher Education, 21*: 342-346, Fall, 1970.

Stiles, L. J.: Certification and preparation of educational personnel in Massachusetts. *Phi Delta Kappan, 50*: 477-480, April, 1969.

Stiles, L. J.: Last may be first. *Journal of Educational Research, 62*: inside cover, January, 1969.

Stiles, L. J.: Teacher Certification and Preparation in Massachusetts, Status, Problems, and Proposed Solutions, Report Number 1, a Report Prepared by the Massachusetts Advisory Council on Education. Boston, Massachusetts Advisory Council on Education, 1968.

Stinnett, T. M.: Trends in teacher certification. *Science Teacher, 38*: 24-25, February, 1971.

Walden, J. C.: Proposal for professional control of educator performance. *School and Society, 99*: 39-41, January, 1971.

second class citizens: 49
the civil rights
of teachers

David Schimmel
Louis Fischer

"Pedagogue" was the Greek word for slave. To us it means "teacher." Although no one contends that teachers in the United States today are treated like slaves, until very recently they were certainly second class citizens.

Several decades ago it was common practice to regulate all aspects of teachers' lives and subject them to conditions of employment that violated the constitutional rights of the general citizenry. Freedom of expression, association, and religion, as well as the rights of privacy and political participation were often curtailed. The following provisions were not uncommon in teachers' contracts in the past:

> I promise to take a vital interest in all phases of Sunday-school work, donating of my time, service, and money without stint for the uplift and benefit of the community.
> I promise to abstain from all dancing, immodest dressing, and any other conduct unbecoming a teacher and a lady.
> I promise not to go out with any young men except in so far as it may be necessary to stimulate Sunday-school work.
> I promise not to fall in love, to become engaged or secretly married.
> I promise not to encourage or tolerate the least familiarity on the part of any of my boy pupils.
> I promise to sleep at least eight hours a night, to eat carefully, and to take every precaution to keep in the best of health and spirits, in order that I may be better able to render efficient service to my pupils.
> I promise to remember that I owe a duty to the townspeople who are paying me my wages, that I owe respect to the school board and the superintendent that hired me, and that I shall consider myself at all times the willing servant of the school board and the townspeople (quoted by Minehan, 1927, p. 606).

Lest the reader dismiss this excerpt as mere historical information, one of the authors had the following conversation in 1969 with the Associate Superintendent of Public Instruction for the State of California:

Superintendent: "Teaching is a privilege, not a right. If one wants this privilege, he has to give up some of his rights."

Author: "Just what constitutional rights does one have to give up in order to enter teaching?"

Superintendent: "Any right his community wants him to give up."

In other words, this educational leader (though no longer an associate superintendent) believes that the civil rights guarantees of the national constitution do not apply to teachers in the same way as to businessmen, physicians, lawyers, or plumbers.

VIOLATIONS OF TEACHERS' RIGHTS

Many parents, administrators, and school board members still believe that local communities can and should control the behavior of teachers. The controls that they seek to impose, though less extreme than those at the beginning of the century, often lead to a partial revocation of the Bill of Rights in the lives of teachers. Particularly invidious are instances where these controls are applied in a covert, unstated fashion.

Practices which occur at the point of *selection* of a teacher or administrator are peculiarly difficult to eliminate or even attack, since selection committees necessarily exercise discretion and make qualitative judgments when hiring people. Thus, for example, in a recent interview for an elementary teaching position in North Carolina, a well-qualified graduate from an excellent school was asked whether or not she smoked. It turned out to be the most dangerous question in the interview. She smoked, she admitted it, and she later learned that "smokers" are not hired there. The wisdom of smoking aside, no school board in the country would propose to dismiss a teacher who, outside the classroom or away from the school, smoked cigarettes. Yet, an "overall qualitative judgment" at the initial *screening* or *selection* stage was used as a cover for the denial of this applicant's constitutional freedom.

A more common example is the current concern with beards and long hair. While courts tend to protect teachers' rights to have a beard, candidates for teaching positions often lose out if their faces are so adorned. Many a young candidate faces personal conflict when his friends or college advisors tell him: "Shave your face and you'll get the job. Once the principal and the community come to appreciate your talents, you can grow your beard again."

Membership in certain controversial organizations carries similar consequences. While we generally proclaim the right of everyone to freedom of conscience and political commitment, an open membership in the Socialist Party or the John Birch Society is an insurmountable bar to initial employment in thousands of school districts throughout the country.

Membership in controversial political organizations can often pose problems for nontenured teachers as well as applicants. Many nontenured teachers, for example, are dismissed for membership in such organizations, though the *stated* reason for the nonrenewal of a contract refers to insufficient knowledge of the "new math," "the new English," or some other apparently legitimate ground.

A known history of social dissent, even though peaceful and lawful, is also commonly viewed with suspicion by school authorities. Whether deciding on hiring or contract renewal, administrators have a concern for the efficient functioning of schools; and they tend to view social activists as potential trouble-makers who will interfere with the running of a "tight ship." Viewed with suspicion is a history of activism in peace movements, Black Power, women's liberation, world federalism, or gay liberation. Open support of such causes by tenured teachers often leads to harrassment, disciplinary action and, at times, dismissal. *Most teachers* do not fight unwarranted disciplinary action but agree to resign with a positive letter of recommendation that might lead to a new job in another community. *Most administrators* would rather settle the matter this way to avoid public controversy and possibly endanger "the next bond issue." Thus, both teachers and administrators contribute to the erosion of civil rights.

Participation in controversial political elections or public criticism of school policies and practices are other legally protected activities which are often abridged. The extent of these infringements is not known. However, inferences can be drawn from the cases which reach the courts, from the countless incidents reported in the newspapers, and from the files of the two major educational organizations, the National Education Association and the American Federation of Teachers.*

The reader will appreciate the difficulties of civil rights problems related to education as he reads the following cases. Each case is on the frontier of current legal thinking in five controversial areas: freedom of speech outside the classroom; classroom speech and academic freedom; organizational affiliation, loyalty oaths, and political activity; personal appearance; and private life.

Freedom of Speech Outside the Classroom: Should a teacher be able to publicly criticize his superiors?

Marvin Pickering was a high school teacher from Will County, Illinois who did not want his criticism of the superintendent and the Board of Education to be restricted to the teachers' lounge. He sent a letter to the local newspaper which criticized the Board for misinforming the public about the allocation of financial resources in a proposed school bond issue. It also charged that the superintendent had threatened to discipline any teacher who refused to support the bond issue. Noting that teachers' letters had to be approved by the superintendent before publication in newspapers, Pickering commented, "That's the kind of totalitarianism teachers live in at the high school, and your children go to school in."†

His letter concluded:

> As I see it, the bond issue is a fight between the Board of Education that is trying to push tax-supported athletics down our throats with education, and a public that has mixed emotions about both of these items because they feel they are already paying enough taxes, and simply don't know whom to trust with any more money.
> I must sign this letter as a citizen, taxpayer, and voter, not as a teacher, since that freedom has been taken from the teachers by the administration.

The Board of Education responded that statements in the letter were false and would disrupt faculty discipline, damage the professional reputation of Board members and school administrators, and impugn their motives, honesty, and competence. After a full hearing on these charges, the Board dismissed Pickering because it determined that publication of his letter was "detrimental to the efficient operation and administration of the schools of the district."

---

*The NEA, for example, has created a special arm, the Dushand Fund, which focuses on the variety of problems and issues dealing with the rights of teachers. The concerns of the NEA and the AFT are broader than the concerns of this paper, since we explore only the *civil rights* of teachers, while these organizations are also concerned with a variety of contractual rights, welfare issues, and other professional matters.

†*Pickering v. Board of Education,* 391 U.S. 563 (1968). The discussion of the *Pickering* case in this article is based substantially on the opinion of the Court by Mr. Justice Marshall.

Pickering contended that his comments in the letter were protected by his constitutional right of free speech, and took his case to court. The Illinois court rejected Pickering's claim, saying that his acceptance of a teaching position in the public schools obliged him to refrain from making statements about the operation of the schools which he otherwise would have the right to make.* Pickering appealed this decision to the U.S. Supreme Court.

The Supreme Court indicated that questions of school funding are appropriate matters for public discussion and should be open to free debate. Since teachers are citizens who are most likely to have informed opinions as to how school funds should be allocated, it is essential that they be able to speak out freely on such matters without fear of retaliatory dismissal. Therefore, the Court ruled that: "a teacher's exercise of his right to speak on issues of public importance may not furnish the basis for his dismissal."

The Supreme Court decision not only led to Pickering's reinstatement, but it also clarified the law on several questions of importance to all teachers.

1. Can a teacher be compelled to give up his First Amendment right to comment on matters of public interest in connection with the operation of the public schools?

The general answer is no. Because a person is a teacher is no reason to compel him to give up constitutional rights that he would otherwise enjoy as a citizen.

2. Is there any time a school board can restrict a teacher's right to publicize his views?

Only if the board can show a compelling need for confidentiality or demonstrate that the teacher's working relationship with his superiors is so close that public criticism would destroy that relationship can it restrict a teacher's right in this way.

3. If some of the statements in a critical public letter are not true, is the school board then justified in dismissing the teacher?

Not just for writing the letter. But if the teacher published a letter that was clearly without any factual basis, questions might be raised about his fitness to teach. In that case the letter could constitute one piece of evidence concerning the teacher's general competence.

4. Suppose the teacher published statements that he *knew* were false about an issue of public importance?

If the school board could prove that false statements were made knowingly or recklessly, then the teacher might legally be dismissed for making such statements.

Classroom Speech and Academic Freedom: Can a teacher use "offensive" language in a high school class?

Robert Keefe taught in a public high school in Ipswich, Massachusetts. He was a creative teacher who wanted to expose his students to relevant and provocative contemporary writing. Therefore, on the first day of school in September, 1969, he assigned his class an article entitled "The Young and the Old" in the current issue of the *Atlantic* magazine that dealt with dissent, protest, radicalism, and revolt (Lifton, 1969). It contained the word "motherfucker" which was repeated a number of times. The teacher

---

*Pickering, said the Illinois Court, "holds a position as teacher and is no more entitled to harm the schools by speech than by incompetency, cruelty, negligence, immorality or any other conduct for which there may be no legal sanction" (*Pickering,* 225 N.E. 2d. 1, 6 [1967]).

explained the article and the vulgar term, its origin, and context. And he told the class that any student who felt the assignment distasteful could have an alternative one.*

While there was no evidence of negative student reaction to the article, several parents found the word highly offensive and protested to the school committee. Members of the committee asked Keefe if he would agree not to use the word again in class. The teacher replied that he could not in good conscience agree. After the meeting, Keefe was suspended and charges were drawn up to dismiss him. Keefe, however, believed that this would violate his civil rights and went to court to stop his dismissal.

This case raises a number of questions regarding controversial speech in a high school classroom. This is the way one U.S. Court of Appeals answered them:†

1. Isn't an article that repeatly uses a vulgar and highly offensive term pornographic and improper?

It depends on the article. In this case the judge read the article and found it "scholarly, thoughtful, and thought-provoking." The court said it was not possible to read this article as an "incitement to libidinous conduct." If it raised the concept of incest, wrote the judge, "it was not to suggest it, but to condemn it"; the word was used "as a superlative of opprobrium."

2. Assuming the article had merit, couldn't the teacher have discussed it without considering this word?

Not in this case. The offending word was not artificially introduced but was important to the development of the thesis and conclusions of the author. Therefore, no proper study of the article could avoid consideration of the offensive word.

3. Can't a school committee protect students from language that the parents of some students find genuinely offensive?

This would depend on the age of the students, the words used, and their purpose. In this case the word was used for educational purposes. Most high school seniors knew the word, and it was used nationally by young radicals and protestors. "If . . . students must be protected from such exposure," wrote Judge Aldrich, "we would fear for their future." Thus he concluded that the sensibilities of offended parents, "are not the full measure of what is proper in education."

4. Does that mean that a teacher could assign any book that is legally published? Are obscenity standards the same for students as for adults?

No, the court does not go that far. The issue is one of degree. Whether the use of offensive language is proper depends on all of the circumstances. In fact, Judge Aldrich

---

*The following excerpts illustrate the language, tone, and style of the article:

> Of enormous importance for these rebellions is another basic component of the protean style, the spirit of mockery . . . .
> The mockery can be gentle and even loving, or it can be bitter and provocative in the extreme. Here the Columbia rebellion is illuminating. What it lacked in graffiti, it more than made up for in its already classic slogan, "Up against the wall, motherfucker!" I make no claim to full understanding of the complete psychological and cultural journey this phrase has undergone. But let me at least sketch in a few steps along the way:
> 1. The emergence of the word "motherfucker" to designate a form of extreme transgression . . . .
> 2. The use of the word in contemptuous command by white policemen when ordering Black (and perhaps other) suspects to take their place in the police lineup, thereby creating the full phrase, "Up against the wall, motherfucker!" . . . .
> 8. Finally, Lionel Trilling's pun, in characterizing the striking students (not without affection) as "Alma-Mater-fuckers" . . . .

†*Keefe v. Geanakos*, 418 F. 2d 359 (1st Cir. 1969).

acknowledged that "some measure of public regulation of classroom speech is inherent in every provision of public education." But the judge concluded that the application of such a regulation in the Keefe case "demeans any proper concept of education." Thus, as the Supreme Court has pointed out, the unwarranted inhibition of the free speech of teachers affects not only the restricted teachers, but it also has an "unmistakable tendency to chill that free play of spirit which *all* teachers ought especially to cultivate and practice" (Frankfurter, 1952).

The concern for the protection of academic freedom, of course, goes beyond the selective protection of offensive language. It is based on an historic commitment to free speech, on the importance of academic inquiry to social progress, and on the need for both teachers and students to operate in an open atmosphere which allows established concepts to be freely challenged.

Membership in Controversial Organizations: Can a teacher be dismissed because he is a member of a subversive organization?

Harry Keyishian was an English instructor at the Buffalo campus of the State University of New York. To comply with the state's Feinberg Law, Keyishian was asked to sign an oath that he was not a Communist. When he refused, his one-year contract was not renewed. As a result, Keyishian challenged the constitutionality of the Feinberg Law, which disqualified any teacher in New York's public educational system who joined any organization that advocated the overthrow of government by unlawful means.

The Board of Regents of New York and several justices of the Supreme Court believed the Feinberg law should be upheld.* They saw the classroom as a sensitive area where the teacher shapes the attitudes of young minds toward society. School officials, therefore, have the right and duty to screen teachers concerning their fitness. Furthermore, teachers may be subject to reasonable terms of employment, such as not belonging to subversive organizations. If they do not choose to work on such terms, they are free to retain their beliefs and associations and seek other employment. The intent of the Feinberg Law is merely to protect society's right to preserve democracy.

A majority of the justices of the Supreme Court disagreed. They held that it was unconstitutional to disqualify a teacher merely because he was a member of the Communist Party or any other subversive organization without also showing that the teacher had the specific intent of furthering the unlawful aims of the party or organization. These were some of their reasons:

1. "Our nation is deeply committed to safeguarding academic freedom, which is of transcendent value to all of us and not merely to the teachers concerned. That freedom is, therefore, a special concern of the First Amendment which does not tolerate laws that cast a pall of orthodoxy over the classroom . . . . The nation's future depends upon leaders trained through wide exposure to that robust exchange of ideas which discovers truth out of a multitude of tongues rather than through any kind of authoritative selection" (*Keyishian,* 1967, 603).

2. While New York has a legitimate interest in protecting its educational system from subversion, that interest cannot be pursued by means that broadly stifle fundamental liberties when the end can be more narrowly achieved.

---

*Keyishian v. Board of Regents, 385 U.S. 589 (1967). For further arguments supporting the Feinberg Law, see especially Mr. Justice Clark's dissent in the *Keyishian* case.

3. Even the Feinberg Law, when applied to public school teachers who have young captive audiences, is subject to constitutional limitations in favor of freedom of expression and association, for the curtailing of these freedoms has a stifling effect on the academic mind.

4. The court rejected the doctrine of guilt by association upon which the Feinberg law was based: "Under our traditions, beliefs are personal and not a matter of mere association, and men in adhering to a political party or other organization do not subscribe unqualifiedly to all of its platforms or asserted principles. A law which applies to membership, without the specific intent to further the illegal aims of the organization, infringes unnecessarily on protected freedoms" (*Keyishian,* 607).

The court concluded that those who join an organization but do not share its unlawful purposes and do not participate in its unlawful activities pose no threat, either as citizens or as public employees. Thus mere membership in the Communist Party is not a constitutionally adequate basis for excluding Keyishian from his teaching position.

Would the Keyishian ruling apply to membership in the John Birch Society, the Ku Klux Klan, the Black Panther Party, or the Weatherman faction of the S.D.S.? The answer is the same whether the teacher is a member of an unpopular or revolutionary organization of the right or the left: a teacher cannot be dismissed for membership in any controversial organization unless it can be shown that he specifically intends to pursue the organization's illegal activities.

Personal Appearance: Does a teacher have a right to wear a beard?

Paul Finot taught government to high school seniors in the Pasadena, California school system for seven years. In September, 1963, when Finot arrived at school wearing a freshly grown beard, the high school principal asked him to shave it off. Upon his refusal, the Pasadena Board of Education transferred Finot to home teaching, despite the fact that he was a challenging and effective classroom teacher. Finot branded his transfer unconstitutional. He went to court to force the Board to change its action.*

The Board said the transfer was justified on the basis of the school's administrative policy as well as the professional judgment of the principal and superintendent. The administrative policy, which had been in force for three years, was based on the city's Teacher Handbook. The handbook called for teachers to practice the common social amenities, as evidenced by acceptable dress and grooming, and to set an example of neatness and good taste. This was related to a student handbook prohibiting beards, mustaches, and excessively long hair as "not appropriate dress for male students." The "professional judgment" of Finot's principal and superintendent was that the appearance of teachers had a definite effect on student behavior—that the well-dressed student generally behaved equally well. They felt that Finot's beard might attract undue attention, interfere with the process of education, and make the prohibition against student beards more difficult to enforce. And they felt that wearing a beard did not meet the school's requirement of acceptable grooming or set an example of good taste.

The trial judge found that the Board's action in changing Finot's teaching assignment was a lawful and reasonable exercise of its discretion. But Finot and the American Civil Liberties Union disagreed, and they appealed to the California District Court.

Here Finot found judicial support for his stand. The Court said that Finot's right to wear a beard was one of the liberties protected by the Fourteenth Amendment, which

---

*Finot vs. Pasadena City Board of Education, 250 C.A. 2d 189, 191 (1967).

prohibits the deprivation of life, "liberty," or property of any person without due process of law. Furthermore, the judges said that "the wearing of a beard is a form of expression of an individual's personality" and that such a right of expression is entitled to the peripheral protection of the First Amendment. In the absence of evidence that a teacher's beard had an adverse effect on the educational process, the Court ruled that beards on teachers "cannot constitutionally be banned from the classroom."

Would the ruling in the *Finot* case apply to clothing as well as beards? If a teacher decided not to conform to a school's dress code, would a court support his argument that the way a teacher dresses is a constitutionally protected personal liberty?

Judging from the court's opinion in the *Finot* case, it is doubtful that courts would be inclined to give equal protection to a teacher's right to dress. This is because clothing can be changed to suit the occasion. In contrast, the court points out that "a beard cannot be donned and doffed for work and play as wearing apparel generally can, and therefore the effect of a prohibition against wearing one extends beyond working hours."

On the other hand, courts might be more likely to protect certain nonconforming clothing under special circumstances. Thus a court might protect a black teacher of African Studies who wore a dashiki as directly relevant to his job or as a matter of academic freedom and racial pride.* But it is doubtful that such protection would be given to a math teacher who insisted on coming to class in jeans, sandals, and a T-shirt because he did not approve of middle class attire.

Personal Behavior: Can a teacher be dismissed for homosexual behavior?

Marc Morrison had been a public school teacher in California for a number of years before becoming friends with Mr. S., another teacher in the system. As a result of this friendship, the two men engaged in a homosexual relationship during a one-week period. About 12 months later, Mr. S. reported the incident to Morrison's superintendent. This led Morrison to resign. More than a year after the resignation, the Board of Education conducted a hearing concerning possible revocation of Morrison's life diploma which qualified him as a secondary school teacher in California. Morrison admitted that he engaged in homosexual acts in his apartment with Mr. S. Although Morrison said he did not regard his conduct as immoral, he testified that he had never engaged in any other homosexual acts before or after this single incident. There was no evidence presented to contradict Morrison's testimony. After the hearing, the Board of Education concluded that the incident with Mr. S. constituted immoral and unprofessional conduct which warranted revocation of Morrison's life diploma. Morrison went to court to set aside the Board's decision.

The Board's reasoning went as follows: (1) A teacher stands *in loco parentis;* he takes the place of parents during school hours and should be an example of good conduct. (2) State law requires all teachers to impress principles of morality upon the minds of their students. (3) Morrison was a potential danger to his students not only because of the

---

*In a 1969 Florida case, a black high school teacher was not reappointed because he refused to remove a goatee which he wore as a matter of racial pride. The court said that when a goatee is worn by a black man as an expression of his heritage, culture, and racial pride its wearer "enjoys the protection of First Amendment Rights." Furthermore, the court ruled that the decision not to reappoint the teacher was racially motivated and was tainted with "institutional racism," the effects of which were manifested in "an intolerance of ethnic diversity and racial pride." Therefore, the court ordered the teacher to be reappointed (*Braxton v. Board of Public Instruction of Duval County Florida,* 303 F. Supp. 958-960, [1969]).

immoral acts which he admitted, but also because he did not regard such acts as immoral. (4) California law provides that the Board of Education shall revoke life diplomas and teaching credentials for immoral or unprofessional conduct. (5) Homosexual behavior has long been contrary to the moral standards of the people of California. It also constitutes unprofessional conduct which need not be limited to classroom misconduct or misconduct with children.*

Despite these arguments, a majority of the California Supreme Court disagreed with the Board of Education.† The Court felt it dangerous to allow the terms "immoral" and "unprofessional" conduct to be broadly interpreted. To many people, "immoral conduct" includes laziness, gluttony, selfishness, and cowardice. To others, "unprofessional conduct" for teachers includes signing petitions, opposing majority opinions, and imbibing alcoholic beverages. Unless these terms are carefully and narrowly interpreted, they could be applied to most teachers in the state. Thus, the Board cannot abstractly characterize Morrison's conduct as "immoral" or "unprofessional" unless that conduct indicates that he is unfit to teach.

The Board of Education should also not be empowered to dismiss any teacher whose personal, private conduct incurs its disapproval. A teacher's behavior should disqualify him only when that behavior is clearly related to his job. If his job as a teacher is unaffected, his private acts are his own business and should not be the basis of discipline.

Before a board of education can conclude that a teacher's conduct indicates he is unfit to teach, its conclusion must be supported by evidence. In making a decision of fitness, the Court suggested that a board consider the likelihood that the conduct may adversely affect students or fellow teachers or that it may recur, when the conduct took place, and the surrounding circumstances.

In this case there was no evidence to show that Morrison's conduct affected his performance as a teacher. "There was not the slightest suggestion," said the Court, "that he had ever attempted, sought or even considered any form of physical or otherwise improper relationship with any student." Furthermore, there was no evidence that Morrison failed to teach his students the principles of morality required by law or that the incident with Mr. S. affected his relationship with his co-workers.

The Court's decision does not mean that homosexuals must be permitted to teach in the public schools of California. It does mean that the Board of Education can revoke an individual's teaching certificate only if "his retention in the profession poses a significant danger of harm to either students, school employees, or others who might be affected by his actions as a teacher" (Morrison, 235). Thus the California Court took a bold and controversial step to protect the private lives of teachers.

SUMMARY AND CONCLUSIONS

The five cases we have considered reflect the increased protection given to the civil rights of teachers during the past decade. In each case, a teacher believed that his constitutional rights were violated, took his case to court, and had his position vindicated. In the process, the courts clarified and extended the rights of other teachers. Thus,

---

*Arguments in support of the decision of the Board of Education are taken largely from the dissenting opinion of Judge Sullivan, *Morrison v. State Board of Education,* 1C 3d 214, 240 (1969).

†These arguments are taken largely from the opinion of the Court by Judge Tobriner, *id.* at 217.

Pickering held that a teacher cannot be dismissed for publicly criticizing his superintendent or school board; *Keefe* upheld the academic freedom of high school teachers to
assign controversial materials and use controversial language when relevant to the subject
and appropriate to the students; *Keyishian* ruled that a teacher cannot be dismissed
merely because of his membership in a "subversive" or "revolutionary" organization;
Finot upheld the right of a teacher to wear a beard as a form of symbolic speech; and
Morrison ruled that a teacher cannot be dismissed for homosexual behavior that has no
relationship to his teaching effectiveness.

These cases, of course, are not representative. Some, like the *Morrison* and *Finot*
decisions, are rulings by state or district courts which are not binding on the courts of
other states or districts. Each case is on the cutting edge of the law and reflects the recent
changes in social and judicial thinking in America.* Teachers, of course, do not always
win in court. In fact, many teachers are often unaware of their rights, and many do not
assert them even when they are openly violated. Thus these cases are intended to suggest
the range of teacher's civil rights and the possibility of judicial protection when a teacher
does know and assert them.

A systematic inquiry into the civil rights of teachers leads to a variety of conclusions,
some of which are encouraging to the civil libertarian. The principle that civil rights do
not stop on the steps of the school has been recognized, so that by becoming a teacher
one does not have to surrender his rights as a citizen. Previously, teaching (and other
public employment) was considered a privilege, not a right, and one who wished to gain
such a privilege had to give up some of his rights. In recent years, this theory has been
repeatedly rejected by the courts. Legally, no conditions may be attached to the
occupation of teaching that limit one's constitutional rights. Pursuant to this principle,
the courts have systematically enlarged and protected the civil rights of teachers in the
areas of religion, speech, organizational membership, political activity, private life and
personal appearance.

Discouraging conclusions fall into three categories. First, illegitimate practices endure
despite court rulings. Many school boards, administrators, parents, and even fellow
teachers participate in practices known to violate civil rights. These practices occur most
often, we suspect, at the initial stage of screening candidates for positions or during the
probationary period, prior to tenure. They also occur despite tenure, and only a small per
cent of such violations surface through legal action or through grievance procedures.

Second, teachers often do not know their rights, either substantive or procedural. A
knowledge of both is crucial: for one who does not know his rights cannot assert and
enforce them; and a right without a known procedure to enforce it is functionally no
right at all.

Third, and perhaps most discouraging, there seems to be a willingness on the part of
teachers, administrators, and the general public to restrict the civil rights of teachers.
Political reasons for this tendency arise from the role of the public schools as a focal
point for ideological conflict. Psychological explanations can be found in the pervasive
concerns parents have in the lives of their children. None of us are pleased when our
private preferences are not served by the public institutions we support.

---

*Other current controversies that are gaining increasing prominence include due process for
untenured teachers, "equal protection" for pregnant teachers, and the special problems of minority
teachers in newly integrated school districts.

If predictions are in order we offer the following: (1) That teachers will become increasingly well organized and more militant in asserting their civil rights; (2) That the more knowledge educators as well as laymen have about civil rights, the less likely these rights will be abridged; (3) That students taught by teachers who know and assert their rights will be more active citizens, because teachers who are less than free cannot produce a nation of free men.

As we enter a judicial era that may be dominated by a conservative Supreme Court, will teachers' rights continue to be protected? Or will a new high court reverse the gains of the past decade? We think not. In the next decade, teachers may not be able to depend on the Supreme Court to further expand their rights, but further expansion of these rights is not the major problem today. Most teachers now have more legal rights than they realize. Therefore, the most urgent task is to make teachers aware of the rights they have and to teach them how these rights can be legally asserted and protected. And the work has only begun.

REFERENCES

Finot v. Pasadena City Board of Education, 250 C.A. 2d 189, 191 (1967).
Frankfurter, J., concurring in *Wieman v. Updegraff,* 344 U. S. 183, 194 (1952).
Keefe v. Geanakos, 418 F. 2d 359 (1st Cir. 1969).
Keyishian v. Board of Regents, 385 U. S. 589 (1967).
Lifton, Robert Jay: The young and the old: notes on a new history, Part 1. *The Atlantic, 224*: No. 3, 47, 1969.
Minehan, T.: The teacher goes job-hunting. *The Nation, 124:* 606, 1927.
Morrison v. State Board of Education, 1C 3d 214, 240 (1969).

50 bridging the gap: teacher aides in the learning environment

James C. Young

The teacher aide is becoming a recognized person on the elementary school scene, and the time has come for the teaching profession and school administrators to realize the potential of aides and to establish provisions for their training, employment, and utilization. By utilizing teacher aides, teachers are freed to spend more time at a professional level of work. Not only does this provide the opportunity for more teaching, but it also assists in bridging the gap between school and community (Shipp, 1967).

The goals of a teacher aide program are to provide more child-adult interaction within the classroom setting; to relieve the teacher of routine clerical duties, thus allowing time for more individualized teaching; to improve communication between the home and the school by involving people indigenous to the community; and to expand part-time employment opportunities for capable adults from the school community (Shipp, 1967). Teacher aides must not replace teachers, but should be regarded as a way of enhancing the learning opportunities for children. How they are used is usually determined by local school systems.

Much of what goes into a teacher aide program can be established only by a school or school system itself. Administrators and teachers should assess the various kinds of tasks performed in the classroom and sort them into categories, i.e., teaching and nonteaching tasks. Based upon the assessment, a decision could be rendered as to whether or not there is a need to establish a teacher aide program (National Commission on Teacher Education and Professional Standards, 1967).

It is also important to consider the relationship of teacher aides to the school's staffing pattern. Differentiated staffing almost inevitably involves teacher aides, as well as a variety of other roles in addition to ordinary teachers. The school considering the use of aides should decide whether merely to add them to the existing staff or to include them in a total reorganization.

The title of teacher aide appears to be a catch-all for any person working with certified classroom teachers, whether a paid staff member or a volunteer. Some definitions might help to clarify their role.

Teacher aides are essentially noncertified persons who assist the teacher directly in his instructional role (Bennett and Falk, 1970). Human service aides are trained in New Careers programs to assume aide responsibilities and assist professionals in the delivery of human services (Gartner, 1969). Paraprofessionals or auxiliary personnel are not professional educators, but work directly under the supervision of a professional, who continues to be the responsible agent in the classroom (Goralski and Hayen, 1968).

Bennett and Falk (1970) see the role of the teacher aide expanding beyond the usual heavy emphasis on menial and housekeeping tasks. Expectations for aides develop in close conjunction with the changing set of expectations that define the teacher's role. Generally speaking, three dimensions emerge when discussing the utilization of teacher aides: first, the teacher aide is viewed as offering technical assistance to the teacher. Second, she has a supportive role and is permitted to carry out supportive educational functions under the guidance and supervision of a certified teacher. Finally, the teacher aide can supplement the teacher, as in the case of an aide possessing a unique talent, e.g., singing or playing an instrument (Klopf, Bowman, and Joy, 1969).

The first two roles include tasks that the teacher previously did (or was unable to do for lack of time or assistance). Technical assistance, such as taking attendance or duplicating classroom materials, relieves the teacher of minor chores that take time from teaching. Supportive work, such as helping children who have been absent catch up with classroom work, can effectively double the instructional manpower and help teaching become more effective. The aide can also bring to the classroom particular skills the teacher might not possess that could supplement instruction. These could range from musical talents to understanding of unique community problems, and the ability to relate directly to parents.

The following lists give examples of how teacher aides can assist classroom teachers.

Instructional Duties
1. Taking charge of the class for short periods of time during the teacher's absence
2. Taking charge of the class as a whole while the teacher is working with a smaller group of children
3. Supervising hallways, lavatories, the lunchroom, recreation periods, field and bus trips
4. Helping children with reading, spelling, arithmetic and word recognition
5. Giving assistance in following instructions
6. Assisting in the development of special classes, i.e., art, music, educational and recreational play
7. Reading stories to the children
8. Making materials to aid fast and slow learners
9. Working with children who have been absent over a period of time
10. Helping children to search for materials related to their work
11. Helping children organize games and other activities
12. Assisting teachers in reading and evaluating children's work
13. Assisting teachers during lab assignments

Housekeeping Duties
1. Preparing play dough, paint, and chalk supplies
2. Obtaining supplies from the storage room
3. Checking for good lighting, ventilation, and seating arrangements
4. Putting out playground equipment and cots for rest
5. Taking children to and from the washroom
6. Helping children take off and put on outdoor clothing, tie their shoes, and wash their hands before lunch and after using the toilet
7. Sitting at the table to help children and talk with them
8. Assisting with the preparation of food
9. Assisting children in getting ready for naps and in putting away toys and other materials
10. Assisting children in cleaning up after painting or playing with dough or similar materials or after juice or lunch
11. General straightening up at the end of the day

Clerical Duties
1. Taking attendance, keeping the roll book, and preparing seating charts
2. Keeping health records up-to-date
3. Assisting in the school's office: sorting and filing
4. Filling out library cards
5. Helping children arrange bulletin boards
6. Grading papers with the teacher's key
7. Preparing duplicating materials
8. Requisitioning materials from the supply room

Mechanical Duties
Operating the movie projector, slide projector, duplicating machine, tape recorder, and record player

General Duties
1. Making home visits
2. Attending staff meetings
3. Attending parent meetings
4. Supporting the staff in their efforts (Steinberg and Fishman, 1968)

THE LEGALITY OF TEACHER AIDES

Nearly half the teacher aide programs operating in large public schools are less than six years old. Using a sample of large districts, a recent study showed that 40 per cent of all such programs were started in the 1965-1966 school year and 36 per cent were started between 1960 and 1964.

Because most states do not have specific statutory provisions pertaining to teacher aides, most of these programs operate under general legislative provisions for school operations. In many cases the question of legality has arisen: "Does a school district have the authority to expend public funds for the hiring of teacher aides in the absence of statutory authority?" (Alexander, 1968).

There appears to be a trend in some states toward legislative action for teacher aides. Several states have specified precisely the purposes of teacher aides, e.g., lunch period supervision (Washington and Massachusetts), and compensatory education programs (California). For the most part, states utilizing teacher aides have issued policy statements on their limitations. Since most state legal codes do not cover the use of teacher aides, school districts should be concerned with the manner in which they are used. Aides are not certified personnel, and school systems could jeopardize state funds if students are permitted to spend time alone with aides for instructional purposes (Alexander, 1968). This is a problem that many states seem to be making efforts to resolve, but state legislatures can be sluggish in responding to changes in educational practice.

THE IMPACT OF TEACHER AIDES

If young people are to grow and develop, they must have an environment conducive to growth. In particular, the pupil-adult ratio should be small. In such a setting the teacher aide assumes a major responsibility in enhancing the development of young children. She usually resides in the neighborhood where she works. She must be a person with infinite patience to deal with the endless questions young children ask. She must be willing to learn how children grow and develop their intelligence. According to Brunner (1962), "A teacher aide does not assume the role of teacher in a professional sense; but by being present and relating to children, she is bound to transmit ideas, feelings, habits and skills that become a part of the behavioral repertoire of children."

There are currently about 300,000 teacher aides in the United States. The Parent Teacher Association magazine estimates that by 1977 the number may grow to 1,500,000. The bulk of the literature on the use of paraprofessionals in schools has focused upon their activities in the classroom, their selection, training, and the question of the effect of their utilization upon teacher activities and upon the aide himself (Reissman and Gartner, 1969).

A study conducted for the United States Office of Education of all compensatory programs for the disadvantaged reported that, between 1963 and 1968, of the 1000 programs examined, only 23 were found to have yielded "measured educational benefits of cognitive achievement." Eleven of these involved the use of paraprofessionals (Gartner, 1969).

To find out if teacher aides really make a significant difference in the classroom, a study was conducted by Central Michigan College. The results of a five year study indicated that teacher aides really do free teachers to teach. The activities conducted by teachers were measured by a stopwatch extensively before and after the teacher aides were brought into the program. During a two year period using aides teachers were able to reduce the percentages of time allotted for routine duties. The following *reductions* were made: correcting papers, 89 per cent; enforcing discipline, 36 per cent; taking attendance, 76 per cent; preparing reports, 25 per cent; supervising the movement of children from class to class, 61 per cent; monitoring classes, 83 per cent. The newly acquired time was put to use in the following *increases:* preparation of lessons, 105 per cent; pupil-teacher interaction, 57 per cent; moving from desk to desk for individual assistance, 27 per cent (U.S. Department of Health, Education, and Welfare, 1967).

During the school year 1965-66 in 217 school systems enrolling 12,000 pupils or more, 44,351 teacher aides were employed. In these 217 systems were 396,028 teachers and 10,181,182 pupils at all levels in the school program. About three-fourths of the school systems used only paid aides, and about one-fourth had both paid and volunteer aides in their schools; only two systems, or less than 1 per cent of the total, used volunteers alone. Of the total number of aides, 29,995 (67.6 per cent) were paid and 14,356 (32.4 per cent) were volunteers (National Education Association, 1967a).

TRAINING OF TEACHER AIDES

Once a school or school system has decided to initiate a teacher aide program, it is up to the professional staff to assemble a group of people to begin planning the program. This group should be representative of teachers, administrators, community people, and paraprofessionals who have demonstrated successful experiences in other schools. During the preplanning phase the planners should be concerned with the following areas:

1. A rationale for the program
2. The role of teacher aides in the school
3. Procedures for recruitment and selection of teacher aides
4. Training: Preservice and in-service
5. Evaluation for growth and progress
6. A plan for career development

All teacher aides should be told what their responsibilities are and cautioned against action that might endanger children. The training should include orientation to the program, the philosophy of the school, the understanding of characteristics of young children, the physical layout of the school and its facilities, and the school's history, purpose, policies, structure, and available resources.

All of this could be accomplished during the preservice training in a total group situation, and at times in sessions with members of the professional staff. Preservice training should give a general overview of the total school program.

The in-service training should be more specific: it should focus on the teacher aide's strengths and weaknesses, his attitudes, values, education, experiences, abilities, work, and teaching style. A multilevel in-service training program should be designed to maximize the effectiveness of the training. Teacher aides will come with varying backgrounds, and the program should be tailored so that each can gain the necessary experiences in order to be effective in the classroom.

The objectives at this stage should be to provide specific instruction in the techniques for conducting or assisting in classroom activities, the use of audio-visual media, the use of the library, or any other area of the school program in which teacher aides will be utilized. Training should occur in small groups because interdependent learning can best take place in such situations. The groups need to be structured in a way that facilitates free exchange of methodological ideas and conclusions among teachers and teacher aides, discussions on classroom management techniques, and the utilization, development, and evaluation of classroom materials. All of the components in the training must relate back to the child, since the entire process is designed to serve his needs.

ATTITUDES OF PROFESSIONAL ORGANIZATIONS

Professional organizations for preschool educators have long endorsed the utilization of teacher aides in such programs. The two largest teacher organizations in the United States have also issued policy statements regarding the utilization of paraprofessionals in the classroom. Research conducted by the American Federation of Teachers (AFT, 1968) has caused this professional organization to adopt the following resolution on paraprofessionals: "That the AFT actively supports the use of both men and women of minority group background in paraprofessional positions; and be it further resolved that the AFT continue to support a program to enable these men and women to participate in paraprofessional duties while improving their educational potential as fully trained and certified professionals in their own right."

The National Education Association (National Education Association, 1969-70) adopted a resolution on paraprofessionals and auxiliary personnel during their assembly meeting in 1969. "The NEA urges local school systems to provide classroom teachers with a supportive staff who will free the teacher from certain nonteaching and routine duties so that he can perform more successfully the primary function of teaching each child." The association also urged its affiliates and local school systems to become involved in the recruitment, orientation, and training of paraprofessionals and auxiliary personnel.

The National Commission on Teacher Education and Professional Standards (1967) sees the addition of auxiliary personnel in the schools as one of the most challenging and hopeful advances in modern education. Auxiliary school personnel are here. They are not an idle dream; they should not be a source of hidden fears. They are here because they are needed, needed by both professionals and children.

A recent report by the NEA (1972) indicated that 250,000 teacher aides proved to be most effective in their roles in school systems throughout the country. However, teachers still feel "threatened" by the presence of teacher aides. The report went on to say that teachers needed retraining in the following areas: (1) classroom management; (2) supervisory skills; (3) diagnostic skills; and (4) human relations skills. The same statement could very well apply to some school administrators.

ISSUES RELATED TO PARAPROFESSIONALS

There is a crucial need for the training of trainers. If the number of paraprofessionals will indeed increase over the next five year period, schools, colleges, universities, and other agencies in the business of training trainers should be cognizant of the fact that existing training programs need to be revamped if their products are going to be sensitive to meeting the needs of teacher aides and other paraprofessionals.

Trainers should be knowledgeable about paraprofessionals and possess skills that would enable them to deal with specific teacher aide issues:

1. How the paraprofessional sees the professional
2. How the paraprofessional can overcome deficiencies
3. Human relations skills
4. How the professional can profit from the paraprofessional
5. Teacher aides as change agents

The effective utilization of teacher aides and other auxiliary school personnel could prove to be a real revolution in American education. The role of the teacher will have to be redefined. New staffing patterns will emerge from schools of varying sizes. What those patterns will be is still an unknown. Effective aide programs may cause teacher training institutes to work more closely with school systems and to design programs of study that will allow teacher aides to receive credit which would lead towards the bachelor's degree. In the meantime, colleges and universities should start immediately to prepare their teachers to work with additional classroom staff.

School administrators should not look upon teacher aides as replacements for teachers. Rather, they should consider how they can effectively employ such a program to increase the learning of the children.

RECENT DEVELOPMENTS

Under the directorship of Dr. Edward Zigler, the Office of Child Development has initiated the creation of a new profession. This new professional would be called a Child Development Associate (CDA). He would work directly with young children in programs such as day care centers, nursery schools, Head Start centers, and so on.

The CDA profession is competency based. That is, a preliminary set of standards of competence has been established by a group of well-known experts in the early childhood field working with officials from OCD. A competency-based profession would assure to some degree that people working directly with young children will be knowledgeable of the major areas of child development—social, emotional, cognitive and psychomotor—and of the kinds of activities and experiences that are appropriate for the young. Moreover, a CDA would also be expected to be able to plan for an organize an environment conducive to children interacting within it.

The Office of Child Development is presently establishing pilot training projects in different regions of the country. It would be wise for teacher training institutes to become cognizant of this project, because a potential CDA does not necessarily have to have college training to be certified in this new profession. If a person can meet the criteria established for certification, he qualifies as a CDA. The CDA Consortium, an independent agent, will be responsible for the development of assessment standards and procedures (Williams and Ryan, 1972).

Additional information can be obtained from the Office of Child Development, Washington, D.C.

REFERENCES

Alexander, S. Kern: What teacher aides can—and cannot—do. *Nation's Schools, 46*: 23-25, 1968.

American Federation of Teachers. Policy Manual. Washington, D. C., 1968, p. 146.

Bennett, William S. Jr., and Falk, R. Frank: New Careers and Urban Schools. New York, Holt, Rinehart and Winston, 1970.

Brunner, Catherine. A lap to sit on—and much more. *Childhood Education, 43*: 20-23, 1962.

Gartner, Alan: Do Paraprofessionals Improve Human Services: A First Critical Appraisal of the Data. New York, School of Education, New York University, 1969. p. 15.

Goralski, Patricia J., and Hayen, F. V.: Teacher Aide Program: 1967-1968. Minneapolis, Minneapolis Public Schools, 1968. (Mimeographed)

Klopf, Gordon J., Bowman, Garda W., and Joy, Adena: A Learning Team: Teacher and Auxiliary. Bank Street College of Education for the United States Office of Education, April, 1969.

National Commission on Teacher Education and Professional Standards (NCTEPS): Auxiliary School Personnel. National Education Association, 1967.

National Education Association: Auxiliary School Personnel. National School Publication Relations Association, 1972.

National Education Association: The Classroom Teacher Speaks on His Supportive Staff. Washington, D.C., National Education Association, 1967b.

National Education Association, NEA Handbook. Washington, NEA, 1969-1970.

National Education Association: Teacher aides in large school systems. *NEA Research Bulletin: 45:* Number 2, May, 1967a.

Reissman, Frank, and Gartner, Alan: Paraprofessionals: the effect on children's learning. *The Urban Review, 4*: Number 2, October, 1969.

Shipp, Mary D.: Teacher aides: a survey. *The National Elementary Principal, 46*: Number 6, 30-33, May, 1967.

Steinberg, Sheldon S., and Fishman, Jacob R.: New Careers: The Teacher Aide. Washington, D. C., New Careers Institute, October, 1968.

U. S. Department of Health, Education and Welfare, Office of Education. Staffing for Better Schools. Washington, D.C., Government Printing Office, 1967.

Williams, C.R., and Ryan, T.F.: Competent professionals for quality child care and early education: the goal of CDA. *Young Children, 28*(2): 71-74, 1972.

Young, James C.: A Regional Investigation of the Effective Utilization of Teacher Aides in Head Start Centers. Dissertation. May, 1971. (Unpublished)

SECTION SEVEN
STUDENTS

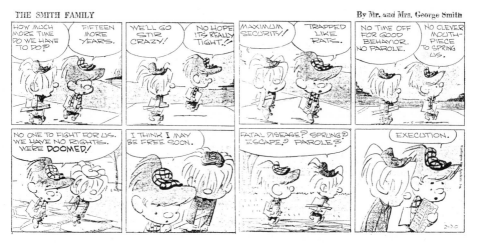

THE SMITH FAMILY   By Mr. and Mrs. George Smith

It is often difficult for an adult to find out what students really think. Put on a jacket and tie, adopt the role of educator, and ask a child what he thinks about school. It's unlikely that you'll receive the same answer that would be given to a friend of his own age.

Students have their own unique reactions to the educational process. They range from the Georgie Smiths who feel "trapped like rats" to those who genuinely enjoy school. The feelings may change because of differences in teachers and the passing of time—a model student in elementary school dropping out in high school, a difficult student being "reached" by a gifted teacher. Their perceptions of what is going on about them are not always correct or even rational. Yet these perceptions are a major factor in determining how well they can function in school.

Much of the problem is unquestionably caused by the fact that schools are designed by adults. Jean Piaget and others have documented some of the ways in which children's thinking differs from that of adults. The differences are subtle yet profound—and as yet only roughly understood. Educators designing programs have taken these differences into account only in a small way. To design institutions for children without determining how children feel about them is to ask for trouble.

Educators like to speak of learning as, ideally, a partnership between teacher and student. Too often the reality is teacher versus student. Listen to the conversations in the teachers' lounge about the "little bastards"—or to the kids walking home talking about "old grouches" and "Gestapo gym teachers." Each group can provide evidence for its own views: kids who actively torment teachers and teachers who actively torment kids.

The lines of antagonism are drawn even more boldly in the difficulties of deviant or delinquent youth in the school *system. Larry Dye and Arthur Eve find that "the lock-step atmosphere and regimentation of many school systems is reminiscent of correctional institutions." The mischievous skirmishes between a normal child and his teachers become a full-scale war when the child is adjudged a "discipline problem." It is in the handling of such children, both in normal schools and in so-called "reform schools," that one frequently sees the causes of student resentment.*

What do kids think of their schools? Read M. del Vecchio's "Bureaucracy in the High School." Smith Public High School is not in an urban crisis zone—it's located in an apparently pleasant city of some 25,000 people, some 30 miles from the nearest larger city. Some of the problems are new: ten years ago heroin was a problem only in Harlem; the main problem elsewhere was the number of expectant mothers in the graduating class. But many problems, like petty tyranny and political infighting, are almost as old as the schools themselves.

Indeed, most of the problems and resentment have not appeared overnight. Students felt trapped in school ten years ago, but they were less articulate and more afraid to express it then (see Noel Novinson's "School is Unconstitutional, 1962-1972"). There have been changes in the schools and in student life in the last decade. Yet these changes are not nearly as shocking as the similarities between high school in the 1920's as described in the Lynds' Middletown* and that of the early 1960's.

For young people, the whole experience of schooling is inter-mixed with our society, and issues on one level relate to both. The President's Commission on Campus Unrest† found that "campus protest has been focused on three major questions, racial injustice, war, and the university itself" (p. 3). In looking at schooling, we must be deeply concerned about society as well, for, as Joseph Rhodes asks, "Is student freedom more important than freedom?"

---

*Lynd, Robert S., and Lynd, Helen Merrell: *Middletown.* New York, Harcourt, Brace, and World Inc., 1929.

†President's Commission on Campus Unrest. *Report.* Washington, D.C., U.S. Government Printing Office, 1970.

51 deviancy: an unknown factor in education

Larry L. Dye
Arthur W. Eve

To deviate: characterized by or given to significant departure from the behavioral norms of a particular society.

Webster's Seventh New Collegiate Dictionary, p. 227.

Behavior that deviates significantly from our society's traditionally acceptable middle-class norms may be either penalized or rewarded. Although deviations that lead to new inventions or discoveries may bring both financial rewards and national recognition, these often occur only after the inventor has been initially scorned. In recent years, some behaviors once considered dangerously deviant, such as certain men's hair and clothing styles, have become socially accepted. At the same time, many other forms of deviant behavior, such as the use of drugs or the violation of various criminal codes, still result in societal sanctions.

Deviant behavior among youth is seldom rewarded. Many public agencies dealing with youth, especially school systems and juvenile correction agencies, systematically punish virtually all behavior that deviates from their rigid expectations, even if such behavior is considered quite normal for adolescents. This reflects an inherent conflict between youths searching for their own unique identity and the institution's traditional treatment of students as identical and interchangeable parts. In attempting to produce "successful" students, the schools have often produced a rigid mold that allows little room for deviation. Though this failure is understandable, the results can be serious for the creative individual who is thus cut off from the larger society.

THE REWARDS OF NONCONFORMITY IN EDUCATIONAL INSTITUTIONS

Although it is quite normal for early adolescents to be highly verbal, hyperactive, and inconsistent in their behavior, school personnel typically identify such students as discipline problems. Since the "discipline problem" cannot "learn to behave," teachers often tend to assume that he simply cannot learn, for reasons ranging from lack of intelligence to brain damage (Rosenthal and Jacobson, 1968, pp. 19-23). This prejudgment often becomes a self-fulfilling prophecy of failure, which can easily be compounded by racial, ethnic, or language differences between the teacher and the students. The problem is effectively illustrated by Clark, who states that:

> These children, by and large, do not learn because they are not being taught effectively and they are not being taught because those who are charged with the responsibility of teaching them do not believe that they can learn, do not expect that they can learn, and do not act toward them in ways which help them to learn (Clark, 1965, p. 131).

Administrative concern over such superficialities as clean halls, outwardly respectful and orderly students, and paperwork tends to aggravate the problem.* Arbitrary school behavior standards, which ignore students' divergent backgrounds, internal needs, and emerging adolescent pressures only encourage the student to rebel (Ross, 1970, p. 225-238). Educators, ever-fearful of losing control, often overreact to such rebellion by imposing even more stringent restrictions upon students. No consideration is given to whether an individual student violates school rules as a result of an internal problem, a conflict at home, a personality clash with a particular teacher, or simply as a means of testing the limits of the system; he is simply punished for his actions. The absence of any effort to identify the causes of such behavior is a major reason why problems intensify. The student, meanwhile, becomes further convinced of the arbitrary nature of school discipline, as he watches the system uphold even blatantly wrong teacher decisions (and, indeed, often punish the students who dared question a teacher's judgment). If he is fortunate, he might be given a few shreds of sympathy and be told that he will just have to live with Mrs. Smith for the remainder of the semester since she has tenure.

Not only does the school make the "discipline problem" feel there is something wrong with him, but it gives the same message to his family and community.** The student does not have many options left. If he remains involved in school, he receives only negative reinforcement. If he resorts to truancy—withdrawing from a painful situation—he is further punished, even though it would be considered appropriate for an adult to similarly withdraw from a painful job situation. Eventually, this leads to more extensive truancy or complete withdrawal from school. As the school comes to classify the youngster as incorrigible, he becomes convinced the system has little to offer him. By this time, he has invested a great deal in his own identity and finds it very difficult to accept the possibility that he may be wrong in any way. He may even be convinced that the school system is actively hostile to his interests, so he does everything he can to obstruct its functioning.

In some respects, the lock-step atmosphere and regimentation of many school systems is reminiscent of correctional institutions. Students are not allowed to talk back, their movements are controlled by centrally regulated bell systems, policemen and other security personnel patrol the halls, doors are locked securely even in the daytime, and a constant state of submerged hostility exists between the student inmates and the

---

*For examples of this preoccupation with order and control on the part of teachers, administrators, and professors of education, see the various essays in *Discipline in the Classroom,* a monograph published by the National Education Association in 1969 (NEA, Washington, D. C.). A number of recent studies highlight the arbitrary dullness and repetitiveness of many classroom environments as well as the narrow range of acceptable classroom behavior that prevails in many schools. See for example: Phillip W. Jackson, Life in Classrooms. New York, Holt, Rinehart and Winston, Inc., 1968; and Charles E. Silberman, Crisis in the Classroom. New York, Random House, 1970.

**For an example of how guidance counselors assist teachers in placing the blame for deviant student behavior on the student's "home life and community environment" see Gerald E. Levy, Ghetto School. New York, Western Publishing Company, Inc., 1970, p. 133.

educators who are responsible for their supervision. Within our society, school systems and correctional institutions are the only two institutions where it remains legal to administer physical punishment to youngsters. In both institutions, the supervisory personnel (both teachers and prison guards) are typically regarded as right even when they are wrong.

Many students identified as deviants are eventually pushed out of school. If the student has reached age sixteen and has not quit school of his own accord, he can simply be expelled or he can be pressured to drop out by poor grades or by teacher or administrative harassment. If he is under sixteen, the job of pushing him out is more complicated. Some administrators, seeking a more direct method, have tried "continuous" or "indefinite" suspensions—usually meaning that the student is suspended for two weeks every two weeks, until he is formally expelled on his sixteenth birthday. Since this violates the spirit, if not the letter, of most compulsory attendance laws, more subtle means are usually used.

A student under sixteen can be sent to another institution if he is classified as a "delinquent" or "chronic truant." Delinquency requires actual commission of some sort of crime, usually outside the school (though crimes inside the school, particularly those directed at teachers, are considered much more heinous, much like crimes against police or prison guards). Delinquents are usually handled like underage criminals, and the institutions they are sent to share most of the faults of adult "correctional institutions."

Truancy is a crime only in that it represents a violation of state compulsory attendance laws. It is a crime that educators can provoke by harassing students until the situation becomes unbearable for them. Usually, very little is done to encourage truants to return to the classroom, either because the school does not want them back, or because the task is beyond the capacity of the attendance officers. Even when conscientious attendance officers are effective in convincing truants to return to school, there is little likelihood that they will stay there, unless the situation has improved (Stein, 1971, p. 195). When and if the truant youth is brought to court, typically by the school attendance officer, he can be adjudged a "chronic truant" and incarcerated in some type of detention center until his sixteenth birthday. This usually is little different from the institutions where delinquents are sent—and frequently the two systems are combined.

COUNTY TRAINING SCHOOLS IN MASSACHUSETTS

The County Training School system in Massachusetts provides one example of what happens after truant youngsters are incarcerated. In the spring of 1971 there were a total of 237 children living in the three such institutions in the state. These training schools were established to house children from seven through 16, committed for school-related offenses such as truancy and school behavior problems. The Massachusetts General Laws state that:

> every habitual truant, (i.e., every child who is required to attend school and who willfully and habitually absents himself therefrom) every habitual absentee, (i.e., every child between seven and 16 years of age who may be found wandering about in the streets or public places of any town or city of the Commonwealth, having no lawful occupation or business, not attending school and growing up in ignorance) and every habitual school offender, (i.e., every child who is required to attend school as aforesaid, but who persistently violates the rules and regulations of the school which he attends, or otherwise persistently misbehaves therein so as to render himself a fit subject for exclusion therefrom, but not for commitment to any one of the institutions, other than a County Training School) shall be liable to arrest as a habitual truant, habitual absentee,

habitual school offender, as the case may be; and shall upon complaint and conviction thereof be committed to the custody of the trustees of the County Training School (Mass. General Laws, Ch. 77, Sec. 3 and 4).

The law also states that school attendance officers shall inquire into all cases and shall alone have authority to make complaints, serve legal processes, and carry into execution judgments on habitual truants, absentees, and school offenders. The youth is then brought before a court or magistrate. It is at the discretion of the court either to place him on probation under the supervision of the school attendance officer or to commit him to a county training school. Once in custody of the county training schools, he starts an indeterminate sentence until his sixteenth birthday. Theoretically, this means a youth could be committed to the county training schools at age eight and incarcerated until his sixteenth birthday—for eight of the most important years of his physical, social, intellectual, and emotional growth. In February of 1971, there was one youth who had entered Essex County Training School when he was eight years old and had been there for a total of five years and nine months.

Representatives of the county training schools can, whenever they think it in the best interest of any child committed to their custody, permit the child to be at liberty or placed on parole and discharged. The requirements for parole are the approval of the school superintendent and at least two county commissioners; in Essex County, parole requires the additional approval of the committing judge and the parent or legal guardian. At any time after the youth has been paroled until his sixteenth birthday, his parole can be revoked and he can be brought back to the county training school without having to return to court. Specifically, the law states that

if any child who is permitted to be at liberty violates, in the opinion of the trustees, the conditions of his parole at any time previous to the expiration of the term for which such child was committed to their custody, they may revoke such parole, and issue an order directed to the school attendants or police officers of any town or city to arrest such child wherever found and return him to the trustees (Mass. Acts and Resolves, 1897).

Although the County Training Schools were initially established to handle truancy and other school-related problems, there is virtually no contact between the school system and the training school. Neither the school systems nor the training schools are concerned about the youngster's life either before or after he is in their custody. Thus, there is very little continuity in dealing with the problems of committed youngsters, and virtually no records concerning their family, health, previous behavior, educational, or delinquency problems.

On the basis of interviews and review of what County Training School records do exist, it appears that only about half of the boys have been committed because of truancy or school behavior problems. In many other instances, the courts have committed boys to remove them from unsatisfactory home situations, mostly involving very poor families. In a number of cases, judges have committed boys involved in nonschool-connected delinquency to a training school rather than branding them as juvenile delinquents.*

---

*These conditions exist not only within Massachusetts but throughout the entire country. As Birch Bayh pointed out in his address to the National Council of Juvenile Court Judges in Washington, D. C. on July 12, 1971, more than one-half of the children presently being held in detention centers, training schools, and other correctional institutions have never even been charged with the equivalent of an adult crime. Children labeled "incorrigible, neglected, truant, run-away and in need of supervision" have come before juvenile courts all across this country in need of attention and guidance, only to be institutionalized and isolated, with little or no hope of ever receiving proper care, simply because it doesn't exist.

Although the three Massachusetts County Training Schools are different in many respects, located in different areas of the state, and under different superintendents, they all reflect the same basic operational philosophy found in most institutions. The institutions' primary concerns are custodial and punitive, not rehabilitative or educationally oriented. Generally, they are run according to a paramilitary model, which is reflected in such things as marching, uniforms, calling cadence, saluting, and addressing staff as "sir."

None of the training schools administer any professional diagnostic, psychiatric, or sociological evaluations to the youths entering the institution, even though such clinical services would provide information regarding background, abilities, interests, attitudes, and problems which are needed to plan intelligently for them. The lack of continuity with the child's previous life is compounded by the hopelessly inadequate records the county training schools keep on their wards. Nor is any attempt made to maintain continuity when a youth is returned to his own community from a county training school.

Most of the youths entering the training schools have had very little medical attention during their childhood; therefore, it would seem imperative to provide up-to-date medical care for them. However, two of the county institutions reported that upon entrance the youths are given only a "general" check-up and that dental work is conducted only upon complaints. The Hampden County Training School revealed that the youths are not even given a general check-up upon entrance and most likely do not receive medical or dental attention unless an extreme emergency occurs. This situation reflects the school's philosophy of being merely a "holding" operation rather than trying to meet not only the educational and rehabilitative but also the basic health needs of its students.

The educational programs being conducted at the county training schools are medieval in theory and practice. They have not established any mechanism for obtaining data or information from the school systems from which the youths came. Their education neither provides for any individual differences nor incorporates any innovative educational techniques. They do not provide any cooperative liaison or follow-up with the school systems upon release of the youths. Essentially, they force the youths to sit silently at their desks during the day and be talked at rather than allow them the opportunity to become actively involved in their own educational process. In an institution which receives youths because they have educational problems, it seems absurdly irresponsibile to take no action to deal with those problems or to equip the youths with the educational skills needed to function successfully in the community.

Instruction is given strictly at a prescribed time. It does not provide the children with the ability or the opportunity or the desire to learn or to return to a regular schooling system of any kind. Because their educational activities are predetermined and strictly supervised, the youths have no opportunity for individualized or extensive study during the evening or other free time.

A discipline-oriented philosophy pervades the classrooms. Teachers use public humiliation and physical force both as a substitute for instruction and for gaining classroom control. Class hours are grossly wasted and the notion that "so long as they are quiet, things are all right" is common. It is a system that discourages creativity and expression on the part of the boys and certainly offers them no encouragement to learn. Since the children are not allowed to deviate, even in a positive manner, the teachers are not encouraged to try innovations within their classrooms. The teaching staff itself includes some well-qualified and well-meaning individuals, but they are stifled within the county training school system. The teachers are forced to uphold the custodial feature of the institution rather than being allowed to fulfill their teaching obligations.

Many factors combine to destroy totally any constructive program of physical education and recreation. Athletic facilities are inadequate and available community resources are not utilized. Indoor sports and recreational programs are limited by the facilities, while outdoor activities are limited by the schools' strict custodial policies. Staff members are not properly trained and thus are generally unaware of the development potential of athletic programs.

One of the resulting failings is an inability to accommodate varying levels of athletic interest and ability. It is blatantly sadistic to match two youths of greatly different size, strength, and skill in the boxing ring. Such a match merely demonstrates the confusion in staff members between constructive athletic programs and corporal punishment as a form of discipline and humiliation. The prevailing use of often debasing calisthenics is meaningless to any constructive program. At best, the combination of athletics and punishment leads to vast amounts of wasted time and meaningless byplay; at worst, it can be highly destructive to the incarcerated youths.

A cursory glance at the individual staff members at the three county training schools reveals that they are lacking in any kind of professional background or experience in dealing with the problems of juveniles. The careers of truck driver, security guard, or farmer do not prepare one to deal with the problems of troubled youths. In fact, there are no requirements or standards for advertising, recruiting, or selecting potential staff members, as well as no specific job descriptions. There is also no preparation or orientation program for individuals joining the staff and no in-service training program.

Essentially, the school is an absolute monarchy with the superintendent as king. He controls staff positions, which are not covered by any kind of civil service requirements and are subject to political patronage. This can lead to nepotism. In one training school the superintendent, his wife, and representatives of his family are all members of the staff. In addition to these inadequacies, the allocation of staff according to function reflects the philosophy of the institutions—there are more staff assigned to institutional maintenance, farm services, and custodial duties than are assigned to essential child care and rehabilitative services.

Youths between the ages of 12 and 15 are going through a very traumatic period in their lives when they are struggling for identity. Every aspect of the county training schools seeks to obliterate that emerging identity. Beginning on the first day the youth arrives, he is stripped of everything that relates to any kind of identity. He is given the same haircut as the other youths; he must surrender his own personal clothing and wear institutional clothing which makes him blend in with the others.

From the day he arrives, he has no choice in determining his activities. He will be on a job at a certain time and in a certain place. He will be in school and at dinner, breakfast, and supper or participating in recreational activities at certain times and in certain places. There are no opportunities for him to either participate in the planning of any activities or to make even the simple choice of going to and from them. The youths are waked up at a certain time and told exactly where to be during the course of the day; then they make those movements in large groups. There are long periods of enforced silence—there are no opportunities to talk while eating at meals, taking a shower, after lights out, or during normal periods of meaningful expression. There are no opportunities to interact, even by letter, with members of the opposite sex.

Living quarters are very sterile and antiseptic. Dormitories hold neat rows of uniformly made beds on the second floor. Lockers for the boys' clothing and any of the minimal personal belongings they are allowed to have are located in the basement. Under surveillance 24 hours a day, youngsters are not encouraged to develop a sense of personality and individuality. These institutions are very deadly and dangerous places which promote conformity, idleness, and a very unrealistic perspective of the way the world is, in fact, run.

It is perhaps unnecessary to say that youths of the type incarcerated in the county training schools need a great deal of individual attention. But they rarely get it. The youths have no privacy and virtually no personal possessions. They spend months or years in a situation of almost total conformity and irresponsibility, with no chance to develop independence of thought, self-reliance, self-knowledge, or creativity.

"These are truly children in bondage, with fewer civil rights than any group in our Commonwealth, even including inmates of our state prisons" (Mass. Dept. of Youth Services, 1971, p. 7). There is no right to parole consideration or any criterion for release upon parole. Youths cannot send or receive mail from anyone, including attorneys or public defenders. They are allowed two visits a month and then only for two hours. There are no dividing partitions around toilets. The youths have no area at all of their own. They spend even their sleeping hours under observation and under lock and key. Within the Massachusetts State Prison, with the exception of prisoners on death row or those being disciplined for some reason, no inmates live under restrictions as severe as those imposed in the county training schools. Yet these children have not been sentenced as criminals, they are simply deviant youths that have been rejected by the educational structure.

Many of the rules of good disciplinary procedures are violated in the training schools; punishment is arbitrary, often cruel, not generally suited to the offense, and not leading to correction of the wrong behavior. In fact, the program of discipline tends to be one of only arbitrary punishment that will not lead to adaptation of desirable behavior. A Harvard University Report on the County Training Schools pointed out that

> Any study of discipline at the training school becomes confused by the fact that staff members, almost universally, confuse and intermingle the meaning of the words discipline and punishment. The staff, for the most part, feels that corporal punishment is the only valid means of gaining discipline in the institution . . . .
>
> In the past two months, alone, we have documented at least eighteen validated affidavits of cases where boys have been physically abused by members of the staff. (Reference here is made to cases where corporal punishment was used as a willful act of punishment involving violence inflicted upon the boys) (Harvard University, 1972, p. 137).

In summary, there is a great deal of confusion with regard to the goals of the county training schools. The confusion begins with the Compulsory Education Laws. Under these laws the juvenile sent to the training schools has committed only a noncriminal offense. The juvenile has not willfully gone out and done bodily harm to another person, nor has he committed mayhem or some other act which violates a criminal law. Instead, he has committed the noncriminal offense of growing up in "ignorance," or of being a "stubborn child," "truant," or "runaway."

The confusion over goals intensifies when one considers the original intent of the county training schools—to remove a juvenile from a bad, or at least socially unacceptable, home situation or general environment and to place him in an environment conducive to his growth and development. This was based on the finding that many behavior problems of juveniles at public schools originated from bad home environments and other family problems.

The confusion grows in complexity when one considers the procedures of the juvenile court system. When a juvenile court judge is faced with the alternative of sending an offender to an industrial school for boys or to a county training school, he often elects to adjudicate the child guilty of the noncriminal offense of truancy even when that child has committed criminal offenses that should lead to an adjudication of delinquency. Once adjudicated as guilty of truancy, the judge may or may not send the child to a training school.

These court procedures destroyed the intent of both the Compulsory Education Laws and the county training schools. Perhaps it should be said that all three—the laws, the training schools, and the court procedures—have moved so far in practice from their original intent that their original intent has been forgotten. What was considered humane and constructive many years ago has now become inhumane and destructive. After a century of existence, as the youths become progressively older, more sophisticated, and simply tougher, the county training schools are now only repressive custodial institutions. They are still receiving youths who come from bad home environments on truancy charges. These youths, who are above all basically dependent and neglected children, are thrust into a hardened institutional environment. From these considerations and from the previous discussions of the inadequacies of staff and facilities and operating philosophy, only one conclusion can be reached, a conclusion stated strongly by a team of researchers from Harvard University:

> An institution with an administration and staff which is poorly trained and poorly motivated and whose function is self-perceived as almost entirely custodial in nature, cannot be allowed to function with regard to the well-being of children. An institution where the problems of children are not only ignored, but are intensified cannot be considered anything but inhumane and destructive. An educational program which ignores the needs of its charges and adds to the growing problems of those children cannot under any circumstances be endorsed. An institution where almost all factors involving health, support and treatment are dealt with inadequately and which ignores the real problems of youth cannot be allowed to stand (Harvard University, 1972, p. 213).

Although this study has focused primarily on conditions within three County Training Schools in Massachusetts, these conditions are not unique to Massachusetts. However, by examining closely what happens within these training schools, we may be able to understand what actually happens to those youths who do not conform to the structure of our existing educational system.

We systematically identify and exclude those students who exhibit deviant behavior from our educational institutions. Once they have been pushed out of school our compulsory attendance laws insure their commitment to training schools where the environment creates even greater despair, hopelessness, and feelings of hostility toward society. By putting these students out of sight, we at least temporarily solve their conflict with school systems and society. But in the process of confining them until the age of sixteen, we increase the probability that they will eventually end up in adult correctional institutions. The high rate of recidivism is guaranteed by training schools because the problems that lead to a youth's initial incarceration are never dealt with, and at the age of sixteen the youth is simply returned to society with a host of additional problems that he acquired while in the training school.

Instead of viewing the student exhibiting deviant behavior as a threat to the school system and to society, we ought to consider the potential for leadership and creativity that is inherent within those youths who are self-assured and confident enough to speak out on their own behalf. By demanding conformity to a predetermined set of behavioral norms and by systematically screening out those youngsters who are unwilling to conform, school systems highlight the narrowness with which they confine their client group. If schools are to become models of the individualization they are supposed to be, then we must judge their ineffectiveness by the students that they presently do not serve.

And we must also raise questions as to why the child who exhibits deviant behavior patterns is often singled out for such harsh and vindictive treatment both by educators and eventually by juvenile detention center and training school personnel. Perhaps our form of civilization is not quite as advanced as we like to think.

REFERENCES

Clark, Kenneth B.: Dark Ghetto. New York, Harper and Row, 1965.
Harvard University: Report on the Status of the Essex County Training School, Lawrence, Mass. Cambridge, 1972.
Massachusetts Department of Youth Services: Report of Special Committee on County Training Schools. 1971.
Rosenthal, Robert, and Jacobson, Lenore F.: Teacher expectations for the disadvantaged. *Scientific American, 218:* 19-23, 1968.
Ross, Donald C.: The psychobiology of underachievement. *Teachers College Record, 72:* No. 2, 225-238, 1970.
Stein, Annie: Strategies for failure. *Harvard Educational Review, 41:* No. 2, 195, 1971.

bureaucracy in 52
the high school

M. Del Vecchio

Webster's Third International Dictionary defines the term "bureaucracy" as a system of administration marked by a constant striving for increased functions and power, by lack of initiative and flexibility, by indifference to human needs or public opinion, and by a tendency to defer decisions to superiors or to impede action with red tape. Webster's definition is being practiced at Smith Public High School.

Mr. X is the illustrious principal of Smith Public High School and Mr. Z is his vice-principal. Together they run the school. Mr. Y is the Superintendent of Schools. He runs the men who run the school.

There is a serious drug problem here. Mr. X denies this problem. He has denied this because Mr. Y has told him to deny it. If this problem were known to the public, the system would look bad. If the public insisted that the problem be corrected, the system would lose power. The system must be preserved at all costs, including the health and welfare of its students.

Only the teachers and students know of this problem. However, the bureaucratic system at Smith Public High School does not recognize the student, and it recognizes the teacher only as a machine that has been programmed by the system. Therefore, at this high school, heroin is sold in left field and students get stoned in the rest rooms.

This school is no different from other schools—on the outside. It comes complete with a student newspaper. To a person on the outside, the newspaper is typical. There are pictures of smiling teachers and captains of football teams. There are articles on homecoming floats. This newspaper has been censored. All attempts to describe and depict the true scene at Smith Public High School have been cut. The pleas for help to correct a desperate situation have been omitted.

Many departments are grossly overlooked, the Art Department for one. Here, there is a shortage of teachers and materials, the rooms are overcrowded and dilapidated, and the tools are old and inaccurate. Art does not count here—it is considered a "busy course." Schools do not become famous for artistic students. They become famous for students who win awards and scholarships. There are no awards and scholarships offered in art at Smith Public High School. There are no awards for people who are able to create, to design, to change the commonplace to the unique. There are only awards for those who memorize textbooks and rewrite them on Friday's tests. Creativity and skills that mold a person's character are suppressed and discouraged.

The system must be preserved at all costs. It must be uniform and obeyed by all. If the rule books say that gym classes must play hockey, the gym classes must play hockey. It is November and the rain is beating the ground. It is 36 degrees outside. The gym classes are playing hockey. They play hockey because the rule books tell them to. They beat each other unmercifully in the pouring rain. The system must go on and the needs of the individuals are irrelevant. The students sustain pneumonia for bureaucracy.

Last year a new position was created at Smith Public High School, namely, that of student affairs coordinator. He is the new "red-tape, run-around man." He receives an annual income of $10,000, which is brought to him by courtesy of the taxpayers. A student who has problems goes to the student affairs coordinator. He, in turn, refers him to a higher official. (A higher official, in this case, is a person who gets paid more than the student affairs coordinator.) This higher official refers him back to the student affairs coordinator. It is an endless circle. Mr. Coordinator, thus far, has not done any actual work, since there was no need for the creation of the position in the first place. It looks good to the public if the school system has a Student Affairs Coordinator whether or not it needs one. It *looks* good. Mr. Y probably owed him a favor, and in a school of robots no one will question him.

There is racial tension at Smith Public High School. This, too, is another problem which has not been exposed. A young black student was recently knifed by a gang of whites. He was hospitalized, and gangs of blacks wait daily to revenge the attack on their comrade. Black students who attend school here appear to belong to another world. There is a wall between blacks and whites. Any attempt to bridge this gap causes the student to be automatically "labeled," labeling being a fundamental part of the bureaucratic system at Smith Public High School.

Another labeled group is the "radicals," who have been stamped by the administration, not by their peers or interested onlookers. On National Moratorium Day forty to fifty students, the so-called radicals, left class to participate in a peaceful demonstration against U. S. involvement in Vietnam. Automatically, the administration and its "puppet" teachers marked these students as hippies, radicals, and trouble-makers in general. Some teachers held this against the students for the rest of the school year, and those teachers' opinions of U. S. involvement in Vietnam were clearly expressed in the students' marks. The teachers' views of mod clothing and hair styles also became evident in the students' marks.

This peaceful demonstration proved that Mr. X and Mr. Z were unfit to run a school. Their qualifications failed and their lack of experience showed. Their true positions of "red-tape men and puppets" confirmed the ever-growing suspicions of the observant. On this day, Mr. X and Mr. Z were unavailable for comment all during the protest. They also did not take any action whatsoever about the protesting students. They did, however, as all puppets should, phone their master, Mr. Y. Mr. Y, of course, had the "leaders" of the demonstration hauled away, and spent the day posing for TV cameras and commenting on the radio. Why are these men, Mr. X and Mr. Z, governing 1300 students when they are incapable of handling 50 students sitting quietly on a lawn?

Mr. Y ended the professional careers of nine teachers, five of whom were from an English Department of eight people. He changed the patterns of nine lives with no more concern than lighting a match or smoking a cigarette.

In a specific case, the Board of Education charged that Mr. J did not follow the curriculum. Nowhere in the State of New York was there a curriculum for an eighth year English course. The teachers had been told previously to this school year that they would have to improvise and teach as they saw fit owing to this lack of curriculum. The principal had given Mr. J a favorable report, but the Board was now firing him.

The lack of curriculum was the official reason for the action. The real reason was that Mr. J took an interest in his students, something that the teaching machines of Mr. Y were not supposed to do. He was very active in staging after-school activities, such as dances and plays. Mr. J felt that these affairs would keep children off the streets, away from drugs, crime, and delinquency. The administration obviously had different ideas, since they soon began to charge each student group for the use of the gym or the cafeteria. They had to rent their own school, which was maintained by their parents the taxpayers. The firing of Mr. J caused many students to miss opportunities to visit museums and other places of interest.

A closer look at the other eight teachers who were fired shows that they too were active in student affairs and activities. They cared for their students. These teachers had one other thing in common—they were young and possessed new, fresh ideas, creative ideas designed to make the student think, which was something that the administration had not allowed. These teachers brought with them the end of the student as a machine and his beginning as an individual.

The system resorted again to labeling. These teachers were labeled "troublemakers." The school wished to go back to peaceful Friday nights when the students would walk the streets and gather on street corners, not dance in the gym or watch a play in the auditorium. These "troublemakers" could be taken care of easily by a simple "resignation." Headed by Mr. Y and his school board of scared machines, the posse gathered and reached the verdict that these teachers should hand in their resignations. The motion was approved with no more concern than tying a shoe.

The highlight of this episode came when Mr. J appeared at a board meeting one evening. Many people present felt that he would probe publicly into the reasons he was asked to turn in his resignation. Tension mounted as Mr. J raised his hand. The board refused to recognize him as Mr. J kept his hand raised for thirty minutes. When Mr. Y attempted to close the meeting rather quickly, an irate parent jumped up and demanded that Mr. J have his right to ask his question. Mr. J calmly asked permission to take one of his English classes on a field trip. A look of relief was thought to be seen on Mr. Y's face.

Why had Mr. J been forced to ask for this permission at a board meeting? It seemed that this type of permission was usually granted by the school's principal. Mr. J had gone through the proper channels and the proper forms. His form, however, had been neatly and quietly misplaced. The local "red-tape" man was at work again.

The dismissal of Mr. J and the other teachers had an unsettling effect on their students. An atmosphere of "what will happen next" prevailed. As they saw their teachers being fired one by one with no apparent justification, they began to fill in for themselves the missing reasons which the Board would not supply. There were rumors throughout the school that many of these teachers smoked pot, drank alcoholic beverages in the teachers' lounge, and egged on student protest groups to the point of picketing the school on school time. No work was accomplished in these classes for the rest of the school year. The students had study halls or played games. The school year was now a total waste.

The ruin of these professional careers did not end with a formal resignation. Other teachers, friends of the teachers who had been fired, felt they could no longer teach in a school where such a situation had occurred. One such teacher went to a nearby town to apply for a new job. The principal of this school called Mr. Y for a record of the teacher's accomplishments and a reference. Mr. Y stated that under no circumstances was one of "his" teachers to be hired by this school. Since Mr. Y's reputation and record were known throughout the state, no one would dare cross him, and this teacher had to remain at Smith Public High School almost as a prisoner.

Many parents and teachers were angered by the dismissal of these nine teachers.

Groups appeared at every meeting to harass the Board of Education, slowly diminishing as Mr. Y threatened every teacher in the group with loss of his job. This was done quietly, and this incident is a thing of the past for some.

The tentacles of bureaucracy do not stop in the high school; they stretch down into the grade school. Mr. Y's power reaches down into the grade school, too. Recently, a busing incident occurred at a school whose principal was planted by Mr. Y. An ages-old school bus law states that students within a mile radius from the school must walk, while students living outside this radius could ride on the school buses. This law has been hidden in a pile of notices for years, and generally has been ignored while the bus drivers pick up students whether they are inside or outside this radius. Mr. Y, however, along with his puppets, devised a way to save money on busing by enforcing this law (the money most likely going to the same fund which bought Mr. Y the two air-conditioned cars which he drives to attend board meetings and P.T.A. meetings). The enforcement of the law forced forty children from kindergarten to fifth grade to walk along a busy highway where the speed limit was 65 miles per hour and ditches instead of sidewalks lined both sides of the road.

There is a club at Smith Public High School called the Committee for Environmental Involvement. On the grounds of the school is a small patch of "forest-type" land where birds and rabbits nest and play. The C.E.I. group is concerned with keeping this section of land undisturbed. Their request was supposedly okayed by the administration, but yesterday a bulldozer plowed through it. If there were any opposition to this event, they would be labeled as supporters of the nine dismissed teachers and "trouble-makers." Who knows, the total of dismissals might grow to eleven. The same bureaucracy that made a promise to keep this land unharmed broke this promise with the action of the bulldozer.

Bureaucracy has taken strong root at Smith Public High School and is spreading and working its way into other schools throughout the nation. It has worked its way down to the kindergarten level and is still growing. The tentacles of bureaucracy are strangling and suffocating thoughts and free ideas. It must be stopped now, or it will produce a generation of machines and robots.

school is 53 unconstitutional, 1962/1972

Noel Novinson

Noel A. Novinson
N.M.B. Junior High School
English, section 9-5
Feb. 9, 1962

School Is Unconstitutional

According to the Fourteenth Amendment of the Constitution of the United States, "All persons born or naturalized in the United States . . . are citizens of the United States . . . ." This means that all people as soon as they are born in the United States are citizens and have all the rights and protections granted all citizens by the Constitution. The Federal Constitution is the "supreme law of the land" and overrules any laws or regulations of lower governments like states or cities. And nowhere in the Constitution does it say anything about people under the age of 21 having less rights than anyone else. People under 21 ("minors") are as full citizens as anyone else according to the Constitution, and any state or local laws taking away their rights are unconstitutional.

The Thirteenth Amendment to the Constitution states that "Neither slavery nor involuntary servitude, except as a punishment for crime . . . shall exist within the United States . . . ." This means that all persons in the United States, except for criminals, are protected against being forced to work against their will. People do not have to do any physical labor, like digging ditches or working on plantations like the slaves had to do before the Civil War, or mental work like being forced to read, write, or add. And according to the Constitution, this applies to all citizens, regardless of race, religion, or age.

Putting the Thirteenth and the Fourteenth Amendments together, compulsory education (being forced to go to school) is unconstitutional! In the first place, all kids, regardless of their age, are full citizens and therefore have all the rights and protections granted by the Constitution. No state law can take away their rights since the Constitution is "supreme" over all other laws. Second, no one can be forced to work against his will. And what is school except work? It is supposed to be for the benefit of the kids being forced to go, but even if this was true the Constitution doesn't say "slavery is illegal unless it's for your own good!" It says all involuntary servitude shall not exist.

457

There are laws in all states, counties, and cities saying kids *have* to go to school until they reach a certain age, usually sixteen. But these laws conflict with the United States Constitution which is "supreme" over them. Therefore the lower laws setting up compulsory education are unconstitutional. If the education laws were not compulsory (if kids could go to school if they wanted to, but were not *forced* to go), the education system would not be unconstitutional.

If schools were not forced on kids, many would probably go anyway. Kids would go when they wanted to learn, and go to the classes they wanted to learn from. I don't think kids can be *forced* to learn anyway. You can force a kid to go to school by threatening him with juvenile hall or reform school or a beating, but if he doesn't want to learn, he won't. You can try to make him learn by threatening him with "flunking" or "bad grades," but you can't scare a kid into being interested in something he isn't already interested in. And I don't think you can learn something if you're not interested in it. Kids can probably be forced to "study" something and then "pass" a test on it, but nothing will be remembered a day after the test. Adults and teachers probably won't admit it, especially to kids, but they probably felt the same way when they were forced to go to school.

But nobody listens to kids or pays any attention to their gripes about school. After all, "they're" only kids and what do "they" know, anyway?

Even though compulsory education is unconstitutional, nothing will ever be done to make school optional because it's the "adults" who make the laws and decide what is legal or illegal, constitutional or unconstitutional, right or wrong, good or bad. Adults run the lives of *all* the people, not just their own, just like the way we learned the slave-owners ran the lives of the slaves. Slaves had nothing to say about what they were forced to do until the Civil War was fought and the Thirteenth Amendment added to the Constitution. Kids today have nothing to say about what they are forced to do. According to the Constitution, kids are as free as everyone else, but it would probably take something like another Civil War before they are really free.

Schools are supposed to be for the good of the students being forced to go to them, so why doesn't anyone ask the students what the good classes are so there could be more of them, or who the bad teachers are so they could be replaced? The only hope for kids is that when they grow up they shouldn't forget how *they* felt when *they* were younger and they should try to change things so that all people of all ages are really free. And when we all get older, we should remember not to treat any person like a slave. It's not only unconstitutional, it's not being human.

GRADE B+ Well written, Noel, except for several grammatical mistakes such as your occasional habit of ending sentences with prepositions. Why do you add those irrelevant comments towards the end of your paper? I'm sure you'll see things in a different light when you become an "adult."

A decade has passed since that essay was written for a junior high school English class. In the interim, I successfully graduated from junior high school, high school, and college, and am now in the midst of my Ph.D. program in social psychology. I have been an official adult for several years and can therefore—by the grace of society's consensual validation—discourse rationally about such matters as education, involuntary servitude, and other, more "irrelevant" topics.

Junior high school—seventh, eighth, and ninth grades—was a very strange subculture comprising puberty, pimples, and a great deal of reliance upon social reality wherein the image was the reality. No longer children in elementary school but not having yet "arrived" in high school, we were too old for bicycles and too young for cars. We occupied ourselves with fist fights after school, looking in the mirror for some sign of fuzz above the upper lip, and proving ourselves persons or else no one believed. Proto-cliques developed on the basis of income, looks, interests, or "coolness." Are you "in" with the "in crowd"? Do you go the junior high dances and make out in the shadows? Do you sneak a smoke in the john or after lunch? A smoke—cigarettes of course; only beatniks or drug addicts used narcotics. Vietnam—what's that, something to eat? And Kennedy's so *cool* for a president.

And the teachers were types displaying a greater variance than the students: the tight-lipped Republican history teacher; the motherly English teacher; the Gestapo gym instructors ("C'mon, dress out! And when I say run around the field, I mean *run* around the field!"); the tolerant shop teacher; the crazy, bespectacled math teacher; the friendly, birdlike music teacher.

We had never heard of Summerhill, the Berkeley Free Speech Movement was two years in the future, and radicals were thought to be like Communists. Maybe it was because of the civil rights sit-ins in Mississippi, or watching the Lone Ranger and Superman battle against oppression and injustice on television, but *something* was in the air, and the only way I could express it was, ". . . try to change things so that all people of all ages are really free."

The television heroes showed us that "truth, justice, and the American Way" were always right and that, in the end, the struggle against oppression was successful. Violence was never glorified for its own sake (after all, the Lone Ranger never shot to kill), but if you were going to win, you had to take a stand sometime (thank you, John Wayne and Davy Crockett). Freedom marches and sit-ins brought the message into a practical context, and we kids, spending twice as much time in front of a television set as in a classroom, began to fantasize with our eyes open: maybe we too can be free from the oppression of schools, parents, and all of adult society.

The relationship of school bureaucracy (and equally, of adults in general) to the student has always been, and still admittedly is, that of a benevolent (usually) dictator to a discontent (usually) peasant. No one, whether because of age or color, wants to wait to become a free and equal member of his society. And having to live with an unpleasant and inefficient rite of passage system, makes the "peasant's" situation that much more irritating. The student, like the peasant under feudalism or the worker under a corporate capitalism, quickly learns to be passive and apparently studious. As long as he agrees not to rock the boat—to hand in his assignments on time, not question authority, and cram the night before exams so that he can demonstrate a reasonable ability to regurgitate "facts"—he will move up one more notch each year toward full membership in society.

However, although social reality in junior high, as in most public schools, tends to be inexorably linked to social image, the student is usually able to discriminate between academic image and educational truth. He knows that even though he received a *B* in History, he actually understands little or nothing. The student knows he is encouraged to be a passive receptacle for facts, and that the school system makes little or no attempt to encourage dynamic, inductive, creative thinking. The very structure of the classroom itself enforces this static, mechanistic process, with the endless repetition of dates, deeds, and data. Students do have an awareness of what, or whether, they are learning, and the ubiquitous public school ennui is a clear manifestation of the whole bureaucratic charade.

We all knew that the classroom boredom we experienced was a boredom of thwarted excitement. We all felt that there were many things we did want to experience (i.e., learn) but that these would be experienced in spite of, rather than because of, school. The most amazing thing about students is that they leave a public educational system and still exhibit signs of intellectual and experiential curiosity. Such is the strength of man's desire to learn about himself and his world.

We knew that we couldn't be forced by the school bureaucracy to learn unless we were already interested in the subject, in which case, of course, it wasn't a matter of coercion. The Summerhill paradigm would have appealed to us immensely, because of its innumerable opportunities—not requirements—to learn. But "education by coercion" seems to be the mainstay of the educational system in America. It is evident on all levels from elementary school through college, which also has its various required courses. In all cases, since learning has become a chore and no longer possesses the pleasure of discovery, everyone postpones as long as possible the unpleasant business of studying and then crams (a word both semantically and onomatopoetically correct) at the last minute for the most barbaric of all modern day atrocities, the exam.

On test day we would all file into the classroom like the prisoners at Dachau marching into the "showers": fingernails chewed to the quick, stomachs churning, hearts pounding, sweat dripping. The saddest aspect of this farce was that little or none of the information so painfully absorbed for the exam would be remembered for any significant length of time after the ordeal. We all knew this—the students, the teachers, and the administration —but we were supposed to pretend that wonderful things were going on in the classroom. And woe to the person who publicly recognized that not only was the Emperor wearing no clothes, but that he was fat and very ugly.

All of public school life wasn't without value, of course. Contact with several truly motivating and humane teachers, exposure to a diversity of other students, and the experience of sudden flashes of insight as veritable encyclopedias of science, math, English, and history were haphazardly and often blindly repeated to us, kept me interested in staying in the game to see what else might come to pass. But it seemed as if these rare occurrences were accidental to the process; that the teachers who could really allow their students to turn on to something new were mavericks in the system. The exquisite but oh-too-fleeting taste of true learning only made the rest of school seem that much more like a mouthful of stale, soggy Saltines.

As luck would have it, I was classified as having high educational potential. I was placed in various "honors" courses and given relatively great latitude in the choice of essay or book report topics or whatever, thereby escaping some (but by no means all) of the duller aspects of the public school experience. This elitist position engendered vague hostility from those classified otherwise, while giving me a slightly better perspective for viewing the ongoing process of public compulsory education.

Thus, in ninth grade, given the assignment of writing some sort of essay, I decided to examine some of the public school's failings, specifically its compulsory and mechanistic structure. I don't quite remember why I approached the essay in a legalistic manner; possibly we were concurrently studying the Constitution in Civics class. In any event, after giving the matter ten years' more thought, I have now come to the conclusion that the Supreme Court would definitely not agree that the compulsory education system is unconstitutional.

However, the entire question of whether or not compulsory education is technically "involuntary servitude" is a moot point, an academic problem which the Supreme Court wouldn't bother to decide one way or another. I realized this in junior high school. More important, the question of how to allow young people to be free to learn, without force, still exists as a real and vital issue.

As I wrote in 1962, "The only hope for kids is that when they grow up they shouldn't forget how *they* felt when *they* were younger, and they should try to change things so that all people of all ages are really free." Possibly for the first time in history, we *haven't* forgotten. We still remember what it was like to be treated as if we were something less than human, something inferior; something to be controlled, coerced, channeled, and tracked; something that has to be forced to sit in a sterile, boring room and be talked at. We were treated by the entire adult world in general, and the school bureaucracy in particular, like something that has to be forced or threatened into doing the most pleasant, natural thing in the world: exploring, experiencing, learning.

But why is it that this generation remembers, generalizes, and acts when so many others have not: is it obsession with youth culture? Mass immaturity due to overuse of drugs? The evolution of Consciousness III? Rebellion against the apathy of previous generations? Belief in the possibility and the necessity of freeing all people from slavery?

"And when we all get older, we should remember not to treat any person like a slave. It's not only unconstitutional, it's not being human." 1962/1972.

54 teachers as cause and cure of student unrest

Edward T. Ladd

It was about 1968 that the roof fell in. Suddenly high school kids all over America were criticizing, protesting, and demonstrating in a way they never had before (Trump and Hunt, 1968 and 1969). Some 500 free, "unauthorized" student publications were started, and more were coming (Divoky, 1969). Right and left, kids were courting tonguelashings and suspensions.

Back in the good old days—a few months earlier—almost all high school kids behaved pretty well. There were rebels, the kids who couldn't see that school was doing much for their lives, present or future (Stinchcombe, 1964; Remmers and Radler, 1957), but school people were able to manipulate things so that usually even they were "good"—those of them that stayed in school—and to impose a climate in the schools that kept things under control. This hadn't been too hard, because in elementary school kids had already been conditioned to the decorous (Henry, 1957), and then in high school the natural leaders could be bought off with big athletic programs and a grading system that had a way of reflecting how "cooperative" they were (Gordon, 1957; Coleman, 1961). Kids who wanted to go to college and cared about their grades thought the schools were good places for building up records for future use. Thus, though few of them developed much interest in the things a school is supposed to be all about, the typical kid who was interested in anything beyond day-to-day pleasures was loyal to his school as it was and blindly confident that everything the school was doing to him was being done for his own good and done well (Rhea, 1968).

Most of the success-bound kids are still like this; in fact, some of them resent the activists and their criticisms and demonstrations (Harris, 1969), but since around 1968 many of them, like their older friends and siblings in college, are openly rebelling. Some of the kids who a little earlier would have been uninterested in school success, especially black kids from the ghettoes, must have begun to dream that success might be possible for them, too, for they, too, came up with ideas for change. Ghetto kids and middle- and upper-class long-hairs sometimes worked separately and sometimes made intriguing alliances. All over the United States they used the mimeograph machine and the loud-speaker to enlarge and "educate" their constituencies. Delegations of kids asked for hearings; some kids went on strike; some occupied buildings; some got their parents on their side. With their parents and often with the help of free legal services, a remarkable number fought the schools in court.

In another country or at another time, kids who were angry with their schools might have wanted to get away from them, but not these kids. Nor did they want to destroy the schools, or even take them over. Part of what they *were* after was more respect, more freedom, fairer treatment, and more say within the system, more sensitivity to human beings as human beings and less of "the student as nigger," as some of them put it (Farber, 1968). A part of this goal was more interesting teaching and a more meaningful curriculum, which for a lot of them meant the inclusion of a good-sized chunk of "black studies." Lumping these things together, they were rejecting blind subjugation to the conventions and values, however benevolent, of the white middle class and the older generation, and insisting that, instead, the schools serve them as clients, responding to *their* ideas and feelings about what would be most useful to *them* (Divoky, 1964; Birmingham, 1970; Libarle and Seligson, 1970; Harris, 1969).

This wasn't always how school people understood their revolt, especially when it was mounted rudely, obscenely, destructively, or illegally. Teachers and principals knew that what they did to educate and control kids was intended for the kids' own good and not as harassment. They didn't realize that in fact they were trying to run kids' lives for them, and doing it more intolerantly and thoroughly, perhaps, than school people did it in any other democratic country in the world. They probably just thought that this is the way it had to be. They knew that if anything, schools had been getting better, so the cause of the rebellion must lie in the kids, or, if not in them, in their families.

The kids had just been spoiled, some teachers and administrators apparently felt, they had never learned self-discipline. As their hairdos and clothing styles showed, their families had allowed them—perhaps encouraged them—to flout convention and had failed to teach them good taste, courtesy, or respect for their elders. How else to explain their idea that they knew more than the older generation about what kind of education they needed and how to run the schools? If they would first show that they could control themselves and conform to the existing society, they then could be trusted to question it, and they would have earned the right. However, the personalities and values of many had been so distorted by their backgrounds, probably, that it was too late; no amount of teaching or counseling could straighten them out. They had to be forced back into line, and control over them had to be tight, so that schools could get on with the job of preparing the other kids for the adult world. Those who wouldn't respond to these measures just had to leave.

The school people weren't completely wrong. Most of the change *had* been in the kids, not in the schools. Perhaps the schools had become a little more bureaucratic year by year, and a little less humane. But there was no question that *these* kids *were* less conventional and more independent—for some that's putting it mildly—and that some of them *were* spoiled.

The changes in kids and their new disposition to revolt, protest, rebel, and become activists or what-have-you are complex and can be attributed to many things, including changes in families and the ways kids are brought up, the technological society, the rapidity of change itself, television, affluence, a general egalitarian trend, and the Vietnam war. Already, books have been written on the subject, as well as hundreds of articles.* In

---

*See, for example, Kenneth Keniston: Young Radicals: Notes on Committed Youth: New York, Harcourt, Brace and World, 1968, Theodore Roszak: The Making of a Counterculture: Reflections on the Technocratic Society and its Youthful Opposition. Garden City, Doubleday and Company, 1969, Margaret Mead: Culture and Commitment: A Study of the Generation Gap. Garden City, Natural History Press, 1970; Jerry L. Simmons and Barry Winograd: It's Happening: A Portrait of the Youth Scene Today. Santa Barbara, Marc-Laird Publications, 1966; Charles A. Reich: The Greening of America. New York, Random House, 1970.

a sense, though, it shouldn't matter to the schools what other forces have helped to make kids what they are, any more than it should matter in a hospital whether a broken leg was caused by a car wreck or a fight. For as an important old educational principle says, you can teach any student if you start with him where he is. The changes in kids needn't prevent the school from selling them on the excitement of learning and providing a positive focus for their lives rather than a cause of resentment. To paraphrase one of the kids' slogans, suppose they gave a student revolt and nobody came. Other educational institutions created by adults, such as youth organizations and camps, have been known to reach the most difficult kids and win great loyalty from them, and the attitudes of a few kids suggest that some schools, too, are achieving this. Yet many bright young people view schools as irrelevant and repressive, the part of the adult society they most want to see changed (Trump and Hunt, 1968, 1969). Whatever it is that has piled up the fuel of revolt, the schools have supplied the kindling and the matches. In this important sense what causes kids to revolt is what schools do to them.

Ironically, the people who do most of what is done to kids in schools are well-intentioned teachers who have wanted to turn kids on, not off, but who, as we shall see, have fallen into a trap. (It makes little difference that the trap is one that nobody ever designed.) Teachers, however, as we shall also see, are also the people in the best position to straighten the situation out again. Happily, there is reason to believe that they will.

WHAT TEACHERS DO TO KIDS THAT BUGS THEM

If you are a teacher you may find the next few pages hard to take. It may be that you yourself haven't done any of the things that will be listed; if so, there's no reason to feel defensive. It may be that you have, but you don't believe you were wrong, again, no reason to feel defensive. If you have done some of these things and wish you hadn't, try to grin and bear it, and later on some things will be said that you may find reassuring. There is a true story of an evening meeting called not long ago to bring about communication between kids and teachers. When, as planned, the kids got up and recited their gripes about the school, a number of teachers said, "We can't take this any longer," and walked out (Postman and Weingartner, 1969, p. 134). If *you* can't take it, walk out now before you get angry. If you stick with it, though, perhaps you'll be glad you did.

There's no need to dwell on kids' objections to the curriculum and the teaching. They're sick of dry facts about things that seem far away. They're sick of dull lectures and recitations and tests that don't allow them to think, and of teachers' careful steering away from controversy. Some are sick of *Silas Marner* (which the curriculum specialists have been trying to get rid of for decades). Some resent the way their grades may bar them from sports or from voting in school elections, or separate them from their friends, forcing them into classes with younger or "dumber" kids. Some don't like the way teachers seem to give the best grades to the kids whose thinking seems to match theirs. The creative ones are angry about the way teachers side-step or put down kids who figure out new approaches or look at things differently—a habit documented by educational researchers several years ago (Getzels and Jackson, 1962, pp. 88-123). They're tired of having "teaching" done *to* them, of teachers acting like academic Simon Legrees: handing out narrowly defined, mechanical assignments, asking questions about snippets of information or empty verbalisms, making threats, giving pop quizzes, and penalizing them for digressions and even plain lack of interest. They resent teachers' unwillingness to explore tricky questions with them in free-wheeling, candid ways, in a teacher-student partnership. Those who have been concerned about the black revolution object to the fact that in the majority of schools the thing that most strongly concerns and moves them has been almost entirely ignored.

With the exception of the last item, these are shortcomings which good teachers have been aware of for years and have been working on, often successfully, tough as it is at times. So it should be not distressing but encouraging that kids themselves have come to see it our way. Maybe they can help. Or at least their pressure will keep us trying to do the thing we want to do.

The rebels' objections to what goes on in their academic life, however, are not as strong as their objections to what might be called the governance aspect of the classroom. The youth counterculture revolves around the repudiation of authoritarianism (Roszak, 1969). Yet American schools, which are supposed to induct kids into the ways of democracy under law rather than inspiring revolt against those ways, are in many respects more authoritarian even than the military—are, in fact, almost totalitarian (Marker and Mehlinger, 1970; Silberman, 1970). (Is the fact that school people call unofficial student newspapers "undergound newspapers" an unconscious admission of this?)

Older people, including most teachers, are so used to schools like this that they don't think what it means for kids to spend their days in large institutions where, day in and day out, their bosses tell them, sit down; sit up; sit still; keep quiet; speak up; write; stop writing; this is not the time to talk about that; get rid of your gum; keep in a straight line; don't talk in the corridors; hurry up; you can't do that without permission; you should have gone to the bathroom before, you can't go now; I'm your friend; don't talk back to *me;* don't tattle; how can you be so stupid; tell me who did it; your dress is too short; your hair is too long; be cooperative; wipe that smile off your face; children don't have rights; develop a better attitude toward school; mind your own business; let me see that piece of paper; don't say things like that; always tell the truth; and say you're sorry. . . .

But those are things teachers say to kids every day. And they represent the kind of governance that prevails in many, perhaps most, classrooms.

What schools do to kids' freedom can be looked at this way. When kids are still so small that they don't go to school, most of them encounter few barriers to doing what they want; they can play with this toy or that kitchen utensil for as long as they want, sing while playing, talk to themselves or whoever is around at almost any time, watch television or not, visit the neighbors', go to the bathroom when they feel like it, and in some families, get something to eat whenever they are hungry. All these are examples of one kind of freedom—the ability to do what one feels like doing. Adults have much less of this kind of freedom, they must meet schedules, wait until lunch is ready, hold their tongues on some occasions, obey the law, live more or less within their incomes, and often not go right after major gratifications, but wait for them or renounce them entirely. To go from infancy to adulthood is to learn to respond less to impulses and more to the logics of different situations; it is to lose a great deal of freedom in this first sense of the word.

Freedom can be looked at in another way, though—as the ability to do a large number of different things. In this sense adults are much more free than little kids. Though there are many limits on what they can do, most of them can choose their style of living and dress, eat or not eat many different kinds of things at meals or between meals, put their personal touches on the work they do, move from one city to another and from one job to another, spend their nonworking time sleeping, working, or playing in any of many ways, take part in the choosing of their governments, and so on. In this sense of being free, to go from infancy to adulthood is to gain tremendously in freedom.

If a school is to help kids make the transition from infancy to adulthood, it should gradually and steadily help them adjust to the narrowing of the first kind of freedom and the widening of the second. Typically, American schools do neither. The typical American kid finds that the first kind of freedom has shrunk suddenly and radically the day he enters school, and, right to the day he leaves, he never finds the second kind appreciably broadened beyond where it started. He is never allowed to do many of the things he might feel like doing, and the number of things he is allowed to do is always kept very small. With respect to either kind of freedom the American school is like the narrow end of a cone into which teachers jam kids when they first arrive and keep them the whole time they're in school. This is one reason why social scientists have recently been comparing schools to the military and to prisons. Kids have been drawing the same comparison.

To get kids to comply with the norms that are prescribed, teachers use influence techniques that are typically as unpleasant as the norms themselves. For performance they approve, teachers hand out practically no rewards other than grades and purely personal favors like smiles and praise. But performance they disapprove brings from them an array of sanctions: physical violence—even in the 1970's, long after being outlawed in the Army and in prisons—expressions of disapproval, rejection, and humiliation; the impugning of motives; the arousing of guilt feelings; such nuisance punishments as assigning sentences to be written a hundred times, detention, or referring the student to the counselor to see if there's a screw loose; and such potentially catastrophic actions as sending students to the principal or landing them in trouble with their parents.

Also, in teachers' dealings with apparent infractions there is not often anything even resembling due process of law. Teachers often berate or even punish the innocent along with the guilty and accuse and punish kids with insufficient evidence. When a serious charge is made, usually the sole provisions for fairness for the kid are the teacher's or the principal's personal reasonableness and sense of justice. That these usually leave something to be desired is shown by teachers' almost universal insistence that principals back them up against kids regardless of whether they are right or wrong, and by principals' tendency to oblige (Becker, 1953).

Teachers harm kids through their omissions, too. Every day teachers stand by while principals treat kids repressively, unprofessionally, and sometimes illegally. However noneducational or countereducational an administrator's way of dealing with kids (he may, of course, be responding to pressure rather than his own good judgment), teachers, who are supposed to be professional educators, usually cooperate. They allow administrators to make the rules which jam kids into the narrow end of the cone we have described, to moralize about behavior instead of teaching understanding about it, to manipulate student councils and censor the guts out of student newspapers, to drive wedges into the cracks between kids and their parents, and to ring down the curtain on kids' schooling, at least temporarily, for tardiness or for offenses which in a plant or office would produce nothing more than friendly laughter or a dirty look.

Principals would be unable to do these things if teachers reacted the way doctors would if a hospital administration tried to subordinate professional procedures to administrative ones; if teachers said, "Stop! As this school's professional educators, we won't stand for such unprofessional treatment of our clients." But most teachers cooperate, or, at best, are silent.

That some kids are breaking the silence themselves should not really be a surprise. It *is* surprising, though, how little of their anger has been turned on teachers. It's as if students thought teachers do what they do and put up with worse because they have no choice. Is this so?

WHY TEACHERS TREAT KIDS THE WAY THEY DO

The case can be made that teachers behave as they do because they don't like kids and don't trust them. For one thing, most teachers seem less concerned with eliminating injustices to kids than with avoiding or suppressing the rebellion that may result (Divoky, 1964, p. 62). And just listen to how teachers talk about kids in the faculty lounge, look at how nervous they are about even letting a kid *into* that secret place, and see how careful they are never to be called by their first names in a kid's presence. Or read how they vote on propositions such as these:

> Pupils shouldn't be allowed to contradict statements a teacher makes in class.
> Sarcasm is a good disciplinary technique.
> Pupils aren't usually capable of solving their problems by logical reasoning (Adapted from Willower, 1967, esp. pp. 47-48).

The fact is, though, that teachers as a group, deep down inside, are warm, human people who would really like to be friends with kids. Most of them chose teaching as a career partly because they didn't want to compete with their fellow men but to share with them the things they love, and sometimes, really, just wanted to help them (Walberg, 1970, pp. 414-415; Jenkins and Lippitt, 1951). Most teachers, in fact, started out being pretty nice to kids. It's after they are on the job that they get inconsiderate or nasty. The change takes place quickly. What is there about the job that does this to teachers and even makes them believe that it's right and proper? (Iannaccone, 1963; Hoy, 1969).

First, while teachers usually start out not liking the uninteresting curriculum they are asked to teach, they have little to say about it. Replacing it with something else would take freedom, time, and expert help. They're not free to junk last year's textbooks and buy a different set, or to say, "No, we won't do algebra: these kids don't even like math yet, so we'll spend the first six weeks on crap games." Time? They're on the front line almost all day every day, and in the little unscheduled time they have, they must grade papers and try to prepare a little for the next class. Members of a fine high school social studies faculty once told the writer that they knew they should overhaul their curriculum, but the only time they could have found for doing that was 7 o'clock in the morning. (School teachers aren't in the same position as college teachers, who have two to ten hours to spend preparing for each scheduled hour with students.) Expert help? Since teachers can't usually take time off during the day to work with an expert, the issue is moot.

So teachers impose on kids a lot of dull, irrelevant stuff. Then, perhaps out of a distorted sense of duty, they feel they must tell the kid it's good for him, and eventually some of them come to believe it is.

Second, teachers really don't know how to teach in any other way than the conventional one that casts them in the role of academic Simon Legrees. Most teachers have never been exposed to exciting, stimulating, interest-centered teaching themselves, let alone shown how to do it, and they're afraid that if they tried it, pandemonium would break out. Because they don't know how to do it, they're probably right (more on that subject shortly).

Third, a lot of teachers don't understand kids very well, especially kids from a different social class or race. Whatever psychology they learned didn't include the fact that the basic learning mechanisms and aspirations of a hood are the same as those of a nice middle-class girl—or teacher—and those of a black the same as those of a white, or the fact that *every* human being wants to learn things only the older generation can teach him, wants his elders' respect, and wants to succeed. Teachers just don't know that it's possible for every kid to start where he is if a good teacher will meet him there, and to go where he needs to go without necessarily "wasting time."

Fourth and most important of all, teachers are tied up in knots about "discipline," so many knots, in fact, that we can talk about only a few.

One of the knots is the instinct of self-defense, which causes trouble in other professions, too, such as psychiatry, politics, and police work. Like people in these fields, teachers *are* insulted, harassed, and attacked, and their usual impulse is to use their position to hit back, which, though entirely human, isn't professional. (Actually, some of this may be educational if it teaches kids what's likely to happen to aggressors, but only in a limited way.)

Other knots derive from the peculiar way school systems are organized. Sociologically speaking, school systems are different from most other organizations rendering professional services directly to the public because they are organized hierarchically like corporations, the civil service, and the army, not professionally like hospitals, universities, architectural firms, and symphony orchestras. Teachers' roles, in turn, are not designed as the roles of professionals but of petty bureaucratic functionaries, and kids' roles are those, not of clients to be served, but of helots at the bottom of the bureaucratic totem pole. The bureaucratic pressure to keep track of what is going on, carry out routines, and keep order inevitably conflicts with the initiative, freedom, excitement, controversy, noise, and confusion needed for learning, and when the conflict becomes the least bit sticky, you-know-which takes precedence (Rhea, 1964; Fuchs, 1967, pp. 86-93). If you are an American school teacher today, almost everyone you deal with professionally except the kids themselves thinks it's so important for you to sit on kids that if it comes down to a choice, you should do it even at the expense of teaching them (Herndon, 1968; Fuchs, 1967). Whereas the federal government tries only to *regulate* General Motors' behavior and yours and mine, the teacher is expected to *control* the kids' behavior and control it *all*—where they sit, when they talk, when they go to the bathroom, whether they visit on the way back from the pencil sharpener, what they read, what they think, the expressions on their faces, their attitudes, and the color of their jeans. No one seems to make any bones, by the way, about actually using that word "control."

You might refuse. Most teachers don't. One reason they don't is that a large and vocal part of the community with strong convictions in favor of autocracy stands ready to pounce (Harris, 1969; Gallup, 1969). At heart these people are still Puritans; they don't know that kids learn to use freedom by having a chance to use and misuse it and see the result, but believe instead that kids must be put in a straitjacket and kept there until they miraculously become "self-disciplined"—which is to say, until they have learned to want to do what the older generation wants them to do. The same people know so little about kids that they also mistrust their very dispositions. Again, as Puritans, they think kids are programmed to like doing bad things more than good things, which makes it essential for teachers to exert every effort to prevent them from doing what they like, from experimenting with doing anything bad, from seeing other people do something bad, and even from finding out about bad things they might do. So, if you're a teacher, they see it as your job to stamp out every trace of unwanted behavior. (There are teachers who themselves are Puritans and for whom this approach comes naturally without community pressures, but fortunately they're a dying, or at least a retiring, breed.)

There is another reason why some people in the community want you to keep tight "discipline" over kids—they are afraid of them and want any older person who's in a position to hold them down to do so.

For both these reasons, if teachers do give kids the freedom they need to learn to regulate their own behavior, pretty soon there's likely to be a meeting somewhere in town about the "erosion of authority" in the school (Libarle and Seligson, 1970, pp. xi-xiii).

Meetings like that give administrators the willies. Administrators, after all, owe their jobs and budgets to the community's leaders. They see themselves as being on the "firing line" and don't relish heavier bombardment, let alone the possibility of unemployment. Even when they don't share the community's anti-intellectual authoritarianism, they act as if they do. So they usually try to carry out the community's wishes and add to the pressure on teachers.

Quite apart from that, they are susceptible to the occupational disease of all administrators, the disposition to give too high a priority to running the organization smoothly, efficiently, and noncontroversially. Their desire to avoid disorder and disruption also makes them force teachers, too, to be autocratic, which they do by subjecting them to "the most intolerant pressure" (Sarason, 1966, p. 133). Administrators usually have relatively few formal powers over teachers—they can't promote, demote, or fire them, or, except in the case of coaches, change their salaries. But the powers they do have are enough to bring woe to the teacher who doesn't exercise complete control over his class.

The greatest pressure on teachers, however, is the pressure they exert on one another. One might expect teachers to band together to resist the outside pressure to be autocratic, but they don't. The system pushes them, instead, to reinforce those pressures. If one teacher were to give kids their heads, they'd be likely to pressure another teacher to do the same, or at least they might carry some of their rambunctiousness with them from one class to the next. Either way, it's trouble for the other teacher. His work is hard enough; one thing he can do to keep it from getting harder is to keep his colleagues from being nicer to kids than he is. It's as simple as that. And teachers have developed a repertoire of ways of giving a hard time to any colleague who steps out of line in this way (Smith and Geoffrey, 1968; Gordon, 1957; Sarason, 1966, p. 102; Willower and Jones, 1967, pp. 424-428; Ryan, 1970; Kohl, 1969).

So every teacher is pressured to sit on kids, even though as a person and an educator he'd like to be friendly with them and has never heard a good educational reason for sitting on them; in fact, he has been taught in college that it's bad professional practice. The teachers who don't give in, who say, "To heck with it, I'm not going to push these kids around," are in trouble before very long and are fired or quit. (For one reason or another, half of our teachers quit the profession after two years or less, and only a dribble of them come back later.) The teachers who stick around are for the most part those who have given in. Some have done so because they felt they had little choice. They wanted badly to teach; if they had tried to move to other school systems, they might not have found jobs, and, even if they had, things probably wouldn't have been any different; they may have felt compelled for family reasons to stay in the community, and teaching was the only thing they were trained to do; they needed the money; they needed to be free during vacations; and so on. Perhaps some would have liked to fight the system but didn't like fighting, or didn't want to embarrass husbands or wives by a fight.

To make matters worse, when a teacher has gone along with autocracy, he almost inescapably feels, consciously or unconsciously, a bit uncomfortable and defensive about his forced conversion. Also, for a number of reasons, a teacher is likely to take kids' resistance to rules and orders as personal attacks. Both these psychological facts make teachers even a little harder on the brats, hoods, militants, and other rebels.

This, then, is how it comes that nice, decent teachers who survive in the schools are pushed into being harsh governors of kids and brainwashed into believing they should be. This is how they get into the trap. It is something which their teacher education programs never prepared them for, let alone taught them how to resist, and something their administrators are not likely to try to reverse.

It is a credit to the high school dissidents' perspicacity that even though the typical teacher administers the resented medicine or stands idly by while it is administered by the principal, the kids seem to sense the trap he's in and direct relatively little of their fire at him (Birmingham, 1970, p. 214; Divoky, 1964; Libarle and Seligson, 1970; "What's troubling high school students?").

IT MIGHT GO ON THIS WAY BUT IT MUSTN'T

If kids aren't soon treated better in school, there's going to be a lot worse trouble, and more people, especially kids, are going to be hurt. Everywhere in the world the spirit of liberty and self-assertion is growing. The present situation is like a guerrilla war and carries with it the same dangers. The kids are the guerrillas, loosely organized but dogged. Most of their "underground newspapers" die at an early age, but new ones spring up. When it comes to action, most kids are careful not to expose themselves too far. When they aren't fighting, they fade back into the general population, and the more they are harassed, the more backing they pick up from their fellows. They feel they have little to lose and a lot to gain—if only the fun of retaliating against us and seeing us overreact. They can keep going indefinitely.

The school's forces are, of course, better organized. There are occupation troops (teachers), commanders (administrators and school boards), and even supporting forces (lawyers, professors, planners of workshops and conferences, and writers of pamphlets and articles). The administrators design the tactics, give the orders, take most of the rocket fire, and drop the big bombs of suspension and expulsion.

More kids may resort to violence. Violence from kids and official reaction to it have already led to police guards in many city schools and police occupation of a few. Wherever, as a result of such practices, the blood of martyrs flows, it will be, as it has been throughout history, the seed of new converts.

Even if our young people could be crushed, though, they shouldn't be. When the older generation and the younger are caught in a vicious circle of mutual frustration and aggression as at present, it is the older generation which has to stop it. We do, after all, have a little more wisdom than our kids, and it is we, not they, who control our schools, our school rules, and presumably our own actions. Moreover, there are educational, moral, and legal reasons why we who purport to educate kids should treat them better.

So far, because high school dissidents have sensed the pressures on teachers, teachers have got off lightly. But, as we have seen, their record is vulnerable. And every year kids become more perceptive. College students have already begun to see that professors have had more to do with the ways colleges treat students than administrators have.

At the same time, teachers more than anyone else have the capabilities and, deep down, the human understanding needed to develop better ways of treating kids; if they can establish the right relationship, kids will put up with a lot of nonsense from others.

Teachers aren't going to find changing easy. Because the public's attitudes are what they are, because school boards exert such control over administrators, and because administrators are trained and hired to be public servants rather than crusaders (and like to eat), it will be a long time before the pressures on teachers let up. But teachers as a group have unusual professional security, enough to face up to and resist these pressures.

WHAT TEACHERS WILL DO ABOUT IT

Many teachers are coming to understand the things we have been describing. Events of the last few years, student revolt, administrators' actions (tyrannical and just, stupid and wise), and court decisions have started teachers thinking about students' feelings and rights and about discipline to an extent they never had before. And many of them are ready to do something to improve the situation. What will they do? What they can. What *can* they do? Here are some possibilities:

1. Teachers can try to become less uptight about disorder in school life, in the curriculum, in teaching, and in conduct, recognizing it as often educationally useful and sometimes necessary. They can quietly stop trying to control kids and can settle for a minimum of regulation. To this end they can subject each rule governing kids' in-school behavior to the clear-and-present danger test: without this rule would someone's health, welfare, or rights be clearly and imminently endangered? They can sit down and list all the kinds of decisions the typical kid is likely to make at age five and those he can make at the age when he leaves school; they can then plot the increasing number of decisions the school should schedule him to make so that, as he approaches that inexorable deadline, he will be as well-prepared as possible. That will mean, of course, steadily widening his prerogatives *whether or not he is ready;* for, ready or not, adult freedom is coming.

2. In three different ways teachers can change the disciplinary practices of their schools. In their own dealings with kids they can gradually give kids more latitude, and they can cut down on threats, reproaches, and punishments, replacing them with rewards for good behavior, the ignoring of disapproved behavior, friendly needling or teasing, bargaining, and other nonauthoritarian influence techniques. Second, they can insist that administrators develop more attractive institutional rewards and less drastic punishments than teachers now have access to. There's no reason why they shouldn't do what private profit-making companies do: reward kids with green stamps and transistor radios. In the high schools teachers can press for repertories of privileges and prerogatives for dispensation to deserving young adults. As for punishments, some kind of on-campus suspension, for instance, is fairer and more educational than putting a kid out on the street. Third, in lots of ways teachers can engage the kids themselves in setting norms and securing compliance with them.

3. Teachers can help students change the roles of student organizations so that they can share in the important decision-making within the school and create significant "student involvement." Whether we like it or not, this means a degree of student power and some sharp disagreements. It also means less use of quasi-police and quasi-legal procedures in dealings with students and more use of the skills of diplomacy and politics.

4. Teachers can try to relate to kids like the persons and professionals they really want to be. As professionals, they can carry out institutional policies and regulations without identifying themselves personally with them, and they can try to avoid taking challenges to their teacherly actions as personal attacks. As persons, they can try to be more open with kids, revealing themselves as human beings who can joke, take a joke, lend one kid money and buy another a coke, and who have doubts, loves, and hates—as far as is compatible with being fair to kids and helping them learn. For example, a teacher can reveal his doubts about a decision he or someone else has made, his love for a certain colleague, or his hate for some of the materials he has to assign. As a person, when a kid is in trouble, a teacher can take his side and show him how to live with the regulations and the personnel of the school, or how to get around them. Teachers can start listening to

kids, really listening, which means letting them say what they want to say, complete with untruths, defamation, profanity, and obscenity, if that's the way the kids want it. (*After* hearing them out, teachers can still talk with them, and talk back to them if they think they should.) Teachers can teach kids about the educational value of more freedom and its risks, too, as well as the forces which incline communities and school officials to be repressive. In this way, teachers may indirectly educate parents. Teachers can encourage kids who oppose school policies to express *their* personal feelings about those policies and to work for change, and can coach them in the proper ways to do it.

5. Teachers can develop a new professional relationship to their administrators—they can stop trying both to please them and to keep them at arm's length, and can, instead, insist on a relationship of mutual respect and support, even mutual use of first names. They can help administrators discharge their administrative responsibilities, including those which make educating kids easier, while pressing administrators to help them, in turn, with their own educational functions. In particular, they can figure out ways of getting principals to lay off trying to keep kids docile, orderly, and quiet. They can do this by sending fewer kids to the office; intervening to protect kids whom principals are treating unfairly; ignoring, if it has to come to that, principals' efforts to interfere with activities which make classrooms, hallways, and cafeterias a little noisy and sometimes a little messy; and joining together to defy unprofessional orders (Ryan, 1970, pp. 106-107). Sometimes they can subtly reeducate a principal (Sarason, 1966, pp. 95-96). They may even be able to force a hopelessly repressive one to resign. There are administrators, by the way, who will welcome this sort of posture on the part of their teachers and will gladly use it as leverage on the school board.

6. Teachers can insist on having time during the work week for study, for planning, and for revising of curricula, teaching methods and materials, and for informal contacts with kids. When teachers insist, most administrators and school boards will soon devise the arrangements. (When they have time for these activities, teachers can get good help from students.)

7. When teachers do the professional things which serve the school's clients—the kids—but which disturb the school's routines, they can give one another support, even when it means that some of them have to face kids who are excited as the result of the activity of the previous hour. Teachers can get their organizations, school-wide, local, state, and national, to give more attention to the causes of student unrest, to ways teachers can deal with kids which are more professional than those most common today, and to teachers' need for support rather than supervision from administrators.

Teachers are already doing things like these, and, as suggested, there are administrators who welcome what they're doing as signs of the dawning of a new day. An administrator can't change the way a school impinges on kids by fiat; it takes a new kind of spontaneous behavior on the part of those staff members whose primary responsibility is to educate.

Some teachers will try these new ways of behaving, find that the schools they're working in aren't ready to live with such professional behavior, and become too frustrated to continue, so they'll give up trying, even if it means putting cans of Mace in their desk drawers. Others will want to keep at it, even if it means looking for jobs in other schools that are ready. A few will make good headway on their first try. The numbers of the determined will grow. Thus teachers will gradually convert student alienation and unrest into loyal opposition, which, when all is said and done, will mean that teachers and kids are mutually respectful members of a significant educational community.

REFERENCES

Becker, Howard S.: The teacher in the authority system of the public school. *The Journal of Educational Sociology, 27*: No. 3, 128-141, 1953.

Birmingham, John (ed.): Our Time Is Now: Notes From the High School Underground. New York, Praeger, 1970.

Coleman, James S.: The Adolescent Society. New York, The Free Press, 1961.

Divoky, Diane (ed.): How Old Will You Be in 1984? New York, Avon Books, 1964.

Divoky, Diane: Revolt in the high schools: the way it's going to be. *Saturday Review, 52*: No. 7, 83-84, 1969.

Farber, Jerry: The student as nigger. *This Magazine Is About Schools,* 1968.

Fuchs, Estelle: Teachers Talk: Views from Inside City Schools. Garden City, Doubleday and Company, 1967.

Gallup, George: How the Nation Views the Public Schools: A Study of the Public Schools of the United States; A CFK Ltd. Report. Princeton, Gallup International, 1969, and succeeding surveys in that series.

Getzels, Jacob W., and Jackson, Philip W.: Creativity and Intelligence: Explorations with Gifted Students. New York, John Wiley and Sons, 1962.

Gordon, C. Wayne: The Social System of the High School. Glencoe, Ill., The Free Press, 1957.

Harris, Louis: The Life Poll. *Life, 66*: No. 19, 22-23, May 16, 1969.

Henry, Jules: Attitude organization in elementary school classrooms. *American Journal of Orthopsychiatry, 27*: 117-133, 1957.

Herndon, James: The Way It Spozed To Be. New York, Simon and Schuster, 1968.

Hoy, Wayne K.: Pupil control ideology and organizational socialization: a further examination of the influence of experience on the beginning teacher. *The School Review, 77*: Nos. 3-4, 257-265, 1969.

Iannaccone, Laurence: Student teaching: a transitional stage in the making of a teacher. *Theory into Practice, 2*: No. 2, 73-80, 1963.

Jenkins, David H., and Lippitt, Ronald: Interpersonal Perceptions of Teachers, Students, and Parents. Washington, National Education Association, 1951.

Kohl, Herbert: The Open Classroom: A Practical Guide to a New Way of Teaching. *The New York Review,* 1969. pp. 83-86.

Libarle, Marc, and Seligson, Tom (eds.): The High School Revolutionaries. New York, Random House, 1970.

Marker, Gerald W., and Mehlinger, Howard D.: Schools, politics, rebellion, and other youthful interests. *In* The Danforth Foundation, and the Ford Foundation: The School and the Democratic Environment. New York, Columbia University Press, 1970. pp. 38-54.

Postman, Neil, and Weingartner, Charles: Teaching as a Subversive Activity. New York, Delacorte Press, 1969.

Remmers, H. H., and Radler, D. H.: The American Teenager. Indianapolis, Bobbs-Merrill, 1957.

Rhea, Booth Buford, Jr.: The myth of institutional paternalism in high school. *The Urban Review, 2*: No. 1, 13-15, 34, 1968.

Rhea, Booth Buford, Jr.: Organizational Analysis and Education: An Exercise in Sociological Theory. Unpublished Ph.D. dissertation, University of Missouri, 1964.

Ryan, Kevin, (ed.): Don't Smile Until Christmas. Chicago, University of Chicago Press, 1970.

Sarason, Seymour B., et al.: Psychology in Community Settings: Clinical, Educational, Vocational, Social Aspects. New York, John Wiley and Sons, 1966.

Silberman, Charles A.: Crisis in the Classroom. New York, Random House, 1970.

Smith, Louis M., and Geoffrey, William: The Complexities of an Urban Classroom. New York, Holt, Rinehart and Winston, 1968.

Stinchcombe, Arthur L.: Rebellion in a High School. Chicago, Quadrangle Books, 1964.

Trump, J. Lloyd, and Hunt, Jane: The nature and extent of student activism. *The Bulletin of the National Association of Secondary School Principals, 53*: No. 337, 150-158, May, 1969.

Trump, J. Lloyd, and Hunt, Jane: Special report: student unrest in public schools. *School Management, 13*: No. 11, 50-92, 1968.

Walberg, Herbert J.: Professional role discontinuities in educational careers. *Review of Educational Research, 40*: No. 3, 1970, esp. pp. 414-415.

What's troubling high school students. *Today's Education, 59:* No. 6, 1970.

Willower, Donald J., and Jones, Ronald G.: When pupil control becomes an institutional theme. *In* Raths, James D., et al. (ed.): Studying Teaching. Englewood Cliffs, N.J., Prentice-Hall, 1967.

Willower, Donald J., et al.: The School and Pupil Control Ideology. University Park, Pa., Pennsylvania State University, 1967. See esp. pp. 47-48.

55 student freedom?

Joseph Rhodes, Jr.

but:
Got no culture
Got no schooling
I got life
I got freedom
I got good times
I got crazy ways

Hair

This is an essay about the importance of student involvement in decision making. Sometimes I wonder how we come up with topics to write about. In this case, I got a letter from an old schoolmate who asked me to write 3000 words about the importance of student involvement in decision making. I wonder how many students were part of the decision to send that letter to me. Probably not many; and it is completely possible that by writing this essay I have already violated the very tenet I hope to establish as vital. Staying alive in America of 1971 isn't easy, but it must be easier than being in Vietnam or Southeast Asia in 1971. And to think that we live in a society regulated more by the outcome of Sunday football games than the weekly death toll. Yet, has there ever been a society that could sustain a preoccupation with death without becoming kind of dead? If I run out before 3000 don't blame me; the Germans proved a long time ago that concentration even in camps is the best sociology. I wonder if to forgive is to forget.

Lost my soul in '68
Where were you?
There must be a reason why
I don't know
(screams)

A song on the radio

Walking along Massachusetts Avenue near Harvard Square you see the people Mr. Capp is so given to describing as "human debris," and you feel nothing. Our Leader decides to invade another country—in this case, Laos—and we do nothing. Visiting Ethiopia last summer I walked past hundreds of wretches huddled in doorways and sidewalks—the homeless—and I felt nothing. Mr. Rockefeller decides to cut down the Attica "jungle creatures," and we feel so very little. Your woman leaves you and you feel less. Is there such a thing as pity? And where does pity end and sympathy begin? If to be alive is to be at the very least unable to stomach outright brutality, how alive are we? Granted, in some ways the System stifles all credible action, so why just frustrate yourself, but then again, why not? Life may not be so smooth when Terrors swirl about, and to deny the Terrors may be only to deny your self. All I'm trying to get at is the question: Is living or surviving getting more or less difficult in these United States? If you walk along the streets and feel nothing are you any better than the cars that pass you?

Now, of course, we will encounter the obvious retort: things are not worse—*you* are worse. Or maybe you are not so much worse as older and more mature, which in this sense means you can stomach more, you dream less. Sometimes I think growing up means to stop dreaming, but certainly we cannot be down on the cynics in a time like this; there is so much to be cynical about. Joel prophesied that in the time of the outpouring of God's spirit the old men will dream dreams. Religion certainly has its place in times of despair. In our modern age personal religion seems strangely out of date, but religion over the centuries has never felt any restraints in assuming that its mission was to deal with the "person" and not just with society.

Educators have not yet made up their minds about this issue. Some imagine education to be merely an institutional process without individuals, and others fight for "individualization of instruction." Aside from static considerations, those who presume to educate must first deal with the issue of social versus personal being, and if America is getting to be a terrifying place to live then ignorance of this fact can only increase our quiet hysteria. If, on the other hand, *we* have only gotten worse, then we need help. But, as a matter of fact, we need help in both cases, so how can we write even thirty words about student freedom when *we* need help? Now, there are all kinds of ways to help people. Our national student strike of 1970 following the Nixon invasion of Cambodia did help the people of Cambodia. Or did it? A generation of Americans will have to grow up wondering or forgetting to wonder whether when their nation conspired to destroy a people, a little brown people, they gave them any help.

On one level it would appear that education began as a decision to help people. Some contemporary critics have made the point that, increasingly, what we regard as education shares the form and sometimes even the content of a ritual and has lost its purpose as an actual and pertinent revelation. People go through the motions of education; in some circles, to be considered educated means to posses an uncanny ability to reproduce those motions on demand. Education may have come to this for many, but it started as the expression of a real concern: a nonreader suffered a disadvantage and compulsory education might remove that disadvantage. Much of what passes for educational criticism these days can be reduced to a search for some device or reliable mechanism for deciding when or when not to intervene in another person's life. That this intervention takes place in the company of other people whom we call students who also suffer or enjoy the intervention does not alter the main point. To presume to educate someone implies that we want "to help them"; it doesn't matter that some of us add on the phrase "to help themselves." In fact, much of education attempts precisely to define what their "selves" really are. Finding yourself is not easy these days. The biggest decision you probably make is who you are.

> To me being free is being myself. I think this is what Sly and the Family Stone meant when they sing in their song: "Thank you for letting me be myself." I just heard this on the radio. This makes a lot of sense to me because if I can't be myself then actually I am not being free.
>
> From a paper by Shirley Moore for my seminar in public policy at Calstate College in California, Pa.

If there is any useful distinction between undergraduate and graduate education it must be that undergraduate education attempts to help the student discover who he is, while graduate education allows him to refine himself. Of course, in many cases students use their graduate educations to establish their identities, and in other cases under-graduates may concentrate on strictly professional preparation. The current popularity of law and medical schools is an example of the former case, and schools like Caltech are examples of the latter. By and large, however, the undergraduate tries to use his four years to select a career and his graduate years to pursue it. Already I have made the mistake of equating one's career with one's self. They are not the same, though we may seek to determine both of them at the same time. We too often lump the two processes together and give students the impression that if they work at finding a profession, somehow magically, they will find themselves at the same time. A particular tendency of our industrialized society is to define a person almost entirely in terms of his employ-ment. We speak of policemen and politicians as though by saying this we have sum-marized them; when you've said "pig," you've said it all. To call this a form of dehumanization probably affirms the obvious, but too often we forget how much this obvious tendency distorts our social relations and conceptualization of education. When a student comes to a counselor and says he doesn't know what he wants to be, the worst possible reply is to list the advantages and disadvantages of the various professions.

Why do we go to college in the first place? Only a few reasons come to mind; peer group pressure is one. Some people go because they think college will insure their financial future. A corollary reason is the desire to acquire a profession: college as preparation for employment. Still another reason might be that college seems a preferable environment, and we would rather spend time in a college than in a factory. In the recent past, and still to some extent, men go to college to avoid the draft.

When you think about it, however, all these reasons can be reduced to the notion of college as a general or specific aid. You go to college to deal with either a specific need such as the desire for professional employment, or for general reasons like finding yourself. Of course, a given individual may have both kinds of reasons; he may enter college to get himself together and to get a good job.

Most colleges have not resolved the issue of whether their students have come to them for a specific or general experience. In some instances a college has avoided this issue by diversifying and increasing the academic freedom of its students. The reasoning goes that if UCLA, for instance, has many options and its students have the freedom to choose, then they really don't have to consider whether they have benefitted from their four years. Of course, such a definition of benefit—the result of a series of individual decisions made in the context of a variety of choices—begs the question. The question of freedom may not be a question of access to decisions. The decisions made by a person which relate to his definition as a student may or may not have anything to do with his being free. Decision making can become so much busy work. We all have our individual histories, which on one level are a history of made decisions, but at the same time we share a social history which in many and devious ways determines the conditions of our freedom. Growing up in America, life sometimes appears as a decision between a racist and a racist being: you can be black or white. But it is very difficult to be human. Dubois' veil has become an Iron Curtain. We confuse employment with being because work is very important; we confuse freedom with loneliness because trust is the most precarious and difficult state of mind to attain.

> Having no obligations to anyone or anything other than yourself = Freedom.
>
> From a paper by Lee for the same seminar at Calstate

General reasons for going to college involve a peculiar paradox because of the nature of general reasons: they are general but are also the most personal. One could argue that going to college to avoid the draft is the most personal of reasons for getting an education. Yet, is it really so personal? The very point of the draft is to reduce a generation of young people to the most impersonal of human classifications: the soldier. If soldiers were people they would be very difficult to kill. Uniforms always remind me of targets pasted on men's backs for some reason (a specific reason). Uniforms are the most shared part of the game of war: both sides agree to wear them so the other side will know who to kill. We certainly find strange ways to communicate in the year of our Lord nineteen hundred and seventy one. We experience the draft and unemployment as a group and that is why so much of the drama associated with wars and work strives to individualize what can only be regarded as an impersonal experience. If you go to college because your father went there, you are instantly part of a definite class of people who made their college decision for that reason. Though individual fathers are unique, fathers are not, and what appears to be a personal decision becomes in fact an impersonal one. There is something inarticulately unique about personal reasons. That is why our attempts to describe them sound so general and universal; on that level of abstraction we can only manage a weak: "I went to college to get an education."

There is no more interesting feature of higher education than the fact that, unlike every other level of education in America, it is not compulsory. You are not required to go to college by law. On the surface this fact may seem extremely arbitrary, but the point of this essay is not to examine its arbitrary character so much as its social character.

It appears that, at the point of transition from high school to college, our society has decided that the system of incentives and subtle forms of persuasion either has reached a sufficiently powerful level or the objects of these measures of coercion (the 18 year old population) have reached a degree of maturity on which the social pressures can have an effect. It never ceases to amaze me how such a massive and diverse society as ours, with so many outward signs of decay and ineptitude, manages to instill in millions of young minds at precisely the same point in time the utter urgency of attending a college or university. The most interesting and therefore least popular proposition put forth by the Newman Committee was a proposal made by Professor Stanley Cavell of Harvard that the federal government simply give 18 year olds a lump sum of money which they could spend any way they wished. I suspect, social pressures being what they are, we would see only marginal changes in behavior if we implemented such a proposal, but the quality of the behavior might be greatly altered.

Last summer I attended a conference in South Africa and at the last meeting of the plenary session, I felt compelled to make the point that at the very least, organizing a society around race was a very crude form of social organization; in the twentieth century we have discovered more sophisticated ways to get people to move from one area to another than by passing Group Areas Acts. It does make a great deal of difference whether I brush my teeth because I want to or because someone holds a gun to my head and threatens to obliterate the area of my anatomy in question if I don't clean it up. Society exerts a great deal of pressure on young people to go to college. There are many conceivable explanations for this, but most of them would escape Society since they do not take note of the fact that society as an abstraction is unable to make conscious choices. The only thing that Society knows is whether it exists. And the only reason Society urges us to go to college is that putting the bulk of our young people through four years of college tends to increase the survival potential of our society. Which is to say that going to college is important in America. At the present time raising an army in America is not so important or a volunteer army would exist. We pay to go to college. If we needed an army as we did during the Revolution, we would have volunteers. It is, of course, true that maintaining an army is important to the government and that is why the government drafts people. But who in his right mind in 1971 would equate our government with our society? If democracy is an ideal we have a long way to go to realize it.

There are many societies in America and to postulate the existence of an American Society that urges us to go to college may seem to belie this obvious coexistence. But all these societies share the ethic of Going To College. Attendance at college remains a common feature of almost every American society. Religion itself does not command as much reverence as college. College attendance seems to be a genuine belief in America. We shouldn't push this point to the extreme of saying that college attendance is a great American myth, because that unfortunate word has almost been twisted out of the English language; but we might say that if Americans believe in anything they believe in college. Somewhere here there must be a connection between the belief in college and the peculiar political role colleges have played in the past decade. Seizing a college building has seemed at times to come close to desecrating a seventeenth century church. This aspect we shall arbitrarily leave undeveloped because our main objective in this essay is to say something about student decision making.

> This article was to adopt the viewpoint that student freedom is extremely important—an idea I've seen you develop well several times.
>
> From a letter received last summer soliciting this essay.

For the past three years I have tried to decide whether racial injustice was worse than injustice; is anything added to the notion of brutality by describing it as racial? When I took a course in English Composition from Professor Edwin Peterson at the University of Pittsburgh, he made a point which has stuck with me over the years—modifiers change the meaning of that which they modify; if you choose the right word in the first place you don't need to modify it. Is student freedom more important than freedom?

Freedom strikes me as inextricably bound up with the process of decision making. When you ask what we have freedom for, the answer that comes to mind is that we have freedom to make decisions. But do we? Or more to the point, do students?

On the surface, at a level of first approximation, students or potential students have three decisions to make: they can decide whether to go to college at all; they can decide what college to go to; and they can decide what to do while at college. Perhaps there is a fourth student decision: whether to remain a student or to leave school. Therefore, one can decide whether to become a student, what kind of student, and for how long.

We have already touched on the issue of whether a person really has any decision to make when it comes to attending college. All the social pressures aim at convincing the ordinary person that he has no real choice if he wants to get ahead—he must go to college or sink into those regions of society reserved for the drudges, those faceless shapes that plod along, racing the treadmill, never having anything approaching recognition except through their organizations. Fine choice we lay out: go to college or kill your self; matriculate or destroy forever a certain potential selfness that only the magic of college can reveal. The Bobby Fischers must give admissions committees the willies. We want our young to be good at some games but not just any game. We aspire to uniformity, but we are not a uniform society.

In any case, the decision to attend or not to attend college operates on the level of the total society. We can only alter the nature of this decision by altering the nature of our society, a proposition which humbles even the most arrogant. Nothing aggravated the Nixon-Agnew portion of the population more than the image of the uninitiated proclaiming their intention to revolutionize society before they had properly experienced it; that is, before they had failed, lost a California election, and learned to maintain the force of restraint. To the credit of this administration, few people in America of 1971 openly demand a revolution. Modern repression works in odd ways. Sometimes it manages only to convince the dissenters that the focus of their dissent does not exist; I wonder whether, if the census were taken in a spiritual dimension, it would indicate that in 1971 the population of the United States had dropped significantly. A nation of ghosts, one way or another, makes for pretty dull living, but if you scream and nobody hears, either you are a ghost or they are.

A man doesn't become a student in the same sense that he becomes a schizophrenic. People don't have schizophrenia; they are schizophrenics. Dr. Alexander Heard once said to the Scranton Commission in closed session that the most startling feature of the "student revolt" was that students were rapidly becoming a class. By this he meant that students increasingly were identifying themselves as students. At a party, when the blond comes up to you and asks what you do, you say, "I'm a student." Or in some circles you just say, "I'm at Calstate or Hampshire." When you've said that you've said it all. Being a student is not an occupation so much as a way of life.

Once you've been one abstraction for a while, like "a student," it is easier for you to become another, like "a teller" or "an engineer." One of the simple influences of a college experience is to convince you that living a slot is not such a bad thing after all. You do fit the slot, but after a while it becomes academic whether you fit it or it fits you. Please don't think this is a version of the great and terrible "They" theory. Society has no mind and that is 90 per cent of the problem. Society doesn't know you; it knows only if it survives. Of course, the other side of this is that the closest we have come to a society with Presence was the State which does know you, but the secret police variety of recognition was not exactly what I had in mind.

The transition from an "it," a student, into another "it," an engineer or accountant, takes place more and more within the confines of college matriculation and graduation. I went to a small college where the operant assumption was that the entire undergraduate student body had decided on their life goals and careers before their eighteenth birthdays. Alias Smith and Jones the other night made the point to a young evangelist that she ought to go back East and live a little. Living a little is about all the living our society can spare you, and if it keeps on demanding earlier and earlier professional choices it will just move the average age of cracking up further back until we become a society of profession-al infants caring for blasted-out 20 year olds. Those Marcus Welby and lawyer shows really give the straight dope. There must be some way to satisfy the decent urge of young people to be recognized other than offering them a scalpel or a code. A society has really sunk pretty far when its youth can tolerate decisions of life and death only when they involve a patient on an operating table. Modern societies kill people in so many subtle and clean ways. The first important and manageable issue related to student freedom is the nature of undergraduate education as it goes about the business of moving people into jobs. The high school counselor tells you that such-and-such a college is for you and the college course tells you that such-and-such a profession is right for you. Nobody stops to ask you who you are.

To the extent that the character of a college is determined by its decision-making process and to the extent that the character of a school determines what kind of student you can be, student involvement in decision making aims at the second "student" decision, the student garment you finally select. Except in the case of the teaching profession, the extent to which an academic program aims at preparing a student for a specific job seems to coincide inversely with the amount of student involvement in decision making. The professions illustrate this point. Medical students have very little to say about the form of their core curriculum; police trainees even less. But when a liberal arts program pretends that it aims only at the broad education of its students, attaining student participation in decision making is much easier, barring special personal or political problems. Many factors influence this condition but one of the most important is the assumed connection between what is taught in a program and its relevance (to use another anti-word) to an eventual occupation. The nature of this connection, as perceived by the faculty or whoever creates the academic program, represents a definite interpretation of some feature of society, that is, if we regard the professions and occupations as features of society.

Education as preparation for employment, then, implies some perception of society. What is true for this narrow view of education is even more true for the "general" view of education, which is an explicit process of formal preparation for a social existence. Any other definition of education would detach it from accessible reality. Education as ecstasy is a most unreal juxtaposition. The question keeps coming back: if we do exist in a social dimension and if some portion of our selves, perhaps the most vital portion, is a functioning internalization of Society, a society which is getting worse, we would then experience that negative process as the personal despair of feeling that it is getting more difficult to live in America, or more directly, America is getting to be a terrifying place in which to live. It is therefore personally destructive to divorce the decision-making process of the university from some understanding or interaction of understandings of the condition of society. The university appears as a haven from the world, but more than any other institution it must remain intimately aware of society; this does not mean that the university simply serves society but that its true service involves in the strictest sense a judgment of society.

The initial interest of students or student leaders in the decision-making process of the university sprang from their disagreement with the particular perception of society represented in the existent programs of the university. Students saw participation in the governing of the academy as a way to improve the quality of the decisions made within the university. The dissatisfaction with the process of decision making began as a negative reaction to the decisions themselves and not to the system of decision making. Few students initially argued for student participation in government on the basis of principle. At first, the basis for political change was a genuine search for truth; the decisions of the faculty and administration were the issue, not the faculty or the administration itself. Gradually this initial argument over objective truth shifted into a political issue: does the student deserve the right to participate in decision making by virtue of being a student? Citizens do not claim the right to vote because of a theoretical conviction that their participation in government will make for the best of all possible worlds. The key assumption of democracy is that the democratic world is the only possible world, a world made possible by virtue of the vote. For this reason, the emphasis on students' rights represents a deterioration, and the only valid principle for the university must remain its dedication to truth, no matter how corny that seems. The Academy is not a Republic. Its object is not the establishment of the only possible world but the contemplation of the virtues of the world as it is, a contemplation that often necessitates the promulgation of various and often contradictory worlds. Surely, if it engenders such judgment, the Academy's ability to denounce that which affronts humanity must motivate its determination to make alternative humanities real to its students. When we denounce inhumanity we assert an alternative, and this alternative, which we for the sake of parity will designate humanity, does not exist for those guilty of perpetrating the inhumanity. Every act of moral courage divides and unites men. Historians may someday describe the decade of the 1960's as the period in American history when the constitutional checks on executive power failed to restrain a President who felt compelled to wage war. Other historians may say that in the sixties the American people faced their most trying moral challenge since the Great War and failed themselves and mankind.

As a matter of fact, young people do not *become* students; their participation in the academic community is only a part of their lives, a part which is becoming increasingly smaller. To grant the right of participation in formal decision making on a campus may improve the quality of decision making but it will in no essential way make the student body more free. The great invention of the nineteenth century was institutional entrapment. To survive these days, you must resist the temptation to define yourself in purely institutional terms. To assert that student freedom is something we can take care of by placing a few students on governing boards includes two assumptions: the notion of the "student" classification as all-inclusive and a peculiar faith in the vicarious character of representative democracy. We don't trust each other very much in this country, and I suppose that is as good a reason as any for student participation in campus government, but this by no means concludes the discussion. We have lives beyond our status as students, professors, Democrats, whites, heads, and pigs. Making students more free in a structural or institutional sense deals with their duties in its narrowest meaning, but it does not deal with their responsibilities.

It never ceases to amaze me how certain officials on a campus make such fun of the rapidity with which students change their political fashions. One year they are tearing up the campus, demanding participation in decision making, and the next year you have to work pretty hard to keep up quorums. Snicker, snicker. And they said that they were responsible. In a floor speech given before six senators who were nodding out, Senator Usual says, "The Republican party ought to take pride in the way it has calmed the country down." I wonder if he means that the President pushes dope. Living in America in 1971 is no joke: some say it's tragic; I think it's pathetic.

> Students making decisions about education is like trying to solve the pollution problem by giving the people the decision to choose between buying a Cadillac or Chevy. Both contribute to the total problem. We would first of all have to find another means of transportation. Dig? We must find another way to spend our seconds, minutes, hours and days. If education is to really *mean* something—four years of something or more—then relate it to life. I mean like real life.
>
> From Lee's paper

Structure is much but it is not everything. Student freedom in the dimension of structure has developed at two levels: students have been placed on governing bodies, and they have sought or received more "freedom" of choice within their academic program. The first part of this essay has stumbled about the first level, and now we will tumble into the latter. There is something very truthful about gravity, but it has an apparent single-mindedness. Pinball machines fascinate me. Curricula sometimes strike me as so many pins which jostle you as you roll toward graduation. If you get enough points you get to replay the game in graduate school. Experience can be narrow or random. It takes so much effort to tilt the machine and so much more to level it, allowing the ball to move only by its spirit; that is to say, it does not move. If you wait for the spirit to move you, motion may become a part of nostalgia.

The St. Johns College approach has one redeeming merit—it unequivocally declares that some of the things written by man do matter. The scholars and teachers of this college clearly believe that the experience of what they collectively believe to be the most important writings of man, the Great Books, does help the student to survive. Without becoming too dualistic, we might say that on one level at least, perhaps what would be called the mortal level, very little has meaning except that which contributes in some way to the enterprise of living. Once the multitude has fallen at Verdun it is too late to talk about the meaning of war; death is not just an extension of life, and too many fall for those who stand to wile away their time. Maybe at the millenium man will enjoy the luxury of a freedom from guilt; living to keep living does seem like a drag, but the alternative (living without mortal purpose) fails to satisfy the prerequisites for Humanity. A line of thinking has it that to make explicit that which remains hidden out of a fear of reducing the most intimate of human secrets to cheap sentiments does have some merit; this society certainly seems to ravage genuine human sympathy. But the size of modern society has left us no choice. We can't afford any misunderstandings these days. Students? Teachers? Freedom? Responsibility?

I've got to get out of this place!
A song on the radio

What would happen if President Bok called the Harvard University community together and said: "This University shall dedicate itself to the improvement of life on this planet. This may sound very general, but if we work together through our various disciplines and professions with the central commitment of exhausting every bit of our energy in the struggle for freedom, justice, and decency in our world, we must rely on our genuine mutual trust. Harvard will leave its previous posture of neutrality. It is up to each member of the community to find the way that he can help move this university into a vital realization of this ideal. Our first job will be to attempt a comprehensive assessment of the current state of affairs. We must find ways to create actual forums in which the real issues of our time have the opportunity for expression." Now this might not change the actual courses, research programs, and departmental arrangements, but the quality of the school might change. The notion of the Revolution, like that of the Enlightenment and the Renaissance, has its physical manifestations, but its critical influence bears on the vision of man. Cynics may scoff and the charge of grandiosity may come down on you, but Elliot Richardson kept saying in Switzerland that "the most important feature of American higher education is its diversity." Structurally speaking, this may be so, but the quality of education doesn't vary that much. Although it seems like the inverse of the truth, the quality of an institution, a living embodiment of an opinion, is determined by what is made explicit or conscious by those who endeavor to achieve some approximation of their institutional ideal in a reality. And we can no longer afford to be unconsciously humane if we hope to free ourselves and to resist the allure of petty distraction. Sometimes it requires arrogance to make a point about the struggle for life; the Black Panthers have made this clear and by doing so have for all practical purposes doomed themselves.

Urgency clears the air, but it also encourages insensitivity. Maybe our society is doing the best it can, in which case urgency is a delusion. But, though the mass media can change its mind pretty fast, Society has no mind to change. A lady in Pittsburgh once asked me on a radio talk show why I was so critical about America and wasn't there anything that I liked about my country. I told her that I loved Pennsylvania, for instance, but if someone you love is trapped in a burning house, you don't shout to her through the flames that she has a great shape and a sympathetic disposition. If you love someone or something which is suffering, you try to do something about the suffering. Part of the storm of despair is an uncertainty over the actual condition of society. Those who live in white houses see one America and those who clean them see quite another. Mr. Nixon offers some solutions, but they all have the ring of deceptions masquerading as remedies. Overstatement only dulls the language, but it is not asking too much of the colleges and universities to try to determine how serious things are. There is no way to avoid personal tragedy in life except by chance, and unless we understand our social obligations and erect convincing devices for discharging those obligations, we will wile away our time within personal dilemmas.

Students cannot be free until man is free. Life sometimes slouches like an eternal laboring excited by a realization of a level of civilization almost impossible to imagine. The most pressing job of the university today is to make that vision a credible one.

As much as we would prefer it otherwise, the world is not a series of fragments but, on one level at least, it is simply what *is*. And what *is* does not exist as a set of mutually indifferent features or qualities. When we ask whether things are getting worse we have merely proposed a dynamic version of the question: what is? Most certainly, the range of apprehension administered within the academy limits the extent to which a college education can help a person know what is; the academy seems to emphasize one dimension of human understanding to the exclusion of others. Unfortunately, at a time when we need intellectual leadership within the university, the trend of recent events has elevated crisis-management ability to the top of the qualities sought in a President. Most likely, the apparent shift toward a service function for the university will occupy the energies of academic leaders for the next period. With so many people going to professional schools, the university might settle back into its old function of servicing society. The painful fact persists that until we have a picture or an understanding of how things are, it is extremely difficult to develop effective and intelligent strategies. There may not be sinister conspiracies, but there most certainly are serious strategies, and if you don't believe that, get in touch with Mr. Nixon's people.

The challenge now facing the university is to find a way to involve its community in a cooperative attempt to determine what is. It may be that much early social action had its motivation in curiosity, and there is nothing wrong with that; it is a natural human desire to want to know what is. One of the elements of the repression that has struck America is the dwindling curiosity of its people.

The trend over the past few decades has been an increasing fragmentation of knowledge within the university. Much of this has been explained as the result of the knowledge explosion; segmentation naturally follows from expansion. If the student's experience of the academy is to be a liberating process, then something must be done to resist this flow toward greater separation of our knowledge. It is not an easy thing to accomplish, this integration of knowledge, and many attempts at "interdisciplinary work" turn out to be disastrous wastes of time, but if a university can accomplish this community-wide, mutual endeavor it will greatly contribute to the accomplishment of its essential mission: the preparation of the citizenry for progressive social existence.

There are all kinds of devices that a university can employ to move in this direction. I have found student-directed research projects a particularly effective device, but there are many others. Whatever the process adopted, it must attempt to raise the difficult questions that so many of us find elusive and frightening. When a school decides to undertake such a process it should find ways to reduce the sharpness of the distinctions which separate its audience from others. Ads can be placed in the paper announcing its intent and inviting the community to participate. Some university people may discover that the realities of life have given certain questions an unreal quality. People who work hard all day may not want to consider what is, but I bet that we would be surprised. We have to start somewhere, again.

SCHOOL/SOCIETY

"We are pleased, Running Bear, that you will attend Harvard Business School. For over 2,600 moons, what our people needed most was a damned good real estate specialist."

Society created our schools. But, the cynics warn, it may not survive them. Ideally, the schools were established to bring opportunity to all. (To all upper middle-class white Anglo-Saxon Protestant males, the cynics mutter.) The public school, early advocates claimed, would eliminate every major social pathology. In the light of current events, that seems a bit of an exaggeration.

One of the original goals of public schools was acculturation —the assimilation of immigrants and other aliens into the mainstream of American life. For many of those who wanted to be assimilated, this was successful, but others saw it as attempted cultural genocide. Simple, gentle people, like the Amish and the American Indian, were dragged into the schoolroom, and told, directly or indirectly, that their way of life was wrong. Is it right or necessary to force "assimilation" on such people?

What of the poor and the racially oppressed? What are the schools' mistakes in trying to help them—or are they really trying? We have a history of racism and discrimination, and it is to some degree involved with the allocation of resources, the planning of programs, and the very educational process itself. Education has tried to cure deprivation with compensatory education, and disorder with "reform" schools. But the ailments persist.

Busing is another attempt to cure some of our social ailments —an attempt that has run into serious opposition. It is largely tied into the issue of discrimination, racial and economic, yet it reaches beyond these into a very difficult area—the control of education.

Who should control education? Although this is the last question to arise in this volume, it is probably the most important. For decisions depend on who decides them. Parents, educators, taxpayers, and students each have different ideas about how the schools should be operated. Each group feels that it has a right to at least a say in school decision making. In practice, however, the situation is usually less complex. Except in rare cases, where the bulk of the community is elderly or childless, parent and taxpayer interests are usually similar. Except to a limited degree at the high school level, students will have very little say in school affairs in the near future. The result is conflict: parents versus educators.

The very wording of the problem is ominous: parents versus educators. This is how it seems to a wide range of people, including such diverse voices as John Coyne, Jr., and Julius Hobson. Coyne feels that our schools are being used to indoctrinate children with values alien to those held by parents. Hobson sees educators as having a tendency to "talk fast, flip charts, and produce 300 page reports while the schools continue to deteriorate." Listen to David Wilson, an editorial writer for the Boston Globe, following a teacher strike in nearby Somerville:

> We are beginning to suspect that the schools are a unionized economic system, the "ed biz," which tends in many communities to support a spurious Civil Service intelligentsia, separated by income and life style from those engaged in humbler pursuits, a special caste of people secure in their jobs and pensions, exulting in their vacations and fringes and devouring tax money at an accelerating rate. . . .
> . . . The "ed biz" has a hammerlock on the taxpayers. It is called fiscal autonomy for school committees. It has this hold whether or not its services are effective, useful or desirable, and even, as in the case of Somerville, whether they are delivered at all. . . .
> What the Somerville strikers and their apologists do not seem to sense is the risk of losing what may be left of traditional respect for education and things of the intellect (Wilson, David: "The 'ed biz' is forfeiting respect," Boston Sunday Globe, September 24, 1972, p. 6-A).

This is probably the most critical problem educators must face. A balance must be struck between professional prerogatives and responsiveness to community concerns. Otherwise, all our efforts at building a system of learning for our young may go to waste.

56 the amish case: a struggle for control of values

William C. Lindholm

The intransigence of the Old Order Amish toward sending their children to high school or employing non-Amish teachers has repeatedly provoked more dramatic controversy than any other problem in educational enforcement in the last 25 years. However, the United States Supreme Court has hopefully settled the long-standing struggle with its May 15, 1972 ruling that states may not constitutionally force the Amish to send their children to high school.

The Amish victory was a significant one: it was the first successful challenge of compulsory education laws in U. S. history. In an opinion written by Chief Justice Warren E. Burger, the U. S. Supreme Court held that "states undoubtedly have the responsibility of improving the education of their citizens, but this interest must be measured against the legitimate claims of the free exercise of religion."

Even though the Amish have been given protection only because they were able to raise a constitutional claim on religious grounds, the decision restricting the threat of state-established values ought to make us sensitive to the needs of all minorities. Whatever else the decision means, it is a warning to state education officials that, just as parents cannot do anything they wish in raising children, now the states cannot do anything they choose in the name of educational standards.

The Amish resistance to mainstream education was simply an act of self-preservation, to avoid the devastating influence of the state's technology and secular values on their ethnic, religious, and social patterns. In short, the problem of Amish education is a clash between those who advocate the forced assimilation of minority cultures such as the Amish, and those who seek to maintain the identity and integrity of the cultural diversity in a pluralistic America; it is a clash between those who assert that the majority and the state bureaucracies should define approaches and values, and those who hold that progress and truth are best found when freedom and diversity prevail. Tied closely to this is the issue of the theoretical basis and the limits of a state's power to compel its citizens to get an education and conform to its values.

488

THE AMISH

In order to understand the problem, it is necessary to know the uniqueness of the culture involved. The Old Order Amish, named after their early leader, Jacob Amman, originated about 1525 in Switzerland as part of the Anabaptist wing of the Protestant Reformation. They sought not church reform like Martin Luther but to restore a lost and "primitive" Christianity. They wanted a simple faith and followed the literal teachings of the scripture: nonconformity to all things worldly and sinful, an austere life style, and a separated community of peaceableness and mutual aid.

The Bible says, "I will destroy the wisdom of the wise . . . has not God made foolishness the wisdom of this world?" (I Cor. 1:21). From this source comes the Amish rejection of speculative philosophy and sophisticated reasoning, as well as their rejection of technology. The violent persecution of the well-educated authorities, who drowned them in sacks and buried their women alive, confirmed their suspicions of worldly learning and made them more determined to stress strict moral principles. Today they shun modern conveniences such as electricity, television, automobiles, and government subsidies and instead drive horses and buggies and wear plain clothing—ankle-length dresses, bonnets, and broad-brimmed hats. They believe in small, close-knit communities and consider farm-related living a religious command for life.

For at least a hundred years, the Amish remained in the public schools. They finally withdrew, not because they wanted religious instruction but because of rigid educational policies advancing a changing culture that was posing a threat to Amish identity and values.

The Amish have a strong desire for education in the basic skills. Often they can tolerate the elementary schools, but they uniformly shun high schools because of the heavy emphasis on socialization into the dominant culture. The materialistic, competitive, highly technological teenage culture of fast cars, rock music, College Boards, miniskirts, and hot pants violates their moral sense. For the Amish are taught slowness of pace, peace, love of hard work, democratic cooperation, and shunning of competition and aggressiveness. Their socialization produces a different personality type—a quiet-mannered, introverted, friendly, feeling individual.

Not only does a regular high school teach things that are irrelevant and antagonistic to their needs, but during the critical adolescent period of religious development it takes them away from the instruction in their own communities that they need to live the Amish life and prepare for their baptism as adults.

In their own schools, the Amish teach their own way of life. This is the mission of their schools; to them it is the only proper mission of schooling. It is something that only they, with their eighth grade educations, can teach. An atheist can teach math, a Ph.D. can teach anthropology, but only an Amishman can teach how to be and live the Amish way.

The goals of Amish schools are to produce Christians who will be "useful, God-fearing, and law-abiding citizens." Thus they are more concerned with teaching character than facts or critical thinking. They stress "believing" revealed truth rather than "questioning." Amish believe that talent is God-given—therefore no slow learner is condemned and no fast achiever is praised. There is no frantic hand waving in response to teacher questions. Every child is called upon and given a chance to answer. They are taught that school is work that must be done whether one likes it or not, and that they should not compete but work so that the whole group will perform well.

Even intellectual training conflicts with the Amish way of life, for you can't learn the love of hard work sitting at a desk, nor can you learn to plow a furrow straight or know the timing of nature by facing forward in a room. Vocational training, whether farming or medicine, is best taught by "doing" in the shops and farms and kitchens. At an early age, Amish youngsters are quite competent in farm and homemaking skills. They can speak three languages—high German, Pennsylvania Dutch, and English—all of which are taught in the home and community. Their society is a school.

The Amish concentrate on the "oral tradition," which includes memorizing and experiencing the example of a humble life. The non-Amish teacher has not undergone this essential training and thus cannot deliver the genuine "education" and the feeling of the good man heaven-bound, accepting the life of hard work on the farm. These Amish teachers are "called" and are not protected by contracts or tenure, nor are they motivated by monetary concerns.

How effective are Amish schools? They are successful when judged by standardized tests or goal attainment, or by the feelings of Amish parents. The tragedy is that some educators have failed to see this. John A. Hostetler, in a three year study under a U. S. Office of Education contract, found that Amish IQ's are normal and, compared to regular rural public school pupils, they perform above the norm on tests of basic skills. In fact, the Amish did better than non-Amish on spelling, word usage, and arithmetic problems (Hostetler, 1969). Significantly, he found that Amish pupils in Amish schools generally outperformed Amish pupils who attended public schools, indicating that the somewhat uncomfortable learning atmosphere may interfere with the learning process. In a mixed public school, the Amish did better than blacks but not as well as whites. The Amish schools are more effective than government schools on Indian reservations, probably more successful than many ghetto schools, and more successful than public schools with Amish pupils—yet the Amish schools have been outlawed in a dozen states.

The Amish belong to a tradition that established schools 250 years before governments became interested in educating their citizens, and they continue to make a profound contribution to education. They emphasize what has become characterized as the *wisdom* dimension, as contrasted with the *technos*. Wisdom is devoted to character, honesty, humility, and long suffering. They have no interest in landing men on the moon—they seek only to produce good men.

Is there some correlation between this approach and their social conditions? The Amish have not recorded a felony since they came to America, nor have any of them been on welfare, while the highly educated mainstream society suffers from drug addiction, crime, and family problems. Are the Amish far out? Perhaps, but buggies and bonnets are less harmful than the tools we have given the "technically competent barbarian" who is raping the land and could very easily blow up the world.

The issue here is a clash between state notions of child rearing and Amish ones, which educate for persistence rather than change, moral values rather than technical competence, and vocational training by involvement with the community's experts rather than confinement to learning within four walls. One thing is quite clear—no power on earth has been able to make the Amish do what their religion forbids, and they are absolutely determined to raise their children to thrive on cooperation and humility rather than competition and pride of achievement.

BACKGROUND OF THE CASE

In the fall of 1968, three Old Order Amish fathers—Jonas Yoder, Wallace Miller, and Adin Yutzy, of rural New Glarus, Wisconsin—were arrested upon the complaint of the school administrator for failure to enroll their three children, Frieda Yoder and Barbara Miller, both 15 years old, and Vernon Yutzy, aged 14, in high school after they had completed the eighth grade in the public schools. Wisconsin law required attendance until the child's sixteenth birthday.

Since the Amish will not defend themselves in courts of law—"turn the other cheek," says the Bible—the National Committee for Amish Religious Freedom, having been organized a year earlier at the University of Chicago by a group of educators, clergymen, and attorneys, decided to defend them. The defense was based on the Constitutional guarantees of freedom of religion. Considerable evidence was introduced in their behalf.

Dr. John A. Hostetler, an anthropologist from Temple University, testified that forcing the Amish to partake of the values in a modern public high school would have the effect of destroying their faith, community, and religious culture. He also introduced a study, made under contract with the U. S. Office of Education, which concluded that Amish youth performed slightly above the norm of regular rural public school pupils on tests of basic skills.

Dr. Donald A. Erickson, professor of education at the University of Chicago, said the Amish received in their own communities what could definitely be called "an education." "The Amish training is the best kind," he said, "they learn by doing, and I would be inclined to say they do a better job than most of us, judging by the fact that they have little unemployment, delinquency or divorce."

A law officer testified that although the Amish do not go to high school the tax structure is not threatened because they have never been on welfare or public assistance.

Frieda Yoder, a 15 year old Amish girl whose attendance was in question (and who was old enough to marry in Wisconsin), testified that it was against her beliefs to attend high school and that she wanted to live the way of her people.

It was also brought out at the trial that the arrests of the Amish were the direct result of the loss of $17,000 in state aid incurred by the local school district when the Amish withdrew to open a private elementary school.

The State of Wisconsin produced no testimony beyond showing that the Amish were not attending a recognized public or parochial school in the area.

On the above evidence, the state was upheld in the county and the circuit courts. The Wisconsin Supreme Court, however, ruled that the state had failed its proofs, stating, "There is not such a compelling state interest in two years high school compulsory education as will justify the burden it places upon appellants' free exercise of their religion."

Wisconsin then was granted a review before the United States Supreme Court. Arguments advanced by the State against the Amish were: (1) Compulsory education laws are necessary for the "very existence" of the political system and have been in practice since colonial days, the first such law being passed in Massachusetts in 1852. Further, "all historical and legal precedent" acknowledges the right of the state to compel school attendance. (2) The state also has a right to insulate a child from the disease of ignorance for his economic survival. (3) The child has a right to know. (This apparently means that he should be socialized into mainstream values.) (4) We must place the same values on our "system of education that we place on military conscription of our youth." (5) Governmental control of education is firmly established and the legislature alone controls educational policy. Privileges, not rights, are granted to private educational agencies, and the Wisconsin Legislature has rejected an exemption for the Amish (Brief of the Petitioner, *Wisconsin v. Yoder*).

William B. Ball, defense attorney for the Amish, argued that the state is "insisting that there cannot be different kinds of education . . . all education must be dictated by the state with values derived from technology or related to consumption and competition and must be imposed upon every child." He asserted that "the state wants to enter the minds of the Amish young people, expose them to worldly education, fill up their minds with state-packaged learning, alien to the Amish way, threatening the privacy of their psyche, and causing a painful personality restructuring by placing them in a high school which places the stress upon competition, ambition, consumerism and speed."

He further argued that if the state was not restrained from its actions, which would prevent Amish youth from following their chosen faith and farm vocation, violate their right of communal association, and interfere with the parental right of nurturing their children, "it would sound the death knell for an old, distinctive and innocent culture."

The ultimate issue was whether our constitutional government could use its secondary school requirements to destroy a church and force people to perform actions which they think will send them to hell.

Since education and religion, or shall we say, education and values are more closely related than people usually realize, a number of religious groups filed friend of the court briefs in behalf of the Amish.

The National Council of Churches of Christ observed that "responsible religious groups have the right in this country to undertake, not just an imitation of conventional education, but a fundamentally different *type* of education from that generally prevailing in a given state . . . if necessary to embody and inculcate their understanding of what the divine Will requires" (*Amicus Curiae* Brief, pp. 2-3). Interestingly, the Council of Churches argued that the state should not tolerate any mode of education which produced criminals or those who would become dependent upon society. It held, however, that competition for jobs in a technologically advanced society "has virtually eliminated the need for compulsory education laws" that largely originated from humanitarian concern over child labor abuses and union desire to keep young people off the labor market

The National Jewish Commission on Law and Public Affairs called the case a "disturbing illustration of an attempt by State authorities to compel nonconformists . . . to adhere to norms which may be entirely sound and desirable for most inhabitants of this country but which are offensive and harmful to the affected religious minority . . . . The Constitution and traditions of this country do not permit this kind of coercion, which endangers all religions and ethnic minorities" (*Amicus Curiae* Brief, p. 15).

The Synagogue Council of America asserted that "eight years of schooling is adequate to assure the informed citizenry upon which democracy depends" (*Amicus Curiae* Brief, p. 13). It noted that in the Civil Rights Act of 1964 Congress decreed that completion of six years of education should be deemed satisfactory for literacy requirements for voting, and that the Voting Rights Act of 1970 abolished all such literacy requirements.

The Mennonite Central Committee also felt that education given to the Amish adequately prepared them for their future and that when the "rudiments of education have been achieved" the state's educational interest has been satisfied.

U. S. SUPREME COURT DECISION

Chief Justice Warren E. Burger delivered the opinion in the Amish case, *Wisconsin v. Yoder,* stating that "the First and Fourteenth Amendments prevent the State from compelling the respondents [the Amish] to cause their children to attend formal high school to age 16."

He wrote the opinion with great care, pointing out that the decision was based on the claim of religious belief—not philosophical, personal, secular, or cultural values—for if the Amish had asserted claims on their "subjective evaluation . . . of the contemporary secular values" they would not have prevailed. The Court kept the decision narrow, apparently fearing the consequences of some extreme group threatening the peace of society, although this narrowness also restricts those who simply want to experiment with a different process of child rearing.

The Court accepted the presently held assumptions that education is necessary to produce self-reliant citizens for the political system and that the state has "a high responsibility for the education of citizens," the right "to impose reasonable regulations for the control and duration of basic education," and the duty to provide public schools. But the high court rejected the notion that the Amish are ignorant or unfit citizens: "Whatever their idiosyncrasies as seen by the majority, this record strongly shows that the Amish community has been a highly successful social unit within our society." The Court also agreed with the expert educational witnesses that the Amish vocational system is an "ideal system." They rejected the argument that the Amish children were being deprived, and that if they left the Amish community they would become burdens on society. Not so, said the Court, because of "their practical agricultural training and habits of industry and self reliance." The Court concluded that there "is strong evidence that the Amish are capable of fulfilling" their responsibility of citizenship without further state-prescribed education.

The Court noted that educational requirements for attendance beyond the eighth grade are recent developments. "When Thomas Jefferson emphasized the need for education as a bulwark of a free people against tyranny, there is nothing to indicate that he had in mind compulsory education to any fixed age beyond basic education."

The Court stated again that it is "now established beyond debate" that parents have the right to nurture and bring up their children, and the duty to prepare them for "additional obligations," meaning moral standards, religious beliefs, and elements of good citizenship. If only a general interest of the parents is involved, it is "beyond dispute that the state acts 'reasonably' in requiring education to age 16 in some private or public school meeting the standards prescribed by the State." This is not so, however, in a case such as that of the Amish, in which the state's requirements are in direct conflict with fundamental religious teachings. The Court concluded: "We accept it as settled, therefore, that however strong the State's interest in universal compulsory education, it is by no means absolute to the exclusion or subordination of all other interests."

The opinion of the Court was unanimous except that Justice William O. Douglas dissented in part, arguing that a child who expresses a desire to attend high school in conflict with his parents' wishes should not be prevented from attending. Since the parents were the only ones being fined in the Amish case, and the children were in agreement with parental desires, the majority of the Court explicitly noted that they were not deciding this point.

The opinion is clearly a strong affirmation of parental rights and religious freedoms when no social, health, or safety hazards are in evidence. It is a significant decision for religious freedom and will undoubtedly aid a number of religious minorities to sustain their religious and cultural integrity. As Justice Douglas pointed out, "What we do here today . . . opens the way to give organized religion a broader base than it has ever enjoyed."

The decision was a narrow one and does not give the Illiches and Goodmans much hope that compulsory attendance laws will soon come tumbling down, but it is a recognition of the rights of one minority and a clear statement that compulsory education is by "no means absolute to the . . . subordination of all other interests." Perhaps it will lead the way to voluntary decisions that will aid other minority peoples.

IMPLICATIONS

The problem of educational policy toward minorities has significant dimensions for everyone. The Supreme Court has ordered that religious dissenters cannot now be assimilated against their will, but what about other minority groups? What about blacks, Chicanos, American Indians and Chinese-Americans? It is obvious that if educational theories with as little scientific basis as patent medicines are enacted into rigid laws, educational experimentation and cultural diversity are stifled.

The Amish case indicates that public schools would be more effective if they respected the identities of minority students. For if the school demands the rejection of one's parents and their values, or if it implies that a student's language, dress, and skin color are somehow wrong, anxiety has been produced and personalities have been crippled. And this cultural violence has existed too long in this country. "Black is beautiful," and the Amish people are a joy to behold. They are different, but we need the richness of diversity.

Even a casual examination reveals that we are not in agreement on educational standards. There is a surprising lack of uniformity in state regulations. For example, only 6 states require nonpublic schools to have certified teachers, 31 states regulate course requirements, and some states have stringent requirements for such things as visual aids, electrical lighting, and indoor plumbing, all of which the Amish religion forbids. Some states require Amish schools to be "equivalent" to public schools. Whoever judges the equivalency always makes sure the Amish schools are not approved. How can vocational agricultural schools be equivalent to college prep schools? Are the requirements for equivalency so rigid as to deny religious liberty? Do we leave all of these decisions in the hands of monolithic government bureaucracies? Can't state administrators look at the goals of various schools and judge their *outcomes* rather than the means of production? As Justice Burger underscored in his Amish opinion, "the value of all education must be assessed in terms of its capacity to prepare a child for life."

The Amish controversy shows that the present pattern of socialization through equivalency requirements really permits very little diversity. Those who can afford to support an almost identical educational program can have a parochial school. Yet Wisconsin would make no accommodation to the important differences in Amish schools that originate from religious reasons and denied approval for the same programs which are approved in Pennsylvania and Indiana. Amish were left with the choice of accepting criminal penalties or casting their children in the mold of somebody else's values and views of child rearing.

The prosecuting attorney wanted to choose the values for the Amish: as he told the U. S. Supreme Court, "What is needed is . . . more pride in intellect, not less." The Wisconsin Supreme Court had clearly seen the issue: "Secondary schools not only teach an unacceptable value system, but they seek to integrate ethnic groups into a homogenized society."

This writer has seen the tears of suffering in the eyes of these "plain people" and has been appalled at case after case of losing farms and suffering heavy fines, jailings, and the threatened loss of children, as well as at the unbelievable lack of understanding by good men—when their only crime was trying to raise their children by peaceful values that they have loved and revered.

We would like to think that our society has moved beyond systematic religious persecution. But we have not—we have only changed its form. Instead of assaulting Amishmen physically, we assault their souls. It is more sophisticated, somehow cleaner, than drowning them or burying them alive, but it is persecution nonetheless.

If the state can choose and mold values, where is the basis of freedom? If the state can regulate requirements for personality formation, awesome consequences appear. And if a state can compel attendance at school beyond the learning of basic skills for citizenship, why not at any age for life engineering?

Whatever else the Amish controversy does, it should cause us to re-examine the reasons for state compulsory education laws, hopefully to draw the line for state regulation nearer specific abuses to children and society, and to make possible various approaches to education rather than permitting the state to be the supreme parent with power to socialize and decide the values for all.

REFERENCES

Hostetler, John A.: Educational Achievements and Life Styles in a Traditional Society: The Old Order Amish. U. S. Office of Education, Washington, D. C., 1969.
Wisconsin v. Yoder, 406 U.S. 205 (1972).

57 the life and education of the american indian*

G. Louis Heath

The American Indian, inspired by the hard-won successes of the black civil rights movement, has recently developed sufficient political consciousness to emulate that great movement. He wants to remove the mask of "Uncle Tomahawk," the facade of the self-effacing and obsequious redskin, much as the black has refused the role of the pliable "Uncle Tom." Although far removed from the militancy and solidarity of the "Black Power" movement, the "Red Power" movement is pulling together the strands of tribal dissent and resistance so that the Indian might compel an amelioration of his condition.

The situation of the Indian is, of course, beyond the thrust for self-determination, quite different from the black's. The Indians number only 600,000 and are scattered over twenty-eight states,[1] thereby drastically diluting their political impact. They would constitute a major political force only if they were all located in one of the most sparsely populated states, like New Mexico or Nevada. Two-thirds of the Indians reside on reservations where the Bureau of Indian Affairs administers educational and welfare services to them in fulfillment of treaty obligations.[2] The Bureau binds its charges into a web of paternalism and discrimination. Most of the other Indians are integrated into the economic underworld of the cities, where they stoically endure privation and cultural shock far from the reservations. The urban Indian experiences the abuse that is doubly the lot of the poor and non-white. But deplorable conditions, both on and off the reservation, have not completely prevented the Indian from challenging the myth of "Uncle Tomahawk."

I visited fourteen reservations and one settlement in the Southwest, Midwest, West, and Pacific Northwest during the summer of 1970, interviewing 147 Indians and other persons somehow knowledgeable or prejudiced in the matter of Indian affairs. My field research provides the substance for this paper's observations.

THE CONFLICT OF CULTURES

Although most Indians do not yet feel competent enough to govern themselves, a good number of young Indian leaders have become militants in the pursuit of Red Power.

*From *Illinois Quarterly*, *33*, No. 3, 1971.

What Stan Steiner calls the "new Indians"[3] have emerged in such diverse and distant places as Rough Rock, Arizona, Tama, Iowa, and Nisqually, Washington. The new Indians aspire for community control of their schools and political self-determination. They demand that their primary identity be Indian; they experience an intense revulsion to the idea of becoming second-class whites, forcibly fashioned by the Bureau of Indian Affairs' xenophobic assimilation. ("The only good Indian culture is a dead Indian culture," according to a distressingly frank teacher on the Northern Cheyenne Reservation in Montana.[4]) They wish to learn the technical skills to participate occupationally in the mainstream society, but they are convinced they need not sacrifice their inner and tribal lives to do so. They insist that being Indian is mutually exclusive with participating in aggressive competition or rampant self-interest, the psychic dynamos of the mainstream. The Indians (save the "Tomahawks") value total human relationships set in a close-knit community. This value orientation aggravates the Bureau of Indian Affairs (BIA) bureaucrats who cannot fathom why the ignorant savages will not exert themselves in an effort to outdo one another.[5] They are about as tolerant of Indian culture as the average American is of the Hippie counter-culture, which, incidentally, accords extraordinary respect to the Indian, particularly for his ecologically sound involvement in nature.

The Indian pupil's communal identity clashes with the school's emphasis on competition and individual rewards. The Indian becomes deeply abashed when he excels. He deliberately fails rather than embarrass his classmates. When a teacher endeavors to goad an Indian student into rivalry, he suddenly becomes "shy and stupid." The school, representing the mainstream values, seeks to assimilate the Indian pupil rather than respect his identity and accommodate him in the curriculum. It rhetorically expounds the vaunted pluralism of America, but refuses to practice it in the classroom. Culturally myopic teacher behavior produces a strongly denigratory impact upon the Indian child. The experience of the Mesquakie children is particularly revealing in this regard. In Iowa's South Tama County District where a few Mesquakie children attend classes, a teacher raised the issue of taxes in a class that included four Mesquakie students. One of the Mesquakies contributed to the ensuing discussion and the teacher responded by berating him: "You Indians don't pay taxes. You're so lazy you have to live off the government." In another instance, a teacher informed the Mesquakie children that they would not be allowed to produce any Indian art in school. The tribal leaders had no alternative (excluding cultural suicide) but to rent a deserted farmhouse so their children could paint and draw in the Mesquakie tradition.[6]

The standard, mediocre teacher in the BIA schools is particularly adept at impugning the cultural integrity of Indian students.[7] Classes often begin with the Lord's Prayer. Some teachers, notably on the Navajo Reservation and at the St. Mary's School for Indian Girls in Springfield, South Dakota, even advocate the free labor of Indian girls in their homes (scrubbing floors, doing laundry, and the like) for the instructional purpose of "teaching the American way of housekeeping." They individualize instruction with such courses as "Laundry" and "Cleaning."[8] This sort of fundamental violation of human rights is especially grievous when one considers that Indians exercise no voice in educational decisions. They elect no school board members in either the public school districts or the BIA school jurisdictions. (There are three noteworthy exceptions which will be discussed later in this article.) The public schools even receive Johnson-O'Malley Act money for their Indian pupils,[9] but they do not expend the federal money to satisfy their Indian charges' distinctive educational needs. The funds accrue insufferable interest as coercive assimilation capital.

The BIA schools function more like child labor and detention camps than educational institutions. The Bureau spends $1,500 on each of the 35,000 Indian pupils housed in the boarding schools.[10] The per capita expenditure must cover a child's entire living and educational expenses for ten months. Such funding affords only elementary institutional care. The available education is simply vocational training that is a by-product of BIA *in loco parentis:* the officials require able students to perform maintenance and repair work on buildings and equipment, particularly carpentry and painting, to help defray operating expenses. Cursory, non-instructional supervision of Indian child labor is intended to legitimize the deception as genuine vocational training. The subterfuge is preposterous: 10,000 Indians annually receive training that has no market value while there are only seven doctors, four lawyers, and two engineers who are Indians in the entire United States.[11] The inference that BIA education does not prepare Indian students to improve the Indian community is empirically valid.

When additional money becomes available for Indian education, it is often spent foolishly. For example, the government paid Westinghouse Electric $2 million to provide experimental computer-aided instruction for fifteen Menominee children in Wisconsin. Although the funds were adequate to supply conventional quality education to every Menominee child, the 900 other Menominee pupils remained trapped in a condition of enforced educational austerity while the government subsidized Westinghouse Electric's research into a potentially lucrative market.[12]

The BIA's pursuit of assimilation is basically a rationalization of the exploitation, decimation, and attempted genocide the white man has organized against the Indian. The historic assumption is that the redskin's culture and character are too defective for him to independently succeed. The schools, the national instruments of acculturation, must integrate the Indian into white culture so he can transcend his innate (whether by culture or by genes) inferiority. This is the racist myth of "compensatory education." It includes a panoply of pseudo-scientific terms like the "culturally deprived" and, more recently, the "socially disadvantaged." Beyond the abstruse verbiage and cultural blind spots, one can detect a sophisticated white racism: Indians must be enriched with the elixir of life, the cure-all of the downtrodden (to paraphrase the frontier mountebank's spiel), and the happy tonic is white folkways and education.

ASSIMILATION AS WHITE SUPREMACY

It is not at all obscure that undergirding the superstructure of assimilation is the doctrine of white supremacy. Thus, in a recent history of the Cherokees, an Oklahoma author writes of the "full-bloods," the genetically pure Indians: "They supplement their small income from farms and subsidies from the government with wage work or seasonal jobs in nearby towns or on farms belonging to white men . . . . Paid fair wages, this type of worker usually spends his money as quickly as he makes it on whiskey, and on cars, washing machines, and other items that, uncared for, soon fall into necessitous disuse."[13] Contrary to that assertion, the Indians are not "paid fair wages." It is my observation that white employers often pay Indians extremely low wages and aver that they are, in fact, performing a millenial missionary work. They claim they provide employment and guidance for an infantile people, too ingenuous to manage for themselves. The BIA employs the same ethic in cunningly commandeering the vestiges of tribal government, including the disbursement of the Indian's own funds to the Indians. For example, the Papagos of Southern Arizona applied for some of their money when a heavy snowfall threatened their livestock. By the time the request had worked its way through bureaucratic channels, 2,000 head of cattle had starved to death.[14] White supremacy and bureaucratic inertia have, *in tandem,* inflicted relentless hardship on the Indian. Cherokee anthropologist Robert Thomas concludes that the BIA is "the most complete colonial system in the world."[15]

White exploitative paternalism has produced the intensely negative self-concept the Indian suffers. The Coleman Report disclosed that American Indians experience more stigma and self-hatred than any other ethnic group.[16] The very process of growing up is absurd for the Indian because it is anti-Indian. The Indians attach little value to themselves, a response inculcated by a school system that infects the children with a virulent form of white racism. The Indian's excessive school dropout rate, his depressing suicide statistics (the teenage rate is over ten times the national average),[17] and his extravagant alcoholism are shameful indicators of the defamatory influences impinging on him. Until recently, no remedy has been in the offing. But the Indian's new antidote for white oppression and the resultant feelings of powerlessness and self-hatred is political organization. He has begun to seriously countervail white discrimination through the National Congress of American Indians, founded in 1944, and regional and local groups. The insidious bite of paternalism has become accordingly less toxic.

Contemporary Indian education is neither Indian nor education. Indian pupil achievement and dropout rates reflect the utter meaninglessness and irrelevance of what passes for education in the BIA schools and the public schools to which many Indians have been transferred. A quarter of the teachers who instruct Indian children admit they would rather teach someone else.[18] Even the job descriptions of the federal boarding schools betray their real purpose: "attendant," "matron," and "guard" are occupational categories for penal and mental institutions—not schools. Bureaucratic absurdities subject Indian pupils to unnecessary misery and anguish. Two hundred and sixty-seven Alaskan Eskimos, who speak no Midwestern Indian language or passable words of English, have been transferred 5,000 miles to Chilocco boarding school in Oklahoma.[19] It is disturbingly apparent that Chilocco will not meet their learning needs. The Indian pupils at Chilocco who can understand English are perhaps even more unfortunate for they can ingest the emetic pabulum that is provided. For example, I saw a cavalry-and-Indian film being shown in one of the Chilocco dormitories. According to the usual format, the Army was heavily outnumbered and held a militarily untenable position. The Indians, assaulting the position, were being killed, one every shot. As they were on the verge of overwhelming the Army troops, a bugle sounded and the cavalry charged to the rescue from behind a hill. The Indian pupils cheered the climax, inadvertently divulging the utter alienation of their education.

The insipid paternalism that induces Indian alienation is evident in the BIA's pamphlet, "Curriculum Needs of Navajo Pupils." From it we learn that the Navajo child "needs to begin to develop knowledge of how the dominant culture is pluralistic and how many people worked to become the culture which is the American mainstream of life . . ."; "needs to understand that every man is free to rise as high as he is able and willing . . ."; "needs assistance with accepting either the role of leader or follower . . ."; "needs to understand that a mastery of the English language is imperative to compete in the world today . . ."; and "needs to understand that work is necessary to exist and succeed. . . ." This manifesto of the American way of life, albeit commendable as a doctrine, completely ignores the fact that there is also an American Indian way of life, as sacred and viable as the mainstream cultural tradition. This cultural insensitivity is exceedingly debilitating to Indian youngsters. Many learn virtually nothing from the white teacher who clings to the antiquated teaching methods and ideas of nineteenth century Middle America. For example, I learned through interviews that at Point Arena, California, white children and the Kashaya Pomo children from the depressed Stewart's Point Reservation attend school together in a climate of intense enmity. The white children habitually challenge Kashaya Pomo children to fights and taunt them mercilessly. The teachers cannot comprehend why the Indians will not behave and toil assiduously on their lessons. They do not realize that few Kashaya youngsters command a working knowledge of English, that the only cues the Kashaya pupils can effectively read are nonverbal, and that quite often those cues happen to be physical insults. The eventual result is that the Kashaya pupils drop out. The "push out" process has been so thorough that no Kashaya child has completed high school in the past five years, I was told.

The Indian child, initially quick-learning, well-adjusted, and eager, does well the first few years of school, achieving commeasurably with white children. But the "crossover phenomenon" soon sets in. The Indian pupil begins to regress rapidly between the fifth and seventh grades. For example, a study of the Stewart Institute in Carson City, Nevada, shows that Indian sixth graders score 5.2 on the California Achievement Test, but score only 8.4 six years later at graduation. The national achievement test average for Indian high school graduates is only the 9.5 grade level.[20] This figure is all the more disconcerting when one considers that sixty per cent of all Indian students do not graduate, but drop out somewhere along the lockstep hierarchy. The typical Indian completes about five years of schooling. The implicit policy is to pass students on until they either graduate or drop out. The ineluctable inference is that the schools actually impair the Indians whom they purport to educate, inflicting severe psychic damage. Educators persist in forcing a square peg into a round hole, despite all the lamentable signs that compulsory assimilation is more alienation than education.

BOARDING SCHOOL LIFE

The non-academic aspects of the federal boarding schools offer no improvement upon the dismal classroom situation. The student's life is regimented by a near-military discipline. In fact, the schools resemble military installations: each is a complex of deteriorating, one-color buildings, the shabby sentinels of the minds and spirits of America's Indian children. A number of condemned buildings are in use, notably at Chilocco, Oklahoma, Tuba City, Arizona, and Fort Wingate, New Mexico. The Brookings Institution's 1928 Meriam Report pointed specifically to the preposterousness of operating Fort Wingate as an elementary boarding school. But forty-two years later, the practice continues.[21]

The impersonal, indecorous and bleak living conditions of the BIA schools in no way replicate a healthy home environment. The dormitories, with their long rows of double-decked iron beds, are strikingly similar to military barracks. I saw iron bars enclosing dormitory windows in several schools, exposing, it seems to me, administrators' distrust of the students and one of the institution's real functions. Most significantly, the school treats everyone identically: each child is repressed into a stultifying conformity. The monolithic process dehumanizes, acting upon each child as if he were an inanimate object. The school programs each hour of the pupil's day into an invariable routine of classes, study halls, meals, chores, and recreation. Rule violators receive demerits that can be expunged by doing extra work or sacrificing privileges. Students at some schools may even be severely beaten or handcuffed for extended periods of time.[22] Punishments often become very physical at Fort Wingate, Tuba City, Northern Cheyenne, and the Inter-mountain Indian School in Utah. For example, Intermountain matrons duck the heads of Indian children suspected of drinking into unclean toilets.[23] The confidential statements of two teachers and three attendants at these four schools, in addition to the undisguised reality of seven children walking about with arms in slings, suggests that much more "discipline" may be operative than cursory investigation can ascertain.

Boys and girls endure a strict segregation in the boarding schools. They deeply resent the isolation and retaliate by making clandestine social contacts that often lead precipitously to premature sexual relations. School officials severely discipline students who defy the sexual repression policy. They seem to believe that sexuality among Indians is a sin. The superintendent at Chilocco even wants to construct a jail and employ additional guards to handle the transgressors of the sexual separatist code.[24]

The boarding schools discourage visits. If a visitor does appear he is dissuaded from talking to the children. The school officials claim visits and conversation render the children hyperactive, particularly if a visitor happens to be a parent. Runaways always seem to increase after visits. Stirred from sensory deprivation, the Indian child seeks out further attention. Since he cannot secure it in the dormitories where one matron attends 100 or more children, he flees his desperate condition. To obviate the upheaval that contact with the outside world engenders, the policy of discouraging visits has become so entrenched at the Fort Wingate school that a sign over a dormitory entrance officially deprecates parental visits. If this deterrent does not work, the often impracticable, always obstructive road to Wingate provides a second line of defense. Wingate is exemplary. I am forced to the conclusion that the objective of the entire boarding school system is to narcotize and arrest the young Indian's developing mind and emotions so that he will not become a trouble-maker.

The boarding schools deny the cultural identity of the Indian. School employees exercise great care to address the Indian children only in English. They scathingly censure the speaking of native languages in both the classrooms and dormitories. This cultural bleaching has been insensately effective. For example, the Indian dormitory attendant scrupulously avoids demonstrating any knowledge of his tribal language. He is religiously convinced that knowing it is shameful, that it is an incubus of inferiority. He represents perhaps the most consummate example of how white-manipulated education defiles the Indian. He is the quintessence of the BIA's "assimilated Indian." Many run away or commit suicide in desperate efforts to assert their dignity, but the attendant has overcome all the degrading obstacles, repressing any tormenting uncertainty he may have about the purpose of his education. He eventually embraces the education the "Great White Father" has provided and assumes the ambivalent status of an "Uncle Tomahawk." He is the inimitable product of the boarding school system.

The young, idealistic teachers, including a sizeable contingent of VISTA volunteers, who gravitate to the BIA schools, become rapidly disenchanted. Their commitment to effective change threatens bureaucratic equilibrium. Once identified as potential disrupters of the status quo, the BIA officials paternalize them much as they do the Indians: they implement a panoply of stinging stratagems to extinguish creative and enthusiastic involvement in the educational process. For example, one Navajo Reservation teacher, a former Peace Corps volunteer, told the Senate Subcommittee on Indian Education that her principal frequently discredited the Indian students in the presence of teachers with statements such as "All Navajos are brain-damaged," and "Navajo culture belongs in a museum."[25] Those who do not leave, disgusted with the cultural assassina-tion and impertinent desecration of teacher professionalism, survive by defecting to the role of eight-to-five bureaucrats and somehow becoming inured to their students' crying needs. The statistical consequence of this negative selectivity is that the turnover rate among BIA teachers is double the national average.[26] To the Indian pupils, the teacher is a stranger passing through. He is a stranger not simply because his sojourn is short-lived, but also for the reason that he is very seldom Indian. Only sixteen per cent of the Bureau's teachers are Indian.[27] The white teachers, even if they are genuinely concerned about the welfare of their students, seldom command sufficient tribal knowledge and ethnic empathy to seriously relate classroom activities to Indian life and culture. An Interior Department report systematically documented this failure in Alaska, finding that "education which gives the Indian, Eskimo and Aleut knowledge of—and therefore pride in—their historic and cultural heritage is almost nonexistent . . . . In the very few places where such an attempt is made, it is poorly conceived and inadequate."[28] The cultural deficiency of the curriculum might be remedied if more Indians taught, but this is an unlikely development since very few Indians graduate from college. Perhaps more para-professions could play a decisive role.

Indian students often react to their dehumanizing living conditions and schooling by committing suicide. For example, twelve of 240 students in the Northern Cheyenne Reservation's Busby School attempted suicides in a recent eighteen-month period.[29] A sixteen-year-old boy, charged with drinking in school, committed suicide in jail at Fort Hall, Idaho.[30] A Crow boy apparently drank himself to death at Chilocco boarding school.[31] A Sioux boy hung himself in the Wilkin County jail at Breckenridge, Minnesota, in December, 1968. He had been held "in virtual isolation," according to a newspaper report, for seven weeks. Only thirteen, he had been accused of complicity in a car theft. No court hearing had been granted during his incarceration.[32] Dr. Daniel O'Connell testified before the Senate Subcommittee on Indian Education that "the situation as far as suicide is concerned is especially acute among the boarding school children, particularly in high school."[33] Unfortunately, the self-immolations do not represent isolated incidents, but fit into a comprehensive pattern of hopelessness and self-estrangement.

Running away, psycho-analytically quite difficult to distinguish from suicide, is another of the Indian student's historic responses to the schools. In 1891, three Kiowa schoolboys froze to death trying to reach home in a blizzard.[34] Indian students still perish in institutional escapes. For example, two Navajo boys recently froze to death attempting to reach their parents fifty miles away and a young, very drunk runaway froze to death at the Albuquerque Boarding School.[35] The impulse to flee is intense among students detained in the boarding schools. The absurdity of their predicament intrudes into consciousness in more aware moments. The agonizing self-admission of living an alien life impels them to abscond, departing the educational limbo that confines them.

TERMINATION AND THE 'MELTING POT'

"Termination," the phasing out of the reservations and the liquidation of the Indian land base, would irreparably shatter Indian communities. American whites exist as atoms in the maws of urban behemoths called megalopolises. They take umbrage at any community, whether Amish, Orthodox Jewish, or Indian, that seeks to hang on to a strand of common humanity among men. Everyone should be an "individual;" so, terminate the reservations. The unhospitalized paranoia over community has incited the destruction or drastic erosion of virtually every ethnic enclave. (A few colorful trappings displayed on the old country's national holidays and infrequent, halting words of Polish or whatever do not constitute tenacious ethnicity.) The Indians seem unwilling to heed the cues as to where rewards reside and how punishments are meted out. They persist in their Indianism.

The present wholesale transfer of Indian students into the public schools. begun in 1965, signifies a powerful impetus toward termination and detribalization.[36] Two-thirds of all Indian students on the reservations have already been transferred to schools that have no idea how to educate them.[37] Very few tribes are sufficiently powerful and political to contest independently the indiscriminate one-way bussing. (One group of Navajos claims "The buses are kidnaping our children.") The Mesquakie Tribe has perhaps most effectually challenged the federal bureaucracy's unilateral actions. They initiated legal procedures to enjoin the BIA from closing their settlement school[38] and transferring all their children to public schools. The regional BIA officials in Minneapolis had become so accustomed to Indian compliance that, when the Mesquakies reacted, they spent several confused days determining a revised policy. Don Wanatee, secretary of the Mesquakie Tribal Council, flatly asserts, "We want the Mesquakie people to operate the school the way they see it." Most threatened tribes have been unable to translate this spirit of participation into purposeful action.

Termination would be tantamount to the abrogation of the government's Indian treaty obligations. It would supply the final solution to the Indian problem. When the Indians relinquished their lands, the federal government signed treaties promising to protect their rights and provide essential services, such as schools and hospitals. These pacts precluded the populist fundamentalists in state and local jurisdictions from inflicting their prejudices upon the "naked savages." The anti-Indian crusaders have been obliged to direct their fervid antagonism through the BIA, which all too often has not altogether fulfilled its guardianship role, but has undoubtedly functioned historically as a significant buffer against avaricious and opportunistic predators. Without the BIA, the reservations long ago would have passed into private ownership and unscrupulous entrepreneurs would have defrauded the Indians of all their alienable properties. Yet today, the BIA's termination policy promises the ultimate depredation that the special interests have been craving for decades.

A majority of white Americans look askance at the Indian. The Indian stress on cooperation and community over competition and possessiveness seems singularly un-American. A white man in Ponca City, Oklahoma, who dresses as an Indian to entertain tourists, shared his expertise: "All they do is sit out there on the reservations waiting to be fed." The charlatan's attitude, especially in view of his unique, seasonal occupation, caricatures white prejudice: exploit the Indian but deny him dignity since he is not really an American. He lives for the community while we, "the Americans" (the supreme ethnocentric arrogation), live for ourselves. Termination of the reservations would force the Indian into the self-interested mainstream and fulfill the "melting pot" prophecy, but it would kill the Indian forever.

Anti-Indian prejudice intensifies as one approaches an Indian reservation. On the Northern Cheyenne Reservation in Montana, a truck driver confided to me, "This state would be a helluva lot better off if we didn't have to take care of so many damned lazy Indians." In Toppenish, Washington, a storekeeper noted that "The Indians waste a lot of our good land just sitting around." In Ponca City, Oklahoma, a realtor opined that "The Indians ought to stop drinking, get off their duffs, and do some work."[39] A shameless sign in front of a general store and gasoline station near the Pine Ridge Reservation in South Dakota restricts its clientele, advising "No Dogs or Indians Allowed." These attitudes are not isolated from local public policy, especially law enforcement. The arrest rate for Indians in towns near reservations is thirty times the rate for whites and six times the rate for blacks.[40] It is little wonder that the Indian has begun to experience an unsettling paranoia. Every force seems to work against his cultural survival. He has witnessed the tragic termination of the Menominee and Klamath Reservations. His most apprehensive and pessimistic inferences do not lack substance.

The plight of the 11,000 Oglala Sioux at Pine Ridge Reservation is typical of the permanent depression that afflicts Indians. About half the families live in small huts covered with boards, sod, or rusted sheet metal. Floors are of tamped earth. A good 90 per cent of the huts have no plumbing or electricity. A few families live in abandoned auto bodies and chicken coops. Most Oglala Sioux must somehow haul water—as much as twelve miles, depending upon their location on the reservation. No bank, hotel, drugstore, or theatre—none of the appurtenances of twentieth century life—embellish the reservation. The unemployment rate among the Oglala varies, but averges about 75 per cent, hitting a peak of 95 per cent in winter.[41] One of the grim anomalies of the Oglala is that sixty-four research projects in progress command an aggregate funding sufficient to solve many of the reservation's problems.[42]

The situation at Pine Ridge is not at all unrepresentative of other reservations. The appalling poverty of the peoples of Asia and Africa is the norm. Over 75 per cent of the housing on the reservations is substandard, with 50 per cent beyond repair.[43] A recent survey on twenty-two reservations showed that the water was 80 to 100 per cent contaminated and more than 70 per cent of the water had to be carried a mile or more.[44] Owing to such primitive living conditions, the reservation Indian is eight times as likely to be infected with hepatitis, seven times as likely to contract tuberculosis, and three times as likely to die of pneumonia and influenza as the non-Indian.[45] In fact, one of every five Indian deaths is attributable to preventable diseases that afflict the reservations on an epidemic scale.[46] The cumulative, toxic effects of misery, want, and high morbidity cut the Indian's life span short by one-third of the white's. The Indian lives a harsh, primitive forty-four years in a pre-industrial subculture; the white, reaping the harvest of the scientific and cybernetic revolutions, is privileged to a comfortable sixty-seven years.[47] Callous WASP values have produced the cruel discrepancy.

RED POWER AT ROUGH ROCK

The Navajos operate their own educational system at Chinle, Arizona. The seven school board members are all Navajos—some with very little formal education. But they govern a successful school, relevant to the Navajo's spiritual and occupational needs, that has attracted international attention and over 12,000 visitors annually. They call their school dine bi'olta,' "the Navajos' school." For Anglos who cannot comprehend Navajo, the school is simply the Rough Rock Demonstration School.

Rough Rock is by every indicator a thoroughly Navajo school. Navajo culture, history, and language contribute the major components to the core curriculum. Sixty-two of eighty-two full-time employees are Navajo. The school's Cultural Identification Center provides facilities for Navajo artists and writers. Recordings of Navajo music and rituals are played regularly in the dormitories. Teachers encourage the children to express themselves aesthetically and culturally as Navajos. They periodically visit pupils' homes to counsel with parents concerning their children. Parents even live in the dormitories for eight-week periods, serving as paid dormitory aides. They comfort children tormented by nightmares and tell others bedtime Navajo folk stories. The children can travel home on weekends. If necessary, the school provides transportation. The Rough Rock experiment substantiates that the involvement of the Indian community, the resurrection of tribalism, is requisite to a truly Indian educational experience.[48]

Rough Rock has not been the only notable success in Indian education. The Pima and Mesquakie Indians similarly have taken control of their schools. An all-Indian school board governs a former BIA school on the Gila River Pima Indian Reservation in Arizona and the Mesquakie Tribal Council now operates the Tama Community School near Tama, Iowa. At the Lukachukai Boarding School, Navajo parents and students have been successful in playing a major role in curriculum development and school governance. Historically, the Choctaw Republic administered its own schools in Oklahoma and Mississippi until the 1890's. It operated 200 schools and academies and sent many graduates to eastern colleges. The Choctaw Nation was much more literate in English than the surrounding white communities in Texas and Arkansas. But Oklahoma politicians, responding to public prejudice, confiscated the Choctaw school in 1907. The Choctaw's educational attainments were rapidly eroded in white schools they regarded as alien and ingermane.[49] The common experience of the Navajo, Pima, Mesquakie, and Choctaw has been that white power trammels educational achievement, but community control of schools generates educational excellence.

CONCLUSION

The Indian student represents the supreme challenge to American education. The black student wants into the mainstream, with but only a little recent backlash, born more out of frustration from not getting in than not wanting in. His culture does not constitute an inversion of the prevailing social values. His challenge is not one of the conflict of cultures but a demand for social justice and equality. But the Indian, unbusinesslike and intent upon interpersonal harmony, has never wanted in; in fact, his values contradict the work ethic of collecting material wealth as a measure of success. A Paiute Indian told me: "I think not only for me, but for all Indians, the basic values are different. The Indian values the forest, the streams, and the animals. But as far as I'm concerned, the only thing the white man can see is a dollar sign." The Indian is not a status-seeker or entrepreneur. This is why he fares so badly in the schools. Only the shaker and maker can satisfy the meritocratic criteria of the contemporary school. The Indian is a failure in the Anglo-controlled schools by virtue of the very fact he was born an Indian. To transform the school into an instrument of equal opportunity for the tiny and weak Indian minority that dissents from our values is the supreme challenge to our schools and culture.[50]

The Rough Rock experiment most clearly demonstrates that the challenge is not unreasonable. In fact, Indian communities can meet it themselves by administering their own educational systems. The white majority need only suspend its bigoted pre-judgments. The actualization of Red Power throughout the nation can extend greatly the brief list of three Indian-controlled schools (Rough Rock, Tama, Gila River Pima). Everything we know about motivation and achievement indicates that Indian involvement in decision-making would produce quality American Indian education within the larger framework of American public education.

The Indian's only tool for building educational excellence is self-reliance. Only by directing his own educational future can he surmount the supercilious, Indian fighter mentality and the devastating psychological impact of conquest. Once he seizes control of his life, he will convert the fifty million-acre ghetto, the reservation system, into a decent place to live and learn. The antidote to the government's emasculating and oppressive paternalism is self-determination. Only Red Power, fiercely unrelenting and intelligently applied, can compel a relevant Indian education.

The BIA should no longer discharge the federal responsibility for Indian education. A new federal commission, composed of nationally recognized Indian authorities and Indian leaders, should administer the reservation schools until they can be completely entrusted to the Indian peoples. The withdrawal should be accomplished within five years. [51] However, the government must continue to fulfill its treaty obligations to guarantee Indian rights and provide essential services. The appropriate federal departments, such as HEW, Interior, and Justice, can execute the commitments, but they will only act at the behest of the tribal councils. Thus, each tribe will enjoy sufficient financial resources and legal safeguards to govern its own educational affairs and sustain its communal life. The hope is that the Indian can eventually develop enough political and economic power so that he need not depend primarily on enlightened policy.

The Report of the National Advisory Commission on Civil Disorders evinced profound insight in its analysis of white supremacy. "What white Americans have never fully understood—but what the Negro can never forget—is that white society is deeply implicated in the ghetto. White institutions created it, white institutions maintain it, and white society condones it." [52] The observation is no less valid for the reservations. White racism, masquerading as assimilation, has isolated the Red Man geographically and defiled him culturally. The Indian has been mythologically portrayed as listless and indolent. A famous anthropologist has even contributed to the basic cultural fable, theorizing that the depressed condition of the Oglala Sioux owes to the fact that they are "warriors without weapons." [53] He says nothing about white supremacist control of Oglala lives. Such myth-making is intended to generate the rationalizations for subordinating the redskin. But, as the National Advisory Commission Report recognized, the recent rebelliousness signifies that the old myths are wearing thin. The WASP no longer wields invincible hegemony. [54] On this incipient pluralism rides the Indian's hope for quality education and life.

NOTES

[1] Lehman Brightman, "Red Power," *The Black Politician,* I, 2 (October 1969), p. 37. *The Black Politician* is a new journal published by the Center on Urban and Minority Affairs, 955 South Western Ave., Los Angeles, California 90006.

[2] Information provided in a letter from the Bureau of Indian Affairs, National Headquarters, Washington, D.C., June 4, 1970.

[3] Stan Steiner, *The New Indians* (New York: Harper and Row, 1968). Some of the more prominent new Indians are: Lehman Brightman, the militant Sioux who presides over the United Native Americans; Sid Mills, the Yakima who demanded a discharge from the Army so that he could fight against the state of Washington's usurpation of Indian fishing rights; Wallace "Mad Bear" Anderson, the Iroquois who appealed to the United Nations to prevent the U.S. Army Corps of Engineers from flooding valuable Seneca Indian lands; and Al Bridges, an organizer of the 1964 Washington fish-in, presently under indictment for defying the State Fish and Game Commission.

[4] Statement to the author.

[5] This assertion is generally my inference, but an interview with Dr. Murray Wax, Indian expert, University of Kansas, served to clarify my summer's research in terms of a dichotomy of competitive and communal cultures. See also Wax *et al.,* "Formal Education in an American Indian Community," *Social Problems,* II, 4 (Spring, 1964), reprinted in Indian Education Subcommittee Hearings, 90 Cong., 1 and 2 Sess., Part IV, pp. 1391, 1403, April 16, 1968.

[6] These incidents were reported to the author in personal interviews with Indians in the community.

[7] See the whole of the following: Stan Steiner, *The New Indians;* Edgar S. Cahn, editor, *Our Brother's Keeper: The Indian in White America* (New York: The World Publishing Company, 1969); and Vine

Deloria, Jr., *Custer Died for Your Sins: An Indian Manifesto* (New York, The Macmillan Company, 1969). There are a number of examples of culturally-callous teacher behavior in these volumes.

[8] Peter Collier, "The Red Man's Burden," *Ramparts,* VIII, 8 (February, 1970). p. 28.

[9] The Johnson-O'Malley Act is intended to provide money specifically for satisfying the distinctive educational needs of Indian pupils.

[10] Dr. Carl Marburger, commissioner of education for the State of New Jersey, former assistant commissioner for the Bureau of Indian Affairs, data furnished at the hearings before the Subcommittee on Indian Education of the Committee on Labor and Public Welfare, United States Senate, Ninety-First Congress, First Session on Policy, Organization, Administration, and New Legislation Concerning the American Indian, Part 1, February 18, 19, 24, and March 27, 1969; April 11, 1969, Fairbanks, Alaska (Washington, D.C.: U.S. Government Printing Office, 1969), p. 315. The 2,371 pages of testimony transcribed in 1969 before the Subcommittee on Indian Education, the "Kennedy Committee," support the allegation that the education provided the Indian is extremely corrosive. The subcommittee's final report, published in November, 1969, offers sixty recommendations for "culturally sensitive" and bilingual programs and Indian participation in educational decision-making to neutralize the contemporary caustic curriculum.

[11] Lehman Brightman, president, United Native Americans, San Francisco, data presented at the hearings before the Subcommittee on Indian Education, *Ibid.,* p. 33.

[12] "Fifteen Little Indians: Westinghouse Computer Project On Menominee Reservation," *New Republic,* June 17, 1967, p. 6.

[13] Quoted in Albert L. Wahraftig and Robert K. Thomas, "Renaissance and Repression: The Oklahoma Cherokee," *Trans-Action,* VI (February, 1969), pp. 45-46.

[14] "Deadly Windfall: Navajo Tribe Suffers From Snowfall," *Time,* Jan. 5, 1968, p. 23.

[15] Collier, p. 31.

[16] James S. Coleman *et al., Equality of Educational Opportunity* (Washington: U.S. Government Printing Office, 1966), pp. 288, 322, and 324.

[17] Brightman, p. 38.

[18] Coleman, pp. 317-319.

[19] Daniel Henninger and Nancy Esposito, "Regimented Non-Education: Indian Schools," *The New Republic,* March, 1968, p. 18.

[20] Collier, p. 31.

[21] Henninger and Esposito, p. 20.

[22] "Official Horror Story of Federally-Run Chilocco Indian School," *Integrated Education,* VII, 4 (July-August, 1969), pp. 48-51. The report concludes that "there is evidence of criminal malpractice, not to mention physical and mental perversion, by certain staff members." It notes that "youngsters reported they were handcuffed for as long as 18 hours in the dormitory . . . or chained to a basement pillar or from a suspended pipe. One team member . . . verified a youngster's hurt arms, the deformed hands of another boy, and an obviously broken rib of another . . ."

[23] Letter from Intermountain School employee to the Citizens Advocate Center, Washington, D.C., March 2, 1969. The letter writer reports that one employee "dunks the students' heads into a toilet bowl which is unfit for even a hand."

[24] Interview with a confidentially-disgusted teacher at the Chilocco Indian School.

[25] Collier, p. 31.

[26] Dr. Alan Sorkin, economist in residence, Brookings Institution, Washington, D.C., data presented at the hearings before the Subcommittee on Indian Education, *op. cit.,* p. 330.

[27] Henninger and Esposito, p. 19.

[28] *Ibid.*

[29] *Ibid.,* p. 21.

[30] William Brandon, "The American Indians: The Un-Americans," *The Progressive,* XXXIV, 1 (January, 1970), p. 37. Mr. Brandon is the author of *The American Heritage Book of Indians.*

[31] Henninger and Esposito, p. 21.

[32] Brandon, p. 38.

[33] Henninger and Esposito, p. 21.

[34] Brandon, p. 36.

[35] *Ibid.*

[36] *Ibid.*

[37] *Ibid.*

[38] The Mesquakie, also known as the Fox, purchased their own land in 1854. Hence, they live on a "settlement" rather than a "reservation."

[39] Statements to the author.

[40] Brandon, p. 37.

[41] Robert G. Sherrill, "Red Man's Heritage: The Lagoon of Excrement," *The Nation,* (Nov. 10, 1969), p. 501.

[42] Brandon, p. 35.

[43] Dr. Alan Sorkin, economist in residence, Brookings Institution, Washington, D.C., data presented at the hearings before the Subcommittee on Indian Education, *op. cit.,* p. 330.

[44]Brightman, "Red Power," *The Black Politician,* I, 2 (October, 1969), p. 37.

[45]*Ibid.*

[46]*Ibid.*

[47]Ralph Nader, "Lo, The Poor Indian," *The New Republic,* March 30, 1968, p. 12. For a detailed analysis of the white colonialism inflicted on the American Indian, see Nader's "American Indians: People Without a Future," *Harvard Law Record,* May 10, 1956, pp. 1-4.

[48]Dr. Robert A. Roessel, Jr., founder of the Rough Rock school, has published the *Handbook for Indian Education* (Los Angeles: Amerindian Publishing Co., 1962), an excellent source book for developing a more practicable, less biased Indian educational program.

[49]White intolerance also collapsed the outstanding educational systems of the four other Civilized Tribes of Oklahoma. The Cherokees, for example, attained 90 per cent literacy in their native language in the 1830's. The Western Cherokee even had a higher literacy rate than the region's white population. The superior quality of the Cherokee Republic schools irritated the white supremacists. They eventually found the embarrassing contrast unbearable and successfully lobbied the Federal government to terminate the Cherokee system in 1898. Angie Debo describes in *And Still the Waters Run* (Princeton University Press, 1940) how the white population closed the Five Civilized Tribes' schools and defrauded them of their resources. Debo's *The Rise and Fall of the Choctaw Republic,* published in 1934, documents in detail the exploitation of the Choctaw Tribe.

[50]Estelle Fuchs, associate professor of education at Hunter College, the City University of New York, has some interesting insights into Indian education. Her article, "American Indian Education: Time to Redeem an Old Promise," *Saturday Review,* Jan. 24, 1970, pp. 54-57 and 74-75, presents an excellent history and analysis of Indian schools.

[51]This proposal is substantially the recommendation of the Carnegie Report on Indian Education.

[52]National Advisory Commission on Civil Disorders, *Report of the National Advisory Commission on Civil Disorders* (New York: Bantam Books, 1968), vii.

[53]Vine Deloria, Jr., former executive director of the National Congress of American Indians, has expressed deep contempt for the anthropologists and ethnologists who practice academic colonialism on Indians. Mr. Deloria is thoroughly a Red Muslim in his *Custer Died for Your Sins: An Indian Manifesto.*

[54]Any WASP or non–WASP who wishes to support the tribal Americans can write letters to his Congressman opposing the federal termination policy. For information about any current, socially-compelling issue, write the National Congress of American Indians (1346 Connecticut Avenue N.W., Washington, D.C. 20036) or the Association on American Indian Affairs (475 Riverside Drive, New York, N.Y. 10027). Both of these organizations are financially malnourished. Contributions are welcome. Your supportive letters on crucial issues contribute to the genuine pluralism the tiny Red minority is vociferantly seeking to mobilize. Those wishing to support the demand of the Indians occupying Alcatraz Island for a culturally-expressive Indian educational complex may send checks payable to "Alcatraz Relief Fund," 3189 16th Street, San Francisco, Calif. 94110. Those who wish to directly financially assist an Indian child, write Futures for Children, 5612 Parkston Road, Washington, D.C. 20016. The commitment is $15 monthly, $45 quarterly, $90 semi-annually, or $180 annually. I am supporting a twelve-year-old Shoshone-Bannock boy and find that the Futures for Children program is very effective. Contributions are U.S. income tax deductible.

compensatory 58 education and powerlessness

Doxey A. Wilkerson

Current discussions of compensatory education tend to focus on two interrelated groups of issues. One includes such narrowly "professional" questions as educational goals, curriculum development, home-school relations, teacher education, and evaluation. The other, professional in a broader sense but also "political," includes such questions as racial and social-class influences in the educational process, school segregation, school-community relations, and the opportunity structure of the society.

The concern here is mainly with issues in this latter political-professional realm. I am increasingly of the opinion that critical problems in the education of disadvantaged children, including gross professional nonfeasance, stem fundamentally from the relationship of the school to the distribution of power in the society it serves. As Bruner noted recently, education "is a deeply political issue . . . ." (Bruner, 1971, p. 29).

The compensatory education movement emerged during the early 'sixties for the avowed purpose of narrowing the gap between the academic performance of middle-class children and children of the poor. It burgeoned with Federal support during the last half of the decade and now includes a vast, widespread, and varied array of special compensatory programs extending from preschool to college. Just what "compensatory education" is, operationally, depends on who does the defining; the term covers an extremely diverse assortment of educational theories and practices.

The main population served by compensatory education, both initially and today, consists of black youngsters attending segregated schools. Large numbers of Puerto Rican and Chicano youth are also served by these special programs, as are some American Indians and substantial numbers of poor whites.

In the course of its controversial development, compensatory education has been characterized as the road to equality of opportunity for children of the minority-group poor, a ruse to circumvent or delay school integration, a catalyst for improving education in general and teacher education especially, a fraudulent waste of money and energy, a notable educational achievement, a massive failure, and much more! In varying degrees, all of these characterizations are apt.

It seems clear that some progressive trends have, indeed, been set in motion or strengthened by developments in and around compensatory education. I would include among them growing public awareness and concern over the crippling of masses of young people by prevailing school practices, new and promising approaches to teacher education, redirection of curriculum-development emphases from the elitist thrust following Sputnik toward pressing problems of education in the ghetto, liberalized college admissions policies favoring disadvantaged high school graduates, and, perhaps, the United States Office of Education's new priority of broadly-based "career" education.

On the other hand, it is quite clear that the specific promise of compensatory education—to enhance substantially the educational development of impoverished children—has not been realized. Dramatic but largely ephemeral gains have been achieved on the preschool level, and outstanding improvements on other levels have been noted in a number of small-scale projects here and there. However, the most common finding of careful and systematic evaluations of compensatory education, especially comprehensive programs in big-city school systems, is that they made "no significant difference." In its efforts to improve the academic achievement of disadvantaged children, the mountainous compensatory education enterprise labored for a decade and brought forth a mouse.

Why compensatory education has failed thus far to change significantly the prevailing pattern of academic retardation among children of the poor is the subject of considerable speculation and debate. Some observers find it inexplicable. The United States Commissioner of Education, for example, is moved to call upon the profession to "solve the mystery of how to bring effective learning to the poor" (Maeroff, 1971, pp. 1, 52). Others seek explanations in the discredited hypothesis of hereditary racial differences in ability to learn. Garret and Shuey, long-time proponents of this idea, are now joined by Jensen in contending that Negro children and others of "inferior stock" do not learn effectively in school because they are poorly endowed by nature (Shuey, 1966; Jensen, 1969). Most professional educators tend to eschew genetic explanations but arrive at much the same operative principle through the sociological doctrine of "cultural deprivation." Positing serious learning deficits induced in disadvantaged youngsters through primary socialization under conditions of poverty and discrimination, they infer—in full accord with the biological determinists—that "these children," almost if not quite irreversibly scarred by their preschool experiences, simply cannot learn effectively (see Frost and Hawkes, 1966; Hellmuth, 1967; and scores of similar publications).

Common to all these points of view is the assumption that persistent academic retardation among children of the poor, including those in programs of compensatory education, is a function of limitations internal to the children involved; they carry within themselves the cause of their own failure. Convincing refutations of this etiological assumption, on both theoretical and empirical grounds, appear increasingly in the literature, and the temptation to review them here must be resisted (see Bodmer and Cavalli-Sforza, 1970 and 1969; Schwebel, 1968; Ryan, 1971; Leacock, 1969; Rist, 1970; Rosenthal and Jacobson, 1968).

In contrast to these "blame the victim" approaches is the view of a growing number of observers that the school itself is the main cause of widespread academic failure among disadvantaged children, and that compensatory education programs tend to share the defeatist theories and practices that make most schools almost, if not quite, counterproductive for poverty populations. Such observers point to negative expectations and low performance standards that prevail in ghetto schools, curricular materials and experiences designed for middle-class white children but largely irrelevant and often offensive to minority-group children and the poor, the predominance of custodial over instructional emphases in classroom practice, the neglect of the elemental health and nutritional needs of impoverished learners, the severe alienation of the school from the lower-class community it serves, and with it all the notorious resistance of the educational bureaucracy to meaningful change (Clark, 1965; Stein, 1971; Silberman, 1970; Ryan, 1971).

This view holds that most special compensatory programs, preoccupied with overcoming presumed defects within disadvantaged children, involve no substantial break with the pattern of noneducation that has long prevailed in poverty-area schools; whereas truly compensatory intervention would have to be directed mainly toward correcting the grossly dysfunctional characteristics of the school as an institution. Thus, as Birch and Gussow put it, "Compensatory education has not really failed; it has just not often been adequately tried" (Birch and Gussow, 1970, p. 272).

I embrace this latter position, but I find little theoretical comfort in doing so, for it opens up an even larger question. If all that has gone into the compensatory education movement—hundreds of books, innumerable journal articles and professional conferences, great numbers of special teacher-education programs and institutes, myriad school-based projects developed mostly by staffs that wanted to succeed, new outpourings of special instructional materials for inner-city schools, billions of dollars from private and public sources, and mostly believable proclamations of serious intent from all levels of the educational hierarchy—if all this has not afforded an adequate test of the corrective potential of compensatory education, then the big question that emerges is: *Why not?*

Perhaps the basic answer does not lie in the ideas and practices, or even the motivations, of educators, however negatively they may be assessed, but rather in the relationship that compensatory education bears to a culture that devalues the humanity of impoverished and minority-group persons, especially if they are black. Given the social setting of the school, especially the derogatory class and racist values and corresponding oppressive structures that prevail in American society, perhaps it is "natural" that special educational programs for the powerless—however noble in purpose—tend to become distorted into means for their continued degradation. Perhaps, further, the destructive society-to-school influences here suggested do not operate mechanistically, "inevitably," but can be mitigated or even reversed by progressive educators acting in concert with other progressive forces in the community.

The American school reflects the characteristics of the imperfect democracy it serves. Nor could it be otherwise. The education of any people at any time or place functions at the heart of their culture, and is influenced decisively by the prevailing values. It is important, therefore, to see the school as a structural manifestation of the commanding attitudes and values of American society. This provides a fruitful theoretical framework for understanding its differential role in the education of affluent whites, poor whites, American Indians, Chicanos, Puerto Ricans, and blacks. Consider briefly some of its implications for blacks.

Ours is still a young nation, having achieved self-determination less than two centuries ago, and our colonial antecedents go back only about three and a half centuries. It is instructive to recall that during two centuries of that period the vast majority of Negroes were slaves—chattel bought and sold on the market, legally bound in total subjection to their owners. Forced to labor without pay on the plantations of the South, they were bereft of all human rights, even integrity of the family, personal dignity, and life itself.

Eight decades after the Declaration of Independence, the Supreme Court, in the famous Dred Scott case, declared in effect that "the Negro, so far as the United States Government was concerned, had no rights that the white man should respect" (Woodson, 1931, 353-354). In so doing, it expressed attitudes and values that were fairly universal in the South and very widely accepted in the North. Black people were perceived by the white masses and intellectuals alike as inherently inferior beings, properly subordinated in the social structure to their "betters."

The brief interlude of radical reconstruction following the Civil War promised to change fundamentally the relations of the Negro people to the nation. Under the protection of Federal troops, coalitions of recently-freed blacks, liberal Republicans from the North, and many poor whites achieved political power in the former slave states and proceeded to install and develop democratic governmental structures for the first time in the history of the South.

Within a decade, however, this progressive trend was reversed. A succession of Supreme Court decisions eroded the civil-rights legislation of the Reconstruction Congresses; Federal troops were withdrawn from the South, and lynch-terror became the law of the land, with thousands of black people murdered with impunity, often at big public orgies of sadistic racism. The franchise was wrested from blacks and poor whites; the still-new democratic state constitutions were replaced by reactionary political instruments, thus re-entrenching the Old South in power; and the masses of Negroes were pushed back into virtual slavery on the plantations. It was during this last quarter of the 19th century that the nearly universal system of racial segregation was established by law, thoroughly supported by effective public opinion, and ruled constitutionally valid by the Supreme Court in the landmark case of *Plessy v. Ferguson* in 1896.

By the turn of the 20th century, 90 per cent of all Negroes still lived in the South, and their status had been definitely "fixed" (many contemporaries thought permanently) as that of an inferior caste, pariahs in the only country they knew, and subject at any time to insult and physical violence to "keep them in their place." This was within the life-span of more than 12 million Americans now living.

There was no substantial change in this state of affairs until World War I. Indeed, more than 1100 Negroes were lynched between 1900 and 1914 (Franklin, 1969, p. 439). But the great migrations of the war years opened up new perspectives of freedom. Mass Negro populations were established in the less oppressive environments of large northern cities. Black workers moved into the manpower-starved war industries. Negroes entered politics, sent their children to school, and built vigorous protest organizations and a vital Negro press. In the process, they developed increasing group consciousness and self-confidence, reflected in a flourishing of the arts.

But this upturn toward freedom was also short-lived; the economic depression immediately following the war triggered an outburst of virulent racist oppression, in the North as well as the South. Most black workers—"the last hired"—were fired from their new-found jobs in industry, forced residential segregation became widespread in the North, and a new wave of bloody race riots burgeoned. From June to the end of 1919, some 25 anti-Negro pogroms were carried out in cities located in all sections of the country. Further, "More than 70 Negroes were lynched during the first year of the post-war period" (Franklin, pp. 480-483). Almost one-half of all Americans living at that time, approximately 50 million, are still alive.

The decade of the Great Depression brought further racist oppression to black Americans, only partially relieved by progressive measures of the New Deal. In the course of and following World War II, however, a strong trend developed toward increased civil rights and opportunities for the Negro people, which persists, although with notable reverses and a generally waning impact during recent years. Highlighting this development and reflecting the enhanced stature of blacks in the society, was the Supreme Court's declaration in 1954 that "in the field of public education, 'separate but equal' has no place. Separate educational facilities are inherently unequal" (*Brown v. Board of*

Education of Topeka). This principle was soon extended to strike down legal sanctions for racial segregation in other areas of social life.

It is important to note that the Court's segregationist ruling in *Plessy v. Ferguson* stood for nearly six decades—until just 19 years ago!—and that since that time school segregation has grown apace, especially in the North. It is also relevant that recorded lynchings of black people continued at least to a little over a decade ago. Tuskegee Institute, which kept the record, reports that 1790 Negroes were lynched between 1900 and 1950, and six more between 1950 and 1959 (*World Almanac, 1961,* p. 459).

This thumbnail historical sketch omits illuminating details and the dynamics of the social developments noted, including the freedom struggles of the Negro people in each period, but accounts of these are readily available elsewhere (Franklin, 1969; DuBois, 1935; Woodward, 1951, and 1955; Meier and Rudwick, 1969). The purpose of this brief outline is to emphasize the subordinate social status of black people through the three and one-half centuries that the cultural values, social patterns, and institutions of our nation have been developing. During almost all of that period, Negroes have been an oppressed and essentially powerless people, and their degradation has been viewed with approval or indifference by the vast majority of white Americans and the Government of the United States.

Marx's observation that "the tradition of all dead generations weighs like a nightmare on the brain of the living" (Marx, p. 13), is apt in relation to the impact of our nation's centuries-long oppression of Negroes on the society in which today's schools function. It is a legacy of deep-rooted and explosive racism, powerfully influencing the behaviors of individual Americans and the roles of all our social institutions.

Carmichael and Hamilton define racism as "the predication of decisions and policies on conditions of race for the purpose of *subordinating* a racial group and maintaining control over that group" (Carmichael and Hamilton, 1967, p. 3). And they differentiate between "individual racism"—overt acts by individuals—and "institutional racism"—more subtle operations of established and respected forces of society. The latter is "less identifiable in terms of *specific* individuals committing the acts," but "it is no less destructive of human life" (Carmichael and Hamilton, p. 4). It is also more pervasive in the society and masked by an aura of blameless "naturalness."

Bruner obviously had both forms of racism in mind when, in "reconsidering" his famous *The Process of Education,* he declared:

> There must be ways in which we can think honestly of reformulation of the institutions into which our schools, as one integral part, fit. Surely it requires that we redirect our resources, reorder our priorities, redefine our national effort, and come to terms with the fact that we have a deep and brutal racism in us—in all of us. We must learn how to cope with that (Bruner, p. 29).

The individual racism in all of us is inescapable for any observer of contemporary American society. It is manifest in impassioned protests against "busing" for school integration, in organized resistance to the "invasion" of residential suburbs by black home-seekers, in the racially restrictive policies of the major unions of skilled craftsmen, in the unprovoked insults and brutality that police and prison guards commonly inflict upon Negro citizens, in the bombing of a Negro church that advocates civil rights, in "Off Duty" signs that frequently flash when blacks hail a taxicab, in the tendency of many teachers to equate pupils' blackness with dumbness, in the racially restrictive cliques of high school boys and girls, in the studied exclusion of Negro work-day associates from after-hours social affairs, in the general apathy with which most citizens accept the well-publicized fact that thousands of black babies die from preventable lead-poisoning in the ghetto, and in countless similar behaviors of white Americans. Most of them are prisoners of deeply entrenched attitudes and values that stem from a past they neither know nor understand.

The more subtle but all-pervasive impact of institutional racism is seen in the consistently inferior position of Negroes in all major areas of social life. Illustrative are the following facts, culled (unless otherwise noted) from a special publication of the U. S. Department of Commerce, *The Social and Economic Status of Negroes in the United States, 1970.*

> The Negro population of the United States in 1970 was approximately 22,600,000, or 11 per cent of the total.
>
> In 1970, the median income among Negro families was 64 per cent of that of white families, a difference of about $3600.
>
> About one-third of the black population and one-tenth of the white population were in the low-income group in 1970 (i.e., less than $3968 for a nonfarm family of four, etc.).
>
> In 1969, 20 per cent of black families and 8 per cent of white families had incomes under $3000.
>
> "Forty-two percent of *all* children classified as poor are nonwhite" (Birch and Gussow, p. 4).
>
> In 1969, the median income of black male *college* graduates was $8669, as compared with the median of $8829 for white male *high school* graduates.
>
> Unemployment rates in 1970 averaged 8.2 per cent for blacks and 4.5 per cent for whites. Corresponding rates among teenagers were 29.1 per cent for blacks and 13.5 per cent for whites.
>
> Negroes constituted 11 per cent of all employed workers in 1970, only 7 per cent of professional and technical workers, but 42 per cent of private household workers.
>
> Negroes constituted 15 per cent of all Federal employees in May 1970, only 9 per cent of those earning $8000 or more, but 30 per cent of those earning $7999 or less.
>
> Among young people 14 to 17 years old and enrolled in school in October 1970, 15.3 per cent of black males and 10.2 per cent of black females were two or more years below modal grade, as compared with 5.7 per cent of white males and 3.3 per cent of white females.
>
> The proportions of 16 year old high school dropouts in 1970 were 10.9 per cent for black males and 11.1 per cent for black females, as compared with 5.0 per cent for white males and 6.7 per cent for white females.
>
> Among persons 14 years old and over in 1969, 3.6 per cent of blacks and 0.7 per cent of whites were illiterate.
>
> Among persons 25 to 29 years old in 1970, 54 per cent of black males and 58 per cent of black females completed four years of high school or more, as compared with 79 per cent of white males and 76 per cent of white females.
>
> Among persons 25 to 34 years old in 1970, 6.1 per cent of blacks and 16.6 per cent of whites completed four years of college or more.
>
> One in six college-age black men was enrolled in college in 1970, as compared with one in three college-age white men.
>
> In 1970, 16.9 per cent of the housing units occupied by Negroes lacked some or all plumbing facilities, as compared with 4.8 per cent of those occupied by whites.
>
> Rates of infant mortality in 1968 (per 1000 live births) were 23.0 for blacks and 14.7 for whites under 28 days old, and 11.6 for blacks and 4.5 for whites between 28 days and 11 months old.

The life expectancy of Negroes 25 years old in 1968 was 68.1 years, as compared with 73.3 years for whites of the same age.

From 1965 to 1966, the numbers of persons per 100,000 population who were victims of crimes of violence (homicide, rape, robbery, and aggravated assault) were 33 per cent larger for black males than for white males, and more than 5 times as large for black females as for white females.

"While the average citizen may be the victim of violent crime only once in 400 years, there are indications that the poor black slum dweller faces odds five times greater—one in eighty" (Clark, 1970, p. 50).

"Negroes are arrested more frequently and on less evidence than whites and are more often victims of mass or sweep arrests" (Clark, p. 51).

Among persons of voting age in 1970, 44 per cent of the blacks and 56 per cent of the whites reported that they voted.

Elected Negro public officials in 1970 included one in the U. S. Senate, 13 in the U. S. House of Representatives, 198 in state legislatures, 81 in mayoralty positions, and 1567 in all other elected offices.

No such tabulation as this, even if more comprehensive, could define the qualitative reality of what it means to be black in the United States. However, the few facts noted are suggestive. As compared with white Americans, the Negro people are disproportionately restricted to low-paying jobs, and they are more frequently unemployed, more impoverished, less adequately educated, more poorly housed, less healthy, more often victimized by crime, and but meagerly represented on all levels of government. Such differences are evident in all areas of American social life; they are systematic, *structural.*

True, there has been "progress" since World War II, but it has benefited mainly the relatively small Negro middle class. Despite unprecedented judicial and legislative enactments and dramatic struggles of the civil rights movement, physical and psychic degradation continues to be the hallmark of the Negro slum. None of the available resources—the economy, political institutions, courts, police, schools, trade unions, churches, or social agencies—has come near to coping with the mass despoilation of human beings that persists in the black ghetto. Indeed, the dominant pattern of functioning among all of these institutions serves to maintain the inferior status of Negroes in the society. This, of course, is hardly surprising, since most of these social institutions emerged and developed during centuries of severe racist oppression of black Americans.

Thus, the conscious forces of individual racism and the largely impersonal forces of institutional racism interact to sustain the traditional subordination of blacks—to "keep them in their place." It is within this context that one must look for fundamental explanations as to why most schools fail to educate impoverished Negro children, including schools with special programs of compensatory education. Consider some of the ways in which this social setting impinges upon the school (Bond, 1966, for overall historical impact of racism on Negro education; Rubinstein, 1970, for first-hand accounts of racism in New York City public schools).

In the first place, the people who staff the schools are carriers of the dominant traits of the culture. Their perceptions, attitudes, values, and overt behaviors are the products of developmental experiences in their homes, their schools and colleges, and the society at large. Probably most of those who are in commanding positions—board members, superintendents, principals, and senior teachers, mainly white—grew up through childhood and adolescence during a period when racist values and practices were even more virulent than they are today. They and the great majority of younger teachers were and continue to be influenced in important ways by the individual and institutional racism of their social environment.

It is probable that a large proportion of white school personnel can honestly disavow deliberate and willful racial prejudice, but that is not the point. More important is the certainty that the vast majority of them have been so conditioned by the culture that their racist behaviors, which correspond to prevailing social norms, may not be perceived as untoward. The prior expectation that black children will not learn effectively; the readiness to accept below-standard academic performance from them; the tendency to counsel black youth toward dead-end curricular and occupational goals; unconcern that ability-grouping in desegregated schools tends to re-segregate white and black pupils at the upper and lower achievement levels; the assumption that white middle-class-oriented curricular materials and standardized tests are valid for pupils from the slums; readiness to condemn black parents (whom most teachers do not know) as debased and not interested in their children's education; almost complete isolation from the ghetto community served by the school—all these, I submit, are objectively racist behaviors. They are commonplace in schools serving masses of poor blacks, and most young teachers entering these schools are quickly socialized by their experienced colleagues into such expected patterns of professional conduct (Fuchs, 1969). The resultant impact upon the process of education is overwhelmingly negative.

This list of behaviors, of course, is not apt for all white school administrators and teachers. Some are deeply motivated by humanistic and democratic values, and try hard—often successfully—to guide their ghetto pupils in effective learning. Some others are consciously and unabashedly bigoted and seem to derive satisfaction from demeaning black youngsters. The difference probably arises from variations in their developmental experiences. Culture is never monolithic but always encompasses contradictory tendencies that have differing impacts upon the behaviors of individual human beings. The fact of such variations is wholly consistent with the tendency of most teachers to behave in accord with prevailing social norms. These norms call for maintaining the inferior status of blacks, preferably through the seemingly "natural" processes of social interaction.

Second, the maintenance of ghetto schools as dysfunctional institutions that further the continued subjugation of Negroes obviously coincides with the interests of those business and political leaders who command real power in the community; otherwise they would effect a change. As Hunter pointed out long ago and others have confirmed (Hunter, 1953), the big-city superintendent of schools ranks rather low in the heirarchy of community power, and this is likewise true of those who serve on policy-making boards of education. Truly decisive issues affecting the public schools—key leadership, administrative organization, plant expansion, overall social conformity, and especially budget—are highly political, and their resolution is effectively influenced by the community power structure.

Clark had this in mind when he looked vainly to the top for a mandate to reform slum schools.

> In New York, a conference of top business leaders like David Rockefeller, John Whitney, Robert Dowling could assume responsibility for deciding what must be done with the city's public educational system if the stability and viability of the metropolis are to be assured. A consensus and commitment for action from such a group—and its counterparts in other cities—would impel political leadership to action (Clark, p. 153).

And, of course, he is right. Those in the top echelon of power could, indeed, effect a change if they so willed; and they would if school conditions seriously threatened their material and political interests. But furthering the subordination of black people through crippling their children in school does not qualify for such action.

Stein makes the point sharply:

> How does it come about that the one institution that is said to be the gateway to opportunity, the school, is the very one that is most effective in perpetuating an oppressed and impoverished status in the society? Every oppressive, racist, and exploitative society *must* use all of its institutions to retain its racist, oppressive, and exploitative character. That is why these institutions were erected (Stein, 203).

Although the main focus of this analysis is the community school system, it is relevant to note that the racial practices of local schools are significantly influenced by national policies, proclaimed and implemented by the Federal Government. Their overall impact, despite tendencies toward liberalism from time to time, is supportive of the racial status quo. And as Mills made quite clear: "In so far as national events are decided, the power elite are those who decide them" (Mills, 1956, p. 18). ·

Finally, the role of educational bureaucracy has been to mediate the racist values of American society. As has often been noted, the vast, "faceless" apparatuses through which large school systems are managed serve most effectively to protect the status quo in all important dimensions. They are impersonal entities in which responsibility is diffuse and accountability practically impossible; and their operation is largely immune to efforts at substantial educational change, whether emanating from policy boards and superintendents at the top or from teachers and parents below. Indiscriminate in its conservatism, seemingly "natural" in its functioning, the educational bureaucracy provides an effective mask for racism in the schools (Rogers, 1968; Gittell, 1967). It is difficult to imagine a more perfect mechanism for maintaining the prevailing system of inferior education for black Americans.

Considering the centuries-old and continuing oppression of the Negro people in the social structure, together with the powerful impact upon schools of the racist society they serve, it seems unduly fatuous for educators to become preoccupied—as large numbers of them are—with fashioning self-serving theories about alleged deficits "within" black children that retard their academic development. They might more fruitfully examine the school environment.

It is said that impoverished children from the black ghetto are "harder to teach" than most middle-class children, and they are, for objectively racist teachers in demeaning institutions using methods and materials designed for white youngsters from affluent backgrounds. But if teaching is a profession and not merely a craft, then educational theorists should begin with the long-honored premise that methods and materials must be adapted to the needs of the learners. They cannot excuse the school's failure to do this by observing that "these children are different."

There is no dearth of effective instructional techniques for guiding the learning of impoverished children and youth. The literature abounds with valid suggestions, and there are humane, dedicated, and creative teachers in almost every school system who use them with good results. Why, then, is effective instruction so rare in ghetto schools? Why, especially, have most programs of compensatory education failed to yield significantly positive outcomes? If it is said that valid compensatory intervention "has just not often been adequately tried," why hasn't it?

The basic answer is not to be found in the characteristics of impoverished Negro children, nor even in the inadequacies that prevail in educational methodology. Rather, it inheres in the school's mediation of racist values and attitudes that are deeply imbedded in our culture. To educate black children well is simply not an imperative value in American society. As was noted at the Brookings Institute's 1968 Conference on the Community School, "a public school system that fails poor black children can be

tolerated, while a public school system that fails white middle-class children cannot"
(Levin, 1970, p. 279).

Programs of compensatory education have been conducted mainly in segregated
ghetto schools that are perceived by the community as acceptably inferior for an
oppressed people without power to effect a change. The relevant behaviors of all
categories of participants have been negatively conditioned by this fact—central administrators, principals and teachers, pupils and parents. Herein lies the basic reason why most
of these programs founder.

Advocates of major school reform, including myself, devote considerable time and
effort to trying to get professional personnel to develop educational programs and
procedures that can substantially improve the academic performance of young people in
ghetto schools. We urge unvarying respect for the personalities of black and other
minority-group children from impoverished backgrounds, as, indeed, for all children and
their parents. We call for drastic curriculum revision, introducing meaningful materials
that are clearly relevant to the lives of the learners, and developing informal classroom
procedures that encourage self-confidence, initiative, and creativity among pupils. We
denounce the vicious practice of ability-grouping. We plead for individualized instruction
to supplant the prevailing lockstep. We advocate direct and positive relations with pupils'
homes. Progressive educators persist in teaching and writing and preaching to effect these
and other innovations in ghetto schools, but nothing much happens.

A few administrators and teachers do respond with serious and effective efforts at
school reform, and it is important to note that "the system" tolerates such individual
initiative more commonly than is often believed. Even institutional structures that are
negatively biased against the minority-group poor still afford substandard margins of
freedom for professionals who choose to use them.

Let it be emphasized, therefore, that dedicated and creative teachers and administrators can indeed significantly improve the quality of educational experience available to
children of the poor in their classrooms and schools; and it is very important that they try
to do so. Thus, efforts by professional educators to improve the effectiveness of
individual teachers and administrators are by no means wasted; they may enhance the life
chances of hundreds and thousands of youngsters from the ghetto. Although limited, this
is a powerfully attractive goal.

It is obvious, however, that professional advocacy of major school reform will not
suffice to transform most slum schools into truly educational institutions. Advocacy
backed by social and political power, as in most middle-class white communities, can,
indeed, achieve large-scale results. But advocacy from ghetto positions of powerlessness is
largely futile. The bulwarks of educational racism will yield when forced to do so by
powerful democratic struggles. Helping to mount and support such struggles are tasks for
all Americans to whom equality of educational opportunity is an important value. The
main thrust, however, must come from those whose children's futures are being distorted
and truncated by schools that fail to educate.

The burgeoning movement for "community control" of schools promises to organize
an important sector of the democratic power that is needed (Levin, 1970). When local
boards truly responsive to the people achieve authority over policy, personnel, program,
and budget in ghetto schools, the quality of education for children of the poor is almost
certain to be enhanced. District superintendents, principals, and teachers who are
appointed by and accountable to such boards are not likely to persist in professional
behaviors inimical to their pupils. Moreover, of necessity, they will develop more
understanding of and cooperative relations with the communities their schools serve.

Needed curricular and related innovations can be introduced without running the usual gamut of red tape at the central bureaucracy. Parents in the ghetto will begin to perceive the schools as "theirs," thus eroding the alienation of school from home that now seriously distorts the educational process. The movement for community control corresponds at this stage of history to the pressing needs of education in the ghetto. It undertakes radically to alter power relationships in the school system.

The struggle for community control of ghetto schools is integral to a much broader political struggle—the fundamental restructuring of American society as a whole, to the end that human development will supplant corporate profit as the prime goal of our major institutions. Discussion of this revolutionary perspective is beyond the scope of this essay. Suffice it to note that the achievement of full equality of educational opportunity for the minority-group poor will always depend upon their winning full equality in the economic, political, and social structures of America. For the Negro people, this means freedom from all of the racist shackles by which they have been hobbled during more than three centuries.

Contrary to the fervent hopes and faith of the Negro masses throughout our history, and despite the fond conceits of many professionals and statesmen, it is not the education of black men and women that will achieve their liberation—it is the liberation of black Americans that will assure their effective education.

REFERENCES

Birch, Herbert G., and Gussow, Joan Dye: Disadvantaged Children: Health, Nutrition and School Failure, New York, Harcourt, Brace and World, Inc., 1970.

Bodmer, Walter F., and Cavalli-Sforza, Luigi Luca: How much can we boost IQ and scholastic achievement: a discussion. *Harvard Educational Review, 39:* 273-356, Spring, 1969.

Bodmer, Walter F., and Cavalli-Sforza, Luigi Luca: Intelligence and race. *Scientific American, 223:* 19-29, October, 1970.

Bond, Horace Mann: The Education of the Negro in the American Social Order. New York, Octagon Books, Inc., 1966.

Brown vs. Board of Education of Topeka, 347 U.S. 483, 495 (1954).

Bruner, Jerome S.: The process of education reconsidered. *In* Leeper, Robert R. (ed.): Dare to Care/Dare to Act: Racism and Education. Washington, Association for Supervision and Curriculum Development, 1971.

Carmichael, Stokely, and Hamilton, Charles V.: Black Power, New York, Vintage Books, 1967.

Clark, Kenneth B.: Dark Ghetto. New York, Harper and Row, 1965.

Clark, Ramsey: Crime in America. New York, Simon and Schuster, 1970.

Du Bois, W. E. Burghardt: Black Reconstruction in America. New York, Harcourt, Brace and Co., 1935.

Franklin, John Hope: From Slavery to Freedom: A History of Negro Americans. Third edition. New York, Vintage Books, 1969.

Frost, Joe L., and Hawkes, Glenn R. (eds.): The Disadvantaged Child. New York, Houghton Mifflin Co., 1966.

Fuchs, Estelle: Teachers Talk. New York, Doubleday, 1969.

Gittell, Marilyn: Participants and Participation. New York, Center for Urban Education, n.d.

Hellmuth, Jerome (ed.): Disadvantaged Child, Vol. 1. Seattle, Special Child Publications, 1967.

Hunter, Floyd: Community Power Structure. Chapel Hill, University of North Carolina Press, 1953.

Jensen, Arthur R.: How much can we boost IQ and scholastic achievement: a discussion. *Harvard Educational Review, 39:* 273-356, Spring, 1969.

Leacock, Eleanor Burke: Teaching and Learning in City Schools. New York, Basic Books, Inc., 1969.

Levin, Henry M. (ed.): Community Control of Schools. Washington, D.C., Brookings Institute, 1970.

Maeroff, Gene I.: Education chief urges more career training. *New York Times,* August 8, 1971.

Marx, Karl: The Eighteenth Brumaire of Louis Bonaparte. New York, n.d.

Meier, August, and Rudwick, Elliott M. (eds.): The Making of Black America, Vols. 1 and 2. New York, Atheneum, 1969.

Mills, C. Wright: The Power Elite. New York, Oxford University Press, 1956.

Rist, Ray C.: Student social class and teacher expectations: the self-fulfilling prophecy in ghetto education. *Harvard Educational Review, 40:* 411-451, August, 1970.

Rogers, David: 110 Livingston Street. New York, Random House, 1968.

Rosenthal, Robert, and Jacobson, Lenore: Pygmalion in the Classroom. New York, Holt, Rinehart and Winston, Inc., 1968.

Rubinstein, Annette T. (ed.): Schools Against Children. New York, Monthly Review Press, 1970.

Ryan, William: Blaming the Victim. New York, Pantheon Books, 1971.

Schwebel, Milton: Who Can Be Educated? New York, Grove Press, 1968.

Shuey, A. M.: The Testing of Negro Intelligence. New York, Social Science Press, 1966.

Silberman, Charles E.: Crisis in the Classroom. New York, Random House, 1970.

Stein, Annie: Strategies for failure. *Harvard Educational Review, 41:* 158-204, May, 1971.

U.S. Department of Commerce. The Social and Economic Status of Negroes in the United States. BLS Report No. 394. Current Population Reports, Series P-23, No. 38. Washington, D.C., Government Printing Office, 1970.

Woodson, Carter G.: The Negro in Our History. Washington, D.C., Associated Publishers, 1931.

Woodward, C. Vann: Origins of the New South: 1877-1913. Louisiana State University Press, 1951.

Woodward, C. Vann: The Strange Career of Jim Crow. New York, Oxford University Press, 1955.

World Almanac, 1961. New York World Telegram and Sun, 1961.

discrimination and desegregation: the education crisis in america today 59

Leon E. Panetta

INTRODUCTION

There is a crisis in American education today. Most educational experts, supported by a good portion of the law in this country, believe that the crisis is largely based on continuing discrimination and segregation in education. A growing number of politicians and disgruntled parents, however, believe that desegregation is the true culprit and that education can be affected only detrimentally by busing and mixing. Whatever the crisis may be, it is obvious that our society has failed even to begin to understand the problems of either discrimination or desegregation, and until we do, the crisis will continue and our children will suffer.

The issue of equal education is one of the most emotional and complex challenges ever to face this country. It can be grossly oversimplified into its most emotional terms, and one word alone, such as "busing" or "neighborhood schools" can blind even the most sensitive parent. In addition, the current political turmoil surrounding this issue results in a confusing barrage of charge and counter-charge, statement and retraction, clarification and re-clarification. The greatest need today is to refocus the attention of the nation on the educational requirements of children and the most hopeful ways of meeting them.

Despite the divisive rhetoric of the past 19 years, the real issue is, and always has been, the provision of equal educational opportunity to all of our children. It was concern for the educational needs of children that marked the federal government's initial involvement with the process of public school integration in 1954, in the Supreme Court's fundamental decision in *Brown vs. Board of Education.* Black children, said the Court, have the "personal and present" right to equal educational opportunities with white children in a racially nondiscriminatory public school system. In a critical passage, the Court stated:

> To separate [children] from others of similar age and qualifications solely because of their race generates a feeling of inferiority as to their status in the community that may affect their hearts and minds in a way unlikely ever to be undone.

Over the years, we have learned that the children who are damaged by segregated education are not just the black, Chicano, Indian, or other minority children—they are only its most obvious victims. Dr. Kenneth Clark has stated that advantaged, white, middle-class children are also damaged by educational systems that fail to practice the principles of racial justice and equality of opportunity that they teach. On another level, our entire society—black, white, and brown, rich and poor—suffers as each year brings us closer to the tragic, divided America foreseen in the report of the President's National Advisory Commission on Civil Disorders.

Although case after case dealing with school desegregation since *Brown* has been rooted in a deep concern for children and their education, the process of school desegregation has resembled too often a vicious game of pressures and politics in which the education of children was a matter of secondary importance.

In the south and in some northern school systems where racial segregation was proscribed by law, we have seen a bitter struggle over what is called compliance with the law. Claims of victory are often sounded when even the slightest token integration is achieved. Often the process has included closing modern black schools, firing qualified black faculty members, or separating children according to so-called "ability groupings" —results that can create a climate of bitterness that can damage the education of children for a generation. School systems frequently strive desperately for the least short-term change possible, without any real concern for the long-range effect of this strategy on the education of the children in their care.

As far as the situation in the north is concerned, the Executive Branch of the government, the Congress, local school officials, and the community at large have hidden behind the legalism of so-called de facto segregation, justifying inaction on the ground that the segregation of schools just happened, and ignoring its obvious effect on children and their education.

Furthermore, throughout the country, discrimination against Mexican-American, Indian, Puerto Rican, and children of other minorities has been largely ignored, and too little attention has been given to their special educational needs.

This article attempts to re-establish a commitment to meet the urgent needs of our nation's single most important resource—its children. In the political turmoil of the present, it is often difficult to remember how this process of desegregation began, why racial segregation is detrimental, and what are the barriers to desegregation and the remedies to segregation. This article is but a small reminder of the promise that was held out by the *Brown* decision. The hope is that there is still time to begin to solve the problem of racial separation in our public schools in a sensitive, humane, and intelligent way, using an understanding of the complex educational issues involved and the strategies developed over the past few years, and maintaining the objective of better education for all children.

EFFECTS OF RACIALLY ISOLATED EDUCATION

Few, if any, educational authorities or statistics are quoted to support the argument that busing is somehow detrimental to education. The fact is that most of the 20 million children who travel to and from school in the country's 256,000 school buses do it because they have to: they live too far from their schools to get there any other way. Busing for the express purpose of desegregation accounts for only a tiny fraction of the actual busing that goes on. Even so, all of the evidence gathered before or since 1954 indicates that the segregated child receives an education that is inferior to that of the integrated child, and that most of the bus trips result in a better education for children.

The Coleman report was commissioned under the 1964 Civil Rights Act to study the equality of educational opportunity—or more precisely, the lack of such opportunity—throughout the country. The report showed, among other things, that test scores of black students in classes with 50 per cent or more white students rose in comparison with those of blacks in totally segregated classes. What seemed more important was that, as Coleman reported, "Those students who first entered desegregated schools in the early grades generally show slightly higher average scores than the students who first came to desegregated schools in later grades." Also emphasized in the Coleman report was the importance of integrating children from different family and socioeconomic backgrounds. Not only was a disadvantaged child of any race likely to achieve much more in a school attended by middle-class pupils than he would in a school attended by other disadvantaged youngsters, but the middle-class child was not likely to suffer from the mix.

Since the Coleman report, other studies have reinforced the basic point. In an appraisal of school desegregation studies by Dr. Meyer Weinberg in 1968, the conclusion was that the black pupil learns more in a desegregated class, while the white student continues to learn at his accustomed rate. Black aspirations, already high, increase in desegregated classes. Other studies, many conducted in desegregated school districts, substantiate the fact that desegregation does improve the overall quality of education for all students. And the principal reason lies in the obvious detrimental effects of a racially isolated education.

There are, of course, a number of factors which influence the education of students, including their home backgrounds, the quality of instruction provided in the schools they attend, and the social background of their classmates. The racial composition of the schools is one of those factors. For the minority student, racially isolated schools tend to lower achievement and restrict aspirations. By contrast, black or brown children who attend predominantly white schools more often score higher on achievement tests and develop higher aspirations.

The educational and economic circumstances of a child's family are other factors that determine the benefits the child derives from his education. The elementary school student from a disadvantaged home, isolated from others with more fortunate circumstances, typically has a lower verbal achievement level than the more advantaged student. Another determining factor is the social class level of a student's classmates. From the early grades through high school, a student is directly influenced by his peers. The evidence has established that the disadvantaged student who is integrated with others performs at a higher level than those isolated by social class level.

There also is a strong relationship between the attitudes and achievements of minority students and the racial composition of the schools they attend, as the Coleman and Weinberg reports substantiate. The simple fact is that the racially isolated schools have fewer library volumes per student, less advanced courses, and more pupils per teacher than integrated or majority white schools. Minority students are more likely to have teachers with lower verbal achievement levels, substitute teachers, and teachers who are dissatisfied with the school assignment.

Racially isolated schools are inferior institutions, and they are regarded as such by the community. Teachers and students locked into these schools recognize the stigma of inferiority attached to their schools, and this has a negative effect on their attitudes and achievement. The longer a student is in a racially isolated school, the greater the negative impact. The longer a student is in a desegregated school, the higher his performance.

The cycle, of course, extends into every aspect of life as these children grow into adults, and it accounts in part for the differences in income and occupation. Isolation is perpetuated in other areas of American life. Black, brown, and red adults who attended racially isolated schools are more likely to develop attitudes that further alienate them from whites, lower their self-esteem, and permit them to accept an inferior status in life.

In like terms, whites attending schools isolated by their race tend to have attitudes that assign inferior status to nonwhites. They are more apt to regard minority institutions as inferior and to resist measures designed to overcome discrimination against minorities.

A federal District Court judge recently rendered a decision to speed integration of a segregated school system. His observations were eloquent:

> In any community where one school is black and one predominantly white nobody needs to be told which is considered the good school. This is the case whether segregation is the result of an old housing pattern, the flight of white residents or the construction of a new school on a site beyond the walking distance of Negro children. The implication, and not infrequently the assertion, that the Negro school is "undesirable" disheartens both pupils and teachers and limits their expectations. Because it saps the pupil's motivation, his achievement level drops below his actual capacity and gives ostensible confirmation to the fear that he is somehow deficient. In other words, the school which should help him to resolve his self-doubts, strengthen his self respect and encourage his aspirations actually does the reverse.

The truth which emerges from the evidence is simply this: minority children suffer serious harm when their education takes place in racially segregated public schools, whatever the source of such segregation may be. The conclusion drawn by the U. S. Supreme Court in *Brown* about the impact upon children of segregation compelled by law—that it "affects their hearts and minds in ways unlikely ever to be undone"—applies also to segregation not compelled by law. Large numbers of minorities reside today in ghettos not as the result of an exercise of free choice, and the attendance of their children in racially isolated schools is not an accident of fate wholly unconnected with deliberate segregation and other forms of discrimination. And, in the end, it is the children who must carry the stigma of a racially isolated education throughout their lives. After San Francisco schools were desegregated, a fourth grade teacher there commented, "One thing is obvious to me that wasn't before, the kids in the ghetto schools really weren't getting a fair shake before." Giving kids that "fair shake" is what *Brown,* desegregation, and busing are all about.

BARRIERS TO UNDERSTANDING AND REMEDY

Many Americans have sensed the grave injustice that racial isolation inflicts upon the children of the poor and minorities. But the need for a remedy sufficient to correct the injustice has been obscured by other factors that contribute to educational disadvantage —factors that are sometimes used as excuses for not dealing with the basic problem of isolation.

Thus, it is said with some degree of truth that minority children often are handicapped in school because they come from poor and ill-educated families. But the conclusion drawn by a few pessimistic educators that the school cannot be expected to deal with these deficiencies is unjust both to the children involved and to American education. The very purpose of American public education from Jefferson's time to the present has been to help youngsters surmount the barriers of poverty and limited backgrounds to enable them to develop their talents and to participate fully in society.

The tributes accorded to public education in this country are based largely on the fact that it has played this role so successfully for so many Americans. This record affords ample grounds for hope that education can meet today's challenge of preparing the children of the poor, the disadvantaged, and minorities to participate in American society. Counsels of despair will be in order only if, after doing everything to create the conditions for success, we fail.

It is also said with some truth that disadvantaged youngsters are in need of special attention, smaller classes, a better quality of instruction, and teachers better prepared to understand and set high standards for them. However, the suggestion that this is all that is needed finds little support in our experience to date with efforts to provide compensatory education.

Many educators believe that the environment of poverty, the lack of cultural stimulation in the home, and the lack of motivation to learn account for a child's failure to achieve in school. Compensatory educational programs that seek to improve the quality of education for disadvantaged children are often predicated on the assumption that deficiencies in a child's background are the main deterrent to learning. The trouble with these efforts is that compensatory programs attempt to instill in a child feelings of personal worth and dignity in an environment filled with visible evidence of denial of his value as a person. This is not a weakness which will yield easily to additional infusions of money, particularly when, as the studies of the Washington Research Project show, much of the money that is available is not being used in accordance with Federal guidelines.

School programs involving expenditures for cultural enrichment, better teaching, and other needed educational services *can* be helpful to disadvantaged children, but the evidence suggests that the better services provided by additional funds and compensatory programs will not be fully effective in a racially isolated environment but will work only in a setting that supports the teacher's effort to help each child understand that he is a valuable person who can succeed.

Finally, it is often held that the problem of educational disadvantage is not one of race but one of class. And, as the Coleman report and others contend, it is true that an important key to providing good education for disadvantaged youngsters lies in giving them the opportunity to attend school with children who, by reason of their parents' education and income, have a genuine head start. Children benefit from association with others more advantaged than they and from a classroom environment that permits the establishment of high standards toward which they must strive. But, as a practical matter, the relatively small number of middle-class minority children in public schools means that it is possible to provide social class integration only by providing racial integration. Even if social class integration could be accomplished without racial integration, the remedy would be partial and inadequate, for children would still be attending schools that are stigmatized because of race. Thus, the complexity of the problem of educational disadvantage should not be allowed to obscure the fact that racial isolation is the heart of the matter and enduring solutions must deal with this basic challenge.

More fundamental, perhaps, than the difficulties of understanding the problem of racial isolation is the belief, held by many Americans, that solutions will require such extensive change and sacrifice that both education and society will suffer. Change certainly will be required. As our cities have grown, increasing distances—both physical and psychological—have separated the affluent majority from disadvantaged minorities. We have followed practices which exclude racial and economic minorities from large areas of the city, and we have created tax structures which, by providing more attractive educational facilities with less tax effort, tend to attract the affluent to the very areas from which minorities are excluded. The facts of racial and economic separation themselves have generated attitudes which make integration increasingly difficult. The lines of separation are now well established, self-perpetuating, and difficult to reverse.

Because change is difficult, it has been tempting to consider remedies which require a minimum of effort on the part of schools and the least disruption of the educational status quo. So it has been suggested that the problem of securing equal educational opportunity is really a problem of housing, and that if discrimination in housing can be eliminated, it will be possible to desegregate the schools without changing existing school patterns. But such a solution would require vast changes in an area in which resistance to change is more entrenched than in education. Although laws designed to secure an open market in housing are on the books, the attitudes fostered in segregated schools and neighborhoods make it unlikely that these laws will be fully effective for years. To make integrated education dependent upon open housing is to consign at least another generation of children to racially isolated schools, thus lengthening the time required to overcome housing discrimination.

Similarly, it has been suggested that if integration were put into effect at the high school level only, it would be accomplished with relative ease and without unduly disturbing existing attendance patterns. But the hard fact is that attitudes toward learning are formed during a child's early years, and it is in this period that the educational process has its greatest impact, positive or negative. Educational remedies that are not instituted until high school are least likely to be successful.

Thus, it appears that an effective remedy will require an alteration in the status quo. In a changing world, change is not likely to be resisted for its own sake, particularly when it is designed to create a more just society, but a more substantial question for many white American parents is whether the measures necessary to right the wrong inflicted upon millions of minority children will impair the interests of their own children.

Such an inquiry may begin by asking whether the racially isolated education most white children now receive causes them any injury. Dr. Kenneth Clark believes the advantaged, white, middle-class child is damaged by a hypocritical educational system that teaches one thing but practices another. Other evidence suggests that children educated in all-white institutions are more likely to develop racial fears and prejudices based upon lack of contact and information. White children are deprived of something valuable when they grow up isolated from children of other races, their self-esteem and assurance resting in part upon false notions of racial superiority, and ill-prepared by their school experience to participate fully in a world rich in human diversity. These losses, although not as tangible as those inflicted upon minority youngsters, are real enough to deserve the attention of parents concerned about their children's total development.

Unfortunately, they do not seem as real to many parents as the fears associated with integration. These fears are most frequently expressed in the concepts of the neighborhood school and the busing of children over long distances. The values of neighborhood and proximity, of course, are relative. In today's world, all of us are residents of many neighborhoods and communities, large and small. People do not hesitate to bus their children long distances in rural areas, or, in cities, to private schools or to other schools offering special advantages. The issue is not really neighborhood schools or busing but whether the interests of our children will be served or impaired by particular proposals or solutions. Will our children be held back by being placed in classes with children of other, less advantaged backgrounds? Will the education provided at the end of the trip be as good as, or better than, that which they are receiving now?

Most often these issues have been debated in the context of the inner city, in circumstances which have made it easy for fears to be magnified and exaggerated. Many parents imagine that their children will be cross-bused to ghetto schools and taught in classrooms populated by large numbers of disadvantaged children and lacking in essential services. Moreover, ethnic and class tensions have been aroused by proposals for partial solutions in which more responsibility is placed upon less affluent whites than upon those who have more advantages.

The fundamental answer to all of these fears is that solutions must be sought that will not only remedy injustice but will improve the quality of education for all children. The evidence from thousands of desegregated school districts is that such solutions are available.

While public attention has been focused upon the more dramatic controversies, these communities have quietly integrated their schools. Using a variety of techniques, they have achieved their goal by substituting community schools for those serving smaller neighborhoods. In most cases, the issue has been approached calmly and compassionately, with the aim of improving the quality of education for all children. Steps have been taken to maintain and improve educational standards, to avoid the possibility of interracial friction, and to provide remedial services for children who need them. And, in most cases, it has been concluded that advantaged children have not suffered from educational exposure to others not as fortunate, and that the results have been of benefit to all children, white and black alike.

In larger cities, although efforts to achieve integration have been fragmentary, the results generally have been the same. The most recent efforts, admittedly embryonic, of the largest city school districts have met with favorable reactions from those involved. Minority parents have reported that the value of better education has not been diminished by the bus trips necessary to obtain it. White parents have reported that their children have benefited from the experience. Administrators and teachers have described the educational results in positive terms.

Listen to some of the voices of those who have led the way:

> Dr. David H. Porter, the superintendent of schools in Harrisburg, Pennsylvania: "The change has been dramatic. Walk into an early childhood center or an elementary school and look at the faces, hear the sounds, watch the kids at work and play. You can't show it on paper yet, but down inside, you know it's working."
>
> Dr. E. Ray Berry, the superintendent of schools in Riverside, California: "I see desegregation as an important element . . . it is the only answer in terms of if we really believe in an integrated society. I don't see any other way to do it."
>
> Donald Abernethy, the superintendent of schools in Hoke County, North Carolina: "I don't think it would ever happen, if we kept the schools segregated and kept pouring in money for compensatory education in segregated schools. But I believe in an integrated system that we will eventually work it out."
>
> Caesar Orsini, principal in the San Francisco school system: "Any black kid who got out of an all-black school is getting a better education now in integrated schools—there's no doubt about it."
>
> Mrs. Amanda Williams, mother of four, in the Berkeley school system: "You have to have an administration that will listen to all concerns and problems and deal with them so that confidence will be built where parents feel they are wanted and needed. I believe that has been one of the things that has made Berkeley's integration in school work."

The statistics from these and other school districts prove that desegregation results in a better education for millions of children. In Hartford, Connecticut, extensive testing of children in a desegregated program has shown that fifth grade students who have been in the program two years are five months ahead of those who have been in the project for only one year, and the chances for significant gains in basic reading and arithmetic skills have also increased threefold for all children in the program. In Hoke County, North Carolina, before integration, white sixth graders were a year ahead of their Indian and black counterparts. By twelfth grade the gap was two full years. At the end of the first year of integration, white students continued to progress as before. Black students gained a year and a half; their rate of achievement was more than 50 per cent better as a result of integrated schooling. Similar results emerge from less comprehensive testing programs in Sacramento, California, and White Plains and Rochester, New York.

Both research and experience show that integrated education—sensitively conducted with community support—can be better education for all children, white as well as black, rich as well as poor. Fears of the unknown, therefore, are being refuted by practical experience. Efforts to achieve integration by establishing schools serving a wider community clearly will be more difficult and costly in large cities than in smaller cities and suburban communities, but there is every indication that they will yield beneficial results.

Thus, although many argue that a wrong which has been inflicted upon minority children must be righted even if it requires real sacrifice, it is not necessary to face this dilemma. The goals of providing equal educational opportunity for black and brown Americans and quality education for all children are consistent, and the measures which will produce both are in many respects identical. The only sacrifice required is that of our resources and energies in securing these goals . . . the will to secure equal justice and to build a better society for all citizens.

CONCLUSION

The education crisis in America today is basically a human crisis. Despite the achievement scores, graphs, and figures, it must never be forgotten that what we have is the brutal and unnecessary damage to human lives. It is tragic and unnecessary at this point in a country as affluent as ours that hundreds of thousands of poor children, a disproportionate number of them from minorities, should be isolated in inadequately staffed and equipped schools—schools which the community has stigmatized as inferior. And, at the same time, we have too long permitted only the advantaged children—most of them white—to attend schools in the suburbs and outlying residential sections of our cities, schools which have a disproportionate share of the best teachers, offer the most advanced curricula and facilities, and provide individualized attention of a kind and quality seldom available to the minority poor.

Segregation is a term at which many northerners wince, but for generations of poor living there, segregation has been a reality which has hardly been mitigated by legalistic distinctions between *de facto* and *de jure.* The courts today are beginning to recognize that segregation, be it *de jure* or *de facto,* north or south, is wrong. Neither the presence of nondiscrimination statutes nor the absence of overtly discriminatory laws has been very effective in erasing the barriers between black and white, advantaged and disadvantaged, educated and miseducated.

It is true that in the past a good many children of minorities have emerged from segregated schools to earn advanced degrees, to acquire comfortable incomes, and to register achievements which are too seldom recorded in the books which most American schoolchildren read. But the fact that the barriers imposed by segregation have been overcome by some of the more talented, determined, and fortunate does not recommend it to thousands of disadvantaged youngsters for whom segregation has already demonstrated its capacity to cripple rather than challenge. Aside from being poor democracy, it would seem to be poor economy and criminally poor educational policy to continue to isolate disadvantaged children by race and class when it is interaction with advantaged children which appears to be the single most effective factor in narrowing the learning gap.

Let us be clear on the issues facing us—the question is not whether, in theory, minority schools can be as good as white schools. In a society free from prejudice in which minorities were full and equal participants, the answer would be positive. But we are forced to ask the harder question, whether in our present society, where blacks and browns are minorities which have suffered discrimination, their children can prepare themselves to participate effectively in society if they go to school and grow up in isolation from the majority group. We must also ask whether we can cure the disease of prejudice and prepare all children for life in a multiracial world if white children grow up and go to school in isolation from other races.

Integration is the most effective course if we are really concerned about the future of American children of all races and classes. As the principal value-bearing institution which at one time or another touches everyone in our society, the school is crucial in determining what kind of country this is to be. If in the future, the adults who make decisions about who gets a job, who lives down the block, or the essential worth of another person are to be less likely to make these decisions on the basis of race or class, the present cycle must be broken in the classrooms.

None of the financial costs or the administrative adjustments necessary to bring about integrated quality education will be as costly to the quality of American life in the long run as the continuation of our present educational policies and practice. For we are now on a collision course which may produce two alienated and unequal nations confronting each other across a widening gulf created by a dual educational system based upon income and race.

Our present school crisis is a human crisis, engendered and sustained in large part by the actions, the apathy, or the shortsightedness of public officials and private individuals. It can be resolved only by the commitment, the creative energies, and the combined resources of concerned Americans at every level of public and private life.

60 message to congress, march 17, 1972*

Richard M. Nixon

TO THE CONGRESS OF THE UNITED STATES:

In this message, I wish to discuss a question which divides many Americans. That is the question of busing.

I want to do so in a way that will enable us to focus our attention on a question which unites all Americans. That is the question of how to ensure a better education for all of our children.

In the furor over busing, it has become all too easy to forget what busing is supposed to be designed to achieve: equality of educational opportunity for all Americans.

Conscience and the Constitution both require that no child should be denied equal educational opportunity. That Constitutional mandate was laid down by the Supreme Court in *Brown* v. *Board of Education* in 1954. The years since have been ones of dismantling the old dual school system in those areas where it existed—a process that has now been substantially completed.

As we look to the future, it is clear that the efforts to provide equal educational opportunity must now focus much more specifically on education: on assuring that the opportunity is not only equal, but adequate, and that in those remaining cases in which desegregation has not yet been completed it be achieved with a greater sensitivity to educational needs.

Acting within the present framework of Constitutional and case law, the lower Federal courts have ordered a wide variety of remedies for the equal protection violations they have found. These remedies have included such plans as redrawing attendance zones, pairing, clustering and consolidation of school districts. Some of these plans have not required extensive additional transportation of pupils. But some have required that pupils be bused long distances, at great inconvenience. In some cases plans have required that children be bused away from their neighborhoods to schools that are inferior or even unsafe.

The maze of differing and sometimes inconsistent orders by the various lower courts has led to contradiction and uncertainty, and often to vastly unequal treatment among regions, States and local school districts. In the absence of statutory guidelines, many lower court decisions have gone far beyond what most people would consider reasonable, and beyond what the Supreme Court has said is necessary in the requirements they have imposed for the reorganization of school districts and the transportation of school pupils.

---

*Excerpts.

All too often, the result has been a classic case of the remedy for one evil creating another evil. In this case, a remedy for the historic evil of racial discrimination has often created a new evil of disrupting communities and imposing hardship on children—both black and white—who are themselves wholly innocent of the wrongs that the plan seeks to set right.

The 14th Amendment to the Constitution—under which the school desegregation cases have arisen—provides that "The Congress shall have power to enforce, by appropriate legislation, the provisions of this article."

Until now, enforcement has been left largely to the courts—which have operated within a limited range of available remedies, and in the limited context of case law rather than of statutory law. I propose that the Congress now accept the responsibility and use the authority given to it under the 14th Amendment to clear up the confusion which contradictory court orders have created, and to establish reasonable national standards.

Busing: The Fears and Concerns

Before discussing the specifics of these proposals, let me deal candidly with the controversy surrounding busing itself.

There are some people who fear any curbs on busing because they fear that it would break the momentum of the drive for equal rights for blacks and other minorities. Some fear it would go further, and that it would set in motion a chain of reversals that would undo all the advances so painfully achieved in the past generation.

It is essential that whatever we do to curb busing be done in a way that plainly will not have these other consequences. It is vitally important that the Nation's continued commitment to equal rights and equal opportunities be clear and concrete.

On the other hand, it is equally important that we not allow emotionalism to crowd out reason, or get so lost in symbols that words lose their meaning.

One emotional undercurrent that has done much to make this so difficult an issue is the feeling some people have that to oppose busing is to be anti-black. This is closely related to the arguments often put forward that resistance to any move, no matter what, that may be advanced in the name of desegregation is "racist." This is dangerous nonsense.

There is no escaping the fact that some people oppose busing because of racial prejudice. But to go on from this to conclude that "anti-busing" is simply a code word for prejudice is an exercise in arrant unreason. There are right reasons for opposing busing, and there are wrong reasons—and most people, including large and increasing numbers of blacks and other minorities, oppose it for reasons that have little or nothing to do with race. It would compound an injustice to persist in massive busing simply because some people oppose it for the wrong reasons.

For most Americans, the school bus used to be a symbol of hope—of better education. In too many communities today, it has become a symbol of helplessness, frustration and outrage—of a wrenching of children away from their families, and from the schools their families may have moved to be near, and sending them arbitrarily to others far distant.

It has become a symbol of social engineering on the basis of abstractions, with too little regard for the desires and the feelings of those most directly concerned: the children, and their families.

Schools exist to serve the children, not to bear the burden of social change. As I put it in my policy statement on school desegregation 2 years ago (on March 24, 1970):

> One of the mistakes of past policy has been to demand too much of our schools: They have been expected not only to educate, but also to accomplish a social transformation. Children in many instances have not been served, but used—in what all too often has proved a tragically futile effort to achieve in the schools the kind of a multiracial society which the adult community has failed to achieve for itself.
>
> If we are to be realists, we must recognize that in a free society there are limits to the amount of Government coercion that can reasonably be used; that in achieving desegregation we must proceed with the least possible disruption of the education of the Nation's children: and that our children are highly sensitive to conflict, and highly vulnerable to lasting psychic injury.
>
> Failing to recognize these factors, past policies have placed on the schools and the children too great a share of the burden of eliminating racial disparities throughout our society. A major part of this task falls to the schools. But they cannot do it all or even most of it by themselves. Other institutions can share the burden of breaking down racial barriers, but only the schools can perform the task of education itself. If our schools fail to educate, then whatever they may achieve in integrating the races will turn out to be only a Pyrrhic victory.

The Supreme Court has also recognized this problem. Writing for a unanimous Court in the *Swann* case last April, Chief Justice Burger said:

> The constant theme and thrust of every holding from *Brown I* to date is that state-enforced separation of races in public schools is discrimination that violates the Equal Protection Clause. The remedy commanded was to dismantle dual school systems.
>
> We are concerned in these cases with the elimination of the discrimination inherent in the dual school systems, not with myriad factors of human existence which can cause discrimination in a multitude of ways on racial, religious, or ethnic grounds. The target of the cases from *Brown I* to the present was the dual school system. The elimination of racial discrimination in public schools is a large task and one that should not be retarded by efforts to achieve broader purposes lying beyond the jurisdiction of school authorities. One vehicle can carry only a limited amount of baggage. . .
>
> Our objective in dealing with the issues presented by these cases is to see that school authorities exclude no pupil of a racial minority from any school, directly or indirectly, on account of race; it does not and cannot embrace all the problems of racial prejudice, even when those problems contribute to disproportionate racial concentrations in some schools.

In addressing the busing question, it is important that we do so in historical perspective.

Busing for the purpose of desegregation was begun—mostly on a modest scale—as one of a mix of remedies to meet the requirements laid down by various lower Federal courts for achieving the difficult transition from the old dual school system to a new, unitary system.

At the time, the problems of transition that loomed ahead were massive, the old habits deeply entrenched, community resistance often extremely strong. As the years wore on, the courts grew increasingly impatient with what they sometimes saw as delay or evasion, and increasingly insistent that, as the Supreme Court put it in the *Green* decision in 1968, desegregation plans must promise "realistically to work, and . . . to work *now*."

But in the past 3 years, progress toward eliminating the vestiges of the dual system has been phenomenal—and so too has been the shift in public attitudes in those areas where dual systems were formerly operated. In State after State and community after community, local civic, business and educational leaders of all races have come forward to help make the transition peacefully and successfully. Few voices are now raised urging a return to the old patterns of enforced segregation.

This new climate of acceptance of the basic Constitutional doctrine is a new element of great importance: for the greater the elements of basic good faith, of desire to make the system work, the less need or justification there is for extreme remedies rooted in coercion.

At the same time, there has been a marked shift in the focus of concerns by blacks and members of other minorities. Minority parents have long had a deep and special concern with improving the quality of their children's education. For a number of years, the principal emphasis of this concern—and of the Nation's attention—was on desegregating the schools. Now that the dismantling of the old dual system has been substantially completed there is once again a far greater balance of emphasis on improving schools, on convenience, on the chance for parental involvement—in short, on the same concerns that motivate white parents—and, in many communities, on securing a greater measure of control over schools that serve primarily minority-group communities. Moving forward on desegregation is still important—but the principal concern is with preserving the principle, and with ensuring that the great gains made since *Brown,* and particularly in recent years, are not rolled back in a reaction against excessive busing. Many black leaders now express private concern, moreover, that a reckless extension of busing requirements could bring about precisely the results they fear most: a reaction that would undo those gains, and that would begin the unraveling of advances in other areas that also are based on newly expanded interpretations of basic Constitutional rights.

Also, it has not escaped their notice that those who insist on system-wide racial balance insist on a condition in which, in most communities, every school would be run by whites and dominated by whites, with blacks in a permanent minority—and without escape from that minority status. The result would be to deny blacks the right to have schools in which they are the majority.

In short, this is not the simple black-white issue that some simplistically present it as being. There are deep divisions of opinion among people of all races—with recent surveys showing strong opposition to busing among black parents as well as among white parents —not because they are against desegregation but because they are for better education.

In the process of school desegregation, we all have been learning; perceptions have been changing. Those who once said "no" to racial integration have accepted the concept, and believe in equality before the law. Those who once thought massive busing was the answer have also been changing their minds in the light of experience.

As we cut through the clouds of emotionalism that surround the busing question, we can begin to identify the legitimate issues.

Concern for the quality of education a child gets is legitimate.

Concern that there be no retreat from the principle of ending racial discrimination is legitimate.

Concern for the distance a child has to travel to get to school is legitimate.

Concern over requiring that a child attend a more distant school when one is available near his home is legitimate.

Concern for the obligation of government to assure, as nearly as possible, that all the children of a given district have equal educational opportunity is legitimate.

Concern for the way educational resources are allocated among the schools of a district is legitimate.

Concern for the degree of control parents and local school boards should have over their schools is legitimate.

In the long, difficult effort to give life to what is in the law, to desegregate the Nation's schools and enforce the principle of equal opportunity, many experiments have been tried. Some have worked, and some have not. We now have the benefit of a fuller fund of experience than we had 18 years ago, or even 2 years ago. It has also become apparent that community resistance—black as well as white—to plans that massively disrupt education and separate parents from their children's schools, makes those plans unacceptable to communities on which they are imposed.

Against this background, the objectives of the reforms I propose are:

— To give practical meaning to the concept of equal educational opportunity.

— To apply the experience gained in the process of desegregation, and also in efforts to give special help to the educationally disadvantaged.

— To ensure the continuing vitality of the principles laid down in *Brown* v. *Board of Education.*

— To downgrade busing as a tool for achieving equal educational opportunity.

— To sustain the rights and responsibilities vested by the States in local school boards.

using the legal 61
process for change

Julius Hobson

Up to now, large urban school systems in the United States have traditionally consigned poor and black children to the social and economic junk heap. This process has been accomplished through a variety of vehicles; some obvious, such as simple segregation by race, others more subtle, such as an unequal distribution of educational resources, rigid tracking, and inferior physical plants.

The Washington D.C. school system has been guilty on every count. My first challenge to the District of Columbia schools (under Superintendent Carl Hansen) occurred in 1953, when I attempted to take my six year old son to the closest elementary school (all white) rather than transport him out of our neighborhood to another school (all black). There were no top level objections then to busing children in order to maintain segregation.

In reality, the whole issue of busing is camouflage, both on the part of Nixon and of the NAACP, to cover what we refuse to deal with—namely, inequality in the distribution of public resources. Integration in public education in the United States has clearly failed to bring us to the millenium. Blacks realize, therefore, that their only salvation is to fight for their equal share under the Fourteenth Amendment to the Constitution, which allows for equal access to public resources and equal protection under the law.

Let us go back through history. Nearly twenty years ago, *Brown v. Board of Education* shook the entire country and exposed the bitter consequences of racism in the United States. Although it was an extraordinary decision, it masked a still greater fight which is now being faced.

Blacks applauded the death of the separate-but-equal doctrine, not because of an enormous desire to integrate as suspected by fearful whites, but because we knew where the real educational resources were—in the white schools. Black schools, such as the one I attended in Birmingham, Alabama were subject to the whim of white officials like the white superintendent who said at my graduation: "You sing so well that God must have set aside a separate place in heaven for you people."

The integration issue only postponed consideration of the more important and revolutionary issues related to the equal distribution of public funds in public programs. We must decide if tax benefits should be disbursed according to the level of payment, or, in a democracy, should we be talking about "one man, one dollar?" It is extraordinary to me that the really significant questions have been ignored for so long, and that only now are we addressing ourselves to what is obvious. The fight for equal resources is not a black/white fight; it is a war perpetuated by those who benefit most from public resources against those who benefit least and are unable to object.

The research leading to Judge J. Skelly Wright's opinion of June, 1967 in the *Hobson v. Hansen* case exposed the different treatment within the District of Columbia school system. It required a two year struggle and a court order to secure data on the average expenditure per pupil in elementary schools. In the 1963-64 school year these data ranged from a low of $216 per child in the poor and black community to a high of $627 per child in the wealthy white community—a difference of 190 per cent. The difference in per pupil expenditures between the lowest school in the predominantly black community and the highest school in the predominantly white community had increased from $411 to $506 by 1968. Data for 1970 showed that the difference had reached an unbelievable $1719.

Judge Wright's 1967 opinion decreed that discrimination in the distribution of public resources based on race or income was unconstitutional and thereby ordered the school system to set about eliminating this differential. The judge stated that:

> The doctrine of equal educational opportunity for Negro and poor public school children of the District of Columbia, under the equal protection clause in its application to public school education, is in its full sweep a component of due process binding on the District of Columbia under the due process clause of the Fifth Amendment.

The D. C. school administration made no attempt to abide by the judge's decree, even though it was upheld at the appeals court level. The plaintiffs had to return to court in 1970, to secure a judgment that directed the school administration to equalize expenditures per pupil based on teachers' salaries from regularly budgeted funds.

It is, however, a difficult problem for parents and other community groups to obtain the type of detailed information that can lead to such a decision. Professional educators, who resent and resist questions and the involvement of noneducators in their special preserve, have refused to release statistical information. Because substantive data are unavailable, interested adults have usually been side-tracked into debating unmeasurable qualities, such as teacher attitudes and sensitivity to children, curriculum content, and the responsibility of the parent versus that of the school. Professional educators, arguing that the educational process is indeed complicated and cannot be understood by non-educators, have been left virtually free to perform their mysterious function in isolation from community accountability.

My work has been directed toward providing parents and community groups with tools to evaluate measurable quantities in the educational process. Although use of these tools will not insure the "quality" of education, once equity in educational resources is established other qualities harder to define can be attacked. Indeed, "attack" is a very appropriate term to parents and community groups, who have discovered the practiced ability of school board officials to talk fast, flip charts, and provide 300 page reports while the schools continue to deteriorate.

The evaluation and analysis of data in this article are presented as examples. Public education can be traced quantitatively from the composition of the Board of Education to "Johnny's" ability to read. Such data have been presented as evidence to the Congress of the United States, the United States District Court, and the United States Court of Appeals of the District of Columbia.

The 1967 *Hobson v. Hansen* school case, upheld in the United States Court of Appeals in the District of Columbia, was based on statistical evidence that measured, among other things, assignment of teachers, expenditures per pupil, distribution of books and supplies, utilization of homogeneous ability grouping methods, and utilization of classroom space. When related to the color of the population and the economic level of the neighborhoods where schools were located, the data showed definite patterns of racial and economic discrimination.

Although many city school systems assert that they do not have these data, it is very likely that they do. To administer large school systems, officials, particularly those overseeing school finances, must have such information. In most states, these data are considered public information by law and can be obtained through legal procedures if necessary. Parent groups and others outside school administrations cannot hope to fully understand what is actually happening to their children without access to such information. Any attack on the deteriorating educational systems in large American cities must begin from a factual basis.

Since unequal conditions have prevailed throughout the entire history of public education in large cities, such conditions appear to show a deliberate design to keep black and poor children in a condition which could be called "programmed retardation." At the same time, professional educators blame the children for their inability to learn under measurably adverse conditions. Indeed, primary and secondary public education in large cities in the United States is the only major industry in which the consumer (the child) is held responsible for the quality of the product.

Since much of the information we use is quantitative rather than qualitative, some authorities on evaluation will probably raise eyebrows, since these are computational data that do not deal with changes in learning, or the dynamics of school curricula or organization. The latter point is valid. However, as a first step, these data readily reveal a measurable flow in unequal practices in public education which can serve as a starting point for parents and lay groups attempting to save the children.

Education is a big industry and should be administered as such. For example, Washington schools have an average annual budget (funds from all sources) of about $150,000,000, approximately 18,000 employees, 150,000 students (about 94 per cent black) and more than 200 school buildings. The following information is based solely upon data collected from the Washington public school administration and the United States Census Bureau. It provides nothing more than an elementary decision-making, management tool essential to an operating organization; such information should become part of the normal computerized collection of data annually made available to parents and taxpayers.

In 1965, elementary schools in lower and moderate income neighborhoods (under $9,000) had average expenditures per pupil substantially lower than those in the higher income areas ($10,000 and above)—$306 contrasted with an average of $396 in the wealthier neighborhoods, about 30% higher. Three years later, in 1968, the general pattern remained the same, although the gap had narrowed. The overall average expenditure per pupil in areas of less than $9,000 income was $391, contrasted with $442 in areas of $9,000 income and more (Fig. 1).

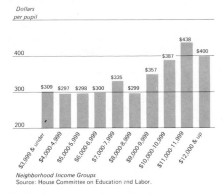

Dollars per pupil

$3,999 & under $309, $4,000-4,999 $297, $5,000-5,999 $298, $6,000-6,999 $300, $7,000-7,999 $335, $8,000-8,999 $299, $9,000-9,999 $357, $10,000-10,999 $387, $11,000-11,999 $438, $12,000 & up $400

Neighborhood Income Groups
Source: House Committee on Education and Labor.

FIGURE 1A Average expenditure per pupil in elementary schools in 1965.

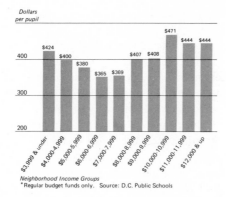

FIGURE 1B Average expenditure per pupil in elementary schools in 1968*.

In 1963-64, the highest expenditure per pupil in any school in the predominantly black community equaled only 81 per cent as much as the lowest expenditure per pupil in the schools located in the predominantly white community. The differential in expenditures per pupil between the lowest school in the predominantly black community and the highest school in the predominantly white community amounted to $411 (Fig. 2A).

In 1968, even though new data showed there had been a striking increase in expenditure per pupil in selected schools in predominantly black areas, ten of the eleven schools listed in the lowest expenditure group were still located in the District's poorest and most neglected area—Southeast Washington (Fig. 2B).

The differential in expenditures per pupil between the school receiving the highest expenditure and the school receiving the lowest expenditure was $506 in 1968, an increase of $95 over the spread which prevailed in 1963-64.

The differences in per capita expenditures were greater than those recorded in the elementary school systems in the States of Alabama, Georgia, Louisiana, or Mississippi in either 1964 or 1968.

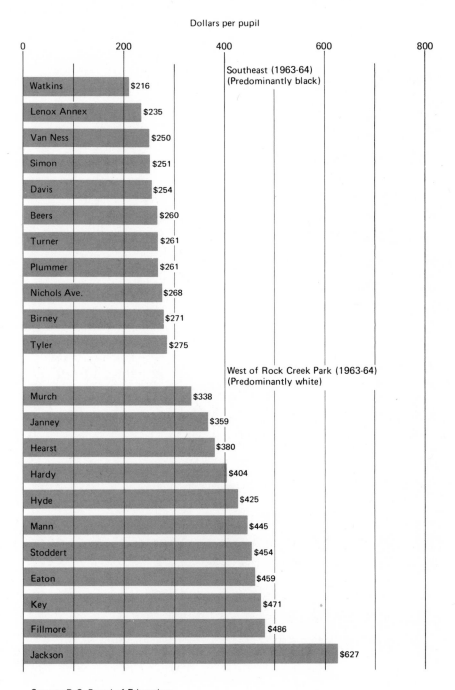

FIGURE 2A   Expenditures per pupil in selected elementary schools.

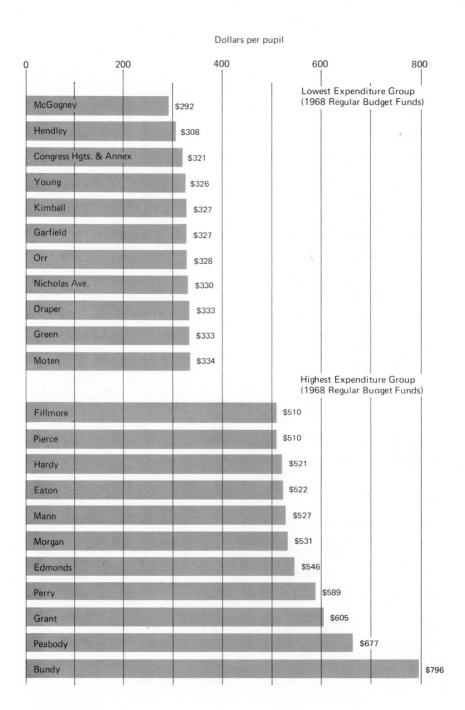

FIGURE 2B Expenditures per pupil in selected elementary schools. (Continued)

There are three main categories of teachers in the Washington public schools: permanent, probationary, and temporary. "Permanent" teachers have passed the qualifying examination, have met all the academic requirements, and have served a specified probationary period. "Probationary" teachers have passed the qualifying examination and have also met all of the academic requirements, but are still serving a specified probationary period. "Temporary" teachers, for the most part, have not passed or cannot pass the required examination to become permanent and may not have the required academic qualifications.

The percent of "temporary" teachers in the elementary schools by neighborhood income groups for the school year 1965 indicates that as the economic level of the neighborhood declined, the percentage of temporary teachers assigned to the schools in those neighborhoods increased. In the poorest community where the income was $3,999 and under, 46 per cent of the teachers were temporary in 1965; while in the community where the income range was from $11,000 to $11,999, only 19 per cent of the teachers were temporary. Temporary teachers, as defined by the school administration, are the least qualified and were assigned primarily to the poorest communities (Fig. 3A).

In 1969, despite a U.S. court order directing the D.C. school board to equalize facilities, and despite an elected board which was 73 per cent Black, the same general pattern of discrimination still prevailed. In 1969, the elementary schools in the poorest communities with income levels of $3,999 and under had 45 per cent permanent teachers. The $6,000 to $6,999 community had a low of 41 per cent permanent teachers assigned to their elementary schools. The elementary schools located in the neighborhood where the income range was $10,000 to $10,999 contained 59 per cent permanent teachers and well over half of the teachers assigned to the $11,000 to $11,999 and the $12,000 and over income communities were permanent (Fig. 3B).

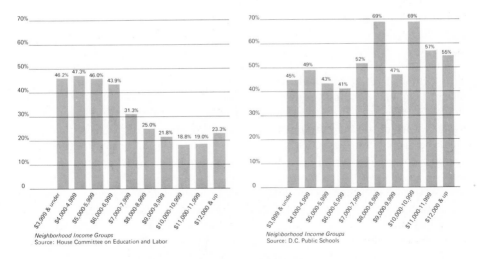

FIGURE 3A   Per cent of *temporary* teachers, 1965.   **B**   Per cent of *permanent* teachers, 1969.

As the income level goes up, the reading levels of the children go up. In the poorest neighborhoods in 1968 96 per cent of the schools reported that their children read *below* the national norm, and that the average expenditure per pupil was about $383. In the richest neighborhoods 94 per cent of the elementary schools reported reading scores *above* the national norm. The average expenditure per pupil for the richest neighborhoods amounted to some $435.

A further analysis of the data on reading scores for elementary school children shows that in 1966-67, 72 per cent of the schools reported that their fourth graders read below the national norm. By 1968-69 these children had reached the 6th grade. The data show that by that time, 77 per cent of the schools these same children attended reported sixth grade reading scores below the national norm. Thus, the longer children remain in the Washington public schools, the lower their reading performance becomes.

Important steps are being made to bring about an equal distribution of educational resources. On August 30, 1971 the California State Supreme Court found that, "the California public school financing system, with its substantial dependence on local property tax and resultant wide disparities in school revenue, violates the equal protection clause of the Fourteenth Amendment." The Court found further, "We have determined that this funding scheme invidiously discriminates against the poor because it makes the quality of a child's education a function of the wealth of his parents and neighbors."

While this is a landmark decision, which, if left standing, will revolutionize funding among school districts within the states, it does nothing about discrimination against individual children or schools within school districts. Thus, school districts maintain the full right to continue discrimination against minorities and poor children under their jurisdiction by distributing disproportionate shares of their resources to certain schools within the district. Parents in California are faced with duplicating the *Hobson v. Hansen* decision in order to assure the elimination of discrimination against minorities and the poor.

It is always surprising to me that so-called "well-meaning" parents, teachers, and citizens who enjoy the greatest share in public resources always defend their position by stating that money doesn't matter, that the real problems of the poor involve broken homes, unruly children, poor habits, alcoholism, and drugs. Yet, I have never heard a poor family say that additional—certainly, *at minimum, equal*—resources would not be of enormous help. At present, as shown in the examples that follow, the record in resource allocation is discouraging.

We must face the problems inherent in inequality in school finances. Indeed, the issue extends beyond the institution of education, for if it is unconstitutional to discriminate in the distribution of public resources in education, might it not also be unconstitutional to discriminate in the distribution of public jobs and other public services, such as health, transportation, and even sanitation?

62 the redistribution of school power: a populist approach to urban education

Harvey B. Scribner
Leonard B. Stevens

At a time when urban social problems are becoming, if anything, more acute than ever, we know little about underlying causes, or about how to increase the capability of cities to govern themselves better. The conventional wisdom of many liberals, that what the cities need most is much more money and more and better programs, may well be hopelessly inadequate. Money and programs would probably help a lot, but not unless accompanied by fundamental changes in the politics and management of cities.

David Rogers

Most city-dwellers in America would probably agree with this observation from the preface to *The Management of Big Cities* (Rogers, 1971). They would agree because the ills of the big cities have become so recognizable, and because "politics" and "management" are ready-made targets in the government reform scenario. The Rogers observation also applies to urban schools. Unfortunately, while the failures of urban schools are now beyond dispute, disagreement continues among school professionals, legislators, academics, critics, and citizens as to the reasons for the failures, and no lasting consensus exists as to precise remedies.

As one pair of critics (Gross and Osterman, 1971) has said, to list the elements of the critique of urban schools is almost too easy—it is a catalogue of clichés. The schools, in the span of a very few years, have been described as boring, joyless, inequitable, discriminatory, anti-intellectual, undemocratic, misdirected, mismanaged, and destructive of children. The critique as a whole, although sometimes overstated and uneven and occasionally shrill, generally has been based on substance and not fantasy. It has served an important function in clarifying the nature of the crisis and focusing public attention on it.

Although the legitimate complaints against the schools are multiple, their failure can be described basically as an inability to deliver services to all their consumers. For in our largest cities the American system of schooling, which has been so unique, so successful, so praised, and so expandable, has not been able to fulfill for all the young who enter it those basic promises that, taken together, constitute their raison d'etre. Because of genuine flaws, because they annually turn off or turn away a frighteningly large percentage of the students they are required to serve, and who are required to attend them, and also because the establishment so often defends the schools instead of attempting to change them, urban schools are in danger of coming apart at their institutional seams.

The widespread inability of the schools to reform themselves is their single most significant defect. It is the ultimate cause of parent and student disaffection. This general tendency to protect and preserve the schools essentially in their present form and for their traditional function not only flows from institutional inertia, but also reflects an important and willful resistance by the special interests comprising the school establishment to legitimate consumer demands for new forms of education and more enlightened educational policies.

Our own beliefs and experience lead us to believe that urban schools are in a more than passing crisis. The kind of trouble they are experiencing cannot be eliminated simply by the infusion of more money. Unless urban schools undergo some radical alterations in the next few years, they may force out an increasingly large percentage of students who are neither dull nor unwilling to learn, *and* who want and need new opportunities for productive learning. Those who remain in the schools may receive an increasingly inadequate education. Our own point of view can be expressed simply by altering a few words of Rogers' observation to make its subject *urban schools* rather than *urban government:*

> At a time when urban *school* problems are becoming, if anything, more acute than ever, we *agree* on little about underlying causes, or about how to increase the capability of *the schools* to govern themselves better *and thus to serve the young more productively.* The conventional wisdom of *the vast majority of school professionals,* that what the *schools* need most is much more money and more and better programs, may well be hopelessly inadequate. Money and programs would probably help a lot, but not unless accompanied by fundamental changes in the politics and management of *urban schools.*

In urban schools (and increasingly, outside the cities as well) the *program approach* to school reform is no longer reform: it is a cosmetic. In fact, it guarantees a deepening of the school crisis by protecting the basic nature of the schools from change while adding new touches to a system that needs, more than anything else, a basic realignment. The program approach—so popular in the past decade—is obsolete. It is no longer enough to speak of reforming urban schools solely by the new math and the new physics, by improving libraries and adding new equipment, or by devising one more special program for yet another special group of students. New school buildings are not the same as better education. More money will not necessarily solve anything. These methods have been tried in recent years and have changed little in the basic nature of schooling—they have simply made the system bigger and more complicated.

School systems are extremely difficult to change, and efforts to change them, however costly, are rarely directed at fundamental reforms. John Fischer, commenting on schools at the end of the nineteen sixties, after extensive new funding was provided, observed, "The atmosphere has changed. Students' hair is longer, their clothing scruffier, and their language less inhibited. The teachers . . . are more outspoken, better organized, and less compliant . . . . *But the institutional character of the schools—their purposes, forms and functions—look . . . much as they did in 1960*" (Fischer, 1970) (italics ours).

What is demanded today is a *structural* approach to urban school reform—the kind of change which deals directly with the distribution of decision-making power and systems of governance. It is only by altering these elements that reformers can hope to obtain such long-term effects on school policies, attitudes, and assumptions as the extent and kind of experiences that the schools provide the young, the style of teaching and learning that the schools encourage and tolerate, the way in which education is defined and measured, the content of individual courses, and the pattern of the programs that make up formal schooling.

To speak of the future of urban schools in a hopeful and constructive vein requires us to speak first of the redistribution of decision-making power, just as it is necessary, as Senator Fred Harris has observed in another context (Harris, 1972), to speak of the redistribution of political power when considering this nation's future progress. For too long, schools have been controlled primarily by professionals and special interests (and often the two overlap). Thus, schools have responded much more to the concerns of such people than to the desires of their consumers—parents and students.

In the cities, this problem is further complicated by the sheer mass of urban education systems—New York City is the prime example—which makes it virtually impossible for the individual parent or student even to find, never mind influence, whoever actually makes the decisions. This central fact accounts for the contemporary demand for decentralization or community control of city schools, the popularity—and legitimacy—of attacking educational "bureaucracy," the movements for parent power and student power, and the origin, at least in part, of the 1969 state legislation which largely decentralized school administration in New York City.

Like virtually all legislative acts, this landmark law was imperfect; it contained ambiguities and inconsistencies attributable for the most part to the many political compromises which led to its passage. Nonetheless, it represented an unparalleled step forward in urban school reform. For, by turning over control of the city's public school system* to thirty-one locally elected Community School Boards, the law brought educational decision-making substantially closer to students and parents, the people for whom schools exist and to whom they belong. (Presently, because of an amendment to the law, there are thirty-two Community Boards.)

There has been considerable debate in New York City as to the value of school decentralization. The critical issue, of course, is (or should be) educational results—better learning opportunities for children. Yet decentralization, since it affects the distribution of power in the schools, is also an intensely political issue, and this has, if anything, caused even more debate. It has been the target of innumerable attacks on both educational and political grounds. Even a strong ally and early supporter of decentralization criticized at one point the power struggles it had caused in some parts of the city (Clark, 1972).

Decentralization, as practiced in New York, is portrayed by some advocates of community control as a meaningless gesture of no real benefit to parents who want and deserve a new voice and a new influence in the way their schools affect their children. These critics see it as a political compromise that uses the word "decentralization" but contains nothing of substance to make it work—an imperfect and misguided experiment doomed to failure.

Opponents of community control, meanwhile, have depicted decentralization as a political give-away to power-hungry individuals and groups who are intent on using the schools as a patronage system rather than an educational one. At best they regard it as a

---

*Except for high schools, special schools, and special education programs, which remain centrally managed.

political pseudo-reform of no educational benefit to children. It is even said that the quality of education in some schools has deteriorated since they were decentralized.

The difference in perception vis-à-vis the educational value of decentralization depends in part on the kind of change that is believed to be most beneficial for children in the long run as well as in the immediate future. Those who hold that the highest priority in urban school reform should be a re-distribution of decision-making authority in order to place parents (and students) in influential roles see decentralization as a step, or at least a gesture, in the right direction. Those who would like to use more professional expertise in re-designing the curriculum see it as having limited potential or none in accomplishing anything meaningful in the classroom.

One of the most vocal opponents of decentralization has been the president of the United Federation of Teachers, Albert Shanker. He has repeatedly attacked it, often by attacking the actions and alleged actions of Community School Boards. His unyielding opposition to decentralization is often viewed as an essentially political posture, taken by the head of organized classroom teachers in order to protect the rights and privileges they have won through many years of persuasion and collective bargaining. Thus, Mr. Shanker has been highly critical of "conflict and violence" in the operation of decentralized schools, the occasional inability of some Community School Boards to function effectively, the alleged "misspending of hundreds of thousands of dollars" in one Community School District, and the recruiting and hiring by Community School Boards of teachers who are "not regularly licensed" while "regularly licensed" teachers go unhired. The last is an indirect but clear suggestion that decentralization and the notion of hiring professionals on the basis of merit and fitness are inherently incompatible (Shanker, 1972).

But there is, it seems, a deeper reason for Mr. Shanker's opposition to decentralization. The reason is more philosophical than political and becomes clear when one considers his declaration that "educational improvements will be made on the basis of educational programs rather than political and administrative ones." He thus assumes that the program approach to urban school reform is useful—more new programs, more spending, an improved teacher-pupil ratio, and perhaps some adjustments in teacher education. Conversely, his argument suggests, the basic structure of the schools is sound, control is appropriately distributed. Parents and students have the rights of clients but not consumers—thereby implying that they should speak out on school issues but not share to any greater extent in decision making.

Despite their different postures, strong advocates of community control and opponents of decentralized schools like Mr. Shanker speak from the same political ground in criticizing decentralization. The former believe a redistribution of educational *decision making* is the reform of highest priority in the urban schools, and they criticize decentralization as a political compromise and cop-out which has failed to accomplish this. The latter believe that educational *programs* are of highest priority, and they attack decentralization and its supporters for pursuing the wrong kind of reform at a time when urban schools are indisputably in extremis. Decentralization is thus the victim of whipsaw attacks.

Given the choice between placing new programs in the existing urban school system with all its infirmities, and trying to remake the system in a lasting way by redistributing decision making to include parents and students, we opt for the latter. In the future, urban education must have maximum public involvement. In the big cities, such involvement of parents and whole communities is virtually impossible until power presently highly centralized is transferred in some fashion to a network of relatively autonomous, locally elected boards of education. Until urban parents achieve a sense of potential influence over the schools which they pay for and their children attend, little can be done to renew their confidence in the schools, confidence which is crucial to school reform.

Decentralization deserves to be evaluated and the test should be whether it delivers an education for children. We should expect schools to help the young to learn to read and think and make rational decisions. We should expect decentralization to produce an educational benefit in the form of improved opportunities, and much wider variety in the styles of learning. But the success or failure of decentralization should be assessed not merely by reading scores but also by such factors as parent involvement in the schools, school responsiveness to the needs of children and communities, the openness of the schools to new forms of education, and the extent to which the schools and their surrounding communities come to view each other not as adversaries but as allies in a common cause.

Decentralization of urban schools will not yield instant benefits in student achievement. The politics of the operation are guaranteed to produce citywide pain and some local trauma. In addition, as Maurice Berube has said, there will remain the always unfinished tasks of generating new financial support and new kinds of educational programs. But, as he has suggested, without the necessary redistribution of decision making, "more money and more imaginative programs will have little effect" (Berube, 1970).

The redistribution of decision making in urban school systems is necessary at two levels. The first is legislative—the highly centralized big-city school system should be administratively decentralized both to thrust policymaking closer to the people the policies affect, and to organize educational systems of more manageable size. The second level is the individual school, where the objective should be parent involvement. This means defining parents as legitimate partners in policy analysis and review, as well as consultation and hearings on proposed policy. It means involving parents in the design, operation, and evaluation of programs. It means volunteer parents working in classrooms —and schools open to parents other than merely during American Education Week (which serves, unhappily, to reinforce the notion that parents belong in schools only one week a year). Involvement means parents (and, in high schools, students as well) actively engaging in the selection of principals; and it means parents becoming part of staff evaluation and school accountability projects. Simply put, urban schools are likely to be improved in a fundamental way only to the extent that parents are able to exert positive and regular influence over them; and this is possible only when the system is of manageable size and the places of decision making are open to and welcome parents.

Such changes in the distribution of educational decision making—at the level of the urban school system and at the level of the individual school—would produce totally different relationships among the constituencies of the schools. Parents and students would gain new influence. The special interests and powerbrokers would undoubtedly (and hopefully) lose their presently massive clout. The school professionals would probably find themselves in situations of higher risk because parents would have broken through the mystique of School and Education and obtained a new voice along with a new comprehension of how and why decisions are made. At the same time, those talented professionals who *want* to be accountable and who are victimized as much as parents and children by the inflexibility and impersonality of large school systems would enjoy their own liberation. While some parents might be overly critical of staff, it seems likely that teachers might well obtain more independence and personal autonomy from parents than they will ever obtain from colleagues who have reached the supervisory ranks. The lesson plan as a check on teachers is the invention of supervisors, not parents.

Dean Corrigan has said that "because of our past evasion of responsibilities, our unwillingness to change schools and colleges, it is now five minutes to midnight" (Corrigan, 1970). What he called the "normal necessary adjustment" can no longer pass for school reform, at least not in the volatile cities. There is the possibility that pressures on the big-city school systems will conspire to produce more defensiveness than creativity, and that urban schools will grow more susceptible to the special interests, more inequitable in the distribution of learning opportunity, more narrow in their vision of what the young want and deserve, and increasingly repressive in their policies. There is also the possibility that these same pressures will produce a burst of renewal—a period in which urban schools will become not only more effective institutions but also more responsive and more humane. The remainder of the nineteen seventies may well tell the story.

REFERENCES

Berube, Maurice R.: Community control: Key to educational achievement. *Social Policy,* July/August, 1970.
Clark, Kenneth B.: quoted in Decentralization of schools fails, Kenneth Clark says. *New York Times,* May 8, 1972.
Corrigan, Dean: Browsing through the bookshelves. *The Journal of Teacher Education,* Spring, 1970.
Fischer, John: Who needs schools? *Saturday Review,* September 19, 1970.
Gross, Ronald, and Osterman, Paul: High School. New York, Simon and Schuster, 1971.
Harris, Fred R.: The real populism fights unequal wealth. *New York Times,* May 25, 1972.
Rogers, David: The Management of Big Cities: Interest Groups and Social Change Strategies. Sage, 1971.
Shanker, Albert: Where we stand. Advertisement in *New York Times,* May 14, 1972.